jazz styles
HISTORY & ANALYSIS

second edition

MARK C. GRIDLEY

Mercyhurst College
Erie, Pennsylvania 16546

prentice-hall, inc. englewood cliffs, new jersey 07632

Library of Congress Cataloging in Publication Data

Gridley, Mark C., 1947–
  Jazz styles.

  Bibliography: p. 406
  Discography: p. 432
  Includes index.
  1. Jazz music.   2. Style, Musical.   3. Jazz
musicians.   I. Title.
ML3506.G74   1985   785.42   84–16068
ISBN 0–13–509134–9

Editorial/production supervision: Fred Bernardi, Elizabeth Athorn
Cover photograph: Dale S. Weiss
Cover design: Diane Saxe
Manufacturing buyer: Raymond Keating

The cover photograph is used through the courtesy of Dale Weiss and Pat McCarty. Portions of pages 69–71 originally appeared in *Jazz Educators Journal*, Vol. XVI (1984), No. 3, as "Why is Louis Armstrong So Important?" and are reproduced here by permission of the editor. Portions of Chapter 19 originally appeared in *Popular Music and Society*, Vol. IX (1983), No. 2, as "Clarifying Labels: Jazz, Rock, Funk and Jazz-Rock," and appear here by permission of the editors. Portions of Chapter 4 originally appeared in *The Black Perspective in Music*, Vol. 12 (1984), No. 1, as "Toward Identifying African Traits in Early Instrumental Jazz," and are reproduced here by permission of the editor. The section called "Popular Appeal," which appears here on pages 171–175, is used by permission of the editors of *Popular Music and Society*, who are publishing the passage as "Why Have Modern Jazz Combos Been Less Popular Than Swing Big Bands?"

Printed in the United States of America

10   9   8   7   6   5   4

ISBN 0-13-509134-9   01

Prentice-Hall International, Inc., *London*
Prentice-Hall of Australia Pty. Limited, *Sydney*
Editora Prentice-Hall do Brasil, Ltda., *Rio de Janeiro*
Prentice-Hall Canada Inc., *Toronto*
Prentice-Hall of India Private Limited, *New Delhi*
Prentice-Hall of Japan, Inc., *Tokyo*
Prentice-Hall of Southeast Asia Pte. Ltd., *Singapore*
Whitehall Books Limited, *Wellington, New Zealand*

CONTENTS

LIST OF TABLES AND ILLUSTRATIONS   vii

PREFACE   x

ACKNOWLEDGMENTS   xiv

AIDS FOR USING THIS BOOK   xviii

1 **INTRODUCTION**   1

part I BASICS OF JAZZ

2 **WHAT IS JAZZ**   4

  Improvisation   4

  Swing Feeling   5

  Defining the Jazz Musician: Four Views   8

3 **APPRECIATING JAZZ IMPROVISATION**   12

  Listening Techniques   13

  Instrument Roles   15

  Alternatives Available to the Improviser   25

  Skills Possessed by the Improviser   27

  Chord Progressions and Tune Construction   30

part II PREMODERN JAZZ

4   **ORIGINS OF JAZZ**   38

5   **EARLY JAZZ: COMBO JAZZ PRIOR TO THE MIDDLE 1930s**   56

6   **SWING: THE EARLY 1930s TO THE LATE 1940s**   86

7   **DUKE ELLINGTON**   107

8   **THE COUNT BASIE BANDS**   128

part III MODERN JAZZ: THE EARLY 1940s TO THE EARLY 1960s

9   **BOP**   143

10   **COOL JAZZ**   177

     Lennie Tristano and Lee Konitz   179
     Birth of the Cool   181
     West Coast Style of the 1950s   182

11   **HARD BOP**   191

12   **MILES DAVIS, HIS GROUPS AND SIDEMEN**   207

part IV MODERN JAZZ: THE EARLY 1960s TO THE MID–1980s

13   **FREE JAZZ**   226

     Ornette Coleman   228
     Albert Ayler   234
     Don Cherry   236
     Cecil Taylor   237
     Free Drummers   238
     Free Bassists   239

14   **CHARLES MINGUS**   **243**

15   **BILL EVANS, HERBIE HANCOCK, CHICK COREA,
AND KEITH JARRETT**   **251**

16   **THE SECOND CHICAGO SCHOOL**   **268**

     Sun Ra   *269*
     Association for the Advancement of Creative Musicians   *273*

       Art Ensemble of Chicago   *274*
       Anthony Braxton   *276*

     World Saxophone Quartet   *276*

17   **JOHN COLTRANE**   **279**

18   **WAYNE SHORTER, RON CARTER, AND TONY WILLIAMS**   **301**

19   **TWENTY YEARS OF JAZZ, ROCK, AND AMERICAN
POPULAR MUSIC: THE MID-1960s TO THE MID-1980s**   **312**

     Distinguishing Jazz from Rock and Funk   *317*
     Blood, Sweat & Tears, Chicago, and Ten Wheel Drive   *317*
     Miles Davis   *321*
     John McLaughlin   *325*
     Larry Coryell   *327*
     Don Ellis   *328*
     Josef Zawinul   *329*
     Weather Report   *331*
     Jaco Pastorius   *336*
     Established Greats Embrace Rock   *338*
     Models for Jazz-Rock Players   *339*
     Popular Appeal of Jazz-Rock   *340*

20   **BIG BANDS IN THE 1960s AND 70s**   **344**

     Stan Kenton   *344*
     Woody Herman   *348*
     Maynard Ferguson   *349*
     Thad Jones-Mel Lewis   *351*

APPENDIX

CHRONOLOGY OF JAZZ STYLES CHART   356

ELEMENTS OF MUSIC   358

Rhythm:
   Beat   358
   Tempo   358
   Meter   359
   Rhythm   359
      syncopation   362
      swing eighths   363

Scales, Keys, Tonality, and Modality   365
Blue Notes   371
Chords and Chord Progressions   372
Chord Voicing   374

The Blues   377
The Thirty-Two-Bar AABA Tune   378
Listening for the Twelve-Bar Blues and Thirty-Two-Bar Forms   378
Detecting Other Forms   382
Modal Forms   384
The Effects of Form on Improvisation   386
Phrasing in Relation to Form   387

Tone Color   388

GUIDE TO RECORD BUYING   392

GLOSSARY   401

SUPPLEMENTARY READING   406

SOURCES FOR NOTATED JAZZ SOLOS   412

FOR MUSICIANS   415

A SMALL BASIC RECORD COLLECTION   432

INDEX   433

TABLES & ILLUSTRATIONS

TABLES

4.1   *Jazz features according to cultures of origin*   55

5.1   *Early jazz musicians*   58

5.2   *New Orleans and Chicago musicians*   60

5.3   *Comparing Louis Armstrong with Bix Beiderbecke*   73

6.1   *Swing-style musicians*   87

6.2   *Fletcher Henderson musicians*   92

7.1   *Duke Ellington musicians*   112

7.2   *Johnny Hodges disciples*   118

8.1   *Kansas City musicians*   132

8.2   *Count Basie musicians*   133

8.3   *Comparing Coleman Hawkins and Lester Young*   134

8.4   *Lester Young disciples*   135

9.1   *Bop musicians*   147

9.2   *Charlie Parker disciples*   152

9.3   *Thelonious Monk disciples*   157

10.1   *West Coast musicians*   183

10.2   *Stan Kenton and Woody Herman musicians*   184

11.1   *Hard bop musicians*   192

11.2   *Comparing West Coast style with hard bop style*   193

11.3   *Philadelphia and Detroit musicians*   *194*

11.4   *Horace Silver musicians*   *197*

11.5   *Art Blakey musicians*   *203*

11.6   *Comparing J. J. Johnson with Curtis Fuller*   *204*

12.1   *Miles Davis saxophonists*   *208*

12.2   *Miles Davis guitarists*   *208*

12.3   *Miles Davis rhythm sections*   *210*

12.4   *Miles Davis disciples*   *212*

13.1   *Ornette Coleman disciples*   *233*

13.2   *Free-jazz musicians*   *240*

15.1   *Bill Evans disciples*   *252*

17.1   *McCoy Tyner disciples*   *293*

17.2   *John Coltrane disciples*   *296*

19.1   *Jazz-rock musicians*   *320*

SPECIAL BOXED FEATURES

Vibrato   *50*

Distinguishing trumpet from cornet   *67*

Listening guide for "Cottontail"   *111*

Listening guide for "Harlem Air Shaft"   *113*

Listening guide for "Take the 'A' Train"   *122*

Listening guide for "Taxi War Dance"   *136*

Listening guide for "Lester Leaps In"   *138*

Listening guide for Kind of Blue   *217*

LINE DRAWINGS AND INSTRUMENT PHOTOS

3.1   *Possible visualizations of tone perceptions*   *14*

3.2   *String bass and electric bass guitar*   *16*

3.3   *Audience view of drum set*   *17*

3.4   *Drums*   *19*

3.5   *Open and closed high-hat cymbals*   *20*

3.6   *Sticks, brushes, and mallets*   *21*

3.7   *Bass drum—foot pedal*   *21*

4.1   *Guitar and banjo*   *46*

4.2   *Drop or fall-off*   *51*

4.3   *Scoop*   *51*

4.4   *Smear*   *51*

4.5   Doit   52

5.1   Clarinet and soprano saxophone   76

5.2   Baritone saxophone—bass saxophone   78

5.3   Tuba   78

6.1   Alto, tenor, and baritone saxophones   89

7.1   Fluegelhorn   117

9.1   Piano keyboard illustration of a whole-tone sequence   155

9.2   Vibraharp   159

15.1   Piano keyboard illustration of a chord voiced in fourths   259

16.1   Kettle drum   271

16.2   Piccolo, flute, clarinet, bass clarinet   271

16.3   English horn, oboe, bassoon   271

17.1   Piano keyboard illustration of fifths in left hand,
fourths in right hand   292

18.1   Piano keyboard illustration of "E.S.P." notes   305

19.1   Chart of parallel streams distinguishing jazz from rock
and jazz-rock   314

MUSICIAN PHOTOS

Jelly Roll Morton band   62

Louis Armstrong   69

Benny Goodman band   94

Coleman Hawkins   98

Duke Ellington band   108

Count Basie band   130

Charlie Parker and Miles Davis   144

Dave Brubeck quartet   187

Cannonball Adderley, Paul Chambers, Miles Davis,
John Coltrane   213

Ornette Coleman Trio   228

Charles Mingus   244

Art Ensemble of Chicago   274

John Coltrane Quartet   289

John Coltrane on soprano saxophone   297

Ron Carter and Wayne Shorter   302

Miles Davis's electric band   323

Weather Report   332

PREFACE

This book is intended as a guide to appreciating jazz and as a historically organized introduction to most styles that have been documented on records. It includes a thorough discussion of how jazz originated, and it covers all periods of jazz history. However, the book devotes proportionally more space to music since 1940, especially the past twenty years, because recent styles have been routinely neglected by other texts, and because recent music occupies the lion's share of available recording, night club, and concert fare that is likely to be encountered by today's readers. This focus also stems from the observation that two thirds of recorded jazz history has occurred since 1940 because jazz has been recorded only since 1917. So to place greater emphasis on the earliest styles would be to neglect most of jazz history, and to omit music of the 1960s and 70s would constitute neglecting an entire third of jazz history.

No technical knowledge of music is required for understanding the contents, and the text's vocabulary has proven to be comprehensible for high school students as well as college students. Though originally conceived as a text for nonmusicians, the first edition has seen considerable use as the single basic text in numerous jazz history courses for music majors. This occurred partly because of the appendix containing notations of basic musical principles and partly because the book is especially concerned with detailing the ways styles sound and how they can be differentiated in terms of preferred instruments, tone quality, melody, harmony, rhythm, and approaches to improvisation.

For readers who are already familiar with jazz, this book offers a considerable amount of new information that has not been presented in other jazz books.

Any individual or class using this book should listen to as much jazz, both recorded and live, as possible. The book will be an effective guide only if reading is accompanied by extensive listening.

This second edition is similar enough to the first edition that it should be interchangeable with the first edition in jazz courses that have already been designed around the first edition. There is very little from the first edition that is missing in the second. Most of what is gone is material that first edition users complained was superfluous and tiring. For example, I took seriously the frequently voiced complaint that the text contained "too many names." The problem was solved in two ways. First, coverage was eliminated for musicians whom surveys showed to be ordinarily ignored by teachers. Second, many lists of names were moved out of paragraphs and placed in the "gray tables," which readers have praised and requested more of. This made them optional reading and allowed the style characterizations to flow in a relatively uninterrupted manner.

In response to the frequently voiced complaint that users of the first edition were handicapped by its reliance on difficult-to-find recordings, this new edition is keyed to the titles found in the *Smithsonian Collection of Classic Jazz.* This set is available in most libraries and hundreds of personal collections. It is also available on cassette. Users of this book are therefore urged to listen to the set so that the discussions in the text make sense. However, because the Smithsonian is not sufficient for illustrating more than about half of the styles in jazz history, page 432 of this text offers a list of additional records which, when combined with the Smithsonian set, constitute the remaining bare essentials. And, to help readers find these recordings, there is a section on how to locate records beginning on page 395. Every recording cited in this book is available by mail from at least one of the sources described there.

In response to requests by the first edition's users, this new edition has

1) twenty-eight new entries in the glossary
2) extended discussion of how jazz originated
3) expanded coverage of 1920s giants Jelly Roll Morton, Louis Armstrong, Earl Hines, and Bix Beiderbecke
4) more about music in the 1970s, including jazz-rock and the AACM
5) chapter-end summaries

6) point-by-point differentiation of styles
7) more analysis of classic recordings
8) additional "gray tables" of personnel and influences
9) more use of boldface to highlight important points that otherwise remain buried in paragraphs and fail to jump out at the reader

To accommodate the expansion while remaining within length restrictions imposed by the publisher, the first edition's fifty-two page discography has been moved to a new, one-hundred page *Teacher's Manual, Discography, and Test Bank.* The record listings in it have been updated and expanded. (This loss to the main text is partly justified by survey results that showed students to hardly ever use the discography.) The *Teacher's Manual* is available, at no cost to instructors, through the publisher's sales representatives.

Eighty percent of the text has been rewritten for greater readability, and, though basically retaining the first edition's content, many sections now include additional observations and summaries of style characteristics.

Many new photos appear in this edition, and, to increase their educational value, many were given captions that convey historical perspective for the pictured players.

The "For Musicians" appendix now contains

1) additional examples of ride rhythms
2) transcriptions of jazz-rock drumming, showing the continuity between Sly Stone and Herbie Hancock bands
3) an additional example of twelve-bar blues comping

Despite the above changes, the layout and content of the text remains basically intact from the first edition. Reorganization has simply moved all chapter numbers one number further after the insertion of the new Origins of Jazz chapter, and it has

1) grouped Sun Ra, The Art Ensemble of Chicago and the AACM together with new sections on Anthony Braxton and the World Saxophone Quartet
2) moved Cecil Taylor to a free jazz chapter with Ornette Coleman, Don Cherry, and Albert Ayler
3) moved Bill Evans to a chapter of his own, with Evans disciples Herbie Hancock, Chick Corea, and Keith Jarrett being pulled out of the second Miles Davis chapter for placement with Evans
4) placed Miles Davis sidemen Wayne Shorter, Ron Carter, and

Tony Williams in a chapter to themselves instead of their being in a second Davis chapter

5) combined Weather Report and the electric Miles Davis material with new sections on jazz-rock, John McLaughlin, Larry Coryell, Don Ellis, Joe Zawinul, and Jaco Pastorius

6) broken coverage of the 1950s into three chapters:
    a) cool (Tristano, Birth of the Cool, and West Coast)
    b) hard bop
    c) Miles Davis

ACKNOWLEDGMENTS

In preparation of this second edition of *Jazz Styles* I was blessed with the kindness of numerous individuals. The following people took time out of their own busy schedules to comment on my ideas and to share their own observations with me. The thinking of Harvey Pekar pervades this book. In fact, the only sections in which discussion with Pekar was not extensive were Appreciating Jazz Improvisation and the appendices. Pekar generously shared his rare records with me and even arranged purchase of collectors' items that helped us pin down obscure details of stylistic influences.

I am very grateful to Chuck Braman, whose musical insights and skillful editing of several drafts reduced the pain of writing.

Throughout the revision process I have been very fortunate to have the friendship and professional support of Bruce Kennan, whose knowledge of the college book publishing business combined beautifully with his love of jazz and understanding of my work. His concrete layout and format ideas provided clarity and practicality precisely when I needed them the most. Bruce also wrote most of the Ellington drummers coverage.

I thank Bill Anderson for keeping me current in the quick-changing jazz record market. He expanded, updated, and proofread the hundreds of record citations for the discography in the teacher's manual. Bill also influenced my thinking about the Second Chicago School chapter.

I thank these people for generously supplying musician photos: Bill Smith and *CODA*, Duncan Scheidt, Frank Driggs, and Mark Vinci.

Appreciation is extended to John Richmond and Victor Schonfield, who kindly detailed errors in the first edition; Pat Rustici and John Koenig, who collected record sales estimates; James Dapogny and Stanley Dance, who clarified details on Earl Hines, Jelly Roll Morton, and Duke Ellington for me; George Simon, who helped me pin down information on the popularity of swing era music; Ira Gitler, who performed an equivalent function for modern jazz; Bill Dobbins, who furthered the accuracy of my modal music discussions; Andrew White, who increased the accuracy of my John Coltrane and Ornette Coleman sections; Wallace Rave, Frederick Starr, and Lawrence Gushee, who helped me lay out the Origins of Jazz chapter and make a very difficult set of ethnomusicological problems comprehensible (Rave also made helpful suggestions for the jazz-rock coverage); Lewis Porter, who detailed problems in the first edition and helped evaluate many of my ideas for the revision; Bob Curnow, who reviewed manuscripts on Stan Kenton and swing eighth notes; Ernie Krivda, who also reviewed the swing eighth-note discussion; Dan Maier and Nancy Gantose, who helped evaluate my ideas about Keith Jarrett; Jonathan Stern, who has been a continual sounding board for my ideas; Tony LaVorgna, whose observations on Don Cherry and Ornette Coleman helped clarify my assessments; David Lee, who helped me gain a better understanding of Charlie Haden's music; Ed MacEachen and Bob Fraser, who helped me evaluate jazz-rock guitarists; Fred Sharp, who helped me clarify the differences between Eddie Lang and Lonnie Johnson, Django Reinhardt and Charlie Christian; Evan Vangar, George Steckler, and Kenny Davis, who helped me characterize Freddie Hubbard's playing; Jay Grills, who provided background on popular jazz-rock groups and got me thinking more systematically about the differences between jazz and rock; Hamiet Bluiett and Oliver Lake, for proofreading the coverage on the World Saxophone Quartet; John Coates, for filling me in on the details of his musical relationship with Keith Jarrett; Jimmy Heath, for giving me further insights about Dexter Gordon's and John Coltrane's styles; Jimmy Giuffre, for detailing his own career and adding information about free jazz; James Patrick, for helping me reorganize the John Coltrane chapter, Jon Goldman and Chuck Mancuso, who influenced my thinking about jazz-rock, leading to my considering ideas that were further refined with the help of Chuck Braman; Kenny Washington, Jerry Sheer, and Mike Wahl, who expanded my appreciation of rhythm-section playing.

I thank the following professors for telling me how the first edition worked for their students, thereby influencing my revision:

Tom Everett	Harvard University
Lewis Porter	Tufts University
Bill Dobbins	Eastman School of Music
John Harding	University of Miami
Richard Davis	University of Wisconsin
Nick Brignola	Russell Sage College
Terry Steele	Slippery Rock State College
Chuck Mancuso	Buffalo State University College
Michael Wright	Buffalo State University College
Wallace Rave	Arizona State University
Anita Clark	University of Nebraska at Omaha
Chris Colombi	Cleveland State University
Chas Baker	Kent State University
Rosemary Snow	John Carroll University
John Specht	Queensborough Community College
Milton Stewart	University of Washington
Ray Eubanks	Capital University
Vaughn Wiester	Capital University
Bud Gould	Northern Arizona University
Maurice McKinley	LaGuardia Community College
James Patrick	State University of New York at Buffalo
James Warrick	Lakewood High School
Tom Knific	Interlochen Arts Academy

George Ward and Chuck Mancuso were helpful in positioning the country music streams within the chart that plots musical streams leading to rock and jazz-rock.

Conversations and proofreading parties with the following people helped tighten the content and improve the phrasing of many pages in this book: Ruth and Lloyd Miller, Sara LaVorgna, Pat McCarty, Anita Clark, Susan Rifas, Morris Holbrook, and Art and Virginia Benade.

In preparing this revision, I am reminded of the help given to me in the first edition by the subjects of my analyses. In person, by phone, or by mail, these musicians helped verify and add to bits and pieces of my original work:

Bill Evans	Gerry Mulligan
Joe Farrell	Jaco Pastorius
Dizzy Gillespie	Wayne Shorter
Benny Goodman	Paul Smith
Herbie Hancock	Eddie Vinson
Stan Kenton	Andrew White
Abe Laboriel	Tony Williams
Al McKibbon	Joe Zawinul

Thanks are due to Pat McCarty and Greg Selker for their music copy work and to Lynn Landy-Benade for graphics in the chart that plots musical streams leading to jazz-rock. McCarty also conceived and constructed the cover art, which was photographed by Dale S. Weiss.

AIDS FOR USING THIS BOOK

Every recording title that appears in this book with an SCCJ designation can be found in the six-LP set of records called *The Smithsonian Collection of Classic Jazz*. Most college libraries and many public libraries own it. The record collection, also available on cassette, can be ordered by writing Smithsonian Performing Arts, Washington, D.C. 20560, or by phoning (toll-free) 1-800-247-5028. Other examples cited in the book are also available from Smithsonian Institution (as cited in the coverage of Louis Armstrong, Earl Hines, Duke Ellington, Dizzy Gillespie, and the chapter on the swing era big bands). The other recordings, however, should not be confused with the titles contained in SCCJ. They are separate collections.

It is promised that eventually every sound on each of the performances in SCCJ will be made available in score form (every horn note, piano chord, cymbal crash in relation to each other). This is a joint venture of the Smithsonian Institution and Schirmer Publishing Company that will probably bear the title *Smithsonian Collection of Classic Jazz Scores*.

The book that you are now holding in your hand means little if it is not accompanied by the sounds it describes. Any class using this book as their basic course text should be given access to the SCCJ and all the albums listed in the Small Basic Collection on page 432. Together, they constitute a bare minimum exposure to the most historically significant jazz styles. See page 395 for an explanation of how to find the records that are cited in this book.

The *Teacher's Manual, Discography, and Test Bank for Jazz Styles, 2nd Ed.* supplies detailed record information for most citations that are made in the text. Sufficient detail is presented to enable you to identify the music when it appears in reissued form under a different album title. The discography also features listings of Count Basie and Stan Kenton records organized by arranger. Some sections of the discography are organized to document origins or influence of a particular style. For example, rare Blue Mitchell, Cal Tjader, and Herbie Mann albums are listed to document the formative years of Chick Corea's style. Other LPs are listed to document the influence of the mid-1960s Miles Davis rhythm section style.

The 100-page Prentice-Hall teacher's manual (free to instructors via sales representatives or by writing College Marketing, Prentice-Hall, Inc., Englewood Cliffs, New Jersey 07632) has a companion volume that is a 200-page book called *How to Teach Jazz History: A Teacher's Manual and Test Bank* (available from the National Association of Jazz Educators, Box 724, Manhattan, Kansas 66502). It details numerous lecture-demonstration ideas as well as providing essay exams and listening exams for every chapter of this textbook.

chapter 1
INTRODUCTION

Jazz is a broad stream of musical styles which originated in America. Though primarily black music and urban, jazz is played by all races and can be found in some rural areas as well as in more than half of the world's major cities.

An essential element of jazz is improvisation. This means that each performance represents an original and spontaneous creation. Improvisation is a very demanding activity which requires highly sophisticated talents, and jazz stands out as the most developed improvisational music of the twentieth century.

Jazz is not popular music, but it has had a significant impact on popular music. For example, combo and big band jazz styles have been employed in the accompaniments for pop singers and dancers, especially in stage shows. The Las Vegas stage show format forms a large portion of night club and television fare, and musicians with jazz backgrounds write, conduct, and perform the music for many of these productions.

Jazz has influenced the styles used in background music for films and television. The influence of jazz on Broadway musical shows is also extensive. Jazz flavor is displayed in accompaniments, especially the melodic figures assigned to trumpets, trombones, and saxophones. The style of drumming employed in most Broadway pit orchestras is also a jazz-influenced style. An entire field of choreography and dance style, called jazz dance, has developed.

Thinking About Jazz History

As you explore the musical relationships between styles you will discover a remarkable continuity. Some developments occurred so smoothly that contemporary observers were actually unaware of them until they had already happened. Few revolutions occur in music. Changes appear sudden only to people not deeply involved with the elements of the styles as their proportions are being altered.

When reading an outline of jazz history, you must remember that the central figures did not create their innovations entirely by themselves. Nor did they invent a style simply by consolidating the one or two primary influences I have listed for them. Their work instead reflects the result of many influences, their own ideas, *and* chance occurrences. Additionally, it may reflect techniques which they picked up from musicians in their own hometowns. (Not all come from New York City!) Many of the musicians who influenced greats-to-be were obscure, part-time players who never got much attention. In reading interviews, we often come across names of local musicians and legendary characters unknown to us. Whenever you come across a name like that and say "Who?" remember that the name might represent a very strong player who is far superior to many well-known players.

Jazz styles do tend to flow one from another, but jazz history cannot accurately be described as a single stream evolving from Dixieland to swing to bop and so forth. Nor can approaches used in playing a given instrument be traced to a narrow line of innovators, each of whom is the sole influence on the next. Nor can jazz history be accurately considered the series of "reactions" to which historians love attributing origins (one style being "a reaction" to another as though musicians collectively became angry and then suddenly fought a style by "inventing" another to oppose it). There are a multitude of styles. Jazz musicians find their own favorite way of playing. Sometimes they are happiest playing within an established approach. (Most musicians simply find an existing style they like and play it.) Sometimes they slightly modify a traditional approach to suit their tastes and capabilities. Sometimes they combine different approaches until the proportions please them. Many players come upon new sounds by accident, find out that they like them, and end up incorporating them into a modification of their past style. Some musicians pursue tangents that interest them and end up with fresher sounds, which, in turn, attract others to collaborate and develop them. What usually lies behind the most substantial and freshest approaches to jazz improvisation is the talent and persistent hard work of a few individuals. A stream may originate in the work of a single individual. Then offshoots of the stream form streams of their own. Sometimes streams remix. To understand jazz history is to hear major styles and then sort out their component parts and begin to realize numerous interrelationships.

Concerning Your Grasp of Musical Terms

An understanding of musical terms will heighten your comprehension of the remaining material, although a technical knowledge of music is *not* required for you to read and understand any of the remaining chapters.

If you find any of the following terms unfamiliar, you might find it helpful to study pages 358–391 before continuing.

atonal	minor
blue note	mode
blues poetry	octave
bluesy quality	orchestration
bridge	polyrhythm
chord	polytonal
chord progression	quarter note
chord voicing	rhythm
chorus	scale
chromatic	scoring
dotted eighth note	sixteen-bar blues
dotted eighth-sixteenth figure	sixteenth note
eighth note	staccato
eighth note triplet	swing eighth note
fifth	syncopation
flat fifth	tempo
flat seventh	thirty-two-bar forms
flat third	tonal
fourth	tone center
intonation	tone color
key	turnaround
legato	twelve-bar blues progression
major	verse
measure	voicing in fourths
meter	waltz

chapter 2

WHAT IS JAZZ?

The word jazz has a variety of meanings, encompassing a broad, changing stream of styles. Definitions of jazz tend to be controversial, partly because people hold different concepts of what jazz is and partly because jazz depends on improvisation, which is often very difficult to notate. The inflections in pitch, variations in tone color, and rhythmic nuances in jazz improvisation must be notated in order to describe and define jazz. This has not been done. The changes which have taken place throughout the history of jazz and the existence of many different jazz styles also make it difficult to arrive at an adequate definition. But there are some traits which characterize jazz of several different eras. Two of these traits are improvisation and jazz swing feeling.

IMPROVISATION To improvise is to compose and perform simultaneously. A great deal of improvised music is spontaneous, unrehearsed, not written down beforehand. Popular synonyms for the verb "improvise" include ad lib, ride, and jam. Some of the vitality associated with jazz may be due to the spontaneity of improvisation. Jazz musicians are so conscious of spontaneity and originality that they try to never improvise in a given context the same way twice. Several versions of a tune played by a soloist during one recording session may be quite different from one another.

For most people, improvisation is an essential element of jazz, and musicians occasionally use the word jazz as a synonym for improvisation. For example, in a music publisher's brochure describing big band arrangements, a note might be included to the effect that "only the tenor saxophone part requires jazz." Or a musician's contractor might phone a player requesting that he play jazz trumpet chair in a big band, meaning the player will be the only man in the trumpet section required to improvise.

The inexperienced listener may have difficulty in differentiating what has been written or memorized beforehand from what is being improvised. If a performance sounds improvised it quite often is, but the best improvisations are so well constructed that they sound almost like written melodies. Many jazz fans solve the problem by knowing that, in most performances when a tune itself ends, what follows is improvised. It is all improvised until that same tune begins again. In the case of large jazz ensembles where written arrangements are required and the players sit down in front of music stands, the audience knows that a player is improvising when he stands up alone and solos. Most of the remaining music in that case is read from written arrangements. And, of course, any lines played in unison by several players must have been prepared beforehand, not improvised in performance. (Do not let the emphasis on improvisation lead you to think that small jazz groups are without arrangements. Though arrangements themselves are often improvised during performance, bands which do not use written arrangements do work out some passages in advance. For example, melodies are often played in unison or in harmony after they have been rehearsed. Introductions and endings are occasionally rehearsed, memorized, and used again and again.)

SWING FEELING The following discussion presents several different views regarding what jazz is. Some of the views allow music which bears no jazz swing feeling to be called jazz. Some views allow nonimprovised music to be called jazz. As a foundation for describing jazz swing feeling, elements are listed which I think contribute to swing feeling in performances of both jazz and non-jazz styles.

If music makes you want to dance, clap your hands, or tap your feet, it possesses what many people call a swinging feeling. This effect can be created in almost any kind of music, not just in jazz. Music that keeps a relatively steady beat and is performed with great spirit seems buoyant. In that sense, many non-jazz performances can be described as swinging. But to specify the unique ways in which an effective jazz performance swings, we must outline both the general characteristics of swinging and those characteristics specific to jazz swing feeling.

Swing is a rhythmic phenomenon which is the sum of several easily defined factors and a few subtle, almost indefinable factors. During the following discussion, the term swing should not be confused with its use as a label for an era in American popular music that began during the 1930s and continued until the late 1940s (swing era, swing bands, King of Swing, etc.). It is also not to be confused with its occasional use as a synonym for jazz itself.

Swing in the General Sense

One of the easily defined factors contributing to the phenomenon of swing feeling is **constant tempo.** In jazz, a steady beat is nearly always maintained. In symphonic music, the adherence to steady tempo is less rigid. Constant tempo brings a certain momentum to music, and the momentum achieved by the jazz practice of rigidly maintaining tempo from start to finish for each piece is essential to swing feeling. (Note that this is not recognized as a factor in swing feeling by those who feel that swinging is achieved partly by slight alterations in tempo and nonsynchronization of players.)

Another easily defined element of swing feeling is **cohesive group sound.** This is achieved when every member's playing is precisely synchronized with that of every other member. The different members need not be playing the same rhythms in unison, but each player must execute the rhythms of his part with great precision in relation to the beat and the sounds of the other instruments. A group cannot swing if its members are not playing closely together. (Note that this is solely a rhythmic concept. Musicians can play out of tune with each other yet still swing.)

Saying that a performance swings means that the group is maintaining constant tempo and that its rhythmic parts are precisely synchronized. But to call music swinging also indicates that the performance features a **rhythmic lilt, something that musicians call edge.** This is a property that is genuine but is very difficult to define. It is also sometimes referred to as a good rhythmic groove. In fact, verbs derived from the nouns "swing" and "groove" are commonly applied to the sound of jazz: "The band is swinging tonight." "That pianist is really grooving." (To a certain extent, swinging simply denotes pleasure, in that a swinging performance is like a swinging party. Both are very enjoyable.)

The **spirit** with which a group plays contributes to swing feeling. Jazz has a reputation for being highly spirited music. In fact, the word "jazzy" is sometimes used instead of the word "spirited." To "jazz up" and to "liven up" are often used interchangeably, and "jazzy" clothes are gaudy or extroverted clothes.

Music that swings, then, is characterized by constant tempo, cohesive playing, and is performed with rhythmic lilt and spirit.

Listeners may be inclined to describe a good performance of any kind of music as swinging if it conveys a feeling of life and energy that compels the listener to respond. This description of swinging applies not only to jazz, but also to lilting performances of polkas, waltzes, flamenco music, Gypsy music, marches, bluegrass, rock, and classical music. This general sense of swing can describe the feeling achieved by a good performance of almost any music that bears constant tempo, cohesive group sound, lilt, and spirit. (Note, however, that to describe a given performance as swinging depends upon the listener. Individuals tend to disagree when asked whether a given performance swung.)

Swing in the Jazz Sense

For music to swing in the way peculiar to jazz, the above characteristics are necessary but not sufficient. Jazz requires additional properties before it can swing in the way that is identified with it.

One important element in jazz swing feeling is the **preponderance of syncopated rhythmic figures** (see pages 360–362 for detailed explanation). Syncopation often takes the form of accenting notes that occur just before or just after a beat. In this way, you might wish to think of syncopation as being off-beat accenting, or the occurrence of stress where it is least expected. Jazz swing feeling requires precisely such off-beat accents. The tension generated by members of a group tugging at opposite sides of the beat is essential to jazz swing feeling. Playing slightly after the beat can lend music a soulful or laid back feeling, and syncopations are especially good at providing this property. Jazz musicians exaggerate this tendency more than classical musicians do, and, if a classical musician were presented with a written syncopation, he would play it slightly earlier than would a jazz musician. (Because rhythm is a matter of timing, we must remember that a player's degree of jazz swing feeling is tied to the success with which he times his syncopations. This means that when a player's quality of swing feeling is appraised, tone quality, note selection, and melodic imagination are all secondary to his sense of timing.)

Another factor contributing to the special kind of swing feeling found in jazz is called the **swing eighth note pattern,** a rather complicated concept that is best described in the appendix for nonmusicians on pages 363–364. If you have not already read that section, you might find that you need that information now.

One more component of jazz swing feeling, this one suggested by Harvey Pekar, is not actually a rhythmic element. It is the continuous rising and falling motion or the alternation of more and less activity in a jazz line that provides **alternation of tension and relaxation.**

Swing in the jazz sense is composed of the elements that comprise swing in the general sense (constant tempo, cohesive playing, rhythmic lilt, and spirit) plus the additional elements of syncopation, swing eighth note patterns, and alternation of tension and relaxation.

As with swing in the general sense, jazz swing feeling exists in the ear of the beholder to the extent that **listeners disagree about whether a given performance swings** at all, and, if so, how much. Note also that within the field of jazz **there are several different types of jazz swing**

feeling. For example, Count Basie swings differently from Bill Evans. Duke Ellington swings differently from Count Basie, even though both players are from the same era. And **not all players associated with jazz manage to swing with equal facility.** Some players sound stiff or stilted in this respect, and the question of whether their performances qualify as jazz becomes controversial.

DEFINING THE JAZZ MUSICIAN: FOUR VIEWS

1) For many people, a musician need only **be associated with the jazz tradition** to be called a jazz musician. He may fall into this category even though he neither improvises nor swings. Defining a jazz musician by association alone is circular, but unavoidable in this discussion.

2) For many other people, a musician must **play with jazz swing feeling** in order to be called a jazz musician. In fact, for these people a musician need only swing in order to qualify as a jazz musician. These people tend to say, "Jazz is a feeling more than anything else."

3) For some people, a musician need only **be able to improvise.** Of course, the people who define jazz this way overlook the Indian, rock, and selected pop musicians who also improvise.

4) Probably the most common definition is that which requires the musician both to **improvise and swing in the jazz sense** in order to qualify as a jazz player.

Much music can be sorted according to the two categories of swing feeling (the general one and the one peculiar to jazz) and the four approaches to identifying the jazz musician. The next few paragraphs illustrate the definitional approaches by highlighting kinds of music in which one or more of the critical elements are absent.

Applications of the Four Definitions

A great deal of music which is not jazz is improvised. Numerous musicians associated with Indian music, African music, rock, American popular music, as well as classical music improvise. The music of India is like jazz in several ways. Much of it is improvised, there is much syncopation, and a performer creates his own personal style. The native music of Africa is also like jazz. It employs improvisation; there is much syncopation. It is characterized by extensive repetition of rhythmic and melodic figures. Question-and-answer format is common (also known as call and response, leader and chorus, or antiphonal form). And two or more moving parts create a complex rhythmic fabric. Some solos at rock performances are improvised (although many are rehearsed over and over, memorized and played almost the same each time). Pop singers often improvise embellishments in the tunes they sing, adding their own personal nuances. J. S. Bach, Franz Liszt, and other classical composers were excellent improvisers.

As interesting as many of these improvisations are, few people would claim that this music is jazz just because it is improvised. The musicians improvise without jazz swing feeling. Their music might definitely swing in the general sense, but the absence of jazz swing feeling is critical. So, though it might be called jazz by our third definition, it usually is not.

Music which has syncopated melodic figures and a bluesy flavor is considered jazz by some people but not by others. George Gershwin's "Rhapsody in Blue" is a written piece with no improvisation. The piece is often performed by symphony orchestra musicians whose playing does not swing in the jazz sense. Yet some people consider "Rhapsody in Blue" to be jazz. This is probably because its melodic figures give it a jazz flavor. Another reason is that the band which first performed the piece was Paul Whiteman's, a band billed as a jazz group. Jazz musicians did not, however, consider it primarily a jazz band. It swung only stiffly, and rarely did such jazz members as cornetist Bix Beiderbecke and saxophonist Frankie Trumbauer improvise more than a very short solo. So perhaps the only way a performance of "Rhapsody in Blue" would qualify as jazz is by association with the jazz tradition (first definition). If it were called jazz because of its syncopations and bluesy melodic figures, any performance of a jazzy piece should also be called jazz. (If Paul Whiteman's band did swing, and the pianist did improvise some portion of "Rhapsody in Blue," then such a hypothetical performance would qualify as jazz by our fourth definition.)

How would you classify an improvisationless performance by a jazz band? Several Stan Kenton big band performances contain no improvised solos (Robert Graettinger's "City of Glass," a Kenton LP of Christmas carols, an album of national anthems, etc.). Yet the band is associated with the jazz tradition and can swing in the jazz sense if it chooses. Kenton's musicians are capable of both improvising and swinging, but on these albums they are not improvising and sometimes not swinging either. Therefore those performances would qualify as jazz by the first definition, but not by the others.

How would you classify those players who swing but have questionable improvisatory skills? In this category fall many nonsoloing members of big bands playing written arrangements which require swing feeling. Some swing well but improvise only a little. Some swing but improvise poorly, lacking originality or authority in their lines. Would you call them jazz musicians because they play with a jazz band (first definition) or because they swing (second definition), even though they do not improvise (third definition)?

How would you classify music which contains swinging improvised solos in a nonjazz context? Most people do not associate the names Guy Lombardo or Lawrence Welk with jazz. That is probably because most of Lombardo's and Welk's music is outside of the swing band category. It is what, during the 1940s, was called the sweet band category. Yet both Guy Lombardo and Lawrence Welk have at various times had good jazz soloists with their bands. Those soloists did not play often, but they did occasionally improvise swinging jazz solos. Here then is an example of jazz (fourth definition) in what, by association alone (first definition), is definitely a non-jazz context.

Lukas Foss and John Cage are mid-twentieth-century composer-performers who employ improvisation in their pieces. Their music is associated primarily with symphony orchestra composers and musicians, the category most people call classical music. (Classical is also a term attached to the period of music during which Mozart, Haydn, and Beethoven were active: the second half of the eighteenth and the early part of the nineteenth centuries.) The improvised portions of their pieces rarely swing in either the general sense or in the jazz sense. Because the music is improvised, someone might want to call it jazz by our third definition. But the music of Foss and Cage is an example of improvisational music which very few people, if any, ever call jazz.

Several important musicians of what was considered the avant-garde during the 1950s and 60s play with unusual rhythmic style. Pianist Cecil Taylor and saxophonists Ornette Coleman and Albert Ayler were all said to have lacked jazz swing feeling. They definitely swung, however, in the general sense of the term (constant tempo, cohesive playing, rhythmic lilt, spirit). These musicians were also definitely associated with the jazz tradition (first definition) and their music was largely spontaneous (third definition). Yet many listeners refused to call them jazz musicians. Perhaps those listeners were using the fourth definition (that requires the musician both to play with jazz swing feeling and to improvise).

So you see that defining jazz and classifying musicians is a sticky matter. However, if you feel compelled to do it, some guidelines are available, and they are routinely used by listeners even when not explicitly cited. Additionally these schemes give us a summary of what makes jazz distinctive from other kinds of music. So, despite the overlaps and the labelling problems, jazz can be defined.

Jazz is a word that has been applied very loosely throughout this century. Musicologists routinely confuse jazz with popular music. Apparently they do not know where to place jazz, but they do not feel comfortable classifying it with classical or "serious" music, and, because they do not give it a category of its own, jazz often gets thrown in with popular music. This compromise is unfortunate because the word "popular" can easily be defined by record sales, and fewer than a couple dozen jazz instrumentals have sold a million or more copies in the entire history of jazz. So, by a statistical definition of "popular," jazz does not fit. Some of the confusion might stem from the fact that, during the 1920s, it was often used as a synonym for popular music as a whole and was not limited to improvised music that swung. For example, a famous Al Jolson movie about a vaudeville singer was called "The Jazz Singer," even though the movie had nothing to do with improvised or swinging music. (Subsequent remakes of the movie starring Danny Thomas and Neil Diamond have also had nothing to do with jazz. They were about pop singers.) Having journalists and fiction writers dub the 1920s as "The Jazz Age" has added to the confusion surrounding what jazz is. (In fact, even today, much of the public thinks jazz is only the music ordinarily associated with "The Roaring Twenties." This conjures visions of musicians playing in speak-easies and wearing red-and-white striped clothing, visions that define jazz to many people at conventions, baseball games, and celebrations for the opening of new auto showrooms.)

Even during the 1960s and 70s, the term jazz was applied to a much broader spectrum of music than most jazz musicians ordinarily include. *Playboy* magazine used to poll its readers for their favorite jazz groups, and, more than once, those readers called the top jazz vocal group Peter, Paul, and Mary—a well-known folk music act that had no connection with jazz. Then, in the popularity rankings in *Billboard* magazine's jazz category, Isaac Hayes records sometimes appeared, despite the fact that Isaac Hayes is a popular singer, not a jazz musician.

Jazz is not folk music. Playing jazz requires far more training than folk music requires, and jazz is more complex than any folk music. Jazz is not African folk music, either, though jazz does have roots in African music. Nor is jazz "black classical music" (a category invented by writers who did not fully understand the musical origins of jazz or the differences between African music and American music). Jazz resulted from mixing black and white musical traditions. It has never been an exclusively black music, though most of the major innovators have been black. Jazz did not come from Africa. It came from America. This will become much clearer once you have studied the discussion of origins on pages 43–54.

chapter 3
APPRECIATING JAZZ IMPROVISATION

Listening to jazz improvisation is a demanding task. But with knowledge and practice, it can also be one of the most pleasurable experiences available to your ears. To appreciate what the jazz improviser does requires knowing some of what he knows. So, in addition to suggesting listening techniques, this chapter provides descriptions of the roles of different instruments in a jazz combo, the skills possessed by an improviser, alternatives available to the improviser and, finally, an introduction to chord progressions and tune construction.

For this information to have any meaning, you should periodically get a record or tape and carefully listen for the aspects being discussed. At the end of each section, or at least as often as every five paragraphs, you should stop reading, and listen carefully to at least one good example of the music. (Albums cited on page 432 are meant for this purpose.) Listen for the concepts you most recently read about. This book means little without the actual music it describes. If you plan to read the book as you might read a novel or as you would read a textbook about economics or history, you are doing yourself a disservice. This book is a guide. Try not to fall into the easy trap of treating it as the content of learning itself. Only a small part of the content of learning is found in this book. The primary content of your learning is in hearing the music. The book is intended to make jazz more comprehensible by improving your listening skills. The most important section of the book is the guide to records and record collecting. You ought to buy at least one record recommended for each chapter before reading that chapter. See the guide to record buying which begins on page 392 and the lists of important albums which appear in the footnotes of each chapter. It might also help to study pages 358 to 391 in the appendix before plunging into this chapter.

LISTENING TECHNIQUES

Before reading the description of instrument roles which follows, get a record or tape made between the middle 1950s and the late 1960s, on which only horn (sax, trumpet, or trombone), piano, bass, and drums are playing. It is important to find a recording on which the bassist and drummer are clearly audible. If you do not already have or know about a record that meets these criteria, glance at the following list of suggestions:

1) Anything Sonny Stitt recorded after 1969.
2) Miles Davis albums made for Columbia, entitled *E.S.P., Sorcerer, Someday My Prince Will Come, Kind of Blue, Basic Miles, Milestones.*
3) Sonny Rollins's "Blue 7" (in SCCJ).
4) Sonny Rollins's "Pent-Up House" (in SCCJ).
5) Miles Davis's "So What" (in SCCJ).
6) Any Dexter Gordon records made for Columbia.

First listen to a selection as you normally would. Then listen an additional four times to that same selection: *first,* concentrate on every sound but drums and cymbals; *second,* listen carefully to the soloist and bassist; *third,* ignore the soloists and listen only to the piano, bass, and drums; and *fourth,* ignore everything except the interaction between the chords the pianist is playing and notes of soloists. Finally, listen four more times, each time concentrating on a single performer.

You may find it helpful to **hum the original tune to yourself while listening to the improvisations which are based on its chord changes.** Synchronize the beginning of your humming with the beginning of a solo chorus and maintain the same tempo as the performer. You might hear snatches of the original tune embedded in the improvisation, and you will begin to hear the chord changes more clearly. You will become aware of two compositions based on the same chord changes: the original tune and the improvised melody.

Try to imagine a graph of the solo line. The horizontal dimension of the graph represents the passage of time. The vertical dimension represents highness and lowness of pitch. Your graph can be embellished by colored shapes and textures representing the accompanying sounds of piano chords, drums, cymbals, bass, and so on. The solo line itself can include all the ornamentations soloists employ: scoops, bends, shakes, doits, drops, smears, trills, vibrato, changes in tone color, changes in sharpness of attack, and changes in loudness (see Figure 3.1).

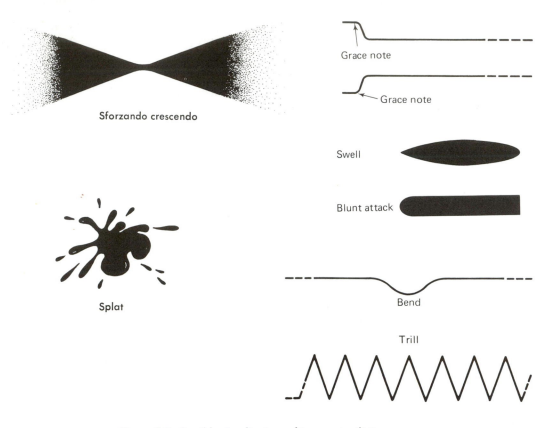

Figure 3.1. Possible visualizations of tone perceptions.

You might be able to imagine layers of sound, one on top of another, all moving forward in time, each layer representing a different instrument. Once you become skilled in visualizing separate sounds, you will begin to observe relationships between those sounds. That, together with hearing chord changes, is an important step in appreciating the interaction between musicians which is so essential to jazz.

Hearing the improvised lines of a jazz soloist as melodies in themselves should help you enjoy the music of most pre-1960s improvisers. Much of the music after that period requires sensitivity to mood and certain specific elements of music. There is less emphasis on clear-cut melody and accompaniment. Sometimes the mood alone may be the single most prominent aspect. The music of Sun Ra, Cecil Taylor, and post-1968 Miles Davis is especially accessible to listeners who are attuned to variations in mood, interesting tone colors, and rhythms. Most jazz, however, can usually be appreciated for a combination of qualities: mood, melody, and particular elements of the sound itself.

Try listening to every note in a soloist's improvisation. You might not be able to detect each note in fast passages, especially those played by saxophonist John Coltrane or pianist Oscar Peterson. But with repeated listening and close concentration, you should eventually be able to hear every note. If this proves difficult for you, do not be upset. Most people can improve their listening skills with practice. It is not uncommon for professional musicians to require repeated listenings before they can account for every note in complex, up-tempo improvisations. Some musicians require years of listening before they appreciate the content of a particular style. Given proper exposure, your ears will get better and better.

INSTRUMENT ROLES   What follows is a general description of some instrument roles that developed during the 1930s and 40s. These roles have to some extent become standardized, although since the 1960s certain jazz groups have made innovations in the use of instruments, so that the roles have not been strictly maintained.

Jazz is partly an ensemble art. The soloist and rhythm section combine to form an ensemble which, though described here in terms of separate roles, attempts to play as a single unit. The *rhythm section* is a group of players, improvising together, who both accompany and inspire the soloist. They provide a setup or a springboard for his lines and can make or break his effectiveness. The following discussion is intended to clarify the role of each instrument in the rhythm section.

The rhythm section usually consists of string bass or electric bass guitar (see Figure 3.2), drums (see Figure 3.3), and an instrument which plays chords, such as a piano or guitar. An organ can be substituted for both the bass and chord instrument, because bass lines can be played on the organ by means of foot pedals. But in spite of this advantage, most jazz organists actually play bass lines with the left hand, using the foot pedals for assistance. This technique restricts the organist to a single hand for playing chords and, consequently, no extra hand for chording behind his own right hand solos. The poor pianos and poor sound systems often furnished by night clubs compel many groups to carry their own portable electric piano or electric organ. Carrying an organ has the additional advantage of saving salary for one man, the bassist, because an organist can supply bass lines together with chords.

Bass   The bassist plucks one note per beat with occasional embellishments added (see p. 426 for notations of typical bass lines). Many bassists pluck the second and fourth notes of each measure harder than the first and third, thus contributing to the creation of a swing feeling. The bassist keeps the beat and gives buoyancy and a low register component to the group sound. This style of playing is called **walking bass.**

Figure 3.2. String bass, also known as acoustic bass, bass viol, or upright bass (left). Electric bass guitar, also known as Fender bass or electric bass (right). Though it looks like a guitar, the electric bass can be differentiated from the solid body electric guitar by having four instead of six tuning pegs, one for each string. Technique used for playing string bass differs from that used with electric bass, but the pitch range and combo role of the two instruments are similar.

The notes played by the bass are chosen from important notes of the chord progression or notes compatible with these chords. The bass clarifies a chord progression by playing its most important notes. Good walking bass lines make musical sense by themselves. In fact, some soloists consider walking bass to be the single most essential sound in the rhythm section. They would play without drums or chording instrument before they would play without walking bass.

Some bassists employ a variety of techniques in their work. Occasionally a bassist will pluck two strings at the same time. That is called a **double stop**. Or he might strum his four strings as though his bass

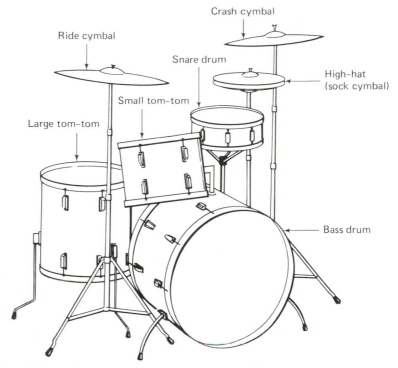

Figure 3.3. Audience view of drum set.

were a guitar. In symphony orchestras, the bass sound is usually extracted by a bow drawn across the strings in the manner of a saw cutting through wood. This technique is called **arco**, not to be confused with plucking, which is also known as **pizzicato** ("pitts-a-cah-toe"). Though most jazz bassists are capable of it, they do not use the bow very often.

Some bassists fill in silences with musical remarks, almost as though they were talking with the rest of the group (sometimes called "broken time"). In some post-1960 groups, these musical remarks have become more important than the beat. The role of the bassist has changed, and now he is often involved in musical conversations as intricate as those typically carried on simultaneously between trumpet, trombone, and clarinet during Dixieland jam sessions. During this period, bassists also played melody more often than they traditionally had. Note also that their accompaniment rhythms became more varied now that they were freed from playing exclusively walking style. (See pages 253–256 for more about this approach, and listen to the bass parts in Bill Evans Trio recordings and Weather Report's first album, Columbia PC 30661.)

Piano The pianist plays chords in a syncopated fashion, providing harmonies and rhythms which complement and support the soloist. These chords are usually played in the middle of the piano keyboard, a pitch range that is easy to hear (see pages 424–425 for notations of typical piano accompaniments). What the pianist does underneath a soloist is called **comping** (ac**comp**anying or **comp**lementing). While playing the chorded rhythms that constitute comping, the pianist uses both hands. But **when taking his own solo, he uses his left hand to comp while his right hand plays melodic lines.**

Comping is an improvised activity intended to enhance the solo line. It also sometimes inspires the soloist, suggesting chords and rhythms for use in his improvisation. Comping involves responding instantaneously to changes in direction taken by a soloist. When the soloist's line suggests a particular sequence of chords, the pianist must follow suit even if that progression is not traditional for the piece and was not discussed ahead of time. The pianist must be inventive when he comps, without getting in the soloist's way. That is a difficult task, requiring a great deal of discretion. Sometimes the pianist may drop out if he feels that the soloist would sound better without him. Piano comping must also relate to the drummer's kicks and prods. Ideally, the pianist and drummer will kick and prod the soloist in some integrated (or perhaps unison) fashion. The members of the rhythm section are constantly providing an accompaniment for the ever-changing melodic and rhythmic directions of the soloist's improvisation. They also underscore rhythms in written melodies and ensemble figures.

Drums The drummer uses his right hand to play rhythms which provide both regular pulse and swing feeling just as the bass often does. The drummer plays these rhythms on the *ride cymbal,* which is suspended to his right over the drum set (see Figure 3.4).

These rhythms are called **ride rhythms.** Occasionally they consist of one stroke per beat (ching, ching, ching, ching), played in unison with the walking bass, but they are usually more complicated, for example, ching chick a ching chick a ching chick a ching OR ching ching ching chick a ching OR ching chick a ching chick a ching chick a chick a ching, etc. (See page 430 for notations.) The drummer may play ride rhythms on other parts of his set, too. In fact, before the ride cymbal came into common use, ride rhythms were played on the snare drum and high-hat cymbals. Note also that the drummer might play ride rhythms on another cymbal suspended to his left, and that the drummer's right hand is not limited to playing the ride cymbal. He can use it on any part of his set, but the ride cymbal gets more of its attention.

The drummer's left hand is free to accent and color the group sound by striking his *snare drum,* on a stand close to his lap (see Figure 3.4). The sounds made by striking the snare drum are often called

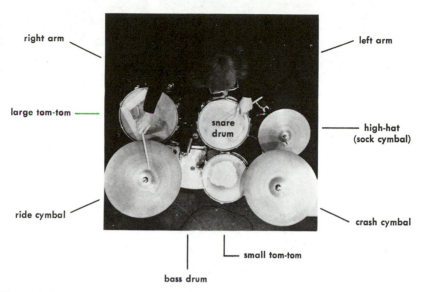

right arm

left arm

large tom-tom

snare
drum

high-hat
(sock cymbal)

ride cymbal

crash cymbal

small tom-tom

bass drum

Figure 3.4. Drums.

"fills" because they fill in a musical gap left by the soloist. The snare drum has a crisp, crackling sound. The ***crash cymbal*** is often struck by the right hand, after a fill, while ride rhythms are interrupted. The crash cymbal is chosen for its tone color and the quickness with which its sound disappears. The ride cymbal is chosen for its tone color and the quality of its "ping." Its sound generally sustains longer than that of a crash cymbal. In addition to "fills," the snare drum is used to provide an undercurrent of activity that seems to be "chattering" while the band is playing. The ***small tom tom,*** suspended over the bass drum, and the ***large tom tom,*** sitting on the floor to the player's right, are also available for accent and coloration.

Accentuating the swing feeling achieved by the bassist's emphasis of the second and fourth beats in each measure, the drummer plays those same beats by pressing his left foot on a pedal which closes two cymbals together making a "chick" sound. This apparatus is called a ***high-hat*** or ***sock cymbal*** (see Figure 3.5). The high-hat will produce a "chick" sound if the pedal is depressed and held in closed position for a second. It can then be opened and closed again for another "chick" sound. A "ching" sound, almost like a chord, can be achieved by bringing the cymbals together just long enough for them to strike each other, and then releasing them to resonate. All this is done by means of the high-hat's foot pedal. The high-hat can also be struck with sticks, wire brushes, or mallets, all of which produce different sounds (see Figure 3.6). The high-hat cymbals can be struck when they are closed or open. Each cymbal in the unit can also be struck in-

Figure 3.5. Open high-hat, closed high-hat.

dependently. Any part of any cymbal can be struck; each part produces a different sound.

The drummer uses his right foot to press a pedal which, in turn, causes a mallet to strike the ***bass drum*** (see Figure 3.7). The drummer sometimes plays the bass drum lightly on all four beats of each measure, and he also uses it for accents.

A drummer can be recognized on a record by the particular instruments he plays and the characteristic ways in which he strikes them. No two drummers have the same cymbal sound, and each drummer has his personal way of tuning his drums, which he does by tightening the drumheads (the plastic or animal hide striking surfaces) by means of adjustment bolts. Drummers acoustically damp portions of their drumheads by attaching gauze and tape. They tune cymbals by critical placement of tape on the underside. To produce a "sizzle" sound they often drill holes in a cymbal and attach rivets that vibrate

Figure 3.6. Sticks, brushes, mallets.

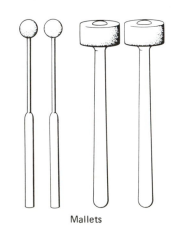

Sticks   Brushes   Mallets

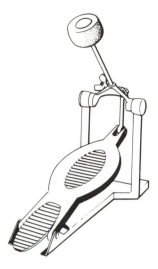

Figure 3.7. Bass drum—foot pedal.

against the cymbal when the cymbal is struck; another technique, one which does not require drilling, is to hang a large key chain across the top of the cymbal which bounces when the cymbal is struck.

Cymbals on a bandstand often appear old and dirty. Very few drummers polish their cymbals because the sound of the cymbal will be changed if any part of its surface is removed, whether it be dirt, corrosion, or the brass itself. In fact, dirt lends a darker sound quality to a cymbal. Many drummers actually let new cymbals age to provide a certain tone.

Even though they come in various brands, thicknesses, and diameters, there is not enough standardization to guarantee perfect cymbals for every drummer. No two are alike, even among the same make and model. Drummers will spend years looking for cymbals which give them the sound they desire. Many drummers collect cymbals, using certain ones for certain jobs, depending on the sound required. When required to play on someone else's drum set, a jazz drummer often removes its cymbals and uses his own. No one knows as much about cymbals as the master jazz drummer.

The drummer can create a huge variety of sounds, depending on what drum or cymbal he strikes, how hard he strikes it, and what part of the surface is struck. Striking the center of the cymbal creates a sound different from that produced by striking half-way out to the edge which, in turn, is unlike striking the edge itself. The sound also varies according to what means are used to initiate it: sticks, wire brushes, mallets, and bare hands all produce different effects. (Listen to Charlie Parker's "Ko Ko" in SCCJ. Drummer Max Roach plays snare drum with wire brushes for the introduction then switches to playing ride cymbal with a drum stick for accompanying the solos. Roach can also be heard contributing spontaneous interjections by striking his snare drum with a drum stick and by striking the bass drum with a mallet that is mounted on a foot pedal.)

What has just been summarized is the basic drum set (also known as a "drum kit" or a "set of traps"). However, most drummers also carry additional instruments such as extra cymbals, tom toms, and Latin American percussion instruments. Until the 1960s, many drummers also had a cowbell (without its clanger) and a wood block.

The public often considers drummers to merely be timekeepers for a band. Though this is true in some bands, throughout jazz history, drummers have also added sounds and rhythms that make music more colorful and exciting. Many of these colorful sounds do make the tempo explicit. However, the point here is that much jazz percussion work does not consist merely of timekeeping patterns. It consists of decoration for the band's sound. In other words, **the drummer acts as a colorist in addition to acting as a timekeeper.** In fact, some bands have employed drummers exclusively for coloristic playing instead of timekeeping.

The drummer not only keeps time and colors the group sound, but **he kicks and prods the soloist** in ways that relate to rhythms the pianist and bassist are using. He also underscores rhythms in the ensemble lines of tunes and arrangements. The conception of jazz drumming changed so much that, by the mid-1960s, the drummer in many jazz groups was as much in the forefront as those instruments traditionally defined as melody instruments. The amount of interplay between drummers and other group members began to equal the amount of interplay previously expected only among front line instruments (trumpet, clarinet, and trombone) simultaneously improvising in Dixieland jam sessions. (Listen to the John Coltrane albums *Live at Birdland*[1] and *Sun Ship*[2] or the Miles Davis albums *Miles Smiles*[3] and *Filles de Kilimanjaro*.[4]) It should additionally be noted that, by his own playing, **a drummer can control the loudness level, sound texture, and mood of a combo's performance,** much as a conductor does with a symphony orchestra. (Listen to the drumming on "Masqualero" in the Miles Davis album *Sorcerer*.[5])

The 1970s saw a large number of combos using two or more drummers. (Listen to the Weather Report albums called *I Sing the Body Electric*,[6] *Black Market*,[7] and *Sweetnighter*[8] or the Miles Davis albums

[1] MCA 29015
[2] MCA 29028
[3] Columbia PC 9401
[4] Columbia PC 9750
[5] Columbia PC 9532
[6] Columbia PC 31352
[7] Columbia PC 34099
[8] Columbia PC 32210

called *Live-Evil*[9] and *On the Corner*.[10]) In some performances, all the drummers would function as colorists. However, in most performances, one player would be explicitly stating the beats on a standard drum set while the other colored the group sound using auxiliary percussion instruments.

Soloist   The improvising soloist learns to be aware of a number of important events. Although he cannot possibly be conscious of all of them all the time, he does manage to respond intuitively to most of them. Much successful jazz improvisation is largely the result of ultra-high-speed intuition. Here are **a few things the improvising soloist tries to do:**

1) *Remember the chord changes common to the tune he is playing*. Occasionally, when the improviser is at a jam session or sitting in with a strange group, he may not know the chord progressions of the tune being played. He might know the melody, but be unsure of some of the progressions. Or he might be requested to play a tune he once knew but whose progressions he has forgotten. In these cases, he listens to the rhythm section and determines the chord changes while he improvises. He can usually guess some of the progressions because he knows certain patterns which recur in hundreds of tunes. He can also determine the chords by listening to other soloists use them. (And even if he does know a tune, he cannot always predict the chord progressions the rhythm section will play. A tune can be harmonized in several different ways which are quite unlike each other. Altering chord progressions, **reharmonization,** is very common in jazz.)

2) *Create phrases compatible with the chord changes*. Both the style of jazz and the individual player determine what notes are compatible with the chord changes. The concept of compatibility is very broad. For example, notes that are definitely compatible for modern jazz of the 1940s are often not at all compatible for jazz of the 1920s. The final decision rests with the improviser.

3) *Edit* his work so that each improvisation represents a clear musical statement.

4) *Think ahead* so that the phrases will fit together well.

5) *Remember what he has played* so that self-duplication does not occur.

6) *Swing* with the tempo of the piece. All jazz improvisers, soloist and rhythm section included, possess the skill of strict

[9] Columbia CG 30954
[10] Columbia PC 31906

timekeeping. When it is said that the rhythm section keeps time for the band, you might assume that constant tempo would not be maintained without a rhythm section, but that is not the case at all. Much jazz was originally dance music, so you might say that the rhythm section was keeping time to make the beat obvious for dancing. The improvising soloist, as well as all the other players, keeps time to himself with a kind of "mental metronome." The ability to keep perfect time with rhythmic vitality enables a soloist to swing without a rhythm section or in spite of a bad one. When the rhythm section is good, it acts as a kind of springboard for the soloist and enhances his sound.

7) *Respond to the rhythmic figures of his accompanists* so that a healthy interaction will occur instead of a monologue.

8) Keep loudness at a level which will *project* out beyond the sound of the band to the audience.

9) *Play in tune and with the desired tone quality.*

10) *Remember how long he has been soloing* so that he can stop before he uses up the time left for other soloists.

11) *Play in the mood of the piece.*

12) *Create something personal and original.*

Rarely are an improviser's lines totally fresh and original. There are recurring themes in the improvisations of every jazz musician. Along with tone color, these themes help us identify an improviser's style. Using recurring themes is an accepted practice. In fact, an aspiring jazz musician is often advised to collect favorite "licks" or "riffs," those very themes and fragments which will later recur in his music and help us identify him. Most improvisers tend to play bits and pieces of lines they have played before, melodic figures they have practiced, and pet phrases of other improvisers. An improviser may actually play portions of a solo he remembers from another musician's recording. (When phrases are lifted intact from another improviser's work, we can often differentiate them from the original by differences in inflection, tone color, and precision.) Sometimes an improviser will quote snatches of a pop tune or a classical piece. The bits and pieces that constitute a solo may not themselves be original, but the way in which they are combined often is.

To understand the mechanics of a sound that a musical model produces and the phrases that he prefers, developing jazz musicians usually analyze, memorize, and then imitate the model's work. Once the player has mastered the techniques required to produce whatever sounds and phrases he wants, he usually develops variations of the learned imitations and mixes them with his own original ideas. The process of artistic development starting with imitation is not exclusive to jazz musicians. It has been employed by artists of all types for centuries. In this way, the same process that allowed Ernest Hemingway to develop a writing style, in part, from the techniques of Gertrude Stein has also allowed modern jazz trumpeter Dizzy Gillespie to develop a new approach using premodern trumpeter Roy Eldridge's style as a foundation.

It may seem curious to the outsider, but the musician's practice of analyzing, memorizing, and imitating is not usually viewed as plagiarism (stealing another's idea and calling it your own), but rather as a necessary first step in the elaborate training process which jazz musicians undergo. If, however, the player never moves beyond the imitation phase and ends up living out his career sounding much like his model, he frequently elicits the dismay of music critics and, to a lesser extent, the disappointment of fellow musicians. But there are exceptions to this. Some players may be so proficient or play with such beauty that they earn admiration despite their failure to develop beyond the imitation stage.

Sometimes imitation itself leads to innovation. For instance, tenor saxophonist Lester Young produced a tone quality that was unusual and highly influential for its time, partly because he was imitating the playing of Frankie Trumbauer, whose instrument was the smaller C-Melody saxophone. Just as important to jazz history as Young was trumpeter Roy Eldridge, who created an innovative style by imitating jazz saxophonists instead of trumpeters.

Jazz improvisations can be very intimate, personal creations. This is especially obvious when a soloist uses his instrument almost as an extension or substitute for his own voice. Pianists, guitarists, and vibraharpists can often be heard humming the lines they are playing. Pianists Keith Jarrett and Oscar Peterson are noted for humming their lines as they play. Drummers can often be seen mouthing their rhythmic figures. Guitarists George Benson and Toots Thielemans purposely incorporate such devices into their styles. Benson scat sings lines in unison with his guitar picking. Toots whistles in unison with his guitar. Bassist Slam Stewart hums his lines in octaves with his bowed bass playing; so does Major Holley. Saxophonist-flutists Yusef Lateef, Roland Kirk, Dewey Redman, Jeremy Steig, and others hum and blow their horns at the same time. The different tone colors a musician creates in this way are part of his personal style.

ALTERNATIVES AVAILABLE TO THE IMPROVISER

Describing what an improvising soloist does must take into account the actual playing situation. Let us examine a few alternatives suggested by three different situations: playing alone, playing with chord instruments, and playing according to chord changes and constant tempo. The following descriptions are separated only for the sake of clarity. The rules listed in each category are not binding and they are not necessarily exclusive to that category. The player probably never thinks in these terms, either. He responds intuitively to the requirements of each situation. Consider these three situations as groups of requirements that build upon each other in the order presented here. In other words, the rules increase as the number of players increase and as the adherence to musical forms and roles increase. The first situation is what has become known as "free jazz," whereas the third situation typifies improvisatory practices employed from the 1930s through many current styles of jazz.

If he is playing alone and not required to follow chord changes or keep time, he is free to play anything that comes to mind:

1) He can organize his notes in a melodic sequence or
2) just place them in a haphazard way.
3) He can use notes common to a single key,
4) switch keys occasionally, or
5) play in no key at all.
6) He can group his notes in a way that implies a tempo, or
7) use no tempo of any sort, either stated or implied.
8) He can play loudly or softly at will.

If he is playing with chord instruments (piano, guitar, etc.), but not necessarily improvising on a tune or chord changes:

1) He must play notes which are compatible and in tune with the other sounds.
2) His notes should not make the ensemble sound cluttered—they must have clarity and balance.
3) He must sequence his notes so that they fit with what preceded them and what is likely to follow. This means paying attention to both the construction of his own line and its relationship to the lines of the other performers. The more he plays with the same musicians, the better he will be able to predict what those musicians are likely to play from moment to moment. That knowledge will increase his ability to construct lines compatible with theirs.
4) He must adjust the loudness of his playing in response to the group sound. Sometimes he may suddenly play louder or softer for the sake of contrast.
5) He might play melodically with such strength that he surfaces to the forefront of the ensemble sound, or

6) he might choose, at any moment, to play notes and rhythms which are subsidiary to those of another group member. Those sounds might help create an ensemble texture instead of a solo line.

If an improviser is playing according to chord changes and constant tempo:

1) His lines must reflect the direction set by the chord progression.
2) He must maintain the tempo of the piece, and
3) swing in that tempo, letting the steadiness of tempo give momentum to his improvisation.
4) He must play notes that fit with the underlying chords. Improvisers are free, however, to initiate lines that deviate from an otherwise strictly defined chord progression. But if the line is to sound good, the improviser's accompanists must listen and instantly follow suit. Frequently a hornman initiates the deviation and the pianist responds with appropriate chords. Or a pianist can suggest alterations in harmony by what he plays. Then the hornman picks up the direction, and the ensemble works together with the alteration. Soloists can also play notes which are incompatible with the underlying chords, while the rhythm section maintains the preset progression. This is called playing "against the changes" or playing "outside," and it is used effectively by some soloists.

Giving the Improviser a Chance

Since jazz is a spontaneous music, dependent on both the inspiration of the soloists and the simultaneous inspiration of musicians in a group, its quality can vary drastically from performance to performance. It is rare for all group members to be equally inspired at the same time. So if you listen to a jazz group playing in a night club, you ought to stay through at least two sets. Give yourself a good chance to hear their best moments. For the same reason, it is also a good idea to hear them on several different nights.

SKILLS POSSESSED BY THE IMPROVISER

Spontaneous music is not totally spontaneous creation. Extensive preparation is required. Before a musician can improvise coherent lines with jazz feeling, he must undergo much training. Some is formal, but most is informal. Jazz players spend years practicing their instruments and learning tunes and the chord changes to them.

Near-effortless command of an instrument is the constant goal of a jazz player, because the ability to play virtually any musical idea that comes to mind, and to play it immediately, is related to instrumental proficiency. It is not unusual for a player to practice by himself for more than two hours a day, and some average four hours a day, five to six days per week. In other words, they play every spare minute. In addition to practicing scales and exercises, the jazz musician invents, collects, and develops phrases he might later use during improvisation. He tries out rhythmic variations of his favorite phrases. He practices to achieve fluency in different keys, in different registers of his instrument, and in different tempos and rhythmic styles.

To adequately respond to the harmonies produced by a rhythm section, **a jazz improviser must be well acquainted with harmony.** So, because the piano keyboard provides a means for seeing and hearing relationships between melody and harmony at the same time, **most jazz soloists know the piano well.** Many jazz musicians who are known best for playing other instruments are good pianists. (On rare evenings, listeners have heard jazz piano playing come from saxophonists Eddie Harris, Gerry Mulligan, Ben Webster, Roland Kirk, trombonist Don Sebesky, trumpeters Dizzy Gillespie and Miles Davis, bassist Charles Mingus, and drummers Art Blakey and Jack DeJohnette.)

Jazz musicians are quite versatile. Most play more than one instrument. For example, tenor saxophonist Stan Getz has played bass and bassoon as well as piano. Drummer Kenny Clarke plays trombone. Tenor saxophonist John Coltrane has played E-flat alto horn (brass instrument of the trumpet and trombone family). Trumpeter Bobby Hackett and tenor saxophonist Paul Gonsalves played guitar. Tenor saxophonist Coleman Hawkins played cello. Pianist Bill Evans played flute and violin. Trumpeter Fats Navarro, pianists Lennie Tristano, Keith Jarrett, Wynton Kelly, and Horace Silver all played saxophone. Pianists Chick Corea and Jan Hammer play drums. Nearly every saxophonist plays clarinet, and, since the 1960s, most also play flute. And each saxophonist also plays saxophones other than the particular one associated with him. Most are capable of performing on soprano, alto, tenor, and baritone saxophone.

To respond in a split second to the rhythm section, the improvising soloist must have **an extremely quick and keen ear for pitch and rhythm.** This ability also helps him imagine a note or phrase and immediately play it. Jazz musicians are so quick to perceive and respond to subtle nuances in style and group direction that they can usually play a respectable performance the first time they work with an unfamiliar group.

Most jazz musicians have remarkably good memories for sounds. The average jazz improviser is able to hear a note or phrase once and then remember it and accurately play it back. In fact, you can often hear an improviser incorporate phrases from the solo that immediately preceded his.

A jazz musician has to **remember hundreds of tunes and chord progressions.** He must be as familiar with pop tunes and jazz standards as he is with his native language, perhaps more so. The convenience of knowing many of the same tunes helps musicians play together without rehearsal.

Another helpful skill is that of **recognizing chord progressions** quickly. Many jazz musicians can play a tune from memory after hearing it only a few times, and they often improvise solos compatible with the tune's chord progression after hearing it only once or twice.

As long as musicians **listen to each other and interact flexibly,** they can play well together. Keeping constant tempo and following agreed-upon chord progressions can help, but the most important ingredient in a good ensemble is each musician's sensitivity to the requirements of the musical situation. An examination of how improvisation relates to chord progressions appears later, but it is important to know that in a performance based on preset chord progressions, each group member is aware of the portion of the tune going by at each moment, whether or not he is actually playing at that moment. This claim also applies to the drummer, a player who need not necessarily know the actual chords.

Even though improvisation is their primary skill, most jazz musicians can also read music. Not all musicians in past jazz history could read, but the widespread use of written arrangements for big bands during the 1930s and 40s made reading an important skill. (This was not necessarily true for drummers and bassists, however. Arrangers tended to write only chord symbols for bassists instead of particular notes. And because arrangers of the 30s and 40s did not know how to write for drums, they often provided no music for drummers at all. So most drummers did not have the same opportunity that hornmen had to become sharp sight readers.)

Basically, **the skills of reading and writing music** can be described as four levels:

1) The **ability to read music** accurately if allowed to practice or look it over ahead of time. Many people call that "reading music."

2) The ability to play a piece of music correctly the first time it is seen. This is called **"sight-reading."** Musicians simply term this skill "reading." When musicians say someone reads, they usually mean he is capable of sight reading. This skill is possessed by all symphony orchestra musicians and by most jazz musicians, but, at least during the 1950s and 60s, it was not a common skill among pop singers or in rock and country and western groups. The ability to sight read saves rehearsal time because it is easier to learn a new piece by reading it than by trial and error ("by ear"). Some people go so far as to say that a player "is not a real musician unless he reads music." I do not agree. Many players who are both instrumentally proficient and compositionally creative are unable to read music.

3) The **ability to make up an original tune and correctly notate it:** "writing music" or "composing." Actually the act of making up a tune is "composing"; notation is more specialized. But the term "writing music" usually refers to the process of making up a tune, and not necessarily to writing it down for musicians to play. Many people who are said to write music actually cannot write down their ideas. In other words, there are composers who cannot read or write music. Pop singers and rock musicians often make up songs and then pay a skilled musician to write them down (not for the singers or rock musicians themselves, but for copyright, sales, and publication—the singers and rock musicians usually teach songs to each other by ear).

4) The highest level of music reading and writing is **the ability to listen to someone else's music and then correctly notate it.** This skill is possessed by people who write down jazz solos they hear on records.

During the 1950s and 60s, it was rare to find rock groups or country groups who could quickly notate their own work or sight read someone else's. Some pop singers can read music, but most are unable to sight read. But it is common for jazz musicians to both compose and notate their own tunes. **Nearly all jazz improvisers are also composers.** Most jazz musicians occasionally write down their improvisations in the form of tunes. Few of the tunes become famous in jazz history, but all serve as vehicles for improvisation. Some jazz players have written every tune on every album they have recorded. It is not unusual to find a jazz saxophonist or pianist who has written more than one hundred original tunes. Though many of them never write a memorable tune, some become so good at writing that they are more important to jazz as tune writers or band arrangers than as improvising players.

CHORD PROGRESSIONS AND TUNE CONSTRUCTION

To improvise is to simultaneously compose and perform. The jazz musician therefore makes up his music as he goes along. **Most jazz, but not all of it, is guided by preset accompaniment harmonies.** The musicians agree beforehand to maintain a given tempo, key, and chord progression. They then proceed to invent their own melodies and accompaniments in a way that is compatible with the harmonies which have been agreed upon. While being invented, these melodies and accompaniments are spontaneously performed. Frequently, the agreed-upon harmonies are borrowed from a familiar melody, and the melody itself will usually be played before the improvisation begins. However, the improvisations usually have little to do with the original melody to the piece except that they have a set of accompaniment harmonies in common. (Jazz musicians often write their own melodies using the harmonies of a popular tune. Then, as a springboard for a session of improvisation, they play their own melody before beginning improvisation based on its harmonies.) Though the original melody is often kept in mind by the improviser as he creates his spontaneous lines, rarely can his lines be conceived as variations on the theme of the original melody itself. The resemblance between his improvisations and the original melody, if there is any resemblance at all, is usually quite remote. (Premodern jazz improvisers have been known to interject fragments of the original melody into their solos.)

To appreciate what the jazz improviser does, it helps to know a little of the improviser's knowledge of forms which, coupled with **adherence to a few unwritten rules, allow him to put together a performance without any rehearsal because**

a) constant tempo is maintained,
b) musicians know many of the same tunes in the same keys,
c) the standard chord changes of these tunes are followed, and
d) traditions regarding the sequence of tune and solos are adhered to.

The remainder of this chapter explains this rule (d).

When a jazz group plays a twelve-bar blues, the entire tune is usually played twice by everyone. Then the soloists improvise on the chord progression of the twelve-bar blues. **One complete twelve-bar progression is called a chorus.** Each soloist ordinarily improvises for several choruses. When he ends his improvisation, another soloist takes over. If anybody misses an entrance or overlaps into someone else's chorus, the chord changes just keep moving along so that the whole group stays together. That twelve-bar progression (and the tempo at which it is played) is law. After all the solos are taken, the whole group concludes by playing the entire tune twice more. (If these terms are new to you, read pages 377–388 in the appendix.)

Some tunes were written in the form of four eight-measure sections. If the piece were in meter of four, and most were, you could imagine each section as a thirty-two beat section (eight measures of four beats per measure). In notating the chords, musicians use a vertical line to separate each group of four beats. That line is called a bar line. (We used the term in our description of twelve-*bar* blues.) The form which has four eight-measure sections is called a thirty-two bar form because it has thirty-two measures in all, each measure separated from the other by a bar line.

The most common arrangement of thirty-two measure forms is one which uses two eight-bar sections, one called the A section, the other called the B section, release, inside, bridge, or channel. The A section is played twice in succession. Then the B section is inserted, followed by the A section again. The sequence is **A-A-B-A**, and thousands of standard pop tunes of the 1920s, 30s, 40s, and 50s were thirty-two bars long in the A-A-B-A form.*

When jazz musicians played a tune of that form, they usually played its melody once before and once after the solo improvisations. Each solo adhered to the tune's chord progression so that a repeating sequence of A-A-B-A was followed over and over again without interruption. The cycle continued A-A-B-A-A-A-B-A-A-A-B-A, etc.

What musicians meant by the term **chorus** was simply that segment of a solo which used the entire thirty-two measure A-A-B-A chord progression or entire twelve-measure blues progression. A soloist might take any number of choruses. The number indicated the duration of his solo. Then he ended on the thirty-second measure of some chorus and was immediately followed by another soloist who started on the first measure of the next chorus. (He ended on the twelfth measure if a blues progression was used.) If a soloist stopped improvising in the middle of a chorus, usually at the end of an eight-measure section, another player would immediately take up where the previous player left off, and the A-A-B-A form was unchanged.

Soloists sometimes trade eight-measure sections with each other: one musician improvises on the first eight measures, another on the second eight, and so on. This is called **trading eights.** The same thing is done with four-measure sections and is called **trading fours.** (Listen to the fourth chorus of "Lester Leaps In" in SCCJ. Pianist Count Basie and tenor saxophonist Lester Young trade fours within the tune's thirty-two bar A-A-B-A construction.) Note that, for a twelve-bar blues, trading fours is more convenient than trading eights because the blues is made up of three four-bar phrases.

---

* A few of the thirty-two bar A-A-B-A pieces found in SCCJ are "Body and Soul" (done once by Coleman Hawkins and once by Benny Goodman), "I Got Rhythm" (done by Don Byas and Slam Stewart), "Lester Leaps In" and "Taxi War Dance" (by Count Basie with Lester Young), "I Can't Believe That You're In Love With Me" (Benny Carter), "Willow Weep For Me" (Art Tatum), "The Man I Love" (Coleman Hawkins), "Moten Swing" (Bennie Moten), and "Smoke Gets in Your Eyes" (Thelonious Monk). If you do not have access to SCCJ, and you do not have examples of any thirty-two bar A-A-B-A compositions listed on page 380, dig through your record collection and look for a copy of "Honeysuckle Rose," "Undecided," "Moose the Mooch," "Roseland Shuffle," "Jumpin' at the Woodside," "Off Minor," "There Is No Greater Love," "Polka Dots and Moonbeams," "Stompin' at the Savoy," "Give Me the Simple Life," or Mel Torme's "Christmas Song" ("Chestnuts roasting on an open fire . . ."). Note that the format followed by musicians recording these tunes might not be identical to the routine described above, but at least their solos will probably adhere to the chord progression of the tune. It should not take much time or thought to determine how the musicians are handling the form. Just listen for such musical landmarks as turnarounds and bridges as described on pages 386–387.

In jazz styles of the 1940s and 50s, it is common for drummers to trade eights or fours with the rest of the group. A soloist, accompanied by the rhythm section, plays for four or eight bars, and then the entire band drops out while the drummer improvises alone for four or eight bars. This pattern repeats over and over so that various soloists are trading fours or eights with the drummer. The form of the tune and its tempo are maintained throughout that sequence, even though no chords or melodies are played during the drum solos. That is how the entire band can begin playing again, precisely after four or eight measures. Each musician is silently counting the beats and thinking of the chord changes passing while he is not playing. At the end of four or eight bars, each musician knows exactly where he is in relation to the beats and chord changes, no matter how complex and unpredictable the intervening drum solo has been.

Manipulations That Throw Off the Listener

When you are listening to improvisations and trying to detect the form of underlying chord progression, look out for three different manipulations which might throw off your counting. First is an **absence of steady tempo.** This is not commonly found in jazz, but introductions and endings sometimes employ it, and ballad melodies sometimes receive this treatment the first time they are played. (Miles Davis uses it for the beginning melody statement on his 1964 recording of "My Funny Valentine.") Jazz musicians use the term **rubato** to indicate the absence of steadiness in tempo. (Classical musicians, however, call that practice "free rhythmic style," and they reserve the term rubato for designating the situation in which the tempo remains steady but part of the time originally occupied by some notes is robbed from them and used to extend the sound of other notes. In other words, classical musicians use the term rubato to indicate that a passage is not played exactly as written and that the relative durations of the notes are rearranged at the discretion of the performer.)

Aside from the infrequent occurrence of rubato, a passage within an improvisation might sound as though its tempo increased simply because of an increased amount of activity. Or, a passage might sound as though the tempo is decreasing simply because of a decreased amount of activity. Most of these situations can be deceiving because, in most of them, each chord lasts exactly the same amount of time as it did when it was accompanying the theme statement, and the chords move at the same rate that was originally set for that piece. **Only the density of musical activity is changing,** not the tempo for the passage of the chords that guide improvisation. It is often difficult to differentiate a true rubato, in the jazz sense of the term, from an alteration in density (what you might call "pseudo rubato"), and some performers use both techniques. (See pages 253–264 for lists of Bill Evans's work in the 1960s and Keith Jarrett's from the 1960s and 70s that contain numerous examples.) But it should not be too difficult to learn to detect two other manipulations: double-timing and half-timing.

When a member of a band starts playing as though the tempo were twice as fast, double the tempo that had been in effect immediately before, the musician is said to be **double-timing.** (Listen to Coleman Hawkins depart from the ballad tempo feeling of the melody in his "Body and Soul" in SCCJ, as does Charlie Parker when improvising on "Embraceable You" in SCCJ.) To create double-time feeling, a soloist might switch from improvising eighth notes to improvising sixteenth notes. A bassist can create double-time feeling by playing eighth notes where he would ordinarily play quarter notes so that he plays two notes on each beat instead of playing only one, and his walking bass pattern might now best be characterized as "running bass." The result of this practice is a feeling that the tempo has doubled, even though there is no difference in the amount of time each chord's harmony is in effect. This can deceive the listener who is trying to keep track of the relation between the improvised solo line and the underlying chord progression because twice as many sounds now occur on each beat, even though the tempo at which the chords pass has not changed. The solution for the listener is to concentrate harder on humming the original melody to himself while the improvisation occurs and to tap his foot at the original tempo to help keep his place in the same manner used before the piece seemed to double its pace.

The opposite of double-timing is **half-timing.** In half-timing the tempo remains the same, but the note values become twice as long, so that the tempo seems to be slower, half as fast as the absolute rate at which chords are passing.

Half-timing is rare, but double-timing is quite common. During the 1950s and 60s, improvisations on ballads were often played in double time. After the tune was played in its original tempo, solo improvisations followed, nearly always in double-time, as though the improvisers wanted to swing hard and were impatient with the slowness of the original tempo. Chord progressions in these performances moved at the same absolute rate during solos as during the tune itself, but the improvisations seemed twice as fast as the tune.

Double-timing is also common in Latin American jazz because the beat in that music is usually subdivided into eighth notes instead of quarter notes. Rock of the 1960s is often in double-time, and some is actually in quadruple-time. **In quadruple-time the beat is divided into four equal parts (sixteenth notes).** Young dancers during the early 1960s often requested "fast music" when in fact they did not want up-tempo performances at all. They wanted rock in double-time or qua-druple-time feel. To the dancers, it was fast.

Another manipulation that often leads the listener to believe mistakenly that the tempo has changed is the **stop-time solo break.** Its name "stop-time" implies that the tempo stops when all group members except the soloist stop playing. (Listen to Louis Armstrong's "Skip the Gutter" in SCCJ.) Actually, however, the tempo and constant passage of chords is maintained, but since everyone except the soloist has stopped playing, we perceive the tempo as suspended (or "the time has stopped"). (Several examples of this can be found in SCCJ. On "Lester Leaps In," listen to the second A section and the final A section of Lester Young's second solo chorus. He is afforded a stop-time solo break in the first two measures of each. The final third of "Cake Walkin' Babies from Home" also features stop-times.)

Stop-time solo breaks are especially effective as springboards for solo choruses. Often, groups finish the opening melody statement with a two-measure break for the first soloist. Many tunes end with a long note held for one or two measures, and this "empty space" in the melody furnishes a good opportunity for a solo break. In other words, a combo might stop playing during the last two measures of a thirty-two-bar tune, giving the soloist for the next chorus a two-measure break to launch his improvisation. If the piece is a twelve-bar blues, the solo break takes place in the eleventh and twelfth measures.

Beginning and Ending a Piece

Other standard alternatives are also available to aid unrehearsed performances. For example, **introductions** are optional. But if a piece is to include one, the performers have at least four stock alternatives:

1) Use the final four or eight measures of the tune, and let the rhythm section rework and play it without the hornmen.
2) Have the rhythm section improvise a common four- or eight-measure progression and, at the same time, a line compatible with it. (Listen to Count Basie's four-measure introduction to "Lester Leaps In" in SCCJ.)
3) Use an introduction that the entire group knows (from a famous recording of the tune, for example) thus including the hornmen in addition to the rhythm section.
4) Let the rhythm section play a one-, two-, or four-bar figure (called a vamp) over and over until the hornmen feel like starting the tune.

Other alternatives exist, but these four seem the most common.

Endings are handled in similar ways. A few of the standard alternatives include:

1) End immediately on the last bar of the tune with no extra notes.
2) Improvise a *ritard* for the last three or four bars, and then sustain the final chord. (Listen to the ending used by Louis Armstrong and Earl Hines on "Weather Bird" in SCCJ.)

3) Sustain a chord or rest while a soloist takes a *cadenza* (an improvisation out of context), then follow it with a final, sustained chord.
4) Repeat the last four bars of the tune, thus creating a tag, and then sustain the tune's final chord.
5) Use a well-known ending.
6) Let the rhythm section play a vamp followed by a final chord.
7) Have the rhythm section improvise some common progression and end with it.

Other styles of ending also exist, but most fall into one of these categories.

Once a progression had begun, its chords and its tempo remained in charge of the situation, providing the organization principles for the entire musical event. Strangers could play with each other and be instantly compatible. Musicians from different eras could play with each other, using the tempo and chord progression as a common unifying principle.

Exceptions to the Rules

Although the tune is usually played as written, before and after the improvised solos, **jazz performers occasionally omit the melody statement.** The 1945 Don Byas–Slam Stewart recording of "I Got Rhythm" (in SCCJ) does not have a return to the melody at the end. Charlie Parker does not completely state the melody in either of his 1947 Dial recordings of "Embraceable You" (in SCCJ). Coleman Hawkins departs considerably from completing an opening melody statement in his 1939 recording of "Body and Soul" (in SCCJ) and never states the melody at the end, either. In 1951, Miles Davis recorded a twelve-bar blues improvisation without a melody, calling it "Bluing," and, in 1956, he recorded another blues improvisation without a melody line, calling it "No Line."[11]

During the 1960s and 70s, much jazz departed from the tradition of improvising within fixed chord progressions and preset chorus lengths. Ornette Coleman and Cecil Taylor popularized such practices. (See pages 230–231 and listen to the excerpt of Coleman's *Free Jazz* album and Taylor's *Unit Structures* album that are in SCCJ.) Miles Davis also explored these practices. (He omitted fixed chorus lengths within one piece on his *Kind of Blue*[12] album–see pages 218–224 for explanation–and he recorded performances that contain prewritten melodies but do not use the chord progressions or lengths of those melodies as strict guides for improvisation—listen to "Hand Jive"

[11] Prestige 24054
[12] Columbia PC 8163

on his *Nefertiti*[13] album and "Dolores" on his *Miles Smiles*[14] album.) Such music is often called "free jazz" because improvisers are free of preset chord changes.

Beginning in the 1960s, **John Coltrane and his disciples recorded pieces whose melodies had chord progressions but whose improvisations were not based on those progressions.** These improvisations were accompanied by extensively repeated, two-chord patterns. In some bands, this approach replaced improvisation guided by standard chord progressions. (Listen to Coltrane's improvisations on "My Favorite Things" in his album of the same title.[15])

[13] Columbia PC 9496
[14] Columbia PC 9401
[15] Atlantic SD 1361

chapter 4
ORIGINS OF JAZZ

It is very difficult to determine exactly how jazz originated. No one knows precisely how the musical culture of African slaves blended with the European musical culture that dominated the American South at the time slaves were first exposed to it. We have no record of how black American music sounded before jazz emerged because little was written down well enough to capture important nuances of timing, pitch, and tone quality and because recording machines were not in common use until it was too late to catch different stages in the blending of African and European musical streams. We will never know for certain how jazz came into being, but the mysteries surrounding it remain fascinating.

Why Did Jazz Originate in New Orleans? New Orleans has always had a unique culture. In the late 1700s and early 1800s New Orleans was largely occupied by the French who maintained a high regard for the arts and enjoyed the pleasures of music and dancing more than their more conservative northern neighbors. In fact, relative to its size, New Orleans had more musical organizations than any other American city during that period.

Another factor that made New Orleans a good place for jazz to form was the city's having been a magnet for freed and escaped slaves in the South throughout the 1800s. New Orleans was especially attractive for its work opportunities, social activity, and diverse ways of life. And the city was convenient to several slave states, actually being closer to several parts of Mississippi and Alabama than to much of Louisiana itself. Much of the South is only a short boat ride or a few days on a raft away from New Orleans because, on its way to New

Orleans, the Mississippi River touches the states of Kentucky, Arkansas, Missouri, and Tennessee as well as Mississippi and Louisiana. Together with the 1809 arrival of many Haitian Creoles and an already high proportion of blacks in the city's population, these geographical conveniences made New Orleans a center for black culture in the United States. And, of course, several types of music were included in that culture.

Not only did New Orleans have a festive French tradition contributing to an atmosphere of pleasure, it also had its role as host to travelers from all over the world because the city was a seaport, and it was a center for commerce because of its nearness to the mouth of the Mississippi River, a flourishing trade route for America and the Caribbean. New Orleans therefore maintained its party atmosphere and had one of America's largest and most famous brothel districts. ("The district," as musicians called it, eventually became known as Storyville, in honor of an alderman named Story whose idea it was to section off a portion of the town in 1897 and limit prostitution to that area. Because of Storyville's legendary importance in jazz history, jazz record companies, book publishers, and night clubs have been given the same name.) The singing and dancing, sex and liquor that was so plentiful in New Orleans was important to the birth of jazz because it generated work for musicians. And, in this way, it furnished a context, in addition to that of church music, for mixing the musical traditions of European colonists with those of African slaves.

New Orleans was a whirlwind of musical activity. Diverse styles bumped into each other, with characteristics of one rubbing off on another. Opera coexisted with sailors' hornpipes. Music for the formal European dances of the minuet and the quadrille coexisted with African music used in voodoo ceremonies. Band music, in the style of Sousa, was especially popular during the late 1800s. There were also the musical cries of street vendors selling their wares.

Another factor that promoted the mixing of African and European traditions was a considerable amount of sex and intermarriage occurring in New Orleans between blacks and whites prior to the mid-1800s. The offspring of these unions, whose ancestry was part African and part French, were called Creoles of Color, or simply *Creoles,* for short.* However, a sharp separation existed between the two groups of New Orleans residents who had African ancestry. Creoles were not referred to as Negro. That term was reserved for blacks who had little or no

---

* Strictly speaking, the term *Creole* originally meant people speaking Spanish and French who were born in the New World. This included French and Spanish American-borns who were white, not just those of mixed blood to whom the term was later applied in a manner similar to mulatto, which means half black and half white.

white blood. Creoles were usually well-educated and successful people such as businessmen, physicians, landowners, and skilled craftsmen. They spoke French. Many owned slaves, and often required their slaves to speak French, too. Children in Creole families often received high quality, formal musical training, some even traveling to Paris for study at a conservatory. Creoles lived downtown in the area of New Orleans today known as The French Quarter. Negroes lived uptown and worked primarily as laborers. Creoles embraced almost exclusively European music. Negroes played less formal music and forms which retained some African elements. Though many uptown musicians received formal training, their music was generally somewhat rougher than that of the Creoles. (Only sketchy information exists about the uptown music of that period, and it remains unclear whether improvisation was used and, if so, how much. According to some reports, however, little improvisation was used, and it was mostly in the form of simple embellishment upon existing material instead of being totally fresh melodic invention.) In summary, some African traditions were preserved in Negro music while many European concert traditions were absorbed and maintained by Creole music.*

The vocal music of the uptown blacks included Afro-American religious music (a compromise between European church music and African vocal style) and work songs that were devised to ease the burden of laborers. Another kind of black vocal music was the cry of the street vendor, a sound which made much use of expressive variations in pitch and voice quality. These kinds of music evolved into another kind of music which was initially an unaccompanied solo form that eventually added the sound of guitar or banjo as accompaniment. Note, however, that accompanying chords were originally almost incidental to the melodic line, being only whatever chords the player could play, not necessarily having the traditional European relationship between melody notes and chords which finally developed into the jazz conception of accompaniment in which the chords actually limit the choices of melody notes which the musician has. Accompanying chords in this early Afro-American vocal style were very

---

* Creole culture is described here instead of black American culture as a whole because jazz first emerged in New Orleans. But it should be noted that New Orleans Creole culture was not the only opportunity for blacks in America to acquire musical training in the European tradition. Long before jazz emerged in New Orleans, there were black opera singers and classically trained black concert musicians in other parts of America. Colonists along the East Coast frequently gave their slaves musical instruction and instruments. (Accounts of talented black fiddlers, for example, are numerous in the history of pre-Civil War America.) Also at this time, scattered about the United States, were black institutions of higher education, most of which offered formal musical instruction. (Wilberforce University, in Ohio, was founded in 1856; Howard University, in Washington, D.C., began in 1867; Fisk University began in Nashville in 1866; Alabama's Tuskegee Institute was founded in 1881.)

simple, and sometimes only two or three were used for an entire song. Lyrics and melody lines were also simple, with long pauses between phrases and much repetition. This is the form of music we now call **the blues**. (See pages 374–379 for explanation of chord changes for the blues and the poetic form commonly associated with it. Listen to Robert Johnson sing "Hellhound on My Trail" on SCCJ.)

Why Did Jazz Emerge Near the Turn of the Century?

The critically integrating factor that might explain the timing for jazz origins is a set of social and legal changes in Louisiana that gradually resulted in assigning the same social and legal status to Creoles that the Negroes had.* Between the beginning of the 1800s and the beginning of the 1900s, distinctions between "pure" and "mixed" ancestry were more and more ignored. *All* citizens with any African ancestry were assigned to the same category. Creoles were forced to give up the favored status that they had acquired during the 1700s and begin living with Negroes. This readjustment was undoubtedly difficult for the individuals involved, but jazz was the ultimate benefactor because the readjustment facilitated the blending of European traditions (as represented by the Creoles) with African traditions (as represented by the Negroes).

---

* As outlined by James Haskins in *The Creoles of Color of New Orleans* (Crowell, 1975) and paraphrased here, France began building New Orleans in 1718, and 147 black slaves were brought there in 1719. There were free blacks there as early as 1722. In the 1750s, France and Spain fought a war against Prussia together and signed a treaty in 1763, with France giving Louisiana to Spain as a gift. But Spanish rule was not firmly established until 1769, and despite Spanish rule, the language and customs remained primarily French in New Orleans. Under Spanish rule, marriage between the different ethnic groups in Louisiana occurred more frequently than it had under the French. Furthermore, the Spanish freed many slaves, thereby increasing the number of free blacks (there were 1,147 by 1789), and, under Spanish rule, free people of color began to be regarded as a class that was separate from the whites and the slaves, with status closer to that of whites. Many light-skinned women of color became mistresses to white men and were set up as second families to the men in separate houses (a relationship called placage). This was especially common when there were more white men than white women. In 1801, Spain ceded Louisiana back to France, but Spain continued to run Louisiana until the United States bought the territory from France in 1803. Another event affected New Orleans Creoles about this time. A slave revolt in Haiti (from 1791 to 1804) against the white French and the Creole planters caused many free people of color from Haiti to move to New Orleans after, in 1809, being forced out of Cuba, which had been giving them refuge. By 1810, the free people of color living in New Orleans had increased to 5,000, making them the majority ethnic group there. The small American white population reacted with fear. They began enacting laws and continued enacting laws for about 100 years which, little by little, eroded the favored status of the Creoles and eventually placed them in the same position as Negroes. The process was slow. As recently as 1830, Creole families owned almost 2,500 slaves and continued to prosper in business. However, by the mid-1840s, life became uncomfortable enough for Creoles that many left New Orleans.

At the same time, the popularity of ragtime music, a syncopated form with Afro-American origins, was influencing the rhythmic character of popular music in New Orleans. Ragtime may have put the finishing touches on the gradual mixing of African and European musical traditions that had been occurring in New Orleans for more than a century already. In other words, the Afro-American vocal techniques affected the way band instruments were played (making them sound bluesy), and ragtime influenced the rhythmic style (making it syncopated).

Ragtime is a label ordinarily used to describe a kind of written piano music that first appeared in the 1890s and was associated with the popular compositions of Scott Joplin (1868–1917). (Listen to his "Maple Leaf Rag" in SCCJ.) It is also a label that has been used to identify an entire era of music, not exclusively written piano music. For example, between the 1890s and 1920s, there were ragtime bands, ragtime singers, ragtime banjo players, and, in addition to ragtime pianists who played only written music, there were also ragtime pianists who improvised.

The word "rag" is a noun identifying a compositional form resembling that of march music and formal West European dance music, but also featuring a distinctive set of elementary syncopations. The word "rag" is also a verb: "to rag" is to alter the rhythms in a piece of music in order to lend it a distinctive ragged-time feeling.

Jazz historians disagree about the role of ragtime in early jazz. Some consider it to have been just one more type of American popular music that influenced the formation of jazz, whereas others consider it the first jazz style. Ragtime was one of the most syncopated kinds of popular music, and, because jazz was known for its syncopated character and emerged about the same time or a little later, it is likely that jazz drew much from ragtime. However, jazz is primarily improvised music, and the extent to which ragtime was improvised is thought to have been limited. Therefore, by the strictest definition of jazz, ragtime does not qualify because jazz must be improvised. And, by the strict definition of jazz which requires that the music possess the swing feeling peculiar to jazz, most ragtime performances again fail to qualify. However, the compositions of ragtime, such as Joplin's "Maple Leaf Rag," did provide material upon which many of the earliest jazz musicians based improvisations, and the polyrhythmic construction of rags may have carried African rhythmic traditions into jazz.

What Is African and What Is European About Jazz?

We do not know how the streams of African and European music blended, nor whether they blended precisely because of the reasons outlined above. In fact, the earliest jazz recordings sound so little like native African music that listeners are inclined to wonder whether jazz had African roots at all, and the earliest jazz sounds so much like rag-time that a few jazz historians simply contend that the European marches and formal dance music, after which ragtime is modelled, are the roots of jazz. ("Tiger Rag," one of the all-time best-selling early jazz pieces, contains entire strains lifted from a piece that had origi-nally been written for a type of French ballroom dance called the quadrille.) Some jazz historians actually consider ragtime to constitute the first jazz style, rather than being only a source. Further confusion arises when it is acknowledged that, in the entire span of jazz history, there are only a few examples of styles which closely resemble pure African instrumental music. We are therefore confronted with the fact that most jazz does not sound like African music. But even the earliest jazz could be distinguished from European music. In other words, jazz has always been unique. Furthermore, most of the earliest jazz musi-cians were black, and almost all historically significant jazz musicians have been black. We are therefore back to the question of what jazz characteristics parallel African traditions and what ones parallel Euro-pean traditions.

To identify the musical influences that probably led to jazz, we must make inferences about forms of music that we know only from a dis-tance. This can be done by piecing together bits of knowledge about musical traditions that we have already studied up close, such as eighteenth- and nineteenth-century music of the English, French, Ger-man, Spanish, and Italian colonists in New Orleans. (European Gypsy music and the various traditions of Eastern European countries such as Yugoslavia, Rumania, Bulgaria, Albania, Greece, or Turkey were not common in New Orleans, and are therefore omitted here.) Al-though we know a great deal about Western European musical prac-tices because we have scholarly documentation, what is said here about African musical customs is based on relatively recent studies of music played in the parts of West Africa known today as Ivory Coast, Guinea, Senegal, and Ghana—music that is thought to typify the cul-tures of blacks who were brought to America as slaves. But because our knowledge is based primarily on observations made during the twentieth century, the following narrative can not perfectly describe the musical tradition that the West Africans brought with them to America in past centuries. It is the best information we have, however.

Let us first consider the question of **improvisation.** Does a Euro-pean tradition for improvisation instead of an African one account for the presence of improvisation as a central element of jazz? The answer is that improvisation probably reflects both West African and Euro-pean practices. The idea of simultaneously composing and performing a fresh melody or accompaniment might stem from the practices of some European-style performers who were active at the turn of the century.

In what ways are African musical performances improvised? The lines of some soloists in West African ensembles are subject to enough variation from performance to performance that we can legitimately label the work as being improvised. This is nowhere near the highly developed level of ever changing improvisation that typified the lines of the earliest jazz hornmen, but it is improvisation nevertheless. Additionally, there is a tradition for improvisation among West African drummers, and because of the drum ensemble's great importance in some West African musical styles, this emphasis on improvisation by drummers might have been transferred to a emphasis on improvisation among early jazz hornmen.

It should be noted that, for the West African singers and the Afro-American blues singers who evolved from them, improvisation did not consist of inventing elaborate melody lines as it did for jazz improvisers. Since West African singers did not usually channel their originality into creating melodies of wide pitch range and changes of direction, they often channeled it toward creatively altering the sound of a single, sustained tone. Improvisation, for them, consisted of beginning and ending notes differently and varying the timing for the alterations of pitch and tone quality which characterized these different beginnings and endings. Improvisation also existed in toying with the rhythms of melodies. Tones would be started a bit earlier or later than expected, or a given tone might be repeated several times in succession instead of being sung only once. Similarly, a tone might be started, then softened, and then pushed again by way of an abrupt increase in volume before it was allowed to end. (Listen to Robert Johnson sing "Hellhound on My Trail" in SCCJ.) These techniques are especially evident in performances of gospel music by Afro-American singers and gospel-influenced styles such as the soul music of James Brown and Aretha Franklin. (It is also likely that such vocal practices influenced the style of jazz musicians who played trumpet, trombone, clarinet, and saxophone. Many listeners feel that instrumental music projects a soulful or jazz flavor when it displays these devices.)

A second feature of jazz is **syncopation** (see pages 360–365 for detailed explanation). Syncopation is the occurrence of accent at times when it is not normally anticipated, and it is the most common rhythmic trait in jazz. Though not unknown in European music (Mozart and Haydn, for example, both used it extensively), it is more likely that the model for syncopation in jazz came from Africa rather than from Europe because it is more prevalent in West African music.

A third feature of jazz is **harmony.** Here, the most likely model is European instead of African. Two- and three-part melodic textures are not unknown in Africa, but African harmonic textures are generally conceived as simultaneous melodies rather than as a progression of chords. European music, on the other hand, has had recognizable chord progressions of the type that jazz uses at least since the 1500s.

The reliance on an often elaborate set of chord changes in most jazz performances is derived from European tradition, but the presence of harmony in much African music probably eased the incorporation of chord progressions into the earliest jazz.

A fourth feature of jazz is the particular way that improvisation is used in it, notably **the collective approach.** The earliest jazz recordings did not contain much solo work. (Listen to the 1917 records of The Original Dixieland Jazz Band, for instance.) In this music, several melodies were often improvised at the same time. To some extent, this resembles selected examples of African music in which each member of an ensemble is free to spontaneously vary his part while performing. It is also reminiscent of informal European dance music and parade music in which spontaneous variation of parts sometimes occurs with more than one musician at a time. This contrasts, however, with formal European concert practice of the time because most improvisation in it was solo, not collective. Note also that most of the improvisation that did occur in turn-of-the-century European concert music was done on keyboard instruments, not on the trumpet, clarinet, and trombone instrumentation that characterized early jazz improvisation. (To hear remnants of the early jazz collective style, listen to the 1924 "Cake Walkin' Babies From Home" by the Red Onion Jazz Babies with Louis Armstrong and Sidney Bechet and the 1923 "Dippermouth Blues" by Joe Oliver's Creole Jazz Band with Louis Armstrong in SCCJ.)

A fifth feature of jazz is **call and response format** (also known as responsorial or question and answer format). (Listen to the antiphonal exchanges between trumpet and trombone sections in Count Basie's "Taxi War Dance" or the "call" of the bassist and the "response" of the horns in the theme statement of "So What" by Miles Davis. Both are in SCCJ.) Jazz historians are fond of citing the Afro-American church as a source for this feature of jazz because the preacher there often sings from the pulpit with the congregation answering. Though this was also common in European church music, the greater predominance of such responsorial singing in African vocal music suggests that the call and response format probably came to jazz more by way of Africa than Europe.

A sixth feature of jazz is the **choice of instruments** used by the earliest jazz musicians. Although African music contains forerunners of practically every twentieth century European instrument, the particular region of Africa that supplied slaves for the New World did not have musical instruments that closely resembled the trumpet, clarinet, trombone, or saxophone which were found in the earliest jazz groups. Flutes and xylophones were common West African instruments. Yet, flute was not used in jazz until the 1930s, and then, even after that time, it remained rare in jazz groups. The xylophone was not common in early jazz groups, either. But its keyboard relative, the piano, was common in early jazz groups, and the percussive, time-keeping role that jazz piano assumed may have been transferred from African xylophone to European piano.

What about stringed instruments coming to jazz from Africa? Evidence exists in that the earliest jazz bands commonly employed banjo, and there are West African stringed instruments such as the halam or molo, which are played by plucking strings which pass over a gourd resonator covered with skin, that are considered forerunners of the Afro-American banjo. There were European stringed instruments found in early jazz, too. The bass viol and the guitar were common (see Fig. 4.1). Interestingly, as with the piano, these European instruments were played in the percussive manner of African instruments. In other words, both Africa and Europe contributed stringed instruments to early jazz.

What about drums coming to jazz from Africa? The drums of West

Figure 4.1. Guitar and banjo (note that the guitar has six tuning pegs, one for each string, and the banjo has four). Guitars appear in a variety of shapes. The one pictured here is a guitar used in early jazz. Electric guitars are usually solid slabs of wood with electronic attachments embedded. Basically, a banjo is a drum with a guitar-like neck and strings. The banjo commonly used in early jazz had four strings, but some banjos have as many as nine strings.

Africa can be found in some modern jazz groups. The drums used in the earliest jazz, however, were European, military-band drums, not African ones. In fact, European military bands and ·Sousa's concert band provided the model for the cornet, clarinet, trombone, saxophone, and tuba instrumentation of the earliest jazz groups. In the 1800s, a substantial number of the black Americans who received formal musical training got it from military bands, all thoroughly European in their tradition and instrumentation. It therefore makes sense that the black fraternal bands that existed near the turn of the century in New Orleans and those which performed for parades, picnics, and funerals, were modeled after European ones.

In summary, **the only obviously African-derived instrument heard in early jazz was the banjo. All other instruments were European, though the manner of playing them does reflect African tradition.**

A seventh feature of jazz is the relative **infrequency of loudness changes** in jazz pieces. Jazz and African music share this trait: performances generally begin, proceed, and end at about the same loudness. European concert music, by contrast, has long explored the dramatic effects of changes in loudness.

An eighth feature of jazz is **counterpoint,** the simultaneous sounding of several different melodic lines. The earliest jazz was conspicuous for the presence of counterpoint and the absence of unison playing. (Listen to the 1924 "Cake Walkin' Babies" by the Red Onion Jazz Babies in SCCJ.) Though it is known for using a variety of simultaneously sounding rhythms, West African music is not distinguished for using several simultaneously sounding melody lines constituting counterpoint. The use of intricately interwoven melodic lines is not common to West African music, although examples can be found. More often, many-part ensembles are made of different rhythm instruments rather than different melody instruments. And, when West African music has more than one melodic line, it is usually created by a leader offering a phrase, and, while the leader pauses, other singers respond to the phrase with one of their own, not with the intricately interwoven style of early jazz lines.

If we cannot trace the presence of melodic counterpoint in early jazz to West Africa, where did jazz get these elements? The answer lies in a kind of music which enjoyed tremendous popularity in America around the turn of the century: the music of John Philip Sousa and other composers who wrote in a similar vein. (Listen to Sousa's "Stars and Stripes Forever," and notice all the different melodic lines which exist at the same time without getting in each other's way. Pay particular attention to the piccolo's intricate melody which is played over that of the brass instruments in the final strain of the piece.)

Techniques similar to Sousa's use of counterpoint had a long history in European music, and it was the Sousa style for this aspect of the European tradition that appeared in the earliest jazz recordings.

A ninth feature of jazz is the **prominent role of percussion.** Most jazz groups include a drummer who plays an entire set of assorted instruments (see page 17 for illustration) and provides almost continuous timekeeping sounds as well as generating musical excitement. Drums are very important in much African music as well. Percussion in formal European concert music, on the other hand, is primarily for emphasis and dramatic effect rather than being a continuous element as it is in African music and jazz. Percussion is important, however, in some European military music and folk dance music. Therefore, the jazz emphasis on percussion is neither entirely African nor entirely European in origin, but its somewhat greater prominence in African music suggests that Africa may have contributed more than Europe did in this respect.

A tenth feature is the attitude toward tempo. The **rigid maintenance of tempo** links African music with jazz. Passages without discernible tempo are almost unknown in most West African music and in most pre-1960s jazz, yet hundreds of European orchestral compositions require speeding and slowing. (In fact, performances of composed solo passages are often praised when they show that the player has taken liberties with the tempo.) Note, however, that European marching band tradition and dance music tradition were both significant influences on jazz and that both traditions emphasize maintenance of steady tempo. Therefore, the jazz preference for steady tempo cannot be said to exclusively reflect African traditions.

An eleventh feature of jazz, one which seems uniquely African, is the attraction for altering sounds by **roughenings, buzzes, and ringings.** Pay close attention to the varied timbres which composer–bandleader Duke Ellington employed in his band's performances, sometimes identifying as "jungle style" the unorthodox growl-style method of playing trumpet and trombone. Witness the jazz musician's fascination for the quality-altering potential which is supplied by mutes for brass instruments (see page 390 for illustrations) and the technique of simultaneously humming and blowing which has been used by some jazz flutists and trombonists. Note the rasping texture favored by many jazz saxophonists in their approach to tone production. Further evidence for this attraction can be found in the quick pace with which jazz musicians began using the instruments of rock music during the 1960s and 70s, incorporating numerous electronic means for altering tone quality. The work of jazz drummers has long been characterized by the use of devices to produce ringings: the positioning of a key chain atop a cymbal used for timekeeping, thereby creating an almost sustained hiss or ringing; the insertion of rivets in a way which allows their vibration to create a sizzle sound.

A twelfth feature of jazz is the **extensive use of short-term repetition.** Though it is found in some passages of formal European concert pieces, extensive repetition of brief patterns is not nearly as prominent in European practice as it is in African and jazz practice. Left-hand figures used by boogie woogie pianists provide a good illustration of this. (Listen to Meade Lux Lewis play "Honky Tonk Train" in SCCJ.) Another example is the jazz drummer's ride rhythms. (See page 18 for explanations and page 430 for notations.) More evidence is offered in the extensive repetition of riffs in the Kansas City big band style (popularized by Count Basie during the 1930s). Repetition of riffs also constitutes an integral device in the jazz-rock style exemplified by Herbie Hancock and Weather Report during the 1970s. In both the Kansas City style and the jazz-rock style, there is often a rocking, back and forth feeling which is projected by the repeating figures, especially when phrases from one section of the band are interlocked with phrases from another. In the Kansas City style, brass riffs are often played against saxophone riffs. In jazz-rock, highly syncopated bass riffs are often pitted against equally intricate drum patterns. These practices probably stem from African music's masterful use of repetition for building and sustaining excitement. In contrast, formal European concert music usually opposes this practice and emphasizes change instead of repetition. It employs change of keys, chords, instruments, rhythms, tempo, and loudness.

A thirteenth feature of jazz is **polyrhythmic construction,** the simultaneous sounding of several different rhythms (see page 365 for detailed explanation). This is more common in jazz and African music than in the concert music of pre-twentieth century Europe. It is therefore more an African than European contribution. Some of this might have filtered into jazz by way of ragtime.

A fourteenth feature of jazz, another that points clearly to African origins, involves the **ways in which tones are decorated.** To help understand what is meant by this and by such terms as tonal inflection, embellishment, and manipulation, keep in mind the several attributes that a tone has:

a) *duration* (How long does the tone last?)

b) *intensity* (How loud is the tone?)

c) *pitch* (Is it high or low, sharp or flat)?

d) *quality*
    1) size (Is it large or small?)
    2) weight (Is it heavy or light?)
    3) color (Is it bright or dark?)
    4) texture (Is it rough or smooth, cutting or blunt, dense or diffuse?)

e) *attack* (How does it begin? Abruptly or gradually? Does it sputter before reaching full force?)

f) *decay* (How does it end? Does it disappear suddenly or gradually? Does its pitch remain constant as it ends, or does the pitch rise or fall?)

g) Using combinations of the above attributes, we can also ask whether a tone has *vibrato* (a regular fluctuation of pitch; see boxed item below) or *tremolo* (a regular fluctuation of loudness).

To understand vibrato, imagine a sustained tone as a straight line.

Now imagine the pitch of that tone oscillating, that is, becoming alternately higher and lower. The up and down motion of the line represents the slight changes in pitch which constitute vibrato.

We often tend to take vibrato for granted, because it can be almost imperceptible. But if you listen carefully to sustained tones in the work of most singers, violinists, saxophonists, trombonists, and trumpeters, you will hear it.

Vibrato can be present or absent, fast or slow, regular or irregular. Many jazz singers and some jazz instrumentalists tend to start vibrato slowly and then increase its rate so that it is fastest at the end of the note.

This contrasts with the practice of musicians in symphony orchestras who tend to maintain an even rate of vibrato through a tone's complete duration. They employ different rates of vibrato for different styles of composition, however, and many use no vibrato at all.

Vibrato is considered an expressive device. It can also be a prime characteristic for differentiating styles. Early jazz players tended to use much quicker vibratos than modern jazz players. The fast vibrato was undoubtedly a characteristic contributing to the popular description of early jazz as "hot," while modern jazz of the 1940s and 50s with its slower vibrato was "cool." During the 1960s and 70s, many jazz saxophonists employed faster vibrato than was common during the 1940s and 50s. Saxophonists of the 1980s often used a regular rate of vibrato, rather than increasing it near the end of the tone. If you compare music from these periods, you will notice distinct differences in feeling, partly due to the vibrato rate.

A decoration of tone that is employed by some African singers, many jazz singers, and a number of jazz instrumentalists is a drop in pitch during a tone's decay. Jazz hornmen refer to this as a *fall-off* (see Fig. 4.2). This is not common in European music.

Figure 4.2. Drop or fall-off

Decorations which precede a tone's fullnes˙ are called methods of "attack." In contrast to the uniformity and simplicity of attacks in European music, some African singers, many jazz singers, and most jazz instrumentalists cultivate an assortment of attacks. One example consists of starting the sound near the tone's pitch, going below it, and then working back up to it before giving the tone its full duration. The result is an effect similar to the arm movements required by a scooping motion, and this tonal decoration *is* called a *scoop* (see Fig. 4.3).

Figure 4.3. Scoop

Some European singers decorate the beginning of a tone by approaching the desired pitch from a pitch that is well below it, then gradually rising to the desired pitch. Though the specifics are precisely dictated for each type of music and identified by technical terms such as glissando or portamento, the effect is essentially that of a *smear* (see Fig. 4.4). Though used in some European singing, it is more plentiful in Afro-American singing and jazz, and, when it is used, it is subject to more individual variation.

Figure 4.4. Smear

Another decoration of tone that occasionally occurs in jazz instrumental practice is a rise in pitch at the end of a tone. (Listen to trumpeter Miles Davis use it in "Solea" on his *Sketches of Spain* album.)

The device is called a *doit*, a term that approximates the sound it describes. (Perhaps you would prefer the spelling to be doyt or "doy-eet." See Fig. 4.5.)

Figure 4.5. Doit

The fall-off, scoop, smear, and doit are all part of the category of manipulations called *pitch bending*. (Listen to Bessie Smith sing "St. Louis Blues" and Sidney Bechet play "Blue Horizon." Both recordings illustrate the Afro-American pitch bending heritage in jazz. Both are in SCCJ.)

What has been said above about differences between European and African treatment of pitch also applies to *manipulations of tone quality*. In fact, such jazz singers as Sarah Vaughan and Al Jarreau are noted for their skills at changing a given tone's quality before letting the tone go. They might, for example, begin the tone with a smooth texture, then make it rough or hoarse, then smooth again. Or they might move from creating a whispery quality to a robust one, then back again. Jazz instrumentalists have long been noted for altering the fullness of the sound as it passes, as well as cultivating varied attacks and decays. Early jazz saxophonist-clarinetist Sidney Bechet is said to have instructed pupils to simply stay alone in a room for several hours and devise as many ways as possible for playing a particular note. Modern saxophonist John Coltrane produced a wide range of sound qualities, from smooth to guttural, from full to shreiking. What these examples illustrate is that jazz carried on the African tradition for improvising on tone quality.

A fifteenth feature of jazz constitutes a primarily African contribution called the **blue note.** This is the sound achieved by playing a few critical notes out-of-tune or "off-key." The blue note's nature and origins are fairly technical, so full discussion of them is found in the more technically geared appendix on page 371. However, a slightly inaccurate but useful idea of what is meant by the term "blue note" can be attained by considering the piano keyboard to represent the entire selection of pitches which musicians are allowed to draw upon. Then also consider that, despite its fairly accurate representation for most European music, the piano's pitch system (of seven white keys and five black ones) does not necessarily match West African pitch systems. Thus, it is likely that when Africans performed European-style music, they probably sang using their own pitch system, and it came out as though they were "playing in the cracks between the piano keys" because that is about where the resulting pitches would be derived if the piano produced finer gradations of pitch than it does. Those notes that came out "in the cracks" are the blue notes. And though not used by all jazz musicians—they are impossible for pianists—they are common in jazz horn playing. (For good examples of such blue notes, listen to Rex Stewart's cornet playing with Duke Ellington, such as "Boy Meets Horn," Miles Davis's Fluegelhorn playing on his *Porgy and Bess* album's "Strawberries" or his trumpet solos on the *Sketches of Spain* album's "Solea." Valve trombonist Bob Brookmeyer frequently records solos with blue notes in them. You might also be able to detect blue notes within the Joe Oliver cornet solo on "Dippermouth Blues" in SCCJ. During the 1970s, Don Ellis played on a specially made trumpet that, by the addition of an extra valve, could produce quarter tones, those notes "in the cracks." Ordinarily, trumpeters had achieved the same sound by depressing their trumpet key half-way, thereby leaving a cocked valve. However, the Ellis trumpet managed the same effect much more reliably.)

It is possible that the blue note does not reflect a compromise between European and West African systems of tuning so much as it reflects the previously discussed tendency for West African musicians to bend a tone's pitch (see page 51). The well-developed African practice of gliding above and below a tone's pitch might have mixed with the less flexible European approach to pitch and resulted in the bluesy quality which much jazz projects. In other words, it might not be flatting of particular scale steps so much as an overall pitch flexibility. By now, it should be obvious that there are several plausible explanations for the origin of blue notes in jazz. But, all the explanations draw heavily from African musical practice. Therefore, the blue note is clearly an African contribution to jazz.

A sixteenth feature of jazz, one whose origins draw upon the same kinds of reasoning required for explaining blue notes, is **the tendency for jazz pieces and improvisations which are in a major key to sound as though they are minor.** There is a fluctuation between major and minor feeling in a sizable number of jazz performances. (Some jazz pianists actually strike several neighboring piano keys at the same time, "crushing" any difference between major and minor.) This also surfaces partly in the practice of jazz musicians and jazz-oriented composers to lower the third and seventh steps of the major scale by one-half step (a chromatic semitone) more often than non-jazz musicians do. (To understand some of these technical terms, you may find it useful to consult pages 369–371 in the appendix.) The possibility exists that in the European piano tuning system, the best way to attain sounds which resemble those of West African music is to emphasize the pitch intervals which the European system calls minor. Therefore, the juxtaposition of major and minor occurs frequently in Afro-American music. (George Gershwin's "Rhapsody in Blue" illustrates the prominent use of this compositional device. It is an especially good example because it manages to sound bluesy without retuning the piano to any West African system of pitch relations.)

A seventeenth feature of jazz is an **attitude of informality** during performance. Both African music and jazz, for example, often have uncertain beginnings and endings for their pieces, uncertainty which would qualify as sloppy performance practice by comparison with European concert music. And during improvised jazz passages, solos often continue long after climaxes instead of stopping, as they would in European composition. Informality is illustrated by the observation that many are welcome to join in making the music. In fact, the communal spirit of jazz and African music often blurs distinctions between performer and listener. Hand clapping and shouting from the crowd are occasionally encouraged, for example. Jam sessions proliferate. Amateurs and professionals often sit side-by-side with the goal of having fun. (The European musician's insistence on perfection and polish make the counterpart of a jam session unknown in formal concert music. The nearest symphony orchestra equivalent to a jam session is a rehearsal, when, oddly enough, jazz jam sessions often constitute paid performances.)

CHAPTER SUMMARY

What?   Jazz resulted from a merging of African and European cultures.

When?   Near the beginning of the twentieth century.

Where?   New Orleans, Louisiana.

Why?   New Orleans possessed a unique combination of
1) a large black population
2) a large French Catholic population
3) much intermarriage between blacks and French Catholics, one group of whom formed the Creoles of Color
4) a large number of musical organizations
5) the city's festive atmosphere
6) a willingness of New Orleans musicians to creatively engage in the intermingling of styles

How?   In New Orleans black music there were African practices such as an emphasis on percussion, manipulations of tone quality and pitch, and a collective approach to improvisation that affected the way European musical forms were performed.

The popularity of contrapuntal march and dance music, band instruments, and syncopated ragtime pieces mixed with the African approaches to performing music.

Elements which European and African music had in common, such as call and response format and different scale types, blended together in original combinations. (See Table 4.1 following and Figure 19.1 on page 314.)

TABLE 4.1. Features of Jazz Arranged According to Cultures of Origin (keyed to pages of explanation)

Primarily African	African and European Blended	Characteristic of Both Cultures	Primarily European
roughenings, buzzes, and ringings (p. 48)	blue note (p. 52)	improvisation (p. 43)	chord progressions (p. 44)
rigid maintenance of tempo (p. 48)	major/minor sound (p. 53)	syncopation (p. 44)	band instruments (p. 45)
infrequency of loudness changes (p. 47)	ways tones are decorated (p. 49)	polyrhythm (p. 49)	counterpoint (p. 47)
extensive repetition (p. 49)		call and response (p. 45)	
prominent role of percussion (p. 48)			

chapter 5

EARLY JAZZ: COMBO JAZZ PRIOR TO THE MIDDLE 1930s

Jazz is the result of a gradual blending of several musical cultures which occurred over a period of a few centuries. The fusion was first recognizable as jazz around the beginning of the twentieth century, but the music did not swing in the jazz sense until the late 1920s and early 30s.

Jazz began as a conglomerate of many styles and continued to absorb new influences and be diversified itself. It drew from twentieth-century classical music during the 1920s and 1940s, from the music of India during the 1960s, and, during the 1970s, from the pop music forms called rock and soul music.

Early jazz musicians often began improvising simply by embellishing the melodies of pop tunes. Eventually, the embellishments became as good as and more important to a performance than the tunes themselves. In some performances, all that remained was the original tune's spirit and chord progressions. What is today called improvising was referred to by early jazz musicians as "messin' around," embellishing, "jassing," "jazzing up."

Early jazz differs from its ragtime, blues, and marching band roots in several important respects:

1) Much of each performance was improvised.
2) Rhythmic feeling was looser and more relaxed, thus anticipating what is called jazz swing feeling.
3) It generated much of its own repertory of compositions.
4) The collective improvisation created a far more complex musical product than was typical in ragtime, blues, or marching band music.

5) There was more vitality and variety in jazz than there had been in its parent idioms.

Combo jazz began in New Orleans, and that city contributed several soloists of far-reaching significance, the best known of whom were Louis Armstrong and Sidney Bechet. The most significant composer-arranger to emerge from New Orleans was Jelly Roll Morton, whose finest recordings were made during the 1920s in Chicago. Regroupings of musicians in Chicago also made several other figures important: Pittsburgh-born pianist Earl Hines and Davenport, Iowa-born cornetist Bix Beiderbecke. Chicago was the site for "The Austin High Gang" to create a white parallel of the New Orleans combo style that is today known as Dixieland. Finally, another important part of early jazz was an East Coast piano tradition that evolved partly from New Jersey-born James P. Johnson and continued through Fats Waller to Count Basie. Let us examine these styles now.

It was in Chicago that important black New Orleans musicians were recorded in the early 1920s. What is usually referred to as New Orleans style is probably not the music that was played between 1900 and 1920 in New Orleans—we have never heard that music because it was not recorded—but rather the music recorded by New Orleans musicians between 1923 and the early 1930s in Chicago. These players, though born and trained in New Orleans, were older and likely to have played differently in Chicago than they had in New Orleans. A major difference is that, according to interview data and a few early records, the earliest forms of jazz placed great emphasis on collective improvisation, with all group members playing at the same time. These early bands tried to have every player simultaneously creating phrases which complemented every other player. We are told that it was common to have performances in which no single instrument took the lead. For many listeners, the greatest appeal of early jazz (or Dixieland, as it has been called) is the activity of several horn lines occurring simultaneously without getting in each other's way. This improvising of complementary lines strongly impressed numerous observers in pre-1920s New Orleans. Eventually, however, roles developed whereby a clarinet would play multi-noted figures ornamenting a trumpet lead, and a trombone would play simpler figures outlining the chord notes, filling in low harmony and creating lower pitched motion.

The black Chicago musicians, most of whom were displaced New Orleans players, strayed from a collective approach to improvisation in favor of a style which featured solos in addition to collective passages. The skills of the improviser who was required to solo dramatically were somewhat different from those of the improviser required to blend with the collectively improvised phrases of other players. The delicate balance and sensitive interplay of collective improvisation

TABLE 5.1. A Few of the Many Early Jazz Musicians

Trumpet	Violin	Piano
Buddy Bolden	Joe Venuti	James P. Johnson
Freddie Keppard		Fate Marable
Joe "King" Oliver	**Clarinet and**	Jelly Roll Morton
Louis Armstrong	**Saxophone**	Willie "The Lion" Smith
Wingy Manone	Johnny Dodds	Fats Waller
Red Nichols	Sidney Bechet	Lil Hardin Armstrong
Bix Beiderbecke	Jimmie Noone	Pete Johnson
Tommy Ladnier	Frank Teschemacher	Clarence Williams
Henry "Red" Allen	Benny Goodman	Meade Lux Lewis
Joe Smith	Albert Nicholas	Albert Ammons
Bubber Miley	Barney Bigard	Cripple Clarence Lofton
Charlie Teagarden	Omer Simeon	Cow Cow Davenport
Jabbo Smith	Alphonse Picou	Elmer Schoebel
Nick LaRocca	Mezz Mezzrow	Pinetop Smith
Paul Mares	Jimmy Strong	Jimmy Yancey
George Mitchell	Sidney Arodin	Earl Hines
Sidney DeParis	Darnell Howard	Frank Signorelli
Muggsy Spanier	Leon Rappolo	Fletcher Henderson
Phil Napoleon	Buster Bailey	Joe Sullivan
Wild Bill Davidson	Don Redman	Jimmy Blythe
Mutt Carey	Bud Freeman	Henry Ragas
	Floyd Towne	
Trombone	Coleman Hawkins	**Guitar and Banjo**
Kid Ory	Jimmy Dorsey	Lonnie Johnson
J. C. Higginbotham	Hilton Jefferson	Johnny St. Cyr
Miff Mole	Stomp Evans	Elmer Snowden
Jack Teagarden	Charlie Holmes	Eddie Lang
Fred Robinson	Larry Shields	Eddie Condon
Charlie Green	Pee Wee Russell	
Jimmy Harrison	Adrian Rollini	**Drums**
Charlie Irvis	Don Murray	
Joe "Tricky Sam"	Tony Parenti	Baby Dodds
Nanton	Izzy Friedman	Papa Jack Laine
George Brunis	Min Leibrook	Paul Barbarin
Bill Rank	Cecil Scott	Zutty Singleton
Tommy Dorsey	Frankie Trumbauer	Sonny Greer
Glenn Miller	Edmond Hall	Dave Tough
Wilbur DeParis	Gene Sedric	George Wettling
Eddie Edwards	George Lewis	Ben Pollack
Honore Dutrey		Andrew Hilaire
	Bass	Chauncey Morehouse
Composer—Arranger		Gene Krupa
	Pops Foster	Vic Berton
Jelly Roll Morton	Wellman Braud	Ray Bauduc
Kid Ory	John Lindsay	Tony Sbarbaro
W. C. Handy		
Clarence Williams		
Fats Waller		

which characterized the earliest form of jazz was, to a certain extent, discarded during the Chicago period of the New Orleans players. Musicians of subsequent eras who played Dixieland tried to recapture the essence of those special skills which make successful collective improvisation possible.

Though much jazz developed in New Orleans, it was not until New Orleans jazz musicians traveled to Chicago and New York that jazz was first recorded. **The Original Dixieland Jazz Band** made those first jazz recordings. This was a white New Orleans band that became popular in Chicago during 1916 and in New York in 1917. Under the leadership of trumpeter Nick LaRocca (1889–1961), the band recorded "Livery Stable Blues," "Ostrich Walk," and several other selections in 1917.[1]

The band usually cited as reflecting the best of New Orleans style in Chicago was a black group led by trumpeter **Joe "King" Oliver** (1885–1938). Having worked with several New Orleans bands, Oliver moved to Chicago in 1918, worked with several more bands, and finally formed one of his own. Oliver's **Creole Jazz Band** was an all-star New Orleans group which, at various times, had most of the best black New Orleans jazz musicians. In 1922 a band led by New Orleans-born trombonist Kid Ory became the first black jazz combo to have its playing issued on record. A group of 1923 recordings made by Oliver's Creole Jazz Band are better known, however, and it is often cited as being the first documentation of black New Orleans combo jazz.[2] This chapter devotes considerable space to the styles of three sidemen in Oliver's band: trumpeter Louis Armstrong, clarinetist Johnny Dodds, and drummer Warren "Baby" Dodds.

During the 1920s Chicago was the center for a very active jazz scene, which could be separated into three main categories. One was the transplanted New Orleans black musicians who were constantly performing and recording. Another contained their white New Orleans counterparts, the New Orleans Rhythm Kings (Friar's Society Orchestra). These two groups of musicians were influencing a third group of younger white musicians, many of whom were Chicago natives. This young white jazz community developed what was called the Chicago style, or the Chicago school. Its music was modeled on the New Orleans style, but sounded less relaxed. Several of these musicians (Jimmy McPartland, Frank Teschemacher, and Bud Freeman) had attended the same Chicago high school, Austin High. They were often called the Austin High Gang—this included Dave Tough, who attended Wayne High. In addition to the Austin High Gang, the white

[1] RCA LPV 547

[2] Milestone 47017 and Smithsonian 2001 (sometimes listed under Louis Armstrong, not Joe Oliver). (*Note*: See page 400 for information about how to get the *Smithsonian Collection of Classic Jazz* and the King Oliver, Louis Armstrong–Earl Hines, and Louis Armstrong–Sidney Bechet sets produced by Smithsonian.)

Chicago scene included Muggsy Spanier, Gene Krupa, Eddie Condon, Mezz Mezzrow, Joe Sullivan, and Ben Pollack, the Chicago-born drummer with the New Orleans Rhythm Kings who became a prominent bandleader during the 1920s. (See Table 5.2.)

Eventually the Chicago musicians and the transplanted New Orleans musicians mixed with New York musicians. By the late 1920s a strong New York scene had developed in addition to the thriving Chicago scene. Key performers in the early combo jazz of New York included trumpeter Red Nichols, trombonist Miff Mole, and violinist Joe Venuti. By the 1930s most of the original Chicagoans had moved to New York.

Many of the Chicago-style players became prominent figures in the next jazz era, the swing era. Benny Goodman and Gene Krupa began their careers playing Dixieland in Chicago. Some big swing bands of the 1930s attempted to orchestrate the style of Dixieland. Singer Bob Crosby had such a big band. The small contingent of it was called the Bobcats, several members of which had worked in Ben Pollack's groups. (With the Bobcats were bassist Bob Haggart and trumpeter Yank Lawson, who, during the 1970s, were joined by tenor saxophonist Bud Freeman, trumpeter Billy Butterfield and others to form the World's Greatest Jazz Band. For the 1970s, that group was one of the most polished organizations of Chicago-style veterans. Their style extended from the Bobcats and its orchestrated Dixieland.)

TABLE 5.2. The New Orleans and Chicago Jazz Styles—Representative Musicians

New Orleans	Chicago
Joe "King" Oliver	Muggsy Spanier
Bunk Johnson	Jimmy McPartland
Freddie Keppard	(Austin High School)
Buddy Bolden	Frank Teschemacher
Louis Armstrong	(Austin High School)
Sidney Bechet	Dave Tough
Jimmie Noone	Bud Freeman
Kid Ory	(Austin High School)
Baby Dodds	Joe Sullivan
Johnny Dodds	Mezz Mezzrow
Zutty Singleton	Eddie Condon
Johnny St. Cyr	Gene Krupa
Lonnie Johnson	
Omer Simeon	
Jelly Roll Morton	
Honore Dutrey	
Albert Nicholas	
Barney Bigard	

Between 1933 and 1935, two other famous swing era figures, trombonist Tommy Dorsey and clarinetist-alto saxophonist Jimmy Dorsey, also employed a big band Dixieland format. The Dorseys became better known as swing bandleaders despite their roots in the Dixieland style.

Early jazz has been identified by many labels which lack standard use. Certain labels have definite meanings for some jazz scholars and musicians, but these labels are not uniformly applied by everyone. Chicago jazz and New Orleans jazz are two of these terms. Ragtime, gut bucket, barrelhouse, Dixieland, classic jazz, and traditional jazz are others. These terms tend to be applied to solo piano styles and combo jazz, to include both black and white musicians, and to refer to music produced by old New Orleans and Chicago veterans as well as revivalist groups. As though this is not already confusing enough, note that the terms "ragtime" and "jazz" have frequently been used to designate all popular music of the period instead of designating just the jazz-related styles discussed here. And the problem has worsened because popular literature frequently calls the 1920s "the jazz age."

Piano We know that jazz piano styles were evolving in places other than New Orleans prior to 1920. In fact, some of the strongest jazz pianists of the 1920s were from the East Coast. Many of them played unaccompanied solo piano. Early jazz piano may have developed apart from jazz band styles.

Early jazz piano styles probably evolved from ragtime. Playing ragtime did not always necessitate reading or memorizing written music. Once the style had been absorbed, skilled pianists emerged who could improvise original rags and embellish pre-written ones. A very powerful style which might have its roots in ragtime piano was **stride style.** Stride piano makes use of percussive, striding, left-hand figures in which low bass notes alternate with mid-range chords together with very active right-hand playing. (Technically: stride style left hand consists of playing a bass note on the first and third beats and a mid-range chord on the second and fourth beats of each measure.) Together, the two hands produced music which you might imagine as a small orchestra with a driving rhythm section. This style is very demanding for the pianist. (Listen to James P. Johnson's "Carolina Shout" in SCCJ.)

Jelly Roll Morton (1890–1941) was a pianist, composer-arranger, and bandleader from New Orleans. Some historians consider him to be one of the first jazz pianists as well as the first jazz composer. Morton was capable of performing in both the ragtime style and the jazz style. He perfected rhythmic techniques that altered the character of eighth-note lines so that they swung. Morton scholar, James Dapogny, has pointed out that Morton used long-short, long-short patterns in playing eighth notes (see page 364 for explanation) and that Morton alter-

Jelly Roll Morton and his Red Hot Peppers, one of the first groups to masterfully combine improvisation and well-developed compositions without losing the spirit of New Orleans jazz. (*Left to right*): Andrew Hilaire (drums), Kid Ory (trombone), George Mitchell (trumpet), John Lindsay (bass), Morton (piano), Johnny St. Cyr (banjo), Omer Simeon (clarinet). Pictured here in 1926. (*Courtesy of Duncan Scheidt*)

nated intensities of eighth notes so that they gave the impression of strong-weak, strong-weak. These tendencies, plus a tendency to reduce the number of notes typically used as adornment, helped lend Morton's playing a lighter and more swinging feeling than was borne by ragtime.

Morton's piano style was quite involved. He often played two or three lines at a time, much in the manner of a band. It was as though trumpet parts, clarinet parts, and trombone parts were being heard coming from a piano! Morton's playing featured a variety of themes and much activity within a single piece using stop-time solo breaks (see page 34 for description) in the same manner as horns in a combo. And Morton mixed ragtime with less formal, more blues-oriented New Orleans musical styles (listen to "Maple Leaf Rag," in SCCJ).

The best-known of Morton's several bands were a series of recording groups in Chicago called the Red Hot Peppers. The imagination of

Morton's compositions and arrangements that is evident on those recordings remains respected by jazz composers and scholars. Morton employed many of the same New Orleans-born musicians shared by other black Chicago groups. However, under Morton's leadership, the resulting sounds were unusually well-organized, though they retained the spirit of music made by less tightly run bands. (Listen to his "Black Bottom Stomp" in SCCJ.)

In summary, Jelly Roll Morton is historically notable because:

1) He was possibly the first jazz composer.

2) He contributed a body of original compositions, several of which became well-known in rearranged form by other bands ("Wolverine Blues," "Milenburg Joys," "Wild Man Blues," "King Porter Stomp").

3) He introduced arranging practices in his small-group performances that became imitated during early stages in the history of big bands.

4) He was one of the first jazz musicians to blend composition with improvisation in an elaborate and balanced way that still conveyed the kind of excitement that had typified collectively improvised jazz. In this way, Morton forecast similar contributions by Duke Ellington, Charlie Mingus, and Sun Ra.

5) He recorded piano improvisations that were well-organized, forcefully executed musical statements with horn-like lines in them.

6) He helped bridge the gap between ragtime piano style and jazz piano style by loosening ragtime's rhythmic feeling and decreasing its embellishments.

(See page 412 for information on how to get James Dapogny's transcriptions and analyses of Jelly Roll Morton solos.)

Earl Hines was born in 1903 in Pittsburgh. (He died in 1983.) He moved to Chicago in 1924, bringing an assortment of different jazz techniques together in the form of one catchy style. Hines's playing had enormous influence during the late 1920s when he recorded with Louis Armstrong and also through his recording of unaccompanied solo improvisations. This impact extended during the 1930s by way of radio broadcasts and tours with his own big band which was based at the Grand Terrace Ballroom in Chicago. He led the band there from 1928 to 1939, and musicians as far away as Kansas and Texas heard his broadcasts. The Hines style affected Teddy Wilson, Nat Cole, and Art Tatum, who themselves became major influences. Hines was also responsible for a portion of the Fats Waller-derived style of Count Basie. And because Hines was a primary influence on Billy Kyle, who in turn influenced Bud Powell, Hines can be said to have affected Powell, the single most imitated pianist of modern jazz.

The physical force Hines employs to strike the piano keys is so great that his music sometimes sounds as though the piano is shouting. (Hines is known to have accidentally broken the large, very strong, bass strings on pianos by sheer force in his left-hand playing. Most people could not break those strings even by smashing a fist down on the piano's bass keys.) Even when Hines plays in a flowery way, a roughness remains in his sound. Rarely is anything sustained, and nearly everything has a punching quality. These properties combine with his method of phrasing to lend a brassy quality to the sound of the piano. Because his right-hand lines sometimes sound like jazz trumpet playing, **the Hines approach earned the title of trumpet-style or horn-like.** His piano lines even seem to breathe at the moments a trumpeter would breathe and contain phrases and rhythms that are ordinarily preferred by trumpeters rather than pianists. This manner stems partly from Hines having originally begun his musical training with the goal of becoming a trumpeter instead of a pianist. And it stems from the piano's inability to be heard over loud band instruments. (This was long before electronic amplification came to the aid of jazz pianists.) To overcome the piano's softness, Hines played very hard, phrased like a trumpeter and began doubling his right-hand melody lines in octaves. (Listen to Hines on Armstrong's recording of "West End Blues" in SCCJ. And see page 366 for explanation of octave.)

The Hines style is the one most commonly associated with the term "trumpet-style," despite Jelly Roll Morton's having previously improvised piano passages in the manner of band instruments. This approach is historically quite significant because, by playing more as a horn and less in the standard piano styles, Hines paved the way for modern jazz pianists who solo with essentially the same conception that is used by jazz trumpeters and saxophonists. It is less flowery and more direct. It is less classically pianistic and more swinging. The Hines approach is more flexible than the rigidly structured ragtime and stride approaches, and, because of this, Hines had greater capacity for conveying a broad assortment of musical feelings.

Earl Hines is known for a sturdy sense of tempo which persists relentlessly despite the many interruptions in melodic flow that he makes. This sense of tempo, plus his insistently percussive attack and varied syncopations, make Hines one of the most rhythmically compelling jazz pianists. (Listen to Hines on Armstrong's recording of "Weather Bird" in SCCJ.)

Hines was prone to introducing new and often jarring ideas into his solos in midflight, departing on tangents the source of which was understood only by him. Instead of maintaining a smooth flow and consistent texture from the beginning of a piece to its end, he filled his work with surprises. In the middle of a piece, he would frequently stop a pattern, cease left-hand accompaniment, employing both hands to seemingly leap all over the keyboard before resuming any repeating pattern. On any of his unaccompanied piano solos, such as "Stowaway," "Caution Blues," "Blues in Thirds," "57 Varieties,"[3] or "Down Among the Sheltering Palms," he pulls a multitude of techniques into play, sometimes all in a single piece:

1) stride style
2) walking tenths (two fingers of the left hand moving in scale-wise fashion, simultaneously sounding tones of about a ten-step interval apart)
3) horn-like lines
4) flowery embellishments
5) octave voicing (see page 366 for explanation)
6) tremolo (see page 50 for explanation)
7) stop-time solo breaks for the right hand (see page 34 for explanation)
8) brief double-time figures
9) off-balance left-hand rhythms which are highly syncopated, seeming to come out of nowhere

Later these techniques prominently appeared in the playing of several generations of jazz pianists. Some historians believe that Hines was the single most pervasive influence on pianists of the swing era (which began in the 1930s and extended into the 1940s), and a few consider him to be the most influential of all jazz pianists. He did not come up with most of these techniques himself, but he combined them in a way that was absorbed by others.

One of the best known products of the stride piano style was New York–born **Fats Waller** (1904–1943).[4] Though his jazz contributions have been overlooked because of his reputation as a popular entertainer, Waller played with excellent technique and a bouncing swing feeling which he used to create countless lighthearted and joyful performances. Aspects of Waller's style were continued in the playing of pianist-bandleader Count Basie. Waller wrote hundreds of tunes, the most familiar of which are "Ain't Misbehavin'," "Honeysuckle Rose," "Squeeze Me," and "Jitterbug Waltz." During the 1970s, an entire Broadway review was devoted to music associated with Waller. This immensely successful show was called "Ain't Misbehavin'," and it revived interest in Waller's work.

[3] *Louis Armstrong and Earl Hines 1928* Smithsonian 2002
[4] *Piano Solos/1929–41* RCA Bluebird AXM2 5518

In addition to ragtime and stride styles, early jazz pianists developed **boogie woogie.** A prime characteristic of boogie woogie is the subdivision of each beat in the left-hand figures so that, in a measure of four beats, there are actually eight pulses in each measure ("eight to the bar"). If you hear a record of boogie woogie, you will have no trouble recognizing it immediately because it has been revived so many times that it has become a well-known and popular jazz piano style. Pianist Pinetop Smith actually entitled one of his tunes "Boogie Woogie," and this piece was later adapted and popularized by trombonist Tommy Dorsey's swing era big band. The leading boogie woogie pianists include Pete Johnson, Albert Ammons, Cow Cow Davenport, and Meade Lux Lewis (listen to Lewis's "Honky Tonk Train Blues" in SCCJ). (Note: Many pieces recorded during the 1960s and 70s whose titles and lyrics contain the word "boogie" do not fit the meaning described here. Like much language in rapidly changing pop music, the meaning of stylistic terms depends on the user and the period of history.)

Trumpet   Trumpeter **Louis Armstrong** was born in 1900 in New Orleans. (He died in 1971.) He left there in 1922 upon the invitation of his former teacher, King Oliver, who had already established a New Orleans band in Chicago. Armstrong eventually spent six years of his career there. His playing with Oliver's band is documented in one of the first recordings ever made by a black jazz band: "Dippermouth Blues" (in SCCJ). The tune's title is derived from Armstrong's nickname, a reference to his mouth being large as a dipper. (His other nickname, Satchmo, is short for a variation on the same idea: Satchel Mouth.)

Before moving to Chicago, Armstrong had been invited to join Fletcher Henderson, leader of the top New York big band. After having played in Chicago for a while, Armstrong accepted a position with that group in 1924, his best-known recording with them being "Copenhagen." In 1925 he returned to Chicago and played with several bands that accompanied dancers and stage shows.

Although some of Armstrong's 1940s and 50s recordings are outstanding, his most significant are the innovative series of recordings made in 1927 and 1928 and billed as Louis Armstrong and his Hot Five (or Hot Seven). Many of Armstrong's earliest recordings displayed him involved primarily with collective improvisation. (Listen to his 1923 playing with Joe Oliver on "Dippermouth Blues" and his 1924 playing with Clarence Williams on "Cake Walkin' Babies From Home" in SCCJ.) But on his Hot Five and Hot Seven recordings of 1925–28, Armstrong's dramatic solo style was showcased more than his collective improvisation skills. The musical approach he refined in them became a model for the swing era.

In the early years of jazz, the cornet was much more widely used than the trumpet. The trumpet's and cornet's tones and ranges are quite similar, and many listeners cannot tell the two instruments apart. Their appearance is also a confusing factor, but one distinguishing feature is the apparent length. The tubing of the cornet, although equal in length to that of the trumpet, is organized so that it looks shorter. Some old jazz cornets are especially compact and stubby.

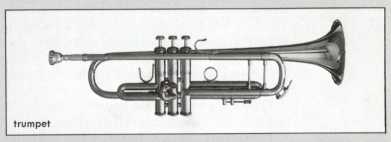

trumpet

cornet

The prime difference between trumpet and cornet, a difference that is difficult to see, is that the inside of the cornet's tubing is cone-like, whereas the trumpet's is more cylinder-like. The technical term for the inside diameter is bore. So, it is said that cornets have a primarily conical bore and trumpets have a primarily cylindrical bore. Although the instruments are played in almost the same way, their mouthpieces are slightly different. The tone color of the cornet is said to be mellow, and that of the trumpet is said to be more brilliant.

Except for Nat Adderley and Thad Jones, most modern players usually use trumpet instead of cornet. Before 1927 nearly all jazz trumpeters used the cornet. The 1930s and early 40s was a period of transition between the two instruments: every band had a so-called trumpet section, but in at least two famous bands, Duke Ellington's and Fletcher Henderson's, the trumpet section sometimes contained more cornets than trumpets. I prefer to ignore this problem and label most cornetists as trumpeters for the following reasons: (a) most listeners cannot detect the difference in sound; (b) it is often impossible to determine from recording data whether a player was using trumpet or cornet on a particular session; (c) the only player I am fairly certain used cornet exclusively throughout his career was Bix Beiderbecke; and (d) trumpet tone colors in jazz vary across a range far greater than that which separates the most pure of cornet from trumpet tones, and actually encompasses the pure tones of both.

The recordings made in 1928 by Armstrong and pianist Earl Hines have continued to impress listeners for decades after their release. By the time these numbers were recorded, both musicians had established well-deserved reputations in Chicago that set them apart from their contemporaries as creators of new methods of improvisation. An especially exciting aspect of the Armstrong-Hines pairing is that, by this time in their respective careers, each man was sporting an original style that had leveled off in its development to the extent that each player had the confidence to confront the other and engage in the give-and-take that is only possible when great self-assurance coexists with sensitivity. Daring explorations resulted as each player pushed the other to take chances while he took chances himself.

One of the most adventuresome of the Armstrong-Hines collaborations is a set of duet improvisations loosely based on the structure of "Weather Bird" (listen to this recording in SCCJ). In this performance, Hines assumes a variety of roles. At different moments, he is an accompanist, a soloist, or a musical dialogist. During the final portion, the syncopations the two men throw each other would probably confuse most lesser musicians. However, these syncopations are handled so well that they increase both the elastic feeling that seems to hold the players on course and the intensity of the entire proceedings. This performance can be listened to over and over again, with each hearing revealing more subtleties.

The first chorus of "Weather Bird" manages to sound like an entire combo because Hines is so firm and insistent in his time-keeping patterns, his unexpected accompanying figures and the countermelodies darting out at the listener and providing a provocative undercurrent for Armstrong's trumpet. When Armstrong lays out and Hines goes alone, as when the two trade briefer and briefer phrases in animated conversation, the pulse somehow manages to maintain the relentless surging that has been apparent every moment since the beginning.

"Weather Bird" demonstrates the communication and remarkably quick thinking the New Orleans collective style required. Yet, it also exhibits a new power and complexity that forecast the next two eras in jazz history. In this way, Armstrong and Hines were leading figures in early jazz and transitional figures at the same time.

At least one more Armstrong-Hines classic is worth mentioning. "Tight Like This," a masterful example of tension building, is a showpiece for Armstrong's huge tone and his slightly behind-the-beat rhythmic approach. Armstrong builds excitement much as though he were ascending a staircase: up two or three steps, down one, then up two again, down one and up two more. It is one of the simplest improvisations he recorded, yet it summarizes one of his greatest skills: tension building with swing feeling.

Armstrong appeared in about fifty movies and sang in most of his

Louis Armstrong, possibly the most influential of all jazz musicians, and clearly the most influential trumpeter in pre-modern jazz. Pictured here at age 27, in 1927, the year several of his classic Hot Five and Hot Seven recordings were made. (*Courtesy of Frank Driggs*)

post-1930 performances. Ironically, most post-1930s fans know Armstrong more as an entertainer than as an innovative jazz improviser who had sweeping impact. However, this also happened to pianist Fats Waller and pianist-singer Nat "King" Cole. And even during the 1970s, examples could be found of the public's love of singing and their relative insensitivity to improvisational quality. It is currently illustrated by guitarist George Benson being better known for his singing than for his excellent work as a jazz guitarist. Listeners who are distracted by Armstrong's success as a singer and entertainer have overlooked or failed to understand his monumental contributions to the history of jazz.

Trumpeter Louis Armstrong is often called the father of jazz. In fact, musicians often refer to him as "Pops." No list of jazz greats omits him, and most start with him. But because Armstrong's career continued successfully four decades after his innovations, the reasons for his importance have become blurred. Some of this is due to the greater familiarity that listeners of the past twenty years had with his work as singer and entertainer, earning him fame by popularizing, for example, the theme song from the Broadway musical "Hello, Dolly!" (his rendition was number five on the 1964 popularity chart). So the question remains, "What exactly did Armstrong do that made him so revered by generations of jazz musicians?" The answers involve appreciation of the following observations:

1) Armstrong showed that the New Orleans technique of collective improvisation need not be the only approach to jazz horn-work. Intelligently developed solos could be improvised in a stirring manner, and the musical effectiveness of such solos need not depend much on ensemble interaction. In other words, Armstrong was one of the first great soloists in jazz history, and, because of him, post-Armstrong styles usually stressed solo improvisation instead of group improvisation. (Of course, Armstrong was not the only reason for this trend, but he was a principal force behind it.)

2) Armstrong was one of the first jazz musicians to refine a rhythmic conception that
   a) abandoned the stiffness of ragtime,
   b) employed swing eighth-note patterns,
   c) gracefully syncopated selected rhythmic figures by use of staggered placement of notes and phrases, suggesting a lag in placement in relation to the beat, as though he were playing behind the beat. This projected a more relaxed feeling than ragtime did.

   These elements combined to produce one of the first jazz styles bearing the rhythmic characteristic that later became identified as jazz swing feeling. Though none of these elements was entirely new with Armstrong, they were more clearly evident as a finished product in his playing than in the playing of either his predecessors or his 1920s contemporaries.

3) Despite the numerous giants who followed him in jazz history, Armstrong remains above most in his ability as a musical architect. He calmly forged sensible lines that had both the flow of spontaneity and the stamp of finality. His improvisations are well-paced, economical statements. Armstrong's phrases suggest that he was always thinking ahead, and yet they manage to sound more natural than calculated.

4) He brought a superb sense of drama to jazz solo conception. His pacing was careful, allowing a solo to build tension. His double-time solo breaks were constructed to achieve maximum excitement, and his high-note endings ensured a properly timed peak of intensity and resolution of tension (listen to "West End Blues" in SCCJ).

5) During a period when most improvisers were satisfied to simply

embellish a tune's melody, Armstrong broke away from the melody and improvised original lines that were compatible with the tune's chord progressions (listen to "Weather Bird" in SCCJ). This became the predominant approach for all improvisation in the next fifty years of jazz history.

6) Armstrong's command of the trumpet was probably greater than that of any preceding jazz trumpeter and became a model to which others aspired. He had an enormous, brassy tone, and remarkable range which, together with his rhythmic and dramatic sense, conveyed a sureness and surging power. Even during the final decades of his career, Armstrong maintained a tone quality that was unusual in its weight, width, and richness.

7) Armstrong popularized the musical vocabulary of New Orleans trumpet style and then extended it.

8) Possibly the most significant reason that Armstrong is important is simply the extent of his influence upon styles that followed his, an influence extending not only to trumpeters, but to saxophonists, pianists, guitarists, and trombonists. In fact, Armstrong was probably the most widely imitated jazz improviser prior to the appearance of modern jazz founders Charlie Parker and Dizzy Gillespie in the 1940s. Armstrong's style is especially easy to detect in three of the most prominent trumpeters of the 1930s and 40s: Oran "Hot Lips" Page, Bunny Berigan, and Buck Clayton. Players within the swing era almost universally cite Armstrong's influence, and segments of his tunes and improvisations continued to be found in the work of such post-swing era innovators as Charlie Parker and Lee Konitz.

9) The Armstrong singing style influenced a number of popular singers and entertainers, including Louis Prima, Billie Holiday, and Bing Crosby.

10) Armstrong popularized scat singing, a vocal technique in which lyrics are not used. The voice improvises in the manner of a jazz trumpeter or saxophonist. (This technique can be heard in his recordings "West End Blues" and "Hotter Than That" in SCCJ.)

Bix Beiderbecke (1903–1931) was a great white trumpeter-composer-bandleader from Iowa. His recordings are important in early jazz, but he fits neatly into neither New Orleans nor Chicago style. He and Armstrong were the leading trumpeters during the late 1920s and early 1930s, and Beiderbecke's style offers an alternative to Armstrong's, though both developed at about the same time.

Beiderbecke was not from New Orleans. So he did not have the opportunity to study the Joe Oliver style in person as Armstrong had done. Instead, Beiderbecke studied the recorded playing of Nick La-Rocca (partly because it was LaRocca's Original Dixieland Jazz Band that began recording in 1917 and gained national attention). Then, when finishing his high school education at a private school near Chicago, Beiderbecke was influenced by and became a part of the flourishing white jazz community there. It remains an open question whether Armstrong influenced Beiderbecke, but the possibility is not to be entirely overlooked. Armstrong had played on Mississippi river-boats that stopped in Beiderbecke's hometown of Davenport, and Beiderbecke did hear Armstrong at least once when a boat stopped, and, of course, after Armstrong began recording in 1923, Beiderbecke was able to study his work closely. When considering these ideas, however, do not forget that, basically, the two trumpeters offered jazz two different approaches.

Beiderbecke first recorded in 1924 with a small group called the Wolverine Orchestra. He became better known when featured, beginning in 1927, with the famous Paul Whiteman Orchestra, a large ensemble, only a part of whose repertory was jazz. Often considered the first great white jazz improviser, Beiderbecke influenced many trumpeters, the best known of whom were Jimmy McPartland, Red Nichols, and Bobby Hackett.

Beiderbecke was almost as original and creative as Armstrong, but he had less command over his instrument and a bit cooler sound. Bix used a less brassy, lighter weight tone that had a softer texture than Armstrong's. His rhythmic approach was also less outgoing. Like most early jazz players, he did not have pronounced jazz swing feeling when he began performing, but later he developed a swing feeling which approached that of Armstrong. Beiderbecke's attitude differs considerably from Armstrong's. He is less dramatic and more subtle. In contrast to Armstrong's assured, outgoing style, Beiderbecke is quieter and sometimes sounds tentative. He plays more in the instrument's middle register than does Armstrong, who likes high notes. Beiderbecke also pays more attention to stringing together unusual note choices and acknowledging every passing chord in the progression—something he knew well because he was also a good pianist. In this way, he anticipated trumpeter-guitarist Bobby Hackett, who also made masterful use of chord notes in his improvisations, acknowledging almost every passing chord. This approach brought acclaim to Hackett in his Beiderbecke-like solo on Glenn Miller's famous 1942 recording "String of Pearls." (For comparison with Armstrong, see Table 5.3.)

Beiderbecke is also known as a composer who blended ragtime with the French Impressionist music of Maurice Ravel and Claude Debussy. His "Flashes," "In the Dark," and "Candlelights" are not well known, but his "In a Mist" has been orchestrated by numerous jazz arrangers, and his own 1927 piano recording of it is especially effective.[5] The piece is distinguished by its use of the whole tone mode, a sound that was favored by Debussy (see page 155 for piano keyboard illustration).

Beiderbecke joined saxophonist **Frankie Trumbauer** for several classic recording sessions. Their 1927 recordings of "Singin' the Blues" and "A Good Man Is Hard to Find" represent two of the most relaxed, melodic, and tender performances in early jazz.[6] Trumbauer's instrument was a C-melody saxophone, which is approximately a size in between the alto and the tenor. It is capable of a very light-colored, light-weight tone. Trumbauer was a very precise and melodic soloist who employed what was an uncommonly slow vibrato for early jazz. Tenor saxophonist Lester Young, a significant figure in the beginnings of modern jazz, has said that he modeled his own light, cool tenor saxophone sound on the playing of C-melody saxophonist Trumbauer. Like Trumbauer, Young also used a slower vibrato than his contemporaries.

The Trumbauer-Beiderbecke "Singin' the Blues" performance is one of the most heralded recordings in jazz history (in SCCJ). Many players have memorized the improvisations on it, and the Fletcher Henderson big band subsequently twice recorded the piece with a har-

TABLE 5.3. Comparing Louis Armstrong with Bix Beiderbecke

	Armstrong	Beiderbecke
command of trumpet	high	moderate
tone quality	full	cotton-like
	warm	cool
	brassy	subtle
	loud	soft
range	wide	moderate
improvisatory character	outgoing	reflective
harmonic thinking	contemporary	advanced
rhythmic conception	swinging	closer to ragtime
influences	Joe "King" Oliver	Nick LaRocca Debussy and Ravel ragtime
birthplace	New Orleans	Davenport

[5] *Bix Beiderbecke Story vol. 3* Columbia CL 846
[6] *Bix Beiderbecke Story vol. 2* Columbia CL 845

monized transcription of Trumbauer's solo. Jazz historians routinely cite Beiderbecke's solo for its advanced use of the tune's harmonies. The notes Beiderbecke chose for his solo go beyond the notes offered by the tune's accompanying chords and reflect a higher level of musical thinking than was common with most other improvisers of the 1920s.

Clarinet Clarinet was more common than saxophone in early jazz. (This situation was drastically reversed during the 1940s when modern jazz emerged. Early jazz combos *without* clarinet were as rare as modern jazz combos with clarinet.) Clarinet usually played countermelodies around the trumpet. Clarinet solos were not usually as dramatic as the trumpet solos. Eventually, however, clarinetists were able to get away from a conception based on embellishment, and by the late 1930s some early players and many swing era players were capable of dramatic, well-paced solo lines.

Johnny Dodds (1892–1940) was one of the leading New Orleans clarinetists who moved to Chicago. He made a large number of recordings with King Oliver, Armstrong, and pianist-composer Jelly Roll Morton there. Dodds and Kid Ory were older than Armstrong, and in New Orleans had often hired him as a sideman, but in Chicago, after Armstrong had achieved a large reputation, the leader/sideman roles were often reversed. Dodds had an edgy tone and very fast vibrato. (Listen to Johnny Dodds on Joe Oliver's "Dippermouth Blues" and on Louis Armstrong's "Struttin' With Some Barbecue" in SCCJ.)

Jimmie Noone (1895–1944) was a more polished player than Johnny Dodds and possessed a greater command of the clarinet. Some consider Noone to be the best New Orleans clarinetist. He had a dark, warm, round tone. He often played jumping staccato lines which had a lot of flash and verve. Noone was a favorite performer of leading white Chicago clarinetists Frank Teschemacher and Benny Goodman. Pianist Earl Hines and Noone made an excellent series of recordings in 1928.

Frank Teschemacher (1906–1932) was the leading white Chicago clarinetist. His technique was excellent, and he swung a bit more loosely than Noone. He also had a somewhat lighter tone and slower vibrato. Teschemacher and Benny Goodman, who became a popular soloist and bandleader during the 1930s, both cited Jimmie Noone as a primary influence.

New Orleans clarinetist and soprano saxophonist **Sidney Bechet** (1897–1959) was one of the most highly regarded musicians in early jazz. In addition to Armstrong, he was one of the first improvisers to display jazz swing feeling. Like Armstrong, he double-timed and created dramatic solos. Bechet had a big, warm tone with a wide and rapid vibrato. He was a very energetic, hard-driving improviser who played with broad imagination and authority. He died in 1959, having spent a large part of his career in France.

Sidney Bechet was one of the first great soloists in jazz. Along with Louis Armstrong, Bechet was among the earliest improvisers to devise a stirringly dramatic way of constructing solos. He and Armstrong cultivated these approaches after they had learned the requirements of collective, nonsolo improvisation which are essential to the New Orleans tradition. (Listen to their playing on "Cake Walkin' Babies From Home" in SCCJ. The recording contains examples of New Orleans style collective improvisation.) In this respect, they introduced a new way for jazz hornmen to be viewed in combo format. Both men eventually became regarded primarily as soloists rather than as ensemble players. This helped make jazz into an improvising soloist's art. For at least the next four decades of jazz, collective improvisation skills remained almost exclusively the domain of rhythm section musicians, not hornmen.

Bechet exerted his impact on solo conception by mastering the timing of central notes and carefully using extended tonal inflections. (See pages 49–52 for details.) His most popular solos are quite simple. Those that journalists discuss the most ("Summertime" and "Blue Horizon" in SCCJ) are slow-tempo performances that exemplify meticulous placement of a few carefully chosen notes. The pitches of these notes are bent in manners that have been perceived as being highly sensual. "Blues drenched" is how some writers like to describe the sounds. The timing of these expressive devices demonstrates the command of restraint necessary for making an emotionally effective climax. This is especially evident in the ornaments he employs to lead up to a central note. The scoop or smear of pitches Bechet uses to introduce a note is essential to the success of his improvisation. The music of swing era saxophonist Johnny Hodges, a Bechet disciple, and modern saxophonist John Coltrane, who was originally influenced by Hodges as well as being aware of Bechet, is characterized by long, swooping lead-ins and tones which arrive at precisely the time best suited for maximum relief of the tension generated by the lead-in. (Hodges prefers to preface an important note with a gradual smearing of pitches, whereas Coltrane usually selects a rapid, scale-like sequence to sweep up to that central tone.) Hodges was featured with the Duke Ellington band for about forty years. His pre-1940s playing displayed some of the double-timing and ebullience of Bechet. For an example of Hodges's double-timing, listen to his solo on Ellington's 1940 recording of "In a Mellotone." For close comparison of the two soprano sax styles, play Bechet's 1938 "Really the Blues" back to back with Hodges's 1938 "Jeep's Blues" and Bechet's 1941 "When It's Sleepy Time Down South" with Hodges's 1938 "Empty Ballroom Blues." Hodges later slowed down and smoothed out considerably but retained the smoothness of tone and extremely expressive inflections of pitch which he had learned from Bechet. During the 1960s, the soprano sax was resurrected by modern jazz saxophonist John Coltrane, one of whose tunes was entitled "Blues to Bechet." (See Figure 5.1 for a comparison of clarinet and soprano sax.)

Figure 5.1. Clarinet and soprano sax. (*The Selmer Company*)

Many of Bechet's solos simply display the reworking of elementary blues phrases. The musical concepts of "bluesy" and "funky" are defined by Bechet's playing. He summarizes the instrumental equivalent of the blues singer. And, in this way, Bechet summarizes what many listeners have come to regard as the essential feeling of New Orleans style: an earthy, warm and full sound. (Listen to Bechet's "Blue Horizon" in SCCJ.)

Trombone In ensemble improvisation, trombonists invented low harmony parts and filled in gaps with devices similar to those played by tuba and trombone in marching band music. With clarinet and trumpet filling out the middle and upper registers, trombone contributed to the combo sound in the lower range. When soloing, early trombonists tended toward a jazz trumpet conception to which they added the trombone's unique capacity for smears and slides. Rarely, however, did they play lines as intricate as those of early jazz trumpeters.

Kid Ory (1886–1973) was one of the first notable New Orleans jazz trombonists. His husky tone and assertive presence were an important part of several early jazz combos. He had a hard, cutting tone and a percussive attack. His work had a boisterous air about it. Ory was also a composer and group leader. His "Muskat Ramble" (later spelled "Muskrat Ramble") became a jazz standard. (Listen to Kid Ory on Louis Armstrong's "Struttin' With Some Barbecue" in SCCJ.)

Miff Mole (1898–1961) was from New York. He and Jack Teagarden were the leading white trombonists in early jazz. His tone was clear and well contained, and his command of the instrument was possibly the best of all early jazz trombonists. Mole's lines were choppy, with frequent wide leaps of range between notes. Melodically and rhythmically, Mole's conception resembled that of trumpeters Bix Beiderbecke and Red Nichols, men with whom he often recorded.

Jack Teagarden (1905–1964) was a trombonist from Texas who paid close attention to producing and maintaining a smooth, full tone which was prettier than that of most other premodern trombonists.[7] His work projected a thoughtful, relaxed quality even though some of his favorite phrases were technically demanding. Teagarden's unique feeling and well-formed phrases were an inspiration to the trombonists of modern jazz. His style was possibly as important to jazz trombone history as Armstrong's was to trumpet. His career was long and productive, running from the 1920s until his death in 1964.

J. C. Higginbotham (1906–1973), a trombonist from Georgia, was a few years younger than Mole and had a larger, harder, weightier tone. Higginbotham projected a very hard-driving, confident presence. His solos bore a trumpet conception, sometimes sounding like Armstong. The rhythms in his phrases were altered so that they did not possess the sameness to which others were prone. He seemed to be treating only one phrase at a time. His work had an overall sense to it. Though 1929 was probably his creative peak, he played until his death in 1973.

Rhythm Section   The front line of most early jazz combos included trumpet, clarinet, trombone, and occasionally, saxophone. The rhythm section was made up of several instruments which might include guitar, banjo, tuba, bass saxophone, string bass, piano, and drums. No bands had all these instruments playing at the same time, but most drew some combination from that collection. It was not unusual for early jazz combos to be without string bass, and many early jazz recordings were made without drums. Some groups substituted tuba for string bass (eventually many tuba players learned to play string bass), and some used bass saxophone (see Figures 5.2 and 5.3). Groups often included both guitar and banjo, though some had only one of these. Usually one player alternated between the two instruments. Piano was absent from some recordings and replaced banjo and guitar on others, though usually both piano and banjo or guitar were used.

The banjo and guitar were often strummed all four beats of each measure. The tuba, bass sax, or string bass frequently played on only the first and third of every four beats. That meant they played on only two beats per measure, a style known as "two-beat" rhythm. Prior to

---

[7] *King of the Blues Trombone* Columbia Special Products JSN 6044

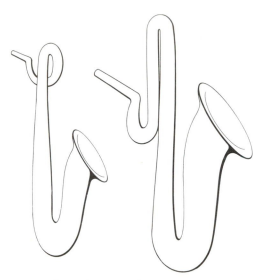

Figure 5.2. Baritone saxophone—bass saxophone. Key mechanisms are omitted so that the distinctive differences in the sizes of the instruments and the shapes of the looped necks will be more readily apparent.

Figure 5.3. Tuba (Besson, BB♭). (*The Selmer Company*)

1927, string bass was often bowed instead of plucked. (See pages 16, 228, 289 and 332 for illustrations of string bass.) Walking bass and two-beat style consisted of sustained tones instead of the staccato sound that is ordinarily produced when the bass strings are plucked. (A two-beat style tuba part can be heard in portions of the 1927 "Potato Head Blues" recorded by Louis Armstrong, found in SCCJ. Walking bass alternating with two-beat style can be heard in the 1926 "Black Bottom Stomp" and "Dead Man Blues" recorded by Jelly Roll Morton and found in SCCJ. A bass saxophone can be heard playing in this rhythm role on the 1927 Trumbauer-Beiderbecke "A Good Man Is Hard to Find" in SCCJ. See pages 78 and 274 for bass saxophone illustrations.)

Sometimes the pianist struck chords in unison with the guitar or banjo, sometimes he played embellishments instead. In many groups, the pianist created countermelodies while the front line instruments were playing melodies and countermelodies of their own. Comping as defined in "Appreciating Jazz Improvisation" did not begin until the late 1930s.

Drums Early jazz drummers are poorly heard on records because early recording equipment was not well-suited to recording drums. At that time, records were made by playing into acoustic recording horns, which looked like the horn that comes out of the phonograph in the famous picture of the Victor dog listening to "His Master's Voice." The small end of the horn was connected to a cutting needle which made grooves in a cylinder or a disc. A blow to the bass drum or any other loud sound could literally knock the needle off the cutting surface. Many recordings consequently represent working bands minus their drummers. Many of the recordings that do employ drummers either omit most drum equipment entirely or muffle it so much that, when combined with terrible recording quality, drum sounds are almost inaudible. We are often left with little more than the clickety clicking sound on several of the earliest jazz recordings that is made by drum sticks striking a wood block (a small block of wood that has been hollowed out to increase resonance). This was one of the only sounds drummers were allowed to produce during the sessions in which recording engineers were afraid of loud sounds. (Listen to Warren "Baby" Dodds play wood block with Oliver's Creole Jazz Band in their 1923 "Dippermouth Blues" in SCCJ, and listen to Tony Sbarbaro play it in the Original Dixieland Jazz Band's 1920 "Margie"[1] or their 1921 "Home Again Blues.") (See pages 413–414 for information on how to get an illustrated history of premodern drumming.)

Though this drumming sound described above was particularly convenient in adapting to the restrictions imposed by early recording situations, it represents only one sample in a range of sounds commonly generated by the earliest jazz drummers. Light, staccato sounds were also produced by striking a cowbell or the bass drum's rim (the shell of the instrument, not the drum head that usually receives the blow). These sounds were also employed in some early record dates, but, at that time, aggressive use of the snare drum and bass drum was generally limited to band engagements. A large cymbal or gong was sometimes used to signal a dramatic height in the music, and some jazz combo drummers of the 1920s also had orchestra and theater band experience, and they accordingly brought an orchestral approach to their combo playing. When playing on the light-sounding instruments, however, many of the earliest drummers chose patterns from military drumming and ragtime drumming, not necessarily from orchestral drumming tradition in which the percussionist only embellishes or reinforces other instrumental activity. The 1917–23 drumming heard in recordings uses more military than orchestral concepts. (If you have a keen enough ear, you might be able to hear these military patterns played on snare drum by Tony Sbarbaro with the Original Dixieland Jazz Band on their 1917 "Original Dixie Jazz Band One-Step"[1] or their 1918 "Clarinet Marmalade" recordings.)

Although we do not know exactly how he sounded, we do know what kind of instruments the early jazz drummer played. He did not have a high-hat. He had a floor cymbal apparatus which enabled him to strike a cymbal with a foot pedal, but it did not allow him to achieve the "chick" sound possible with the high-hat. He also had a bass drum, almost marching band size, two to three times as large as that which became popular during the mid-1960s. A snare drum mounted on a stand and a cymbal suspended above the set were also at his disposal. Wood block and cowbell were attached to the bass drum.

New Orleans drummer **Warren "Baby" Dodds** (1898–1959), brother of clarinetist Johnny Dodds, has been credited with pioneering the use of the ride rhythm which he played on the snare drum. Later in jazz history, ride rhythms were played on the high-hat. Eventually in the 1950s and 60s, they became the primary timekeeping rhythms, and drummers played them on the ride cymbal.

Arthur "Zutty" Singleton (1898–1975), another leading New Orleans drummer, was among the first to use wire brushes to strike his drums. Brushes did not totally replace sticks, but they offered a lighter, softer sound, as well as the capacity to produce sustained sounds if dragged across and around a drum head or cymbal. Zutty also pioneered the use of bass drum on all four beats of each measure. Many drummers had struck the bass drum primarily on the first and third beats. (Singleton can be heard playing brushes on Louis Armstrong's 1928 recordings of "St. James Infirmary" and "Tight Like

This." He can be heard playing a suspended cymbal on "Skip the Gutter." And, on "No, Papa, No," Singleton can be heard briefly playing ride rhythms on a cymbal, thereby predating, by about a decade, the sound that was to characterize modern jazz timekeeping style. All these examples can be found in the same album: *The Louis Armstrong Story Vol. 3* Columbia 853. The material might be cross listed with Earl Hines because it is work that Armstrong and Hines recorded together in 1928.) Singleton influenced George Wettling and Sid Catlett. Catlett played a transitional role in jazz, helping jazz drum conceptions move from early jazz to modern jazz.

The point of the foregoing listening and reasoning is to help us form a notion of how jazz drumming usually sounded at live band engagements in New Orleans and Chicago before the 1920s. Throughout all this guesswork, however, keep in mind that it is dangerous to generalize backwards in history from 1920s recordings because drum-making technology and jazz playing were both evolving so rapidly at this time that what finally got recorded when record companies better recorded drummers might reflect a later stage in its evolution. And remember, as explained above, that what happened in the recording studio was not necessarily what might have been happening on the bandstand, even when the musicians, the tunes, and the arrangements were the same.

There are significant similarities and differences between the roles assumed by the earliest jazz drummers and the roles that jazz drummers assumed later in jazz history. For example, on some of the earliest recordings, horn lines often existed without drum accompaniment. That these lines could exist and often did exist without drum accompaniment is especially important when combined with the observation that, on some of the pieces in which drum lines were present, drum lines constituted an additional instrument line rather than the timekeeping or "swing machine" function that drums provided for some later styles. The earliest jazz drummers could also perform in timekeeping style and often did. However, the point here is an additional one: the earliest jazz drummers often devised lines of activity bearing rhythmic and melodic contours that were distinctly different from the contours of lines being contributed by their fellow musicians. The practice of playing an independent line of activity was suppressed in swing, the primary jazz style of the 1930s, but it enjoyed a resurgence in bop, the primary modern jazz style of the 1940s. In modern jazz, this independent line of activity has sometimes been termed "chatter," and it provides a layer of boiling sounds that increases the excitement of the combo sound. The use of this activity continued throughout the 1950s and 60s, increasing in density and importance. It has been an accepted practice for all modern drummers of the 1970s and 80s. The rhythms used by the modern drummers were not those of ragtime, but the spirit in which they were played is analogous to the conception shown by the earliest jazz drummers.

Another important comparison can be made between early jazz drumming and later styles. Spontaneous interaction between soloist and accompanist was limited to the extent that the earliest drummers did not necessarily alter their playing from moment to moment to try inventing sound patterns that would complement every nuance of the improvised solo lines. These drummers did sometimes change loudness, rhythm, and/or instrument for each successive soloist. Many of their accompaniment patterns, however, usually remained patterns rather than deriving spontaneously from rhythmic ideas heard in the improvised solo lines they accompanied. This varied from drummer to drummer and from band to band, but the earliest drummers tended to demonstrate less spontaneous interaction with their fellow musicians than modern drummers did.

The foregoing discussion will be almost meaningless unless you hear examples of the sounds that are described. Listen to the playing of Baby Dodds on "Dippermouth Blues" in SCCJ and that of Zutty Singleton with Louis Armstrong in "West End Blues" in SCCJ. In those examples, Dodds plays wood block and Singleton plays a pair of small, hand-held cymbals. It would also be helpful to sample recordings that are not contained in SCCJ. For instance, Singleton can be heard on other Armstrong recordings of 1928: "My Monday Date" and "Sugar Foot Stomp." Dodds is best heard on the recordings that Oliver's Creole Jazz Band made for the Gennett company, not those made for Okeh, which Smithsonian has reissued in their Oliver set. (The 1923 "I'm Going to Wear You Off My Mind" has particularly distinct wood block playing, in which Dodds's accompaniment rhythms show considerable variety, seeming to constitute a response to the rhythms of the solo lines. This might, however, have been worked out ahead and not be purely improvised for this particular recording.) Tony Sbarbaro can be heard on the 1917 recording of "Dixie Jazz Band One Step" by the Original Dixieland Jazz Band. After a passage of snare drum, bass drum, and cymbals, he plays wood block and cowbell. This combination can also be heard in the 1918 recording of "Clarinet Marmalade." Note that, despite what is said above about drummers not having entire drum sets in the studio, most all of Sbarbaro's instruments can be heard in these recordings, if the listener is alert and patient enough to seek them. (The Creole Jazz Band recordings for Gennett have been reissued as *Louis Armstrong and King Oliver* Milestone 47017. The Original Dixieland Jazz Band recordings for Victor have been reissued in an album called *The Original Dixieland Jazz Band* Victor 547.)

Guitar   During the 1920s, most guitarists confined themselves to timekeeping, or, when they played exposed parts, they used simple, chorded solos. Guitar was generally ignored as a jazz solo voice until the late 1930s, partly because of the limited loudness that guitarists could generate before the electric amplification of the instrument became common. But two significant guitar soloists did record: Philadelphia-born **Eddie Lang** (1902–1933) and New Orleans-born **Lonnie Johnson** (1899–1970). Lang's work can be heard in recordings by violinist Joe Venuti, and in recordings made by the Beiderbecke-Trumbauer team, such as "Singin' the Blues" (in SCCJ). Good examples of Johnson's music exist in combo recordings with Louis Armstrong such as "Hotter than That" (in SCCJ) and a few moments with Duke Ellington such as the 1928 Okeh version of "The Mooche."

The guitar styles developed by Johnson and Lang contrast markedly. Johnson was a bluesier player than Lang. A favorite means for creating the earthy flavor in his work was to let a tone ring while he glided up to desired pitch. Both men were well organized in their solos, but, in his execution, Lang goes further than Johnson and projects an almost classical conception. (It is notable that he was first trained as a classical violinist.) His technique was excellent, and his lines were executed more cleanly than Johnson's. Listen to the counterlines which Lang improvises delicately under the horn lines in "Singin' the Blues" (in SCCJ). Their construction and execution is almost like that of classical chamber music. Although both players are historically significant, Lang has been the more influential of the two.

CHAPTER SUMMARY

1) The first forms of jazz resulted from blending improvisational approaches to ragtime, blues, spirituals, marches, and popular tunes.

2) The first jazz bands used the instruments of marching bands: trumpet, clarinet, trombone, tuba, drums, and (occasionally) saxophone.

3) The earliest jazz was not recorded. We can only infer how it sounded on the basis of recordings made by New Orleans players after they had moved to Chicago.

4) The first jazz group to record was the Original Dixieland Jazz Band in 1917.

5) Chicago was the jazz center of the world during the 1920s, comprised of
   a) all-star black groups such as Oliver's Creole Jazz Band which had moved from New Orleans,
   b) white bands from New Orleans such as the New Orleans Rhythm Kings,
   c) Chicago-born imitators of the New Orleans Rhythm Kings such as the Austin High Gang.

6) One of the most historically significant New Orleans natives to first record in Chicago was pianist-composer-bandleader Jelly Roll Morton.

7) Morton was the first great jazz composer. Several of his tunes became standards: "Wolverine Blues," "King Porter Stomp," "Milenburg Joys."

8) Morton devised a piano style that featured horn-like lines and long-short, strong-weak eighth note patterns that swung more than ragtime.

9) Morton blended New Orleans improvisational approaches with elaborately arranged, prewritten passages.

10) The single player who stands above all others in jazz history is New Orleans-born trumpeter Louis Armstrong.

11) Armstrong possessed a large tone, wider range, and better command of the trumpet than most early players.

12) Armstrong's improvisations were especially well constructed.

13) Armstrong was one of the first combo players to effectively demonstrate solo improvisation instead of retaining the New Orleans tradition of collective improvisation.

14) Armstrong is possibly the most influential of all trumpeters, having been imitated by saxophonists, trombonists, and pianists as well as by trumpeters.

15) Next to Armstrong, Bix Beiderbecke was the most influential brass player of the 1920s, and he was harmonically more advanced than Armstrong.

16) In addition to a cool, thoughtful style, Beiderbecke was a composer in the tradition of French Impressionists Maurice Ravel and Claude Debussy.

17) Soprano saxophonist-clarinetist Sidney Bechet helped move jazz horn conception from collective improvisation techniques to a dramatic solo style.

18) Bechet influenced Johnny Hodges and John Coltrane, especially in the expressive timing of ornamentations which precede important notes.

19) Earl Hines helped take jazz piano conception from a traditionally pianistic orientation to a horn-like conception.

20) Hines influenced numerous other piano greats, including Teddy Wilson, Art Tatum, and Nat Cole.

21) The stride piano tradition of James P. Johnson was continued by Fats Waller, who, in turn, became the principal influence on Count Basie.

22) Waller was an excellent composer who wrote several tunes that have become jazz standards, such as "Honeysuckle Rose," "Ain't Misbehavin'," and "Jitterbug Waltz."

chapter 6
SWING:
THE EARLY 1930s
TO THE LATE 1940s

With the adoption of swing eighth-note patterns and a looser, less stiff rhythmic feeling, jazz began to swing more. This was a gradual change which began during the late 1920s and continued into the 1940s. Most jazz from this period is called swing music, and, since much of it was played by bands of ten or more men, it is often called the big band era. Swing differs from early jazz in several ways:

1) The preferred instrumentation for swing was big band rather than combo, and greater use of written arrangements therefore occurred during the swing era.

2) Saxophones were more common in swing.

3) Bass viol appeared more often in swing.

4) High-hat cymbals experienced greater use.

5) Collective improvisation was rare in swing.

6) Overall rhythmic feeling was somewhat smoother in swing performances.

7) Swing musicians usually showed a higher level of instrumental proficiency in terms of speed, agility, tone control, and playing in tune.

Swing was possibly the most popular style in jazz history, and it attracted millions of dancers. It also produced several excellent big bands, including those of Fletcher Henderson, Duke Ellington, Count Basie, Jimmie Lunceford, and Benny Goodman. Several soloists with these bands went on to influence the development of modern jazz: saxophonists Coleman Hawkins and Lester Young, guitarist Charlie

TABLE 6.1. A Few of the Many Swing Style Musicians

Composing— Arranging
- Fletcher Henderson
- Eddie Durham
- Benny Carter
- Sy Oliver
- Don Redman
- Duke Ellington
- Billy Strayhorn
- Eddie Sauter
- Will Hudson
- Budd Johnson
- Edgar Sampson
- Jimmy Mundy
- Deane Kincaide

Drums
- Jo Jones
- Sid Catlett
- Chick Webb
- Gene Krupa
- Sonny Greer
- Cozy Cole
- Louis Bellson
- Buddy Rich
- Dave Tough
- Jimmy Crawford
- Ben Thigpen

Trombone
- Lawrence Brown
- Dicky Wells
- Trummy Young
- Jimmy Harrison
- Benny Morton
- Vic Dickenson
- Joe "Tricky Sam" Nanton
- Bill Harris
- J. C. Higginbotham
- Jack Jenney
- Tommy Dorsey

Saxophone
- Coleman Hawkins
- Johnny Hodges
- Benny Carter
- Willie Smith
- Chu Berry
- Herschel Evans
- Dick Wilson
- Ben Webster
- Lester Young
- Georgie Auld
- Don Byas
- Russell Procope
- Illinois Jacquet
- Hilton Jefferson
- Tab Smith
- Flip Phillips
- Pete Brown
- Buster Smith
- Tex Beneke
- Jerry Jerome
- Boomie Richman
- Vido Musso
- Ernie Caceres
- Earl Bostic
- Joe Thomas
- Budd Johnson
- Jimmy Dorsey

Trumpet
- Roy Eldridge
- Cootie Williams
- Bunny Berigan
- Harry James
- Buck Clayton
- Charlie Shavers
- Frankie Newton
- Henry "Red" Allen
- Oran "Hot Lips" Page
- Harry "Sweets" Edison
- Rex Stewart
- Harold "Shorty" Baker
- Jonah Jones
- Taft Jordan
- Jabbo Smith
- Herman Autrey

Clarinet
- Benny Goodman
- Artie Shaw
- Barney Bigard
- Woody Herman
- Buster Bailey
- Jimmy Hamilton

Guitar
- Django Reinhardt
- Charlie Christian
- Eddie Durham
- Oscar Moore
- Irving Ashby
- Al Casey

Piano
- Art Tatum
- Teddy Wilson
- Billy Kyle
- Mary Lou Williams
- Milt Buckner
- Count Basie
- Duke Ellington
- Nat Cole
- Erroll Garner
- Clyde Hart
- Johnny Guarnieri
- Jay McShann
- Mel Powell
- Jess Stacy

Bass
- Walter Page
- Jimmy Blanton
- John Kirby
- Israel Crosby
- Wellman Braud

Vibraharp
- Lionel Hampton
- Red Norvo
- Adrian Rollini
- Tyree Glenn

Bandleaders
- Duke Ellington
- Count Basie
- Bennie Moten
- Benny Carter
- Chick Webb
- Andy Kirk
- Jay McShann
- Cab Calloway
- Tommy Dorsey
- Benny Goodman
- Jimmy Dorsey
- Glenn Miller
- Charlie Barnet
- Boyd Raeburn
- Woody Herman
- Stan Kenton
- Gene Krupa
- Artie Shaw
- Fletcher Henderson
- Lionel Hampton
- Bunny Berigan
- Harry James
- Earl Hines
- Billy Eckstine
- Jimmie Lunceford

Christian, and trumpeter Roy Eldridge. The two most formidable pianists of the era were Art Tatum and Teddy Wilson.

**Big Band
Instrumentation**

Big bands were made up of ten or more musicians whose instruments fall into three categories: brass, saxophones, and rhythm section. The brass section included trumpets and trombones. Although saxophones are also made of brass, they are technically called woodwinds because they originated from instruments traditionally made of wood (clarinet, flute, and oboe) and are played in the manner of traditional wooden instruments. Because most saxophonists also play clarinet, and both sax and clarinet have cane reeds attached to their mouthpieces, the sax section was often called the "reed section," a label which was retained in later decades even when saxophonists began adding flute, a non-reed instrument.

The alto and tenor saxophones were the most frequently used saxes, and, by the late 1930s, most bands had also adopted the baritone saxophone (see Figure 6.1). The soprano and bass saxophones were not especially common.

The sax section contained from three to five men. Saxophonists did not usually play one instrument to the exclusion of the others. Some men, for instance, were required to alternate from clarinet to alto and baritone saxophones. Eventually a section of two altos, two tenors, and a baritone became standard. The leader of the sax section, an alto saxophonist, sat in the middle, with the baritone on one end, tenor on the other.

The size of the trumpet section varied from two to five men, three being the standard number during the late 1930s and early 40s. The lead trumpeter usually sat in the middle. The trombone section ranged from one to five men, two or three being standard. The lead trombonist was in the center.

The growth of big bands was accompanied by an increase in the use of written arrangements, which had not been necessary with small combos. As bands became bigger, it was more difficult to improvise a respectable performance. Many big bands did succeed in playing without written arrangements, but eventually considerations of convenience and variety forced musicians to learn to read and write arrangements. A newcomer had much less difficulty adapting to a band whose materials consisted of written arrangements rather than memorized routines.

The compositional devices employed in a large portion of the arrangements were quite simple. Melodies were played by the entire band in unison or in harmony. Then jazz improvisation followed, accompanied both by the rhythm section and by figures scored for other members of the ensemble. The melodies and accompanying figures were passed from one section of the band to another. Saxes might state

Figure 6.1. Alto (on left), tenor (on right), and baritone saxophone (lying down). (*Photo courtesy of Barry Perlus*)

the A section, brass state the bridge, and so forth. In addition to pop tune melodies, arrangements often contained variations on those themes, some of which were actually as good as transcriptions of improvised solos. These were offered as passages for one section of the band to play while another remained silent or accompanied them. Sometimes, portions within the passages were passed back and forth, so that it sounded as though one section of the band posed a question and another section answered it. This technique, also common in other forms and eras of world music, is called question and answer, call and response, or antiphonal (an-TIFF-on-ull) style.

Short, simple, phrases called riffs were used by some big bands as essential elements of their style. At times, different riffs were assigned to various sections of the band, and played antiphonally. Properly timed, these antiphonal passages could swing a band buoyantly and give jazz improvisation a good send-off. Sometimes entire arrangements were based on such riffs. Woody Herman's "Woodchopper's Ball," Count Basie's "One O'Clock Jump" and "Jumpin' at the Woodside" are well-known examples of that technique. (Listen to Count Basie's "Taxi War Dance" and "Doggin' Around" in SCCJ.)

The Rhythm Section

The rhythm section ordinarily contained piano, guitar, bass, and drums. Rhythm guitar remained a part of Count Basie's band through the 1980s, but disappeared from most other big bands during the late 40s. Although the banjo had preceded the guitar in many bands, it dropped out of sight during the 1930s. Tuba had preceded string bass in some bands, but had been abandoned by the mid-1930s. Before the guitar and string bass became firmly established, guitarists were often required to alternate guitar and banjo, while bassists were required to alternately play both tuba (also called brass bass) and string bass (also called bass viol).

The pianist in the rhythm section occasionally played melody instead of just chords and embellishments. Comping (as described on pages 18–24) was not the common accompaniment style during the swing era, though Count Basie did use it during the late 1930s. The pianists of the swing era used stride style or played a chord on every beat or every other beat. They did not necessarily improvise new rhythms to flexibly fit those of the solo line, as did their successors in modern jazz.

The sound of the guitarist percussively strumming a chord on each beat was prominent on most swing recordings. So was the sound of the bassist who was playing a note on the first and third or all four beats of each measure. (See page 129 for discussion of Count Basie's bassist Walter Page and pages 121–122 for discussion of Duke Ellington's bassist Jimmy Blanton.)

The majority of drummers who played with big bands during this period tended to limit themselves to making the beat obvious for dancers and lending swing feeling to the band instead of doing as the earliest jazz drummers had done and creating a separate line of rhythmic activity that coexisted with the melodic rhythms of the horns. With the exception of striking cymbals and gongs for dramatically timed effects, many of the big band drummers played lengthy passages without doing much more than stating each beat on the bass drum and reinforcing this with a simple timekeeping pattern played on the snare drum with wire brushes or on a closed high-hat with sticks. Sometimes the second and fourth beats of each measure were emphasized by striking the snare drum with sticks. (This is called a "back beat.") Deviations from these patterns usually constituted simple embellishments of the beat or busy patterns that were quickly played when the horns were pausing between ensemble phrases. Swing drummers tended not to play new and provocative rhythms that ran counter to the horn lines. Listeners had to wait until modern jazz developed during the 1940s before they could hear drummers again offering a parallel line of activity instead of just keeping time. Listeners also had to wait to hear a substantial amount of interaction between improvising soloist and accompanying drummer. For the most part, swing drumming was quite conservative and not very light or swinging. It was not until the late 1930s that a lighter and more graceful sound was heard from big band drummers. And, even then, it was only heard in the few bands that were lucky enough to boast such drummers as Jo Jones or Dave Tough (see page 129 for more about Jones).

Jazz drumming authority Denny Brown has pointed out that the nature of the 1930s big band style restricted the jazz drummer's activity, decreasing the rhythmic freedom that combo drummers had. The riff-based format used by big bands discouraged swing drummers from playing complex rhythmic patterns because such complexity might conflict with the melodic rhythms of the written horn parts. Brown contends that the 1930s swing era originated the idea that a jazz drummer should only be felt, not heard. Exceptions to this rule are notable, however, and Gene Krupa's popularity during this period might stem partly from his violating the norm. Brown suggests that Krupa's playing forecast aspects of modern drumming by being heard and by including patterns that responded to horn lines as well as building excitement. Some of Krupa's accompaniments are like solos. In that respect they are a throwback to the methods of the earliest jazz drummers and a contrast to the typical approach of swing drummers. (See pages 413–414 for information on how to get Brown's excellent history of premodern drumming.)

During the late 1930s, a contrast to the Krupa style was offered by Count Basie's drummer Jo Jones. In place of the loud and insistent pounding of the bass drum on each beat that Krupa did, Jones often omitted bass drum playing altogether. In contrast to striking his high-hat while it was closed, Jones continued a ride rhythm on it while it was continuously opening and closing. He let the cymbals ring, thereby making a more sustained and less abrupt sound pattern. This technique, together with an unusually close coordination with the bassist, projected a more flowing feeling than had typified other swing rhythm section sounds. Jones also gave each beat more equal treatment than his contemporaries had done. The feeling Jones conveyed, and the precision with which he played, eventually transferred to the modern jazz drummer's approach to playing timekeeping rhythms on a suspended cymbal that is now known as the ride cymbal. (It is also notable that Jones steered clear of cowbell and wood block, sounds that today help us identify the corny aspects of premodern jazz drumming.)

Bandleaders   Some of the best swing bands were led by Fletcher Henderson, Count Basie, Duke Ellington, Jimmie Lunceford, and Benny Goodman. Following this discussion are entire chapters devoted to Ellington and his musicians and Basie and his musicians. The Henderson and Ellington bands bridged the gap between the styles of early jazz and the swing approach. Each had begun during the early 1920s and grown larger and more sophisticated by the late 1930s.

A very large portion of great early jazz and swing era improvisers worked with **Fletcher Henderson** (1897–1952) between the early 1920s and late 30s (see Table 6.2). Henderson's was an all-star band somewhat comparable to that of the all-star combos led by trumpeter Miles Davis between the late 1940s and late 60s. Together with saxophonist-arrangers Don Redman and Benny Carter, pianist-arranger Henderson created big band arranging techniques which eventually became standard. (Listen to Fletcher Henderson's "The Stampede" featuring saxophonist Coleman Hawkins. It is found in SCCJ.) His style represented one major stream of big band jazz; Ellington's represented another. In his arrangements, Henderson pitted saxes against brass. He also perfected techniques of block voicing, in which the melody is the top voice of a series of chords in parallel motion (in other words, assigning notes in a chord to different instruments, rhythm of the melody played in unison by the entire band). It produced a thicker sound than if the line were not harmonized. Ellington used block voicing, but he also added an assortment of other special

TABLE 6.2. Musicians Prominent in the Fletcher Henderson Bands

Trumpet	Saxophone and Clarinet	Trombone
Louis Armstrong		Jimmy Harrison
Rex Stewart	Coleman Hawkins	Charlie Green
Roy Eldridge	Chu Berry	Dicky Wells
Tommy Ladnier	Don Redman	J. C. Higginbotham
Cootie Williams	Benny Carter	Benny Morton
Joe Smith	Ben Webster	
Bobby Stark	Russell Procope	
Henry "Red" Allen	Hilton Jefferson	
Emmett Berry	Buster Bailey	
Drums	**Bass and Tuba**	
Sid Catlett	John Kirby	
Kaiser Marshall	June Cole	
	Bobby Escudero	
	Israel Crosby	

SWING: THE EARLY 1930s TO THE LATE 1940s **93**

techniques (discussed in the next chapter). Part of Henderson's arranging reputation resulted from the Benny Goodman big band's use of his work on "King Porter Stomp," "Blue Skies," "Down South Camp Meeting," "Sometimes I'm Happy," "Japanese Sandman," "Wrappin' It Up," and "When Buddah Smiles." (Listen in SCCJ to Henderson's own band play "Wrappin' It Up," one of the arrangements that was used by Benny Goodman's band.)

Jimmie Lunceford (1902–1947) led one of the most polished-sounding big bands. His records placed more emphasis on ensemble playing than on improvising; jazz improvisation was more common in the Fletcher Henderson and Count Basie bands. One of Lunceford's biggest strengths was the team of arrangers writing for his band. Will Hudson, Eddie Wilcox, Gerald Wilson, and Sy Oliver all contributed good big band arrangements. Will Hudson's "Jazznocracy" and "White Heat,"[1] and Sy Oliver's "Swingin' Uptown" are attractive features which displayed the precise ensemble playing of the band. (Listen to Lunceford's "Lunceford Special" in SCCJ.)

A distinctive feature in some Lunceford performances was unusually high trumpet playing. The style soon became essential to the excitement of the big band sound (notably in the work of Cat Anderson in Ellington's band and Maynard Ferguson in the Charlie Barnet and Stan Kenton bands). By the 1960s, the average high-register capability of big band trumpeters had improved considerably over that of early jazz trumpeters.

Benny Goodman (b. 1909) led the most well-known jazz-oriented big band of the swing era. The band showcased its leader's swinging, technically impressive clarinet playing.[2] It must be noted that, although it was a well-rehearsed, hard-driving band, Goodman's group did not generate as relaxed and easy a swing feeling as the Count Basie band did. Because of this, many musicians have felt that the promotional banner carried by Goodman, "The King of Swing," is not appropriate.

Part of Goodman's historical significance derives from his providing exposure for other outstanding swing style improvisers. His small combos were especially effective situations for featuring such players. (Listen to his trio play "Body and Soul" and his sextet play "I Found a New Baby" in SCCJ.) The most innovative players he featured were guitarist Charlie Christian (see pages 103–104) and pianist Teddy Wilson (see pages 100–101). Several of those players whom Goodman spotlighted also led their own swing bands at one time or another:

[1] *Willie Bryant and Jimmie Lunceford and Their Orchestras* RCA AXM2 5502. All the big bands cited in this chapter can also be heard on *Big Band Jazz* (Smithsonian 2200, a six LP set available from Smithsonian Performing Arts, Washington, D.C. 20560).

[2] *The Complete Benny Goodman Vol. 1 1935* RCA AXM2 5505

Benny Goodman, the best known of all clarinetists and swing era bandleaders. Pictured here in 1936 (standing in front, playing clarinet), Gene Krupa (drums), trumpets (left to right): Nate Kazebier, Pee Wee Erwin, and Chris Griffin; Jess Stacy (piano), Allan Reuss (guitar); reeds (left to right): Hymie Schertzer and Bill DePew (both are playing clarinet, with alto sax in lap), Art Rollini (playing clarinet, with tenor sax in lap), Dick Clark (playing bass clarinet, with tenor sax and clarinet on a stand); trombones (left to right): Red Ballard and Murray McEachern; Harry Goodman (bass). (*Courtesy of Duncan Scheidt*)

1) trumpeter Bunny Berigan (see page 97)
2) trumpeter Harry James (1916–1983, who continued to lead big bands for decades after the end of the swing era)
3) trumpeter Cootie Williams (see Duke Ellington chapter for more about him)
4) vibraharpist Lionel Hampton (b. 1909; see page 159 for illustrations of the vibraharp, and listen to his "When Lights Are Low" in SCCJ)
5) drummer Gene Krupa (1909–1973; listen to his "Rockin' Chair" in SCCJ), whose drum solos helped emancipate jazz drummers from their restricted role of being merely timekeepers

Tommy Dorsey (1905–1956) developed a method of playing trombone which produced an extremely smooth, clear tone. His high-register work became the model for a later series of highly skilled trombonists who had glossy tones and meticulous technique (Urbie

Green, Si Zentner, Carl Fontana, Bill Watrous, Phil Wilson, and others). One of his best big bands had trumpeter Charlie Shavers and Sy Oliver, who contributed numerous arrangements ("Easy Does It," "We'll Get It," "Opus 1"). Dorsey also had powerful rhythm sections with such drummers as Louis Bellson, Buddy Rich, and Dave Tough.[3,4]

Artie Shaw (b. 1910) was an exceptionally explorative bandleader. In addition to standard big band instrumentation, he also employed a string quartet (two violins, viola, and cello) in one of his bands, and led a combo, the Gramercy 5 (named for a telephone exchange—it was actually a sextet). Shaw composed some of his own material, which, especially in the string writing, was innovative for 1936.

Shaw achieved considerable popularity; his 1940 "Frenesi" recording sold approximately four million copies. Shaw was also an accomplished clarinetist. His tone was bigger and smoother than Goodman's, and his solos were melodically more adventurous. But in spite of his advanced technique, Shaw did not seem to swing as much as Goodman.[5,6]

Trombone Many of the leading trombonists of early jazz were also leading trombonists in the swing era. Their styles became somewhat more refined, and they were found more often in big bands than in Dixieland combos. (See page 77 for coverage of Jack Teagarden, page 77 for J. C. Higginbotham, and page 94 for Tommy Dorsey.)

The swing era spilled into the decade of the 1940s and produced an important trombonist who did not already have a reputation in early jazz. **Bill Harris** was probably the most original and influential of the brass soloists featured in the Woody Herman band of the 1940s. Harris (1916–1973) is often thought to be a transitional figure in the development of modern jazz trombone, coming after J. C. Higginbotham and before J. J. Johnson. He had a broad, thick tone and quick vibrato which remained for the duration of each tone. Harris played with pronounced authority and employed good high range, by 1940s standards. Harris's solos made use of staccato, punching figures in addition to slides and smears. The construction of his solos was clearly thoughtful.

Trumpet Trumpeter **Roy Eldridge** (b. 1911) was one of the most advanced improvisers of the swing era. He is often considered a link between swing and modern jazz. Eldridge had a very aggressive style and un-

[3] *This Is Tommy Dorsey Vol. 1* RCA VPM 6038 and *Vol. 2* VPM 6064
[4] *The Best of Tommy Dorsey* MCA 2 4074
[5] *The Complete Artie Shaw Vol. 1* RCA AXM2 5517
[6] *This Is Artie Shaw* RCA VPM 6039

precedented instrumental proficiency. His imaginative choice of notes and sax-like lines provided continuity in the history of jazz trumpet from the style of Louis Armstrong to the modern approach pioneered by Dizzy Gillespie. Eldridge creatively varied the size, texture, and vibrato of his tone. Sometimes it was clear and warm, at other times brittle and edgy. His high-register playing had a sweeping scope; in that register, his entrances and syncopations were timed with a rhythmic feeling which suggested the modern jazz inflections that replaced early jazz rhythmic style. (Listen to his blazing 1941 solo on "After You've Gone" with Gene Krupa's band,[7,8] his unorthodox note choices in the 1937 "Blues in C-sharp Minor" with Teddy Wilson,[9] or his work with Benny Carter on the "I Can't Believe That You're In Love With Me" in SCCJ.)

New with Eldridge was the idea that a trumpeter could improvise long, sinewy lines which, though easy to execute on saxophone, do not lend themselves to the mechanics of the trumpet. Eldridge's influence caused modern trumpeters to cultivate considerably more instrumental facility and to improvise in more intricate and unpredictable ways than their early jazz counterparts. His conception also extended the average phrase length used by improvising trumpeters. Eldridge's influence extended into the 1950s by way of Dizzy Gillespie, who built his own influential style of modern jazz trumpet playing upon the foundation of Eldridge's bristling high-register playing, unorthodox choice of notes, and saxophone style of phrasing. (To detect the Eldridge character in Gillespie's earliest playing, listen to Eldridge's solo on the Gene Krupa band recording of "After You've Gone," then listen to Gillespie's playing on the 1939 Cab Calloway recording of "Pickin' the Cabbage."[10])

Eldridge was prominently featured with several big bands, including those of Fletcher Henderson, Gene Krupa, and Artie Shaw. His most creative period was probably 1936 to 1941, but he was still performing during the 1980s.

Charlie Shavers (1917–1971) was another brassy swing trumpeter with outstanding instrumental proficiency. He had a brittle tone and quick vibrato. Shavers improvised interrupted phrases of short, clipped notes, occasionally jumping into the high register for an exciting effect. Toward the middle and late 1940s, when he was in Tommy Dorsey's band, he showed a preference for saxophone-like phrasing and the high register that became standard in modern jazz trumpet. Like Eldridge, Shavers exerted an impact on the beginnings of modern

[7] *Gene Krupa-Drummin' Man* Columbia C2L29

[8] *The Early Years* Columbia C2 38033

[9] *Teddy Wilson and His All Stars* Columbia CG 31617; also in *Jazz Critics' Choice* Odyssey (Columbia) PC 37012

[10] *Sixteen Cab Calloway Classics* French CBS 62950

jazz trumpet style. (Shavers also wrote arrangements which adapted classical pieces for one of the most popular of all jazz combos, a sextet led by bassist John Kirby.)

One of the most famous swing era trumpeters was **Bunny Berigan** (1908–1942). His 1937 "I Can't Get Started" solo was well loved, and his improvisation in the Tommy Dorsey band's recording of "Marie" was transcribed and included in subsequent arrangements for other bands. Berigan was a very proficient trumpeter with a clear tone and remarkably clean articulation. He could play quite well in the trumpet's lowest register and still maintain a full, consistent tone in the high register. His playing seemed almost effortless because it was so relaxed and assured. Louis Armstrong's approach was evident as a source for Berigan's solo conception.

Saxophone   The man generally considered to be the father of jazz tenor saxophone playing is **Coleman Hawkins** (1904–1969). Prior to his arrival on the jazz scene in the 1920s, the saxophone had not attained much more than novelty instrument stature. Hawkins's deep-toned, husky command of the horn brought it recognition. Tenor sax became one of the most popular instruments in jazz. In fact, for many people, tenor saxophone symbolizes jazz.

Hawkins not only had exceptional command over his instrument and an aggressive delivery for his lines, but he also demonstrated an understanding of and interest in chord progressions which was substantially more advanced than that of most other premodern saxophonists. His improvisations revealed a greater attraction to investigating the chord progressions that could be added to a tune's original accompaniment than to devising new melodies. Hawkins is therefore known primarily as a harmonic improviser rather than a melodic improviser. He devoured complex chord progressions, such as those of "Body and Soul" (listen to his 1939 recording of it in SCCJ) and added chords to pieces which did not already have enough harmonic activity for him. In this respect, his improvisations resembled those of pianist Art Tatum (see pages 99–100).

Hawkins was a featured soloist with the Fletcher Henderson band from 1923 to 1934. After that he worked mostly with small groups. Though primarily associated with the swing era, he was also a respected figure at modern jazz sessions of the 1940s. In spite of the fact that he lacked the smoothness and fluid swing of modern jazz soloists, his skill with difficult chord progressions helped him adjust to newer styles. A surging energy continued to flow unquenched from his horn for decades. Hawkins was one of the most intense and consistent saxophone soloists in jazz history. His influence was not limited to his swing era contemporaries. Such modern tenor saxophonists as Sonny Rollins and John Coltrane were also influenced by him. Along with

Coleman Hawkins, father of jazz tenor saxophone. Pictured here at age 45 in 1949. (*Courtesy of Duncan Scheidt*)

Coltrane and Lester Young, Hawkins was the most influential tenor saxophonist in jazz history. Though his influence did decline somewhat after the 1940s, Hawkins remained an active performer until his death in 1969.

Don Byas (1912–1972), together with Lester Young (see Chapter 8), was more advanced than most swing tenor men and could hold his own with many modern jazzmen of the late 1940s. Byas incorporated the harmonic advances made by Hawkins, as well as elements of Art Tatum's complex piano style (discussed later in this chapter). Byas had fire, technical proficiency, harmonic sophistication, and melodic daring. He loved to double-time and run through every note in each chord. More significant was his tendency to add new chords to a tune, and to use both the original and new chords in his improvisations. The richness of his lines easily matches that of many solid 1950s modern jazz saxophonists. Byas swung more easily than Hawkins, but not quite as easily as Lester Young or the modern jazz players of the late 1940s. (Byas lived in Europe from 1946 until his death in 1972.)

It is difficult to classify the Byas style neatly as either a swing style or a modern style. In fact, some of his best recorded solos were made during the mid-1940s with the modern combo of trumpeter Dizzy Gillespie. Byas is best seen as a transitional figure, viewed as Lester Young is viewed. Both men had styles which shared elements of pre-modern and modern jazz, and both men influenced modern saxophonists. Lucky Thompson and Benny Golson are outstanding modern tenor saxophonists who drew from the Byas approach. (Listen to Byas and bassist Slam Stewart in their 1945 performance of "I Got Rhythm" in SCCJ.)

Benny Carter (b. 1907) and Johnny Hodges were the most influential alto saxophonists of the swing era (see pages 75–76 and 218–219 for more about Hodges). The first elements of Carter's playing that usually strike listeners are the precision of his execution and the glow of his tone quality. (Listen to Carter's "I Can't Believe That You're In Love With Me" in SCCJ.) His solos flow with grace and lightness. Both Hodges and Carter had rich, full-bodied tones, but the two players had different rhythmic styles. Carter tended to divide the beat precisely and evenly into legato eighth notes. Hodges had a more natural rhythmic feel, and the placement of notes in relation to the beat was far less obvious in Hodges's playing. Though both Carter and Hodges imparted a luxurious feel to their playing, Carter was more obvious in his constructions, Hodges more subtle. (And Hodges had a strikingly original way of placing accents, which set him apart from most swing and early jazz players. His style of accenting was unusual and imaginative, but he made it sound easier and more natural than it was.) Both Hodges and Carter swung easily, and Carter paved the way for modern jazz alto sax styles with his intelligently conceived, harmonically oriented solos.

Carter was also a good trumpeter, clarinetist, and a top-notch arranger (and, sporadically, a bandleader). He contributed arrangements to several good bands besides his own: Fletcher Henderson's, McKinney's Cotton Pickers, Benny Goodman's, and Chick Webb's. In 1960 and 1961, Carter composed and arranged the music for two outstanding Count Basie albums: *Kansas City Suite* and *The Legend*. Carter has continued his writing and playing in the 1980s.

Piano   **Art Tatum** (1910–1956) was one of the most widely admired pianists in jazz history. (Listen to Tatum's "Willow Weep for Me" and "Too Marvelous For Words" in SCCJ.) Even compared with all the very fast, imaginative modern pianists who have emerged since the 1940s, Tatum still stands out with his incredible power and technical facility. His style contains elements of stride piano combined with horn-like lines. Tatum's playing was quite flowery, with long, fast runs which sometimes overlapped each other. He was important in the development of modern jazz because he became a master at spontaneously adding and changing chords in pop tunes. Another device of his, picked up by modern alto saxophonist Charlie Parker and trumpeter Dizzy Gillespie, was to change keys several times within a phrase and still resolve the harmonic motion, neatly getting out of what often seemed like a precarious position.

Rhythmically Tatum was also very inventive. His left-hand rhythms were full of surprises. He is also known for changing tempo in mid-solo, sometimes leaving the intent listener dangling on an unresolved pattern while Tatum pursues another tangent. Tatum's right-hand playing sometimes seemed to throw showers of notes upon the listener, as though Tatum were shaking a tree branch and loosening leaf-like notes down upon us. These groups of notes often departed from simple patterns of eighth notes and sixteenth notes. But despite their complexity, Tatum runs have been memorized by hundreds of pianists and used to decorate solos for both jazz pianists and popular pianists.

The fast lines and added chords of Tatum were a direct influence on tenor saxophonist Don Byas, another swing era figure prominent in the transition from swing to modern jazz. Tatum was also an influence on two innovative modern jazz pianists: Bud Powell and Lennie Tristano, both of whom went on to influence countless pianists of the 1950s. (Oscar Peterson picked up techniques from both Tatum and Powell. Peterson is often compared with Tatum because Peterson has come closer than anyone else to achieving Tatum's impressive speed and power. During the late 1970s, Peterson performed Tatum-like solo improvisations bearing far less modern jazz character than Tatum character. It was as though Peterson were going backwards in jazz history after having established a modern style of his own.) Tatum's influence continued long after the swing era. For example, in the 1970s there emerged a young Polish pianist named Adam Makowicz who sounded very much as Tatum had during the 1930s.

The bulk of Tatum's work was done as an unaccompanied soloist or as a trio player. His bassist on many recordings was **Slam Stewart,** who was a good timekeeper, a responsive accompanist for Tatum's melodic flights, and an inventive soloist. During solos, Stewart often bowed the strings while he hummed in unison (or in octaves). The combination of voice and bass produced a rough-textured and original tone color. (Listen to Slam Stewart's solo in the Don Byas "I Got Rhythm" recording found in SCCJ.) He humorously slid from note to note, but always managed to make as much melodic sense as most swing hornmen. Stewart's solo playing moved jazz bass a step further away from its rigid role of being only a timekeeper. (See page 414 for information on how to get Joe Howard's analyses of more than 200 Art Tatum solos.)

With the exception of Tatum, **Teddy Wilson** (b. 1912) was probably the most innovative pianist in the swing era. He, too, contributed to the development of modern jazz. In fact his lighter lines influenced a whole school of modern pianists. Wilson could be flowery also, but when he chose to create horn-like lines, he refined the best of Earl Hines. Wilson's work on the 1936 "Blues in C-sharp Minor"[9] provides an excellent demonstration of his precisely executed, intelligently conceived horn lines. The whole feeling of Wilson's sound was that of lightening the early jazz and swing weightiness, and making way for the fleet smoothness and streamlined quality of modern jazz piano soloing and comping. Listeners are often impressed by the grace and evenness with which Teddy Wilson improvises even the fastest passages. It was as though equal attention was focused on every note, no matter how brief. His work could be dazzling.

Wilson and Tatum were contemporaries, but their styles differ. Tatum was less predictable than Wilson. Tatum frequently interrupted the direction of his own lines. He seemed to indulge his impulses and go off on musical tangents, instead of doing as Wilson did and seeing each idea through. Rhythmically, Tatum was far more varied than Wilson. Tatum was full of surprises. (Tatum died in 1956, but Wilson continued to play during the 1980s.)

Wilson was featured in Benny Goodman's small combos (listen to Wilson with Goodman on "Body and Soul" in SCCJ) and in his own bands. Like Tatum, Wilson is often mistaken for the type of pianist who usually plays in cocktail lounges and is therefore referred to as a cocktail pianist. This is partly due to the pleasantness of his style. Both Tatum and Wilson influenced countless cocktail pianists but do not themselves fall into this category. As their 1930s and 40s recordings show, melodic meat, variety, swing, and refinement distinguish Wilson and Tatum from the countless less-gifted pianists who have incorporated portions but not the completeness of either style.

Techniques of Earl Hines were especially evident in the early 1940s work of **Nat Cole** (1917–1965) and Erroll Garner, who were also important figures in the transition from swing era styles to modern jazz. Cole was one of the first pianists to extensively incorporate spare, horn-like lines in his playing, which exhibited a lightness not typical of the heavy-handed and flowery styles of premodern jazz. Cole also perfected a style of accompanying in which chords are played in brief, syncopated bursts, a style which eventually became known as comping.[11] Oscar Peterson, Bill Evans, and Horace Silver have all cited Cole as an early influence on their own musical thinking. In fact, Cole had a more pervasive influence than most people realize. His piano style received little attention after he became a popular singer, and it is often overlooked because of that.

[11] *Trio Days* Capitol M 11033

Erroll Garner (1923–1977) is a unique figure in jazz piano history because he does not fit neatly into either the swing era or the bop era and because he originated a relatively unorthodox style. He attained recognition at a time when swing had already peaked and modern jazz had been launched. Garner influenced several important modern jazz pianists, including George Shearing and Ahmad Jamal, and he recorded with saxophonist Charlie Parker, who was a founder of modern jazz.

Garner's greatest popularity occurred during the 1950s, even though his style was rooted in the swing era of the 1930s. He had a simple, swinging, easy-to-follow style, and his piano trio interpretations of popular songs, including his own composition "Misty," made him one of the best known of all jazz musicians to record during the 1950s.

The origins of Garner's approach are far flung. (Listen to "Fantasy on Frankie and Johnny" in SCCJ.) The sound of Earl Hines is suggested by Garner's octave-voiced right-hand lines and his pounding approach, though Garner's melodic sense is much simpler than Hines's, and he showed nowhere near the quantity of rhythmic surprises that typified Hines. It is notable that Garner's style evolved over the years, but he never relaxed his eighth-note conception to the streamlined feeling that was employed by modern pianists or by such advanced swing pianists as Teddy Wilson and Nat Cole. Several aspects of Garner's approach have assumed trademark quality for his name. One is that his left hand played a chord on each beat as a rhythm guitarist might, but each chord was played slightly late. Another is a skillful use of loudness changes. (This is a trait that Ahmad Jamal might have learned from Garner.) A third prime aspect associated with Garner is a flowery manner that seems to almost drip with extensive use of tremolo and grace notes.

Some of Garner's playing is richly orchestral, and it is harmonically like music of Claude Debussy and Maurice Ravel, a style called French Impressionism. Garner often voiced his melodies chordally instead of letting melody notes sound by themselves. This has led jazz historian Harvey Pekar to feel that Garner's historical impact may have been to get pianists to think more in terms of chordal playing. Pekar suggests that, through a concern with chordal playing and Impressionism, Garner may have begun a stream of styles which ran from Ahmad Jamal to Red Garland, and from Garland to Bill Evans and McCoy Tyner. Pekar also notes that Garner's regular statement of the beat with his left hand influenced—possibly through Jamal—Red Garland, though Garner played on all four beats whereas Garland punctuated just twice per measure. (See page 209 for more on Jamal, pages 214–215 for more on Garland, and pages 291–294 for more on Tyner.)

Though not notably innovative as a creater of melodic lines, **Milt Buckner** (1915–1977) influenced pianists of the 1940s through his use of block chording, or the so-called locked-hands style which is a method of voicing a chord and making the top note of it the melody note.[12] Buckner created piano solos that were like the four-, five-, and six-part horn voicings in band arrangements of the 1930s and 40s. It was as though each finger was playing the part that a saxophone would ordinarily play. This is in contrast to a style of playing in which one hand plays a single melodic line, while the other plays occasional chords. In locked-hands style the pianist uses both hands as though they were locked together, all fingers striking the piano keyboard at the same time. During the late 1940s and early 50s, Lennie Tristano, George Shearing, Ahmad Jamal, Oscar Peterson, and others used this technique, as did Red Garland and Bill Evans in the late 1950s. During the 1960s many pianists, including McCoy Tyner, made use of block chording. Each pianist's technique of block chording, particularly the voicings employed, was a distinctive aspect of his style. (**James P. Johnson,** Willie "The Lion" Smith, and other early pianists **had contributed the stride style. Earl Hines was a pioneer in playing horn-like lines. Meade Lux Lewis,** Pinetop Smith, Cow Cow Davenport, and others **introduced boogie woogie. Tatum had explored reharmonization.** And now **Milt Buckner had added locked-hands style** to the list of alternatives available to the modern jazz pianist.)

Guitar During the swing era, guitar was beginning to be viewed as more than a timekeeping member of the rhythm section. Part of this change was due to work done by Charlie Christian (1916–1942) and Django Reinhardt. **Charlie Christian** mastered what was then the almost unexplored world of electric guitar. (Listen to Christian with the Benny Goodman sextet on "Blues Sequence From Breakfast Feud" in SCCJ.) His long, swinging, single-note-at-a-time lines became models for modern jazz guitarists. Some of his phrasing had the fluid swing and freshness of tenor saxophonist Lester Young (see Chapter 8). Christian was featured with the Benny Goodman combos and big band. His work is also available on some amateur recordings of jam sessions with modern jazz trumpeter Dizzy Gillespie and pianist Thelonious Monk. Christian died in 1942 at the age of twenty-six, having been an active influence for no more than three years.

Django Reinhardt (1910–1953) was a Belgian Gypsy guitarist who had at least as much influence on modern jazz guitar playing as Charlie Christian. Reinhardt was based in France, played mostly within Europe, and visited America only once, but his recordings were available here. Prior to Reinhardt, most jazz guitarists had played brief, chorded solos which were quite modest compared to piano and horn solos. Reinhardt had a technical command of his guitar equal to Art Tatum's virtuoso piano technique. In fact, both men were fond of fast, flashy, cleanly executed runs. Reinhardt's playing was ornate and flamboyant with a

---

[12] Lionel Hampton *Steppin' Out Vol. 1* MCA 1315

prominent vibrato.[13] He combined the spirited flavor of Gypsy music with the equally spirited sound of jazz. His lines could have the intelligence of a master composer or simply could be a sequence of flourishes.

Reinhardt's influence on American musicians reversed a typical pattern. Being primarily an American art form, jazz was usually exported rather than imported. The memory of Reinhardt has inspired compositions by pianist John Lewis ("Django") and guitarist Joe Pass ("For Django"). Reinhardt's composition "Nuages" continues to be performed by jazz musicians. And Reinhardt's influence remains current in the person of Bireli Lagrene, a young guitarist recording during the 1980s, sounding remarkably like Reinhardt.

Charlie Christian[14] can be contrasted with Django Reinhardt in that

1) Christian's pace within solos was usually steady, whereas Reinhardt's was uneven and marked by sporadic flashiness;

2) Christian's lines were hornlike, whereas Reinhardt's were more pianistic;

3) Most of Christian's recordings were made with amplified hollow-body guitar, whereas most of Reinhardt's were made on hollow-body acoustic guitar;

4) Christian's tone was usually round and soft, whereas Reinhardt's possessed a bite and was often metallic sounding;

5) Christian drew more from blues tradition, whereas Reinhardt drew from Gypsy music and the French Impressionist composers Ravel and Debussy;

6) Christian used long patterns of swing eighth notes, whereas Reinhardt used somewhat jumpier sequences, with interruptions for drawn-out pitch bends;

7) Christian preferred eighth-note lines, whereas Reinhardt often leaned more toward triplet and sixteenth-note lines;

8) Christian used very little vibrato, whereas Reinhardt employed vibrato as a key element in his approach.

Popular Appeal   The swing era was one of the few periods in jazz history when jazz had wide popular appeal. Much big band music was not improvised—it was written music—but hundreds of improvising musicians were employed in the swing era big bands, so it was a good era for jazz. However, in describing the era as a good period for jazz, a few qualifications must also be considered.

1) A significant portion of swing era hits contained vocals, and many of those that did not have singing were at least based on

---

[13] *Parisian Swing: Reinhardt/Grappelly* GNP Crescendo 9002
[14] *Solo Flight—The Genius of Charlie Christian* Columbia CG 30779

songs that listeners had previously learned by way of a vocal rendition. This alerts us to consider that jazz value might not have provided the primary appeal of the pieces. The popularity of those pieces might just reflect the same appeal that songs have had throughout history.

2) Most of the swing era hits that were jazz-oriented contained only a few solo improvisations, and sometimes they contained only one.

3) The amount of improvisation in most swing era hits was small, sometimes being only sixteen measures, rarely more than a thirty-two bar chorus.

4) The construction of improvised solos in most hits was melodically conservative.

A note about instrumentation is necessary here. There were big bands prior to the swing era (Fletcher Henderson, Duke Ellington, and Paul Whiteman, for example) and after the swing era (Dizzy Gillespie, Gerald Wilson, Stan Kenton, and Thad Jones–Mel Lewis, for example), but the swing era was a peak for the popularity of this instrumentation. During the 1930s and 40s, it seemed that almost every other big-name jazz musician was leading or playing in a big band. In fact, big bands were more common in the 1930s than jazz combos were the 1950s and 60s. Big bands provided the popular music medium during the late 1930s that rock combos provided during the 1950s and 60s.

Some big bands, especially Count Basie's, placed great emphasis on improvisation, but numerous bands were not as concerned with jazz. Therefore, some listeners (disc jockeys, journalists, and musicians) drew a distinction between swing era big bands which emphasized improvisation and those that did not. The very popular Glenn Miller band, for instance, was a swinging band, but it placed much more emphasis on pretty arrangements and vocals than on improvised jazz solos. Therefore, despite its swinging qualities, the Miller band was sometimes classified in the "sweet band" category (as in the 1940 and 1941 popularity polls run by *Down Beat* magazine). This distinguished it from the "hot band" or "swing band" classification that was applied to Count Basie and Duke Ellington. Note, however, that many listeners still class the Miller band as a "swing band" even though it was not deeply involved in jazz.

Like rock combos of the 1950s and 60s, a principal function for swing bands of the 1930s was to provide dance music. Though jazz had been danced to for most of its history, it functioned more as dance music during the swing era than before or since. Another similarity with popular rock combos is that swing era big bands usually had at least one singer, and some routinely carried several singers. The lyrics of the songs, together with the personality and good looks of the singers, were primary attractions for a sizable portion of the band audiences. Only occasionally during the swing era did jazz musicians perform just for listening as later became the custom for most jazz groups. It is unlikely that those millions of swing band fans were attracted primarily by the jazz improvisation in the music. The popular success of jazz during the swing era was partly a result of its appeal to the eyes and feet of fans instead of to the ears alone.

CHAPTER SUMMARY

1) Swing differs from early jazz in
   a) greater use of arrangements
   b) less emphasis on ragtime-like compositions
   c) rejection of collective improvisation in favor of solo improvisation
   d) increased use of string bass instead of tuba
   e) greater swing feeling, achieved by increased use of swing eighth-note patterns
   f) increased use of high-hat cymbals
   g) replacement of banjo with guitar
   h) big band rather than small group instrumentation
   i) saxophone becoming the most plentiful instrument
2) The most historically important big bands were led by Duke Ellington, Count Basie, Benny Goodman, and Jimmie Lunceford.
3) The most influential saxophonists were Coleman Hawkins, Lester Young, Benny Carter, and Johnny Hodges.
4) The most influential pianists were Art Tatum and Teddy Wilson.
5) Tatum possessed phenomenal speed and was known for spontaneously increasing the number of chords in some compositions and completely reorganizing others.
6) Wilson was known for his grace and his streamlining of jazz piano style.
7) Nat Cole influenced modern jazz piano style by reducing left-hand activity and making right-hand lines more horn-like.
8) Milt Buckner perfected the technique of harmonizing melody lines in a block-chord fashion that became known as "locked-hands" piano style.
9) Bunny Berigan and Buck Clayton, two of the most widely admired swing trumpeters, both drew from the Louis Armstrong style.
10) Roy Eldridge paved the way for modern jazz trumpeter Dizzy Gillespie by improvising fiery saxophone-like lines on trumpet.

chapter 7
DUKE ELLINGTON

Duke Ellington (1899–1974) is one of the most outstanding figures in jazz history. He was not only a bandleader and pianist, but also probably the single most creative and prolific composer-arranger. He wrote over a thousand tunes and probably one and one-half times that number of arrangements and rearrangements. He began composing and arranging well before 1920 and continued until his death in 1974. Recorded more than any other jazz group, the Ellington band can be heard in hundreds of 78 r.p.m. recordings and long-play albums.

Pianist Although piano playing was the least of his great talents, Ellington was both a flashy and original solo player in the percussive stride style of James P. Johnson and Willie "The Lion" Smith. As an accompanist he developed a spare manner which framed phrases in arrangements and embroidered the solos of his sidemen. Ellington's piano playing was full of vitality and imagination.

Composer Ellington wrote many tunes which, with the addition of lyrics, became popular songs, such as "Satin Doll," "Sophisticated Lady," "I'm Beginning to See the Light," "Solitude," "Mood Indigo," and "Don't Get Around Much Anymore." He also wrote hundreds of three-minute instrumentals such as "Concerto for Cootie," "In a Mellotone," and "Black and Tan Fantasy." The lengths of these pieces average three minutes because that was standard time length for one side of a 78 r.p.m. record, the primary recording medium until the early 1950s. (Listen to "Concerto for Cootie" and "In a Mellotone" in SCCJ.)

Ellington also wrote many longer pieces, including "Creole Rhap-

Duke Ellington's 1941 band, the mobile laboratory for explorations in varied tone colors and the multilayered weaving of improvisation and composition. *Left to right:* Otto Hardwicke, Juan Tizol, Harold Baker, Ray Nance (directly behind Ellington, who is seated at the piano), Harry Carney (directly behind Betty Roche), Rex Stewart, Johnny Hodges (alto sax), Ben Webster (tenor sax), Chauncey Haughton, Joe "Tricky Sam" Nanton (trombone), Wallace Jones (trumpet), Lawrence Brown (trombone), and Sonny Greer (drums). (*Courtesy of Frank Driggs*)

sody," "Reminiscing in Tempo," "Harlem," "New World a' Comin'," etc. He even wrote a fifty-minute tone parallel to the history of the American Negro ("Black, Brown and Beige").

Ellington composed and his band played several film scores (movie sound tracks): *Paris Blues, Anatomy of a Murder, Asphalt Jungle, Assault on a Queen,* and *Change of Mind.*

Many of Ellington's pieces depict real personalities: "Bojangles" (the famous black tap dancer, Bill Robinson),[*] "A Portrait of Bert Williams" (a leading black comic), "Portrait of Ella Fitzgerald," "The Shepherd Who Watches Over the Night Flock" (for Reverend John Gensel), and "Portrait of the Lion" (Willie "The Lion" Smith, a great stride pianist).

[*] Not the "Mr. Bojangles" by Jerry Jeff Walker that became popular during the early 1970s, though both the Ellington piece and the pop tune were inspired by Bill Robinson.

Other pieces paint musical pictures of places and sensations: "Warm Valley," "Transbluency," and "Harlem Air Shaft." (Listen to "Harlem Air Shaft" in SCCJ.) Ellington composed the entire 11½-minute "Perfume Suite" not to describe the various labels of the commercial perfumes, but rather to delineate the character a woman assumes under the influence of them. He also put together an album inspired by Shakespeare sonnets: *Such Sweet Thunder.*

Nearly every jazz musician has played at least one Ellington tune during his career. The respect Ellington received from other jazz musicians is demonstrated by the fact that no other jazz composer has had as many albums devoted to his music. Ellington tunes have comprised entire albums for more than twenty jazz greats, including musicians as stylistically diverse as Dizzy Gillespie, McCoy Tyner, and Dave Brubeck. A vocal group—Lambert, Hendricks, and Ross—recorded an entire LP of transcriptions of famous Ellington recordings, providing lyrics for the written and the improvised lines. During the 1980s, an entire Broadway review, "Sophisticated Ladies," was devoted to the music of Ellington.

Arranging Style   One of Ellington's greatest skills as an arranger was that of capitalizing on the uniquely personal sounds of individual players. Instead of writing for an anonymous group of instruments ("lead trumpet, second trumpet, third trumpet," etc.) as most arrangers do, **he actually wrote parts suited to particular players** (Cat Anderson, Cootie Williams, Rex Stewart, etc.). He carried this technique one step further by indicating sections of each piece where certain players were to improvise solos accompanied by prewritten ensemble passages. Ellington matched the improviser with the ensemble so carefully that the resulting sound was unusually effective, and his sidemen improvised so thoughtfully that it was often difficult to know which parts were improvised and which were written.

While most arrangers, including Ellington, write passages that pit the sound of one section against that of another (sax section against brass section, for instance), Ellington often wrote passages to be played by **combinations of instruments drawn from different sections of the band. This is called voicing (or scoring) across sections.** In his 1940 "Concerto for Cootie" (in SCCJ), Ellington voiced pizzicato bass notes in unison with the horns. On Ellington's 1940 "Jack the Bear," bassist Jimmy Blanton played pizzicato melody statements both alone and with horns. Voicing across sections was unusual in most 1930s and 40s big bands; the bass was primarily a member of the rhythm section and rarely played horn parts.

In his 1930 "Mood Indigo," Ellington voiced clarinet with muted trumpet and muted trombone; this is an example of combining instruments from three different sections of the band: trumpet section, trombone section, and sax section. During the late 1950s, Ellington achieved an unusual color by voicing clarinet with tenor sax and fluegelhorn. The three instruments played unison lines while three trombones accompanied them with punching back-up figures (in *Cosmic Scene;* "Newport Up," in *Ellington at Newport;* and "Idiom '59," in *Festival Session*).

Occasionally Ellington added another unique tone color by placing a **wordless vocal (also called instrumentalized voice)** in an arrangement. His 1927 "Creole Love Call" (*This Is Duke Ellington*), 1946 "Transbluency," 1968 "Too Good to Title," and 1947 "On a Turquoise Cloud" all use wordless vocals. "Transbluency" combines muted trombone with wordless vocal, and, later in the arrangement, clarinet is paired with the vocal. His "On a Turquoise Cloud" blends vocal, clarinet, and muted trombone; vocal, bass clarinet, and violin are combined in another passage.

One of the Ellington band's first important jobs was playing at the Cotton Club in New York where the floor shows placed great emphasis on "jungle sounds." To create these sounds, Ellington used the **growl style** associated with trumpeter Bubber Miley and trombonist Joe "Tricky Sam" Nanton. The growls were achieved by a combination of mutes and unorthodox methods of blowing. The most common mute was a plumber's plunger (rubber suction cup, also known as a plumber's helper). This was used to open and close the bell of the horn. Occasionally an additional mute was secured inside the horn's bell, lending a buzz to the sound. Voice-like effects were created by Miley and Nanton in this way. The growl style could be very expressive. (Listen to "East St. Louis Toodle-Oo" in SCCJ.)

Other elements of the jungle sound were supplied by certain voicings of clarinets. (Sometimes everyone in the sax section would be playing clarinet at the same time.) Ellington assigned notes to each clarinet which, in combination, produced unusual harmonies and wailing, intensely emotional effects. Together with his unorthodox practice of voicing across sections and his use of the growl styles, these clarinet techniques added to the broad color range of his band arranging style.

Voicing across sections is Ellington's best-known arranging technique. However, **he also scored in the conventional big band manner that pitted the saxophone section against the trumpet and trombone section.** But even when he did that, there always seemed to be more imagination, more variety, and fewer clichés in the finished product than were ordinarily present when other bands tried it. His antiphonal passages boasted themes that were better developed and more substantial. A shining example of this is found in his 1940 recording of "Cottontail." In the sixth chorus, Ellington pits brass against saxes by assigning musical questions to the brass and answers to the saxes. (Listen to "Cottontail," and follow the listening guide on page 111.)

Listening Guide for "Cottontail"

The piece is based on the chord progression to George Gershwin's "I Got Rhythm." The fresh melody that Ellington wrote in harmony for saxophone section to play in the fifth chorus has some of the melodic and rhythmic character of a modern jazz improvisation. It remains one of Ellington's most famous passages. Its popularity among musicians rivals that of the often-quoted Ben Webster improvisation from the same recording. This compositional device is technically known as a saxophone soli. When it is performed, traditionally the entire saxophone section stands up to allow the audience to focus on them.

FIRST CHORUS

A   Melody stated by saxes and trumpets with rhythm accompaniment.

A   Sax and trumpet melody repeated with trombone section figures added to the accompaniment.

B   Saxes ask musical questions, muted trumpet (Cootie Williams) answers them.

FOUR-MEASURE INTERLUDE

This consists of a brief conversation between the sax section and brass section with rhythm accompaniment.

SECOND CHORUS

A-A   Improvised tenor sax solo (Ben Webster) with rhythm accompaniment.

B   Tenor sax talks for a while with the brass section.

A   Brass depart, leaving tenor to continue improvising with rhythm section accompaniment.

THIRD CHORUS

A-A   Tenor continues improvisation accompanied by rhythm section.

B   Brass return to talk more with tenor sax.

A   Brass depart and tenor finishes his improvisation accompanied by rhythm section.

FOURTH CHORUS

A-A   Brass play alone, accompanied by rhythm section.

B   Improvised baritone sax solo (Harry Carney) accompanied by rhythm section.

A   Improvised piano solo accompanied by rhythm guitar, bass, and drums.

FIFTH CHORUS

A-A-B-A   Sax section plays the whole chorus accompanied by rhythm section.

SIXTH CHORUS

A-A   Brass section shouts questions and sax section answers, accompanied by rhythm section.

B   Brass section takes over loudly with rhythm section steaming forward.

A   Saxes and trumpets play the melody to its end with rhythm section accompaniment and no trombones.

During the 1940s, Ellington's writing influenced Charlie Barnet's band and Woody Herman's band. (Herman's band even recorded with Ellington sidemen.) Gil Evans used Ellington techniques in writing for the recordings of Claude Thornhill and Miles Davis. During the 1950s and 60s, Ellington's influence could be heard in the compositions and arrangements of Charles Mingus, Sun Ra, George Russell, Clare Fischer, and Lalo Schifrin. During the 1970s, Ellington's impact was surfacing in the writing of Thad Jones and Toshiko Akyoshi. Anthony Davis, a leading avant-garde composer and pianist of the 1980s, cites Ellington as his main influence. Ellington's piano style influenced many players, including two very significant modern pianists: Thelonious Monk and Cecil Taylor.

TABLE 7.1. A Few of the Musicians Most Significant to Ellington

Clarinet and Saxophones	Trumpet	Quentin "Butter" Jackson
	Louis Metcalf	Tyree Glenn
Rudy Jackson	Bubber Miley	Buster Cooper
Barney Bigard	Arthur Whetsol	
Jimmy Hamilton	Cootie Williams	**Bass**
Russell Procope	Rex Stewart	
Willie Smith	Taft Jordan	Wellman Braud
Otto Hardwicke	Ray Nance	Billy Taylor
Johnny Hodges	Willie Cook	Jimmy Blanton
Harry Carney	Cat Anderson	Oscar Pettiford
Ben Webster	Clark Terry	Wendell Marshall
Al Sears	Harold "Shorty" Baker	Jimmy Woode
Paul Gonsalves	Johnny Coles	Aaron Bell
Harold Ashby	Money Johnson	Ernie Shepard
		Piano
Drums	**Trombone**	
		Duke Ellington
Sonny Greer	Joe "Tricky Sam" Nanton	Billy Strayhorn
Louis Bellson	Lawrence Brown	
Sam Woodyard	Juan Tizol	
Rufus Jones	Britt Woodman	

SIDEMEN   Duke Ellington's band was one of the first big bands. In fact, Ellington, Fletcher Henderson, and Don Redman are often considered largely responsible for the birth of big band jazz. Ellington not only helped create the big band idiom, but also led the most long-lived and stable band in jazz. He started in 1923 and never broke up his band. Many players remained with him for twenty to thirty years at a stretch. Drummer Sonny Greer remained with Ellington from 1919 to 1951. Baritone saxophonist Harry Carney played with him from 1927 until Ellington's death in 1974. Carney himself died five months later.

Nearly all the members of Ellington's band had strong, unique styles of their own; together they made up an all-star unit. Most of Ellington's soloists were exceptionally deliberate players. Their self-pacing was nearly always tasteful. Thoughtfully constructed improvisations were the rule. In certain arrangements their solos often became crystallized and then recurred almost note for note in subsequent performances. These pieces then became much like written compositions, entirely unimproviseed.

Clarinet   Clarinetist **Barney Bigard** (b. 1906) and his successor Jimmy Hamilton are considered by some to be as creative as Benny Goodman and other swing era clarinetists. Both Bigard and Hamilton developed unique styles based on their excellent command of the clarinet. (Both men doubled on tenor saxophone, also.) Bigard brought an expansiveness to the feeling of an Ellington piece. His long, sweeping, legato lines swooped and darted through the ensemble sound. Listen to his contributions on Ellington's 1940 "Jack the Bear" and "Harlem Air Shaft." (Listen to "Harlem Air Shaft" in SCCJ.) Or study his improvisation in the 1936 "Clarinet Lament," which Ellington wrote especially for him. His was a New Orleans style adapted to the swing era.

Jimmy Hamilton (b. 1917) is an original improviser with a style less intense than Bigard's. His sound is well manicured and lighter than most swing clarinet sounds. Hamilton's conception is precise and articulate, with a cool, floating quality that suggests elements of modern jazz. Listen to his work on the 1956 Bethlehem records he made with Ellington, the 1956 and 1958 Newport Jazz Festival LPs (*Newport 1958, Ellington at Newport*), and Ellington's 1959 *Festival Session*.

Listening Guide for the Version of "Harlem Air Shaft" Found in SCCJ

INTRODUCTION
Four Measures

> The brass instruments call in harmonized, sustained tones, and the saxes respond with an active figure. Then, while they are silent, you can hear a full rhythm section sound with prominent rhythm guitar, walking bass, and Sonny Greer using brushes on snare drum for timekeeping. Ellington inserts a brief piano fill.

Four Measures

Saxes now have the lead. Listen to their harmony. Notice more piano fills.

Four Measures

Now the trombones take the lead for about a measure and a half with the baritone saxophone coming in with a response at the end of that second measure. Trombones instantaneously return for two measures of punching figures. (Ellington called them his "pep section" because of the function these figures served.)

FIRST CHORUS

(The remainder of the piece follows a repeating, thirty-two bar A-A-B-A form.)

A Saxes play a simple melody in unison while muted trumpets repeat a more complex background figure in harmony as an answering embellishment.

A Repeat the above.

B Saxes take the foreground by playing a harmonized part in the high register, alternating their calling with trombonist Joe "Tricky Sam" Nanton responding in plunger-muted growl style. Then saxes tie it up with a quick, little, low-register figure at the end of the bridge.

A Repeat of A, but this time, with a tie-it-up figure from the trumpets to get ready for the upcoming stop-time. Sonny Greer ends the figure by striking a cymbal, then quickly grabs it to prevent ringing. (The sound and timing of this technique is effective for closing a musical idea in an abrupt way.)

SECOND CHORUS

A *First Four Measures*

The rhythm section stops playing. This creates a four-measure stop-time break. The saxes use it to play a high-register, harmonized part with sustained tones. This evokes a suspended feeling, partly because the rhythm section is no longer stating each beat, and partly because there is suddenly very little movement in the sax sound. Then Sonny Greer uses sticks to play rolls and rim shots, "breaking things up," to enhance the band's transition from the suspension to a rough and tumble trumpet solo by Cootie Williams.

Second Four Measures

Cootie Williams opens his trumpet improvisation by percussively stating the same note repeatedly in an off-the-beat fashion. He creates excitement by using the high register and by shaking his tones as they end. Notice the sax activity underneath Williams.

A Same strategy as for the first A section. Williams continues with more repeated and shaken high notes, and Greer uses cymbal clasp to end this section of the piece.

B Sax part becomes more intricate, repeating a climbing figure while Williams continues his improvisation against sax lines. Greer's cymbal clasp ends this section, too.

A   Same strategy as for the first and second A sections. Notice how Williams dramatically slides down from his last high note. Listen to Greer's activity. It almost constitutes another line added to those of Williams and the saxes.

THIRD CHORUS

A   Trombones play a harmonized melody in the foreground while clarinetist Barney Bigard improvises around it, and saxes play yet another series of interjections underneath. Pay attention to Bigard's swoops and the New Orleans flavor of his playing. Imagine having to invent all those lines and colorations to spontaneously embroider the trombone and sax parts without clashing. This is not an ordinary jazz solo.

A   Same formula as for the first A section.

B   Trumpets join trombones to repeat a sustained tone while Bigard continues his improvisation and answers them. Saxes make periodic interjections. Listen to Bigard's shake at the end of the bridge.

A   Same formula as for the first A section. Note Bigard's blue notes. Drummer Sonny Greer becomes louder, striking high-hat while it is in partially opened position.

FOURTH CHORUS

(Though it starts softly, this chorus gets louder and louder, gradually raising excitement for the climax.)

A   Band softly plays a syncopated, low-register melody while Bigard's solo from the previous chorus overlaps into the first three measures of this one, with him entering clarinet's lower register. Listen to the rhythm guitar and Jimmy Blanton's driving bass sound. They are easier to hear now that the band has quieted down. Cootie Williams begins a muted trumpet solo where Bigard leaves off. Williams starts softly, but, as he proceeds, note how he changes the size and texture of his tone.

A   Pay attention to the finish of his solo in which Williams taps out the last four notes in the manner of a drummer.

B   The arrangement builds excitement by increasing loudness, adding instrumental activity, and going higher in register. The band calls, and Bigard repeatedly climbs out of the ensemble sound in response. The brass sound becomes clearer. Note the relationship between Bigard's improvised figures and the composed ones being played by the rest of the band. It all fits together despite the spontaneity.

A   Saxes call, and the brass answer repeatedly. A high level of excitement is reached. Bigard is improvising throughout the sounds of several written themes. Saxes repeat a new riff of their own. Bigard enters the high register. Brass begin repeating a new riff. The several levels of competing activity threaten to result in chaos by becoming more and more active at the end, but it all is resolved just in time to prevent an explosion. It ends with the brass sustaining a chord and the baritone sax sounding a low note at the finish.

Trumpet   **Bubber Miley** (1903–1932) and **Cootie Williams** (b. 1910) were known for the growl style of trumpet playing and the unorthodox use of rubber plunger mutes. Miley was one of Ellington's leading soloists from 1924 to 1929. His style furnished a playful voice for such classic Ellington recordings as the 1927 "East St. Louis Toodle-Oo" and "Creole Love Call." (Listen to "East St. Louis Toodle-Oo" in SCCJ.) Cootie Williams was Miley's successor in the band, playing from 1929 to 1940 and then rejoining in 1962 to remain until Ellington's death in 1974. Williams was Ellington's main trumpet soloist. Ellington wrote his 1936 "Echoes of Harlem" and his 1940 "Concerto for Cootie" to feature Williams. (Listen to "Concerto for Cootie" in SCCJ.) "Concerto for Cootie" was later rewritten with lyrics and became the popular tune "Do Nothin' 'til You Hear From Me." (When Williams returned in 1962, Ellington wrote an entirely new piece called "New Concerto for Cootie.")

Some of Cootie Williams's most inventive playing was captured in Ellington's 1940 recording of "Harlem Airshaft." (Listen to this in SCCJ, and follow the listening guide on page 113.) His work on this number demonstrates his mastery of wide-ranging techniques for colorfully altering pitch and tone quality. He is very calculating in the way he reaches notes, but his sound projects a searing sensuality that projects great naturalness rather than cold calculation. His solos on the piece combine a diversity of blues singing techniques and trumpet techniques to conjure peaks of raw excitement. Another asset is a keen sense of rhythm. Sometimes his notes are so well timed and percussively executed, the listener might assume Williams to be a drummer.

Rex Stewart (1907–1967) played cornet for Ellington from 1934 until 1944 and contributed humorous solos, colorful sounds, and blue notes that were produced by pressing his cornet valves only half way down (sometimes called "half valve" or "cocked valve"). Ellington wrote "Boy Meets Horn" to feature Stewart. He was also prominent on "Morning Glory" and "Portrait of Bert Williams."

Cornetist **Ray Nance** (1913–1976) has contributed very individualistic violin solos to Ellington's "Black, Brown, and Beige," "Lonesome Lullaby," "C-Jam Blues," and "Mr. Gentle and Mr. Cool." Prominently featured as a cornet soloist after Cootie Williams left, Nance created the warm, romantic solo on the famous 1941 recording of "Take the 'A' Train." His solo was so melodic and fit so well with the composition and arrangement that other musicians frequently quote it when they play the tune. Even Cootie Williams quoted it when he performed the tune with Ellington during the 1960s and 70s. Nance played with the band for most of the period 1941 to 1963.

Cat Anderson (b. 1916) is one of a long line of big band trumpeters who play stratospherically high notes. It has been playfully stated that

Anderson plays notes so high that only dogs can hear them. (Listen to Anderson's solos on "Coloratura" in Ellington's 1945 "Perfume Suite," Ellington's 1955 "La Virgen de la Macarena," and "Summertime.") It is the sound of Anderson that is heard capping off the endings of many exciting Ellington big band pieces of the 1950s. His clear, powerful sound was the lead trumpet position for the band on and off from 1947 to 1971.

Clark Terry (b. 1920) is a modern trumpeter who was featured by Ellington from 1951 to 1959. Probably the most technically gifted of all Ellington's brass soloists, Terry has excellent instrumental facility and a happy, swinging style that is easy to recognize. He also helped popularize the fluegelhorn, an oversized cornet, played in much the same manner as required for cornet and trumpet (see Figure 7.1). Terry blows the horn so well that he achieves a brassy edge along with a distinct fullness that is quite round. His fluegelhorn sound is unique. Most players extract the instrument's naturally soft, dark tone quality. (Listen to Terry's solo improvisations on four Columbia recordings made with the Ellington band: *Ellington at Newport, Cosmic Scene, Newport 1958,* and *Festival Session.*)

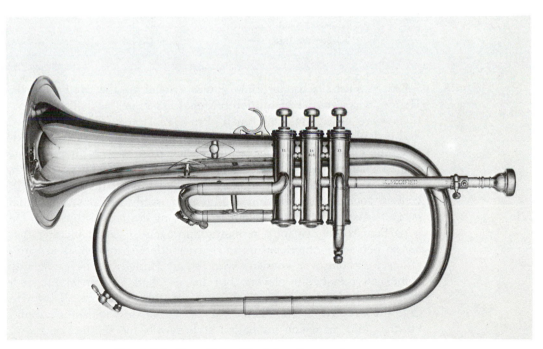

Figure 7.1. Fluegelhorn. (*The Selmer Company*)

Saxophone   **Johnny Hodges** (1906–1970) was the best known of Ellington's side-men. He often played position of lead alto, which is the saxophonist who plays the highest notes in the section and who leads the other saxophonists in timing and interpretation of written sax parts.* His solos and his style in leading the sax section were a vital part of the Ellington sound from 1928 until 1970 (with an absence from 1951 to 1955). Hodges produced such an unusually deep and lush tone that his recorded alto sax has sometimes been mistaken for tenor saxophone. He developed a remarkable way of gliding from note to note very gradually and smoothly. It was almost as if his instrument were equipped with a slide, like a trombone. This technique is called porta-mento, but jazz musicians generally refer to it as smearing. Hodges used it to great advantage in ballad playing. Ellington wrote numerous pieces tailor-made for that well-known Hodges approach. (Listen to Hodges play "Passion Flower" in *Jive at Five*, New World 274.)

TABLE 7.2. A Few of the Many Saxophonists Influenced by Johnny Hodges

Tab Smith	Bobby Plater
Louis Jordan	Charlie Barnet
Earl Bostic	Woody Herman
Johnny Bothwell	Eddie Vinson
Willie Smith	John Coltrane
Ben Webster	Jan Garbarek

An exquisite sense of timing was crucial to the Hodges style. Hodges was a master of subtlety in tonal inflections, and his syncopations were especially well timed. Pre-1942 Hodges often displayed flashy double-timing like Sidney Bechet, his primary influence, but after the mid-1940s, Hodges tended to lay back very deliberately, no matter what the tempo. Nearly every Ellington album features Hodges, and he was such a consistent player that almost all these recordings contain good Hodges playing. Hodges is possibly the most influential jazz alto saxophonist to come out of the swing era (see Table 7.2). He is particularly known for a romantic approach to ballad playing that has so pervaded American music that countless saxophonists are imitating it without even knowing who Johnny Hodges was. He not only influenced premodern players, but he also had an impact on such modern saxophonists as Eddie Vinson and John Coltrane. (Listen to Coltrane's recording of "Theme for Ernie," on his *Soultrane* album, Prestige 7531, in which his ballad style recalls the fullness of sound

* In Ellington's arrangements the lead sax part was not always given to Hodges. Otto Hardwicke and Russell Procope played lead in some pieces.

and timing of ornaments that Hodges refined.) Even as recently as the 1970s and 80s there was a continuation of the Hodges influence: saxophonist Jan Garbarek cited Hodges as a source for his own style.

Harry Carney (1910–1974) is usually considered the father of the jazz baritone saxophone, which almost puts him in a class with Coleman Hawkins, the father of the jazz tenor saxophone and a soloist who influenced Carney. Carney's ensemble playing in Ellington's sax section often vied with that of Hodges himself, providing a rock-solid foundation, often as important as that of the band's bassist. Inspired by Carney's playing, Ellington occasionally scored for baritone sax lead. Few baritone saxophonists have been able to match the size and strength of Carney's mammoth, rich sound. He also played clarinet and bass clarinet for Ellington, each of which, in his hands, became a strong, thick-toned voice in the Ellington ensemble. Although primarily an ensemble voice, Carney occasionally received feature numbers, including "Serious Serenade," "Frustration," and "Chromatic Love Affair."

Ben Webster (1909–1973) and the saxophonist who took his place seven years after Webster left Ellington, Paul Gonsalves, were two of the most skillful tenor saxophone ballad players to be influenced by the Coleman Hawkins approach. Webster solos on the Ellington recordings of "All Too Soon" (1940), "Just A-Settin' and A-Rockin'" (1941), "I Don't Know What Kind of Blues I've Got" (1941), and "Chelsea Bridge" (1941). He played with a breathy tone and a slow, marked vibrato which was especially distinct at the end of sustained tones. He also employed a hoarse, rasping sound to create a rousing effect in selected portions of a solo, as on the 1941 recording of "Raincheck," the 1942 recording of "Mainstem," and the 1941 recording of "Blue Serge" (in SCCJ). For an example of the masculine, laid-back approach to medium-tempo improvisation that Webster developed, listen to Ellington's 1940 recording of "Cottontail." His 1939–43 recordings with Ellington represent the peak of his career. He died in 1973, having been an influence on such modern tenor saxophonists as Charlie Ventura, Eddie "Lockjaw" Davis, and Archie Shepp. During the late 1970s, modern tenor saxophonist Lew Tabackin, who had already molded his own style from John Coltrane methods, began injecting aspects of Webster's approach. Tabackin ultimately changed his own style so drastically that little of Coltrane's remained and much of Webster's was prominent. It was as though Tabackin was traveling backwards in tenor saxophone history. In 1977, a young saxophonist named Scott Hamilton appeared on records, playing in a style that bore uncanny resemblance to Webster's. This was very unusual because it made no reference to the modern styles which had become the primary influences on saxophonists for three decades after Webster's peak.

Paul Gonsalves (1920–1974) was Ellington's main soloist during the 1950s, 60s, and 70s. He began as a disciple of Ben Webster, but also showed hints of the Don Byas–Lucky Thompson approach. Despite these roots, Gonsalves had a unique style, one aspect of which was a very unusual and fluid conception for medium- and up-tempo playing. He had a soft, diffuse tone without edge. But, in spite of his soft tone, his playing almost had the urgency of John Coltrane's, and Gonsalves's choice of notes was so unusual that it is amazing he could deliver them as fluently as he did. Listen to "Take the 'A' Train" on Ellington's 1950 *Hi-Fi Ellington Uptown,* and his solos on *Ellington at Newport, Newport 1958, Cosmic Scene,* and *Festival Session.* Gonsalves played with Ellington from 1951 until his death ten days before Ellington's in 1974.

Trombone   Trombonist **Joe "Tricky Sam" Nanton** (1904–1946) was master of the growl style. With his plumber's plunger and unorthodox blowing, he came very close to pronouncing words with his trombone. From 1926 until 1946, Nanton gave Ellington a provocative sound to voice in arrangements, as in the 1940 "Ko-Ko" and "Harlem Air Shaft" (in SCCJ). Quentin "Butter" Jackson perfected the growl style in Ellington's band from 1948 to 1959 and carried it with him into the modern Thad Jones–Mel Lewis band of the 1970s.

Lawrence Brown (b. 1907) was one of the first trombonists of the swing era to play with a very smooth, large, consistent sound. His tone added a great deal of body to the Ellington trombone section, and Brown had an aggressive solo style. Ellington wrote "Blue Cellophane" and "Golden Cress" as features for Brown.

Drums   There have been only a few drummers in the long history of the Ellington band: Sonny Greer (1919–51), Louis Bellson (early 1950s), Sam Woodyard (mid-1955 to 1963), and Rufus Jones (1968–73). Others played briefly with the band, but remained relatively unknown. Ellington's drummers have performed a relatively unobtrusive role in creating the band's sound. Although all were swinging drummers, none were as historically significant as Jo Jones with Count Basie, Gene Krupa with Benny Goodman, Max Roach with Charlie Parker, Elvin Jones with John Coltrane, or Philly Joe Jones and Tony Williams with Miles Davis. All Ellington drummers were primarily timekeepers, and there are four eras of this role in the band, reflecting Ellington's adapting to the strengths of four different drummers.

The classic tradition of **Sonny Greer** (1903–1982) lasted for more than half of the band's fifty-year history. Being Ellington's first drummer, Greer used drumming techniques in the manner of early jazz drummers. He kept time on the snare drum with sticks and brushes, sometimes moving to high-hat during the 1940s recordings. Though simple in style and technique, Greer was dramatic in presentation. His equipment included tympani, gongs, vibraphone, and wood blocks. (His showmanship with this auxiliary percussion is displayed on "Ring Dem Bells" found in *This Is Duke Ellington.*)

A new era began in 1951 when Greer left and **Louis Bellson** (b. 1924) joined Ellington. In his two-year stay, Bellson changed the technique and technology of Ellington drummers. Like a bop drummer, Bellson kept time with his ride cymbal, and used his left hand for playing musical punctuations on his snare drum. (Listen to "The Hawk Talks" in *The World of Duke Ellington Vol. 2.*) Blessed with enviable technique, he was a precise and tasteful accompanist. Bellson also added a second bass drum and small tom-tom to his drum kit (see illustration on page 17). Ellington took advantage of Bellson's capabilities by giving him solos. The recording of Bellson's solo on his own composition "Skin Deep" in *Hi-Fi Ellington Uptown* furnished a means for demonstrating sound quality in high-fidelity equipment that was just then becoming popular. The piece became a crowd-pleasing part of Ellington's repertory. Bellson's showmanship revitalized the band's appeal when all big bands were experiencing a declining audience size and Ellington was particularly low due to the temporary loss of Lawrence Brown and Johnny Hodges. After he left, his successors on the drum throne were required to perform the often-requested "Skin Deep." They also employed the modern timekeeping techniques that Bellson had first brought to Ellington.

Replacing Bellson was **Sam Woodyard** (b. 1925), Ellington's drummer of eleven years, who supplied a special spark to the band with his hard-swinging style. On special occasions, Ellington added a second drummer. (Listen to Woodyard and Jimmy Johnson, "Dual Fuel" in *Festival Session;* Woodyard and Steve Little, "The Biggest and Busiest Intersection" in *Second Sacred Concert.*)

The Bellson–Woodyard contributions to Ellington's style were expanded by **Rufus Jones** (b. 1936) between 1968 and 1973. Jones added African, Latin American, and oriental rhythms to suites that Ellington composed on his world tours during this era (*Far East Suite, Latin American Suite, Afro-Eurasian Eclipse, Goutelas Suite, Togo Brava-Brava Togo Suite,* and *Uwis Suite*). Jones played rhythms that were new to the Ellington sound, and, as in the earlier years, Ellington incorporated his drummer's ideas.

Bass   Over his long career of bandleading, Ellington had several outstanding bassists. The greatest standout among them was **Jimmy Blanton** (1918–1942), who played with the band from 1939 to 1941. Blanton shattered traditional conceptions of jazz bass playing with his impressive instrumental proficiency and musical imagination. **His cleanly executed melodic solos demonstrated that, in the hands of a virtuoso, the string bass can contribute much more to a band than timekeeping.** Though Blanton's sound was also a powerful component of Ellington's rhythm section, he is best known for the ways Ellington capitalized on his unique talents. **Ellington spotlighted Blanton in solo roles, and he arranged parts for Blanton's bass that were like horn parts.** Blanton played melody on Ellington's 1940 "Jack the Bear," played in unison with ensemble horn lines in the 1940 "Concerto for Cootie," and he soloed on the 1940 "Sepia Panorama." (The idea of voicing pizzicato bass with horns was later used in arrangements by Thad Jones, and it became quite common in modern jazz of the 1970s. Few of the musicians who use the technique today realize that Ellington had been doing it in 1940.) Blanton and Ellington also made a series of historic duet recordings, including their 1940 "Pitter Panther Patter" and "Mr. J.B. Blues." Blanton died in 1942 at the age of twenty-three, having received public exposure only briefly, but in that short time he profoundly shaped the next twenty years of jazz bass styles. (Listen to Blanton's work on "Concerto for Cootie" in SCCJ and on "Pitter Panther Patter" in *Jive at Five*, New World 274.)

Composers in the Band

Not all of Ellington's recordings represent entirely his own musical ideas. Numerous tunes were written by his sidemen or in collaboration with them. Bubber Miley was involved in composing "Black and Tan Fantasy" and "East St. Louis Toodle-Oo." (Listen to "East St. Louis Toodle-Oo" in SCCJ.) Barney Bigard worked on "Mood Indigo," Otto Hardwicke collaborated on "Sophisticated Lady," and Harry Carney coauthored "Rockin' in Rhythm." Valve trombonist Juan Tizol wrote several exotic pieces, including "Caravan," "Bakiff," and "Conga Brava." Tizol also wrote "Perdido," a melody often mistakenly credited to Ellington.

From 1939 until 1967, Ellington worked closely with another very creative pianist-composer-arranger, Billy Strayhorn (1915–1967). The two men collaborated on countless pieces, and their styles were so similar that most listeners never knew which of them contributed the larger portion of any particular arrangement. There are, however, several pieces usually credited just to Strayhorn. The most famous is "Take the 'A' Train," a classic which Ellington used as his band's theme. But ballads were Strayhorn's real forte. "Chelsea Bridge" and "Lush Life" are gorgeous examples.

Listening Guide for Billy Strayhorn's "Take The 'A' Train"

The melody fits a thirty-two bar A-A-B-A form and the chord progression of "Exactly Like You." While you listen to this famous work, examine the following guide:

FOUR-MEASURE PIANO INTRODUCTION

FIRST CHORUS

A-A Saxes state the melody (key of C) in unison and are answered alternately by muted trumpets in harmony and trombones in harmony. Rhythm section accompanies. Drummer is using wire brushes on snare drum.

B Saxes continue with the melody and are answered by trombones only.

A Saxes finish the melody and are answered by a new figure played by muted trumpets and trombones together. Piano comments near the end of the section.

SECOND CHORUS

A-A-B-A Ray Nance improvises a solo on muted trumpet while harmonized saxes are talking underneath. It sounds like the saxes are having an entire conversation filled with original, nonrepetitious lines. Rhythm section continues as before.

FOUR-MEASURE INTERLUDE

This interlude has the feeling of being in meter of three. However, you will notice that you can also organize the passage in groups of four instead of three if you count very precisely, noting that the boldfaced numbered beats are loudest:

1 2 3 **4** 1 2 **3** 4 1 **2** 3 4 **1** 2 3 **4**
(1 2 3) (1 2 3) (1 2 3) (1 2 3) (1 2 3 4)

In each unit of three beats, trumpets and trombones together play a question and saxes answer. Bass plays only on the first of every three beats (in boldface above). Guitar is silent. Drummer makes syncopated cymbal splashes. By the time this waltz section is over, the band has changed from the key of C to the key of E-flat.

THIRD CHORUS

A *First Four Measures*
Saxes enter for a harmonized melody statement answered by unmuted trumpeter Ray Nance improvising.

Second Four Measures
Nance continues his solo while saxes accompany with sustained chords. Drummer Sonny Greer is now using sticks on snare drum.

A *First Four Measures*
Saxes pose the same harmonized question again, but Nance improvises a new answer for them.

Second Four Measures

Nance continues while saxes return to playing sustained chords underneath him.

B *First Four Measures*

Nance continues while saxes state a theme independently and trombones carry an additional theme in harmony of their own. Then saxes comment briefly.

Two Measures

Nance continues while trombones accompany him with chords.

Two Measures

A fanfare, each note drawn from instruments in a different section of the band. Rhythm section does not play timekeeping patterns, but cymbal crashes punctuate the fanfare.

A Rhythm section returns to timekeeping. Original A section is played by saxes in unison, but now in the key of E-flat instead of the original key of C. Brass punctuate the sax statements by alternating open-horn notes in harmony with muted-horn notes in harmony.

ENDING

A Same as previous eight measures, but softer.

A Same again, softer still, but piano answers sax figures, and saxes finally add a "tie-it-up" figure to end the piece.

DIVERSITY OF THE ELLINGTON BAND

Most pieces in Ellington's repertory were filled with variety. The lack of repetition within each piece is striking. When compared with the arrangements of most swing bands, Ellington's possessed a larger number of different themes and rhythmic figures. (Listen to "Harlem Air Shaft" in SCCJ.) Accompanying figures also reflected a greater assortment than was customary. The repertory for Ellington's band was unusually diverse for a big band. One might describe the Ellington repertory as a number of separate books, each of which was both large and distinctive. Here are six categories which come to mind, most of which occasionally overlap:

1) An impressionistic book with arrangements that place more emphasis on orchestral colors and shading than on swinging: from his pre-LP work: "Transbluency" and "On a Turquoise Cloud." From his LP work there are portions of *Anatomy of a Murder* and *Paris Blues.*

2) A book of romantic ballads: from his pre-LP work: "Daydream," "Prelude to a Kiss," and "Sophisticated Lady." From his LP work: *Ellington Indigos, At the Bal Masque,* etc.

3) An exotic book: "Caravan," "Flaming Sword," "Bakiff," etc. from pre-LP work; and entire LPs such as *Latin American Suite* and *Togo Brava Suite,* etc.

4) A concert book, each piece a long work with much less improvisation than his usual repertory contained. "Reminiscing in Tempo," "Black, Brown, and Beige," "Deep South Suite," etc. for his pre-LP work and *Such Sweet Thunder, Suite Thursday, A Drum Is a Woman,* etc., for his LP work.

5) A book of concertos, each piece framing the style of an Ellington sideman. "Clarinet Lament" (Barney Bigard), "Echoes of Harlem" (Cootie Williams), "Boy Meets Horn" (Rex Stewart), etc., for his pre-LP work and "Cop-Out" (Paul Gonsalves), "Lonesome Lullaby" (Ray Nance), etc., for his LP work.

6) A book of music for sacred concerts, a context that brought Ellington to present new shows and use choirs, new vocal soloists, organ and dancers. It inspired writing for different moods, such as that of prayer. It also inspired extensive lyrics (*Duke Ellington's Concert of Sacred Music*).

Among the hundreds of Ellington recordings there are numerous masterpieces which have not been extensively described, including the 1941 "Raincheck" by Strayhorn, the 1939 "The Sergeant Was Shy," and the 1941 "I Don't Know What Kind of Blues I've Got." The vastness of Ellington's contribution becomes evident when you explore a few hundred different selections. In addition to all that material, Ellington also composed several operas, a couple of ballets, and about ten shows.

Many listeners believe that Ellington's peak of creativity was in the years 1939–41 when his band members included Ben Webster, Johnny Hodges, Barney Bigard, Jimmy Blanton, Tricky Sam Nanton, Harry Carney, Cootie Williams, and Rex Stewart. His 1956–59 band was also exceptional, featuring Clark Terry, Jimmy Hamilton, Paul Gonsalves, Harry Carney, and Johnny Hodges. When the band's personnel changed, the band's sound changed correspondingly. Every five to ten years there was a difference in the band sound.

The Ellington band never really fell into any fixed category—early jazz, swing, or modern. It was always unique. Ellington created a jazz classification which was practically his own. Not only did the Duke Ellington band present a very colorful and more varied sound than is usually heard, but it maintained a consistent level of creative energy for more than four decades.

ELLINGTON RECORDINGS: HOW AND WHERE TO FIND THEM

The performances cited in this chapter come into and go out of print at a furious pace, but all of them are available through importers and rare record dealers even when U.S. companies have discontinued them. See pages 395–399 for instructions on how to use such record sources. The teacher's manual for this text also has a detailed Ellington record list with dates and contents for the cited music.

The best place to start an acquaintance with Ellington's work is SCCJ because it has "East St. Louis Toodle-Oo," "Creole Rhapsody," "Harlem Airshaft," "Concerto for Cootie," "In A Mellotone," "Ko-Ko," and "Blue Serge." The next best place is the RCA *This Is Duke Ellington* (VPM 0642) because it has many classics that SCCJ omits: "Take the 'A' Train," "Cottontail," "Mood Indigo," "Creole Love Call," "Black and Tan Fantasy," and "Don't Get Around Much Anymore." However, the RCA collection is more likely to go out of print than the Smithsonian collections. Therefore it might be helpful to seek a few of these special Ellington compilations prepared by Smithsonian. (For brevity, only selections cited in this chapter are listed. The contents of each album include additional riches.)

Duke Ellington 1938 Smithsonian 2003
"Prelude to a Kiss," "Boy Meets Horn."

Duke Ellington 1939 Smithsonian 2010
"Portrait of the Lion," "The Sergeant Was Shy," "Sophisticated Lady."

Duke Ellington 1940 Smithsonian 2015
"Jack the Bear," "Ko-Ko," "Morning Glory," "Concerto for Cootie," "Cottontail," "Never No Lament (Don't Get Around Much Anymore)," "Bojangles," "A Portrait of Bert Williams," "Harlem Air Shaft," "In A Mellotone," "Warm Valley," "Pitter Panther Patter," "Sophisticated Lady," "Mr. J. B. Blues," "Sepia Panorama," "Conga Brava."

Duke Ellington 1941 Smithsonian 2027
"Take the 'A' Train," "Blue Serge," "Solitude," "Bakiff," "Just A-Settin' and A-Rockin'," "Chelsea Bridge," "Raincheck," "I Don't Know What Kind of Blues I've Got," "Perdido," "C-Jam Blues."

Note: Most of the 1956–59 albums cited with Clark Terry, Jimmy Hamilton, and Paul Gonsalves are Columbia records.

Note: See pages 399–400 for information about ordering from Smithsonian. These albums are not carried by record stores.

CHAPTER SUMMARY

1) Duke Ellington is among the most significant of all figures in jazz history.

2) As a pianist, Ellington initially reflected the James P. Johnson stride tradition, though he also developed original methods for setting the pace and mood of his pieces and ornamenting the solos of band members.

3) As a bandleader, Ellington maintained a large ensemble continuously from the early 1920s to his death in 1974, with many musicians remaining for ten to twenty years at a stretch.

4) As a composer, Ellington wrote about a thousand pieces, many eventually being turned into popular songs such as "Satin Doll," "Mood Indigo," "Do Nothin' 'til You Hear From Me," and "Don't Get Around Much Anymore."

5) As an arranger, Ellington was known for
   a) including a diversity of themes within a single piece,
   b) drawing instruments from different sections of the band to play a part together, a technique called voicing across sections,
   c) assigning a part to female voice as though it were an instrument, also known as wordless vocal.

6) Ellington pioneered the use of lengthy composition in jazz, in such works as "Black, Brown and Beige," "Reminiscing in Tempo," and "A Drum Is a Woman."

7) Ellington showcased his improvisers in pieces tailored to their unique musical personalities, having written "Clarinet Lament" for Barney Bigard, "Concerto for Cootie" for Cootie Williams, and "Boy Meets Horn" for Rex Stewart.

8) Ellington's writing capitalized on the strengths and weaknesses of each player, thereby orchestrating for particular musicians' sounds instead of just for anonymous instruments.

9) Ellington's most famous sideman was alto saxophonist Johnny Hodges, a Sidney Bechet disciple whose romantic style was widely imitated.

10) Bassist Jimmy Blanton was showcased in the band from 1939 to 1941. His great imagination and unprecedented instrumental command revolutionized jazz bass conception by making the bass a horn-like solo instrument.

11) A distinctive feature in the Ellington sound was the plunger-muted growl style of brass playing, as perfected by trumpeters Bubber Miley and Cootie Williams and by trombonists Charlie Irvis and Joe "Tricky Sam" Nanton.

12) Ellington's main soloist during the 1950s and 60s was tenor saxophonist Paul Gonsalves, who had a unique style, diffuse tone, and intense delivery.

13) Ellington is historically significant for achieving a successful integration of improvised lines and prewritten parts.

14) Billy Strayhorn was Ellington's coauthor from 1939 to 1967, having contributed several originals, including the band's theme, "Take the 'A' Train."

chapter 8

THE COUNT BASIE BANDS

The public thinks of Benny Goodman as the "King of Swing," but most jazz musicians agree that the title should go to Count Basie (1904–1984). When compared with all the other swing bands, Basie's band never seems out of breath nor the least bit frantic, and it always seems to swing more. Basie led a big band continuously from 1937 until his death, with the exception of the years 1950–51 when he had to reduce the size of his group to a combo. Nearly every edition of the band had one or two players who made important contributions to jazz history, and some editions had four or five.

Basie the Pianist   Basie was originally a Fats Waller–influenced stride pianist and a prominent soloist with some of his own bands. After the 1940s, however, he often played through an entire selection without the audience's hearing more than his piano introduction and a few characteristic "plink plink" interjections during dramatic silences. Succinct and compact statements are hallmarks of Basie's style. When he soloed, he artfully used silence to pace his lines while guitarist Freddie Green strummed his supple four strokes to the measure over quiet bass and drums. Basie's touch was unique among jazz pianists. It was very light yet extremely precise. His choice of notes was near perfect, as was his impeccable sense of timing that was as good as any drummer's. (In fact, Basie originally began his musical career as a drummer, not a pianist.) Basie's piano usually set the mood and tempo for each of his band's pieces.

Basie's Rhythm Section during the Late 1930s and Early 40s   Basie led the first rhythm section in jazz history that consistently swung in a smooth, relaxed way. That famous rhythm section consisted of Basie himself (piano), Freddie Green (rhythm guitar), Walter Page (string bass), and Jo Jones (drums).

The special qualities of the Basie rhythm section were:

1) An excellent sense of tempo.
2) The ability to keep time without using a hard-driving, pressured approach.
3) Quiet, relaxed playing, which conveyed a feeling of ease.
4) A fairly even amount of stress on all four beats.
5) Emphasis on buoyancy rather than intensity.

Bassist **Walter Page** (1900–1957) contributed:

1) A supple walking bass.
2) A strong tone, an articulated sound with life in it, not the dead thud common to many premodern bassists.
3) Playing all four beats evenly.
4) Balancing his sound with piano, bass, and guitar.

Guitarist **Freddie Green** (b. 1911) was noted for:

1) His crisp four strokes to the measure on unamplified guitar.
2) His close coordination with drums.

The style of drummer **Jo Jones** (b. 1911) consisted of:

1) Precise playing, but not stiff precision. Jones displayed precision within a loose, assured manner.
2) Quieter bass drum playing than was common in the swing era, much softer, for example, than Gene Krupa's. Jones sometimes omitted bass drum entirely.
3) Quiet use of wire brushes on high-hat.
4) Ride rhythms played on high-hat while the apparatus was opening and closing. Jones let his cymbals ring prominently between strokes, thereby creating a sustained sound that smoothed the timekeeping instead of leaving each stroke as an abrupt sound. Jones also maintained this conception when using sticks to play ride rhythms on a suspended cymbal (also known as a "top cymbal"). (For greater understanding of high-hat cymbals and ride rhythms, see illustrations and explanations on pages 19–20 and 430.)

The Basie rhythm section was noted for achieving a balance among the sounds of each member. The four parts were so smoothly integrated that one listener was inspired to describe the effect as similar to riding on ball bearings. If you listen carefully to recordings of the band, you will notice that it is unusual for one member to stick out. Guitar, bass, and drums are carefully controlled to avoid disturbing the evenness and balance of sound.

Count Basie Band, perhaps the best of swing era big bands. Its rhythm section style and the innovative sax style of Lester Young bridged the gap between swing and modern jazz. They are pictured here at the Famous Door, in 1938, with (from left to right): Walter Page (bass), Jo Jones (drums), Freddie Green (guitar), Count Basie (piano), Bennie Morton (trombone), Herschel Evans (tenor sax), Buck Clayton (trumpet with cup mute), Dicky Wells (hidden), Earle Warren (alto sax), Ed Lewis (hidden), Harry "Sweets" Edison (trumpet), Jack Washington (playing alto with his baritone sax at side), Lester Young (tenor sax). (*Courtesy of Frank Driggs*)

In Basie's interjections, jazz piano had the bounce, syncopation, and flexibility that characterized what became known as **comping**, a very important element in modern jazz. Listen very carefully to the faint piano sound during Carl Smith's trumpet solo on the 1936 "Shoe Shine Boy" by Jones-Smith Inc., a Basie combo. You will hear Basie comping in the manner adopted by modern jazz pianists years later. Throughout his career, Basie also mixed Fats Waller stride style with "plink plink" interjections, but his accompaniment for Smith is **one of the earliest recorded examples of modern jazz comping.** Even during the 1940s, many excellent jazz pianists had not learned to comp. They continued in the accompaniment styles of the 1920s and 30s, which included

1) stride style,
2) playing a chord on each beat in the manner of a rhythm guitarist, or
3) playing flowery countermelodies and embellishments.

For greater understanding of comping, see pages 18–23, and, for musical notations, see page 424. To hear Basie do it, listen to "Lester Leaps In" on SCCJ, and ignore the saxophone solo so you can focus on the piano accompaniment. To hear it on "Shoe Shine Boy," get *The Lester Young Story Vol. 1* (Columbia JG 33502) or any equivalent collection of the earliest Lester Young recordings. Note that Basie probably did not invent comping. For example, a 1928 recording exists in which Duke Ellington briefly comps. The point to remember is that Basie did it so well, and with such relaxed swing feeling, that he is probably the one who provided the most used model for the technique.

Arrangements   During the 1920s and 30s there was a thriving jazz scene in Kansas City, Missouri. A number of historically significant jazz musicians worked there and are associated with "Kansas City style jazz," though few were born there (see Table 8.1). Their music was not as glossy or elaborate as that of their New York counterparts, but it was noted for how well it swung. Its being a lighter and more relaxed sound partly explains its capacity for swing feeling.

Kansas City style was not based on the interweaving lines of the collectively improvised New Orleans style. Instead it provided a fundamental model for big bands that is called the **riff band style.** The arrangements in this style are based on simple musical phrases called riffs that are repeated again and again. Riffs serve the double function of being ensemble statements as well as being backgrounds for improvised solos. Some of these riffs were written down, but many were created spontaneously during a performance ("off the top of someone's head"), learned by ear, and kept in the heads of the players. Arrangements of this kind are called **head arrangements,** and they are basic to the riff band style.

Many riff-based pieces that band members at first identified only by numbers were eventually given names and composer credits. Count Basie's "One O'Clock Jump" and "Jumpin' at the Woodside" are bestselling examples.[1] Listen to this style illustrated by "Moten Swing," as recorded by the Bennie Moten band in 1932 and preserved in SCCJ. The piece is a thirty-two measure A-A-B-A form based on the chord

[1] *The Best of Count Basie* MCA 2 4050

TABLE 8.1. Musicians of the 1930s Kansas City Style (birthplaces in parentheses)

Count Basie (New Jersey) pianist-bandleader	Mary Lou Williams (Georgia) pianist-composer-arranger
Gus Johnson (Texas) drummer	Buddy Tate (Texas) saxophonist
Walter Page (Missouri) bassist-bandleader	Pete Johnson (Missouri) pianist
Coleman Hawkins (Missouri) saxophonist	Charlie Parker (Missouri) saxophonist-composer
Lester Young (Mississippi) saxophonist	Jay McShann (Oklahoma) pianist-bandleader
Buck Clayton (Kansas) trumpeter	Budd Johnson (Texas) saxophonist-composer
Andy Kirk (Kentucky) bandleader-saxophonist	Hot Lips Page (Texas) trumpeter
Ben Webster (Missouri) saxophonist	Jo Jones (Illinois) drummer
Herschel Evans (Texas) saxophonist	Jesse Stone (Kansas) pianist-arranger-bandleader
Eddie Durham (Texas) guitarist-arranger-trombonist	George Lee (Missouri) saxophonist-pianist-bandleader
Buster Smith (Texas) saxophonist	Harlan Leonard (Missouri) saxophonist-bandleader
Bennie Moten (Missouri) pianist-bandleader	

progression to a song called "You're Driving Me Crazy." (Count Basie had been a member of both Moten's band and the Blue Devils, led by bassist Walter Page. These two groups eventually fused to become Basie's first Kansas City band.) A combo example of the riff style is "Lester Leaps In." Listen to it in SCCJ while you follow the Listening Guide found on pages 138–139.

1930s and 40s Sidemen

Many of the best jazz trumpeters and saxophonists of the late 1930s and 40s played with Count Basie at one time or another—the list of notables is extensive. In that respect, his band was similar to Fletcher Henderson's in that Henderson had employed most of his best soloists available during the 1920s and early 30s (see Table 8.2).

The most notable soloist Basie had during the 1930s and 40s was tenor saxophonist **Lester Young** (1909–1959). He was so good that he was nicknamed "Pres" (or "Prez"), short for president of tenor saxophone players. Young played lines which were fresher, longer, more concise and smoothly swinging than those of any previous improvisers. He paved the way for modern saxophone tone color, vibrato, rhythmic conception, and phrasing. **Young offered a clear alternative to the heavy tone, fast vibrato, and richly ornamented style of Coleman Hawkins.** (See Table 8.3.)

TABLE 8.2. A Few of the Many Musicians Who Have Been Important to Basie

Trumpet	Saxophone	Composer-Arranger
Carl Smith	Lester Young	Eddie Durham
Hot Lips Page	Herschel Evans	Don Redman
Buck Clayton	Jack Washington	Jimmy Mundy
Harry "Sweets" Edison	Tab Smith	Don Kirkpatrick
Shad Collins	Earle Warren	Ernie Wilkins
Emmett Berry	Buddy Tate	Thad Jones
Clark Terry	Jack Washington	Frank Foster
Thad Jones	Wardell Gray	Frank Wess
Joe Newman	Lucky Thompson	Neal Hefti
Al Aarons	Don Byas	Quincy Jones
Sonny Cohn	Illinois Jacquet	Benny Carter
Snooky Young	Serge Chaloff	Billy Byers
Wendell Culley	Paul Gonsalves	Chico O'Farrill
	Eddie "Lockjaw" Davis	Sammy Nestico
Trombone	Frank Foster	Al Grey
	Eric Dixon	
Dicky Wells	Jimmy Forrest	**Drums**
Benny Morton	Billy Mitchell	
Vic Dickenson	Frank Wess	Jo Jones
Al Grey	Marshall Royal	Shadow Wilson
Henry Coker	Charlie Fowlkes	Gus Johnson
Curtis Fuller	Bobby Plater	Sonny Payne
Benny Powell	Paul Quinichette	Louis Bellson
		Harold Jones
	Bass	Butch Miles
		Rufus Jones
	Walter Page	
	Eddie Jones	
	Buddy Catlett	

Young's light tone, slow vibrato, and loping, buoyant phrases became the model for an entire generation of saxophonists (see Table 8.4). These saxophonists often copied Young solos note for note. Complete choruses of famous Lester Young improvisations can occasionally be heard in their playing.

Although his playing did not match the complexity of Hawkins, Young's melodic ideas were at least as advanced. Listen to his 1939 "Taxi War Dance" (in SCCJ and outlined on pages 136–138), where he seems to play against Basie's rolling piano figure, or his improvisation on Basie's 1939 "Jive at Five"[1,2] which anticipates the fluffy tone

2 *Jive at Five* New World 274 (a collection available in libraries and schools)

TABLE 8.3. Comparison of Coleman Hawkins with Lester Young

	Coleman Hawkins	Lester Young
tone quality	warm	cool
	dark-colored	light-colored
	heavy-weight	light-weight
	full-bodied	hollow
rate of vibrato	medium to fast	slow
swing feeling	early jazz style	more relaxed and grace-ful than Hawkins
intricacy of solos	much	less than Hawkins
tunefulness of improvisations	little	much
came to prominence with	Fletcher Henderson (1923–34)	Count Basie (1936–44)
influenced	Herschel Evans	Charlie Parker
	Chu Berry	Wardell Gray
	Dick Wilson	Stan Getz
	Ben Webster	Lee Konitz
		Sonny Stitt
		Woody Herman band's "Four Brothers" sound and West Coast style' players (see Table 8.4)

and melodic approach Stan Getz was to display eight years later with the Woody Herman band.

Whereas Hawkins was bound up in complex chord changes and busy ornamentation, **Young implied new and additional chords in standard pop tune progressions and treated them with a cool, extremely concise approach.** But he did have moments of many notes, too. Listen to his famous 1939 "Lester Leaps In" solo recorded with a combo of Basie sidemen (in SCCJ and outlined on pages 138–139). It is nearly all eighth notes, but the sequences are clear in spite of the number of notes and surprises they contain. (See Table 8.3 for Hawkins comparison.)

Instead of incorporating afterthoughts into every other phrase, as Hawkins was prone to do, Young concerned himself with only a core of melodic material. He possessed the virtue of deliberate restraint. He could pace a solo so well that it seemed an integral part of the written arrangement. Young seems to have possessed a musical storytelling talent which surfaced in nearly every solo. His clarinet solos on the 1938 "I Want a Little Girl" and "Pagin' the Devil"[3] are good examples,

[3] *Kansas City Six* Columbia Special Products 15352

TABLE 8.4. A Few of the Many Saxophonists Influenced by Lester Young

Charlie Parker	Gene Ammons
Brew Moore	Sonny Stitt
Paul Quinichette	Stan Getz
Dave Pell	Herbie Steward
Bob Cooper	Richie Kamuca
Bill Perkins	Al Cohn
Wardell Gray	Jerry Jerome
Allen Eager	Don Lamphere
Zoot Sims	Jimmy Giuffre
Lee Konitz	Buddy Collette
Warne Marsh	John Coltrane
Dexter Gordon	

as are his tenor sax solos on the 1939 "Pound Cake"[4] and "Ham 'n' Eggs."[5] (On "Ham 'n' Eggs" his is the *second* tenor solo; Buddy Tate takes the first, a solo whose style is distinctly different from Young's.)

The advanced level of Young's conception was evident in his easy swing and in his placement of phrases that seemed unhindered by turnarounds and bridges within chord progressions. Young transcended the phrasing of many premodern players who had organized lines around the two- and four-bar sequences of chord progressions. He improvised long lines which had a fresh, expansive feeling. It would be difficult to derive a crowded feeling from a Young solo. **Another aspect of Young's advanced conception was his ability to play against the chord changes instead of playing directly through their tones.** The internal logic of his lines took precedence over strict adherence to the underlying harmonies, a characteristic of the approach taken by hundreds of good improvisers later in jazz history.

Young's playing was strongest during the late 1930s, and his very first recordings were probably the best of his entire career. When he left Basie in 1940, his tone began to darken, his vibrato quickened, and his rhythmic precision decreased. This process began well before 1944, the year most fans cite as the beginning of a serious decline for him. His playing seemed to lose energy steadily until his death in 1959. Yet Young's work remained intelligent and swinging all those years, and he never played badly. In fact, his loyalty to storytelling type improvisations increased. But after 1940, he seemed unable (or unwilling) to jump into his solos with the animation and freshness of his early work.

---

[4] *Lester Young Story Vol. 3* Columbia JG 34840
[5] *Lester Young Story Vol. 4* Columbia JG 34843

A representative of one major branch of the Coleman Hawkins school of tenor saxophone style was **Herschel Evans** (1909–1939). A smoother, more graceful player than Hawkins, he rejected the intricate approach to improvisation favored by Hawkins. Evans played with a fast vibrato and about as deep and dark a tone as any swing tenor, even darker than Hawkins. (Listen to Basie's "Doggin' Around" in SCCJ.) One reason for his dark tone color was his preference for the saxophone's low register. His lines were neither as long nor as ornamented as Hawkins. Yet neither were they as concise as Lester Young's. Like Ben Webster and Hawkins, he excelled in ballad work. His 1938 recording of "Blue and Sentimental" with Basie was widely imitated.[1] He influenced Buddy Tate, Illinois Jacquet, Ike Quebec, Arnett Cobb, and others. Evans was with Basie from 1936 until he died in 1939.

Listening Guide for Count Basie's "Taxi War Dance" Recording Found in SCCJ

INTRODUCTION

Four Measures

Basie's rolling left-hand figure with no bass, rhythm guitar, or drums accompaniment.

Four Measures

Trumpets punctuate in unison with piano as a set-up for the piece, all the while trombones are "walking" underneath them, and Jo Jones has begun playing ride rhythms.

FIRST CHORUS

A Tenor saxophonist Lester Young opens his improvisation by quoting the first line of "Ol' Man River." Listen to Freddie Green playing rhythm guitar, Walter Page playing walking bass lines, and Jo Jones playing ride rhythms on opening and closing high-hat. Basie stops his rolling figures and moves to comping.

A First four bars Basie returns to his rolling piano figures underneath continuation of Young's solo. After that, Basie returns to comping. Note how Young's lines relate to these changes in accompaniment patterns.

B Continuation of Young with rhythm section accompaniment.

A Continuation. (This is a good example of Basie's big band functioning as a combo, something they were particularly distinguished for.)

SECOND CHORUS

A *First Two Measures*

A return to the brass figure that originally opened the piece. Basie's rolling piano figure is also included. The walking trombones are missing, however.

Remaining Six Measures

Trombonist Dicky Wells improvises a solo. He is very melodic and sounds like he is poking fun. Pay attention to how he bases his solo on simple phrases to be developed by repetitions and slight alterations. Note how clear and logical his lines are.

A Solo continues with rhythm section accompaniment, again returning to a small combo performance.

B Continuation.

A Continuation.

THIRD CHORUS

A *First Four Measures*

Band returns, Basie abandons comping for patterned figures. Trombones call and trumpets respond.

Second Four Measures

Tenor saxophonist Buddy Tate begins a solo improvisation. He can be distinguished from Lester Young by having a coarser tone that is darker and has faster vibrato. Tate's execution is less poised and has less swinging rhythmic feeling.

A Repeat of layout for first A section.

B Piano solo by Basie. Notice his light touch, use of the piano's upper register, and impeccable timing.

A *First Four Measures*

Trombones call and trumpets respond.

Second Four Measures

Tate solos with a rapid pattern repeated.

FOURTH CHORUS

A *First Four Measures*

Basie plays a boogie woogie figure underneath ensemble figures by trumpets and trombones.

Second Four Measures

Tenor saxophonist Lester Young returns with a light feeling. He plays an upper register solo.

A *First Four Measures*

Repeat of the pattern used in the first A section, but this time Young enters his solo space early by using a bit of the four-measure lead-in to get started.

Second Four Measures

Young completes his solo remaining with upper register tones.

B Basie solos in the upper register, playing lightly and staccato.

A *First Four Measures*

Trombones call, and the trumpets respond with a simple, syncopated figure which uses alternation of muted and unmuted sound in rapid succession.

Second Four Measures

Lester Young improvises by rapidly alternating his tone quality.

ENDING

Two Measures

Stop-time solo break for Count Basie.

Two Measures

Stop-time solo break for Lester Young (this is called "trading two's").

Two Measures

Walking bass unaccompanied.

Two Measures

Sticks on drums unaccompanied.

Two Measures

Brass play a tie-it-up figure, and Jo Jones strikes a cymbal and grabs it to abruptly prevent it from ringing. This technique effectively closes up the sounds and provides a dramatic means for ending a performance.

Listening Guide for the 1939 Recording of "Lester Leaps In" Found in SCCJ

FOUR-MEASURE PIANO INTRODUCTION

FIRST CHORUS

A-A Muted trumpet, trombone, and tenor saxophone play a single four-measure melodic figure four times with rhythm section accompaniment (a typical riff band device).

B Count Basie piano solo, very spare, just indicating the moments during which chords change. He allows plenty of space for us to hear bass and drums.

A The three horns state original theme (that same riff) two more times.

SECOND CHORUS

A-A-B-A Lester Young tenor sax solo accompanied by drummer Jo Jones playing ride rhythm on opening and closing high-hat. Nice comping by Basie. Walking bass by Page.

THIRD CHORUS

A Young and Basie improvise counterpoint around each other.

A Rhythm section creates stop-time solo breaks for Young during first six measures. Rhythm section resumes normal timekeeping patterns for last two measures while Young keeps on improvising.

B Young continues solo with rhythm section accompaniment.

A Rhythm section creates more stop-times for Young.

FOURTH CHORUS

A Basie solos the first four measures, Young does the second four.

A Basie solos the first four measures, Young does the second four.

B Basie solos the first four measures, Young does the second four.

A Basie solos the first four measures, Young does the second four. (This is called "trading four's.")

FIFTH CHORUS

(This chorus uses another typical riff band device.)

A *First Four Measures*
Ensemble calls, "BOP   BOP   BOP-BOP   BAAH!"

Second Four Measures
Young responds with improvisation.

A *First Four Measures*
Ensemble calls, "BOP   BOP   BOP-BOP   BAAH!"

Second Four Measures
Basie responds with improvisation.

B Basie continues his improvisation.

A *First Four Measures*
Ensemble calls, "BOP   BOP   BOP-BOP   BAAH!"

Second Four Measures
Young responds with improvisation.

SIXTH CHORUS

A *First Four Measures*
Ensemble calls, "BOP   BOP   BOP-BOP   BAAH!"

Second Four Measures
Basie responds with improvisation.

A *First Four Measures*
Ensemble calls, "BOP   BOP   BOP-BOP   BAAH!"

Second Four Measures
Basie responds with improvisation.

B Basie continues his improvisation.

A Ensemble calls, "BOP   BOP   BOP-BOP   BAAH!"
Then the band members collectively improvise a closing by simultaneously playing different lines in Dixieland style.

From 1937 to 1943 trumpeter **Buck Clayton** (b. 1911) played with Basie. Widely considered to be one of the greatest swing era trumpeters, he was probably the best Basie had until the 1950s. He played the most intelligent lines of any early Basie trumpeter. His clear, warm tone and relaxed, graceful command of the trumpet's full range was almost as inspiring as the work of Louis Armstrong, one of Clayton's major influences. (He had memorized Armstrong solos during the early 1930s.) He often played with a cup mute, yet for a muted sound, his tone was unusually full. Listen to his sensitive cup-muted playing at the beginning, and gorgeous open-horn sound at the end of the 1938 "I Want a Little Girl";[3] also note his muted work on the 1938 "Good Mornin' Blues." Clayton was a very consistent player. He maintained an excellent technique and remained active as a trumpet player during the 1970s.

Kansas City Five; Jones-Smith, Inc. Several records were made by combos composed of Basie band members. Variously called the Kansas City Five, Six, or Seven, depending on how many musicians were used, these combos often included the entire Basie rhythm section plus Lester Young, Buck Clayton, and Dicky Wells. Their 1939 recordings, such as "Dickie's Dream"[5] and "Lester Leaps In," are combo classics which historically rank alongside Louis Armstrong's Hot Five and Hot Seven recordings and the Miles Davis album series *Steamin'*, *Cookin'*, *Workin'*, and *Relaxin'*.

One of the first of these combos included drummer Jo Jones and trumpeter Carl Smith, and was given the group name Jones-Smith, Inc. The 1936 recordings made by Jones-Smith, Inc., which include "Shoe Shine Boy" and "Lady Be Good,"[6] are masterpieces.

Basie After the 1940s In the 1950s, 60s, 70s, and 80s, Basie retained many elements of his swing style rhythm section. His own piano style remained constant, and guitarist Freddie Green was still with him, playing in the same style as when he first joined the band in 1937. Basie's drummers kept time more on the ride cymbal now than on the high-hat, and they played far more fills than Jo Jones had. However, his drummers were not performing in contemporary styles after the 1940s. They kept to what worked best for the Basie big band approach.

After the 1940s, Basie carried many excellent soloists. But none were stylistic pacesetters of the magnitude shown by Lester Young or Jo Jones. One trumpeter, however, was of that caliber. **Thad Jones** (b. 1923) was the most uniquely original improviser to play with Basie after Lester Young. In fact, he is considered to be among the handful of trumpeters to offer fresh methods after the dust had settled from 1940s innovations introduced by Dizzy Gillespie. The lines im-

---

[6] *Lester Young Story Vol. 1* Columbia JG 33502

provised by Jones are often composed of unusual intervals that are not natural to the trumpet. They are therefore as difficult as they are unique. Jones is a storehouse of imagination, rarely playing his featured solos in anything resembling the same manner from one night to the next. His lines are compositionally unorthodox and daring. Jones was with Basie from 1954 to 1963, and he also wrote some of Basie's most provocative arrangements. (They can be heard on the 1959 *Chairman of the Board*[7] album.)

For twenty years the Basie band has had the unusual distinction of being practically the only big band that swings *while* playing softly. The band maintains precision and balance without losing the subtle drive that is expected of jazz performances. And the band is precise without sounding mechanical. Much of the music written for Basie during the 1950s and 60s capitalizes on the band's skill with dynamic contrasts: loud passages which instantaneously get soft; soft passages interrupted momentarily by very loud chords; passages which rise and fall in volume so gradually that one wonders how it is possible.

Count Basie's band has always placed more emphasis on simplicity and swing feeling than on complexity and colorful sounds. Simple, catchy riffs were the rule even during the 1950s and 60s when sophisticated composers and arrangers were writing for the band. Remember that the band had been run like an oversized combo during the late 1930s and early 40s. Basie placed much more emphasis on swinging solo improvisations than on fancy arrangements. His approach provided a contrast to the highly polished, well-arranged Jimmie Lunceford band and the elaborate embroidery of written music and improvisation in Ellington's band. Basie's was primarily a soloist's band, and Lunceford's was more an arranger's band.

Basie's emphasis on a combo style decreased during the 1950s (and especially thereafter) when the band performed slick, swinging arrangements in which solos were sometimes rare and usually short. They occasionally constituted inconsequential portions of a recording. Basie's band achieved a very high level of polish and, like Lunceford's band of twenty years earlier, it became known as a swinging showcase for glossy ensemble sound.

CHAPTER SUMMARY

1) Count Basie is a Fats Waller-derived stride pianist who has a light, precise touch and impeccable sense of tempo.

2) Count Basie's accompaniment style constituted one of the first examples of comping: nonrepetitive, syncopated chording

[7] Roulette R 52032 and Emus 12023

which flexibly relates to the melodies and rhythms of the improvised solo line instead of just striking a chord on each beat.

3) Count Basie remains one of the few pianists to make silence almost as important as the notes he plays, thereby allowing the rhythm guitar, bass, and drums to be heard and a relaxed feeling to be evoked.

4) The 1937–40 Basie rhythm section helped bridge the gap between premodern and modern methods of timekeeping and accompanying:
    a) Drummer Jo Jones often omitted pedalling of bass drum on every beat.
    b) Jones lightly played ride rhythms on his high-hat cymbals while they were opening and closing.
    c) Bassist Walter Page played with a large and buoyant sound on all four beats of each measure.
    d) Rhythm guitarist Freddie Green strummed crisply in coordination with Page.
    e) Pianist Basie offered brief musical punctuations.

5) Basie's band played in the Kansas City style using simple figures called riffs which were played repeatedly atop pop tune and 12-bar blues progressions.

6) Basie's chief soloists for the 1930s were tenor saxophonist Lester Young, trumpeter Buck Clayton, and trombonist Dicky Wells.

7) Lester Young offered a light-toned alternative to the deep, heavy sound of Coleman Hawkins.

8) Young was very melodic and fresh in his improvisations, becoming the major model for hundreds of modern jazz saxophonists in
    a) tone color
    b) phrasing
    c) rhythmic conception
    d) vibrato

9) Basie always stressed simplicity and swing instead of complex arrangements, and he retained the same gentle, unhurried feeling throughout his bandleading career.

chapter 9

BOP:
THE EARLY 1940s
TO THE MIDDLE 1950s

Jazz historians tend to date the beginning of modern jazz in the 1940s ("early jazz" is sometimes referred to as the "classic period"). Styles which have emerged since 1940, except those that are revivals of previous styles, are classified as modern jazz. The first modern jazz musicians were alto saxophonist Charlie Parker, pianist Thelonious Monk, and trumpeter Dizzy Gillespie. By the middle 1940s, they had inspired a legion of other creative musicians including trumpeter Miles Davis and pianist Bud Powell. By the late 1940s Parker and Gillespie had also influenced the big bands of Billy Eckstine, Claude Thornhill, and Woody Herman.

Modern jazz did not burst upon the jazz scene as a revolution. It developed gradually through the work of swing era tenor saxophonists Lester Young and Don Byas, pianists Art Tatum and Nat Cole, trumpeter Roy Eldridge, guitarist Charlie Christian, the Count Basie rhythm section, bassist Jimmy Blanton, and others. Parker and Gillespie themselves began their careers playing improvisations in a swing era style. They expanded on this music and gradually incorporated new techniques; their work eventually became recognized as a different style, which, though departing appreciably from swing era approaches, was still linked to the swing era. Rather than being a reaction *against* swing styles, modern jazz developed smoothly *from* swing styles.

Modern jazz improvisers were also inspired by contemporary classical music. The work of Béla Bartók and Igor Stravinsky was favored by many musicians of the 1940s, just as the music of Claude Debussy and Maurice Ravel influenced Bix Beiderbecke during the 1920s.

Charlie Parker (alto sax) and Miles Davis (trumpet), two of the most influential men in modern jazz. Parker devised the bop approach, and Davis went on to develop cool, modal, and jazz-rock approaches. Pictured here in 1949 when Parker was 29 and Davis was 23. (*Courtesy of Duncan Scheidt*)

The new music was primarily a combo style. But modern jazz and its combo format did not emerge solely because young improvisers disliked swing era big band playing. The big bands and written arrangements certainly imposed restrictions on the amount of solo time and on the spontaneous musical interaction between soloist and accompanist. But both combo and big band formats have existed in most eras. Apparently both have been useful. In fact, Parker developed part of his advanced improvisatory style while playing with the big band of Jay McShann. He later recorded with Machito's Latin American big band and sat in with the big bands of Gillespie and Woody Herman. Gillespie played in Cab Calloway's big band, and both Parker and Gillespie worked with the 1940s big bands of Earl Hines and Billy Eckstine. If modern jazz represented a rejection of big bands, why would such leading modern jazz musicians like Gillespie, Thad Jones, Clark Terry, Miles Davis, Gil Evans, Gerry Mulligan, and others endure great hardships to lead their own? The scarcity of big bands in modern jazz compared to their proliferation during the swing era could be due to a number of factors, a small one being the possible distaste some jazz musicians had for big bands. But we should take care to avoid overrating the influence of that factor. Eventually combos became the standard band size for popular music. Jazz was not the only type of music which moved away from large ensemble format.

Bop is considered the first modern jazz style. It was considerably less popular than swing, and it failed to attract dancers. However, it did contribute several impressive soloists who gained disciples for decades to follow: trumpeter Dizzy Gillespie, saxophonists Charlie Parker, Dexter Gordon, and Stan Getz, and pianists Thelonious Monk and Bud Powell. They contributed a vocabulary of musical phrases and distinctive methods of matching improvisation to chord progressions, thereby creating the most substantial system of jazz for the next forty years.

How the names bop and bebop originated is uncertain. But they might have come from the vocabulary of nonsense syllables which jazz musicians use to sing jazz phrases. Instead of singing "la, la, la" or "da, da, da," they might sing "dwee li du be bop oolya koo" or a similar sequence. It is also possible that the style's name was derived from the title of a Gillespie tune: "Bebop."

Bop differed from swing in a number of performance aspects:

1) Preferred instrumentation for bop was the small combo instead of big band.
2) Average tempo was faster in bop.
3) Clarinet was rare in bop.
4) Average level of instrumental proficiency was higher for bop players.
5) Rhythm guitar was rare.
6) Less emphasis was placed on arrangements in bop.

Bop differed from swing in a number of stylistic respects:

1) Melodies were more complex in bop.
2) Harmonies were more complex in bop.
3) Accompaniment rhythms were more varied in bop.
4) Comping was more prevalent than stride style and simple, on-the-beat chording.
5) Drummers played their timekeeping rhythms primarily on suspended cymbal, rather than primarily on snare drum, high-hat, or bass drum.

6) Phrase lengths within solos were longer in bop.
7) Bop tunes and chord progressions projected a more unresolved quality than swing tunes and chord progressions.
8) Bop was a more aggressive, hard-hitting style than swing was.
9) Bop improvisation was more complex because it contained
   a) more themes per solo,
   b) less similarity among themes,
   c) more excursions outside the tune's original key, and
   d) a greater scope of rhythmic development.
10) Surprise was more highly valued in bop.

Bop made its first appearances during the late 1930s and early 1940s in the playing of alto saxophonist Charlie Parker, pianist Thelonious Monk, and trumpeter Dizzy Gillespie, whose approaches were originally begun independently but were compatible and mutually inspiring. Parker, Gillespie, and Monk played together and refined a very complex kind of music. Their improvisations were composed mostly of eighth-note and sixteenth-note figures which seemed jumpy, full of twists and turns. The contours of the melodic lines were jagged; there were often large intervals between the notes and abrupt changes of direction. The rhythms in those lines were quick and unpredictable, with more syncopation than any music previously common in Europe or America.

Modern jazz performers overcame the tendency of premodern improvisers to stop phrases at or before turnarounds (see pages 387–388 for explanation of turnarounds). Bop players took a cue from Lester Young and often began phrases in the middle of eight-bar sections, continuing them through the turnarounds, past the traditional barriers of the eighth bar (twelfth bar in the blues). They planned ahead further and mastered the improvisation of extended lines which reflected a tune's underlying chord progression less and less.

For the basis of their lines, bop musicians did more than embellish the melody. They usually departed from the melodies and retained only the chord progressions. Often they enriched a progression by adding new chords. Swing players and early jazz players might have employed fewer than five or ten chord changes in a twelve-bar blues, but a bop player might want ten or twenty chord changes (see third example under "Chord Progressions for the Twelve-Bar Blues" on page 416). Art Tatum had previously explored reharmonization of melodies and had added chords to existing progressions. Lester Young and Coleman Hawkins had been so fluent in devouring every existing chord change that they and Tatum had set the stage for addition of chords and the related melodic complexity of Parker and Gillespie. Addition of chords is often called substitution because, in place of a single chord or a common chord sequence, new chords are substituted. Some bop

TABLE 9.1. A Few of the Many Bop Style Musicians

Trumpet

Dizzy Gillespie
Fats Navarro
Howard McGhee
Miles Davis
Kenny Dorham
Red Rodney
Benny Harris
Sonny Berman
Freddie Webster
Conte Candoli
Clark Terry
Idrees Sulieman
Benny Bailey

Trombone

J. J. Johnson
Kai Winding
Bennie Green
Frank Rosolino

Bass

Oscar Pettiford
Ray Brown
Tommy Potter
Curly Russell
Nelson Boyd
Al McKibbon
Gene Ramey
Red Callender
Teddy Kotick
Chubby Jackson
Eddie Safranski

Saxophone

Charlie Parker
Dexter Gordon
Lucky Thompson
Stan Getz
Wardell Gray
Allen Eager
Herbie Steward
Brew Moore
Gene Ammons

Sonny Stitt
Flip Phillips
James Moody
Charlie Ventura
Zoot Sims
Al Cohn
Ernie Henry
Leo Parker
Sonny Criss
Serge Chaloff
Don Lamphere
Charlie Rouse
Sonny Rollins
Phil Urso
Boots Mussulli

Vibraharp

Milt Jackson
Teddy Charles
Terry Gibbs

Drums

Kenny Clarke
Max Roach
Joe Harris
Tiny Kahn
Don Lamond
Roy Haynes
Osie Johnson
Denzil Best

Piano

Bud Powell
Thelonious Monk
Al Haig
Dodo Marmarosa
Joe Albany
Walter Bishop, Jr.
Duke Jordan
George Shearing
Oscar Peterson
Billy Taylor
Hank Jones

Argonne Thornton
   (Sadik Hakim)
Hampton Hawes
John Lewis
Tadd Dameron
Ahmad Jamal

Guitar

Arv Garrison
Tal Farlow
Bill DeArango
Jimmy Raney
Johnny Collins
Barry Galbraith
Chuck Wayne
Barney Kessel
Billy Bauer
Johnny Smith

Composer-Arranger

Gil Fuller
George Russell
Neal Hefti
Dizzy Gillespie
Charlie Parker
Thelonious Monk
Tadd Dameron
John Lewis
Shorty Rogers
Ralph Burns
Gil Evans
Gerry Mulligan

lines implied chords which were not originally in a tune; these lines were sometimes played against a tune's original harmonies to achieve purposely clashing effects. In other cases, the rhythm section would instantaneously change chords and chord progressions to fit the new harmonic directions implied by an improvised line. Bop rhythm sections learned to be quite sensitive and resourceful.

Bop players also altered existing chords, and they often based their lines more on the alterations than on the fundamental tones. So, by comparison with their predecessors, bop musicians not only used more chords, they used richer chords, and they created lines that drew from the enrichments. The most common alteration was the flatted fifth (also known as the lowered fifth or raised eleventh). It soon became as much identified with modern jazz as the lowered third and lowered seventh were identified with premodern jazz. Today all three intervals are basic to the tonal character of jazz. (Dizzy Gillespie's 1945 arrangement of "Shaw Nuff" ends on a flatted fifth. Listen to it in SCCJ, and see pages 369–371 for explanation and keyboard illustration.)

Because bop musicians liked to improvise on difficult chord progressions, they sometimes wrote original progressions themselves; Dizzy Gillespie's "Con Alma" is an example. But a more common practice was to improvise on popular song progressions that were more challenging than average. "All the Things You Are" served this purpose. "Cherokee" became a favorite because the progressions in its bridge are unusual. (Listen to "Ko-Ko" in SCCJ. Charlie Parker improvised this atop the chord changes of "Cherokee." Humming the melody to "Cherokee" while listening to "Ko-Ko" should help you follow the harmonic basis for the melody of "Ko-Ko" and the improvisations which follow it because the same chord progression originally intended to accompany "Cherokee" is used here to accompany Parker's fresh improvisations, which are collectively called "Ko-Ko." It is as though Parker's improvisations were new melodies with "Cherokee"'s accompaniment.)

Bop players often wrote original tunes based on standard pop tune progressions, and many of these new tunes went without names. The leader just called out the key and the name of the pop tune which had originally provided the chord progression. In that way, members of the rhythm section could immediately play a tune they might have never previously heard. This technique was not new to bop. It had already been used in swing and early jazz. For example, the twelve-bar blues progression had been used in that way for decades. And Count Basie's 1930s recordings are filled with loosely arranged performances in which improvisations are placed atop the chord progressions of such popular songs as "Lady Be Good," "I Got Rhythm," and "Honeysuckle Rose." This provided a common ground for situations such as jam sessions, in which not all the participants knew the same tunes and arrangements, but most knew the chord progressions to a few commonly played pieces. "Indiana," "What Is This Thing Called Love," "Whispering," and "How High the Moon" respectively provided chord progressions for the bop compositions "Donna Lee," "Hot House," "Groovin' High," and "Ornithology." "Crazeology" (listed as "Little Benny" in SCCJ, elsewhere as "Bud's Bubble") is based on the chord progression to "Lullaby in Rhythm." The chord progression of George Gershwin's "I Got Rhythm" was used so much that musicians just called the chord changes "rhythm changes" ("I Got Rhythm chord changes" was probably abbreviated as "I Got Rhythm changes" which in turn was abbreviated as "rhythm changes" or just "rhythm").

Charlie Parker The musician who contributed most to the development of bop was alto saxophonist Charlie Parker (1920–1955). Going beyond the advances made by Lester Young, Coleman Hawkins, and Art Tatum, Parker built an entire system, the innovative conceptions of which were conveyed in his improvisations and compositions. It was a system that specified

1) new ways to construct improvisations on top of chord progressions;

2) new ways to accent particular notes within phrases and form a highly syncopated character that is immediately recognizable as bop;

3) methods for adding chords to existing chord progressions and implying additional chords within improvised lines.

Charlie Parker also influenced his colleagues and followers in another way. Because his favorite tempos were faster than those of most swing era pieces, Parker helped cause an increase in average tempo for modern jazz pieces. Another tempo-related impact of Parker was spawned by his tendency to intersperse his solos with double-time and quadruple-time figures. Even in his ballad renditions, Parker tended to ornament slow lines with double-time lines. It should also be noted that even when he was not double-timing, his lines still bore a rhythmic undercurrent that suggested he was going twice as fast. Though such practices had been employed by some jazz soloists since the 1920s, it was probably the added inspiration of Parker's use that supplied the impetus for modern soloists to routinely employ double-timing. Such techniques soon came to characterize most ballad playing as well as medium tempo work in modern jazz, and the breakneck tempos employed by Parker during the 1940s established an upper limit for most jazz performances of the next forty years. Musicians were astonished by the ease, high speed, and clarity with which Parker improvised. (For a sample of Parker's phenomenal speed, listen to "Ko-Ko" in SCCJ, or "Bird Gets the Worm" in *The Savoy Recordings*, Savoy 2201. "Ko-Ko" can also be found in *Bebop*, New World 271, a record series donated to schools and libraries by the Rockefeller Foundation.)

Parker's sound departed from standard swing era models. In place of the lush, sweet tone preferred by Johnny Hodges and Benny Carter, Parker used the dry, biting tone preferred by Kansas City saxophonist Buster Smith, an early model for Parker. Though Parker's tone had considerable fullness, it possessed a lighter color than the tone of Hodges. In place of the pronounced vibrato of Hodges and Carter, Parker used the slower, narrower vibrato preferred by Smith, and Parker was less prone to dwell on a few choice notes than Hodges was. By comparison with Hodges, Parker sounded more hurried. Rather than an easygoing romantic, Parker sounded like a modern composer who was improvising at lightning speed.

(Listen to "Embraceable You" in SCCJ or in New World 271. This is based on a thirty-two bar A-A-B-A song by George Gershwin, and it became one of Parker's most acclaimed improvisations. Notice that Parker engages in much quadruple-timing while the rhythm section remains in a ballad accompaniment style. Parker's improvisation is rich with ideas that are complex and unpredictable. Compare Parker's dense, multinoted style with that which Coleman Hawkins uses on "Body and Soul" in SCCJ. Both Parker and Hawkins were especially interested in playing many notes and sequencing the notes to indicate not only each chord that occurred but also many other chords that might fit the progression, even though their accompanists did not sound them. Both men were doing more than simply double-timing. They were quadruple-timing. It is notable that, even though Parker has the Kansas City tone color and rhythmic swing feeling of Lester Young, he leans more toward the Hawkins preference for complex improvisation than toward the Young preference for singable melody.)

Charlie Parker's improvisations were inspired by many sources.

1) He quoted Lester Young solos. (Listen to Parker's 1940 recordings with Jay McShann: "Moten Swing," "Coquette," and "Lady Be Good" on *First Recordings.*)

2) He quoted traditional melodies such as "Reuben, Reuben I've Been Thinking," and "In a Country Garden."

3) He quoted opera themes such as Bizet's "Carmen."

4) He quoted twentieth-century European composers' themes, such as Stravinsky's "Petrouchka."

5) He used the melodic fragments and inflections that were traditional in the music of blues singers and early jazz hornmen. (Listen to his "Parker's Mood" in SCCJ or in New World 271.)

(See pages 412, 413, and 414 for information on how to get transcriptions for hundreds of Parker solos.)

Parker wrote a sizable body of compositions. These were Parker improvisations which had been memorized and written down. They had the same style as his spontaneous lines, but they were now available for two horns to play in unison as a jumping off point for improvisations. The rhythmic and melodic character of Parker's tunes set the flavor for bop as much as his improvisations did. They were not melody-like in the pop tune sense, but they were catchy lines in a jazz vein. These phrases were memorized and analyzed by hundreds of jazz soloists. This was the musical language of bop.

Most of Parker's tunes were based on chord progressions from popular songs. Many were based on the twelve-bar blues chord progression ("Billie's Bounce," "Cheryl," "Barbados," "Au Privave," "Bloomdido," "Bird Feathers," "Now's the Time," "Air Conditioning," and others). Several Parker tunes were commonly played at jam sessions for decades after he introduced them: "Now's the Time," "Billie's Bounce," and "Confirmation." (During the 1970s and 80s, Parker's "Donna Lee" enjoyed a resurgence of use in that setting.)

After co-leading a combo with trumpeter Dizzy Gillespie (listen to their 1945 "Shaw Nuff" in SCCJ), Parker led a series of his own groups, using several of the best players in bop—trumpeters Miles Davis, Red Rodney, Fats Navarro, Howard McGhee, and Kenny Dorham; pianist Al Haig; drummer Max Roach; and others. Not only was Parker heard with his own combos, but also on occasion with Dizzy Gillespie's big band, Woody Herman's big band, Machito's Latin band, all-star jam sessions organized by Norman Granz, and groups employing violin, viola, cello, oboe, and rhythm section. Each recording sounded as though Parker were just sitting in and so happy to be playing that he was practically blowing the roof off.

Parker's impact on jazz was immense. The Parker methods of improvisation were adopted by numerous saxophonists during the 1940s and 50s (see Table 9.2). Several highly influential improvisers of the late 1950s and early 1960s owed part of their approaches to Parker. John Coltrane, the leading tenor and soprano saxophonist of the 1960s, displayed Parker's mannerisms in some his own recorded improvisations of the 1950s. Parker's tunes and phrases were sometimes heard in the earliest recordings of saxophonists Ornette Coleman and Albert Ayler, two leading innovators of the 1960s. Bop trumpeter Dizzy Gillespie cites Parker as a primary influence on his own style, and bop pianist Bud Powell modelled some of his lines after those of Parker. Jazz clubs were named for him: Birdland in New York and Birdhouse in Chicago. Bop singer Eddie Jefferson performed Parker's "Billie's Bounce" and "Parker's Mood" with lyrics which had been written for both the melodies of the tunes and Bird's improvisations on them. (When you hear Parker's work set to lyrics, Parker's melodic skills become all the more evident.) During the 1970s, bassist Buddy Clark

TABLE 9.2. A Few of the Many Saxophonists Influenced by Charlie Parker

Phil Woods	Jackie McLean
Charlie Mariano	Cannonball Adderley
Sahib Shihab	Eric Dolphy
Ernie Henry	John Coltrane
Sonny Criss	Sonny Rollins
Charlie McPherson	Ornette Coleman
Frank Strozier	Albert Ayler
Jimmy Heath	Wardell Gray
Lou Donaldson	Dexter Gordon
Davey Schildkraut	Art Pepper
Sonny Stitt	Bud Shank
James Moody	Joe Farrell

and alto saxophonist Med Flory started a group called Supersax which consisted of five saxes and rhythm section playing harmonized transcriptions of Parker solos. Supersax treats Parker's improvisations as written compositions.

Dizzy Gillespie Louis Armstrong was the jazz trumpet virtuoso of the late 1920s and early 30s. Roy Eldridge held a similar position in the late 30s. But the innovative melodic concepts, high-register playing, and overall instrumental proficiency achieved by Dizzy Gillespie (b. 1917) were not only phenomenal for the 1940s, but have rarely been matched since. Great instrumental proficiency seems to have been a necessary prerequisite for bop improvisation, and Gillespie's awe-inspiring command of the trumpet accounts for only part of his impact. His stirring musical ideas and the blazing force with which they were delivered account for much of his influence. In addition to absorbing the saxophone-style lines and excitement of Roy Eldridge's approach, Diz contributed what was probably the most rhythmically varied style in jazz. He invented intricate syncopations which, though extremely complex, sounded both natural and vital. (Listen to Gillespie's 1945 "Shaw Nuff" in SCCJ.)

Dizzy Gillespie's harmonic skills were startling, and he flaunted them. His phrases were full of surprises and playful changes of direction. He could precariously go in and out of keys within a single phrase, always managing to resolve the unexpected at the next chord. He often zoomed up to the trumpet's high register during the middle of a phrase and still managed to connect the melodic ideas logically. Quotes from non-jazz pieces occurred in Gillespie's improvisations. (Bizet's opera "Carmen" was a favorite for him as it also was for

Charlie Parker.) Gillespie often built a line by going higher and higher by means of syncopated notes played staccato and then coming down from the high register by means of legato lines that resolved the tension that had been built by his going up. Yet Gillespie's lines made sense even when he played these rapid cascades of notes. And despite its complexity, his work bristled with excitement.

Like Roy Eldridge, Gillespie would occasionally toy with a single note, playing it again and again, each time in a different way, creating different rhythmic patterns and using changes in loudness and tone color to achieve variety in his sound. One Gillespie method which is especially reminiscent of Eldridge is to make the trumpet tone brittle and then crack it resoundingly in a burst of high notes. Also, like Eldridge, he could channel all his terrific energy into a ballad, using his exceptional skill with harmony, his fertile imagination, and virtuoso technique to mold a unique, personal creation. A masterpiece of this kind was his 1945 "I Can't Get Started" solo. (Listen to "I Can't Get Started" in SCCJ or in *Dizzy Gillespie: The Development of An American Artist, 1940–46* Smithsonian 2004. The latter also contains "Night in Tunisia," "Salt Peanuts," "Woody 'n' You," as well as Gillespie's solos with the Cab Calloway big band.)

Gillespie exerted sweeping influence on modern jazz. His pet phrases became stock clichés for two generations of jazz trumpeters; these phrases can also be heard in the playing of pianists, guitarists, saxophonists, and trombonists. During the 1940s, he influenced countless trumpeters including Howard McGhee, Red Rodney, Benny Harris, Conte Candoli, Kenny Dorham, Fats Navarro, Miles Davis, Thad Jones, and Clark Terry. Some of these players had originally derived their styles from premodern sources, but they incorporated Gillespie devices after hearing him. Though only a year or two older than several of them, Gillespie exerted the influence of a classic model rather than a mere contemporary. His influence did not end in the 1940s. During the 1970s, trumpeter Jon Faddis appeared, often quoting Gillespie recordings of the 1940s note for note.

As a composer, Gillespie also made lasting contributions to modern jazz ("Birks Works," "Emanon," "Groovin' High," "Blue 'n' Boogie," "Salt Peanuts," "Woody 'n' You," "Con Alma," "A Night in Tunisia," and others). "Con Alma," "Groovin' High," and "A Night in Tunisia" became jazz standards and have been played for decades.

After co-leading a combo with Charlie Parker and leading a few small bands of his own, Gillespie began a series of modern jazz big bands. He did some of the writing himself and assigned some to such excellent composer-arrangers as Gil Fuller, Tadd Dameron, and John Lewis. (Listen to the Gillespie big band's "Things to Come" in New World 271.)

One of Gillespie's special interests, Afro-Cuban music, was explored in the big band numbers "Manteca" and the two-tune combination "Cubano Be" and "Cubano Bop." These pieces, for which Gillespie employed conga drummer Chano Pozo, are among the earliest appearances of Latin American music in modern jazz.

Gillespie kept his big bands going through most of the late 1940s and then formed another during the mid-50s for a foreign tour sponsored by the U.S. State Department. The Gillespie combos and big bands saw a powerful flow of strong players, many of whom went on to lead their own groups. Gillespie sporadically led big bands after the State Department tour, but usually remained in a small combo format. He did not drastically alter his trumpet style after 1947, but he has remained an active performer into the 1980s.

In summary, Gillespie contributed

1) a model of unparalleled trumpet mastery: speed, agility, and a high register that set the upper limit for almost all jazz trumpeters who followed;

2) a body of original compositions including several that remain jazz standards;

3) a string of high quality combos and big bands featuring numerous jazz stars-to-be (such as John Coltrane and Milt Jackson);

4) the use of Afro-Cuban music in jazz;

5) a new musical vocabulary of phrases and new ways of matching solo notes to accompanying chords, both of which became second nature to most modern jazz musicians.

Thelonious Monk Though the emphasis of bop was on improvisation, there were a few outstanding bop composers. Pianist-composer Thelonious Monk (1917–1982) contributed distinctive tunes to the bop repertory, his chord progressions being among the most difficult of all jazz bases for improvisation. Monk's "Straight, No Chaser," "Well, You Needn't," and "'Round Midnight" are jazz standards. The extent of his influence is indicated by noting that bop pianist Bud Powell recorded an album called *Portrait of Thelonious*, modern soprano saxophonist Steve Lacy led a band whose repertory consisted exclusively of Monk compositions, post-bop pianist Chick Corea used Monk pieces for half of his 1982 two-record set called *Trio Music*, and a 1980s band called Sphere (Monk's middle name) specialized in Monk's music.

Monk's tunes have a logic and symmetry all their own. Monk was expert at placing accents in irregular order. He was especially skilled in ending phrases on the least expected notes, yet making the piece sound as though those phrase endings had been expected all along. His "Off Minor" is a good example.

Monk employed simple compositional devices with very original results. His "Straight, No Chaser"[1] employs a single phrase played over and over again, each time in a different part of the measure. It has a few connecting passages, but it consists basically of a series of rhythmic variations on a single phrase. The shifting accents reflect a craftsmanship which can produce depth in simplicity. "Straight, No Chaser" is an ingenious invention based on the twelve-bar blues progression. Find a recording of it; no words can describe it well.

Monk's "Misterioso" (found in the SCCJ) is another masterpiece of simplicity. A twelve-measure sequence of almost unending eighth notes, it has no rests, no sustained tones, just legato eighth notes. These eighth notes are not arranged in the bop manner, either. They are smooth alternations of low and high notes. Pairs of notes in the interval of a sixth, gradually move up and down a scale, never stopping to rest, constantly moving in stepwise fashion. "Misterioso" has exquisite simplicity.

A large portion of Monk's compositions are in thirty-two-bar A-A-B-A form: "Epistrophy" and " 'Round Midnight" are two examples. "Epistrophy" is one of those Monk tunes which is simultaneously simple and quite original. It is usually played in medium tempo. " 'Round Midnight" is one of the most frequently played ballads of the bop era. Although it is one of Monk's prettiest melodies, it is not at all conventional. Some measures contain four different chords. The tune does not even start on the first beat of the chord progression. It begins on the second beat and has four notes on that single beat. Again, you must hear the tune to understand that description.

Monk was one of the most original of all jazz improvisers. His lines often display jagged contours, and the construction for some of his improvisations is quite playful. For example, he loved to abruptly insert a whole-tone scale (see Figure 9.1). Monk is particularly known for playing combinations of tones that clash with each other. (It has been playfully said that Monk could make an in-tune piano sound as though it were out of tune.) Combined with an uneven rhythmic style, these tonal characteristics made his music quite jarring.

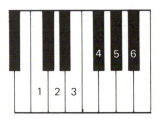

Figure 9.1. Piano keyboard illustration of a whole-tone sequence.

---

[1] "Epistrophy," "Misterioso," "Well, You Needn't," "Off Minor," and "Straight, No Chaser" are all in *Complete Genius* Blue Note LA 579 and Mosaic MR 4-101.

Another prime trait in Monk's music is that Monk is extremely economical. Silence is as important as sound in his improvisations. He uses notes sparingly. His marked deliberation seems to preclude the long, bouncing, horn-like improvisations typical of most other modern jazz pianists. Monk's work sounds very calculated.

As a pianist, Monk was a curious mixture. His use of stride piano techniques suggests Fats Waller. Some of his horn-like lines are reminiscent of Earl Hines. In some voicings, Monk's playing suggests Ellington's. Monk's style also resembles Ellington's in the percussive way both men strike the piano keys, the dark and rough tone quality they extract from the piano, and the way that both men allow notes to ring long after the keys are struck. Monk also likes the lower register, another Ellington preference.

Monk does not swing in the easy, relaxed manner of Teddy Wilson or Nat Cole. In fact, some people feel that Monk does not swing at all, although, as historian Harvey Pekar has pointed out, his groups often swing because of his swinging bassists and drummers. Monk simply plays as a composer who is always concentrating on choosing notes and chords. Some of his rhythmic conception is anti-swing. He often builds tension with little attempt at subsequent relaxation of that tension. Monk's approach is very intense and percussive. He often strikes a note or chord several times in sequence as though knocking on a door. (Listen to Monk play "Criss Cross," "Evidence," and "I Should Care" in SCCJ.)

Monk's comping was not like conventional bop comping style. It was not much like the light and bouncing approach that had developed out of Count Basie's methods. It seemed more like composition than the flexible chording provided by most modern pianists. It served a function more like that ordinarily served by a drummer's snare drum than like that of a guitarist's chording. Monk's comping seemed to be setting up spaces framed by resounding punches. Note also that Monk often stopped comping for considerable lengths of time during performances. The soloist was then consequently left to improvise with only bass and drums accompaniment.

Monk has influenced the compositional and improvisational flavor of much modern jazz. His jazz piano style has had a direct influence on a few pianists and an indirect influence on many more (see Table 9.3).

Monk rarely recorded with Parker or Gillespie. He usually led his own groups, one of which almost attained the status of a jazz institution. This was the group he led between 1959 and 1970 with tenor saxophonist **Charlie Rouse** (b. 1924). Together with bass and drums, they made several outstanding records for Columbia and a few for other companies. Rouse, though rooted in bop tenor style, often sounded like Monk playing sax. Instead of the long, eighth-note lines of bop, Rouse often used a Monk-like approach to phrasing, being biting and

TABLE 9.3. A Few of the Many Pianists Influenced by Thelonious Monk

Randy Weston	Misja Mengelberg
Herbie Nichols	Anthony Davis
Cecil Taylor	Karl Berger
Mal Waldron	Chick Corea
Andrew Hill	Dollar Brand
Bud Powell	

percussive, often engaging in the insistent, staccato hammering of notes characteristic of Monk. He had very little vibrato and rarely sustained his tones. Rouse's style was dark, dry, and blunt.

Composer-Arrangers One of bop's favorite composers was pianist **Tadd Dameron** (1917–1965). His work covered a broad range—from a bop melody based on a pop tune chord progression ("Hot House," based on "What Is This Thing Called Love") to a simple, catchy line with interesting chord changes ("Good Bait") to a pretty song scored for wordless vocal in the manner of Duke Ellington ("Casbah"). Dameron was an exceptional songwriter. His "If You Could See Me Now" was set to lyrics, and it was eventually recorded by Sarah Vaughan. Dameron's "Hot House," "Our Delight," "Good Bait," and "Lady Bird" became standard repertory for generations of bop musicians. (Listen to "Lady Bird" in SCCJ.) In fact, Miles Davis based his own "Half Nelson" on the chord progression of "Lady Bird." In 1956, tenor saxophonist John Coltrane and Dameron recorded an entire album of Dameron tunes, including Dameron's attractive ballads "On a Misty Night" and "Soultrane."[2] In the 1980s, an all-star New York group called Dameronia formed to regularly perform Dameron's compositions and arrangements.

Much of Dameron's most distinctive work appeared in the form of arrangements for medium-sized bands. Dameron was good at getting a big band sound from a small band. His arrangements had voicings with the thick textures and the rhythmic style of bop piano. He would use a strong, clear-toned lead trumpet like Fats Navarro, and then assign melody notes in a block chord-fashion to alto sax, tenor sax, trombone, and baritone sax. The range of the voicing might encompass three octaves. Dameron's arranging concepts turned up in later work by Benny Golson, Gigi Gryce, and Sun Ra.

The Dizzy Gillespie big band boasted several imaginative writers: Gil Fuller, George Russell, Gillespie himself, and pianist **John Lewis** (b. 1920), who contributed "Two Bass Hit" (also known as "La Ronde")

[2] John Coltrane *On a Misty Night* Prestige P 24084

and "Toccata for Trumpet and Orchestra." Lewis became better known, however, for later works such as his waltz "Skating in Central Park" and his tribute to Django Reinhardt called "Django" (in SCCJ). He has written hundreds of tunes in a variety of contexts, ranging from ballet music to film scores, with instrumentations ranging from jazz combos to symphony orchestras.

A special interest for John Lewis is combining classical music with jazz. This style is called **Third Stream music.** It usually consists of mixing the instrumentation and forms of classical music with jazz improvisation and jazz swing feeling. The man who coined the term is Gunther Schuller, another composer interested in pursuing that combination. His "Concertino for Jazz Quartet and Orchestra" was written especially for the group John Lewis directed, the Modern Jazz Quartet. (Note that this concept was not new. The idea of combining jazz and classical music has influenced bandleaders and composers in every era of jazz: Paul Whiteman in the 1920s; Artie Shaw in the 30s; Duke Ellington and John Lewis beginning in the 40s; and Charles Mingus, Gunther Schuller, Stan Kenton, John Lewis, George Russell, Jimmy Giuffre, Miles Davis, and Gil Evans beginning in the 1950s. The Don Ellis big bands of the 60s and 70s also explored Third Stream techniques.)

In 1952 Lewis and three other former Gillespie sidemen formed what was originally called The Milt Jackson Quartet but soon became the Modern Jazz Quartet. Vibraharpist Milt Jackson, pianist John Lewis, bassist Percy Heath, and drummer Kenny Clarke created a subdued, cool sound in a bop context. The group had a delicate, chamber music sound which was polished and dignified. Because of this sound, their good management, and large following, they were one of the first jazz groups to play concert halls almost exclusively. Over the years the Modern Jazz Quartet won many popularity polls sponsored by jazz magazines. (Kenny Clarke left in 1955, and Connie Kay took his place. Jackson, Lewis, Heath, and Kay remained intact as a quartet until the fall of 1974 when they disbanded. They have occasionally regrouped for tours.)

Vibraharpist **Milt Jackson** (b. 1923), nicknamed "Bags," who had previously been featured in several Dizzy Gillespie groups, became recognized in the 1950s as the leading vibraharpist in modern jazz. Not until the 1960s, when vibraharpists Gary Burton and Bobby Hutcherson began performing, was his pre-eminence seriously challenged. (But Jackson, Burton, and Hutcherson do not really compete with one another because each has chosen a distinctly different area within modern jazz. Jackson is a bop player, whereas Burton and Hutcherson developed styles which reflected the significant changes that occurred in jazz of the late 1950s and early 60s.)

In spite of the mechanical and percussive nature of the vibraharp,

Jackson manages to extract a warm sound and project remarkable presence by bluesy melodic figures and a careful regulation of the vibraharp's tremolo speed (he uses especially low rates of tremolo). He often adjusts the tremolo rate while playing, just as a saxophonist alters his vibrato and blowing pressure for expressive purposes (see Figure 9.2).

Jackson's lines are richly ornamented in a graceful, relaxed way. He ties up each phrase neatly. Jackson paces the notes within his

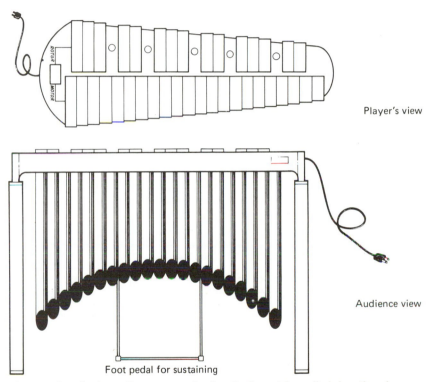

Player's view

Audience view

Foot pedal for sustaining

Figure 9.2. Vibraharp. To most people, the vibraharp (also called the vibraphone or vibes) looks like a marimba or a big xylophone with tubes hanging under its keys. The vibraharp is played similarly to the marimba and xylophone, but it is constructed differently. Its keys are metal; those of the xylophone and marimba are wooden. The vibraharp's resonating tubes are like those of the marimba, but each tube contains a disc that twirls by means of an electric motor. The twirling discs enable the sound of ringing keys to project and sustain. The discs give the vibraharp sound a wavering character, an even pulsation called a tremolo. The sound reaches our ears in alternating pulses (wuh . . . wuh . . . wuh . . .). Tremolo is not to be confused with vibrato. Tremolo is an alternation of loudness, whereas vibrato is an alteration of pitch. Some vibraharps allow the player to control the rate of tremolo by means of a dial attached to the rotor motor. All vibraharps allow the player to start and stop sustaining the sound by means of a foot pedal.

phrases and the phrases within his choruses. Catchy melodic figures fill his lines and seem to swing effortlessly. Subtlety is a prime characteristic of Jackson's approach. (Listen to "Django" in SCCJ.)

Jackson's style is not exclusively idiomatic to the vibraharp. His lines would also sound good played by a jazz trumpeter or flutist. The unhurried, but simmering feeling conveyed by his lines would enhance any number of styles. Jackson is a very fluid, clear-thinking improviser able to articulate his ideas beautifully through the vibraharp. His refinement of bop phrasing is a solid contribution which should not be viewed solely as the product of jazz vibraharp.

In the MJQ, Lewis and vibraharpist Jackson occasionally improvised different lines at the same time (counterpoint). Sometimes the result was balanced and provocative, but often the two lines simply got in each other's way. Lewis sometimes accompanied Jackson's improvisations with piano comments which seemed almost pre-written and did not flexibly relate to directions in Jackson's lines. It might seem that because of this situation, Jackson's work with less rigid pianists should be superior to that with Lewis. But, paradoxically, Jackson's work with the Modern Jazz Quartet is better than most recordings he has made outside of its context. Jackson has also played brilliantly with Thelonious Monk ("Misterioso" in SCCJ), another pianist who presents difficulties to the soloist because of his style as an accompanist. Jackson probably works well with Lewis and Monk because, in spite of their occasional lack of flexibility, they are two of the most freshly inventive pianists in jazz. Their accompaniment figures probably inspired Jackson more than they hindered him.

Rhythm Section Concepts of rhythm section playing did not advance as rapidly as those of solo playing. In fact, some pre-1947 Gillespie and Parker recordings have bop melodies and bop improvisations accompanied by pianists, bassists, and drummers who are stylistically rooted in the swing era. Like Louis Armstrong during the 1920s, Gillespie and Parker during the mid-1940s were more advanced than their accompanists. However, bop pianists eventually evolved the accompaniment style known as **comping,** spontaneous chording that flexibly interacted with the improvised solo lines. (Count Basie had demonstrated this as early as the mid-1930s, but it was not common until the late 1940s playing of bop pianists.)

Duke Ellington's innovative bassist Jimmy Blanton inspired many bop bassists. Most had first begun in pre-modern styles, such as the swing era style of Count Basie's Walter Page, but they also tried to learn Blanton's techniques. Few, however, could match Blanton's tone or agility, and fewer had his drive. But, over the twenty years following his death, Blanton's ideas became a standard part of modern jazz bass playing. **Oscar Pettiford** and **Charles Mingus** were Blanton's most outstanding disciples. (Listen to Pettiford with Coleman Hawkins on "The Man I Love" in SCCJ. See pages 243–247 for more on Mingus.)

Jo Jones and Sid Catlett are the swing drummers most frequently cited as influences when bop drummers are interviewed. Jones eliminated bass drum playing in some contexts and recorded some of the earliest examples of flexible interaction between soloist and drummer. Catlett kept time with a more swinging feel than was common to drummers in the 1930s. (He was one of the few who was able to play with bands from both the swing and bop eras.)

The advances made by Jones, Catlett, and others became crystallized in the playing of bop drummers **Kenny Clarke** (b. 1914) and **Max Roach** (b. 1925), who evolved from swing approaches in at least three fundamental respects. First, they **increased the frequency and spontaneity of kicks and prods**, those sounds that deviate from timekeeping rhythms. (When these extra sounds were extracted from the bass drum, they were called "bombs.") Bop drummers were not merely timekeepers. The kicks and prods were means that they developed for spontaneously accenting and coloring solo lines. (These sounds served at least two important purposes. First was a kind of communication between the drummer and the solo improvisers they were accompanying. Second was what has been called "chatter," the assortment of pops and crashes that provide an energetic layer of activity, thereby increasing the excitement of the band sound. For examples of these practices, listen to Max Roach's playing on Charlie Parker's "Klactoveesedstene" in SCCJ.)

A second advancement was made when **Kenny Clarke and Max Roach took a cue from Jo Jones and altered the manner of timekeeping on the bass drum by playing more gently, "feathering" the bass drum instead of pounding it.** This was a practice that became standard for at least one generation of jazz drummers beyond its originators. However, it is difficult to detect in recordings because not all the combo drummer's instruments were equally well recorded during the first two decades of modern jazz. (Even in the late 1960s, it was still difficult to clearly hear the bass drum on jazz combo recordings because engineering expertise was slow in developing.)

A third advancement occurred in the choice of percussion instrument used for timekeeping. In swing style, tempo had been reinforced by the drummer striking the bass drum and by playing a timekeeping rhythm on snare drum or high-hat. In the bop era, Kenny Clarke and Max Roach extended ways in which Jo Jones and Dave Tough had already been getting away from these devices in the swing era. During the late 1930s, Jones had occasionally played ride rhythms on a single cymbal, as in Count Basie's 1937 recording of "One O'Clock Jump," and Dave Tough had already been playing ride rhythms on a large cymbal that was not part of his high-hat apparatus. (See pages 19–21 for illustrations of these instruments and pages 429–430 for notations of the rhythms.) Kenny Clarke is generally credited with influencing the widespread adoption of **playing timekeeping rhythms on a cymbal suspended up over the drum set.**

Not only the instruments on which timekeeping rhythms were played, but also the way they were executed was different in bop. Modern drummers continued the sustained cymbal sound popularized by Jo Jones. However, they did this on neither the opening and closing high-hat, nor a single cymbal of the high-hat apparatus. They kept time on a large, thick, heavy cymbal which allowed them to extract a "ping" that would sustain until the next "ping." In other words, Jo Jones had smoothed out the manner for playing timekeeping rhythms, and bop drummers extended this to achieve an even more continuous (legato) sound. (Note also that bop drummers emphasized the practice of snapping the high-hat shut sharply on the second and fourth beats of each measure. Many swing drummers had not used the instrument in that way at all.)

Bop drummers, especially Max Roach, had better instrumental proficiency than the average swing drummer. Increased instrumental command was a common trait for bop players in general, but in the rhythm section, its effects were to lighten the group sound and propel it with greater momentum. Many bop tunes were taken very fast, the average tempo being greater than in swing. Bop drummers had to have more technique so that they could handle those tempos with ease.

Most of the foregoing discussion will mean nothing to you unless you are listening to the sounds while reading the descriptions. It helps to have a drummer demonstrate all these practices in person, and it is essential that you hear recordings of those historically significant drummers mentioned. All can be heard in SCCJ: Jo Jones in Count Basie's "Doggin' Around," "Taxi War Dance," and "Lester Leaps In," Sid Catlett in Dizzy Gillespie's "Shaw Nuff," Kenny Clarke in Miles Davis's "Boplicity" and Tadd Dameron's "Lady Bird," Roach in Parker's "Klactoveesedstene" and "Ko-Ko" as well as Sonny Rollins's "Blue Seven" and "Pent-Up House."

Piano   As bop styles developed, jazz piano arrived at the level of jazz trumpet and saxophone in improvisational conception, and it developed from the point of just "playing with a band" to the level of sophisticated skill required for comping. By the standards of early jazz and swing, all good bop pianists were very exceptional musicians. They took up where Earl Hines and Teddy Wilson left off.

Swing piano styles began to take advantage of the widening use of string bass. Pianists placed less emphasis on the left hand for supplying chorded or single note bass lines. By the time bop was under way, pianists had almost entirely abandoned the left hand's bass functions that were so common in stride, boogie woogie, and swing piano; a new left-hand style evolved which was to characterize jazz piano for several decades.

Bop pianists had to be musically well-rounded and very quick-witted. Bop hornmen were breaking records for speed and complexity, and the bop pianists had to do more than just solo effectively; they had to keep up with and anticipate the hornmen. They had to understand all the harmonic and rhythmic innovations of Bird and Diz, and anticipate the soloists in order to comp for them. Bop pianists had to use chords imaginatively, rhythmically set up and underscore both solo and ensemble figures, and inspire the entire group.

Bud Powell (1924–1966) is the most imitated of all bop pianists. When bop piano style is discussed, Powell's name comes to mind as quickly as Charlie Parker's name occurs at the mention of bop saxophone style. Powell crafted his approach from Art Tatum's, with the addition of borrowings from the styles of Billy Kyle and Nat Cole. Atop the Tatum foundation, Powell then laid out the favorite phrases of Charlie Parker and Dizzy Gillespie. The result was one of the first modern jazz piano styles. (Powell also contributed several original compositions to bop: "Tempus Fugit," "Parisian Thoroughfare," "Celia," "Dance of the Infidels," and "Hallucinations," which is also known as "Budo.")

Powell de-emphasized the activity of the left hand, thereby departing from the stride tradition and the "chomp, chomp, chomp, chomp" style of chording used by many swing pianists. This served to lighten the way pianists had begun playing, even more than the streamlining introduced by Teddy Wilson and Nat Cole. In place of the striding left-hand figures, **Powell's left hand inserted brief, sporadically placed two- and three-note chords that reduced his statement of harmony to the barest minimum.** Sometimes the chords sustained for a few beats. Sometimes there was no left-hand sound at all. This comping style became the standard means modern pianists used to suggest the chords underlying their own solo lines. This development was almost as significant within the history of solo piano conception as the emergence of comping had been for rhythm section pianists who were accompanying horn solos. In other words, **the breakthrough that Count Basie had made in lightening the manner in which a pianist supplied chords and support for an improvising soloist was paralleled in the way Powell lightened the manner in which a pianist accompanied his own solo lines.** (Listen to "Un Poco Loco" in New World 271.)

In his prime (prior to the mid-1950s), Powell had the speed and dexterity to create piano solos that matched the high-powered inventions of Bird and Diz. He mastered the erratically syncopated rhythms of bop and charged through his solos with terrific force. He employed the octave-voiced horn lines of Earl Hines and the complex runs of Art Tatum. **Powell was the model for hundreds of pianists during the 1940s and 50s, as James P. Johnson had been during the 1920s and Earl Hines had been after Johnson.**

Though Powell lived until 1966, he was only sporadically active throughout most of his career. He did not appear on nearly the number of recording sessions that pianist **Al Haig** played. Haig (1924–1982) was the most in-demand bop pianist. He traveled with many of the top groups, including Parker's and Stan Getz's, and made hundreds of recordings. His flowing solos and tasteful comping made him a figure on the bop scene who paralleled Tommy Flanagan's position during the middle 1950s and early 60s and Herbie Hancock's position throughout the 60s.

Though still a developing bop pianist when he recorded with Diz in 1947, Haig was a very solid craftsman by the time he began recording with Stan Getz in 1949. He never seemed at a loss for ideas. His touch was light and clean. In some ways he resembled Teddy Wilson. Haig could play hard, driving pieces or slow, pretty ballads. On occasion he could be quite flowery, but usually he was a very direct, swinging player.

Two bop pianists who found much larger popular audiences than Haig or Powell were **George Shearing** (b. 1919) and Oscar Peterson. Shearing became known primarily for the group sound he perfected: soft, polished ensemble statements voiced for piano, guitar, vibraharp, bass, and drums. Peterson's reputation was established in a trio format (piano, guitar, and bass; and later, piano, bass, and drums).

Shearing has what is probably the cleanest, lightest piano sound in bop. His music is so refined that it has been called polite bop. In addition to playing single note lines and octave-voiced lines, he helped popularize the locked-hands style first heard in Milt Buckner's playing of the mid-1940s. Shearing's voicings contrast markedly with those of Buckner, however. Shearing brought a very sophisticated harmonic conception to jazz piano. Shearing often voiced melodies so that chording was achieved by ensemble playing of a line in harmony or in octaves. Piano, guitar, and vibes might play a melody in unison or in harmony while bass and drums underscored critical figures and kept time. Individual solos followed, framed by ensemble fills and endings, all well rehearsed and precisely performed. Everything swung and was well controlled.

Shearing also achieved a successful integration of Latin American elements and bop. Armando Peraza played auxiliary percussion in Shearing's group from 1954 until 1964. Shearing's bassist Al McKibbon had developed Latin American bass figures while playing Afro-Cuban music in Dizzy Gillespie's big band with Cuban drummer Chano Pozo. McKibbon had brought Peraza to Shearing's attention and then collaborated with Peraza to integrate Latin rhythms with Shearing's techniques.

Shearing also wrote many interesting jazz tunes. His "Conception," with its difficult chord changes, was recorded by Miles Davis twice, though the name was changed to "Deception." "Local 802 Blues" was popular with late 1940s and early 50s musicians. Shearing's "Lullaby of Birdland," a theme song for the New York jazz club, Birdland, became a very popular jazz standard.

Oscar Peterson (b. 1925) is one of the most widely envied pianists in jazz history. His extraordinary pianistic facility and endurance enable him to take incredibly fast tempos which bassists and drummers can barely maintain. Peterson has a distinctive style stemming from the approaches of Nat Cole, Bud Powell, and Art Tatum. He has the combined drive of Powell and Tatum yet lacks the originality they brought to jazz. He also has incorporated the funky, gospel-flavored figures popularized by Horace Silver during the 1950s. Peterson's ballad style is full and orchestral. He sweeps the entire keyboard with astounding command. Since the late 1940s, Peterson has been a solid force on the modern jazz scene whose surging power and vitality never seemed the least bit diminished.

Clarinet   The clarinet has not been an important instrument in modern jazz. One of the most popular instruments during the swing era, it became one of the least popular during the bop era. Clarinet has almost disappeared as a jazz instrument. It is easy to name ten to twenty bop saxophonists and at least ten good bop trumpeters, but few people can name more than two bop clarinetists. Tony Scott, Stan Hasselgard, and Buddy DeFranco made valiant attempts to adapt bop to the clarinet, but their efforts did not catch on.

Guitar   Guitar disappeared as a member of the rhythm section during the bop era, but it returned as a solo instrument. Bop was a style pioneered by Bird and Diz which was soon assimilated by players of other instruments. Guitarists were among the last to play in a bop style, and when they did, they still were not improvising with the originality of Parker and Gillespie. The strongest bop guitarists were more active during the late 1940s and early 50s than during the developmental period of the mid-40s. Jimmy Raney and Tal Farlow were outstanding bop guitarists. They remained excellent performers during the 1980s.

Trumpet   Dizzy Gillespie was the leading trumpeter at the beginning of the bop era. But by the late 1940s, Gillespie's disciples Miles Davis and Fats Navarro were also offering models for bop trumpeters to follow.

When Charlie Parker and Gillespie separated, **Miles Davis** became Parker's new trumpeter. Davis and Parker recorded together from

1945 to 1948, but only sporadically thereafter. Counting alternate takes and recordings for both Savoy and Dial record companies, Davis recorded more than one hundred selections with Parker. In these recordings, Davis displayed elements of both Gillespie's and Parker's styles, though he used a lighter, softer tone and played less in the high register than Gillespie. (Other players also seem to have influenced Davis. Trumpeters Freddie Webster and Clark Terry had previously played in styles not unlike that of Davis in the Parker sessions, although it is difficult to be certain of the extent to which Davis drew on the styles of these performers.) Even in 1945, Davis was important as an original and gifted improviser. Evidence of this is found in his combo recordings with Parker and the impact they had on the styles of trumpeters Shorty Rogers, Chet Baker, and Jack Sheldon. (See pages 209–212 and 324–325 for more on Davis.)

The trumpeter most often mentioned as a match for Gillespie was **Fats Navarro** (1923–1950). The tremendous high range, speed, and instrumental proficiency of Gillespie were equalled by Navarro. In addition to that, he had a fuller, brassier tone which he used more smoothly than Gillespie. His tone was a bit clearer and more even: Navarro was not prone to alter his tone size or color as did Gillespie and Roy Eldridge. However, Navarro did not have the rhythmic imagination and daring of Gillespie. There is no question that Gillespie developed the style in which Navarro played, but Navarro offered Gillespie competition. Navarro used vibrato more than Gillespie and Davis did, and this element became an essential aspect in the style of Navarro's influential disciple Clifford Brown. Navarro died in 1950, and Brown went on to directly spread the Navarro style to far more trumpeters than Navarro did himself. (See pages 412–413 for information on how to get Miles Davis, Fats Navarro, and Clifford Brown solo transcriptions and analyses by David Baker. Listen to Navarro on Tadd Dameron's 1948 recording of "Lady Bird" in SCCJ.)

Trombone   The bop style was so instrumentally demanding, that it is surprising that it could be adapted to so difficult an instrument as the slide trombone. And it is a paradox that the two major bop trombonists, J. J. Johnson and Kai Winding, did not use the easier valve trombone, and that Bob Brookmeyer, a performer who specialized in valve trombone, actually preferred a conception that was slower and more easygoing than the high-speed style mastered by Johnson and Winding. (For a comparison of Johnson and Curtis Fuller, see pages 203–204. For description of Bill Harris, see page 95. For discussion of Frank Rosolino and the Stan Kenton band trombone style, see page 347.)

There were several trombonists in the earliest days of bop, but **J. J. Johnson** (b. 1924) is the musician who is most prominently identified with playing bop on the trombone.[3] Note, however, that despite

---

[3] *First Place* Columbia Special Products JCL 1030

the position he occupied, Johnson rarely improvised lines which were as complicated as Parker's or Gillespie's. Johnson's lines were often simple and tune-like. Many of his solos are quite singable. Incidentally, this gift for melody was not restricted to jazz improvisation. Johnson was very active as a composer. His jazz albums from the 1950s and 60s are filled with originals he penned, and he spent most of the 1970s writing and arranging music for movies and television instead of playing jazz.

J. J. Johnson departed from several traditions of jazz trombone playing by having an unprecedented command over the instrument and by

1) using very little vibrato

2) producing a smooth, consistent sound (in place of the more guttural tone quality that many premodern trombonists favored): Johnson attacked each note cleanly and maintained consistent size and quality throughout its duration.

3) avoiding the dependence on wide, drawn-out slurs and rips which typified many early players. (When Johnson used inflections at all, they were clipped, and they ornamented his main tones in a well-manicured way.)

4) playing with a rhythmic regularity and evenness that lent his music a bounce and a smooth swing feeling, especially evident in his eighth-note lines.

Many earlier players had given their trombones a highly extroverted role in jazz by using a choppy melodic style, rough tone, and extensive pitch inflections. Johnson, on the other hand, brought subtlety to the instrument's role and increased its politeness. Consistent with this stance, Johnson's choice of mute was not the rubber plunger favored by growl-style players. It was a cup mute that made his already dark, subdued sound even more gentle and clean. Johnson narrowed the emotional range of the jazz trombone while taking on the quick pace and increased complexity of bop. In other words, he streamlined jazz trombone conception. (See page 413 for information on how to get transcriptions of J. J. Johnson solos.)

Tenor Saxophone Bop tenor saxophonists drew their styles from two primary sources: Lester Young and Charlie Parker, and several secondary sources including Coleman Hawkins, Herschel Evans, Illinois Jacquet, and Don Byas. Some preferred to play the phrases of Lester Young almost unmodified, while others simply adopted the phrases of alto saxophonist Charlie Parker and played them on tenor sax. The most original players mixed several sources with a quantity of their own ideas.

It is possible to classify bop tenor saxophonists in several ways, but the most direct approach lies in the dimension of tone. Bop tenor saxophonists preferred either light-weight, light-colored tones or heavy-weight, dark-colored tones. There are gradations within these categories, of course, but it might be helpful to first describe players in terms of the two extremes, and then form your own descriptions to increase and refine your perceptions. The light-toned players include Stan Getz, Herbie Steward, Allen Eager, Brew Moore, and several players of a somewhat later style (West Coast): Buddy Collette, Bill Perkins, Bob Cooper, Richie Kamuca, and others. The heavy-toned players include Dexter Gordon, Gene Ammons, Lucky Thompson, Wardell Gray, Sonny Stitt, and others.

Dexter Gordon (b. 1923) was one of the least stereotyped bop tenor saxophonists. He used a large variety of melodic devices to create his lines. His phrase lengths and rhythms were varied, and he combined bop clichés with his own inventions. Gordon loved to quote from pop tunes and bugle calls. His tone was deep, dark, and full. Although his style was quite aggressive, his work conveyed great ease. He used the entire range of the tenor but had a special love for its low register. Gordon was a favorite player for many saxophonists who were later called hard bop tenors. Gordon has had a strong recording career from the 1940s to the present, and his playing has displayed depth and swing for over four decades. From 1962 to the mid-1970s, Gordon was based in Denmark. (Listen to "Bikini" in SCCJ.)

Lucky Thompson (b. 1924) was significantly different from Gordon. Instead of using Lester Young, Thompson used Don Byas as a model. He swung more easily than Byas, and had more consistent facility, and used a slower vibrato. Thompson's lines were very long and harmonically rich. He seemed to be using as many chords as he could imagine fitting in a chord progression. Though not as melodic as Gordon, he constructed solos which displayed a lot of continuity. Like Gordon, Thompson has remained active into the 1980s and spent considerable time in Europe.

For flowing, powerfully swinging solos, very few modern saxophonists can compete with **Sonny Stitt** (1924–1982). His instrumental speed and precision are awesome. During the late 1940s and early 50s, Stitt was second only to Charlie Parker as the leading bop alto saxophonist, and his recordings with Bud Powell placed him in the highest rank of bop tenor saxophonists. Stitt's playing has a consistently logical construction and rarely lacks continuity. Though he made more than one hundred albums under his own name, Stitt recorded some of his most outstanding solo improvisations under the leadership of other musicians, including Dizzy Gillespie ("Eternal Triangle"[4]), Bud Powell

---

[4] Dizzy Gillespie *Rollins/Stitt* Verve 2505

("All God's Chillun"[5]), and fellow saxophonist Gene Ammons ("Blues Up and Down"[6]).

Stitt was not an originator in the sense of Don Byas or Dexter Gordon, but he still managed to influence and inspire modern saxophonists with his own style. Frank Foster, George Coleman, and Joe Henderson are among the saxophonists who have cited Stitt as an influence. Stitt inspired many players partly because he had enviable command over the saxophone, playing with great ease, and an unusually high level of precision and consistency, and partly because he systematized a set of patterns which characterized bop approaches to improvisation. These patterns became formula for countless players in the mainstream of modern jazz. It was much easier to learn these patterns than to learn the less predictable and rhythmically more complex inventions of Parker. In essence, Stitt formalized a mixture of Parker, Lester Young, and his own ideas into a homogeneous method that satisfactorily handled the entire range of tempos and common bop chord progressions.

Stan Getz (b. 1927) was one of the most distinctive tenor saxophonists to emerge during the 1940s. Unlike most bop tenors, he used few of Parker's and Gillespie's pet phrases. He developed an original melodic and rhythmic vocabulary. His phrasing and accenting were less varied and less syncopated than Parker's or Gillespie's. At times, pre-twentieth century classical music seems to have influenced him more than bop. His main influences were Lester Young and Herbie Steward. (Getz and Steward played together in the sax section of Woody Herman's band. Steward had an original approach inspired by Lester Young.) Some 1949–50 Getz recordings also sound a bit like Lee Konitz, a modern jazz alto saxophonist not influenced by Parker (see pages 179–180). Getz played in a style rhythmically more like that of Lester Young than like Bird. Getz did not usually sound as relaxed as Dexter Gordon, but he was just as melodic as Gordon, perhaps more melodic. His improvisations were less like bop melodies than like melodies in classical music. Some were quite pretty. That aspect of his style fit well with his light, fluffy tone and graceful approach to the sax.

Stan Getz was one of the few bop musicians to become popular with the general public. One of the prettiest pieces the Woody Herman big band ever recorded was "Summer Sequence" by Ralph Burns. It was rearranged several times during the late 1940s. One segment often lifted out was "Early Autumn,"[7] a feature for the inventions of

[5] Sonny Stitt *Bud's Blues* Prestige 7839, and *Genesis* Prestige 24044

[6] Gene Ammons/Sonny Stitt *Prime Cuts* Verve 2V6S 8812

[7] Woody Herman *Early Autumn* Capitol M 11034, and Woody Herman *Greatest Hits* Columbia 9291

Stan Getz. That piece became a thirty-two-bar A-A-B-A pop tune and brought Getz to national attention. With that recording, Getz proved that he was one of the most sensitive and resourceful ballad players in jazz history.

The other Getz hits also took the form of slow, pretty pieces. His 1952 "Moonlight in Vermont" with guitarist Johnny Smith was quite popular. His 1962 "Desafinado" with guitarist Charlie Byrd was a major event in the popularization of bossa nova, a cross between Brazilian music and jazz. His 1964 recording of "Girl From Ipanema," with a vocal by Astrud Gilberto, became one of the best-selling records in jazz history.[8,9]

Popular Appeal   Bop was not nearly as popular as swing had been. When Charlie Parker died in 1955 he was an obscure figure compared to Benny Goodman, whose name was a household word. And yet Parker was musically a more significant force in jazz than Goodman. Several swing records sold more than a million copies, yet no bop instrumentals ever came close to that mark of popularity. There are several possible explanations for this. Many of them not only touch the differences between swing and bop, but they also constitute observations which help explain the historically low popularity of jazz as a whole.

One account for why bop was less popular than swing is that bop players presented a more serious appearance, one that was perhaps less inviting to all but the most devoted jazz fans. **Bop did not have as much visual appeal as swing.** Most swing bands carried singers, and many also carried dancers and showy staging. Bop combos, on the other hand, rarely carried singers, dancers, or showy staging. To appreciate modern jazz, people had to listen instead of watch.

Another factor affecting bop popularity is that, by comparison with swing, **bop had a scarcity of singers.** The bop listener was rarely offered song lyrics or the good looks and personality of the singer delivering them. More than ever before, jazz fans now had to follow melodies that had no words. This made jazz more abstract and less enjoyable. (Singers have traditionally been more popular than instrumentalists. Perhaps people like music with lyrics more than they like purely instrumental music because when someone sings a song, it is as though the singer is talking directly to you. This occurs because lyrics are in a language that is common for both the performer and the listener. Jazz instrumentals, on the other hand, are in a language that is known to only a tiny portion of the listening public. In addition to offering familiarity in the form of words, vocals also offer familiarity in the sound source itself. The human voice produces a sound that is

[8] *Getz/Gilberto* Verve 68545

[9] But do not overlook his medium- and up-tempo style: *Best of Stan Getz* Roulette SR 59027

far more familiar to listeners than that of any instrument. And, because of this greater familiarity, music made with the voice can be expected to achieve greater popularity than music made with instruments.)

Listeners have historically shown that they like relatively uncomplicated music. Furthermore, they like music to be fairly predictable. They especially like themes that they can sing along with, remember, and hum by themselves. **In comparison to swing, bop is neither uncomplicated nor predictable, and the written melodies in many bop performances are difficult to follow.** A sizable percentage of bop tunes are so complicated that, even if a listener became familiar with them, it is unlikely that he could sing along with them.

It is essential to note that when we say that "bop is complicated and unpredictable," we are talking about accompaniment styles as well as solo styles. The point is important when explaining popularity because relatively simple accompaniments backed even the most complicated swing era improvisations. Piano, guitar, bass, and drum parts were relatively simple, and they followed fairly predictable patterns that were quite steady. On the other hand, rhythm section accompaniment in bop style was less regular and therefore less predictable. Then as the 1940s progressed, drummers began to break up their timekeeping patterns and cultivate more and more musical surprises. Therefore the decreasing popularity that was associated with the development of jazz styles during the 1940s might be partly explained by the increasing complexity of solo improvisations and the decreasing predictability of accompaniment rhythms.

Danceability was another problem for bop. **People chose not to dance to bop.** Bop combos sometimes played for dances, but they were invited to do this far less often than they were hired to play strictly for listening. This is curious. People could have danced to bop. It had a steady beat and great rhythmic vitality. But somehow, this was not enough. Here are a few ideas that might account for this situation:

1) Perhaps bop's faster tempos scared away some dancers.
2) Perhaps the beat was not stated simply enough. It had to be made extremely obvious as it was in most swing band performances.
3) Perhaps arrangements provided insufficient repetition to make dancers feel comfortable.
4) Perhaps dancers wanted singable melodies in their ears before they felt like dancing.

The next four explanations are all part of the idea that **jazz improvisation is too abstract for the average listener** to enjoy. First, most bop melodies and improvisation resembled little or nothing that the average listener had heard before. (Listen to Dizzy Gillespie's "Shaw Nuff" or Charlie Parker's "Ko-Ko" in SCCJ, and ask yourself what common popular music it suggests to you.) **The less something sounds familiar, the more abstract it is to the listener.** It is harder to follow when it does not resemble a familiar pattern. The harder it is to follow, the more abstract the listener perceives it to be. And, as a rule, the more abstract something is, the less popularity it receives.

A second aspect of bop that makes it abstract is that the **relation between an improvisation and a tune's original melody is almost nonexistent.** This could upset the listener who expected jazz improvisation to simply consist of variation on a familiar theme, in the manner that singers toy with melodies or the manner in which some popular instrumentalists "interpret" current songs. This problem could be especially acute to the listener who asks "Where is the melody?" and who must be told that, in jazz, the improvisation itself is the melody. (Note that this was not new with bop. Nonthematic improvisation had been done in jazz at least as early as the 1920s by Louis Armstrong and Sidney Bechet. But it was more abundant and more drastic in bop.)

Jazz scholar Harvey Pekar has suggested a third aspect of bop that makes it abstract. He observes that **it is extremely difficult for the inexperienced listener to follow the relationship between improvised lines and chord changes in a typical bop performance.** His argument implies that listeners expect to hear particular relationships between notes in a solo line and the notes in the accompanying chord, and that listeners will notice the presence or absence of these expected relationships. As support for this argument we find that Charlie Parker and Dizzy Gillespie are especially known for stretching the conventional ties between solo notes and accompanying notes and that Parker and Gillespie were less popular than their predecessors. In other words, the relationship between melody notes and accompaniment notes sounded unfamiliar to those who heard bop, and that lack of familiarity decreased the amount of popularity that bop had.

A fourth element of abstractness that might account for bop's low popularity is the **relative absence of formal packaging for improvisation.** (A related factor is the greater length and amount of solo improvisations.) To begin appreciating this, first note that the most common size for jazz groups during the swing era was the ten to sixteen piece big band, but that the most common size for bop was the four to six piece combo. Also note that big bands, no matter what the era, tend to use more elaborate arrangements than combos use. Arrangement style that typified swing era big band performances used simple riffs to frame improvisations. The riffs accompanied improvisations, and they occurred before and after improvisations. They also interrupted long improvisations, thereby providing reference points which were especially effective for those listeners who might otherwise be overwhelmed by the newness and unpredictability offered in a jazz improvisation. In the swing format, then, improvisations were made somewhat comprehensible because the listener was required to only briefly cope with the unexpected. The riffs that accompanied the improvisations were simple and familiar, and there was a return to familiar material after each improvisation. (Listen to Count Basie's "Taxi War Dance" in SCCJ, and compare it with Dizzy Gillespie's "Shaw Nuff" in SCCJ.) In the bop format, on the other hand, musicians usually preset only the introduction, the theme, and the ending. Sandwiched between the theme and the ending was uninterrupted solo after solo. In other words, the amount of improvisation was less and the arrangement was more in swing era big bands than in bop combos. When improvisation must stand by itself because accompaniment is minimal, it is more difficult to grasp than when it is frequently interrupted and framed by familiar material. Bop was accordingly less popular than swing.

Another packaging asset available in swing format is that big band listeners are presented with much of the same music in live performances as in broadcasts and recordings. This is because using written arrangements allows reproducibility that a dependence upon improvisation does not allow. Remember that the accompaniments as well as the solos are improvised fresh during every bop combo performance but that swing big bands use preset arrangements for most of their accompaniment. These facts are relevant to popularity because the listener who had been exposed to the music ahead of time would find greater familiarity (hence, less abstractness) in a swing performance than in a bop performance of the same tune by the same musicians. The smaller amount of repetition in the bop performance would therefore present greater listening difficulty and, hence, less popularity for bop than for swing.

There is at least one problem with these explanations, however. If we use them to account for the difference in popularity between bop and swing, we must assume that jazz fans actually follow the improvisations. Yet a sizable portion of swing fans probably follow only the prewritten parts, and a sizable portion of bop fans probably grasp only the overall feeling of the music and not each and every note in the improvised lines. But, of course, this is something that we can never know. Therefore it is offered here simply as a qualification attached to the overall argument about jazz being too abstract to be popular.

Further support for these arguments comes when we look at those few bop combos that did achieve commercial success: The George Shearing Quintet, The Modern Jazz Quartet, and The Charlie Ventura Boptet. All three groups used formats that frequently interspersed tightly arranged and well-rehearsed ensemble statements among the improvisations. All offered a greater proportion of simpler, more sing-able melodies than most other bop combos used. Their repertories contained many well-known songs. The Boptet had the additional as-set of singers Jackie Cain and Roy Kral, and the Modern Jazz Quartet generally produced improvisations that were simpler and easier to fol-low than those ordinarily found in other bop combos. Two points are being made here. First, despite the generally low popularity of bop, there were a few groups and a few records that did become commer-cial successes. Second, the music within those successes prominently features some of the same characteristics that are outlined above for explaining the popularity of swing. As further support for these points, it should be noted that high among Charlie Parker's best-selling rec-ords were those he made of well-known songs with prewritten orches-tral accompaniments. It should also be noted that the greatest hits for Stan Getz have been recordings of singable themes such as "Moon-light in Vermont," "Desafinado," and "Girl From Ipanema." As a final consideration, combine these two observations: first, that the Getz re-cording of "Girl From Ipanema" contains a vocal, and, second, that it represents the largest selling record in the Getz career.

After considering the preceding arguments, you can see that differ-ences in **the amount of popularity enjoyed by different styles of music can be partly explained by differences in performance practices and differences between the ways each style treats basic elements of music.** In comparing the relative popularity of bop with swing, these perfor-mance practices are relevant: appearance, amount of improvisation, repetition, the amount of packaging for improvisation, and presence of words in the music. The musical elements of melody, harmony, and rhythm are also treated differently in the two styles. Bop offered higher, faster, more complex playing. Bop featured more variety of rhythms in melody lines and in accompaniments. Bop used richer chords, more chord changes, and a more elaborate relationship be-tween the notes of the melody and the notes of the accompanying chords. Throughout jazz history the differences between jazz and pop-ular music have echoed the same differences that are listed here be-tween bop and swing. Therefore, because jazz has traditionally been less popular than most other forms of American music, its low popu-larity is probably due, in part, to these same differences in perfor-mance practice and use of musical elements.

With the advent of bop, the status of jazz began to resemble that of classical chamber music more than that of American popular music. It became an art music in the sense that its performance required highly sophisticated skills and its popular appeal was limited. Jazz had always required special skills, and, as far as American popular music went, it had long been in the elite because of its demand for so much spontaneous creativity. Yet bop seemed to crystallize those tendeñcies and remove jazz further from the mainstream of American popular music. It is important to note, however, that like all jazz styles, bop had fans who could not follow every note and chord, but loved it anyway. Most jazz appeals to thousands of fans who like its sound but who may not have a sophisticated understanding of its structure or historical significance. The fans of jazz proportionally include far more musicians than the fans of pop, rock, and country music, but even musician-fans do not technically understand what every improviser does. Musicians do have a greater appreciation for the underlying complexities of music, but that appreciation must be coupled with an attraction to the sound before they will spend time and money to hear it. (No understanding is necessary for a listener to enjoy jazz—modern jazz or any other style. But it is reasonable to assume that knowledge of musical techniques will increase a listener's appreciation.)

Modern jazz continued the jazz tradition of influencing American popular music and symphonic music, but it seemed to carve its own sturdy path for musicians and a small segment of the listening public. Bop became parent for a series of styles (discussed in the next several chapters) which were also less popular than swing. Jazz did not regain its popularity until the 1970s when a jazz-rock fusion brought millions of new fans.

CHAPTER SUMMARY

1) Bop differed from swing in several respects:
   a) The common instrumentation was small combo rather than big band.
   b) The standard tempo was quicker.
   c) Instrumental virtuosity rose.
   d) More chords were used per tune, and more complex chords were preferred.
   e) Improvisatory style evolved from Roy Eldridge, Lester Young, and Art Tatum.
   f) Phrases were longer and less evenly organized than in swing.
   g) Composers and improvisers drew more from such twentieth-century symphonic composers as Béla Bartók and Igor Stravinsky.
   h) Less emphasis was placed on large, rich tone colors while more was placed on speed and agility.
   i) Priority in improvisation was placed on creating surprise rather than on devising easily singable lines.

2) The originators of bop were alto saxophonist Charlie Parker, trumpeter Dizzy Gillespie, and pianist Thelonious Monk. Their favorite phrases became the stock vocabulary of bop.

3) Parker wrote numerous tunes based on popular song and twelve-bar blues chord progressions. His "Billie's Bounce," "Now's the Time," "Confirmation," and "Donna Lee" were standard repertory for generations of jazz musicians.

4) Gillespie led a string of big bands in addition to his combos.

5) Two pieces by Gillespie using original chord progressions became jazz standards: "Night in Tunisia" and "Con Alma."

6) Monk's very unusual and difficult chord progressions were displayed in many compositions, " 'Round Midnight" and "Well, You Needn't" becoming jazz standards.

7) The ideas of Tatum, Parker, and Gillespie appeared in the much-imitated piano style of Bud Powell who reduced the activity of the left hand in modern jazz.

8) The most distinctive bop tenor sax styles were those of Stan Getz and Dexter Gordon.

9) Getz blended Lester Young, bop, and classical music to create an original style.

10) Dexter Gordon extended the deep, dark-toned, swing era style and mixed it with bop approaches and his own unique gift for lyricism.

11) Pianists John Lewis and Tadd Dameron were important bop composers, and Lewis continued writing for the Modern Jazz Quartet long after the bop era.

12) The MJQ's vibraharpist Milt Jackson devised a warm, swinging style by way of
   a) a slow tremolo rate
   b) intelligently constructed bop lines
   c) relaxed delivery
   d) funky melodic figures

13) Bop drummers differed from swing drummers by
   a) increasing the frequency and spontaneity of kicks and prods
   b) feathering the bass drum instead of pounding it
   c) playing timekeeping rhythms on a suspended cymbal
   d) snapping the high-hat shut sharply on the second and fourth beats

chapter 10
COOL JAZZ

Rarely do jazz musicians classify their own music. Some players are even reluctant to call what they play "jazz." Labels for the different styles usually come from the people who listen to them rather than coming from the players who originate them. One of the least clearly defined styles is what many listeners have come to call "cool jazz." The term actually encompasses a group of diverse styles rather than just one approach. It has been applied to musicians influenced by Miles Davis, Count Basie, and Lester Young. It has been attached to the music of white musicians, black musicians, and musicians from the East Coast and the West Coast. It has been primarily applied to the work of a jazz musician whose playing is perceived as subdued and understated. Some historians consider cool jazz to be quite separate from bop. However, many of the players ordinarily dubbed "cool style" are bop musicians, and many cool style players tend to use bop melodic and harmonic style. Cool jazz has somewhat more emphasis on written arrangements and counterpoint, but solos often differ little from bop style. The next few sections introduce styles that have attracted the "cool jazz" label, but keep in mind that many of them have more in common with bop than with any post-bop developments in jazz.

A confusing aspect of "cool" is that the term described an attitude more than a style of music. A musician was said to be "cool" if his feelings were held firmly in check and he remained unruffled and unexcited while playing. It is confusing to use this term to distinguish a particular group of players because professional musicians of many periods had always prided themselves on being in control of their feelings. Most musicians performing symphony orchestra music, bop, or any of several post-bop styles remain quite businesslike throughout their performances, and they keep their feelings to themselves.

The ideas expressed in the preceding paragraph are not meant to oppose the belief that a player's feelings are evident in his music. People who hold this belief think that a loud or high-pitched note indicates rage, lust, or some other intense emotion. It is plausible that cool jazz earned its title by offering only a relatively small portion of loud or high notes. (Why not be the judge of that yourself? Have someone play you a variety of recordings without telling you what period of jazz they represent or what musicians are playing. Then, if you guess cool jazz for the same music that has been historically called cool jazz, your experience would support the argument.)

Two cool jazz groups have already been described: the George Shearing Quintet and the Modern Jazz Quartet. With respect to Shearing, it seemed best to describe his style at the same time as Bud Powell's and Oscar Peterson's. In the case of the Modern Jazz Quartet, it was more convenient to discuss Dizzy Gillespie's former sidemen at the time Gillespie was discussed. Both the Shearing Quintet and the Modern Jazz Quartet, however, are often classed with cool jazz rather than being included with the bop pioneers.

The first musicians to be discussed in this chapter, Lennie Tristano and Lee Konitz, were passionate players who do not fit the characterization of being "cool": detached and subdued in their work. Their music is quite intense. However, they are treated here because they had an impact on a group of Miles Davis recordings collectively known as The Birth of the Cool. Another reason for including them here is that some historians have called their sound cool.

After the Lennie Tristano school and the Miles Davis Birth of the Cool recordings, there is another category of cool jazz known as West Coast style. This label has been problematic because it contains several implications that contradict facts about the modern jazz scene of the 1950s. First is the implication that the West Coast style originated with California-born players, when, in fact, a substantial number of players who are ordinarily lumped with West Coast style were not California natives. Several significant "West Coast" figures were from the East Coast and played only briefly on the West Coast. Second is the implication that cool jazz is all that was played by California jazz musicians during the 1950s, when in fact, some excellent bop was being played by California musicians at the same time that many people were mistakenly assuming that the West Coast jazz scene was almost exclusively comprised of cool style players. Third, by focusing primarily on West Coast musicians during the 1950s, when discussing cool jazz, the public was overlooking Boston and New York musicians who were playing in a similar manner at the same time. In other words, the West Coast being so prominently associated with cool jazz during the 1950s allowed people to form the mistaken impression that bop was limited to the East Coast, and cool jazz was limited to the West Coast. This caused listeners, journalists, and record companies to neglect the excellent bop musicians playing in Los Angeles and the excellent cool style musicians who were playing in New York and Boston during the same period.

Lennie Tristano and Lee Konitz

Lennie Tristano (1919–1978) was a pianist, composer, and bandleader who created a modern jazz alternative to bop during the late 1940s. At that time, it was the strongest alternative available. Although rarely a performer since then, he impressed his students enough to inspire them to carry on his style.

Tristano was a pianist so skilled he could play impressive Art Tatum runs. (Tatum and tenor saxophonist Lester Young were both important influences for him.) Another technique he perfected was improvising in the locked-hands style of Milt Buckner, though his work was more varied and daring than Buckner's.

Tristano's long lines were less jumpy than Charlie Parker's and Dizzy Gillespie's, with smoother, more straight-line contours than bop improvisation. They often seemed not to stem directly from the chords, either. Tristano's lines often seemed a step or a half step away, creating an unresolved feeling. His lines were not melodic in the pop tune sense or in the bop sense.

Like bop, Tristano's music was harmonically complex, often employing several chord changes in a single measure. Yet the pet phrases of Charlie Parker and Dizzy Gillespie did not find their way into his improvisations. Tristano's playing seemed full of precisely calculated complexity. Bop had moments of calculated complexity also, yet seemed to generally flow naturally and warmly from Parker's and Gillespie's horns.

Tristano's most talented students during the late 1940s were alto saxophonist Lee Konitz, tenor saxophonist Warne Marsh, and guitarist Billy Bauer. Together with bass and drums, these musicians made recordings displaying technical feats which still dazzled other musicians decades later.

As in the subsequent West Coast style, bass and drums played a very conservative role in Tristano's music. In fact, on several recordings, they can hardly be heard. Timekeeping seemed to be their only function. But keeping time for the Tristano groups was no easy job: some tunes were played at furious tempos.

Alto saxophonist Konitz (b. 1927) played lines very similar to those Tristano used, and his instrumental technique was as impressive as Tristano's. Konitz's tone color was quite unlike the lush sound of his predecessors Benny Carter and Johnny Hodges, or the bittersweet style of his contemporary, Charlie Parker. Konitz played with a dry, light tone and slow vibrato reminiscent of Lester Young.

It is quite important to realize that Konitz was developing and maintaining his own Tristano-inspired, modern jazz alto style at a time when nearly every young alto saxophonist was imitating Charlie Parker, not only in tone, but in bop rhythmic and melodic conception. Konitz was almost totally unrelated to Parker. He was much more a product of Tristano's piano style. That piano style was, in turn, unlike most of bop piano. In fact, Tristano did not swing in the customary bop manner. He tended instead to be tight, very much on top of the beat rather than laid back of the beat, with less pronounced syncopation than Parker and Gillespie used. Tristano's playing lacked the rhythmic variety of bop; his improvisations were characterized by long strings of uninterrupted eighth notes. His style swung, but in a much tighter way than bop. (Listen to Tristano's "Crosscurrent" in SCCJ.)

Lee Konitz went on to influence many alto saxophonists during the 1950s. Although Konitz was based in New York, his influence was strongest in California. West Coast alto players Bud Shank and Lennie Niehaus absorbed portions of both Konitz and Parker to create their own styles. Art Pepper developed the strongest West Coast alto style by combining the influences of Konitz, tenor saxophonist Zoot Sims, and Charlie Parker.

During the middle 1950s, especially after 1954, Konitz initiated a gradual change in style which continued through the 1970s. It resembled a dilution of his previously full, meaty lines inspired by Tristano; Konitz apparently lost some of his speed and tone as well. Silences became more common in his playing, which was more varied rhythmically than it was with Tristano. His music was also a bit bluesy on occasion.

Some of Konitz's best work, apart from his playing with Tristano, can be found in the 1949–50 Miles Davis *Birth of the Cool*[1] recordings, the 1953 Lee Konitz–Gerry Mulligan–Chet Baker recording *Konitz Meets Mulligan*,[2] and his 1947 recordings with Claude Thornhill.[3]

In addition to adapting melodic concepts unusual in jazz playing, Tristano was also one of the first to record collective improvisation free of preset melody and preset chord progressions ("Intuition" and "Digression").[4] The music was not totally free of form (large portions of it approximated constant tempo and key feeling), but it was quite free compared to most jazz of the 1940s. (During the 1960s and 70s, Ornette Coleman, Cecil Taylor, and others commonly improvised without preset chord progressions.)

Lennie Tristano recorded very little in his career—the equivalent

---

[1] Miles Davis *The Complete Birth of the Cool* Capitol N 16168
[2] Gerry Mulligan and Lee Konitz *Revelation* Blue Note 532
[3] *The Memorable Claude Thornhill* Columbia KG 32906
[4] *Crosscurrents* Capitol M 11060

of approximately seven albums. Since his work does not sell at all well, his recordings are collectors' items. Tristano remained active as a teacher, and, in fact, teaching was his primary occupation from 1951 to his death in 1978.

Through Konitz, Tristano has influenced Bill Evans, a pianist who became very important during the 1960s. Although very much his own man by 1959, Evans displayed Tristano-like phrases in his work with George Russell and Tony Scott during the late 1950s. Tristano's piano style has directly influenced two strong jazz pianists, Sal Mosca and Ronnie Ball. (Mosca has appeared on several albums with Konitz and Marsh.) Tristano has additionally influenced pianists Wally Cirillo, Connie Crothers, trumpeters Don Ferrara and Cy Touff, and saxophonists John LaPorta, Teo Macero, and Ted Brown. Cecil Taylor, a leading avant-garde pianist of the 1960s and 70s, has said that, in the early 1950s, Tristano was a strong influence on him. (The Tristano approach has also had an impact on a number of European jazz musicians.)

Birth of the Cool

After leaving Charlie Parker's group, Miles Davis rarely appeared as a sideman. In 1949 and 1950, he recorded for Capitol record company with a nine-piece band of his own. That work has become known as *The Birth of the Cool*, and it was to have an important influence on jazz in the 1950s. Its sound stemmed partly from concepts pioneered during the 1940s by pianist-composer-arranger-bandleader Claude Thornhill (1909–1965) and arranger Gil Evans. But there were other ingredients as well. Lee Konitz's lines, inspired by Lennie Tristano, and his light, dry, almost vibratoless tone were fundamental to the *Birth of the Cool* sound. In addition to Konitz on alto sax and Davis on trumpet, the session included Gerry Mulligan, a baritone saxophonist who also had a light, dry tone and had played and arranged for Thornhill. A departure from convention was made in that neither tenor saxophone nor guitar was used, and the instrumentation was filled out by French horn, tuba, trombone, and rhythm section.

Miles Davis consolidated the influences of Thornhill, Evans, and Tristano in his high-quality *Birth of the Cool* sessions. Of all the late 1940s recordings made by groups employing these concepts, the Davis nonet recordings are remembered and cited the most. This was the first of many instances in which Davis was closely involved with major innovations in jazz. (Listen to "Boplicity" in SCCJ.)

The subdued feeling that Davis, Konitz, and Mulligan brought to their solos and the dry, mellow textures achieved by the nonet's unique instrumentation created a truly delicate, cool sound. The band was not loud, brassy, or massive sounding. The music was light, sophisticated and, at times, resembled classical chamber music. Recordings by Lennie Tristano-led groups of the same period also achieved that effect. The influence of Claude Thornhill, Gil Evans, and Lennie Tristano was strongly felt by young jazz arrangers during the late 1940s. It was the freshest sound in the air during that period.

The tunes played by the Davis nonet, however, were more within the bop idiom than within the Tristano idiom or the swing idiom. But emphasis on arrangements was not frequent in bop, and the nonet's arrangements gave bop tunes distinctive twists. Most bop groups assigned the melody to the horns, playing in unison before and after a series of long, improvised solos with the rhythm section, but the Davis nonet replaced that with a scheme which wove short, improvised solos into written arrangements much as Duke Ellington had done. Some arrangements also placed attractive melodic figures underneath some of the solos. Orchestral textures were occasionally altered within a single arrangement, also. The alterations were always made gracefully. Davis, Gil Evans, Gerry Mulligan, John Lewis, and Johnny Carisi wrote for the nonet. Mulligan wrote the largest number of arrangements: a total of five.

As early as 1946, pianist Dave Brubeck had recorded work similar to the *Birth of the Cool*. During the 1950s, baritone saxophonist Gerry Mulligan, French hornist-composer John Graas (also a veteran of the Thornhill band), composer-trumpeter Shorty Rogers and others composed for, arranged for, and led bands similar to the Miles Davis nonet. Davis himself abandoned the nonet approach not long after beginning it. Except for his late 1950s big band collaborations with Gil Evans, Davis subsequently remained with small groups and concentrated almost exclusively on improvisation instead of arranging.

WEST COAST STYLE OF THE 1950s

The Birth of the Cool was an important influence in the development of the so-called West Coast style, which seemed to dominate the playing of California musicians during the 1950s. (See Table 10.1.) It employed light-weight, light-colored tones which had soft, dry textures. Although incorporating the melodic and harmonic advances of bop, the West Coast style had a smoother, more tune-like sound than bop improvisation. The music often projected a relaxed feeling, in contrast to the intensity of bop. Drummers in this style played quietly and less interactively than bop drummers did. West Coast style was a restrained, understated approach that was labeled "cool" by many listeners.

Lester Young, Miles Davis, and Lee Konitz were important in influencing the West Coast style. West Coast trumpeters mixed larger portions of Davis in their styles and smaller portions of Gillespie. Tenor saxophonists seemed more inspired by Lester Young than by Dexter Gordon or Lucky Thompson. Alto saxophonists mixed large portions of Lee Konitz with the ideas of Charlie Parker. (Different

TABLE 10.1. A Few Of The Many West Coast Style Musicians Of The 1950s

Trumpet

Chet Baker
Conte Candoli
Jack Sheldon
Shorty Rogers
Stu Williamson

Trombone

Bob Brookmeyer
Frank Rosolino
Bob Enevoldsen
Milt Bernhart

Tenor Sax

Bill Perkins
Richie Kamuca
Bob Cooper
Jack Montrose
Buddy Collette
Dave Pell
Bill Holman
Jimmy Giuffre
Zoot Sims

Alto Sax

Art Pepper
Bud Shank
Herb Geller
Lennie Niehaus
Paul Desmond

Baritone Sax

Gerry Mulligan
Bob Gordon

Guitar

Howard Roberts
Barney Kessel

Piano

Hampton Hawes
Claude Williamson
Russ Freeman
Pete Jolly
Vince Guaraldi
Carl Perkins
Andre Previn
Dave Brubeck

Bass

Red Mitchell
Red Callender
Leroy Vinnegar
Buddy Clark
Carson Smith
Howard Rumsey
Curtis Counce
Joe Mondragon
Monty Budwig

Drums

Shelly Manne
Mel Lewis
Stan Levey
Larry Bunker
Chico Hamilton

Composer-Arrangers

Gerry Mulligan
Dave Brubeck
Shorty Rogers
Dave Pell
John Graas
Jimmy Giuffre
Bill Holman
Marty Paich
Dave Brubeck

TABLE 10.2. A Few of the Many West Coast Style Players Who Played With the Woody Herman and Stan Kenton Big Bands. (The two bands used many of the same musicians. Most were white. Most were good sight readers. Most played in similar styles.)

Kenton	Herman
Lee Konitz	Bill Perkins
Art Pepper	Richie Kamuca
Bud Shank	Shorty Rogers
Lennie Niehaus	Jimmy Giuffre
Bill Holman	Conte Candoli
Richie Kamuca	Stan Levey
Conte Candoli	Shelly Manne
Jack Sheldon	Red Mitchell
Mel Lewis	Stu Williamson
Stan Levy	
Shelly Manne	
Bob Cooper	
Frank Rosolino	
Stu Williamson	
Milt Bernhart	

proportions surfaced in the playing of each musician.) Arrangers adopted the approaches of Claude Thornhill and Gil Evans. Several bands were modeled after the 1949–50 Miles Davis nonet.

The style of jazz known as West Coast was played far more by white than by black musicians. A number of these musicians had been members of the predominantly white big bands of Woody Herman and Stan Kenton (see Table 10.2).

It is important to remember that West Coast was not the only style of jazz being played in California during the 1950s. Charlie Parker and Dizzy Gillespie both performed there, and tenor saxophonists Wardell Gray and Dexter Gordon spent more time there than Bird and Diz. Dixieland was also popular. Remember also that the sound was not exclusive to the West Coast. The light, dry, melodic playing characteristic of West Coast players could also be heard on the East Coast in the Basie-derived approaches of saxophonist Al Cohn, pianist Nat Pierce and others, as well as several Konitz-influenced players.

Gerry Mulligan (b. 1927) was the baritone saxophonist and the primary composer-arranger in the 1949–50 Miles Davis nonet sessions. (Mulligan contributes the first improvisation in the nonet performance of "Boplicity" that is found in SCCJ.) He also wrote for the Claude Thornhill and Stan Kenton big bands. Mulligan had a dry, light-weight, light-colored tone and an unhurried and subdued approach to improvisation. In 1952, Mulligan moved to California and began a series of piano-less quartets consisting of himself on baritone sax, another horn, bass, and drums. The piano-less quartets of Mulligan have a lighter, clearer, simpler sound texture than any quartets that use the piano.[5] Additionally, they allow greater appreciation for bass playing than is allowed by groups that also have piano in them. This is because when chord notes are shared by piano and bass, or the low pitch range of sounds is shared by piano and bass, piano sounds often overshadow the contributions of the bassist. (Note that, although much attention was gained by Mulligan's abandoning the piano, other groups in the late 1950s and early 1960s also omitted piano and created far more radical sounds. See pages 230–235 for coverage of Ornette Coleman and Albert Ayler.)

Mulligan's compositions are neither as complex as Lennie Tristano's nor as full of the twists and turns that typified bop writing. A few are quite song-like. They have the same soft, calm character that is projected by Mulligan's improvisations.

Mulligan's sidemen were similarly cool in their playing. Compared to East Coast contemporaries Art Blakey and Philly Joe Jones, Mulligan's drummers Chico Hamilton and Larry Bunker played conservatively. One of Mulligan's trumpeters, **Chet Baker,** also had a soft, mellow approach. Baker's cool, relaxed style is often considered a parallel to those of Bix Beiderbecke and early Miles Davis.

Mulligan considers his best recordings to include some 1953 material produced by a ten-piece band employing tuba and French horn, an instrumentation similar to that of the 1949–50 Miles Davis nonet. Mulligan's writing also played a significant role in his East Coast-based big band called The Concert Jazz Band, which employed simple, relaxed playing with a light, dry sound. It was one of the most unusual bands to appear during the late 1950s and early 1960s.

Valve trombonist **Bob Brookmeyer** (b. 1929) was a frequent member of Mulligan's piano-less quartets and The Concert Jazz Band. His melodic, often humorous lines and relaxed, laid-back style were quite compatible with Mulligan. Brookmeyer is one of the few modern players whose work strongly suggests early jazz and swing. He loves bending notes and altering tone color. Brookmeyer's arranging is clear and intelligent, sometimes reminiscent of Gil Evans (see pages 215–216). Brookmeyer and Mulligan were The Concert Jazz Band's primary soloists, although trumpeter Clark Terry, tenor saxophonist Zoot Sims, and others were sometimes featured. Brookmeyer later wrote for and played with another big band: the Thad Jones-Mel Lewis band of the 1960s and 70s. Then Brookmeyer wrote for the Mel Lewis big band of the 1980s.

[5] *Freeway* Liberty LT 1101

One of the most novel West Coast combos was led by former Mulligan quartet drummer **Chico Hamilton** (b. 1921). Like the Mulligan quartet, Hamilton's quintet had no piano. It consisted of guitar, cello, bass, drums, and a hornman who played saxophones, flute, and clarinet. With tightly arranged pieces and excellent musicianship, Hamilton's quintet created a jazz style which resembled classical chamber music. Its textures were light and pretty, and the arrangements displayed variety, too. Several melodies were sometimes played at the same time. That technique is called counterpoint, and it characterized early jazz improvisation. (Mulligan and his hornmen had also shown interest in reviving counterpoint as a jazz device.)

Hamilton's quintets were also notable for their leader's drumming. Chico Hamilton was one of the first modern drummers to get away from nearly always playing conventional ride rhythms as the undercurrent for a group sound. A remarkably original drummer, Hamilton is known for generating unusual and catchy patterns on his drums and maintaining them as consistent accompaniment figures for a given piece. And, instead of depending primarily on the ride cymbal and high-hat sound, Hamilton is just as likely to use a snare drum or tom-tom sound as the primary voice in his accompaniment pattern. Hamilton's style is a gentle approach to creating unusual rhythmic textures instead of simply defining the beat and kicking the soloists. Each piece features a separate rhythm pattern and percussion color. Hamilton's imagination is fertile, orchestral, and subtle.

The Hamilton quintet employed cellist Fred Katz, guitarist Jim Hall, bassist Carson Smith, and reedman Buddy Collette—all careful, understated improvisers who were attuned to the general feeling of West Coast style. Eventually Chico altered the character of his group and employed such outgoing improvisers as saxophonists Eric Dolphy[6] and Charles Lloyd,[7] and guitarist Larry Coryell.

California pianist-composer **Dave Brubeck** (b. 1920) led a series of small bands during the late 1940s which employed approaches similar to the 1949–50 Miles Davis nonet. From 1951 to 1967 Brubeck led a quartet with alto saxophonist **Paul Desmond** (1924–1977). This group was possibly the best-known modern jazz combo of the 1950s and 60s.

Desmond's light, dry tone resembled that of Lee Konitz, but Desmond's approach to improvisation was his own. He was extremely economical, very cool, and quite melodic. Desmond was one of the first jazz alto players to explore the instrument's extreme high register, the altissimo range. Some of Desmond's solos contained notes far higher than the normal high range of the alto saxophone. (Desmond

[6] *Gongs East* Discovery 831
[7] *Passin' Thru* MCA 29037

Dave Brubeck Quartet, one of the few jazz combos to achieve wide public apprecia-
tion without singing or including rock. *Left to right:* drummer Joe Morello, bassist Gene
Wright (hidden), pianist Brubeck, and alto saxophonist Paul Desmond. (*Courtesy of
Duncan Scheidt*)

also composed "Take Five," the Brubeck quartet's biggest hit.[8] This
piece was based on a very simple accompaniment rhythm which was
extensively repeated under a funky and engaging little theme. Departing from the jazz tradition of poor sales, the record sold more than
a million copies in 1961 and remained popular into the 1980s.)

Though he briefly studied composition with the world-renowned
symphonic composer Darius Milhaud, Brubeck is not, and never was,
a classical pianist. It remains a widely held misunderstanding that
Brubeck was trained in the classics. There are several reasons why
it is not hard to understand that listeners maintain this impression.
Brubeck is one of the few modern jazz pianists to clearly avoid standard bop melodic conception and rhythmic feeling. He is very inventive and depends almost exclusively on original melodic lines instead

[8] *Gone With the Wind/Time Out* Columbia CG 33666

of the repertory of Charlie Parker, Dizzy Gillespie, and Bud Powell phrases used by most of his contemporaries. And despite his lack of classical piano lessons, much of his invention has a distinctly classical flavor. In other words, Brubeck is a modern jazz musician who is not really a bop player.

Brubeck is a prolific composer, and the melodic quality of his tunes and improvisations is outstanding. Some of Brubeck's popular appeal must be due to the simple and tuneful quality of his compositions and improvisations. His lines are much easier to follow than bop lines. Brubeck's creations are orderly, and they project a freshness and clarity that makes the listener's job easy. In addition, most of Brubeck's pieces are pretty, and they convey a light and pleasant mood.

Brubeck's drummer for many years, **Joe Morello** (b. 1928), had considerable speed and precision and was quite successful mastering unusual meters. He became known to thousands of young musicians during the 1960s because of the Brubeck quartet's immense popularity, but it is ironic that he received more notice than other, more historically significant drummers such as Max Roach, Art Blakey, Philly Joe Jones, Tony Williams, and Elvin Jones. Like another very popular drummer, Buddy Rich, Morello had impressive facility, but was conservative as a rhythm section member. It is also ironic that Morello and Rich both gained great response for soloing, an aspect of modern jazz drumming which was secondary to the advances being made at that time in loosening traditional roles within rhythm section playing.

An interest of Brubeck's which brought him a large amount of publicity was the use of meters unusual to jazz, such as three, five, and seven. His albums *Time Out* and *Time Further Out,* which explored those meters, were very popular. His recording of Desmond's "Take Five," in a meter of five, was also issued as a single, an unusual occurrence for jazz of the late 1950s and early 60s. Brubeck was one of the most popular jazz musicians of the 50s, and "Take Five" carried his commercial success well into the 60s.

Jimmy Giuffre (b. 1921) is a saxophonist-clarinetist who composed the famous "Four Brothers" for the Woody Herman band and wrote much West Coast style music. Based on the West Coast from 1946 to 1960, he definitely qualifies for the cool jazz label because he produced a stream of original compositions and jazz improvisations which represent the essence of cool jazz. He produced a soft, diffuse sound on all the instruments he played. And, in keeping with cool style, his lines were understated and melodic. Giuffre also qualifies for the cool label because he ranks with Count Basie and Miles Davis in his mastery of silence and economical attitude in constructing solos. (An outstanding undertaking for Giuffre was a trio he led with trombonist Bob Brookmeyer and Jim Hall during 1958 and 1959. Their music was light and lyrical.[9] It featured close, three-way cooperation in the creation of gentle, contrapuntal improvisations. Despite the absence of bass and drums, the trio generated jazz swing feeling and group improvisations that were very cohesive and highly unique. Another standout among Giuffre's endeavors was a trio he led with pianist Paul Bley and bassist Steve Swallow from 1961 to 1963. It had the flavor of twentieth-century classical approaches, and it used improvisation that was often free of preset chord progressions.[10] Despite the conservatism associated with West Coast style musicians, the Giuffre-Bley-Swallow music was quite adventuresome.)

One more prominent figure associated with West Coast style is trumpeter-composer-arranger **Shorty Rogers** (b. 1924), who wrote for Woody Herman. He led jazz quintets and produced music (with his Giants) which was similar to that of the 1949–50 Miles Davis nine-piece and the 1953 Mulligan ten-piece bands.[11] (A little-known sidelight to Rogers's well-known arranging contributions is that some of the most adventurous products of West Coast players are recordings made by Rogers, Jimmy Giuffre, and vibraharpist Teddy Charles, apparently the first after Lennie Tristano's "Intuition" and "Digression" to display improvisation which had no prearranged chord progressions. Their 1954 work[12] predated the Ornette Coleman recordings of 1958 and 1959 which launched an entire style centered around the "free jazz" concept. Rogers also recorded pieces in which improvisation was based on modes[13] instead of frequent chord changes. These predated the 1958 Miles Davis "Milestones," which launched the popular mode-based improvisatory styles of the 1960s and 70s. The connection with Davis is especially intriguing because Rogers derived his trumpet style primarily from the late 1940s approach of Miles Davis, and, like Davis, he used the fluegelhorn long before it became common among trumpeters.)

[9] *Western Suite* Atlantic 1330
[10] *Free Fall* Columbia CL 1964 and CS 8764
[11] *Shorty Rogers and His Giants* RCA 1195
[12] Shelly Manne *"The Three" and "The Two"* Contemporary M 3584
[13] Teddy Charles/Shorty Rogers *Collaboration: West* Prestige 7028

CHAPTER SUMMARY

1) Although the "cool" label is probably the least descriptive of all the terms imposed on jazz styles by nonmusicians, it does denote a particular group of styles and is widely used.

2) Cool jazz usually contains

a) subdued playing

b) light-weight, dry, or pastel tone colors

c) a slow vibrato or no vibrato at all

d) softer, less wide-ranging sounds than bop used

3) Sources for the cool style include

a) the 1930s band of Count Basie and tenor saxophonist Lester Young

b) bandleader-composer-pianist Claude Thornhill

c) trumpeter Miles Davis and his nine-piece band of 1949

d) pianist Lennie Tristano and alto saxophonist Lee Konitz

4) Two groups associated with cool jazz that actually have closer ties with bop are The Modern Jazz Quartet and The George Shearing Quintet.

5) West Coast style is one subcategory of cool, and the term usually identifies the white modern jazz musicians who played in California during a portion of the 1950s.

6) Among the better-known West Coast groups were

a) baritone saxophonist Gerry Mulligan's piano-less quartet

b) pianist Dave Brubeck's quartet with alto saxophonist Paul Desmond

c) The Giants, led by trumpeter Shorty Rogers

d) drummer Chico Hamilton's quintet

7) Many players classed in West Coast style were veterans of the Balboa Beach-based Stan Kenton big band and the Lester Young-influenced Woody Herman bands.

8) West Coast groups placed more emphasis on written arrangements than did bop groups, and they were more interested in counterpoint, in improvised as well as written form.

chapter 11
HARD BOP

The 1950s was dominated by two jazz styles: West Coast and hard bop (also called bop or bebop). Hard bop began somewhat later than West Coast style and lasted proportionately longer (see Table 11.1 for a list of hard bop musicians). It differed from West Coast style in several respects:

1) West Coast style was characterized by light-colored, light-weight, soft-textured tone colors; hard bop employed dark-colored, heavy-weight, raw-textured tone colors.

2) In contrast to the light, cool, melodically simple improvisation of West Coast style, hard bop employed hard-driving, fiery, melodically complex improvisation.

3) The West Coast style evolved from the tone and mood of Lester Young, Count Basie, Lennie Tristano, Lee Konitz, and the Miles Davis *Birth of the Cool* sessions; hard bop evolved directly from bop. (See Table 11.2.)

4) In contrast to the polite, chamber music feeling projected by much of West Coast style, *some* hard bop projected a funky, earthy feeling with elements similar to black gospel music.

Hard bop players can be distinguished from West Coast-style players by the models they chose. The leading West Coast alto saxophonists were Art Pepper, Bud Shank, and Paul Desmond. All showed some similarity to the sound of Lee Konitz. Pepper was the most respected of altoists, and he combined Konitz traits with traits of a Lester Young disciple named Zoot Sims. (Sims had devised what was

TABLE 11.1. Hard Bop Style Musicians—A Partial Listing

Trumpet	Trombone	Drums
Clifford Brown	J. J. Johnson	Philly Joe Jones
Kenny Dorham	Curtis Fuller	Roy Brooks
Miles Davis	Jimmy Knepper	Louis Hayes
Blue Mitchell	Jimmy Cleveland	Art Taylor
Donald Byrd	Frank Rehak	Roy Haynes
Thad Jones	Tom McIntosh	Roger Humphries
Art Farmer		Elvin Jones
Bill Hardman	**Piano**	Lex Humphries
Joe Gordon		Max Roach
Carmell Jones	Tommy Flanagan	Art Blakey
Lee Morgan	Barry Harris	Mickey Roker
Freddie Hubbard	Cedar Walton	Al Heath
Wilbur Harden	Duke Pearson	Ben Riley
Tommy Turrentine	Bobby Timmons	Jimmy Cobb
Benny Bailey	Red Garland	Frankie Dunlop
Booker Little	Wynton Kelly	
Nat Adderley	Joe Zawinul	**Composer-Arrangers**
	Junior Mance	
Baritone Sax	Kenny Drew	Horace Silver
	Horace Parlan	Benny Golson
Pepper Adams	Les McCann	Gigi Gryce
Cecil Payne	Gene Harris	Oliver Nelson
Nick Brignola	Ramsey Lewis	Cannonball Adderley
	Horace Silver	Nat Adderley
Tenor Sax		Wayne Shorter
	Alto Sax	Bobby Timmons
Sonny Rollins		J. J. Johnson
John Coltrane	Cannonball Adderley	Jackie McLean
Jimmy Heath	Jackie McLean	Tom McIntosh
Frank Foster	Lou Donaldson	
Clifford Jordan	Gigi Gryce	**Organ**
Teddy Edwards	Frank Strozier	
Benny Golson	Phil Woods	Jimmy Smith
Billy Mitchell		Jack McDuff
George Coleman	**Bass**	Richard "Groove"
John Gilmore		Holmes
Oliver Nelson	Paul Chambers	Don Patterson
Stanley Turrentine	Sam Jones	Jimmy McGriff
Junior Cook	Doug Watkins	Shirley Scott
Booker Ervin	Wilbur Ware	
Joe Henderson	Bob Cranshaw	**Guitar**
Wayne Shorter	Gene Taylor	
Hank Mobley	Reggie Workman	Wes Montgomery
Harold Land	Percy Heath	Kenny Burrell
J. R. Monterose	Jymie Merritt	Grant Green
Tina Brooks	Butch Warren	
Yusef Lateef		

TABLE 11.2. Comparing Styles of the 1950s

	West Coast	Hard Bop
tone color	light	dark
tone weight	light	heavy
tone texture	soft	raw
melodic conception	simple	complex
overall character	relaxed	hard-driving
	cool	fiery
principal influences	swing and bop	bop
sources for alto saxophone styles	Lee Konitz	Charlie Parker
sources for trumpet styles	Miles Davis	Dizzy Gillespie
		Fats Navarro
		Miles Davis
sources for tenor saxophone styles	Lester Young	Dexter Gordon
		Sonny Stitt
		Don Byas
sources for arranging practices	Claude Thornhill	Tadd Dameron
	Gil Evans	

probably the funkiest of all variants on Lester Young's style, and he preferred short phrases and fragmented lines.) Hard bop altoists, on the other hand, usually chose Charlie Parker as their model. However, despite the Konitz versus Parker split that usually helps distinguish West Coast from hard bop altoists, many West Coast players were also touched by the Parker style.

Hard bop tenor saxophonists drew their inspiration from Charlie Parker, Don Byas, Dexter Gordon, and Sonny Stitt. West Coast tenor saxophonists tended to be more interested in Lester Young, though they were not untouched by Parker. Hard bop trumpeters were influenced largely by Fats Navarro's disciple Clifford Brown and by Miles Davis. They were also affected by Dizzy Gillespie, but not so much as by Brown and Navarro. West Coast trumpeters were also affected by the playing of these giants. However, they preferred Miles Davis over the others.

Hard bop evolved smoothly from bop. Trombonist J. J. Johnson, trumpeter Kenny Dorham, tenor saxophonist Sonny Rollins, and drummer Max Roach were among the musicians who earned reputations in bop and maintained them in hard bop, adding to their styles and changing various aspects. One of the prominent features of hard bop styles was the use of funky, earthy phrases and harmonies derived from gospel music. Not all hard bop players used these devices, but a sizable portion did.

Though played all over America, hard bop gathered its strongest proponents from Detroit and Philadelphia, instead of Los Angeles and San Francisco, and although hard bop was played by both black and white musicians, there was as much a black dominance in hard bop as white dominance in the West Coast style. (See Table 11.3.)

Standard format for hard bop performances required trumpet and tenor saxophone to state the theme in unison, and sometimes in harmony. Execution of these themes usually projected a hard-driving and insistent character, hence the name "hard bop." Pauses in the melody were often filled by rhythm section routines which were worked out in advance. Hard bop performances were usually more tightly organized than those of many bop groups, though by comparison with West Coast style, hard bop tended toward less elaborate arrangements.

A sizable portion of the average hard bop group's repertory was usually composed by band members. Sometimes the pieces contained tricky chord progressions, as in Clifford Brown's "Joy Spring." Most tunes derived their character from bop melodic conception, but they had somewhat less stop-start quality than had typified Charlie Parker's and Dizzy Gillespie's tunes. Jazz historian Harvey Pekar has observed

TABLE 11.3. Two Cities Contributed Many Leading Hard Bop Players

Philadelphia	Detroit
Clifford Brown	Thad Jones
Lee Morgan	Elvin Jones
McCoy Tyner	Hank Jones
Philly Joe Jones	Barry Harris
Jimmy Heath	Charles McPherson
Percy Heath	Roland Hanna
John Coltrane	Tommy Flanagan
Bobby Timmons	Paul Chambers
Benny Golson	Ron Carter
	Louis Hayes
	Yusef Lateef
	Kenny Burrell
	Donald Byrd
	Billy Mitchell
	Doug Watkins
	Pepper Adams
	Curtis Fuller

that the form for many of the pieces departed from bop's reliance on twelve-measure blues and thirty-two measure A-A-B-A constructions. For example, Gigi Gryce's "Minority" and several Sonny Rollins pieces are sixteen measures long: "Valse Hot," "Pent-Up House," and "Doxy." Benny Golson's "Stablemates" has a form of two fourteen-measure sections separated by an eight-measure section. Horace Silver's "Nica's Dream" is an A-A-B-B-A construction in which A is sixteen measures, and B is eight. In other words, variation in construction and chord progressions marked a departure from the bop practice of borrowing chord progressions from popular songs. With less standard compositional form, the hard bop improviser was less prone to rely on bop formulas in constructing his solos. This led to greater variety, which, in turn, ultimately led to new forms of jazz in the 1960s, forms that depended little upon bop conception.

A principal musician in hard bop of the 1950s and 60s was pianist, composer, and bandleader **Horace Silver** (b. 1928). After playing with the bands of Stan Getz and Art Blakey, Silver began leading a series of quintets with trumpet, tenor saxophone, bass, and drums. His impact was felt both through his compositions and his piano style. A major characteristic was the use of funky melodic figures and gospel-influenced harmonies. (As a young player, Silver had learned, note-for-note, the Avery Parrish piano solo on the 1940 Erskine Hawkins recording of "After Hours." This then became a source for funky piano solos adapted to modern jazz.) The earthy, gospel quality that Silver incorporated into his style became a model for pianists and hornmen alike. Pianists Gene Harris (of the Three Sounds), Ramsey Lewis, Les McCann, organists Jimmy Smith, Richard "Groove" Holmes, Jack McDuff, and others based their styles on the funk devices which Silver popularized, and even pianists of the 1950s whose styles had not originally been funky absorbed his influence. During the 1960s, such major stylists as Bill Evans, Herbie Hancock, McCoy Tyner, and Chick Corea occasionally used Silver's funky figures. (Corea has cited Silver as an influence on his composing as well as his piano playing.) In addition, hundreds of small-time pianists and organists who played in taverns and hotel cocktail lounges incorporated Silver's bluesy devices. Big band arrangers also added them to their repertory.

In addition to his impact on the funky brand of hard bop, Horace Silver perfected a unique piano style by replacing bop's preference for long, complicated phrases with his own simple, tuneful phrases. He made considerable use of silence as well as an exacting deliberation in the timing for the starting and stopping points of his phrases. His improvised melodic figures are rhythmically compelling, and they unfold with logic that is obvious even to the novice listener. His solos are like his tunes: filled with simple, catchy ideas that are easy to remember. It is as though, while improvising, Silver keeps on composing at the same level of creativity and clarity that he maintains in his writing. (Silver's composition "Nica's Dream" can be heard played by the Art Blakey group in *Nica's Dream*—volume 242 of the New World collection that has been donated to libraries and colleges by the Rockefeller Foundation.)

The Horace Silver tunes that are most frequently played outside of Silver's groups have a bluesy flavor: "Doodlin'," "Sister Sadie," "The Preacher," "Filthy McNasty," and "Song for My Father." It should be noted, however, that only a portion of Silver's output was funky. He was possibly the most prolific composer in hard bop, having penned most of the tunes for over twenty-five years of albums on the Blue Note record label,[1] and the immense library he composed cannot be accurately described by a single characteristic.

Horace Silver had used Bud Powell as a source for his piano style, but like John Lewis's playing in the Modern Jazz Quartet, Silver's piano accompaniment figures sounded like prewritten set-ups for his soloists instead of spontaneous chording that flexibly followed the shifting directions taken by the solo improvisations. In this way, then, the soloists in Silver's quintets were supported by backgrounds similar to those in big bands where written arrangements supply the same accompaniment figures each time the soloist improvises. This resulted in music having more continuity than the music produced by the less formally organized procedures used in most modern jazz groups. The Silver accompaniment figures may have given listeners something to cling to, and, despite the fact that these same figures decreased the range of moods an improvising soloist could create in the band, this aspect of the Silver sound might account for Silver's achieving somewhat greater popularity than most hard bop bandleaders.

Horace Silver quintet arrangements were generally more elaborate than those of other bop-influenced groups. The arrangements often contained ensemble strains in the middle of a piece as well as combinations of Latin American rhythms and gospel music. Silver often voiced trumpet and tenor saxophone in intervals of a fourth or fifth apart, an especially successful way to achieve fullness and make the quintet sound as though it contained more than five musicians. In addition to this compositional technique, Silver often wrote bass figures and used his left hand on the piano to play them in unison with his bassist. These figures had an engaging quality that, when reinforced by Silver's playing, offered an expanded resource to the usually limited scope of bop bass lines. These figures fit into an overall design that integrated Silver's repetitive chording with the rhythms of his drummers. It is partly for these reasons that his quintet's identity was unlike that of any other bop or hard bop group's. Performances by

---

[1] *Best of Horace Silver* Applause 2321

TABLE 11.4. A Partial Listing of Former Horace Silver Sidemen

Blue Mitchell	Junior Cook
Art Farmer	Joe Henderson
Tom Harrell	Michael Brecker
Woody Shaw	Roy Brooks
Randy Brecker	Louis Hayes
Hank Mobley	Al Foster
Bob Berg	Billy Cobham

Silver's quintets were consistently swinging and polished, and they featured many of the most outstanding musicians of the 1950s and 60s (see Table 11.4). His best-known and longest-lived quintet lasted from 1958 to 1964 with trumpeter Blue Mitchell and tenor saxophonist Junior Cook.

Trumpet The historical order of major influences on modern jazz trumpeters begins with Dizzy Gillespie and then moves to Miles Davis and Fats Navarro, with Clifford Brown arriving a little later. The 1940s belonged to Gillespie, with Davis exerting an impact in the last few years of the decade. Brown and Davis together were the primary sources for most trumpeters developing during the 1950s, though Brown probably influenced as many as or more trumpet players than Davis did. Then came Freddie Hubbard during the 1960s. By the late 1970s, the majority of developing trumpeters were choosing Hubbard as a model. (In fact, three of the most successful players in the 1970s—Woody Shaw, Randy Brecker, and Tom Browne—were all influenced by Hubbard, and during the 1980s, Wynton Marsalis carried on this tradition, combining Miles Davis methods with Hubbard methods.)

Clifford Brown (1930–1956) molded a style from the combined influences of Fats Navarro and Miles Davis. Clifford Brown's tone was warm and supple with a wider, more deliberate vibrato than Gillespie or Davis used. Brown's use of a slow, even vibrato may be responsible for its renewed use by jazz trumpeters. Brown had superior speed and stamina. Jazz historian Harvey Pekar has observed that Clifford Brown's solos are similar to those of Miles Davis in that they jump into the high register less often than Dizzy Gillespie's and Fats Navarro's, and that the contours of Brown's and Davis's lines are usually smoother than Gillespie's and Navarro's.

Brown manages to suggest relaxation in his playing even when executing intricate melodic figures. This is partly because of the perfection he achieved in making the trumpet obey his wishes and partly because his style was concerned with simplifying bop instead of blazing new trails in the way that Parker and Gillespie had done. Brown placed more emphasis on swinging than on bop's practice of trying to cleverly throw off the listener with surprise after surprise. Tuneful improvisations were more common in Brown's recordings than were those that clashed and jarred. (Listen to "Pent-Up House" in SCCJ, and see pages 412–414 for information on how to get David Baker's and Milton Stewart's book-long analyses of Clifford Brown's playing.)

Though his earliest playing drew from Clifford Brown, Miles Davis, and Chet Baker, **Freddie Hubbard** (b. 1938) had developed a relatively original approach by the early 1960s. Like Brown, his sense of time is very precise. Hubbard sticks close to the beat and likes to double-time as Brown did. Although he has incorporated some Miles Davis methods of tonal manipulation, he steers clear of the ways in which Davis gets away from the beat (technically termed "rubato playing"). Hubbard's solos during his creative peak of the mid-1960s were stocked with phrases of his own invention as well as reworkings of saxophonist John Coltrane's ideas. His playing on albums made at that time with Herbie Hancock[2] and Eric Dolphy is especially rich with invention.

Freddie Hubbard is almost universally envied among trumpeters for his frequent use of a very demanding musical device called a lip trill (in which, without changing fingering or shaking the trumpet, Hubbard rapidly alternates, in legato fashion, intervals of a minor third, moving the bottom note in stepwise fashion). This trademark, together with his squealing into the high register, is part of what makes Hubbard's style so extroverted that it bristles with excitement. At times, his playing suggests the good-natured sparring of a prize-fighter.

Tenor Saxophone Hard bop produced a large number of excellent tenor saxophonists. Tenor sax was a key instrument in the hard bop style, as trumpet had been in early jazz, and drums were to become during the 1970s. Though there were at least twenty important tenor saxophonists, there is little dispute that Sonny Rollins and John Coltrane were the two most outstanding performers. (See page 282 for a detailed comparison of Sonny Rollins and John Coltrane.)

Sonny Rollins (b. 1930) would undoubtedly have been an exceptional jazz musician no matter what instrument he had chosen. Many of his virtues are not exclusive to tenor saxophone playing. The Rollins solos have a well-reasoned quality. His clarity of mind, even at furious tempos, enables him to transcend the cliché figures and technically accessible melodic patterns most saxophonists must employ when high speeds press their skills.

[2] Herbie Hancock *Maiden Voyage* Blue Note BLP 84195

Rollins was one of the ultimate masters of jazz improvisation. He had exquisite command of the tenor saxophone, and his solos easily incorporated every chord, even in the fastest progressions. And, what is most important, he transcended the chord progressions and spontaneously set new melodies to them. The improvisations of Rollins abounded in melodies and were possibly as inventive as those of any saxophonist to appear since Charlie Parker.

Sonny Rollins was within the first group of musicians to play the Charlie Parker style on tenor saxophone. Dramatic support for this contention can be gained by simply listening to Parker play tenor instead of his alto saxophone (the 1947 Savoy recording of "Half Nelson"). Then listen to any records that Rollins made with Bud Powell in 1949 or with Miles Davis in 1951.[3] Back to back, the sounds are so similar that you might even confuse the two tenor saxophonists. Rollins went on to devise his own musical identity, but the point here is that his Parker roots should not be overlooked.

In addition to recordings with Miles Davis and others, Rollins made several outstanding records as a member of the Clifford Brown–Max Roach quintet. The Brown–Rollins "Kiss and Run," "Pent-Up House," and "Valse Hot" recordings were among the best trumpet–tenor sessions to come out of the 1950s. Both Brown and Rollins played with wonderful ease and great imagination. (Listen to "Pent-Up House" in SCCJ.)

Rollins mastered the rhythmic devices necessary to swing, and he swung when he wished, but he played against or apart from the tempo at other times. He could go in and out of tempo with amazing skill. He seems to have gotten inside the beat one moment and ignored it the next. But he always treated a piece as though it, its tempo, chord changes, and melody were to be toyed with, quickly and effortlessly redesigned from moment to moment. (Listen to his "Blue Seven" in SCCJ.)

Rollins differed from the majority of bop tenormen in that he often used staccato phrasing instead of an exclusively legato style. He could manage a blunt, brittle attack, move to legato and back again to staccato. His vibrato was slow and very deliberate. The Rollins tone is rough but not as deep or richly textured as Coltrane's. It is brittle and quite unique among tenor saxophonists.

Rollins could deliver bursts of rich, swinging phrases or short spurts within long pauses. His use of silence was an important aspect of his skill in pacing. Rollins used silence to set off short phrases, some of which were repeated in varied form. Sometimes he repeated a single note, attacking it with different rhythms and tone colors. Like West Coast baritone saxophonist Gerry Mulligan, Rollins played so

[3] Miles Davis *Dig* Prestige 24054

clearly that it was as though you could hear him thinking. There was a logical development within each solo. It was especially obvious when he played a figure and then, using the same rhythm but different notes, played it again. He also repeated figures using the same notes but varying the rhythm in their repetition. Rollins began recording actively in 1949 and had considerable impact on tenor saxophonists of the 1950s. His influence is difficult to pinpoint in the playing of others, however, because some of his virtues were also possessed by Charlie Parker, whose influence was also strong at that time. The Rollins name often appears next to those of Charlie Parker, Sonny Stitt, and John Coltrane in lists of saxophonists favored by saxophonists themselves. For example, such prominent saxophonists of the 1970s as Pat La Barbera, John Klemmer, and Billy Harper have all cited Rollins as a favorite.

Rollins's compositions, like those of Monk, are deceptively simple. Their architecture embodies odd placement of accents and many other surprises. Yet, his unusual compositions sound so logical that the most remarkable features of their construction may not immediately be obvious. "Valse Hot" is an example of Rollins's cleverness in this regard. The piece is syncopated in the most basic sense of the term: accents fall on beats or portions of beats expected to be weak. The phrases in "Valse Hot" start and stop in unusual places.[4]

Several Rollins tunes have become jazz standards: "Airegin" (Nigeria spelled backwards), which has an unusual construction; "Doxy," a sixteen-bar A-A-B-A tune with a common chord progression; and "Oleo," a very syncopated line with no melody in its bridge, based on the chord progression of "I Got Rhythm."

During the 1970s and 80s, Rollins ordinarily played in a way that differed significantly from his style of the 1950s and 60s. He used a tone that was broader, more coarse and guttural than his tones of the 1950s and 60s. He also lost the speed and agility that had characterized his 1950s playing. The razor sharp precision of his command over the saxophone was gone. His lines recalled those of saxophonists associated with the popular style known as rhythm and blues. His playing was simpler and funkier. The Rollins allegiance to lyricism was retained from his past, but his roots in Charlie Parker were often only barely detectable. The tunes he performed were simpler, too. The accompaniments he employed resembled those common to popular dance music styles known as disco, funk, and Latin. Occasionally Rollins returned to more bop-like playing, as when working with the Milestone All-Stars, but his preferred approach during this period usually remained so simple and funky that his playing fit perfectly with the Rolling Stones, a blues-

[4] *Saxophone Colossus and More* Prestige 24050

oriented popular group that used him in some of their music. In summary, we find that, twenty years after being the top hard bop tenor man, Sonny Rollins had mastered a new style and gained a fresh audience. (See page 412 for information on how to get David Baker's book-long analysis of the Sonny Rollins style.)

A man whose playing is sometimes reminiscent of Rollins, sometimes suggests Coltrane, but usually exemplifies his own personal style, is **Joe Henderson.**[5] Along with Wayne Shorter (see Chapter 18), Henderson (b. 1937) is probably the most original tenor saxophonist produced by hard bop after Rollins and Coltrane. He has a hard, shiny tone with a razor-sharp edge. The biting effect of his playing is enhanced by his ability to subdivide each beat very precisely. This, combined with a high level instrumental proficiency, enables him to play extremely quick figures with uncanny accuracy. The sharpness of his attacks and releases also contributes to the biting effect.

Like Rollins, Henderson can play intense, provocative lines. Some contain syncopated staccato figures alternating with churning legato lines. Henderson can swing conventionally, playing perfectly within tempo, or he can play against the tempo, over the beat, as though free of it. He alternates swing eighth-note figures with straight eighth notes, sometimes interjecting bursts of sixteenth notes. Dramatic use of shakes and trills is also characteristic of Henderson and is consistent with his love of variety. Sometimes he employs shrieks which sound like animal cries. He varies the speed of his vibrato, also.

Henderson began his career in the mainstream of hard bop, but blended well with newer styles introduced during the 1960s by Ornette Coleman, Albert Ayler, and John Coltrane (see Chapters 13 and 17). He has led an assortment of groups, appeared on numerous albums with other leaders, and written tunes which are quite distinctive. His influence could be heard during the 1970s in both the style of tunes being written and in the playing of young tenor saxophonists who had chosen not to base their approaches entirely on Coltrane's. (See page 412 for information on how to get Don Sickler's transcriptions of Joe Henderson solos.)

Alto Saxophone

Cannonball Adderley (1928–1975) was one of the best improvisers to play alto saxophone after Charlie Parker died. In fact, Adderley's style was partly derived from Parker's. Though he led several good hard bop combos, some of the most popular of that era, Cannonball's most outstanding recorded solos were made as a member of the Miles Davis group. When Adderley was playing with Davis, tenor saxo-

[5] *Power to the People* Milestone 9024

phonist John Coltrane was also in the group.[6] The fact that Adderley could keep up with Coltrane and sometimes surpass him is a measure of Adderley's improvisational prowess.

Cannonball had an inventive mind combined with the high-level instrumental proficiency of Parker and Coltrane. His tone was so deep and full that it sometimes sounded like a tenor sax. He had an earthy, legato style and amazing energy. Adderley's style displayed the influence of Parker (as early as 1955), some Coltrane devices (after 1958), and his own unique, bouncing rhythmic conception. A trait which served to distinguish him from Coltrane and Lee Konitz, and to a certain extent from Parker, too, was his use of funky melodic figures. Cannonball bent his huge, flowing tone with blue notes and wails. Bits of pop tunes crept into his lines. Humor was also part of his outgoing style. (See page 412 for information on how to get David Baker's book-long analysis of Adderley's style.)

Jackie McLean (b. 1932) was another highly respected alto saxophonist. Originally a Parker protégé, McLean developed his own style and eventually incorporated elements of new styles which became prominent during the 1960s. He had a dry, biting tone and very insistent delivery. His style was unusually intense. Also a solid hard bop composer, McLean wrote numerous tunes for his own albums, some of which were also recorded by other leaders. Miles Davis recorded McLean's "Donna" (also known as "Dig"), "Little Melonae," "Minor March," and "Dr. Jackle" (also known as "Dr. Jekyll").

Drums Drummer **Art Blakey** (b. 1919) paved the way for conceptions of jazz drumming which called for active interaction with soloists. Blakey's drumming was often as much in the forefront of his combo sound as were trumpet and sax. His rhythm section playing was so vital and dynamic that for him to solo was almost anticlimactic. His 1954 work[7] with trumpeter Clifford Brown and pianist Horace Silver shows him engaged in volatile rhythm section drumming years before such activity was common practice. He also is significant for leading a series of hard-driving quintets and sextets containing a stream of outstanding hard bop players. (See Table 11.5.) (One of Blakey's great bands can be heard in *Nica's Dream* New World 242.)

Max Roach is one of the giants of jazz drumming, and his intelligently developed solos are often melodic. He is also routinely cited for his clean touch and discreet accompanying. Unlike many drummers, Roach does not flaunt his proficiency; his technique never overshadows his musical sense. By the time he joined Clifford Brown, he had already made many of his historically significant advances (evident in recordings from the 1940s with Charlie Parker, such as the 1945 "Ko-

[6] Miles Davis *Milestones* Columbia PC 9428
[7] *Night at Birdland* Blue Note 81521

TABLE 11.5. A Partial Listing of Former Art Blakey Sidemen

Clifford Brown	Junior Mance
Donald Byrd	Keith Jarrett
Bill Hardman	Curtis Fuller
Lee Morgan	Wynton Marsalis
Freddie Hubbard	Bobby Timmons
Woody Shaw	George Cables
Jackie McLean	Reggie Workman
Hank Mobley	Jymie Merritt
Wayne Shorter	Lou Donaldson
Benny Golson	Dave Schnitter
Johnny Griffin	Bobby Watson
Chuck Mangione	James Williams
Horace Silver	Valerie Ponomarev
Cedar Walton	Ira Sullivan

Ko" in SCCJ). For more on bop drumming, see pages 161–162; for notations of drumming, see page 430.

Max Roach co-led a quintet with Clifford Brown from 1954 to 1956.[8] The two saxophonists most prominently featured in the group were Sonny Rollins and Harold Land. Land played in a manner that exemplifies what jazz musicians term "straight ahead": his improvisations place high priority on swinging and incorporating each new chord as it comes along, stressing continuity and flow over uniqueness. It is as though Land is snaking through the rhythm section sound, hardly ever pausing from his determination to generate long phrases in evenly paced lines.

The Brown–Roach quintet was among the most widely respected units in modern jazz. Many listeners ranked it higher than the Miles Davis groups, the Horace Silver groups, or the Art Blakey groups of the same period. Its recordings remain a definitive product that epitomizes hard bop for many listeners. (Listen to "Pent-Up House" in SCCJ.) As recently as the 1970s and 80s, young musicians were emulating this combo. Some of the tunes which the quintet recorded remained favorites among musicians of the 1980s: "Jordu," "Joy Spring," and "Daahoud."

Trombone   There were nowhere near as many trombonists in hard bop as there were saxophonists and trumpeters. And the leading trombonist in hard bop, J. J. Johnson, did not appear first during this era, he had already been established in the bop era. The next best-known hard bop trombonist, **Curtis Fuller** (b. 1934), did emerge first during the hard bop

[8] Clifford Brown *Jordu* Emarcy EXPR 1033

era. Though there were other trombonists, Johnson and Fuller were about the only ones to receive much recognition, and because Fuller rarely recorded under his own name, his reputation derives most from his playing as a sideman. Johnson, on the other hand, made numerous records and tours as a bandleader and attained proportionally more recognition. (See pages 166–167 for more about Johnson.)

At times, Curtis Fuller sounds a lot like J. J. Johnson, but careful listening will reveal considerable difference between the two styles. (See Table 11.6.) Fuller uses a softer, more diffuse tone quality, and he prefers lines which are constructed more subtly. He is melodically more adventurous than Johnson and is neither as tuneful nor as economical as Johnson. He plays as fast or faster than Johnson, but his attacks and releases (the ways he begins and ends his notes) are not as clipped as Johnson's. Some of Fuller's best work is available on records made with Art Blakey, the Art Farmer–Benny Golson Jazztet,[9] and a variety of bandleaders who recorded for Blue Note record company during the 1950s and 60s.

Bass   Hard bop produced a number of very solid bassists, some of whom were remarkably melodic soloists. **Paul Chambers** (1935–1969) was the first choice for many hard bop record dates. His large, dark sound and horn-like bop solos, both pizzicato and arco, impressed many leaders. Chambers expanded the solo potential of jazz bass with his instrumental proficiency and unique bop horn approach to bass solos. Though active for approximately eight years in Miles Davis's groups, Chambers also appeared on numerous records with other leaders.

Sam Jones (1924–1981) was another skillful hard bop bassist. Together with drummer Louis Hayes, he gave the Cannonball Adderley Quintet a buoyant yet driving foundation. Like Paul Chambers, Jones

TABLE 11.6. Comparing J. J. Johnson with Curtis Fuller

	Johnson	Fuller
tone quality	full	airy
	fat	diffuse
	dark	light
methods of starting notes	clipped	relaxed
harmonic thinking	simple	complex
tunefulness of improvisations	high	low
rhythmic conception	percussive	legato
	obvious	subtle
quantity of notes per solo	moderate	large

[9] Art Farmer *Meet the Jazztet* Cadet 664

and Hayes were in constant demand at jazz recording sessions. Jones continued to be in demand during the 1970s.

Guitar   The peak creative period of hard bop's leading guitarists, **Kenny Burrell** (b. 1931) and **Wes Montgomery,** was in the late 1950s and early 60s. Burrell blended characteristics of Charlie Christian, Django Reinhardt, and Oscar Moore with bop horn lines. The funky melodic figures of Horace Silver slipped into Burrell's work often, but Burrell was also capable of nonfunky solos which contained meat and depth.[10]

Wes Montgomery (b. 1925) was probably the best hard bop guitarist.[11] It is ironic, though, that his widest exposure came with recordings for Verve and A & M which did not reflect much of his great talent. He played tastefully on these records, but his work of the late 1950s and early 60s is a far richer jazz vein.

Montgomery created a relaxed, melodic style derived from Charlie Christian. His tone was round and full, cleanly articulated, and not edgy or excessively percussive. He had a well-paced style where everything swung comfortably.

The Kenny Burrell style differs from the Wes Montgomery style in several respects. Montgomery's playing exudes naturalness, whereas Burrell's is somewhat more self-conscious. Montgomery's tone is larger and rounder, partly because he uses his thumb instead of a pick to pluck the strings. His lines have somewhat more continuity and seem a bit more relaxed. Burrell's lines jump around more than Montgomery's and resemble trumpet more than sax lines. Though not the first jazz guitarist to do it, Montgomery popularized the playing of lines in octaves. Many of his best-known recordings of the 1960s consist of pop tunes voiced in octaves. Though both men were widely respected during the 1960s, Montgomery was probably the more influential of the two. Montgomery died in 1968, but Burrell remained active during the 1980s.

Popular Appeal   As with bop, hard bop accumulated a relatively small audience. Most of the public never knew who Clifford Brown or Max Roach were, and Dave Brubeck and Stan Getz were far better known than Sonny Rollins or Curtis Fuller. Freddie Hubbard was relatively obscure until he began recording albums that had more orchestration than improvisation, and his best improvisations sold poorly. There were fewer singers in hard bop than in bop, and dancing was almost unknown. Except the relatively successful Miles Davis groups of the 1950s and 60s, the very few hard bop groups that gained a large audience featured music that bore considerable repetition mixed with the improvisations. Their

[10] *Kenny Burrell/John Coltrane* Prestige 24059
[11] *While We're Young* Milestone 47003 or *The Incredible Jazz Guitar of Wes Montgomery* Fantasy OJC 036 or Riverside 9320

music was characterized by simple, easily singable tunes plus repetitive accompaniment rhythms. These properties seemed to help counter the difficulty that listeners experienced in following jazz improvisation. Thus the few hard bop pieces of the 1950s and 60s which rose to popularity outside of the limited jazz audience were simple, funky tunes such as Horace Silver's "Señor Blues" and "Song for My Father," Cannonball Adderley's "Sack o' Woe," Nat Adderley's "Jive Samba" and "Work Song" (later popularized by Herb Alpert and the Tiajuana Brass), Bobby Timmons's "Dat Dere" and "Dis Here," Joe Zawinul's "Mercy, Mercy, Mercy," Lee Morgan's "Sidewinder" (later recorded by Quincy Jones), and Ben Tucker's "Comin' Home Baby."

CHAPTER SUMMARY

1) The hard bop style evolved from bop during the 1950s.

2) Some hard bop groups incorporated earthy feeling and elements of gospel music to create a funky variation of bop, especially evident in pieces by pianist Horace Silver, saxophonist Cannonball Adderley, trumpeter Nat Adderley, and pianist Bobby Timmons.

3) Hard bop departed from the bop practice of basing most compositions on pop tune progressions. Most groups featured original compositions with original progressions, and many of their pieces boasted forms other than the traditional 12-bar blues and 32-bar A-A-B-A constructions.

4) Hard bop groups used more preset introductions, endings, and accompaniment figures than bop groups used.

5) Hard bop drummers played more actively, with Art Blakey, Philly Joe Jones, and Louis Hayes being especially volatile.

6) The musicianship of bassists rose with hard bop, as exemplified in such capable timekeepers and soloists as Paul Chambers and Sam Jones.

7) Clifford Brown was the most influential hard bop trumpeter. He had a fat, warm tone and slow, even vibrato which was a departure from bop custom.

8) Sonny Rollins and John Coltrane were the most imitated of the hard bop saxophonists. Rollins developed from Charlie Parker, but added his own touches to contribute an original and influential style.

9) Late in the hard bop period the most influential trumpeter was Freddie Hubbard, and a model for many saxophonists was Joe Henderson.

10) The leading guitarists of this style were Wes Montgomery and Kenny Burrell.

chapter 12
MILES DAVIS, HIS GROUPS & SIDEMEN

Miles Davis (b. 1926) is known to many people primarily as a trumpet player, but he has probably had more influence as an innovative band-leader and composer. A large portion of modern jazz history is documented in Davis-led recording sessions. In fact, Miles was bandleader at several major landmark recording sessions: the 1949 *Birth of the Cool* (see pages 181–182), which influenced West Coast Jazz styles;[1] the 1959 *Kind of Blue*,[2] which was important in the development of improvisation techniques using modes instead of chord changes (see pages 216–224); and the 1969 *In a Silent Way*[3] and *Bitches Brew*,[4] which were influential in the fusion of jazz with rock (see pages 321–325). After the recording of *In a Silent Way* and *Bitches Brew*, many of the participants formed important jazz-rock groups: Joe Zawinul's and Wayne Shorter's Weather Report, Tony Williams's Lifetime, John McLaughlin's Mahavishnu Orchestra, Herbie Hancock's Head Hunters, and Chick Corea's Return to Forever.

Davis was not personally responsible for all the ideas at these recording sessions, but he was the overseer, and much in the progression of modern jazz styles has occurred within Davis-led groups. Because Miles has been innovative for so long, many fans are not familiar with every phase of his career. Music from one of his stylistic periods often sounds quite different from that of another period. The *Birth of the*

---

[1] *The Complete Birth of the Cool* Capitol N 16168
[2] Columbia PC 8163
[3] Columbia PC 9875
[4] Columbia PG 26

Cool was the first of a series of Davis recordings which helped bring about new styles in jazz. Davis has kept his ears open so that, at crucial times, he has chosen leading innovators as composers, arrangers, and players for his bands.

Miles Davis has composed tunes which have become standard repertory for modern jazz musicians, including "Nardis," "Milestones," and "So What."

Miles Davis has popularized and mistakenly been assigned composer credit for several modern jazz standards, including "Blue in Green" by Bill Evans and "Tune-Up" and "Four" by Eddie Vinson. His treatment, on records, of popular tunes such as "Bye Bye, Blackbird" and "On Green Dolphin Street" has made them into jazz standards. Several jazz tunes also became jazz standards after he recorded them (Richard Carpenter's "Walkin'," Jimmy Heath's "Gingerbread Boy," Eddie Harris's "Freedom Jazz Dance," etc.).

The quality of Davis's recordings usually reflects his collaboration with great sidemen, some of whom were directly responsible for many of the innovations of his groups; but since he chose them and provided an excellent working environment, he gets and deserves much of the credit. He has an uncanny knack for choosing the best sidemen. (See Tables 12.1, 12.2, and 12.3.)

TABLE 12.1. A Few of the Many Well-Known Saxophonists Who Worked With Miles Davis

Lee Konitz	Joe Henderson
Sonny Rollins	Sam Rivers
Jackie McLean	George Coleman
Gerry Mulligan	Wayne Shorter
Sonny Stitt	David Liebman
Jimmy Heath	Steve Grossman
Bennie Maupin	Gary Bartz
John Coltrane	Cannonball Adderley
Hank Mobley	Sonny Fortune

TABLE 12.2. A Few of the Many Well-Known Guitarists Who Worked With Miles Davis

George Benson	John Scofield
John McLaughlin	Barry Finnerty
Larry Coryell	Mike Stern

With only a few exceptions, recordings led by Miles Davis are full of sensitivity and stand out above most other jazz records made during the same years. There is a feeling of intelligent, well-measured musical creation throughout the Davis recording career. This feeling prevails even in performances for which he did not write the tunes and in which he is only one of several soloists. Balance and concentration pervade Davis-led sessions, even when he does not solo at all ("Two Bass Hit" on *Milestones*,[5] and "Pee Wee" on *Sorcerer*[6]).

Miles Davis as a Trumpet Player

Miles is generally a very melodic soloist. Much of his work is characterized by unusually skillful timing and dramatic construction of melodic figures. Davis, like pianists Count Basie and Thelonious Monk, is a master of self-restraint in construction of improvised lines. Much of his improvising gives the impression that Davis must be carefully editing his solos as he is performing them. (For outstanding examples of this, listen to his solos on the 1954 session with Milt Jackson and Thelonious Monk that produced "The Man I Love" and "Bags' Groove."[7] Other good examples of his self-restraint and dramatic timing occur in "Eighty-One" on the 1965 *E.S.P.* album,[8] side one of the 1970 *Jack Johnson* album,[9] "Sivad" on the 1971 *Live-Evil* album,[10] "So What," and "Boplicity," in SCCJ.)

By his placement of silence as well as his choice of notes, Davis has created logical and dramatic solos. During his solos, Miles often lets several beats pass without playing. During that time, the sound of bass and drums comes clearly to the listener. This is an especially dramatic technique employed by few other improvisers. (One other musician who does this is pianist Ahmad Jamal, whose light touch and use of silence enhanced his well-known 1958 recording of "Poincianna" on *Ahmad Jamal at the Pershing*, Argo or Cadet LP 628. The amount of variety and contrast in Jamal's solo work provides another point of similarity with Davis, who is an open admirer of Jamal's playing.)

Few improvisers invent phrases as well thought out as those of Miles. He rarely plays an obvious phrase or cliché. Subtlety is central to the Miles Davis style. To say "his solos make sense" is to sum up much of it.

During the 1940s and 50s, and on many albums of the 60s (*Seven Steps to Heaven, E.S.P., Sorcerer, Miles Smiles, Nefertiti*), Miles played with a lighter, softer, less brassy tone than was common for

---

[5] Columbia PC 9428
[6] Columbia PC 9532
[7] *Modern Jazz Giants* Prestige S 7650, or *Tallest Trees* Prestige 24012
[8] Columbia PC 9150
[9] Columbia PC 30455
[10] Columbia CG 30954

TABLE 12.3. The Evolution of Modern Jazz Rhythm Section Styles Documented by Miles Davis Recordings

1950:	Pianist John Lewis, bassist Al McKibbon, drummer Max Roach on *Birth of the Cool.*
1951:	Pianist Walter Bishop, Jr., bassist Tommy Potter, drummer Art Blakey on "Conception"; "Denial"; "Paper Moon."
1956:	Pianist Tommy Flanagan, bassist Paul Chambers, drummer Art Taylor on "No Line"; "Vierd Blues"; "In Your Own Sweet Way."
1955–58:	Pianist Red Garland, bassist Paul Chambers, drummer Philly Joe Jones on *The New Miles Davis Quintet; Steamin';*[11] *Cookin'; Workin'; Relaxin'; 'Round About Midnight; Milestones.*
1959–63:	Pianist Wynton Kelly, bassist Paul Chambers, drummer Jimmy Cobb on *Someday My Prince Will Come;*[12] *In Person at the Blackhawk; Miles Davis at Carnegie Hall.*
1963–68:	Pianist Herbie Hancock, bassist Ron Carter, drummer Tony Williams on many albums, including *My Funny Valentine;*[13] *Sorcerer; Miles in the Sky; Nefertiti.*
1971:	Pianist Keith Jarrett, bassist Mike Henderson, drummer Jack De-Johnette, percussionist Airto Moreira on "Sivad" from *Live-Evil.*[14]
1969–72:	Groups whose rhythm sections sometimes included two or three keyboards[15] (Miles drew from a pool of pianists which included Joe Zawinul, Chick Corea, Keith Jarrett, Herbie Hancock, Larry Young, Harold Williams, Hermeto Pascoal, Lonnie Liston Smith, and Cedric Lawson).
1970s:	Groups whose rhythm sections sometimes included two or three guitars (Miles drew from a pool of guitarists which included Reggie Lucas, Pete Cosey, David Creamer, Dominique Gaumont, Cornell Dupree).[16]
1970s:	Groups including sitar and tabla.[17] Use of instruments native to India, such as the sitar (a stringed instrument) and tabla (drums), was as unusual in jazz rhythm sections as using two and three keyboards at once.

[11] *Workin' and Steamin'* Prestige 24034
[12] Columbia PC 8456
[13] Columbia PC 9106
[14] Columbia CG 30954
[15] *In A Silent Way* Columbia PC 9875
[16] *Agharta* Columbia PG 33967
[17] *On the Corner* Columbia PC 31906

bop and hard bop trumpeters. He used almost no vibrato and favored the trumpet's middle register over its flashier and more popular high register. Double-timing was rare in his playing. The Miles Davis trumpet style of the 1940s and 50s was gentle.

During the 1950s, Miles was one of the few modern trumpeters to employ colorful alterations of pitch and tone color reminiscent of pre-modern trumpeters. His ways of varying the pitch, color, and size of his tone constituted critical dramatic devices in his playing on *Porgy and Bess* (especially "Fishermen, Strawberry and Devil Crab")[18] and *Sketches of Spain* (especially "Saeta").[19]

Miles created a personal sound by playing through a Harmon mute without its shank (or stem). These muted solos were amplified by placing the mute very close to the microphone. The result was a wispy quality, delicate and quite intimate, as on the down-tempo pieces in the 1963 *Seven Steps to Heaven*[20] and the 1959 *Kind of Blue*.

During the 1960s, Miles began to reach into the high register more often. (Listen to the 1963 *Miles in Europe*[21] and the 1964 *Four and More*.) During the 1970s, he developed a more explosive and violent style which, like his 1960s developments, also emphasized the trumpet's high register. This style also employed long bursts of notes, splattered tones, electronically produced echo, and electronic "wah wah" alterations of the trumpet tone. (Listen to *Bitches Brew, Live-Evil,* and side one of *Jack Johnson*.)

In spite of his strikingly original phrases and his unusually skillful pacing, Miles Davis does not possess the awesome instrumental proficiency of trumpeters Dizzy Gillespie, Clifford Brown, and Maynard Ferguson. He does not play as fast, as high, or as clearly as these performers. Davis occasionally cracks his tone or misses a note he intended to reach. He often attempts trumpet lines which are faster than he is able to play, as on *Miles in Europe, Miles in Berlin, Miles in Tokyo,* and *Four and More*. He does, however, maintain the momentum of even the fastest tempos, whether or not he succeeds in sounding every single note he attempts. Miles is seldom unable to express his ideas because of technical limitations.

Many listeners are so obsessed with the limitations of Davis's trumpet technique that they fail to recognize his assets. They ignore not only his tremendous skills as an improviser but also his talents as a composer and bandleader. The fact that Davis occasionally fluffs notes should not be allowed to obscure the fact that he improvises lines which are more varied and original than those of most other trum-

18 Columbia PC 8085
19 Columbia PC 8271
20 Columbia PC 8851
21 Columbia PC 8983

peters. He has a great melodic gift, and he is one of the few jazz musicians who can improvise swinging figures in constant tempo ("Freddie the Freeloader" on *Kind of Blue*, "Sid's Ahead" on *Milestones*, "Devil May Care" on *Basic Miles*) as well as figures which imply freedom from strict tempo and swing feeling (second selection on second side of *Kind of Blue*, "Fishermen, Strawberry, and Devil Crab" on *Porgy and Bess*, the first few measures of "My Funny Valentine" and "Stella by Starlight" on *My Funny Valentine*[22]). When Miles plays a tune, he makes it completely his own, but, at the same time, he expresses its essential character (his 1956 recording of "It Never Entered My Mind," his 1963 recording of "I Fall in Love Too Easily," and his 1964 recordings of "My Funny Valentine" and "Stella By Starlight" on his *My Funny Valentine* album).

Miles Davis has continued to influence jazz trumpet styles from the 1940s to the 1980s (see Table 12.4).

The Classic Miles Davis Quintet For Prestige record company, Miles Davis recorded five albums with one of the most exciting combos in jazz history. Those albums were *The New Miles Davis Quintet*, recorded in 1955, and *Steamin'*, *Cookin'*, *Workin'*, *Relaxin'*, all recorded in 1956. Davis put together a rhythm section consisting of pianist Red Garland, bassist Paul Chambers, and drummer Philly Joe Jones; he chose tenor saxophonist John Coltrane as his front line partner (see Chapter 17).

After leaving Prestige, Davis signed with Columbia records and has remained with them as of this writing. With Columbia, the Coltrane-Garland-Jones quintet made *'Round About Midnight* in 1956[23]

TABLE 12.4. A Few of the Many Trumpeters Influenced by Miles Davis

Clifford Brown	Blue Mitchell
Chet Baker	Lester Bowie
Shorty Rogers	Tom Harrell
Jack Sheldon	Randy Brecker
Nat Adderley	Mark Isham
Charles Moore	John McNeil
Johnny Coles	Terumasa Hino
Eddie Henderson	Kenny Wheeler
Stu Williamson	Wynton Marsalis
Ted Curson	Terence Blanchard
Luis Gasca	Herb Pomeroy

[22] Columbia PC 9106
[23] Columbia PC 8649

Cannonball Adderley (alto sax), Paul Chambers (bass), Miles Davis (trumpet), and John Coltrane (tenor saxophone). Each man was a modern jazz giant on his respective instrument, and all were present on the historic *Milestones* and *Kind of Blue* recording sessions. Pictured here at the 1958 Newport Jazz Festival. (*Courtesy of Frank Driggs*)

and, with the addition of alto saxophonist Cannonball Adderley, *Milestones* in 1958. The period of Adderley's association with Davis and Coltrane marked his creative peak. His solos on the 1958 *Milestones*[24] album and those on a 1959 quintet recording made with the Davis group minus Davis ("Limehouse Blues," "Grand Central," "The Sleeper," etc.)[25] are rich in melodic material and infused with tremendous energy.

Most of the tunes Davis recorded before 1958 were written by either pop song composers or bop-oriented writers. Many are in twelve-bar blues form or thirty-two-bar A-A-B-A form. They were the basis for bop-style improvisation guided by chord progressions. But with the "Milestones" selection, for which the *Milestones* album was named, Davis broke away from the tradition of improvisation guided by chord progressions. Davis was one of the first and most important

[24] Columbia PC 9428
[25] *Cannonball Adderley Quintet in Chicago* Mercury EXPR 1014

musicians to move away from jazz improvisation based on chords. Instead of using chord changes, "Milestones" used two different modes, the first lasting sixteen measures, the second for another sixteen measures, followed by a return to the first for a final eight measures. The use of modes in "Milestones" was a prelude to Davis's *Kind of Blue* album, which contained several modal pieces (see pages 368 and 418 for explanations of modes).

Red Garland (1923–1984) played in a style derived partly from Bud Powell and other bop pianists and partly from the locked-hands style typical of Milt Buckner. His playing of "Billy Boy" on the *Milestones* LP contains passages identical to Ahmad Jamal's 1951 Epic recording of the same tune, which also employs the locked-hands style. Garland's comping was not as sensitive or imaginative as that of subsequent Davis pianists, yet his solos were quite creative within the bop context. He sometimes improvised his solo lines in the lower register of the piano, a very unusual practice (the 1956 Davis recording of "Oleo").[26] Garland also recorded solos in which he did not comp for himself. His horn-like lines were supported only by string bass and drums. This device had previously been used by Lennie Tristano ("Line-Up" on a 1955 Atlantic record). It was subsequently used by Herbie Hancock with Miles Davis on "Orbits," "Dolores," and "Gingerbread Boy" (*Miles Smiles*, 1966) and "Hand Jive" (*Nefertiti*, 1967).

Bassist **Paul Chambers** (1935–1969) was a driving and buoyant force in the Davis group. Much of the momentum generated by the group can be attributed to Chambers, who remained with Davis through many changes in quintet personnel. He was the last original Miles Davis Quintet sideman when Davis disbanded in 1963. Though he did not solo much with Davis, Chambers was one of the foremost bass soloists of the 1950s. His lines were rich with bop figures and melodic continuity. This trait, together with his large, dark tone, and a very muscular approach, made him widely admired among jazz musicians. He was also one of the few to explore bowed bass solo technique as a jazz device. Many musicians consider Chambers to rank with Oscar Pettiford and Charles Mingus as the top bassist of his era.

Philly Joe Jones (b. 1923) was possibly the most adventurous rhythm section drummer of the 1950s. His crisp snare drum fills, bass drum accents, and cymbal splashes were so well-conceived that he became far more than a mere timekeeper. Philly Joe's playing conveyed a constant excitement. He helped emancipate drummers by showing how active they could be without disturbing the pulse. His playing interacted intelligently with the solos of Davis, Coltrane, and Garland. His solos and solo-like fills retained the character of a piece; they did not seem isolated from what the rest of the group was doing, as did

[26] *Miles Davis* Prestige 24001

the drum solos in much pre-1960 jazz. His fills on "Two Bass Hit" in the 1958 *Milestones* album and in "Budo"[27] are models of originality and assured execution. (Listen to his melodically conceived fills played with wire brushes on "Billy Boy" in the *Milestones* album.)

Collaborations with Gil Evans

In 1957, Miles renewed his association with former *Birth of the Cool* arranger Gil Evans (b. 1912). Together they produced several Columbia albums on which Miles was the only soloist playing with a large band. Evans conducted his own arrangements for groups of brass, woodwinds, string bass, drums, and occasionally, harp. The brass section included French horn and tuba in addition to trumpets and trombones. The woodwind section consisted of flutes and clarinets in addition to saxophones; bassoon was added for *Sketches of Spain*. The arrangements reflected the prolific imagination and high-level workmanship of Gil Evans and produced several fresh, well-balanced recordings: *Miles Ahead, Porgy and Bess*, and *Sketches of Spain*.

Miles Ahead[28] was recorded in 1957 with Davis playing fluegelhorn throughout. This was previously an uncommon instrument to find in jazz (see illustration on page 117). By the 1970s, many jazz trumpeters were doubling on fluegelhorn, and arrangers who worked for popular singers and put together night club acts were frequently including fluegelhorn parts in their scores. Although trumpeters Clark Terry and Shorty Rogers had played fluegelhorn prior to 1957, Miles's use of the instrument probably provided the impetus for its ensuing popularity.

The program of *Miles Ahead* includes popular tunes and jazz tunes. The pieces are connected by brief interludes which Evans composed specially to bridge the gaps between selections. *Miles Ahead* contains writing which ranges from the subtle, unforced swinging of the *Birth of the Cool*, to lush pastels in slow tempo, to moments of brassy excitement. Compared to other big band writing of the 1950s and 60s, it was far more reflective. Here Evans mastered the effective use of shading and contrast of both rhythmic and tonal dimensions. Probably the only arranging style of similar character and quality was Ellington's. Like Ellington, Evans also freed himself of the formula writing which pitted brasses against saxes. He freely voiced across sections and assigned different parts of a melody to different instruments. Like Ellington's writing and his own work on *Birth of the Cool*, Evans's arrangements for *Miles Ahead* managed to weave improvisation into the framework of a piece without sounding contrived or awkward. There were brief passages in which Davis interpreted pop tune themes, or in which he improvised on the chord progressions in the arrangements. In either

[27] *Basic Miles* Columbia PC 32025
[28] Columbia PC 8633

case, the scoring was perfectly conceived to match the mood and color of Davis's style.

Porgy and Bess,[29] recorded in 1958, is a lush scoring of music from George Gershwin's opera, "Porgy and Bess." Evans created sweeping colors and breathtaking drama. Miles plays some numbers on trumpet and others on fluegelhorn, reworking the frequently played Gershwin melodies so that they acquire a new quality. That flavor of sweet sadness so characteristic of Davis's style is especially noticeable in his work on "Summertime," "Fishermen, Strawberry and Devil Crab," and "My Man's Gone Now." (Listen to "Summertime" in SCCJ.)

Sketches of Spain,[30] recorded in November, 1959, and March, 1960, is nearly a classical album. Except for "Solea," in which Miles develops a long modal improvisation, the music on this recording was almost exclusively prewritten. The "Concierto de Aranjuez" for guitar and symphony orchestra by Joaquin Rodrigo was rescored by Evans for trumpet and wind orchestra; there are no strings. "Pan Piper," "Saeta," and "Solea" are developments of Spanish folk themes. Evans embroidered the melodies in a delicately beautiful way, and then he placed the haunting sound of the Miles Davis trumpet on top.

Sketches of Spain is a truly unique album. It easily qualifies as Third Stream because it combines jazz improvisation with the forms and instrumentation of classical music. Yet it has a more soulful punch than do most Third Stream efforts. The subtleties of the Evans arrangements—the voicings of tuba, harp, bass clarinet, snare drum, trumpets, and French horns—combine with the understated approach of Miles Davis to create very unusual music.

Kind of Blue   During the time between the *Porgy and Bess* sessions and the *Sketches of Spain* sessions, the Miles Davis sextet recorded what turned out to be an historically pivotal album: *Kind of Blue*.[31] Each player on *Kind of Blue* had already made or would soon contribute approaches which dominated jazz of the 1960s. Davis, alto saxophonist Cannonball Adderley, tenor saxophonist John Coltrane, pianist Bill Evans, bassist Paul Chambers, and drummer Jimmy Cobb comprised the group. On one track, "Freddie the Freeloader," Wynton Kelly replaced Evans, thus forming the Kelly-Chambers-Cobb rhythm section that Miles retained until 1963. (Bill Evans had been with Miles for an eight-month period after Red Garland left. Evans was replaced by Wynton Kelly and had been gone for a few months but returned for this record date. Philly Joe Jones and Jimmy Cobb had alternated as Miles's drummer until the *Kind of Blue* session, when Cobb became the permanent drummer until Davis disbanded in 1963.)

[29] Columbia PC 8085
[30] Columbia PC 8271
[31] Columbia PC 8163

Nearly every selection on the album represents a "first take." This means that the musicians themselves were so pleased with their first improvisations that they decided to release them instead of trying again for better ones. It rarely happens that so many soloists are all playing in excellent form at the same time. The music is a model of pacing and spontaneous balance. The mood of the album is one of calm, consistent thoughtfulness.

The construction of pieces on *Kind of Blue* marked a departure from pre-1959 jazz albums because the dominant flavor of the album was modal. This approach was a continuation of the modal interest Davis had shown on the title track of *Milestones* (an interest he was to display in "Solea" on the *Sketches of Spain* LP) and the interest shown by his pianist Bill Evans. (Evans's "Peace Piece," which he recorded as an unaccompanied piano solo four months before *Kind of Blue*, is based exclusively on a repeating two-chord pattern identical to the beginning of the second selection on *Kind of Blue's* second side. The primary difference between the two performances, aside from personnel and instrumentation, is that "Peace Piece" is based on a single mode, whereas its counterpart employs four additional modes.) The role Bill Evans played in working out the style of the 1959 *Kind of Blue* was similar to that of Gil Evans in the 1949 *Birth of the Cool* and that of Joe Zawinul in the 1969 *In a Silent Way* and *Bitches Brew*. Miles Davis and Bill Evans collaborated on all the pieces, with the exception of "Freddie the Freeloader," a twelve-measure blues composed by Davis, and "Blue in Green" (also called "Blues in Green"), which was written by Evans and mistakenly credited to Davis.

Listening to *Kind of Blue*

"So What" begins with a slow, written introduction played by pianist Evans and bassist Paul Chambers (listen to it in SCCJ). It is not in strict tempo. It is played rubato. The introduction conveys a mood of quiet anticipation. The theme, a new melodic figure in strict tempo, is then stated by the bass played pizzicato.* It is a thirty-two-bar A-A-B-A form with a question and answer pattern: the bass states a question, and the answer is stated by piano and drums during the first eight bars, and then by horns and piano together through most of the remaining question-answer segments. The bridge of the tune is identical to the A section, but it is played a half step higher.

---

* "So What" popularized a relatively new style for jazz pieces because it was modal. It was also unusual because it had an out-of-tempo, prewritten introduction followed by a theme statement in the form of a call by pizzicato bass and a response by horns and piano. Duke Ellington had used bassist Jimmy Blanton in a similar capacity for his 1940 "Jack the Bear" and other recordings. The Davis recording of "So What," however, caught on more with the mainstream of jazz bassists.

Instead of using a variety of chord changes within each few measures, "So What" employs a single chord or mode for eight or sixteen consecutive measures. (See page 423 for modes used on "So What.")

One mode is the basis for the first sixteen bars, the A section and its repetition. The same mode is raised a half step for the eight-measure bridge, then lowered again to the original mode for the final eight-bar A section.

The Bill Evans composition **"Blue in Green"** is ten measures long, an unusual form for jazz. The improvisational technique used on it is even more unusual. Each soloist is free to halve or double the duration of the chord progression and use that alteration as the harmonic basis of his improvisation.

The first selection on the second side (entitled either "All Blues" or **"Flamenco Sketches"** depending on what album copy you have) is basically a twelve-bar blues in meter of six. Unlike most modern jazz blues, this piece does not have a variety of chord changes in the first four measures. Instead, the first four measures are dominated by a single mode (centered on the I chord of the piece). The absence of harmonic movement helps create a calm feeling. The entire blues progression is treated in this manner, with the exception of an interesting chord progression in the ninth and tenth measures (the V chord moves up one half-step then back down again). The reduced number of chord progressions together with the swaying feeling created by meter of six, gives the piece a calm, almost hypnotic quality. Vamps sandwiched between theme statements and solos help maintain the effect. (If any of the musical terms here are unfamiliar to you, study pages 358 to 388.)

At the beginning, the rhythm section plays a figure (one two THREE four five SIX one two THREE four five SIX) for four measures. The saxes then join them for an additional four measures prior to Miles's solo entrance. This vamp is employed frequently throughout the performance. It provides time for things to air out. It accompanies the first four bars of Davis's melody statement, and it is inserted as a four-measure breathing space between the first and second choruses of the theme. It is played for an additional four bars after the theme statement and before Miles begins his improvised solo. The vamp is always inserted between soloists thereafter. (It is a calming device typical of Miles Davis's skill in pacing. It also provides a graceful transition, setting the stage for a new voice instead of making the awkwardly quick shift in style which occurs in many jazz performances when several soloists improvise choruses back to back.)

Evans is the final soloist. His improvisation is followed by the four-bar vamp. Then Miles returns with the theme statement, accompanied by the saxes and rhythm section playing the vamp. Finally the performance fades out on the beginning of a new improvisation by Miles. (A year earlier Miles had also used a fade-out to conclude his "Milestones" performance, but the device was uncommon until the 1960s. Here it adds further to the calm achieved by the vamps, the slow tempo, the meter of six, and the modal approach to harmony.)

The second selection on the second side of *Kind of Blue* is known by two different titles because many records were released with the second side's tune titles interchanged. The name that seems to have stuck for the *second* selection is "Flamenco Sketches." Bill Evans's album jacket notes indicate that the piece was supposed to be called **"All Blues."** But several subsequent Davis versions of the second side's *first* selection have been released using the "All Blues" title. Other groups have also recorded the tune, a blues in meter of six, with that title. The title "All Blues" seems to have stuck as the name of the *first* selection, leaving "Flamenco Sketches" as the title for the *second*.

The second selection on *Kind of Blue*'s second side was created by an interesting improvisational technique. No melody or chord progressions were written. Instead of playing a melody and improvising on its chord changes, the sextet followed a preset sequence of five modes. Each mode served as the harmonic guide for improvisation as long as a soloist wanted to use it. Then, whenever he wanted a change, he moved to the next mode. Although there were no restrictions on the duration of any mode, the soloists tended to use each mode for an even number of measures. In fact, most soloists used each mode for four measures and then moved to the next. So, in spite of the increased freedom allowed by this technique, the players usually chose duration patterns which typically occur in conventional jazz improvisation.

Suggestions for keeping your place while hearing "All Blues" and following the modal construction.

1. Remember that the second track on the second side of *Kind of Blue* has been mislabeled "Flamenco Sketches" on many copies of this album. So, if you hear a feeling of "ONE two three Four five six ONE two three Four five six" instead of a very slow "ONE two three four ONE two three four," then you are listening to the wrong selection.

2. To begin synchronizing your counting with the record, notice that the piece starts with a bass note on the fourth beat of a measure that actually precedes the beginning of your counting. If you are to count accurately, you must say "FOUR" when that first note is sounding, then say "One" when the next bass note sounds. That note lasts three beats, so you must continue counting even though there is no clear statement of any beats until the pattern is repeated. In other words, to get you through the introduction and well synchronized with the tempo of the piece, you need to count "FOUR One two three FOUR One two three FOUR." When you say "FOUR One," you are acknowledging the bass notes. When you say "two three," you are acknowledging the middle of the measure, a time when the bass note is still ringing and no clear statement of beats is coming from the musicians. Eventually, you should be able to count "ONE two three four ONE two three four" with or without assistance from the musicians. This will become important later because bassist Paul Chambers sometimes plays figures that purposely delete the simple pattern outlined above and leave the listener to fill in the beats. You will have some assistance, though, beginning with John Coltrane's entrance, because drummer Jimmy Cobb starts using a wire brush to play ride rhythms on the ride cymbal. If you still have yet to figure out where the beats are by the time you are near the end of the selection, simply listen to Cobb's playing under the final Miles Davis solo. It is almost exclusively quarter notes, one note on each beat.

3. Remember that the tempo is very slow, and that you should therefore take care to not be counting twice as fast or four times as fast as the beats are passing.

4. If your mind wanders, let the sound of mode #4 refocus your attention. It has a Spanish flavor that differs noticeably from the flavors of the other modes. It has also attracted the longest improvisations from the musicians and can therefore give you the most time to get back with it. In fact, if you lose your place and all of a sudden find yourself in the middle of that mode, you can restart your counting when that flavor disappears. The disappearance of that flavor will signal the beginning of mode #5.

5. Start counting anew when a different solo voice enters. Remember that the sequence is four measures of piano and bass introduction followed by these sounds each running five modes in sequence: muted trumpet, tenor sax, alto sax, piano, and muted trumpet.

6. Listen carefully for the bass notes that begin the measures. If a new mode is starting, this will often be signalled by the sound of a NEW bass note on the first beat of the measure.

7. To help you anticipate each new mode within a single musician's solo, keep in mind that *generally*
   a. Miles Davis lets bassist Paul Chambers lead him to each new mode. Chambers plays the important note of the mode while Davis is silent, then Davis enters with a new melodic idea to fit the mode.
   b. Coltrane tends to increase the number of notes played per beat just before beginning a new mode. In other words, if you hear Coltrane sound like he is going faster and faster, consider the likelihood that he is requesting the next mode.
   c. Adderley suggests the upcoming mode by a peculiar choice of notes in his line. The flavor of his melody line shifts when he is about to change modes.

8. Once you know where you are, if it is the beginning of a mode, count "1234   2234   3234   4234" in order to keep your place by tallying beats as they pass. Each group of four beats ("1234") accounts for one measure. You tag the measures by saying a number to yourself at the beginning of each one. If it is the first measure for the mode, you say, "ONE two three four." If it is the second measure of a given mode, you say, "TWO two three four." If it is the third measure, you say, "THREE two three four."

Eventually you should be able to follow the changing modes without referring to the guide. Your ears will tell you what mode is in effect at a given moment. The whole point of this exercise is to help you peek into what the jazz improviser is doing. By being able to identify the same sounds that the improviser is using as basis for his solos, you will lessen the mystery of how solos are put together and how musicians manage to play well together without having to discuss their parts or use prewritten themes. The more you recognize in the sounds, the better prepared you are to go on to an appreciation of the compositional beauties present in the improvised lines. Listening for modes to change at the slow pace used by these performers should better equip you for listening to chords changing in conventional jazz pieces. The better you get at accurately anticipating chord changes, the more you will realize how the improviser's lines reflect his own appreciation of how the chords are progressing in a given piece. To a great extent, the progress of a melody line mirrors the progression of harmonies that lies beneath it in the accompanying chord changes. The improvised line reflects the flavor of the underlying chord, and a line improvised in "All Blues" often bears the same character as the mode that is implied in that moment's accompaniment harmonies. Once you begin confidently following the music in this piece, it will be as though you are peering through a microscope. But instead of tiny things being made to appear large, ordinarily quick-paced improvisational processes have been slowed down for your calm examination.

MODAL CONSTRUCTION OF "ALL BLUES"

(See page 421 for musical notations and technical names of these modes.)

INTRODUCTION

Four measures of mode #1. The sound of this mode is indicated by bass notes and chord voicings set in a pattern previously used by Bill Evans for his "Peace Piece." What were originally left-hand parts for pianist Evans are given here to bassist Paul Chambers. The pattern has Chambers playing on only the first and the fourth beats of each measure. Pianist Evans plays chords whose harmonies flesh out the rest of the mode's flavor.

MILES DAVIS MUTED TRUMPET IMPROVISATION
(with only piano and bass accompaniment)

mode #1	mode #2	mode #3	mode #4
four measures	four measures	four measures	eight measures

mode #5
four measures

JOHN COLTRANE TENOR SAXOPHONE IMPROVISATION
(with piano, bass, and ride cymbal accompaniment)

mode #1	mode #2	mode #3	mode #4
four measures	four measures	four measures	eight measures

mode #5
four measures

CANNONBALL ADDERLEY ALTO SAXOPHONE IMPROVISATION
(with piano, bass, and cymbals accompaniment)
Notice that Chambers plays less predictably during this solo.

(one-measure introduction by piano and bass using mode #5)	mode #1 eight measures	mode #2 four measures	mode #3 eight measures
mode #4 eight measures	(Drummer Jimmy Cobb plays double-time and adds high-hat closings during the middle of Adderley's treatment of this mode.)		mode #5 four measures

BILL EVANS PIANO IMPROVISATION
(with bass and ride cymbal accompaniment)

mode #1 eight measures	mode #2 four measures	mode #3 eight measures	mode #4 four measures
mode #5 four measures			

MILES DAVIS MUTED TRUMPET IMPROVISATION
(with piano, bass, and ride cymbal accompaniment)

mode #1 four measures	mode #2 four measures	mode #3 four measures	mode #4 eight measures
mode #5 two measures			

Historical Significance for *Kind of Blue*

In bop and bop-influenced styles, the chords were basically prescribed before improvisation. Each chord also lasted a specific number of beats before moving to the next. Constant tempo was also maintained, and rarely was a meter other than four employed. In bop, the chords changed quickly and often moved in directions less predictable than most pop tune progressions. (The chord progressions of Dizzy Gillespie's "Con Alma," George Shearing's "Deception," Clifford Brown's "Joy Spring," and John Coltrane's "Giant Steps" are quite difficult.)

When a jazz musician improvises at a constant tempo but does *not rely on preset chord progressions* which have *preset durations*, at least four alternatives are available to him:

1) He can invent his own chord progressions while he improvises. The progressions need not repeat nor fall into four- or eight-measure phrases.

2) He can follow a preset sequence of chords or modes whose durations are not fixed, employing each chord or mode only as long as he wishes and moving to the next at his own discretion.

3) He can follow a preset sequence of modes in which each mode has fixed duration.

4) He can base his entire improvisation on a single chord or mode.

(See pages 25–27 for more details about alternatives available to the improviser.)

For more conventional jazz forms, in which chords change frequently and have preset durations, Miles Davis substituted forms in which a single chord might last four or more measures. He then preset the durations ("Milestones," "So What"), left the durations up to the spontaneous discretion of the soloist (second selection on second side of *Kind of Blue*), or produced music with a preset chord progression whose total duration might be altered during improvisation ("Blue in Green").

The same time that Miles Davis was altering the bop approach (1958–59), Ornette Coleman, a saxophonist known for improvising without preset chord changes, was making his first recordings. Their techniques had similarities. Both Davis and Coleman maintained constant tempo during most improvisations, for example (although Coleman occasionally changed meters spontaneously). Instead of setting certain chord progressions in advance, Coleman preferred to invent them while improvising. Miles Davis used this technique to a limited extent in "Dolores" (1966 *Miles Smiles*), "Hand Jive" and "Madness" (1967 *Nefertiti*), and in his post-1969 work. Ornette Coleman occasionally avoided improvising in four- and eight-measure phrases. For example, he might switch keys after the first twenty-nine measures of a piece instead of switching after the first thirty-two measures ("Dee Dee," *At the Golden Circle*). His improvisations moved freely from key to key, following only the logic of the line or the impulse of the moment rather than adhering to a single key or changing keys at predetermined times.

Much post-1959 improvisational music employed the alternatives demonstrated by Davis and Coleman. During the late 1960s and 70s, numerous players rejected the bop convention of frequent chord changes which bore preset durations. Entire performances were sometimes based on a single chord instead of an involved progression of different chords. Some performances contained spontaneous chord changes and spontaneous key changes. But in spite of these new aspects, much free-form music retained the sound and feeling of bop-influenced performances. Bop phrases and melodic devices continued to appear.

Lennie Tristano, Lee Konitz, et al. ("Intuition" and "Digression"), and Jimmy Giuffre, Shorty Rogers, et al. ("Abstract #1," "Etudiez Le Cahier") had employed the techniques of free jazz years earlier. But with the work of Miles Davis and Ornette Coleman the approach caught on in the mainstream of jazz. During the late 1960s and 70s, more than half of all jazz and jazz-derived performances contained either modal or free-form improvisations. During the 1970s, fewer than twenty prominent modern jazz combos played selections which fit neither modal nor free-form styles.

The 1959–63 Rhythm Section

The rhythm section employed by Davis from 1959 to 1963 consisted of pianist **Wynton Kelly** (1931–1971), bassist Paul Chambers, and drummer Jimmy Cobb. This was the rhythm section that played on *At Carnegie Hall*,[32] *In Person at the Blackhawk*,[33] and *Someday My Prince Will Come*. Wynton Kelly derived his style primarily from Bud Powell, but there was also a funky, bluesy quality which might be attributed to the influence of Horace Silver. Kelly's playing on *Someday My Prince Will Come* also displays some of the voicings, sustained, ringing tones, and feeling of Bill Evans. Kelly influenced a number of pianists, including Herbie Hancock, Warren Bernhardt, and Keith Jarrett.

Drummer **Jimmy Cobb** (b. 1929) was more conservative than Philly Joe Jones but contributed a significant characteristic to modern jazz drumming. **His ride rhythms were placed toward the front edge of the beat,** so that they seemed to be pulling it. Philly Joe Jones, Art Taylor, and Art Blakey had tended to play more toward the center of the beat. Cobb took that tendency a bit further. This aspect of timekeeping is subtle but quite significant. Tony Williams, who replaced Cobb, played consistently on the leading edge of the beat. That technique, coupled with its counterpart in walking bass, became a prime characteristic of the Davis Quintet sound.

Note: For discussion of the 1960s Miles Davis combo style, see pages 301–306. For his 1970s and 80s style, see pages 321–325.

[32] Columbia PC 8612
[33] Columbia C2S 820

CHAPTER SUMMARY

Miles Davis is historically significant for

1) creating an influential and original style of modern jazz trumpet playing, using
    a) a softer and darker tone than his bop contemporaries
    b) varied rhythms and effective placement of silence

c) a refinement of bop harmonic conception
d) a more melodic and song-like approach to improvisation than his bop contemporaries
e) less upper register playing than was popular in modern jazz

2) organizing landmark recording sessions for at least five major modern approaches
   a) cool style
   b) modal style
   c) modern big band
   d) post-bop small group style
   e) jazz-rock

3) writing several compositions which have become jazz standards

4) leading a string of outstanding jazz combos which gave wide exposure to numerous jazz innovators when they were at their creative peak

5) popularizing the use of fluegelhorn and the Harmon mute (without stem)

chapter 13
FREE JAZZ

Free jazz is the name for an approach to improvisation made common by Ornette Coleman (b. 1930) and Cecil Taylor (b. 1929). The term derives from the observation that performances of this style are often free of preset chord progressions. A model for much of this music is a 1960 Coleman album called *Free Jazz*.[1] Its music consists of simultaneous collective improvisation by two bands attempting to remain free of preset key, melody, chord progressions, and meter. (Listen to the excerpt from this album found in SCCJ, but note that the excerpt omits much of what is later described here.) During the 1960s, aspects of these methods were also incorporated into the styles of John Coltrane, Albert Ayler, and a few of the groups they influenced. (Incidentally, Coltrane's name has become prominently associated with free jazz despite the relatively small representation of these kinds of approaches in his recorded output and the fact that almost none of his music is free of preset musical organization.) Scattered instances of methods like those of Coleman and Taylor had previously been recorded, and free jazz methods were occasionally employed by modern groups which were not necessarily affected by Coleman or Taylor, but it was Coleman's work of the late 1950s and early 1960s that is usually called to mind when free jazz is discussed.

When considering the implications of the free jazz label, it is important to acknowledge that, in contrast to their freedom from bop traditions of melody and chord progression, some of the free jazz players rarely played free of many other basic jazz traditions such as

[1] Atlantic 1364

226

the feeling of tempo or the practice or assigning horns to solo roles and assigning bassists and drummers to accompaniment roles. (See pages 15–24 for an explanation of what standard jazz improvisation entails.)

Most groups in the free jazz category omitted piano. This was primarily because historically the jazz pianist had assumed a role of provider for chord progressions, and the harmonic restrictions created by the organization that came with preset chord progressions was exactly what free players were trying to escape. Another reason for the scarcity of pianists is that, until recently, few pianists were comfortable improvising without the suggestion of chords or key. It was as though, having been the harmonic gatekeepers for so long, jazz pianists could not function when such gates and fences as chord progressions and song forms were removed.

The next three characteristics of free jazz are incidental to the idea of freedom from preset chord progressions, but they happen to be identified more with free players than with bop or cool players. First, many free players earned a reputation for more extensive manipulations of pitch and tone quality than players of any other style since early jazz. Ultra-high register playing ("altissimo" is the technical term for it), plus shrieks, squawks, wails, gurgles, and squeals were common. Second, the improvisation of textures seemed to assume greater importance for some free players than did the development of melodies. The free jazz label became attached to music of high energy and dense textures which maintained turbulent activity for lengthy periods. Some free players became so firmly identified with "energy playing" that the free jazz label often became applied to high energy, nonelectronic music even when preset key and form were present. Third, the free players' conception of melody displayed a loosening of bop melodic and rhythmic practices. Free jazz signalled an end to long, convoluted streams of eighth-note figures which reflected the movement of favorite chord progressions in stereotypic bop ways. Phrasing tended toward greater fragmentation. Sustained tones alternated with screeches and moans.

Another trend identified more with free jazz than with bop or cool was the examination of non-European musical approaches which neither rely extensively on chord progressions nor use much harmony of any kind. This includes some types of music from Africa, Indonesia, China, the Middle East, and India. Not much distance was covered between the move away from piano and preset harmony that was seen in free jazz to the adoption of those non-European forms of music that ignored chord progressions and chord instruments. So it was logical for such development to have occurred with these players. This interest led to an amalgamation of jazz with music of cultures in the Third World (non-Western, non-Soviet), and it resulted in a form

Ornette Coleman, alto saxophonist and the leading figure in free-form jazz. Pictured here at age 42 in 1972 with bassist Charlie Haden and drummer Eddie Blackwell. (*Courtesy of Bill Smith and* CODA)

of music simpler than bop. It manifested itself in the use of non-Western instruments and the cultivation of non-Western approaches to playing European instruments. In this way, it considerably extended the range of sounds used by jazz musicians. Free jazz players were not the only jazz musicians who showed this interest, but the persistence of these elements in 1970s and 80s music by free jazz players and those affected by them marks one of the first such lasting blends since the periodic infatuations jazz had had with Latin American music. (See pages 236–237 and 325–327 for examples of the Third World influences in jazz.)

ORNETTE COLEMAN   One of the most influential forces in jazz of the 1960s and 70s was Ornette Coleman. Some consider him to have been as historically significant as Charlie Parker and John Coltrane.

Sound   Though he also plays trumpet and violin, Coleman is primarily an alto saxophonist. On his 1958–59 recordings, he displayed a soft, pure tone and moved from note to note in legato fashion, as if smoothly sliding along small subdivisions of pitch. His tone did not have the edge of Charlie Parker's or the body of Cannonball Adderley's. Coleman began his notes more bluntly and used a slow vibrato. Later he made his tone somewhat brighter and gave it an edge. Though he seems able to play almost everything he attempts, he lacks the instrumental proficiency of such virtuosos as Parker, Adderley, and Lee Konitz. (Listen to Coleman's sound on "Lonely Woman," and compare it with Parker's on "Embraceable You" and Konitz's on Tristano's "Crosscurrent," then with Adderley's on the Miles Davis "So What." These are all in SCCJ.)

Writing   Coleman is one of the freshest, most prolific post-bop composers; he has written every tune on each of more than twenty albums. His style is quite original, and he has an exceptional gift for melody. Some of his tunes are quite catchy, and, like those of Thelonious Monk, sound simple, in spite of their unusual rhythmic and harmonic qualities. The playfulness of Coleman's tunes is also reminiscent of Monk's work.

A number of musicians have shown interest in Ornette Coleman's compositions. Coleman's impact has been especially notable in pianist Keith Jarrett, who has written and improvised in the style of Coleman as well as dedicating a tune to him: "Piece for Ornette." Further acknowledgment to Coleman has been indicated by fellow saxophonist Roscoe Mitchell, who titled one of his pieces "Ornette" and by bassist Charlie Haden, who wrote another called "O.C."

Though many of Coleman's pieces are simply springboards for improvisation, some have been arranged for ensembles. His "Forms and Sounds" was scored for flute, oboe, clarinet, bassoon, and French horn. Coleman's "Saints and Soldiers" and "Space Flight" were arranged for two violins, viola, and cello (*The Music of Ornette Coleman*).[2] "Skies of America," which he considers one of his best works, was scored for symphony orchestra (*Skies of America*).[3]

On some pieces in his first album (*Something Else*),[4] Coleman used a pianist and improvised to preset chord changes. Except for that work, however, and a recorded concert with pianist Paul Bley (*Paul Bley at the Hillcrest Club*),[5] Coleman generally stayed away from using preset chord changes for his improvisation, and he omitted chording instruments (piano, organ, guitar, etc.). Because his improvisations were free of preset chord changes, Coleman's music became known as *free jazz*. (See pages 30–32 for further coverage of chord progression-based improvisation methods.)

[2] RCA LSC 2982
[3] Columbia KC 31562
[4] Contemporary 7551
[5] Inner City 1007

HOW FREE IS FREE JAZZ? Although often called "free jazz," Coleman's music actually has quite a bit of self-imposed structure. Constant tempo is usually employed. Written and memorized tunes are usually used during some portion of his performances. And, of course, there is nothing haphazard about the use of the freedoms with which he and his sidemen play. They are limited by their own **decision to listen to each other** carefully and plan their music while they improvise.

In addition to the discipline of prewritten melodies, constant tempo, key feeling, conscious self-editing, and sensitivity to fellow group members, Coleman's "free jazz" also uses instruments in conventional solo and accompaniment roles. In his trio, Coleman usually seems to be soloing while his bassist and drummer accompany. Of course there is interaction, give-and-take, and mutual stimulation, but there is little doubt that Coleman is the soloist. (Listen to "Congeniality" in SCCJ.)

If a performance were truly free of role conventions, the three instruments would be undifferentiated in that respect. The absence of solo voices would occur as often as the presence of a single voice. Why should the horn necessarily be a solo instrument and the bass and drums accompanying instruments? In a truly free situation the drums would be accompanied by sax and bass just as often as the sax was accompanied by bass and drums.

Why should there be any solos at all? For me, free means the absence of prescribed roles or prescribed forms. The concepts of solo and accompaniment are roles, just as the use of constant tempo, meter, key, and chord changes (and their chorus lengths) constitute forms.

True musical freedom can indicate the ability to play whatever is in the musician's head, regardless of its relation to

a) intonation
b) key
c) expectations of melodic continuity
d) chord changes
e) tempo
f) instrumental proficiency
g) the playing of other group members
h) the expectations of the audience
i) the characteristics of a fixed style

That describes a nonexistent situation. It is not humanly possible to be that free. Musical conditioning prevents so great an independence from rules, skills, and habits. Therefore, this extreme definition of musical freedom is clearly not a description of Coleman's music.

In short, Coleman's music is free in some respects: it is free of preset chord progressions and their chorus lengths. Some of his work is also free of meter and constant tempo, though that is not characteristic for most of his recordings. Coleman freely changes keys, but he usually stays in each one long enough for us to hear that he is, indeed, in a particular key. And his key changes are logical and obvious; they reflect harmonic planning. The music does not lack key feeling, it is not atonal, and it is certainly not random (see pages 365–369 for discussion of scales, modality, tonality, and atonality).

Coleman attempts a difficult task when he rejects the use of preset chord changes. Without the rise and fall of musical tension indicated by chord changes, Coleman still has the rise and fall of tension generated by his bassist and drummer. But that is all he has to musically support and inspire his creations. Outside of that, every measure is taxing his imagination, requesting that it be filled with interesting and meaningful lines. Yet none of those measures is supplying any organizational ideas in the form of chord changes. Coleman has chosen a situation in which his improvising cannot fall back on the underlying musical motion of chord changes or on the supportive sound of a pianist's comping. With the absence of preset chord changes, and the regular chorus lengths, turnarounds, and bridges indicated by them, Coleman has brought us an especially abstract form of musical experience.

Despite the freedom of his improvisational approach, Coleman improvised lines which often resembled chord progression-based lines. For Coleman, melody is primary and harmony secondary. So it may sound as though he is inventing chord progressions as he improvises lines, but this is only because the harmonic logic of those lines resembles that of chord progression-based lines which we have previously heard in non-Coleman performances. The construction of his lines is ruled by his musical past in the way that our perception as listeners is ruled by our past listening experiences. Coleman plays freely, but in his lines we can hear organization resembling that which characterizes improvisation based on preset harmonies. The feeling of a definite key is present in each portion of his solos, though he changes keys at will. (For example, he used nine different keys in improvising on "Dee Dee," found in his album *At the Golden Circle*.)[6] And part of the chord progression feeling in Coleman's music stems from the approach taken by his bassists, especially Charlie Haden. Though Coleman's bassists follow the harmonic directions indicated by his improvisations, at times they also take the lead. Coleman's line may suggest a chord progression which the bassist will complete, or the bassist's line may suggest a chord progression which Coleman picks up. Coleman and his bassist remain alert to each other's patterns of harmony.

[6] Blue Note 84224

Comparing Coleman With the Past

It is important to note that Ornette Coleman was not the first soloist to suggest new chord progressions during improvisation. Lester Young and Coleman Hawkins had done it as early as the 1930s, and added chords are also implied by Louis Armstrong's lines of the 1920s. During the 1940s Art Tatum, Don Byas, Charlie Parker, Dizzy Gillespie, and their disciples also invented and substituted chord progressions while they improvised. The difference between their approach and Coleman's is in the starting point. Tatum, Parker, et al. began with preset chord progressions and then added to those progressions. Coleman starts with only a key, a tempo, and the mood of the tune. Nevertheless, if Charlie Parker had returned to life during the 1960s and walked into a free-form jam session of Coleman or his disciples, he probably would have fit in quite well. Parker would have been able to retain his own style because he had been an extremely versatile and imaginative improviser, and because he would have had no trouble inventing original lines regardless of the session's lack of preset chord progressions. He had invented his own chord progressions during the bop era; he could do so again within the free jazz style of the 1960s.

It is also important to note that Coleman is neither the first nor the only person to improvise jazz without the use of preset chord progressions. Many musicians quite unself-consciously improvise without giving thought to a preset melody, key, or chord progression. Little of this has been commercially recorded. But it has gone on for decades, continues to occur, and it is not revolutionary at all. Many people played free jazz long before they discovered Ornette Coleman, and many of them undoubtedly remain unaware of his work.

It is interesting to compare Parker and Coleman. Both played alto saxophone. Both were energetic improvisers. Both had a gift for melody. On his first few recordings, Coleman's tonal inflections and their timing resemble Parker's. Much of Coleman's early alto work contains tonal inflections derived from black vocal styles, and his playing is quite bluesy, more so than Parker's. Coleman's tone was unique, but it resembled Parker's more than it resembled that of Johnny Hodges, Benny Carter, or Lee Konitz. Coleman also used a few bop phrases in his improvisation and recorded Parker's tune, "Klactoveesedstene" (*Paul Bley at the Hillcrest Club*). His playing had the soulfulness of Bird's and the explosions of slippery notes which can be found in some Bird improvisations. Like Bird, Coleman also liked to quote pop tunes briefly. Themes from "If I Loved You," "Hawaiian War Chant," "Cherokee," and "Blues in the Night" ("My Mama Done Told Me") have all been interjected in his improvisations at various times.

Although I disagree with the statement, I have heard Coleman called "just another bebop alto player." For me, the rhythmic complexity of bop makes Coleman's less complex music easily differentiable. But I understand how the bop tonal inflections, bop phrasing, steady tempo, and bluesy melodic figures in Coleman's playing might lead a listener to call him a bebop player. A striking aspect of this perception is that it coexists with a completely different response to Ornette Coleman's style: many people, after all, consider him a revolutionary figure. There are valid reasons for both reactions. Coleman was genuinely innovative, but he built on a bop foundation; he did not step out of thin air. Coleman drew from Bird just as Bird drew from Hawkins and Young. Coleman is innovative, but has not shown the genius of Bird.

Coleman's Historical Impact

Coleman's tunes are original and his saxophone style is unique, but it is with his approach to improvisation that he has had the most impact on modern jazz. Coleman's decision to discard chord changes, and the style he developed without them, influenced the playing of numerous improvisers during the 1960s and 70s—not only saxophonists but also trumpeters, trombonists, and composers (see Table 13.1). Though it is not his best album, Coleman's 1960 *Free Jazz* paralleled Miles Davis's *Kind of Blue* in its historical effect on improvisational approaches. *Kind of Blue* popularized modal approaches, and *Free Jazz* contributed to more frequent use of free-form, collective approaches. Coleman used two pianoless quartets. The personnel of the first included Coleman's regular quartet: trumpeter Don Cherry, bassist Charlie Haden, and drummer Eddie Blackwell. The second was made up of alto saxophonist-bass clarinetist Eric Dolphy, trumpeter Freddie Hubbard, bassist Scott LaFaro, and drummer Billy Higgins. The eight musicians played together, sometimes improvising all at

TABLE 13.1. Some of the Many Musicians Influenced by Ornette Coleman

John Tchicai	John Coltrane
Marion Brown	John Carter
Dewey Redman	Charles Brackeen
Jimmy Lyons	Keith Jarrett
Sonny Simmons	Bobby Bradford
Prince Lasha	Don Cherry
Henry Threadgill	Charlie Haden
Carlos Ward	Pat Metheny
Archie Shepp	Joseph Jarman
Oliver Lake	Paul Bley
Roscoe Mitchell	James "Blood" Ulmer
Jan Garbarek	Ronald Shannon Jackson
Anthony Ortega	Jamaaladeen Tacuma
Albert Ayler	Saheb Sarbib

once. There was no preset arrangement of themes, chord changes, or chorus lengths. Tonal centers were used, though they were not agreed upon in advance. (Listen to the excerpt from this album that is in SCCJ.)

Despite the album title, the music on *Free Jazz* is not haphazard, random, uncontrolled, without pulse, or atonal. There are prearranged ensemble passages, solos with rhythm section accompaniment, as well as a string bass duet. Some of the solos, especially Freddie Hubbard's, sound as though they were based on a preset chord progression, but the progression is actually being composed spontaneously during the solo and is only being implied (no chording instrument is stating it). Brief themes recur in the improvisation and are passed back and forth among group members. Rarely are all eight men improvising at the same time. Both bassists and both drummers play throughout most of it, but usually a single horn (Coleman, Dolphy, Hubbard, or Cherry) surfaces while the others lay out. Occasionally all the horns return to embellish the prominent voice.

Other jazz groups had recorded collectively improvised free pieces at about the same time and prior to Coleman's first recordings. But they were isolated efforts, and the approach did not catch on in the jazz mainstream. After Coleman's *Free Jazz*, however, a number of other musicians also recorded collective improvisations without pre-written melodies, chord changes, or chorus lengths (see following discussions of Sun Ra, Cecil Taylor, and John Coltrane). Members of the Chicago-based Association for the Advancement of Creative Musicians (AACM) have recorded free-form collective improvisations which sound similar to Coleman's *Free Jazz*. Although they may have come up with these approaches on their own, it is likely that, having appeared after Coleman's work, the AACM members were at least influenced in part by *Free Jazz*.

ALBERT AYLER   One of the most original saxophone styles to emerge after Parker, Rollins, Coltrane, and Coleman was that of tenor saxophonist Albert Ayler (1936–1970). Some listeners heralded his music as revolutionary and more important than John Coltrane's. However, like Coleman, Ayler also used a Parker tune, "Billie's Bounce," on one of his first recordings (*My Name Is Albert Ayler*).[7] And, like Coleman, he followed its harmonies only loosely. In other words, he acknowledged bop but did not actually play in the bop style. Ayler's rhythmic conception was unlike bop rhythmic conceptions and perhaps unlike any swinging jazz style. His melodic and rhythmic approaches had more in common with classical music and folk music than with jazz. (See pages 5–8 for more about different types of swing feeling.)

Ayler swung in a manner which only approximated conventional

[7] Fantasy 86016

jazz swing feeling. Much of his work did not swing at all. The lack of swing feeling was often caused by a continuously high level of tension, in place of the constant alternation of tension and relaxation characteristic of bop. Ayler definitely swung in the general sense of the term but not in the conventional jazz sense typified by swing era, bop, West Coast, or hard bop styles.

Like Coleman, Ayler followed preset harmonic and rhythmic structures only loosely, and he preferred groups with no chording instrument. His bassists were some of the same gifted men employed by Bill Evans and Ornette Coleman. His drummers were of the "free" school, little concerned with simple timekeeping, and very interested in group interaction and the creation of varied sounds and textures.

Ayler was one of the most unusual tenor saxophonists jazz has ever known. He perfected an approach to improvisation that was technically very demanding. Ayler's lines ran the entire range of the tenor saxophone and through at least one additional octave of pitches beyond the conventional "highest note." He played throughout that range with swooping, swirling legato figures, and a light, slippery tone, at times reminiscent of the C-melody saxophone. Ayler made moans and wails an essential part of his musical vocabulary. Much of his music was strikingly voice-like. His vibrato was sometimes slow, at other times moderately fast, but always very natural in a driven sort of way. There was never anything mechanical or academic about Ayler's playing.[8]

In his extended high-register, Ayler played with the ease that good players exhibit only in the conventional mid-range of the tenor saxophone. His playing often sounded like rapid, legato violin-playing. These elements contributed to an overall feeling which had an other-worldly quality to it. Whether listeners enjoyed his music or not, it provided an intensely emotional experience for them.

Like those of many innovative jazz figures, Ayler's career was very short. His first American recording came out in 1964, and he died in 1970 at the age of 34. And like many other great American musicians, he was more popular in Europe than at home.

Ayler's style lived on in the playing of tenor saxophonist David Murray, whose first album, his 1976 *Low Class Conspiracy*,[9] demonstrated that he had learned the Ayler techniques and begun to use them masterfully. Murray further honored Ayler by writing a composition titled "Flowers for Albert." (In listening to the Ayler connection in Murray's playing it is important that Murray's first two albums, not his later works, be heard. This is because after those first albums, Murray's playing began to sound less and less like Ayler's.)

---

[8] Though it has been out of print for a long time, Ayler's *Spiritual Unity* album (ESP Disk 1002) is probably his best and is well worth searching for.

[9] Adelphi 5002

DON CHERRY

Don Cherry (b. 1936) is a trumpeter, composer, bandleader, and a leading figure in free jazz. He was a regular member of Ornette Coleman's groups in the late 1950s and early 60s, having played on all of Coleman's important early recordings including *Something Else,*[10] *Change of the Century,*[11] and his widely discussed *Free Jazz.* Though strongly influenced by Coleman, Cherry also cites bop trumpeters Fats Navarro and Clifford Brown as influences. And, consistent with this connection, Cherry has recorded improvisations which closely follow preset chord progressions and contain phrasing and note choices which derive from bop methods (listen to "Jayne" on Coleman's *Something Else*). However, like Coleman, most of Cherry's recorded improvisation spontaneously goes its own way instead of relying on a preset form and its accompanying chords. Don Cherry's improvisations are strikingly original, filled with lines and melodic fragments which draw little from standard jazz cliché. (Listen to Cherry on Coleman's "Congeniality" and "Lonely Woman" in SCCJ.) Cherry does not ordinarily use chord instruments in his bands, and he has devoted a considerable portion of his career to playing types of Oriental, Turkish, and Indian music that also omit chord instruments and chord progression-based compositional forms. (During the 1980s, however, Cherry began playing piano and organ on his recordings.)

Cherry is quite flexible as an improviser, able to construct logical solo lines as well as spontaneously construct parts for collective improvisation, as he did on Sonny Rollins's *Our Man in Jazz.*[12] In this way, Cherry is a throwback to the earliest improvisers, for whom sensitivity and instantaneous flexibility were essential in making good collective music. He can successfully improvise lines which swing and stick close to the beat, but he can also play against meter, as though ignoring the beat and resisting swing. In this way, what Cherry does rhythmically is analogous to what he does harmonically. Musicians term the conventional playing as "inside" and the other approach as playing "outside." Because many modern musicians are comfortable playing only in one of the two ways, it is notable that Cherry can play in both.

Since the mid-1960s, Don Cherry has spent considerable time in Europe and has devoted much of his recording to music which is not closely related to the jazz tradition. This is a body of music that is frequently dubbed "Third World Music," partly because it comes from nations which are neither in the European-American nor the Soviet groups of countries, but are in a third group or "third world" of countries. Cherry's interests have led him to compose and perform extensively in groups using such instruments as the tambura, sitar, finger

[10] Contemporary S 7551
[11] Atlantic SD 1327
[12] RCA 2612

cymbals, conch horn, African finger piano, gong, etc. Cherry learned to play flute, bamboo flute, and assorted percussion instruments at this time. The music makes much use of drones and extensively repeated accompaniment figures. Some pieces are based entirely on chants in which the same few notes are played over and over again. For the jazz listener, there is often little in this music which truly distinguishes it from its non-jazz sources. Although there are genuine differences, the methods Cherry has adopted often bear less resemblance to jazz than to the music of non-Western cultures.[13]

CECIL TAYLOR Cecil Taylor is a pianist, composer, and bandleader who developed a unique and specialized style of modern jazz during the late 1950s and early 60s. His style is not simply different, innovative, or unconventional; it is, rather, a major alternative to the mainstream of modern jazz styles.

Taylor does not play with modern jazz swing feeling, and he emphasizes musical textures rather than musical lines. Although quite syncopated, his rhythms tend to be played ever so slightly ahead or on top of the beat and lack the lilt and buoyancy of conventional jazz rhythmic style. As jazz scholar Harvey Pekar has noted, Taylor does not try to swing. His music is too tense to swing.

Taylor's notes often seem to be generated in layered groups, designed to create textures of sound rather than singable phrases. The textures are rich in internal movement; they seem to shimmer and explode. In fact, much of Taylor's music is very percussive and quite violent. There is little serenity. Many of his performances seem to draw on a continuous source of high energy; they maintain a feverish intensity which seems to never let up. (Listen to "Enter Evening" in SCCJ.)

During the late 1950s, Taylor based his improvisations on tunes and chord changes and employed conventional hard bop bassists and drummers (*In Transition*).[14] Then, during the 1960s, he began playing with neither preset chord progressions nor constant tempo, and frequently he did not use a bassist. He played free of the harmonic restrictions imposed by preset chord changes. Brief portions of some Taylor improvisations are genuinely atonal. This is unusual in jazz, and in Taylor's work as well, because even the most adventuresome, freeform improvisations are usually organized around tone centers, keys, modes, or shifting tone centers. But Taylor followed only his inspiration, thus producing harmonies which were truly spur-of-the-moment (*Silent Tongues*).[15]

When Taylor plays horn-like lines, they sound unlike any other

13 *Eternal Now* Antilles 7034
14 Blue Note LA 458 H2
15 Arista 1005

style in jazz. They may have some hint of Thelonious Monk or Duke Ellington, but actually seem more like twentieth-century composers Stockhausen, Ives, and Berio. Taylor's style is orchestral rather than horn-like. Taylor's comping, even in conventional jazz settings, is jagged and dense, and does not provide the springboard for soloists that hard bop comping usually does. When Taylor plays at the same time as the soloist in his group, his work is more like a separate and contrasting activity, which increases the density of the group sound because it does not parallel the soloist.

Some of Taylor's performances begin with a theme loosely stated by horns and accompanied by his orchestral piano improvising. Then a collective improvisation begins, in which nearly everyone participates. The emphasis is on creating textures. The style is not melodic in the pop tune sense, the swing era sense, or the bop sense. Some textures change gradually, others abruptly. Occasionally a preorganized ensemble portion erupts. Usually the group creates a whirlpool of sound and maintains a frantic pace.[16]

FREE DRUMMERS

Cecil Taylor employed several imaginative drummers, including **Sunny Murray** (b. 1937) and **Andrew Cyrille** (b. 1939), who developed a style which did not rely on steady ride rhythms, high-hat closings, and bass drum patterns. Though much of their work did imply tempo, the rhythms they invented only sporadically stated it. The drummer's four limbs in this "free drumming" style served a function similar to that which was assumed by bop drummers for the left hand on snare drum (see page 18 for further explanation). Instead of "chattering" just with the left hand on snare drum while the right hand stated a consistent timekeeping rhythm and the high hat snapped shut on the second and fourth beats, the "chattering" came from the entire drum set, all four limbs being devoted to generating an undercurrent of activity that popped and crackled with unending energy. By comparison with bop and swing era methods of rhythm section drumming, this style produced unpredictable sound patterns and great varieties of color and shading. This represents a complete departure from the marching band and dance band tradition of jazz drumming. It is closer to an orchestral concept of percussion because it emphasizes color and shading instead of timekeeping. (Listen to Murray's playing with Cecil Taylor on the 1962 recording of "Trance"[17] or on the 1964 Albert Ayler album *Spiritual Unity*. Or listen to later examples of a similar style in

[16] Taylor's records go in and out of print so fast that it is almost futile to recommend anything to readers who might not see this book until years after it goes to press. However, these albums were still in print during 1984: *Looking Ahead* Contemporary 7562 (a quartet session) and *Fly, Fly, Fly* Pausa 7108 (unaccompanied solo piano). Also see footnote 17.

[17] *Live at the Cafe Monmartre* Fantasy 86014

the drumming of Barry Altschul on "Q & A" and "Interception" on Dave Holland's 1972 album *Conference of the Birds*[18] or on "Thanatos" and "Vendana" in Chick Corea's 1971 album *A.R.C.*[19])

FREE BASSISTS   **Charlie Haden** (b. 1937) is the bassist who was most prominently associated with Ornette Coleman during the 1950s and 60s. He has also received wide exposure as a member of the Keith Jarrett Quartet during the 1970s, a band which draws much from the Coleman style. Though usually classed with free jazz, Haden's playing is firmly tied to the movement of harmonies which are fundamental to nonfree styles. In fact, his work is usually more bound to jazz traditions than the work of those he accompanies. One of his greatest contributions was to translate what free hornmen were doing into a more conventional jazz time feeling. This helped unify the group sound by anchoring creations of the hornmen which were frequently without feeling of formal meter. This also brought swing feeling to many musical ideas that probably would not have swung by themselves. (Listen to Haden on Coleman's "Congeniality" and "Lonely Woman" in SCCJ.)

Haden's accompaniment lines move with unerring logic, no matter how quickly directions change in the solo lines. Haden manages to pick up direction that momentarily occurs in solo lines and instantaneously align himself with it. This is a bond of skill and intuition he shares with the playing of fellow bassists Dave Holland (b. 1946) in Sam Rivers's groups and Malachi Favors (b. 1937) in the Art Ensemble of Chicago. All three bassists represent the strongest connection with conventional jazz that their respective groups have. They are also distinguished by a higher level of formally accepted instrumental facility than their hornplaying colleagues display. Haden, Holland, and Favors use very full and warm tones. Their sounds are clean and firm instead of favoring the rough hewn, explosive quality used by the hornmen they accompany. Haden makes the richness of his tone an element in his vocabulary of musical devices. He attaches more importance to single tones and the ways they can be manipulated than became the fashion with most bassists during the 1960s and 70s. He is concerned more with sound than speed and is not interested in improvising bass solos in the style of hornmen. Each note reflects intense deliberation. Haden contrasts with most of his contemporaries in that he is not concerned with intricacy. He is concerned with simplicity.

Dave Holland is known for music he played with such chord progression-based musicians as Miles Davis and Chick Corea as well as being known for his free playing. He has a sweeping conception, an imagination which rivals Scott La Faro's, and a swinging timekeeping

[18] ECM 1027
[19] ECM 1009

TABLE 13.2. Some of the Many Musicians Who Have Improvised Without Preset Chord Progressions

Saxophonists	Drummers Associated with Free Jazz
Ornette Coleman	Milford Graves
Eric Dolphy	Sunny Murray
Albert Ayler	Andrew Cyrille
Archie Shepp	Rashied Ali
Bill Smith	Beaver Harris
Henry Threadgill	Barry Altschul
Sam Rivers	Charles Moffett
David Murray	Don Moye
Oliver Lake	Steve McCall
Anthony Braxton	Dennis Charles
Roscoe Mitchell	Ed Blackwell
Joseph Jarman	Billy Higgins
John Coltrane	Paul Motian
Dewey Redman	
John Gilmore	**Pianists**
Danny Davis	Lennie Tristano
Marshall Allen	Keith Jarrett
Pharoah Sanders	Paul Bley
Sonny Rollins	Sam Rivers
Gato Barbieri	Sun Ra
Marion Brown	Cecil Taylor
John Tchicai	
Jimmy Lyons	**Bassists**
Ken McIntyre	Charlie Haden
Steve Lacy	Dave Holland
Pat Patrick	David Lee
	Malachi Favors
Trumpeters	Fred Hopkins
Bobby Bradford	Jimmy Garrison
Freddie Hubbard	Scott LaFaro
Don Cherry	Charlie Mingus
Don Ayler	Buell Neidlinger
Lester Bowie	Bob Cranshaw
Bill Dixon	Henry Grimes
Dewey Johnson	David Izenzon
Eddie Gale Stevens	
Ted Curson	

foundation. Holland's playing exudes strength and confidence. His tone glows with a unique color and the vibrato he gives to many long tones. Naturalness is a pervasive feeling in his sound. He can take racing tempos and still swing and sound pretty. Ballads are a joy for his approach. In addition to being present in many ground-breaking recordings of Miles Davis and Chick Corea, Holland was also leader on an important record session that has been associated with free jazz: *Conference of the Birds.* His work with numerous Sam Rivers groups parallels the work Haden did with Ornette Coleman and Keith Jarrett, however Holland has more speed and agility and uses those capabilities in ways that are not part of Haden's orientation. Holland can play horn-like bass solos in the bop manner as well as generate action-filled textures for use as accompaniment in free jazz contexts.

Popular Appeal Free jazz ranks as one of the least popular jazz styles in history. During its earliest years, free jazz was not wanted by jazz clubs, few record companies showed any interest in recording it, and twenty years of free jazz has done little to affect this situation. Most of the pivotal recordings by Don Cherry, Albert Ayler, and Cecil Taylor are no longer in print, and many have not even sold well enough to absorb production costs. Not much modern jazz is played on the radio, but the situation is especially unfortunate for free jazz. Some major cities never heard more than a few free jazz recordings during the entire decade of the 1960s. Although musicians usually blame their fate on a lack of promotion, several other styles of modern jazz had managed to sell without much promotion. This suggests that even if free jazz had been promoted, its popularity would still have been limited. The problem is that most listeners found free jazz difficult to follow and considered it chaotic and nerve wracking. The particular brand of free jazz is irrelevant. Lennie Tristano's pioneering free recordings of 1949 had been held back by his record company and were not released until several years later because the company did not like them. Even Jimmy Giuffre's relatively gentle, free jazz recordings remained in print only briefly. So, ironically, this period of great innovation was also a period of low exposure.

CHAPTER SUMMARY

1) Free jazz is a style in which improvisations do not adhere to preset chord progressions and such divisions as bridges, turnarounds, and fixed chorus lengths.
2) Some free jazz also dispenses with preset melody and steady timekeeping.

3) Free jazz has a reputation for wider variation in pitch and tone quality than bop and cool styles used.

4) Some free jazz involves lengthy collective improvisations that are loud and frenzied.

5) Alto saxophonist Ornette Coleman is the most influential free jazz musician, having begun recording during the late 1950s.

6) Coleman's saxophone style and composing were as influential as his departure from preset chord changes.

7) Pianist Cecil Taylor is also influential in free jazz and is known for improvising dense textures and much turbulence.

8) The leading bassists in free jazz are Charlie Haden and Dave Holland, Haden having been a long-time member of both Ornette Coleman's and Keith Jarrett's groups.

9) Albert Ayler created a unique and otherworldly tenor saxophone sound, featuring high-register playing and a rapid vibrato.

10) Trumpeter Don Cherry was Ornette Coleman's sideman for the late 1950s and early 1960s, one of the most original improvisers to appear since bop.

11) Since the mid-1960s, Cherry has explored the music of India, Turkey, South America, and Africa, helping launch a series of groups performing Third World Music.

12) Free jazz drummers such as Sunny Murray and Andrew Cyrille have perfected approaches which depart from marching band and dance band tradition by simply generating an ever-changing undercurrent of activity instead of using standard timekeeping patterns.

chapter 14
CHARLES MINGUS

Charles Mingus (1922–1979) is historically significant as

1) one of the first virtuoso bass soloists to appear after Jimmy Blanton,
2) a bandleader who employed unorthodox techniques and all-star personnels,
3) a prolific composer-arranger who
   a) created unique blends of premodern and modern jazz traditions, ranging from Jelly Roll Morton and Duke Ellington to free jazz,
   b) drew from such diverse sources as Negro gospel music, Mexican folk music, and twentieth-century European concert music,
   c) wrote distinctive melodies.

Mingus did not become widely known until the late 1950s, but he had been making highly creative recordings under his own name since the mid-1940s. By the late 1950s, when his work began to be issued by major record companies, he had already recorded with such modern giants as Miles Davis, Charlie Parker, and Dizzy Gillespie.

As a bassist, Mingus stands out historically for several reasons. First is the timing of his career, and second is the quality of his solos. He began by memorizing Blanton solos from Ellington records and then became one of the first bassists to record horn-like solos in a technically assured manner after Blanton's pioneering records. The earliest Mingus solos are especially significant because they are among the first on

Charles Mingus, bassist-bandleader-composer, second only to Duke Ellington in achieving colorful integration of composition and improvisation. Pictured here at age 50. (*Courtesy of Bill Smith and* CODA)

record to go beyond Blanton and incorporate bop. And it is not just the historical position occupied by these solos that is notable, it is also their quality. Mingus extracted a large, percussive sound from his bass, and his solos exude strength and sureness. The Mingus improvisations were developed in a compositionally sensible way that was forceful and wasted very few notes.[1]

Though one of the more adventuresome string bass soloists in modern jazz, Charles Mingus is best known as a composer and bandleader. This chapter is devoted to music which is separate from the mainstream of modern jazz. For the 1950s, 60s, and 70s, this music could be

---

[1] The earliest examples of this that are generally available are in the 1947 "Mingus Fingers," a composition by Mingus in which he solos with the Lionel Hampton big band (*The Best of Lionel Hampton* MCA 2-4075).

identified by pronouncing just one word, Mingus. The jazz mainstream during this period included the groups and sidemen of Art Blakey, Horace Silver, Miles Davis, and John Coltrane. Though there is some overlap in personnel and style, Mingus created a whole stream of approaches apart from that mainstream. Like Ellington, he represents an idiom which, though rooted in idioms which span large periods, is uniquely his own. His music is described here because it represents a variety of original sounds widely respected by musicians and because it has included the work of many exceptionally creative sidemen. Whether his music influenced other bandleaders or composers is not our chief interest in this chapter.

Mingus has written more than one hundred and fifty pieces, many of which have been re-arranged and recorded several times. The Mingus career has explored styles as diverse as:

1) program music ("Pithecanthropus Erectus,"[2] the story of man)
2) funky, bluesy, gospel-oriented music, with shouting and hand clapping ("Better Git It in Your Soul")[3]
3) Third Stream music ("Revelations")[4]
4) hard bop (recordings with pianist Don Pullen and tenor saxophonist George Adams)[5]
5) jam sessions (Massey Hall concert with Charlie Parker, Dizzy Gillespie, Bud Powell, and Max Roach)[6]
6) free jazz (portions of "What Love")[7]
7) music for film ("Shadows")

Mingus has employed diverse instrumentations:

1) his own solo piano (*Mingus Plays Piano*)[8]
2) jazz quintets of trumpet, tenor saxophone, piano, bass and drums (*Mingus Moves*)[5]
3) pianoless quartet (with Dannie Richmond, Dolphy, and Curson)[7]

---

[2] Atlantic 1237
[3] Columbia CG 30628
[4] *Modern Jazz Concert* Columbia WL 127. This has been out-of-print for ages, and when you look for it among rare records, do not look under "Mingus," look under "Anthologies and Combinations." Reissued as *Jazz Compositions* Columbia PC 37012.
[5] *Mingus Moves* Atlantic 1653
[6] Prestige 24024
[7] *Charles Mingus Presents Charles Mingus* Jazzman 5048
[8] MCA 29067 (Impulse A60)

4) five trumpets, four trombones, tuba, cello, oboe, flute, six saxophones, piano, bass, and three drummers ("Half-Mast Inhibition" and "Bemoanable Lady")[9]

5) two trumpets, trombone, French horn, flute, bassoon, two saxophones, harp, piano, guitar, vibraharp, two basses, and drums ("Revelations").[4]

Throughout his career, Mingus displayed the influence of Ellington. The methods of Ellington are obvious in one of the earliest Mingus recordings, "Bedspread," made in 1946 as a 78 r.p.m. single for a company called Four Star. Even the style of improvisations on "Bedspread" shows a similarity to the Ellington approaches. Mingus has composed and recorded pieces dedicated to Ellington, such as "Duke's Choice" and "An Open Letter to Duke." Ellington-like use of plunger-muted brass playing has appeared in Mingus works. The Johnny Hodges alto saxophone style has, at the request of Mingus, been incorporated into the playing of such otherwise non-Hodges-styled saxophonists as Charlie Mariano, Jackie McLean, and John Handy. Mingus has also recorded several Ellington compositions.

During the 1940s, Mingus was attracted to some of the same approaches that the big bands of Boyd Raeburn and Stan Kenton were exploring. For instance, the 1947 Mingus recording "Inspiration" features weighty orchestration, prominent baritone saxophone sound and a sustained sonority of low brass sounds. Clarinet and flute sounds climb out of the ensemble momentarily as they might in a piece by Stravinsky or Bartok. (Unfortunately, this piece, like "Bedspread," is almost totally unknown to jazz fans. It appeared only as a 78 r.p.m. single for the Rex label.) In 1949, Mingus recorded his "Story of Love" (another single for another small company, Fentone). The piece is a loud big band work that is bursting with activity and suggestions of Latin American and bop rhythms. It includes the Kenton trademark of high-register trombone playing. This recording is especially notable for a brief bass solo by Mingus, performed in the Blanton style of eighth notes and eighth-note triplets.

Mingus is far better known for his combo recordings than for his big band material. The Mingus combo approaches are distinguished because they seldom resemble the jam session format adopted in most modern jazz concerts and recording sessions. Instead of being restricted to only a unison theme statement, a string of improvised solos with improvised accompaniments, and another theme statement, the average Mingus rendition illustrates the capacity which composition and preset accompaniments have to relieve the listener from extended concentration. Also to Mingus's credit is that, despite the amount of

---

[9] *Pre-Bird* Mercury EXPR 1015

planning in his performances, a looseness prevails, and a feeling of naturalness is conveyed by his music. In many performances, Mingus rejected conventional bop accompaniment patterns in favor of preset statements which broke the flow of music by introducing stops and changes of style in mid-performance. Portions of some solos were accompanied by nothing more than hand clapping and shouting. Drumming might use a waltz pattern one moment and a conventional jazz pattern the next moment. Passages might contain many stop-time solo breaks. The tempo might be slow one moment and doubled the next. In fact, Mingus is one of the few bandleaders in jazz history to explore the gradual speeding and slowing of tempo. These procedures are similar to those used by Jelly Roll Morton and Duke Ellington. And, like the finished products of Morton and Ellington, the Mingus material rarely sounded anonymous or mistakable for an ordinary recording session run in a more conventional fashion.

The first album Mingus made for Columbia, *Mingus Ah Um* (later reissued as *Better Git It in Your Soul*), contains examples of the varied accompaniment devices Mingus used. The version of "Fables of Faubus" in this collection switches accompanying style several times. It goes beyond the more subtle alterations in comping, bass lines, and drum fills which occur routinely in most modern jazz combo performances. "Bird Calls" from the same album shows an integration of collective improvisation with more structured approaches. It is so well managed that, as with his 1957 "Ysabel's Table Dance" from the *Tia Juana Moods*[10] album, listeners are often unable to determine what elements are improvised and what elements are composed.

Mingus's unorthodox approaches to combo performance had several significant impacts. They forced improvisers away from producing purely bop-styled solos in an uninterrupted stream. They gave improvisers a varied background which elicited more varied solos than conventional settings would have elicited. They gave listeners brief, reassuring chunks of music in the form of figures that became familiar because they regularly recurred during the piece. This allowed listeners to latch onto something familiar amidst the flow of freshly improvised solos. This is an important observation because, in most bop performances, familiar material was offered only at the beginning and the end of a piece. The Mingus technique of placing recurring devices *within* the piece offered listeners something that they could not ordinarily expect from other kinds of modern jazz (though this approach later became associated with bands led by former Mingus sidemen Thad Jones and Ted Curson).

To achieve a successful integration of composed and improvised music, Mingus obtained a high degree of artistic cooperation from his

[10] RCA APL1 0939

musicians. As a bandleader and arranger, Mingus had a sense of what players to cast in what roles and how to pry out maximum distinctiveness in a performance. He colorfully mixed snips of improvisations with his prewritten ensemble sounds to weave unusual textures. Then, instead of thrusting their favorite phrases unthinkingly onto his music, the players were forced to appreciate his musical wishes and give those wishes higher priority than they gave their own. Players had to interpret his demands as well as contribute original twists of their own. Performance was often indistinct from rehearsal. The music amounted to a workshop endeavor in that Mingus gave his musicians sketchily written parts, dictated parts to them by playing phrases on the piano or the bass, and described in words the conceptions which he wanted converted to music. (Listen to "Hora Decubitus" in SCCJ.)

From 1960 until 1964, flutist-clarinetist-saxophonist **Eric Dolphy** (1928–1964) recorded with Mingus. He had previously played with the Chico Hamilton quintet and others. In 1961 and 1962, Dolphy toured and recorded with John Coltrane. The arrangements for Coltrane's *Africa/Brass* album[11] were written by Dolphy. Solos on Coltrane's "India" (*Impressions*)[12] and "Spiritual" (*"Live" at the Village Vanguard*)[13] are by Dolphy. Coltrane's *Olé* album[14] uses Dolphy, but lists him as "George Lane" on the album jacket. Before his death in 1964 he also made a number of albums himself, but some of his best work was documented in Mingus recordings.

Modern jazz has known countless virtuoso reedmen: alto saxophonists Charlie Parker, Sonny Stitt, Lee Konitz, Cannonball Adderley; tenor saxophonists Sonny Rollins, John Coltrane, Albert Ayler, and others. But few could be called virtuoso on three different instruments: flute, alto saxophone, and bass clarinet. Eric Dolphy mastered the complete range of every instrument he played, and then he capitalized on almost every sound it could produce. He even studied bird calls and mimicked them in his solos. Slides and smears connected Dolphy's notes. He sounded like a frantic version of Johnny Hodges—bouncing and twittering exuberantly, animal cries interspersed with bop licks.

Dolphy's 1958–59 work with Chico Hamilton's group was rooted in bop phrasing and swing feeling. Some of his alto saxophone playing of that period sounds like Charlie Parker and Cannonball Adderley. His later work, however, is characterized by explosive torrents of notes, bearing neither conventional melodic development nor bop phrasing. Though much of his work had quite irregular contours, he could play with swing era lushness, approximating the romantic feeling projected by alto saxophonists Benny Carter and Johnny Hodges. Dolphy's un-

[11] MCA 29007
[12] MCA 29014
[13] MCA 29009
[14] Atlantic 1373

accompanied alto saxophone solo on "Tenderly" (*Far Cry*)[15] is reminiscent of Benny Carter. The long duet between flute and bowed bass on "You Don't Know What Love Is" (*Last Date*)[16] is so richly tonal, it is as though Dolphy savors the vibrations of each note before proceeding to the next.

In the 1960 pianoless quartet of Mingus, Dolphy, trumpeter Ted Curson, and drummer Dannie Richmond, an exceptional level of empathy existed between Mingus and Dolphy. There is an extended dialog between the two of them on "What Love" which is filled with humor and flexible interaction, free jazz at its best.[17] The conversation between Mingus's pizzicato bass and Dolphy's bass clarinet is so human that it almost makes you think words are being exchanged. It is very coherent and skillful—without the haphazardness which a dependence on luck brings to much free jazz.

An invaluable asset to many of Mingus's groups was drummer **Dannie Richmond** (b. 1935). He was employed by Mingus more frequently than any other drummer. Richmond is one of the most sensitive and tasteful of all post-bop drummers, supplying the varied rhythms and textures demanded by Mingus's unusual music. A marvelously loose and imaginative drummer, his drums provide a crisp, happy sound.

During 1954, 55, and 56, Mingus collaborated with trumpeter **Thad Jones.** Together, they made several albums, some with Mingus as leader and some with Jones.[18] Mingus and other musicians consider Jones's creative ability to be at the genius level. If you listen to his work with Mingus, you will probably agree that few trumpeters can match his melodic ingenuity, unpredictability, and command of the instrument. He even rivals Dizzy Gillespie, one of his influences. Jones is often listed along with Miles Davis, Clifford Brown, Art Farmer, and Freddie Hubbard as the best post-Gillespie trumpeter. He went on to co-lead the Thad Jones–Mel Lewis big band, thus nurturing an interest kindled by playing in Count Basie's big band from 1954 until 1963. Interestingly, a few key members of the Jones–Lewis band were also with Mingus: pianist Roland Hanna, saxophonist Jerome Richardson, baritone saxophonist Pepper Adams, and trombonist Jimmy Knepper.

During 1961 and again in 1974, saxophonist **Roland Kirk** (1936–1977) recorded with Mingus. Kirk led several popular combos with strong, but relatively unknown sidemen. He was a very outgoing player, quite aware of showmanship and maintaining excitement. Besides flute, clarinet, and all the saxophones (sometimes two or three at

[15] Prestige 8270, also 7747; and it comprises half of *Magic* Prestige 24053.
[16] Mercury EXPR 1017
[17] See footnote 7.
[18] *Charlie Mingus* Archive of Folk and Jazz FS 235

a time!), Kirk played nose flute, siren, and numerous unusual wind and percussion instruments. His music was as varied as that of Mingus: running from simple pop tunes and funky, gospelish twelve-bar blues to freer forms with techniques similar to these of Coltrane, Dolphy, and Ornette Coleman (*The Best of Rahsaan Roland Kirk*).[19]

[19] Atlantic 1592

CHAPTER SUMMARY

1) Charles Mingus was one of the first modern bass soloists.
2) He was a prolific and versatile composer-arranger who showed the influence of Duke Ellington as well as symphonic music, folk music, and many jazz traditions.
3) Though active as a leader, a composer, and a bassist during the 1940s, Mingus did not receive acclaim until the late 1950s and early 1960s.
4) Like Duke Ellington, Mingus was a master at combining composition and improvisation in his bands.
5) Mingus creatively altered accompaniment patterns during solos, thereby
    a) inspiring original improvisations
    b) supplying listeners with more variety than standard bop approaches offer
    c) devising a distinctive combo style
6) Mingus employed several outstanding, historically significant soloists who improvised in unorthodox manners:
    a) Thad Jones, who remains one of the most original of all modern trumpeters;
    b) Eric Dolphy, who had virtuoso command over the flute, alto saxophone, and bass clarinet, as well as inventing a unique style;
    c) Roland Kirk, who played unusual woodwind instruments, sometimes blowing two and three at the same time.

chapter 15

BILL EVANS, HERBIE HANCOCK, CHICK COREA, & KEITH JARRETT

The most influential jazz pianist to emerge after Bud Powell is Bill Evans, and the combined influence of Powell and Evans is apparent in three of the most widely imitated pianists to follow Evans: Herbie Hancock, Chick Corea, and Keith Jarrett. Each of these players toured and recorded with Miles Davis, and each became an important composer and bandleader in his own right. Hancock, Corea, and Jarrett enjoyed large popular followings and accumulated record sales and concert receipts that far outdistanced the recognition accorded to Powell and Evans. This chapter is devoted to the piano styles of Evans, Hancock, Corea, and Jarrett, their respective group styles, and the innovations in rhythm section playing that Evans pioneered.

BILL EVANS   Bill Evans (1929–1980) played with Miles Davis for only about nine months during 1958 and 1959, but that tenure and his contributions to the classic Davis album *Kind of Blue* brought his style the recognition of jazz musicians and fans.

By May of 1958, when he first recorded with Davis ("Stella by Starlight," "Put Your Little Foot Out," "On Green Dolphin Street," available on *Basic Miles*),[1] Evans had already impressed the jazz community with his "All About Rosie" solo (*Modern Jazz Concert*,[2] George Russell's work for a 1957 Brandeis University commission) and made a 1956 trio record with bassist Teddy Kotick and drummer

---

[1] Columbia PC 32025

[2] Columbia WL 127. This has been out-of-print for ages, and if you look for it in rare record lists, do not look under "Bill Evans," look under "Anthologies and Combinations." Reissued as *Jazz Compositions* Columbia PC 37012.

Paul Motian (*New Jazz Conceptions*).[3] Before making *Kind of Blue*, he had recorded another trio LP, *Everybody Digs Bill Evans*,[4] which, as late as the mid-1970s, he still considered one of his very best recordings. (One of the selections on that album, "Peace Piece," is the all-time favorite Evans performance for many listeners.)

Kind of Blue and *Everybody Digs Bill Evans* are classic examples of his style. His tone and conception were delicate without being fragile. He strikes single tones and lets them ring, as though to savor each vibration before proceeding to the next. The effect is harp-like. Listen to his work on "Blue in Green" (*Kind of Blue*); "Young and Foolish" (*Everybody Digs*); second selection on *Kind of Blue*, second side; "Peace Piece"; and "What Is There to Say" (*Everybody Digs*). That way of playing was later picked up by pianists Herbie Hancock and Chick Corea (as in Hancock's "Pee Wee" solo on the 1967 Miles Davis *Sorcerer*[5] and Corea's playing on his own *Piano Improvisations Vol I.*)[6] Keith Jarrett displays this manner in his "Rainbow" on the *Byablue*[7] album, his *Staircase*[8] album and on "Ellen David" in Charlie Haden's *Closeness*[9] album.

Evans's influence has been evident at various stages in the careers of many modern pianists (see Table 15.1). Chick Corea learned Evans solos while developing his own style. Corea's "Song for Lee Lee" (*Piano Improvisations Vol. II*) bears a distinct resemblance to "Peace Piece." There is also much Evans-like playing in Corea's work on the Stan Getz LP *Sweet Rain*.[10] Evans's influence on Herbie Hancock was very strong, as is apparent on "Pee Wee" (*Sorcerer*), "My Funny Valentine" (*My Funny Valentine*),[11] and "He Who Lives in Fear"

TABLE 15.1. A Few of the Many Pianists Influenced by Bill Evans

Herbie Hancock	Warren Bernhardt
Chick Corea	Denny Zeitlin
Keith Jarrett	Clare Fischer
Wynton Kelly	Steve Kuhn
Paul Bley	Don Friedman
Jan Hammer	Cees Slinger

[3] *Conception* Milestone M 47063
[4] *Peace Piece and Other Pieces* Milestone 47024
[5] Columbia PC 9532, listed under "Miles Davis," not Herbie Hancock
[6] ECM 1014
[7] MCA 29047
[8] ECM 1090
[9] A & M Horizon SP 710
[10] Verve 2510
[11] Columbia PC 9106, listed under "Miles Davis," not Herbie Hancock

(*The Prisoner*). Obvious Evans characteristics are employed by Wynton Kelly on "Drad Dog" (*Someday My Prince Will Come*)[12] and by Keith Jarrett on "Pretty Ballad" (*Somewhere Before*). Evans's influence on four successive Davis pianists (Wynton Kelly, Herbie Hancock, Chick Corea, and Keith Jarrett) is interesting because the history of the modern jazz rhythm sections is well documented by Davis recordings and provides strong evidence for the significance of Evans.

Prior to 1959, Evans displayed considerable dexterity, and his style included elements from several sources. His long, fast, smoothly contoured eighth-note lines were reminiscent of alto saxophonist Lee Konitz, one of his early favorites. Because Konitz derived his style from pianist Lennie Tristano, the Evans approach exhibits recognizable Tristano influence. Evans's piano solos also contain elements borrowed from bop pianist Bud Powell, another Evans favorite. Occasionally, Evans used some bluesy figures which might be traced to pianist-composer Horace Silver, a far-reaching force during the 1950s.

After *Kind of Blue*, Evans made the first of four LPs with bassist Scott LaFaro. Evans developed a very personal style during that time. He began ridding himself of typical bop clichés and common jazz piano devices. His left hand gained importance and was soon sustaining chords in almost every measure instead of merely punctuating right-hand lines. He worked out a style of voicing his chorded lines in terms of modes and used tight clusters of notes.

Most of Evans's lines were composed of smoothly connected notes. Rarely after 1959 did he play lines with disconnected or staccato notes. He tended instead to favor a legato style. The melodies he improvised were frequently chorded, note for note, in the locked-hands style.

Evans often chose pretty melodies which were economical in their construction yet provided interesting chord progressions for the improviser. His best-known composition, "Waltz for Debby," embodies the essence of his style. He liked waltzes, an unusual preference for a jazz musician. Among the waltzes to which he gave his tender treatment were "Someday My Prince Will Come" (recorded two years before the Miles Davis version), "Alice in Wonderland," "Tenderly," "Skating in Central Park," and "I'm All Smiles." (An attraction to pretty waltzes later appeared in Chick Corea, who wrote "Windows," "Desert Air," "Song of the Wind," and who honored Evans by writing "Waltz for Bill Evans.")

Rhythm Section Innovations   During 1960 and 1961, **Scott LaFaro,** Evans's bassist, effectively did for modern jazz bass styles what Jimmy Blanton had done for swing era bass playing: he reminded us that, in the hands of a virtuoso, the bass can contribute exciting solo lines and ensemble interplay that provide

12 Columbia PC 8456, listed under "Miles Davis," not Wynton Kelly

a feeling of grace and freedom for the underpinnings of a group sound. LaFaro is also influential for having pioneered the use of all fingers to pluck the bass strings in the manner of a classical guitarist. Earlier bassists had primarily employed only one or two fingers. LaFaro's new technique lent added speed and continuity to his lines.

The idea of pianists and bassists engaging in active musical conversation had been explored by Duke Ellington and Jimmy Blanton in their 1940 duets, "Mr. J.B. Blues" and "Pitter Panther Patter." Evans and LaFaro refined this idea, together with drummer Paul Motian. LaFaro sometimes walked and soloed, but more often he vigorously interacted with piano and drums. While Evans was playing melody or improvising, LaFaro contributed a great diversity of musical ideas. He would throw in melodic figures, mimic Evans or answer Evans, and underscore the figures which Evans and Motian played. In addition, LaFaro often fed ideas to Evans. LaFaro was not merely a timekeeper or even a timekeeper capable, on occasion, of impressive solos. He was a melodic player at least as important to the Evans trio as a hornman was to the standard jazz quintet.

The use of silence, which is essential to the economical Evans style, made LaFaro's contributions possible. In the context of a Bud Powell-style trio, where very little piano silence ever occurs, the amount of melodic and rhythmic interaction between bassist and pianist is negligible. The bassist must focus on explicitly stating the beats, and he has no option for loose, flexible interaction with the pianist. In this way, the Evans piano style provided the perfect context for refinement of LaFaro's highly interactive style because it allowed the bass sound to enter the forefront and engage in sympathetic interactions, a context not provided by pianists who fill up all the spaces with long, uninterrupted lines. (Listen to the Evans-LaFaro recordings back to back with work by the trios of Art Tatum, Bud Powell, Oscar Peterson, or Ramsey Lewis.) Note that this was the way Evans approached the use of LaFaro's most gifted successors, Eddie Gomez and Marc Johnson, and that it allowed them to attain far greater flexibility and creativity than they were allowed to attain working for most other bandleaders.

Some Evans trio passages, instead of treating all four beats of each measure, tend to concentrate on the first and third ("All of You," *The Village Vanguard Sessions*).[13] LaFaro's playing often seemed to decorate the first and third beats and let the second and fourth beats pass. A rhythm section which pronounces primarily the first and third beats is playing what is called a two-beat style. Even though four beats are present, only two are emphasized; musicians would say the music is "in two." What LaFaro frequently did is called a "decorative two feel."

[13] Milestone 47002

When he died in 1961 at the age of 25, LaFaro had been an active influence for less than three years. In this short period of time he set the pace for a whole school of modern jazz bassists characterized by the enormous instrumental facility typical of LaFaro. And like LaFaro, they interacted with pianists and drummers in an imaginative and highly active manner.

Drummer **Paul Motian** contributed an approach of great imagination and discretion. He colored the combo sound and produced accents which complemented the rhythms of LaFaro and Evans. Motian masterfully employed wire brushes to obtain light, crisp sounds from his snare drum and cymbals. He controlled the degree to which his high-hat cymbals opened, so that they would swish and zing, chick and splash. He interacted as sensitively and inventively as any previous drummer in jazz history. His style of interactive coloring in the intimate trio context became a model for drummers playing in similar settings and contributed to the emancipation of the rhythm section.

The post-1959 Bill Evans trios are a great deal more than a piano accompanied by a walking bass and a timekeeping drummer. Instead, there are three constantly shifting parts which sway together. Constant tempo is usually employed but not manifested by explicit statement of each separate beat. The trio members often seem to be carrying on three-way musical conversations in tempo ("Solar," *The Village Vanguard Sessions*). The musical words and phrases are both long and short, fluid and abrupt; they are not necessarily made up of the intricate eighth-note figures typical of bop or the long, smoothly contoured, eighth-note lines typical of Tristano and Konitz. In other words, much rhythmic and melodic variety is present. If the music swings, it is because that is what happened at the moment, not because swinging is the prime goal. Music is the goal. Jazz swing feeling is one of a number of rhythmic possibilities, and it is a means to a musical end rather than being an end in itself.

The most historically significant contributions of the Evans-LaFaro-Motian trio was to loosen the bop formula patterns which had become standard during the 1940s and 50s (walking bass, drummer playing ride rhythms and closing his high-hat cymbals on the second and fourth beats, pianist playing long, eighth-note lines with little interruption, etc.). Though they occasionally played in conventional bop style and they frequently hinted at it, their impact was to help emancipate the piano, bass, and drum roles from traditional conceptions. (A vivid illustration of this influence is provided by listening to the rhythm section style of pre-1963 Miles Davis records such as the 1958 *Milestones* or the 1961 *Miles Davis at Carnegie Hall*, then listening to the Bill Evans 1961 *Village Vanguard Sessions* before listening to the rhythm section on any post-1963 Davis albums, particularly the playing on "All of You" in the 1964 *My Funny Valentine*, or "Circle" in the 1966 *Miles Smiles,* or "Pee Wee" in the 1967 *Sorcerer.* The difference between pre- and post-1963 styles was made by the influence of the 1961 Evans trio conceptions.)[14] The calm thoughtfulness, subtlety, and delicate interaction among the members of the Evans trio provided a solid alternative to the incessantly hard-driving, straight-ahead style of the Oscar Peterson trios or the simple, gospel-like orientation of such groups as The Ramsey Lewis Trio and The Three Sounds.

HERBIE HANCOCK

Herbie Hancock (b. 1940) was with Miles Davis from 1963 to 69 and became the most sought-after band pianist of the 1960s. His work suggests the light, brisk comping of Tommy Flanagan and the chord voicings of Bill Evans. His gentle, even touch resembles George Shearing's. Hancock apparently absorbed several influences while he was developing during the late 1950s and early 60s. Some of his playing has the funky, bluesy figures and the rhythmic bounce which typified Horace Silver and Wynton Kelly. But Bill Evans probably had the greatest influence on Hancock. Evans's harp-like, ringing tones surrounded by silence, his chord voicings, smooth legato lines, and locked-hands style—all of these can be heard in Hancock's playing on the Miles Davis albums *Four and More* and *My Funny Valentine.* And, at times, the Tristano-like approach to constructing lines is also evident in Hancock's work, as on his solos in "The Sorcerer" (*Sorcerer*), "Agitation" (*E.S.P.*), and "Orbits" (*Miles Smiles*). The flexible and intelligent interaction between Hancock, Ron Carter, and Tony Williams on "Pee Wee" (*Sorcerer*)[15] and between Hancock, Buster Williams, and Al Heath on "He Who Lives in Fear" (*The Prisoner*)[16] is reminiscent of the sensitive interactions which typified the 1961 recordings of Bill Evans, Scott LaFaro, and Paul Motian.

Hancock's playing nearly always has a meticulousness and finished quality. His execution is firm and swinging without being violent or insistent. Both his solo work and his accompanying project a politeness and sensitivity. Hancock has shown broad scope and versatility: his style is compatible with several different streams of modern jazz. He has contributed immeasurably to hundreds of records—not only those of the Miles Davis Quintet, but also those of Joe Henderson, Joe Farrell, Freddie Hubbard, Paul Desmond, Milt Jackson, and others.

Hancock was not as innovative as Bill Evans or McCoy Tyner. His special achievement was the creation of a very convincing synthesis of pre-1960 jazz piano styles. Many good pianists, including Larry Willis, George Cables, and others, sounded like Hancock but this may have been that, rather than drawing directly from his style, they drew from

[14] These are all Columbia albums. For catalog numbers see Chapters 12 and 18.
[15] See footnote 14
[16] Blue Note BST 84321

the same sources as he did: Bill Evans, Wynton Kelly, and so forth. What distinguished Hancock was that he created consistently stimulating, swinging, and polished piano improvisations, something that cannot always be said even for the most innovative of his contemporaries.

There is no doubt about Hancock's creativity as a composer and arranger. By the early 1970s, he had written every tune on eight of his own albums, and written or coauthored many of the tunes on seven more of his own. His funky, bluesy piece called "Watermelon Man" became very popular, especially in Mongo Santamaria's version, during the mid-1960s. The big bands of Woody Herman, Si Zentner, and Maynard Ferguson all played their own arrangements of it. Hancock's "The Sorcerer," "Little One," "Riot," and "Madness" were all recorded by the Miles Davis Quintet.

Among the many idioms which Hancock has employed as a composer are:

1) the lush, classical music style of "Suite Revenge" on *Death Wish*;[17]
2) the rock-influenced *Fat Albert Rotunda*;
3) the funky, hard bop approach of *Taking Off*;[18]
4) Gil Evans-like work on *The Prisoner*;
5) writing like that of Sun Ra on *Sextant*[19] and *Crossings*;
6) the style of the 1960s Miles Davis Quintet on *Maiden Voyage*[20] and *Empyrean Isles*;[21]
7) the Sly Stone-influenced style of *Head Hunter*[22] and *Thrust*.[23]

Hancock did much of his creative writing after he left Miles and began leading his own groups. (Hancock had led groups in recording studios before and during his years with Davis, but they were not usually working bands. Most were put together solely for the recordings.) The music produced by Hancock's first post-Davis group capitalized on some of the advances made in the Miles Davis groups of the 1960s. In *The Prisoner*, Hancock wrote lines for trumpeter Johnny Coles, trombonist Garnett Brown, and tenor saxophonist Joe Henderson which had few eighth-note figures or jumpy syncopations and were full of legato passages employing sustained tones. Hancock, bassist Buster Williams, and drummer Al Heath generated considerable

---

[17] Columbia PC 36825
[18] Blue Note 84109
[19] Columbia 32212
[20] Blue Note 84195
[21] Blue Note 84175
[22] Columbia PC 32731
[23] Columbia PC 32965

stimulating accompanying activity in the manner that Hancock, Carter, and Williams had done in the Miles Davis quintet.

Hancock's second band recorded *Mwandishi, Crossings,* and *Sextant,* albums which employed concepts similar to those used on the Davis LPs *Nefertiti, In a Silent Way,* and *Bitches Brew.* The presence of synthesizer, the extensive use of other electronic instruments, and exotic percussion effects also suggest the early 1960s work of Sun Ra. Each of Hancock's group members was responsible for creating a larger assortment of sounds than were traditionally required of most jazz musicians. Eddie Henderson doubled on fluegelhorn and percussion. Julian Priester played tenor trombone, baritone trombone, bass trombone, and percussion. Bennie Maupin played alto flute, soprano saxophone, piccolo, bass clarinet, and percussion. And Hancock often electronically altered the sound of his piano, creating echo and fuzz. The group was rounded out with Buster Williams (bass), Patrick Gleeson (synthesizer), and Billy Hart (drums). Sometimes every member of the band was playing percussion, and there was no instrument which suggested harmonies. Because of the electronically synthesized sounds, the legato lines of sustained tones, and the exotic percussion sounds, Hancock's style on *Sextant, Mwandishi,* and *Crossings* was often referred to as "space music."

Hancock's next band was a quintet with saxophonist Bennie Maupin, bassist Paul Jackson, drummer Harvey Mason, and auxiliary percussionist Bill Summers. The style of this group was much like the funk styles of Sly Stone and Curtis Mayfield. Hancock retained a high level of musicianship, but spent more time constructing funky rhythmic effects, with their repeated piano and bass figures, than he spent inventing long jazz piano solos. The music was tightly organized and hard driving. Syncopated rhythms were laid layer upon layer, and there were colorful, electronically produced sounds and percussion effects. (For more about Hancock's jazz-rock, see pages 340–341. For more about his work with Miles Davis, see pages 301–306.)

CHICK COREA   Chick Corea (b. 1941) followed Herbie Hancock as pianist in the 1968 Miles Davis Quintet. Corea had previously worked with Willie Bobo, Blue Mitchell, Cal Tjader, Herbie Mann, Mongo Santamaria, and Stan Getz. Along with Hancock, Bill Evans, and McCoy Tyner, he became a leading pianist of the 1960s and 70s.

The piano style created by Corea was an interesting blend of McCoy Tyner, Bud Powell, Bill Evans, and others. The mid-1960s recordings he made with Blue Mitchell show the influence of bop piano styles, which he might have absorbed from Powell and Horace Silver. His work with Mann and Tjader points up his use of Evans and Tyner as sources. He favored the voicing in fourths (see Figure 15.1) and flashy

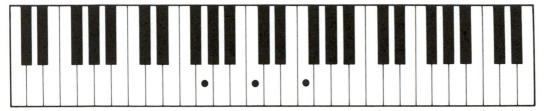

Figure 15.1. Piano keyboard illustration of a chord voiced in fourths.

lines which typify Tyner. His composition "Litha" uses fourths in the melody line, and his left-hand comping on the album *Now He Sings, Now He Sobs*[24] uses fourths. Voicing chords in fourths was especially appropriate for the electric piano. The overtones produced by an electric piano make chords voiced in the manner of bop pianists sound muddy. The open quality of voicing in fourths partly eliminates this problem and, to my ears, the fourth voicings actually sound better on electric than on acoustic piano.

The chord voicings in *Now He Sings, Now He Sobs* are reminiscent of work by the twentieth-century classical composer Paul Hindemith, who also explored the sounds of fourths. Corea may have absorbed ideas for the use of fourths from Horace Silver, also. Prior to 1959, Corea had studied Silver solos and compositions. In fact, he demonstrated a few typical Silver devices in his work on Blue Mitchell's album *The Thing to Do*. (See pages 292, 304–305, and 417–418 for greater coverage of sounds created by fourths.)

Corea also displayed Evans characteristics, having memorized some of Bill Evans's solos while developing his own style. The influence of Evans is most noticeable in Corea's work on the Stan Getz album *The Chick Corea/Bill Evans Sessions*, and in Corea's unaccompanied acoustic piano solos on his *Piano Improvisations Vols. 1 & 2* and *Where Have I Known You Before?*[25] Corea's "Tones for Joan's Bones" and "Windows" reflect the way Evans voices things.

Another prominent source from which he drew was Latin American music. Four of Corea's previous employers, Willie Bobo, Cal Tjader, Herbie Mann, and Mongo Santamaria, were quite fond of Latin American rhythms. Corea's playing, even in otherwise conventional modern jazz contexts, bears a distinctly double-time feeling, and that feeling is a prime characteristic of Latin American music. It is as though each beat is being subdivided over and over. Corea's crisp, percussive attack enhances the Latin feel. (The percussive aspect of

[24] Pacific Jazz LN 10057; also Blue Note LA 395 and Solid State SS 18039
[25] Polydor PD 6509. This is not always listed under "Chick Corea"; look under "Return to Forever."

his style may be related to the fact that he also plays drums.) He is very precise and even in his execution. Corea loves to play swift, multi-noted lines. His comping is bright and very spirited. Corea does not pace his improvisations quite as well as Hancock or Evans, but is, by far, a match for the best hard bop pianists.

Chick Corea's piano style was a strong force during the 1970s. Hundreds of pianists admired his approach. Jan Hammer, Richard Beirach, Jeff Lorber, Andy LaVerne, and Masabumi Kikuchi were among those who exhibited his influence. But, as with Hancock, it is uncertain whether pianists sound like Corea because they have studied his work or because their styles stem from the same sources as his: Evans, Tyner, etc.

In 1968, Corea recorded an album of original compositions and improvisations using bassist Miroslav Vitous and drummer Roy Haynes. This album, *Now He Sings, Now He Sobs*, became a staple in the record collections of modern jazz musicians, and it brought Corea's style under intense scrutiny and wide imitation. (Some musicians learned to play its music note for note.) In 1981, the players on that album regrouped, made another album (*Trio Music*),[26] then began touring during the 1980s.

On and off between 1969 and 1972, Corea led a trio with bassist Dave Holland and drummer Barry Altschul. Free-form improvisation was featured on two of their albums: *The Song of Singing* and *A.R.C.*[27] In some settings, they were joined by saxophonist Anthony Braxton, and with Braxton their group was called Circle. During this time, Corea also appeared on the Miles Davis albums *In A Silent Way*, *Bitches Brew*, *Live at the Fillmore*, and *Black Beauty*,[28] though *Black Beauty* is the only album in which Corea solos at length (and it constitutes some of the best work of his career). This period of Corea's output reflects the influence of pianist Paul Bley, bassist Gary Peacock, and saxophonists John Coltrane, Albert Ayler, and Ornette Coleman. The music also drew from twentieth-century composers John Cage and Karlheinz Stockhausen. Corea's use of the free-form approach resulted not only in the turbulent music found on *A.R.C.* and *The Song of Singing*, but also in the serene pieces he freely improvised within his *Piano Improvisations Vols. I & II*.[29] (All selections there were spontaneously conceived and performed, with the exceptions of "Song for Sally," "Song of the Wind," "Some Time Ago," "Trinkle Tinkle," and "Masqualero.")

After Circle disbanded, Corea formed a new group with bassist

---

[26] ECM 2-1232

[27] ECM 1009

[28] At press time it remained available only as a Japanese import: CBS SONY SOPJ 39–40.

[29] ECM 1014 and 1020

Stanley Clarke, Airto Moreira—a Brazilian drummer who had been with Miles Davis at the same time as Corea—and singer Flora Purim, Airto's wife. Airto had played auxiliary percussion with Davis and Weather Report, but he used a conventional drum set with Corea's new group. The group's sound was light and happy, full of Latin American rhythms and Spanish themes. It was a very energetic band, whose flashy technical feats impressed musician and non-musician alike. The group was called Return to Forever, also the title of their first album. Their second LP was titled *Light as a Feather*.[30] After Corea disbanded the group, he retained the Return to Forever group name. It was with this band that two of Corea's most popular tunes became known: "Spain" and "La Fiesta."

The group Chick Corea carried through the middle 1970s was strongly influenced by rock, often displaying the insistent, machine-like sound of hard rock. In fact, he employed rock-influenced electric guitarists. The first was Bill Connors, then Al Dimeola took his place. Corea retained bassist Stanley Clarke, now playing Fender electric bass guitar more than acoustic string bass. Drummer Lenny White rounded out the group. White's style was a very full, active approach which seemed to blend aspects of the Tony Williams techniques with those of modern rock drummers. Like most of these musicians, he also had played with Miles Davis. Some of the group's material was orchestral, very involved, highly imaginative, slipping back and forth from rock to classical to jazz idioms. White and Dimeola left Corea during the summer of 1976. During 1977, Corea toured with a nine-piece band which, in addition to himself and bassist Stanley Clarke, included a vocalist-pianist, a drummer, two trumpeters, two trombonists, and saxophonist-flutist Joe Farrell. The Return to Forever group name was retained. Thereafter, Corea appeared in a wide assortment of contexts. Al Dimeola, Stanley Clarke, and Lenny White went on to lead groups of their own. Then, in 1983, the Corea-Dimeola-Clarke-White personnel regrouped for a tour.

Corea was an influential composer during the 1960s and 1970s. His style was quickly absorbed by many others. His "Windows" and "Crystal Silence" became jazz standards. Like much of Horace Silver's work, many of Corea's compositions are not simply tunes which only furnish a set of chord changes for improvisation. Some are pieces with assorted sections, each having a distinctive rhythmic and tonal flavor. Several Corea works ordinarily considered "tunes" are actually melodies and arrangements all rolled into a single package. (Listen to "Windows," "Spain," or "Litha."[31]) Within a few tunes, not only do keys and

---

[30] Polydor 5525. This is not always listed under "Chick Corea"; it is often listed under "Return to Forever."

[31] "Windows" and "Litha" are in Stan Getz's *Corea/Evans* Verve 2510. "Spain" is in Return to Forever's *Light as a Feather* Polydor 5525.

melodies change, but meter changes, also. (His "Litha" alternates between meter of six and meter of four.) Also like Silver, Corea writes pieces that make good use of preset bass lines, Latin American-flavored lines in particular. For example, the bass lines that accompany his "Senōr Mouse"[32] are central to the composition. Without them, the melody would not convey the flavor that it does. In fact, a feature of many Corea pieces is bass doubling the melody that is carried by piano and horn parts, no matter how rapid and intricate the line. This arranging practice took advantage of the high-level instrumental proficiency being demonstrated by jazz bassists during the 1970s. The practice became widely imitated in jazz-rock groups of the 1970s and 80s.

KEITH JARRETT

When Chick Corea left Miles Davis, pianist Keith Jarrett (b. 1945) took his place. Like a few other Davis sidemen, Jarrett had also played with Art Blakey. But Jarrett's widest pre-Davis exposure had come as a member of saxophonist Charles Lloyd's quartet beginning in 1966. In recordings with Lloyd, Jarrett had proven himself a powerful improviser paralleling Herbie Hancock and Chick Corea. Jarrett had as much or more command over the piano as they, but more importantly, he had his own distinctive approach. He was a piano original. Jarrett's playing demonstrated imagination of enormous scope. His sources were numerous and separated by wide gaps of idiom. Keith Jarrett seems able to draw from any musical idiom and incorporate its elements in a convincing way. To hear Jarrett play was to hear bits of Bill Evans, twentieth-century classical composers Béla Bartók, Alban Berg, and Maurice Ravel, American gospel music, country music, and Ornette Coleman.

Often Jarrett's lines project a singing quality (and sometimes you can hear Jarrett humming the lines as he plays them). These lines have the sweep of an inspired human voice or a surging saxophone improvisation. In fact, Jarrett plays soprano saxophone in some of his concerts. He is quite accomplished on sax. The long, legato sax lines he creates are mirrored by his long, legato, sax-like piano lines. (Chick Corea is far more crisp and percussive in his approach than Jarrett. Perhaps this is due to Corea's experience as a drummer, whereas Jarrett's preference for legato lines could be related to his saxophone playing.)

During the 1970s, Jarrett made many albums and concert appearances as an unaccompanied solo pianist. It is notable that Jarrett was one of the few pianists of that decade who did not regularly play electric piano. It is also noteworthy that Jarrett's improvisations were more spontaneous than those of most jazz pianists because he simply sat

---

[32] In Gary Burton's *Crystal Silence* ECM 1024

down at the piano and played whatever he felt like playing, rarely using prewritten melodies or preset chord progressions. His playing could be funky, earthy and gospelish, or pretty and orchestrally lush. Sometimes he clearly stated a tempo. Other times he implied only a momentum.

Like Herbie Hancock and Chick Corea, Jarrett is a prolific and quite original composer. He has written mounds of material for his own albums and contributed significantly to the records of Charles Lloyd and Norwegian saxophonist Jan Garbarek. Some of his albums contain extended performances with little or no improvisation; in these compositions the line between classical music and jazz is blurry.

Pianist Keith Jarrett's style is a curious blend of influences. Bill Evans and Ornette Coleman are obvious. Paul Bley, another pianist, should not be overlooked. The work of Bley, saxophonist John Gilmore, bassist Gary Peacock, and future Jarrett drummer Paul Motian (on the 1964 recordings issued as *Turning Point*[33] and *New Music: Second Wave*) suggest both the piano style and the quartet sound that Jarrett demonstrated during the 1970s. A combination of influences converged in a musical friendship that Jarrett began with pianist John Coates around 1957. Jarrett listened extensively to Coates in person as well as becoming interested in a few of the same favorites that Coates had: Paul Bley, Ornette Coleman, black gospel music, and early white American music. The blends of these styles that occurred in the playing of Coates have also emerged in the playing of Jarrett. In other words, Coates and Jarrett had some of the same tastes at the same time and, additionally, Jarrett later displayed some of the same amalgam of these styles that Coates was perfecting in the early 1960s. It is notable that both Coates and Jarrett were making albums during the 1970s that reflected those influences cited above, and that the music of the two men is clearly similar.

Jarrett is one of the few pianists to show extensive Ornette Coleman influence. On one album in particular (Jan Garbarek's *Belonging*),[34] he improvised solos in a style remarkably close to Coleman's. Neither musician uses staccato phrasing often, and both have a way of bursting forth with slippery streams of notes. Both also display a twangy flavor reminiscent of country music. Jarrett's methods also resemble those of Coleman and other free jazz players because, in his solo concert format, he improvises without preset chord progressions. What further helps us hear Jarrett's debt to Coleman is Jarrett's tendency to entirely omit left-hand playing and improvise lengthy, saxophone-like solos with his right hand. The phrasing and note choices in these solos often recall Coleman. When accompanied only by bass

[33] Improvising Artists Incorporated 373841
[34] ECM 1050

and drums, and not playing in a traditional, two-handed pianistic style, Jarrett often sounds like Coleman transferred to the piano. (For more comparisons between Coleman and Jarrett, listen to Jarrett's soprano saxophone playing on "Pocket Full of Cherry" in his *Bop-Be*[35] album and "Part a" of "Encore (a-b-c)" in his *Eyes of the Heart*[36] album. If you have difficulty comparing Jarrett's piano lines with Coleman's saxophone lines, these examples should make the comparison more obvious because both men are now playing saxophone.)

Despite all the similarities between styles, even to the extent of employing the same sidemen (Dewey Redman and Charlie Haden), differences between Coleman's and Jarrett's approaches do exist. First, Jarrett is more complex than Coleman. He is more varied in his improvised lines and draws upon a wider selection of moods and tempos. Secondly, Jarrett possesses very high-level technique, and because of the uniformity in touch afforded by this, Jarrett plays more smoothly than Coleman. Thirdly, Jarrett is less prone than Coleman to move outside of key feeling. (Jarrett's improvisations stick to the same key proportionally longer than Coleman's do, and the notes in the lines seem more loyal to the original key that a given piece is in.)

Keith Jarrett devised a distinctive quartet sound from 1971 to 1976 with tenor saxophonist Dewey Redman, bassist Charlie Haden, and drummer Paul Motian. Redman and Haden were regulars in Ornette Coleman's group, and the two bandleaders had to juggle concert dates to obtain services of their mutual saxophonist and bassist. (Motian had been the drummer with the influential Bill Evans trio of 1960–61.) The Jarrett group arranged a unique combination of:

1) elements from the Coleman approach (Jarrett wrote melodies in the Coleman style as well as soloing in it. Redman soloed in the Coleman style, and Haden's unique approach was central to both the Coleman and the Jarrett group.)

2) elements of the Bill Evans style (Listen to Jarrett's up-tempo piano lines on "Shades of Jazz" in Jarrett's *Shades*[37] album and the slow, sustained tones, and chord voicings on "Rainbow" in Jarrett's *Byablue* album. Compare this with Bill Evans's *Village Vanguard Sessions* or *Peace Piece And More Pieces*.)

3) extension and development of rubato style

4) long, vamp-based improvisations which were funky in Jarrett's unique way

5) Third World approaches (Redman playing musette, the group using several unusual instruments such as steel drums, finger cymbals, etc.)

[35] MCA 29048
[36] ECM 1150
[37] Impulse ASD 9322

6) unique, non-bop timekeeping techniques used by Motian and Haden

7) group improvisations which use rubato.

As an unaccompanied solo pianist, Keith Jarrett has created one of the first jazz sounds since the Modern Jazz Quartet's whose appeal crossed the line from jazz audiences to audiences customarily more fond of symphonic music. He is one of the first jazz solo musicians to consistently pack auditoriums throughout the United States and Europe and earn a satisfactory living as an improviser while gaining business status and audiences comparable to a nonimprovising classical virtuoso. Among the explanations for his success are:

1) a rhapsodic style (A warm, sweeping mood is evoked by much of Jarrett's unaccompanied solo playing.)

2) seemingly effortless control over the piano keyboard (Jarrett has such unusual command that he counts concert pianists among his admirers.)

3) accessibility that comes with vamp-based passages in which brief accompaniment figures repeat again and again (His most popular concert albums are those with the largest number of repeating figures.)

4) non-jazz feeling (In a substantial portion of his unaccompanied solo improvisations, the musical vocabulary is classical. Much of this work sounds like piano sonatas by Maurice Ravel. This sound might provide a bridge for listeners who are unaccustomed to jazz but acquainted with symphonic music, especially the familiar works of French composers Ravel and Debussy. For many such listeners, the only aspect that separates Jarrett's music from classical music is that Jarrett's is largely improvised.)

Listen to his *Staircase*[38] album for illustration of the above points.

Jarrett's influence on jazz pianists has been slower to take hold than was the influence of Herbie Hancock and Chick Corea. However, the work of these players recalls Jarrett's sound: Art Lande (especially on his own album *Red Lanta*[39]), Richard Beirach (most noticeably on David Liebman's album *Forgotten Fantasies*[40]), and Lyle Mays (who played on numerous albums under Pat Metheny's name during the 1970s and 80s). Other pianists, less gifted than Lande, Beirach, and Mays, have begun imitating the most easy to learn aspects of Jarrett's style, the lengthy, vamp-based improvisations which meander and seem soothing. The improvisations of these latter imitators can be

[38] ECM 1090
[39] ECM 1038
[40] A & M Horizon SP 709

distinguished from those of Jarrett because the lines are far less rich with melodic ideas, and the rhythms are simpler. Rarely do Jarrett's imitators attain the sweeping feeling that Jarrett can elicit in the listener. Nor do they play with quite the smoothness and vitality that Jarrett displays.

Comparing Evans, Hancock, Corea, and Jarrett by Rhythm Section Style

One of the most historically significant aspects of the Evans trio is its loosening of instrument roles, and it is instructive to examine Evans disciples in terms of this. For example, Corea, the least Evans-like of the three pianists, usually projects the impression that his lines breathe less often and that he is using his bassists mostly as accompanists or soloists rather than as comrades in flexible conversation. (Listen to *Now He Sings, Now He Sobs.*) Jarrett, on the other hand, seems a bit more involved with his bassist because he shows more Evans influence and more use of silence. (Witness the exchanges between Jarrett and bassist Charlie Haden on "Prayer" in *Death and the Flower.*[41]) The most interactive of the three pianists is Hancock. In the 1963–68 Miles Davis rhythm section, Hancock demonstrated how far flexibility can be taken in a graceful and highly musical way. The conversation-like interplay between Hancock, bassist Ron Carter, and drummer Tony Williams on the slow pieces recorded during this period display refinement of the very difficult Evans-LaFaro-Motian collective improvisation methods. (Listen to "My Funny Valentine," "Stella By Starlight,"[42] and "Pee Wee."[43]) Its musical success speaks well for Hancock's openness to suggestion and the instantaneously reciprocal responsiveness of his colleagues in the Davis quintet.

CHAPTER SUMMARY

1) Pianist Bill Evans came to attention during the late 1950s and had considerable impact on jazz pianists of the 1960s and 70s.

2) Though derived partly from the Tristano approach, Evans was relatively original, especially in his voicings and his modal thinking.

3) With bassist Scott LaFaro and drummer Paul Motian, he devised a fresh approach to trio playing in which explicit statement of every beat was replaced by a highly flexible and varied group style, and the roles of soloist and accompanist were often blurred.

[41] MCA 29046
[42] Miles Davis *My Funny Valentine* Columbia PC 9106
[43] Miles Davis *Sorcerer* Columbia PC 9532

4) LaFaro's immense speed and imagination pushed jazz bass playing ahead as Jimmy Blanton's had twenty years earlier.

5) Among the countless musicians influenced by Evans were three of the most important pianist-composers of the 60s and 70s: Herbie Hancock, Chick Corea, and Keith Jarrett.

6) Hancock refined the Evans style, added Wynton Kelly as a source, and raised accompanying techniques to a high level while with Miles Davis.

7) Hancock led several groups of his own that played his many original compositions, including "Maiden Voyage" and "Watermelon Man."

8) Hancock's mid-seventies group The Head Hunters became a model jazz/rock band and enjoyed very high record sales ("Chameleon" was a big hit).

9) Chick Corea employed Bill Evans as only one of many sources for his original piano style. Horace Silver, Thelonious Monk, Bud Powell, McCoy Tyner, and several nonjazz styles were combined. His playing is more crisp and staccato than that of Hancock or Evans, and he favors Spanish themes and Latin American rhythms.

10) Corea, along with McCoy Tyner, popularized the use of fourths in compositions and piano voicings.

11) Corea's tunes were very popular. "Spain," "La Fiesta," and "Windows" became jazz standards.

12) Keith Jarrett added Ornette Coleman to Bill Evans in developing his own piano style.

13) Jarrett was one of the most original composer-pianist-bandleaders of the 1970s, combining free jazz, funk, and a rhapsodic classical piano flavor that made him the most successful solo concert pianist in jazz history.

14) Jarrett's quartet of the 1970s mixed Ornette Coleman sidemen with Evans sidemen and added Third World music and funk to their respective styles.

chapter 16

THE SECOND CHICAGO SCHOOL

Jazz historians use the term "Chicagoans" or "Chicago School" to indicate a group of white Dixieland musicians who emerged during the 1920s in Chicago. Bud Freeman, Frank Teschemacher, Jimmy McPartland, and others are usually identified with their hometown of Chicago as much as Louis Armstrong and Sidney Bechet are pegged with New Orleans. After the 1920s, Chicago was not particularly known for any single style of jazz until a distinctive stream of black musicians began gaining attention during the 1950s and 60s and finally received wide critical recognition during the late 1970s. Where Detroit and Philadelphia had produced a significant number of outstanding players who defined the hard bop mainstream during the 1950s, Chicago was the home for a small stream of musicians who embraced the avant-garde. Their form of avant-garde music coexisted with and drew upon the work done by Ornette Coleman, first in Los Angeles, then in New York, and by Cecil Taylor, who was exploring his own new approaches in New York. First, Chicago produced the fresh orientation that Sun Ra developed during the 1950s. Second, Chicago was home for the Association for the Advancement of Creative Musicians, which was an alliance of black players spearheaded by pianist Richard Abrams in the mid-1960s. Third, Chicago spawned the most well-publicized of all AACM members: The Art Ensemble of Chicago and saxophonist-composer Anthony Braxton, who became well known in the 1970s. This chapter outlines these three parts of this "second Chicago school," and it touches on their St. Louis relatives, the Black Artists Group.

SUN RA   Sun Ra (b. 1915) is an immensely creative pianist, composer, arranger, and bandleader. He has written and performed in a kaleidoscopic range of musical styles. But in spite of the unusual breadth and depth of his music, he is relatively unknown. His recordings probably number over one hundred, but, because most were made on his own poorly distributed Saturn record label, few have received any attention. Even during the 1970s when the well-distributed Impulse label bought and reissued many Saturn LPs, Sun Ra remained an obscure name.

Active as a professional musician since the 1930s, Sun Ra formed his own big band during the mid-50s. Actually, it might be more accurate to refer to his personnel as the Sun Ra bands, because the size and instrumentation vary from one player (his solo piano) to over fifty musicians. He draws from a pool of musicians who have rehearsed with him over the years. Like Duke Ellington's, many of Ra's principal sidemen stayed with him for more than twenty years at a stretch. His sidemen are unusually dedicated and especially loyal to him.

Most of the music performed by the Sun Ra groups is original material put together by Sun Ra himself. But, as is true of Duke Ellington, another prolific composer-arranger, Sun Ra occasionally performs the compositions of others, also. He has performed Ellington's "Lightning," Jelly Roll Morton's "King Porter Stomp," and pop standards such as "Just in Time." Whenever he performs a piece composed by someone else, however, the arrangement bears his own distinctively original style.

As a pianist, Sun Ra resembles Ellington in his rich imagination and unpredictability. Both Ellington and Sun Ra are often underrated as pianists because the work of their bands overshadows their piano playing. But careful listening reveals not only the importance that their keyboard techniques have in the band sound, but also the uniquely creative approaches they have devised for the piano.

Sun Ra's output is uniquely his own music, but its diversity is most expediently characterized by mentioning similar work of better-known musicians and styles:

1) Some pieces resemble the chant music of Africa.
2) Some suggest the mode-based work of 1960s John Coltrane (*Nubians of Plutonia*[1]).
3) Some of Sun Ra's mid-1950s work almost sounds like a modern jazz version of 1940s Duke Ellington big band music (*Sun Song*,[2] *Super-Sonic Sounds*[3]).

[1] Impulse AS 9242 and El Saturn 406
[2] Delmark 411 and Transition J 10
[3] Impulse AS 9271 and El Saturn 216

4) In the mid-1960s, some of Sun Ra's music had much in common with contemporary classical composers who use electronically altered and synthesized sounds (*Astro Black,*[4] *Magic City*[5]).

The orchestrations of Sun Ra transcend the stock arranging practices that were first identified with Fletcher Henderson and Don Redman. And, in their originality, Sun Ra's orchestrations also go beyond the work ordinarily featured in the Stan Kenton, Woody Herman, and Maynard Ferguson big bands. Many of the differences between Sun Ra's writing and that used by conventional big bands can be summarized by merely saying that Sun Ra capitalizes on the diversity that is possible with big band instrumentation, diversity which was overlooked by so many other bandleaders. Sun Ra

1) creates many different combinations of trumpets, trombones, saxophones, piano, bass, and drums;

2) extends the range of tone colors by adding electronic instruments (Sun Ra employed electric piano and synthesizers long before rock groups made their use common);

3) makes imaginative use of tympani (see Figure 16.1), celeste, xylophone, bass marimba, bells, and chimes;

4) uses saxophonists who play instruments unusual in jazz, such as piccolo, oboe, bassoon, and bass clarinet (see Figure 16.2 and 16.3);

5) requires nearly all his sidemen to double on percussion instruments (long before this became a common practice in modern jazz groups);

6) sometimes creates passages by means of simultaneous collective improvisation instead of composition (a practice that is almost unknown among big bands);

7) runs performances in which pieces are not separated; the entire evening is an uninterrupted sequence of unusual sounds;

8) bases pieces on chants instead of chord progressions.

Sun Ra's use of synthesizers and the overall conception for many of his 1960s albums, especially *Heliocentric Worlds of Sun Ra Vol. 1 and 2,*[6] suggest the work of twentieth-century classical composers Edgard Varèse and Krzysztof Penderecki. Central to the conception of such work is the notion that music can consist of sound by itself instead of sound in the conventional form of melody and harmony. Chunks of sound are sequenced in place of the standard ideas of melody and chord progression. When Sun Ra and his improvisers address them-

[4] Impulse AS 9255
[5] Impulse AS 9243
[6] ESP Disk 1014 and 1017

Figure 16.1. Kettledrum. Two or more kettledrums are called tympani.

Figure 16.2. Left to right: Piccolo, flute, clarinet; bass clarinet lying in front. (*Courtesy of Barry Perlus*)

Figure 16.3. English horn, oboe, bassoon. (*Courtesy of Barry Perlus*)

selves to this style the result has a more natural and flowing character than similar music performed by symphony orchestra musicians.

Sun Ra has also been active in the "free jazz" approach. Portions of his performances are collectively improvised with little apparent pre-arrangement (*Astro Black, Magic City, Heliocentric Worlds of Sun Ra Vol. 2*). His free jazz passages differ from those of Ornette Coleman and John Coltrane in that, in spite of the leadership qualities of Coleman and Coltrane, Sun Ra exerts a stronger, more pervasive artistic control over the proceedings. The music has a continuity and compositional organization superior to most free jazz of other groups. It is important to note that Sun Ra has succeeded with free-form collective improvisation in large ensemble contexts, a situation which poses great difficulty because of the problems musicians must overcome, listening to a large number of simultaneous lines while constructing their own improvisations to be compatible with those lines. Problems are considerably augmented as the size of the group increases. Dixieland combos rarely numbered more than seven men. Coltrane's *Ascension* used eleven musicians, and Ornette Coleman's *Free Jazz* used eight musicians. Sun Ra's works within free jazz are not all great successes, but most outshine similar attempts by other leaders.

In many ways, Sun Ra is like Ellington. His fascination with widely diverse tonal textures and his unconventional arranging methods strongly suggest the work of Ellington. Sun Ra has the rare skill, also possessed by Ellington, of being able to oversee combinations of improvisation and composition and blend them in a unified form. Sun Ra and Ellington both bring out the best in their sidemen. And those players, in turn, adapt their improvisatory styles to the varying moods within each of their leader's compositions. Respect for Sun Ra's musical conception and artistic control is evident in his sidemen's sensitive ensemble improvising.

Saxophonists **Marshall Allen** (b. 1924) and **John Gilmore** (b. 1931) are probably the band's strongest improvisers, and both have remained with Sun Ra for more than twenty years. Marshall Allen plays all the woodwind instruments and has contributed extremely imaginative oboe and piccolo solos to Sun Ra's recordings. Gilmore has recorded with the bands of drummer Art Blakey and pianist Andrew Hill, among others. John Coltrane took an interest in Gilmore's 1960 style; he later recorded solos in which some of the melodic figures bear a discernible resemblance to a few favorite Gilmore melodic devices. Gilmore stands out among late 1950s–early 60s tenor men. Like Marshall Allen, he is an intelligent, imaginative improviser.

A few musicians who have worked with Sun Ra have also played with better-known groups. For example, trombonist Julian Priester worked with the band of drummer Max Roach, and he was part of an innovative septet led by pianist Herbie Hancock during the 1970s. This brings to mind the observation that Hancock's group, like Sun Ra's, used synthesizer, varied percussion sounds, piccolo, and bass clarinet, and often produced music resembling that of Edgard Varèse. That Varèse-like style, as practiced by Hancock and Sun Ra, resembled background music for science fiction and space travel films, and it was popularly labeled "space music."

Sun Ra's live performances are accompanied by singing, dancing, costumes, and unusual lighting. Attending a Sun Ra concert is a multimedia experience. Perhaps many people have failed to recognize the variety and depth of Sun Ra's music because they were paying more attention to the visual aspects than the musical aspects. Perhaps some listeners fail to take Sun Ra's music seriously partly because it is mixed with theater and partly because he attaches a strong emphasis on philosophy, astrology, space travel, and astronomy. Another factor explaining his lack of widespread audience appeal is Sun Ra's diversity. People who hear a single performance and do not enjoy it fail to realize that what they have heard represents only a small portion of what Sun Ra has to offer. It is possible to hear five different Sun Ra approaches and still not to be acquainted with all of his facets. Sun Ra's musical world is vast, and it is unfair to judge him on the basis of just a few performances or a few albums.

Members of the Chicago-based Association for the Advancement of Creative Musicians have presented concerts which resembled those of Sun Ra in that theatrical aspects were stressed, sound was often employed simply for sound's sake, free-form passages were employed, conventional jazz swing feeling was often missing, and unusual wind and percussion instruments were liberally employed. The fact that Sun Ra was based in Chicago for many years prior to the emergence of the AACM suggests that the AACM resemblance to Sun Ra is no coincidence.

THE ASSOCIATION FOR THE ADVANCEMENT OF CREATIVE MUSICIANS

The Association for the Advancement of Creative Musicians (AACM) is a Chicago-based collective of modern jazz musicians begun during the early 1960s by saxophonist Fred Anderson and pianist Muhal Richard Abrams. The organization set up concerts, recordings, training, and promotion for black musicians who had an affinity for jazz that was not squarely within the bop tradition. Their music was almost exclusively nonelectronic, and it was quite separate from jazz-rock. A large portion of the AACM's music was reminiscent of Sun Ra's and Ornette Coleman's. The music also recalls the work of Charles Mingus from the late 1950s and early 60s in several respects. First, the rhythmic feeling lacks the flowing, easy character of conventional jazz. (It has more the unpredictable nature of modern concert music.) Second, solos are often freely improvised and tied more to the mood of the piece than to standard bop patterns. Third, there is a larger assortment of accom-

Art Ensemble of Chicago. *Left to right:* Roscoe Mitchell, Lester Bowie, and Joseph Jarman, 1973 (the large sax in foreground is a bass sax). (*Courtesy of Bill Smith and CODA*)

paniment rhythms than was common to bop. And fourth, the proceedings display a rough quality, as in the Mingus concept that each performance is really a public workshop rather than a polished product.

The Art Ensemble of Chicago: Roscoe Mitchell, Joseph Jarman, Lester Bowie, Malachi Favors

During the late 1960s an interesting group emerged in Chicago. It had much in common with Sun Ra's ensemble, which had been based in the same city. The group performed in a broad range of styles, some of which, like those of Sun Ra, were not squarely within the jazz tradition:

1) They mimicked street bands of foreign countries,
2) performed light-hearted dramatic sketches,
3) made sounds for sound's sake (as opposed to traditional concepts of melody and harmony),
4) recited poetry,
5) improvised without preset harmonies, in addition to
6) applying conventional jazz approaches.

Some of their work is similar to that of Ornette Coleman, Don Cherry, and Albert Ayler. Their jazz solo conceptions owe much to

Coleman. No piano is used, and, although all group members play percussion instruments, many of the Art Ensemble's recordings dispense with the conventional jazz drum set. Timekeeping and a harmonic background are provided by bassist Malachi Favors, who has outstanding technique and distinctive improvisational flexibility. Without his strength and imagination much of the Art Ensemble's music would be weak.

Although the Art Ensemble members seem to play almost every instrument, Lester Bowie (b. 1941) is primarily a trumpeter, Malachi Favors concentrates on bass, and Joseph Jarman (b. 1937) and Roscoe Mitchell (b. 1940) are primarily saxophonists. In addition to percussion instruments, Mitchell plays soprano, alto, tenor, and bass saxophones, clarinet, and flute. In addition to percussion instruments, Joseph Jarman plays soprano, alto, tenor and bass saxophones, clarinet, bassoon, flute, oboe, and vibraharp. Since 1970, drummer Don Moye (b. 1946) has also been recording with the Art Ensemble.

The Art Ensemble of Chicago uses musical elements that have been relatively neglected in the mainstream of modern jazz styles. The group has repackaged ideas that the originators of free jazz had pioneered, presenting them in a less frantic and more humorous way. A notable contribution is the group's practice of taking a brief melodic fragment and altering it over lengthy stretches within a performance. Another feature is that, in place of rapidly flowing bop lines, the group offers unusual instruments and varied tonal inflections. Strict tempo is often rejected. The group stands out in their avoidance of traditional format in which improvised solos are strung together one after another, without a storytelling quality to unify the piece.

In place of complex chord progressions and virtuoso displays of technical prowess, the Art Ensemble offers simplicity and careful use of silence. In fact, the group has made more use of silence and changes in loudness than most jazz-oriented groups have shown since Jimmy Giuffre's work of the 1950s and 60s. This puts them in direct contrast to John Coltrane's high energy, dense-textured music of the 1960s and the loud and repetitive jazz-rock of the 1970s. The Art Ensemble is one of the first groups since the Modern Jazz Quartet to become known for exploration of soft and gentle sounds.

The Art Ensemble of Chicago makes music which does not follow any strict set of rules. They choose styles freely, and they refuse to base their music on the expectations set by a particular idiom or a particular audience. The Art Ensemble embraces the music of the whole world as its repertory.[7] In that way, their musical viewpoint is similar to Sun Ra's.

---

[7] *People In Sorrow* (Nessa 3) is their most highly acclaimed album. *A Jackson in Your House* (Affinity AFF 9) offers a broad sampling of their approaches. *Nice Guys* (ECM 1-1126) and *Urban Bushmen* (ECM 2-1211) have received much publicity and are therefore easier to locate.

Anthony Braxton

One of the most broadly talented figures in the second Chicago school is Anthony Braxton (b. 1945). If ever there was a jazz-oriented musician whose work resists categorization, it is this one. He performs on almost all the woodwind instruments ever invented, yet the tone color he extracts is unlike the accepted model for each. He sometimes improvises solos with conventional modern jazz accompaniment, yet his solo lines do not resemble standard modern jazz approaches offered by Charlie Parker or John Coltrane. Braxton is usually classed within the jazz idiom, but very little of his music swings in the jazz sense (see page 5 for explanation of swing feeling). Though sometimes suggesting atonality, Braxton's lines resemble less the truly atonal music of Arnold Schoenberg than an odd blend of Lee Konitz and Eric Dolphy. Additionally, some of his unaccompanied work draws upon Oriental methods of tone alteration, timing, and motivic development. His large-scale work for symphony orchestra, however, clearly displays the influence of his favorite nonjazz composers Karlheinz Stockhausen, Krzysztof Penderecki, and John Cage.[8] Braxton organizes groups whose instrumentation is unusual, such as two unaccompanied saxophones or simply saxophone and trombone. Yet when employing big band instrumentation, his orchestrations dance back and forth between parade music, snatches of jazz history, and twentieth-century concert music.[9] In summary, Braxton seems to be tireless and blessed with endless imagination, but because his music goes far beyond jazz idioms, he should not be viewed only as a jazz musician.[10]

THE WORLD SAXOPHONE QUARTET

The Black Artists Group was formed in St. Louis during 1968 along the same organizational lines and musical views that inspired the AACM in Chicago. Three saxophonists coming from this organization became prominent in the late 1970s and early 1980s: Oliver Lake (b. 1942), Julius Hemphill (b. 1940), and Hamiet Bluiett (b. 1940). These men recorded in numerous combinations and performed extensively on their own during that period, but their highest critical acclaim was earned when they performed in combination with saxophonist David Murray (b. 1955) within a group they had founded in 1976 called the World Saxophone Quartet (WSQ). Though flute and clarinets are also used, basically the WSQ consists of Lake and Hemphill on alto, Murray on tenor, and Hamiet Bluiett on baritone saxophone.

The WSQ drew from the approaches of Ornette Coleman and Albert Ayler, but they placed a greater emphasis on composition. The diversity of tone colors associated with free jazz players and such

[8] Arista A3L 8900

[9] *Creative Orchestra Music* Artista 4080

[10] A quick sampling of Braxton's work might include *Five Pieces 1975* (Arista 4054), *For Alto Saxophone* (Delmark DS 420), and *Three Compositions of New Jazz* (Delmark DS 415).

earlier bands as Duke Ellington's recurred and was extended. The free-form collective approaches of Coleman inspired the WSQ, but a greater balance of contrasts was achieved by WSQ because they carefully alternated prewritten parts with improvised solos and simultaneous collective improvisations. Greater clarity of sound was also achieved because the WSQ performed without piano, guitar, bass, or drums.

The music of the WSQ is especially distinctive because much of it is delivered in a light-hearted manner. Diversity and activity seem the key guidelines. Some passages recall Igor Stravinsky's writing for woodwinds, while others suggest Ellington's saxophone writing. Like the Art Ensemble of Chicago, the WSQ is significant for offering a unique refinement of free-form methods combined with numerous traditions of jazz and nonjazz sources.[11]

[11] *World Saxophone Quartet* Black Saint BSR 0046; *Revue* Black Saint BSR 0056; *Point of No Return* Moers Music 01034; *Steppin' With the World Saxophone Quartet* Black Saint 0027

CHAPTER SUMMARY

1) Taking a cue from free jazz, Sun Ra and many AACM players departed from bop practices of melody and chord progressions in addition to incorporating Third World music and unusual instruments.

2) Conventional jazz swing feeling was usually discarded.

3) The tone colors and instrumental technique of bop were replaced by a wide variety of approaches which often cultivated roughness and the tonal manipulations associated with free players.

4) Continuity between composition and improvisation was stressed more than it had been in most modern jazz styles.

5) Group approaches such as those of the Art Ensemble of Chicago often succeeded in improvising story-like pieces

6) Development of themes was stressed more than were complex chord changes.

7) Beginning with recordings in the 1950s, pianist Sun Ra's big band methods demonstrated some of the most varied voicings that had been seen since Duke Ellington's 1940s recordings.

8) Sun Ra explored collective improvisation in big band music during the 1960s and 70s.

9) Sun Ra was one of the first jazz composer-arrangers to extensively use synthesizers and electric keyboard instruments.

10) The Art Ensemble of Chicago became prominent during the 1970s and was comprised of trumpeter Lester Bowie, saxophonists Roscoe Mitchell and Joseph Jarman, bassist Malachi Favors and, eventually, drummer Don Moye.

11) The AEC's performances contain humor and theatrics, with bandmembers wearing costumes and war-paint-like face make-up.

12) The World Saxophone Quartet is made up of David Murray, Julius Hemphill, Oliver Lake, and Hamiet Bluiett. It has demonstrated a successful integration of prewritten passages and freely improvised parts without rhythm section accompaniment.

13) The WSQ pieces offer significant expansion of the existing repertory of written music for saxophone quartet as well as mixing premodern saxophone styles with classical and free styles.

14) Multi-instrumentalist Anthony Braxton is a composer and improviser of sweeping scope who does not play in bop style and whose music usually shows ties to non-Western music plus Eric Dolphy, Lee Konitz, and twentieth-century symphonic music.

chapter 17
JOHN COLTRANE

If you had to make a list of the greatest musicians in jazz history, you would undoubtedly include those whose playing directly influenced generations of improvisers, those who possessed extremely creative talents, and those who played with such awesome power that people sometimes looked upon them as almost superhuman.

The 1950s and 60s produced a man who fits all three classifications: John Coltrane (1926–1967). As a saxophonist, composer, and bandleader, he has had profound influence on jazz of the 1960s, 70s, and 80s. The improvisational concepts he introduced were absorbed by pianists, trumpeters, and guitarists in addition to saxophonists.

Coltrane was unknown by the public during the early 1950s, but he had developed his own powerful style by the time he first recorded with Miles Davis in 1955, and he continued to develop it until his death in 1967. The product of that activity was a stream of recordings in which can be distinguished at least two, perhaps three or four, robust styles of saxophone playing and several styles of composing.

THE COLTRANE SAX STYLE By the early 1950s, Coltrane already had an unusually vigorous style. His tone was rough-textured and biting, huge and dark. Coltrane gave it a massive core and a searing intensity. Some saxophonists lose the body of their tone when they play in the high register, and lose definition and agility in the low register. But Coltrane's tone was full and penetrating in every register. He improvised with such proficiency that his work even impressed listeners who were already accustomed to the phenomenal speed and agility of saxophonists Lee Konitz, Charlie Parker, and Sonny Rollins. Coltrane was more than mere tone and speed, however. He played with an urgency which reflected a severely critical craftsman; his music was very serious, almost devoid of humor. Throughout his career, Coltrane's recordings displayed a consistency of strength and inspiration, quite rare even among jazz greats. Along with Charlie Parker, Coltrane was among the most consistent and intense soloists jazz has known.

During the late 1950s, Coltrane frequently improvised densely organized streams of notes, quadruple-timing solo after solo. Notes cascaded from his horn at a furious pace. They were not thrown casually at the listener, either. Each note was carefully chosen to fit a melodic idea or to become an essential element in a sweeping run. Even Coltrane's most elementary phrases were delivered with such intensity that the surging power used in their execution lifted them beyond any ordinariness they might have if used as a practice routine. The patterns Coltrane refined during this period became stock repertory for hundreds of saxophonists playing the 1960s, 70s, and 80s. (For a sample from this period, listen to his solo on the Miles Davis "So What" in SCCJ.)

Primary Influences Because recordings of Coltrane's pre-1950s work have yet to be discovered or distributed, there remains some mystery about his primary influences. We do know, however, that he absorbed much from Lester Young and Charlie Parker. Interviews with him and with people who heard his pre-1950 playing indicate an attraction to Parker and Young and also to Coleman Hawkins. Parker phrases were evident in his late 1950s recordings, although you might have difficulty detecting them because they are played so fast, they are played with Coltrane's own twists, and, of course, they are on tenor instead of on alto saxophone. Coltrane's preference for intricate chord progressions has much in common with the Hawkins style, as does his deep, dark, and richly textured tone.

Alto saxophonist Johnny Hodges, Duke Ellington's star soloist, was one of Coltrane's earliest idols. Coltrane had played alto before concentrating on tenor. (In fact he played lead alto in Dizzy Gillespie's 1949 big band.) Even if Coltrane did not learn the Hodges style as a young man, he definitely had an extended opportunity to study it later because he played tenor in a Hodges combo during 1953 and 1954, a period when Hodges was separated from Ellington. The two players share several traits. Coltrane's unusual depth and fullness of tone recall Hodges, and an exquisite timing of ornaments might reflect the influence of Hodges. (For more about Hodges, see pages 75–76 and 118–119). Coltrane's scale-wise lead-in to a dramatically placed high note is analogous to the long, drawn-out smear (portamento) that was a trademark of the Hodges approach. Both men also handle ballads with exceptional care. In summary, it might be said that, by listening to Hodges, Coltrane learned how to make the saxophone sing.

Comparison with Earl Bostic

Coltrane cultivated several expressive techniques. On a 1954 Johnny Hodges combo recording, for example, he sounds like Earl Bostic milking high notes in a very emotional way. (See pages 298–299 for album titles and catalog numbers of this and most other musical examples cited in this chapter.) This style of wailing into the high register—"the cry"—became a Coltrane signature during the 1960s. He eventually employed notes far above the saxophone's conventional limit. Coltrane may have learned these techniques in 1952 and 1953 as a member of Bostic's band because Bostic himself had exceptional command over the saxophone and explored techniques of high-register playing. These devices of Bostic, along with several of Bostic's favorite phrases, are strikingly similar to some of Coltrane's work recorded during the 1960s.

Multiphonics

Coltrane sometimes produced sounds in which several different frequencies could be heard simultaneously. These multiphonics (to give them their technical name) occasionally sound like chords. In his "Harmonique" on the 1959 *Coltrane Jazz* album, Coltrane uses the method simply to harmonize a melody note, but during the mid-1960s he used multiphonics for controlled screeches during peaks of musical excitement, as found in his albums *Meditations, Expression*, and *Live in Seattle*. (An isolated earlier example occurs in his solo on the 1961 "Chasin' the Trane," however.) Together with Albert Ayler, Coltrane extended the popularity of ultra-high-register playing and multiphonics, especially for moments of high tension that were stirred up in many so-called "free jazz" performances.

Comparison with Lester Young, Dexter Gordon, and Sonny Stitt

The earliest recorded examples of Coltrane's playing (in rare 1951 Dizzy Gillespie records) show a few methods similar to those used by Lester Young on his 1943–44 recordings and Dexter Gordon on his 1947 recordings. Some of Lester Young's favorite phrases and his peculiarly expressive way of bending pitch and tone quality can be detected. There is also a hint of Dexter Gordon's style in the dark, full-bodied tone (aspects not common to Lester Young) and legato style and phrasing (aspects shared with Lester Young). Coltrane, Gordon, and Young all linked long strings of notes together without a break, almost devoid of staccato playing.

Coltrane cited Dexter Gordon as an influence. Aspects of Lester Young's style and Dexter Gordon's Lester Young-influenced approach are evident in the sound of the earliest commercially available Coltrane solo ("We Love to Boogie" from Dizzy Gillespie's 1951 recording session, included in the package called DEE GEE DAYS—Savoy 2209). However, in acknowledging Gordon's effect on Coltrane, we must not overlook the originality in Coltrane's earliest playing. To help us fully credit Coltrane for his own creativity, keep in mind the facts that, by comparison with Coltrane, Dexter Gordon's and Stan Getz in

1) tone is not as dark, as rough, or as cutting,
2) impact is more relaxed and less urgent,
3) improvisations are more graceful and have contours that are less jagged,
4) solos are more tuneful, and
5) improvisations are sprinkled with phrases from popular melodies and bugle calls, a practice that Coltrane hardly ever indulged in.

Coltrane also cited Sonny Stitt as an influence. Stitt's methods can be heard in the earliest recordings that Coltrane made with Miles Davis. For an easy comparison, play Coltrane's solos on "Oleo" from the Miles Davis RELAXIN', an album made for Prestige record company in 1956, back to back with any Sonny Stitt tenor sax improvisations that are based on the same chord progressions ("I Got Rhythm"). Both Dexter Gordon and Sonny Stitt were influenced by Lester Young. So it is difficult to determine what Coltrane derived directly from Lester Young and what aspects of Lester Young's approach Coltrane absorbed through Gordon and Stitt. To illustrate the devices that Coltrane learned from all three men requires musical notation and technical analyses that are beyond the nontechnical scope of this textbook. But careful listening will reveal the interrelationships to anyone who wants to find them, even if that person has no technical knowledge of music. The best Gordon recordings for this purpose are those he made during the 1940s (in a package called LONG TALL DEXTER—Savoy 2211). The best Lester Young recordings for this purpose are those he made between 1936 and 1944, available in reissues by Columbia. Sonny Stitt was so consistent from performance to performance, decade to decade, that almost any tenor sax improvisations recorded by him will be sufficient to reveal what Coltrane drew from the Stitt approach.

Comparison with Sonny Rollins

Coltrane was infrequently recorded during his pre-Miles Davis years, yet his strongest contemporary, tenor saxophonist Sonny Rollins, had already made his mark on the record scene. By the time Coltrane began to record, Rollins was a major figure, even though Rollins was four years younger than Coltrane. This may partly explain the widespread feeling that Rollins came first. The fact is that Coltrane was an outstanding, but underrecorded, player at the same time that Rollins was a heralded soloist on recordings with Miles Davis and others. Then, when Coltrane came along—with a style drawn from some of the same sources that had influenced Rollins—people thought of Coltrane as being directly influenced by Rollins. If you listen carefully to early Coltrane and early Rollins, you can easily tell them apart. Both had unique styles. For example, Coltrane

1) employed a tone that was
   a) larger
   b) coarser
   c) darker
   d) more weighty
2) played with a more searing quality
3) improvised with less of a stop and go quality (made less use of silence)
4) adhered less to Charlie Parker style
5) projected a less light-hearted and playful feeling
6) was less tuneful in his improvised lines
7) used staccato less

The Influence of Monk

Coltrane played with Thelonious Monk during part of 1957 while he was separated from Miles Davis. Coltrane claims that he learned from the experience, but he was not specific about what he learned, except to say that Monk was one of the first to show him how to make two or three notes at one time on the tenor saxophone (these are called multiphonics) and that Monk got him into the habit of playing long solos and playing the same piece for a long time to find new conceptions for solos. It can also be noted that Coltrane's work on the Davis *Milestones* album—recorded directly following his stint with Monk—shows a bit more assurance and increased instrumental proficiency over that on his pre-Monk albums made with Davis—*Steamin'*, *Cookin'*, *Workin'*, and *Relaxin'*. This change might be due partly to his experience with Monk, but it can also be attributed to improved health and much practicing that occurred during the same period.

INFATUATION WITH CHORD CHANGES

Coltrane's pre-1960s playing showed an infatuation with chord changes rivaling the interest in harmonic complexity which had previously characterized bop pianists. Coltrane loved to add chords to a tune's existing chord progression, a practice that had previously distinguished Art Tatum and Don Byas, to name a few pre-modern players. For instance, Coltrane took "Tune-Up," Eddie Vinson's sixteen-measure composition, and almost doubled the original number of chords in it. Then, with a somewhat different melody, he called it "Countdown" and included it on his *Giant Steps* album. What is most significant here is not simply that he added chords to an existing progression, it is the manner in which he chose the ones he added and the way he improvised solos over them. This was a great contribution to jazz that Coltrane made. His system involved stacking distantly related chords on top of each other. Then when he improvised solos, Coltrane devoured the tune's chord changes, trying to acknowledge every note in every chord and every scale which might be compatible with it.

A peak for Coltrane's infatuation with frequently changing chords and rapid playing came in his 1959 album titled *Giant Steps*. The quick tempo and unusual construction for two pieces in it, "Count-down" and "Giant Steps," make exceptional demands on the impro-viser. Their chords seldom last more than two fleeting beats, and each chord stakes out new territory. The title for the "Giant Steps" piece derives from Coltrane's having originally written it as a means to gain mastery over improvising through chord progressions in which large intervals separate the roots of successive chords, and few notes are held in common from one chord to another. In other words, the chords move so frequently and leap such "giant steps" that the improviser is given almost no chance to develop an idea on a given chord or to take an idea and stretch it across common tones of successive chords. In "Giant Steps," the chords change at the same pace as the melody notes.* The piece met Coltrane's practice needs, and it became a pop-ular test piece for improvisers, thereby serving the same function that "All the Things You Are" and "Con Alma" had previously served. Col-trane's improvisations based on the pieces in this album summarized his high level of technical proficiency and the period of his career during which he improvised furiously paced streams of notes with little use of silence.

PEDAL POINTS The pedal point is a device in Coltrane's compositional sound and combo approach that became popular among jazz musicians of the 1960s and 70s. Coltrane's ballad, "Naima," has a single note, the drone note (pedal point) repeated continuously for the first eight measures underneath the melody. Then a new pedal point accompanies the sec-ond eight measures. This device achieves an effect similar to that of a drone that sustains despite shifts in the tune's harmony. Repeating bass notes of this sort came to be strongly identified with Coltrane's sound of the 1960s. They were especially common as part of the ac-companiment to improvisations in pieces with Spanish and Indian flavor, pieces which were labeled "modal." ("Naima" can be heard in the *Giant Steps* album.)

TONE QUALITY
AND
SPIRITUALITY During the early 1960s, Coltrane's tone became smoother. It retained the edge and bite of his pre-1960s sound, but the texture was not as rough and the color was brighter. The confidence projected by his sound increased. Perhaps it was the terrific presence projected by this tone and its delivery that led some listeners to feel a spiritual force in Coltrane's music. His sound was so overwhelming and his solos main-

---

* The number of measures in "Giant Steps" is also noteworthy because the piece is not thirty-two measures, not A-A-B-A, not A-A-B-C, and it is not a twelve-measure blues. It is a sixteen-measure chord progression that is relatively original in jazz. Coltrane wrote many pieces which failed to fit standard song forms, and, though many listeners overlook it, Coltrane made major contributions to jazz history by way of his compositions.

tained high energy for such long periods (sometimes more than an hour), it was difficult to believe a mere mortal capable of such power.

BALLADS A large number of listeners know only the hard-driving Coltrane reflected in medium- and up-tempo pieces. But Coltrane was also one of the strongest ballad players that jazz tenor has known. When Coltrane played slow melodies, he was usually more economical than when involved in full-blown improvisation. It seemed as though he harnessed all the energy customarily released in dense, multinoted passages, and channeled it into a few deep, full-bodied tones. He breathed through long tones, and flawlessly slid from one interval to another. There was special warmth and tenderness in his ballads which was less obvious in his nonballad performances. Like alto saxophonist Johnny Hodges and tenor saxophonist Ben Webster, Coltrane could bring a glowing fullness to the phrases of a slow song.

Coltrane's albums for the Prestige record company usually contained a ballad or two. The 1956 *Mating Call*, an album recorded under Tadd Dameron's leadership (later reissued under Coltrane's name and the new title *On a Misty Night*), has several lush ballads. And Coltrane's *Soultrane* album featured the gorgeous "Theme for Ernie" and "I Want to Talk About You."

Some of Coltrane's best compositions took the form of ballads. There is the haunting beauty of his "Naima" (*Giant Steps*), his "After the Rain" (*Impressions*), his 1964 "Wise One" and "Lonnie's Lament" (*Crescent*), his "Dear Lord" (*Transition*), and his "Ogunde" (*Expression*). (Listen to his "Alabama" in SCCJ.)

WAS COLTRANE A MELODIC IMPROVISER? Despite the melodic gift demonstrated in his tune writing, Coltrane was only sporadically melodic when improvising. In the pop tune sense of melody, Coltrane's improvisations were rarely melody-like. Compared with bop melody style, as conceived by Charlie Parker, Dizzy Gillespie, and Thelonious Monk, Coltrane's improvisations were sporadically melodic before 1960 and rarely melodic after that. In his work both before and after 1960, there was a tendency to alternate between technical complexity and the lyricism which is characteristic of his compositions. If you slow down his most complex improvisations (or speed up your hearing so that every phrase is very clear to you), you will find that his work is often melodic in the bop sense but only sporadically melodic in the simple, singable melody sense. It takes an exceptionally quick ear to keep up with Coltrane, but once you have attained the necessary listening pace, you will notice more melodic tendencies than were apparent at first. However, Coltrane's lines do not possess the songlike quality or bop lyricism typical of Charlie Parker and Sonny Rollins. Harmonic development received a higher priority than melodic development.

**INFLUENCES
ON COLTRANE
IN THE 1960s**

**Ornette
Coleman**

In 1960, Coltrane recorded an album, *The Avant-Garde,* with Ornette Coleman's group minus Coleman (trumpeter Don Cherry, bassist Charlie Haden, and drummer Eddie Blackwell). Three Coleman compositions were included: "Focus On Sanity," "The Blessing," and "The Invisible." Then, again in 1965, Coleman's influence seems to have asserted itself in Coltrane's recording of *Ascension,* an album whose approach and sound resemble Coleman's 1960 *Free Jazz. Ascension* employed high-intensity, collective improvisation with four other saxophonists, two trumpeters, and a rhythm section. Most significant was use of a less restricting form than either John Coltrane or Miles Davis had previously used. (Listen to *Free Jazz* excerpt in SCCJ.)

Improvisation on *Ascension* was not totally collective nor totally free of prearrangement. Nor was it atonal (see pages 365–369 for explanation of scales, tone center, and atonality). Careful listening will reveal a few changes of chord or tone center. (Coltrane preset four scales for the musicians to use.) The changes do not occur often, but they do occur. So it is not totally free of form. Brief, loosely stated ensemble passages separate the solos. Those solos, in turn, receive rhythm section accompaniment. (The roles of soloist and accompanist are jazz traditions. Their separation here therefore demonstrates an absence of freedom from tradition despite the "free jazz" label that was frequently applied to this music.) Collectively improvised sections are balanced in duration and texture. Coltrane preset the order for the solos so that no two similar instruments played back to back. That procedure, for example, allowed a trumpet solo to follow a saxophone solo instead of following another trumpet solo.

During the 1960s and 70s the use of collective improvisation in the context of harmonic bases freer than chord progressions or modes was tried by many jazz musicians. The impetus for this could be attributed to the work of Ornette Coleman, Sun Ra, John Coltrane, or any combination of those leaders. But because Coltrane was the most prominent bandleader engaging in that new style, much of it caught on probably because of his *Ascension, Meditation,* and other albums that used similar approaches. (Note that Coleman and Coltrane each recorded large ensemble collective improvisation only once. They otherwise limited this technique to quartet and quintet format instead of the eight- and eleven-men groups of *Free Jazz* and *Ascension,* respectively.)

John Gilmore

During the early 1960s, Coltrane was interested in the music of Sun Ra and Sun Ra's powerful tenor saxophonist, John Gilmore. Coltrane's influence surfaced in Gilmore's work during 1960. But now it was Gilmore's turn to contribute to Coltrane's own work. Coltrane's solos on "Impressions" (*Impressions*), and "Chasin' the Trane" (*Live at the Village Vanguard*) contain melodic figures which bear a discernible resemblance to a few favorite Gilmore melodic devices used in his own solos on Sun Ra's *The Futuristic Sounds of Sun Ra*. (These are different devices than those of Coltrane's which Gilmore employed.)

SIMPLE HARMONIC BASES AND COLTRANE'S MODAL WORK

Coltrane and his 1965–67 associate, tenor saxophonist Pharoah Sanders, influenced the adoption of modal approaches to improvisation. Although Miles Davis had been one of the first to introduce modal methods, he emphasized them far less during the early 1960s than Coltrane did.

It must be remembered, in discussing the modal pieces of Coltrane and Pharoah Sanders, that, by strictly legitimate musical terminology, the Coltrane-Sanders playing was not entirely modal. It was only loosely based on the critical intervals that are characteristic to certain modes. (A mode is a scale containing a limited number of notes. If notes other than those defined by the mode are used, the resulting music is not strictly modal.) Coltrane adhered to the general harmonic orientation and flavor of certain modes, but he also employed notes outside of the mode. For that reason, his playing was not modal in the strictest sense of the word; only modal in the loose sense which jazz musicians and jazz journalists use. It is therefore accurate to speak of the Coltrane and Sanders work as simply being based on the repetition of one or two chords. Strictly speaking, you need not bring in the word modal at all.

One of Coltrane's most popular records was his 1960 *My Favorite Things*. The improvised portions of the title track were based primarily on the repetition of a few chords with which a single scale or mode was compatible. Toward the end of the improvisation, the chord and its corresponding scale were changed (the first part was minor tonality, the last part major tonality—see pages 370–371 for explanation of major and minor tonalities). The piece was a waltz, a fact which, coupled with the extensive repetition of those few chords, gave the piece a swaying, hypnotic quality. It provided an easy basis for improvisation because its construction was as undemanding as "Giant Steps" had been demanding. In 1961, he recorded "Olé" and "Impressions," both based on only one or two modes. In 1962, he recorded "Tunji," "Miles Mode," and "Out of This World," improvisations which were also mode-based. (See pages 384–386 for further explanations about mode-based improvisation, and see pages 419–421 for notations of several modes.)

Coltrane sought uncluttered harmonic bases which provided exotic colors and moods—those of Spain and India were favorites of his— and which allowed him great freedom in adding and altering harmonies within his improvisation. Especially uncluttered were the very loose harmonic formats Coltrane adopted in his 1965 duet with drummer Elvin Jones ("Vigil" on the *Kulu Sé Mama* album) and his 1967 duets with drummer Rashied Ali, which comprise the *Interstellar Space* album.

In light of his obvious search for simple harmonic bases, it is paradoxical that Coltrane continued to create harmonic complexity even when he steered clear of formats having complex chord changes. There was a lessening of the pre-"My Favorite Things" style characterized by its barrage of notes, and there was simple melodic development in some of his lines (especially in the 1961 "Chasin' the Trane" and "Impressions" solos in which Coltrane demonstrated methods he attributed to John Gilmore). But those aspects were revealed in only part of his work. Coltrane's infatuation with harmonic complexity did not cease with "Giant Steps." Many of Coltrane's solos showed harmonic complexity even when the primary basis of improvisation was a single mode or a repetitive bass figure. Sometimes the improvisations sounded as though Coltrane had determined how many chords could fit the mode and then improvised on all of them in the manner he might apply to a chord progression-based piece. And, by the method he had already developed previously, he stacked chords on top of distantly related chords, thereby lending the music a unique quality that became associated with him. It can be said, then, that Coltrane was spontaneously inventing additional chord changes whenever the musical situation did not already provide a large quantity. This made his improvisations harmonically rich even in pieces whose harmonic bases were not rich. After 1959, Coltrane alternated between simplicity and complexity, never entirely abandoning his infatuation with harmonic richness even though, on occasion, he exhaustively worked over a simple melodic idea, playing it long and short, forward and backward, up higher, down lower, etc.

What was the source for Coltrane interest in mode-based improvisation? First, he might have become interested in them entirely by himself or recalled the musical training he had received during the 1940s. Second, his interest might have arisen from his work with Miles Davis on the 1958 "Milestones" recording which was mode-based and the 1959 *Kind of Blue* album, which was also mode-based. (Coltrane's 1961 "Impressions" is based on the same modes with the same relative durations as the Davis composition "So What" from the *Kind of Blue* album—see notations on page 423.) Third, Coltrane's interest in modes might have resulted from his studying the native music of Africa, India, and other cultures. (He spent considerable time researching the use of modes in music outside of jazz.)

Contrary to the pronouncements of many jazz journalists, it is not accurate to call all of Coltrane's 1960s music "modal" or "free jazz." Coltrane's 1960s output continued to contain popular songs and twelve-bar blues pieces in addition to his modal pieces and the few pieces which were somewhat freer of conventional jazz approaches.

Left to right: McCoy Tyner (piano), John Coltrane (tenor sax), Jimmy Garrison (bass), Elvin Jones (drums), 1962. *(Courtesy of Duncan Scheidt)*

(In 1960, he recorded an entire album of blues tunes, *Coltrane Plays the Blues.* In 1964, he recorded his *Crescent* album with "Bessie's Blues" and his *Love Supreme* album with another twelve-bar blues titled "Pursuance.")

THE COLTRANE QUARTET   Coltrane was a member of the Miles Davis groups on and off for almost six years. (He made his earliest Davis recording in 1955, his last in 1961.) During this period, Coltrane also recorded with a few other leaders, and he recorded under his own name, but he did not lead a group of his own with a consistent personnel and a sound that was uniquely identifiable until 1960 when he was no longer touring with Davis. Coltrane first tried several changes of personnel, then settled with pianist McCoy Tyner, bassist Steve Davis, and drummer Elvin Jones. He used a number of bassists during the 1960s, but he used Jimmy Garrison most after Steve Davis had played with him on several albums in 1960 and 1961. Garrison was with Coltrane for most of the 1960s recordings and remained even after McCoy Tyner and Elvin Jones had left. The quartet had wide influence during the 1960s and continued to exert an influence more than ten years after it disbanded. Its effect is especially notable in records by Pharoah Sanders, the Bobby Hutcherson–Harold Land groups, and those of David Liebman, McCoy Tyner, Charles Lloyd (1966–69), John Handy (mid-1960s only), and Gato Barbieri.

Elvin Jones   As far as some listeners are concerned, Elvin Jones (b. 1927) has proven himself to be the most overwhelming drummer in jazz history. He has established a position on the drums that equals the power and innovation established by Charlie Parker and John Coltrane on the saxophone. Like Parker and Coltrane, Jones is a remarkably consistent performer. He seems to play every tune as though it is his last chance. An almost superhuman energy and endurance is associated with him. And his imagination seems to match his energy.

Elvin avoids the relative simplicity and repetition of most pre-1960 drummers. He rarely plays the obvious. In fact, in his most adventuresome work, he even avoids directly stating the first beat of each measure. His conception of the beat is a wider unit in time than had been usual with previous drummers. His timekeeping is steady, but loose, filled with rhythmic subtleties. He roams through his drums and cymbals distributing portions of triplets. He phrases in three's instead of two's and four's. He often begins his triplex division of time at the middle or end of a beat, and continues to juxtapose a staggered waltz feeling across the duration of several measures (for explanation of triplets, waltz meter, etc., see pages 358–362). During all that time he would still be maintaining a basic meter of four.

With Coltrane's group, Jones was able to play many rhythms at once and have the entire sound swell and heave like an ocean of activity under Coltrane's playing. Elvin Jones was one of the first drummers to play polyrhythmically and still swing hard in a loose, flowing way (for definition and explanation of polyrhythm, see page 364). Earlier drummers who attempted to use polyrhythms had sounded stiff and self-consciously calculating.

While listening to Elvin Jones, you might get the impression that he is juggling. Things seem forever in the air, never sharply defined in exact, predictable proportions. But the different rhythms played simultaneously were not just randomly different. Like those in an African drum ensemble, they were constructed to complement each other. And, in a broad sense, they fit together. It might not be obvious unless you listen carefully to four- and eight-measure sequences in their entirety. Some of his figures purposely omit a stroke or two but let you feel the missing stroke in the overall pattern. He distributes the parts of his triplets so that perhaps the first third is silent and next two are sounded on snare drum. Or perhaps the middle member is omitted. Sometimes the first two members of a triplet will sound on the snare drum and the third on the high hat or the bass drum. It might be because of his complexity and lack of predictability that few drummers in the 1970s managed to sound like him. It is also possible that the Jones orientation is rare because bandleaders find it difficult to play with, and little demand for it exists. A greater number of drummers, it seems, sound like more basic drummers such as Tony Williams (Miles Davis Quintet, 1963–69) and Billy Cobham (John McLaughlin's Mahavishnu Orchestra). In place of Elvin's broadness, Williams gives the impression that the beat is sharply defined. He seems to divide rhythmic figures into two's, four's, and eight's instead of Elvin's three's. Elvin is clearly more difficult to imitate than Williams, even though both styles are intricate and varied.

What bassist Scott LaFaro was doing with Bill Evans, drummer Elvin Jones was doing with John Coltrane's quartet. Jones interacted in as important a way as any front-line hornman at a Dixieland jam session, exemplified by his work on "Sun Ship" (*Sun Ship*) and "My Lady" (*Live at Birdland*). The whole character of the Coltrane quartet reflected the highly interactive style of Elvin Jones. Jones played with the surging power and imagination of two or three drummers combined, and his force was absorbed quite musically into the quartet concept. In fact, the style of Elvin Jones was possibly the most indispensable part of that ensemble concept. Can you imagine any other drummer with the 1961–65 Coltrane quartet? Even as dynamic and versatile a modern drummer as Roy Haynes was unable to supply the texture that Elvin Jones created ("My Favorite Things" in the *Selflessness* album uses Haynes in place of Jones).

When drummer Rashied Ali joined Coltrane, Elvin Jones left. There apparently was not room for both of these drummers, though Coltrane had imagined a new ensemble concept in which there was. But it is very difficult to find two drummers, each with a complete drum set, who can comfortably improvise together in a group with sax, piano, and bass.

Elvin proceeded to form a sequence of high-quality groups which, during the late 1960s and throughout the 1970s, offered some of the rare jazz neither significantly influenced by rock or electric instruments nor predominantly modal in orientation. He usually employed two tenor saxophonists and a bassist, but no piano. He employed some of the best saxophonists playing at that time (most of his tenor men were influenced by Coltrane): Joe Farrell, George Coleman, Frank Foster, Steve Grossman, David Liebman, and others. His groups almost achieved the solemn urgency possessed by the Coltrane quintet.

McCoy Tyner Coltrane's pianist from 1960 to the end of 1965 was McCoy Tyner (b. 1938). Creating an original approach from the linear style of Bud Powell, the block chording of Red Garland, and the voicings of Bill Evans and Horace Silver, he achieved a fresh approach to jazz piano.

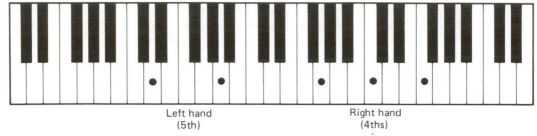

Left hand
(5th)

Right hand
(4ths)

Figure 17.1. Piano keyboard illustration of fifths in left hand and fourths in right hand.

He had been a distinctive and aggressive stylist in the Art Farmer–Benny Golson Jazztet, but carved a very personal style for himself within the Coltrane quartet. Along with Bill Evans and Herbie Hancock, he was a prime force in 1960s and 70s jazz piano styles. In fact, he was possibly as influential as Evans. Tyner's extensive use of chords voiced in fourths was widely adopted (see Figure 17.1). His comping style became a model for pianists of the late 1960s and the 1970s, especially those pianists playing in Coltrane-inspired groups. His fast solo lines also inspired numerous pianists, though few could match his imagination. The patterns he perfected soon became stock solo vocabulary for numerous pianists (see Table 17.1). He even affected pianists who already had established styles of their own.

McCoy Tyner's playing furnished a center for the quartet sound. It was as though he established a pivot for the seesawing of sounds that were being generated around him in the quartet. His stability in this capacity was partly due to his frequent use of a loud, held note (technically called a pedal point) or a loud, held interval (usually a fifth) played by his left hand while his right hand sounded several repeating chords (often voiced in intervals of a fourth). See Figure 17.1, and try it out for yourself on the piano. If you press the keys hard enough, you can sound like McCoy Tyner. These clear, ringing, open-voiced chords usually represented much less activity and more stability than was occurring in the saxophone, drum, and bass sounds. It was simpler and easier to follow than the surrounding activity. In most groups of this period, it was the bass part that was the simplest and steadiest. But in the Coltrane quartet, it was the piano part that was the most reliable sound. (See pages 417–418 for a technical explanation of these harmonies, and listen to Tyner play them on "The Promise" and "Afro-Blue" in Coltrane's album *Live at Birdland*.)

After leaving Coltrane, Tyner led a series of his own combos. He continued to play in the style he had employed with Coltrane and remained an exceptionally forceful player. But he often seemed as though he were spinning his wheels when not in the equally energetic and inspired context provided by Coltrane and Elvin Jones. Much of

TABLE 17.1. A Few of the Many Pianists Influenced by McCoy Tyner

Chick Corea	Ronnie Mathews
Alice McLeod Coltrane	Stanley Cowell
Kenny Gill	Hilton Ruiz
Bobo Stinson	Michael Cochran
Joe Bonner	Joanne Brackeen
Bill Henderson	John Hicks
Lonnie Liston Smith	Hal Galper
Onaje Allan Gumbs	Gil Goldstein
Harold Mabern	

his work continued the modal tradition extended by Coltrane, and Tyner continued to write compelling tunes in a style which was frequently imitated. (Incidentally, by the mid-1980s, neither Tyner nor pianist Keith Jarrett had adopted the electric piano. Though nearly every jazz pianist was using it, both these leading figures on the piano scene remained with the conventional piano.)

Jimmy Garrison Jimmy Garrison (1934–1976) was an imaginative bass player, one who held his own within the fiercely active Coltrane quartet. He invented rhythms which countered and complemented those of Tyner and Jones. Occasionally, Garrison took to strumming his bass as though it were a guitar. His use of double stops (two strings sounding together) and his strumming have been widely imitated. He was not the first to use such techniques, but his particular handling of them might have been the stimulus behind their popularity with jazz bassists of the 1960s and 70s.

Some of Garrison's double stopping may have had its source in Coltrane's interest in drones and in music employing two tones sustained together, a fifth apart. In the modal music of their native cultures, bagpipes, sitars, and tambura achieve exactly that effect. Coltrane's use of two bassists on "Olé" (on his *Olé Coltrane* album) and "India" (on his *Impressions* album) might have also stemmed from that interest.

THE SWEEP One of the most significant advances made by the 1960s Coltrane Quartet was a pioneering move toward a sweeping, broadly paced organization of parts, a change in feeling that was partly due to **a departure from:**

1) explicit statement of the markers for each measure,

2) accompaniment style in which chords changed frequently,

3) dependence on simple ride rhythms and walking bass patterns,

4) bouncing solo lines of eighth-note sequences with few sustained tones.

This new, widely imitated approach produced music which seemed to breathe more deeply and build excitement more broadly and solemnly than earlier jazz styles usually did. Phrases spanned larger units than the four- and eight-measure progressions that typified most jazz improvisation. There was more creation of a suspended feeling, which, each time it resolved, proved to be dramatic in its effect. Much of the new feeling was directly caused by **the particular collection of techniques** which the group refined:

1) Sustained and repeating sustained tones in the bass part (pianist's left hand, bassist's plucking) which are technically termed pedal points.

2) Drum patterns whose basic unit occupied several measures instead of just a few beats.

3) Sustaining piano chords (sounding them loudly and letting them ring).

4) Using a single mode (or a two-chord pattern) for a long time, instead of using numerous changes in harmony.

5) Long saxophone glissandos which were carefully timed and spanned a large portion of the saxophone's pitch range:
   a) sometimes used to preface a dramatically placed high note.
   b) sometimes evoking a rhapsodic effect.
   c) sometimes snaking in and around a central idea.
   The rhythmic construction of these glissandos departed from swing feeling and approximated an orchestral concept reminiscent of music that is not as rigidly tied to the beat as are marching and dancing traditions.

6) Use of sustained tones in saxophone solos (allowing listeners a point of focus and relief from having to follow ever-changing melodic contours).

7) Long-term continuity of mood, as though the composition and lengthy improvisations were conceived in their entirety rather than being a sequence of tune and solos that simply strung together swinging phrases in jam session manner.

COLTRANE'S IMPACT   John Coltrane exerted a striking effect on his listeners. People who hated his music fought in print with those who were impressed by it. Some felt jazz history ended with Coltrane, whereas today many feel it only just started with Coltrane. Not long after Coltrane formed his own group, there were so many saxophonists imitating him that jazz journalists began complaining about a general lack of originality as vehemently as they had responded to the wave of Charlie Parker disciples that rose during the 1950s. Coltrane was the subject of numerous scholarly analyses, and the 1980s saw an increased flow of publications which evaluated Coltrane's work from a technical standpoint. Saxophonist Andrew White was so inspired by Coltrane's music that he transcribed more than four hundred recorded Coltrane solos note for note. (See page 412 for information on how to get the White transcriptions.)

Each of Coltrane's periods caused many musicians to try out the techniques that Coltrane had popularized. First it was multi-noted playing and difficult chord progressions. Coltrane's manner for replacing the chord changes from standard tunes was adopted by many. Musicians began making their own chords move in the manner demonstrated by Coltrane in his "Giant Steps" and "Countdown" progressions. Then it was modal style and pedal points. After that, it was simultaneous collective improvisation and the creation of frantic turbulence that emphasized textures more than lines. (Sometimes it appeared as though a large community of musicians had decided that Coltrane was their guide, and they postponed generating ideas of their own until they could see what he was going to do next.) Even musicians who are known for considerable originality themselves felt the impact of Coltrane's work. Chick Corea credits Coltrane for the inspiration behind the compositions "Litha" and "Straight Up and Down." Corea also cites Coltrane's *Meditations* and *Ascension* for influencing his own free-form approach used on the *Is* album. "A Love Supreme" was recorded by jazz-rock stars John McLaughlin and Carlos Santana. "Naima" and "Giant Steps" were standard repertory for jazz musicians of the 1980s (even the big band of Woody Herman had recorded them).

Influence on Saxophonists
Coltrane had a marked influence on saxophonists during the 1960s (see Table 17.2). Along with Ornette Coleman, Coltrane became the primary model for new saxophonists to study, and several older players also incorporated his techniques in mid-career. Such established players as Frank Foster, Harold Land, Teddy Edwards, and Cannonball Adderley all demonstrated the acquisition of Coltrane techniques. Adderley absorbed some of the Coltrane approach while playing in the Miles Davis band with him during the late 1950s. (A particularly Coltrane-like Adderley solo can be heard in "Fun" on Adderley's *Mercy, Mercy, Mercy* album.) Coltrane's influence even showed up in the unlikely context of Woody Herman's big band, a group whose saxophone section had been previously identified with the sound of Stan Getz and cool jazz. Many of Herman's players of the 1970s and 80s have used Coltrane's methods (In tallying Coltrane's disciples, it must be remembered that Coltrane was rarely the only influence that

TABLE 17.2. A Few of the Many Saxophonists Influenced by Coltrane

Pharoah Sanders	Pat LaBarbera
Charles Lloyd	Bob Berg
Joe Farrell	Sonny Fortune
Wayne Shorter	Jan Garbarek
Gato Barbieri	Michael Brecker
John Klemmer	Andrew White
Nathan Davis	James Spalding
Lew Tabackin	Ernie Krivda
Robin Kenyatta	Joe Lovano
Steve Grossman	Charles B. Owens
Billy Harper	Bob Mintzer
David Liebman	Manny Boyd
John Surman	Bill Evans
Bennie Maupin	Frank Foster
Carlos Garnett	Joe Henderson
Steve Marcus	David Young
Teddy Edwards	Harold Land
Cannonball Adderley	Frank Tiberi
Steve Lederer	Gregory Herbert
Rich Perry	

these players had. Woody Herman's 1970s saxophonists, for example, drew from a variety of sources, and the most outstanding players who were affected by Coltrane have shown marked individuality as well as showing the influence of other sources. Joe Farrell, for example, also cites Charlie Parker as a primary influence, and Michael Brecker cites King Curtis and Junior Walker in addition to citing Coltrane.)

Soprano Saxophone About the time he formed his own groups (1960–61), Coltrane began playing soprano saxophone in addition to tenor. (Coltrane plays soprano on the title track of *My Favorite Things*, "India" on *Impressions*, and "Afro-Blue" on *Live at Birdland*.) Soprano saxophone had been previously used on recordings by Sidney Bechet, Johnny Hodges, Charlie Barnet, and Steve Lacy, but it had yet to catch on as a standard jazz instrument. But a few years after Coltrane first used it, the soprano saxophone had become quite popular with jazz saxophonists, and, by 1970, most tenor saxophonists were performing on it. By the early 1970s, even players who were not necessarily followers of Coltrane also used soprano. Such men as alto saxophonist Cannonball Adderley and tenor saxophonist Sonny Rollins, who had established

John Coltrane, playing soprano saxophone, the instrument he helped popularize during the 1960s. (*Courtesy of Bill Smith and* CODA)

unique, well-known styles on their chosen saxes, also began recording with soprano sax. Some players adopted it almost to the exclusion of their tenors. On their post-1968 Miles Davis recordings, Coltrane disciples Steve Grossman and Dave Liebman played more soprano than tenor. Saxophonist Joe Farrell, another player who absorbed portions of the Coltrane style, recorded an entire album, *Moon Germs,* without using his tenor, and Wayne Shorter recorded *Super Nova* without his. Coltrane's popularization of the instrument coincided with a practical problem that 1970s saxophonists encountered: trying to be heard over loud rhythm sections. The range and tone quality of the soprano saxophone helped saxophonists cut through the sound created by increasing numbers of drums and amplified instruments which comprised groups of the 1970s. The attraction to soprano saxophone then can be attributed partly to the attraction that players had to Coltrane, partly to the practical advantages of its sound, and partly to the search for fresh sounds that has traditionally characterized jazz musicians.

Rare Recordings Valuable for Documenting Coltrane's Pre-Miles Davis Work

(*These are the earliest examples of Coltrane on record.*)

Great Moments in Jazz Vol. 2 Alto Masters Swing Treasury 109. This is usually cataloged under "Anthologies and Combinations," not under "Johnny Hodges" or "John Coltrane," even though it is cited here for a 1954 Hodges combo selection that features Coltrane.

Dizzy Gillespie *Dee Gee Days* Savoy SJL 2209 (Coltrane solos on the 1951 "We Love To Boogie.")

Johnny Hodges *At a Dance, In a Studio, On Radio* Enigma 1059 (1954 sessions)

John Coltrane *Coltrane 1951* (also known as *First Broadcasts*) Oberon 5100 (1951 sessions with Dizzy Gillespie combo)

John Coltrane *First Steps* Jazz Live 8039 (1951 with Gillespie, 1954 with Hodges)

Cited Recordings Made Under the Leadership of Miles Davis

Milestones Columbia PC 9428

Miles Davis Prestige 24001 (includes all contents of albums formerly called *Cookin'* and *Relaxin'*)

Workin' and Steamin' Prestige 24034

Kind of Blue Columbia PC 8163

Cited Recordings Made with Coltrane as Leader Before He Permanently Left Miles Davis

Coltrane Jazz Atlantic 1354

Soultrane Prestige 7531; *John Coltrane* Prestige 24003 (includes contents of 7531), Fantasy-Prestige-Milestone OJC 021 and Prestige 7142 (these are alternate issues of 7531)

Giant Steps Atlantic SD 1311

Cited Recordings of the First Quartets With Tyner and Jones Before Jimmy Garrison Joined

My Favorite Things Atlantic SD 1361

Coltrane Plays the Blues Atlantic SD 1382

Cited Recordings by the Classic Quartet
(Coltrane, Tyner, Garrison, and Jones)

Impressions MCA 29014 and Impulse 42
Crescent MCA 29016 and Impulse 66
Transition MCA 29027 and Impulse 9195
Live at the Village Vanguard MCA 29009 and Impulse 10
Love Supreme MCA 29017 and Impulse 77
Sun Ship MCA 29028 and Impulse 9211
Live at Birdland MCA 29015 and Impulse 50

Cited Recordings of Coltrane-led Sessions
of Simultaneous Collective Improvisations ("Free Jazz")

Meditations MCA 29022 and Impulse 9110
Live in Seattle MCA 24134 and Impulse 9202
Ascension MCA 29020 and Impulse 95

Albums Cited in This Chapter
That Do Not Fit the Preceding Classifications

Expression MCA 29032 and Impulse 9120
On a Misty Night Prestige P 24084
The Avant-Garde Atlantic S 1451
Olé Coltrane Atlantic SD 1373
Kulu Sé Mama MCA 29021 and Impulse 9106
Interstellar Space MCA 29029 and Impulse 9277
Selflessness MCA 29026 and Impulse 9161

Note: Though not cited in this chapter, Coltrane's *Blue Train* album (Blue Note 81577) has remained a favorite among musicians. Recorded in 1957 with trumpeter Lee Morgan, trombonist Curtis Fuller, pianist Kenny Drew, bassist Paul Chambers, and drummer Philly Joe Jones, it features excellent solos and it exposes two of Coltrane's most masterful compositions "Moment's Notice" (whose chord progression is as difficult as his "Giant Steps" progression) and "Blue Train" (a minor blues that became popular at jam sessions of the 1960s).

Note: The recordings cited in this chapter represent only a fraction of Coltrane's recorded output. For a more thorough listing, see the discography in *Chasin' the Trane* by J. C. Thomas (Doubleday hardcover, 1975 and Da Capo paperback).

CHAPTER SUMMARY

Coltrane contributed

1) a repertory of patterns which became basic routines mastered by hundreds of young players during the 1960s, 70s, and 80s. (This paralleled the imitation that Parker's and Gillespie's favorite phrases experienced during the 1940s and 50s and Armstrong's experienced during the 1920s and 30s.)

2) a popularization of the soprano saxophone

3) a popularization of modal improvisation

4) a new rhythm section concept for accompaniment

5) an emphasis on improvisational speed and intensity

6) the sweep

7) a body of original compositions, many of which introduced new methods

8) a model for tone color and rhythmic conception on saxophone

9) a system of juxtaposing distantly related chords and improvising on the least related tones in the juxtaposition, thereby going beyond the bop practice of concentrating on the ninth, eleventh, and thirteenth intervals of the original chord.

chapter 18
WAYNE SHORTER, RON CARTER, & TONY WILLIAMS

In 1963, Miles Davis hired a new rhythm section comprised of pianist **Herbie Hancock**, bassist **Ron Carter**, and drummer **Tony Williams**. The members of Davis's new band were as young as the *Birth of the Cool* musicians had been; Williams was only seventeen years old. By the summer of 1964, the quintet had made one-half of a studio album, *Seven Steps to Heaven*, and three live concert albums: *Miles in Europe*, *My Funny Valentine*, and *Four and More*.

The Hancock–Carter–Williams rhythm section had the excitement of the Garland-Chambers-Jones rhythm section and the sensitivity and delicate interaction which typified the Bill Evans-Scott LaFaro-Paul Motian unit. The Davis rhythm section remained intact, at least on records, from 1963 until 1968. It was probably the smoothest rhythm section sound jazz had experienced. Along with the 1961–65 John Coltrane rhythm section (pianist McCoy Tyner, bassist Jimmy Garrison, drummer Elvin Jones), the Davis rhythm section was a leader during the 1960s. Both the Davis and the Coltrane rhythm sections consolidated the innovations of modern jazz and became far more than simply accompanying units.

Hancock, Carter, and Williams maintained excellent rapport. They were able to play cohesively at breakneck tempos ("Walkin'" on *Four and More*), or, in the context of a slow piece, they could avoid stating tempo, and thus sound as though someone were conducting them through gradual accelerations and decelerations ("My Funny Valentine" on *My Funny Valentine*, "Madness" on *Nefertiti*, and "Masqualero" on *Sorcerer*). Their rapport and high level of musicianship allowed them to change rhythms, textures, and moods spontaneously at

Bassist Ron Carter and tenor saxophonist Wayne Shorter photographed here while with the mid-1960s Miles Davis group. (*Courtesy of Bill Smith and* CODA)

any moment of a performance, at any tempo, and on any chord progression. Their versatility and lightening quick responsiveness were extraordinary.

Hancock, Carter, and Williams were all exceptionally skilled on their respective instruments. Hancock seemed to combine all the best qualities of an improviser: a clear conception, fertile imagination, a sense of continuity, and excellent instrumental proficiency. He had a quick, precise touch and comped briskly. These qualities put him in great demand as a recording pianist. Hancock appeared on more record dates than any other jazz pianist of the 1960s. (See pages 256–258 for more about Hancock.)

Carter (b. 1937) had a slick, round tone. He walked with uncanny perfection and buoyancy. Both his tone and his sense of timing exhibited a uniformly high level of quality. Carter played more toward the front of the beat than Chambers did. He provided a sturdy, yet responsive foundation for the quintet. Miles Davis was not the only leader who appreciated Ron Carter's skill and reliability. By the mid-1970s, Carter had been employed on more than four hundred records.

Bassist Ron Carter did not always restrict himself to walking. He incorporated figures similar to those used by Scott LaFaro and other inventive bassists. Carter embellished walking sequences and set up new rhythmic patterns. He constantly thought of new ways to both underpin the group sound and enrich the musical events that occurred around him. Listen to his playing on "Pee Wee" and "Masqualero" (*Sorcerer*), "Freedom Jazz Dance" (*Miles Smiles*), and "Riot," "Fall," and "Nefertiti" (all on *Nefertiti*).

Tony Williams (b. 1945) represented the very highest level of drum technique, and he was possibly the most influential jazz drummer of the 1960s. He was very fast and his cymbal tones were separated with crystal clarity. Williams provided a model of light, sharp sounds. His ride cymbal sound was very crisp and distinctive, and, because he used a smaller bass drum than most pre-1960s drummers, the low register component of his sound was well articulated.

Drummer Tony Williams was an extremely sophisticated rhythm section player, looser and more daring than Paul Motian. Williams did more than kick and prod the hornmen. By the time *Filles de Kilimanjaro* was recorded, he had assumed a role so prominent that he often overshadowed the other sounds in the group. His was a very assertive style, quite the opposite of Kenny Clarke's or the conservative mid-1950s West Coast style drummers. (Compare Clarke's performance on the records Miles Davis made during the early 1950s with Williams's playing on *Filles de Kilimanjaro* or *Miles Smiles*. You will hear a drastic difference between the two.)

The members of Davis's rhythm section employed many unusual devices. As early as the 1964 *Four and More*, Tony Williams had played pieces without consistently closing his high-hat on the second and fourth beats of each measure. He kept time with the ride cymbal and used the high-hat only for bursts of color. Then on the 1966 "Freedom Jazz Dance" (*Miles Smiles*), he closed his high-hat on every beat, a timekeeping device later adopted by hundreds of jazz-rock drummers. He also colored the group sound with an endless variety of cymbal splashes, snare drum fills, and imaginative rhythmic patterns played on all of his drums and cymbals, extending the techniques which had been employed by Philly Joe Jones, Art Blakey, Louis Hayes, and Paul Motian. These are just a few of the numerous devices which Williams employed. Only by listening to the recordings can you appreciate his tremendous inventiveness and understand how his creations fit with those of his fellow bandmates.

The 1963–68 Davis rhythm section style was heard later in recordings by Joe Henderson (*Power to the People; Tetragon; In Pursuit of Blackness; The Kicker; If You're Not Part of the Solution, You're Part of the Problem*) and Joe Farrell (*Joe Farrell Quartet*). The rhythm section style of *Miles In Europe* and *Four and More* was later heard in records by Freddie Hubbard, Jackie McLean (*Right Now*), and others. The Davis quintet approaches on *Miles Smiles, Miles in the Sky,* and *Nefertiti* influenced Kenny Cox and the Contemporary Jazz Quintet (*Multidirection*), as well as Art Lande (*Rubisa Patrol*).

Compositional Style

Most tunes Davis played during the 1950s fit conventional song forms. An examination of the tunes on his 1961 *Someday My Prince Will Come* and *In Person at the Blackhawk,* his 1963 *Seven Steps to Heaven* and *Miles in Europe,* and his 1964 *Four and More* and *My Funny Valentine* reveals that, after the departure of Bill Evans and prior to his work with Wayne Shorter, Davis had not explored much new territory in the area of song forms. After Shorter joined him, however, Davis recorded very few conventionally constructed pieces. After 1964, Davis favored tunes which did not have bridges, complex turnarounds, or any section demarcations which can easily act as barriers to an unencumbered, free-flowing sound. Most of his recordings were made up of tunes which had fewer chord changes than the pop standards of Richard Rodgers or George Gershwin, or the jazz standards by Charlie Parker, Dizzy Gillespie, Tadd Dameron, John Lewis, or Thelonious Monk. In fact, some tunes recorded by Davis from 1965 to 1968 have no preset chord changes. Their function is only to set tempo, key, and mood. The choice of chord changes is left to the inspiration of the improviser.

A large number of post-1964 compositions are all A instead of A-A-B-A, A-B-A-B, or A-B-A-C. Shorter's "Iris" is a sixteen-bar waltz, all A (*E.S.P.*). His "Prince of Darkness" is sixteen bars long with very few prearranged harmonies (*Sorcerer*). Shorter's "E.S.P." is sixteen bars long, all A, with important and frequent chord changes. It is played twice, as:

twelve bars + four-bar turnaround
twelve bars + four-bar conclusion.

The four-bar sections differ, but the twelve-bar sections are identical. Incidentally, "E.S.P., displays what became a characteristic sound in much late 1960s and 70s music, the fourth (see Figure 18.1 and pages 376 and 418).

Another trait which lent the 1965–68 recordings their distinctive flavor was the use of space in tune construction. Several measures of the melody were filled with silence. Quite often, trumpet and tenor would lay out while the rhythm section continued to play and generate a mood. For example, Shorter's "Dolores" is thirty-eight bars long, divided into phrases of two, two and one-half, three, and three and one-half measures (*Miles Smiles*). These phrases are separated by spaces in which the horns do not play. Only the rhythm section is heard, continuing and developing patterns they played underneath the horns.

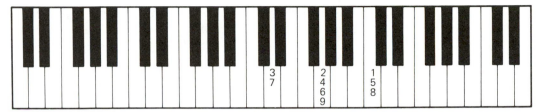

Figure 18.1. Piano keyboard illustration of "E.S.P." The first nine notes of "E.S.P." are separated by the interval of a fourth.

One other important aspect of the group's compositional style was the small number of rapid, jumpy eighth-note figures and highly syncopated lines which had been typical of bop. Of course they still used eighth notes and syncopation, but many of the post-1964 tunes were constructed of smoothly contoured lines of connected, sustained tones. The tunes had fewer changes of direction than bop melodies, with their many twists and turns. Shorter's "Nefertiti" (*Nefertiti*) is a good example. It is a sixteen-bar tune, all A. There is a new chord in nearly every measure, but the motion always has a slow, floating quality. Nothing abrupt or jumpy happens in either the melody or the chord changes. This style places the burden of complexity on the rhythm section, quite the reverse of bop tendencies. In fact, with no improvised solos by anyone else, the 1967 version of "Nefertiti" is practically a feature for Tony Williams. The melody is repeated again and again, a device later employed extensively by post-1968 Davis groups and spin-offs from those bands. The lazy, expansive feeling evoked by the performance of "Nefertiti" suggests the impressionistic classical music of Claude Debussy ("La Mer," "Prelude to the Afternoon of a Fawn") and Ravel ("Daphnis and Chloe"). The melody's silences and sustained tones produce an effect quite the opposite of that created by typical bop melodies such as Charlie Parker's "Confirmation" or Tadd Dameron's "Hot House." The melody's accompaniment, a loose but highly active rhythm section improvisation, contrasts sharply with the bop accompaniment style of walking bass and ride rhythms. The post-1964 Davis quintet discarded the bop formula of quick, jumpy melodic figures on top and stable, metronomic pulse patterns on the bottom. Shorter's writing brought stable simplicity to the top, and Williams's drumming brought super-charged rhythmic complexity to the bottom. This reversal of roles became especially common later in jazz-rock groups, especially Weather Report.

Varied Approaches   In addition to high-level instrumental proficiency, improvisatory freshness and their unique contributions to the development of jazz accompaniment style, Hancock, Shorter, Carter, and Williams managed to ensure that the variety of moods and rhythmic styles employed in the 1964–68 Davis Quintet was vast. They recorded

1) waltzes, including Davis's "Circle" and Shorter's "Footprints" (both on the *Miles Smiles* album), Hancock's "Little One" and Carter's "Mood" (both on the *E.S.P.* album), and Williams's "Pee Wee" (on the *Sorcerer* album);

2) fast pieces, including Jimmy Heath's "Gingerbread Boy," Shorter's "Dolores" and "Orbits" (all on the *Miles Smiles* album), Williams's "Hand Jive" (on the *Nefertiti* album), Hancock's "The Sorcerer" (on the *Sorcerer* album), Carter's "R.J." and Shorter's "E.S.P." (both on the *E.S.P.* album);

3) slow, reflective pieces, including Shorter's "Fall" (on the *Nefertiti* album) "Masqualero" and "Vonetta" (both on the *Sorcerer* album);

4) pieces in which a sequence of different rhythmic styles are created, as in Davis's "Country Son" (on the *Miles in the Sky* album) and in the Davis-Carter "Eighty-One" (on the *E.S.P.* album).

WAYNE SHORTER

Between 1964 and 1969, Miles Davis employed Wayne Shorter (b. 1933), one of the most outstanding tenor saxophonists in jazz. Shorter was also a composer whose work dramatically changed the sound of the Davis Quintet. His writing and playing later became central to the work of Weather Report, a creative jazz-rock group of the 1970s.

Shorter had a gray tone with a broad-textured surface and soft edges. It was a hard sound, but he could temper that hardness according to the mood of the music. Until the 1970s, his tone rarely had vibrato. Though most saxophonists depend partly on vibrato as an expressive device, Shorter cultivated so many other expressive devices, you did not miss the vibrato. He made masterful use of various attacks and releases. He could slide up into the pitch of a note or strike it head on. He could release a note by carefully tapering it or by bending its pitch up or down. The note might trail off and disappear or it might fall and then slide up to another note. He could flit from note to note like a bird going from branch to branch. Though his technique was primarily legato, he sometimes gave out stark announcements consisting of brief tones.

Wayne Shorter brought a gift for melody to his solos. Listening to him improvise is like looking over the shoulder of a composer as he invents and develops themes. Shorter was a very intelligent improviser who brought a strong sense of continuity to his lines. He played unusual intervals in a manner which was somehow graceful and ferocious at the same time. Almost every chorus was a coherent and concise melodic statement.

By the early 1960s, Shorter had abandoned the bop approach to melody. The pet phrases of Parker and Gillespie were absent from his playing. The intricate, bop eighth-note figures with their never-ending twists and turns were disappearing from his work. Shorter played lines of smoother contours. His melodic approach often recalled the concise floating themes of turn-of-the-century French composers Maurice Ravel, Claude Debussy, and Erik Satie.

His early playing had shown a Coltrane influence, but his tone color and texture were unlike Coltrane's. And Shorter's rhythmic conception was looser than Coltrane's; he seemed to be floating around the beat rather than precisely subdividing it. He also played fewer notes in his lines.

By 1964, Shorter had become an extremely fresh improviser. He had eliminated most of the bop influence in his lines and reworked so much of Coltrane's style that he presented a sound which was almost entirely his own. His playing was almost free of clichés. He could handle hard, raw playing, and yet his ballad work was as tender as that of Stan Getz. His best improvisations are to be found in the 1965 Miles Davis LP *E.S.P.* Listen to his solo on "Eighty-One." Note the middle section which is so melodic that it could be taken out of context and used as a tune. Yet in spite of its very deliberate construction, it carries an emotional impact of searing depth. Listen to his improvisation on "Pee Wee" on Davis's *Sorcerer*. It is haunting in its otherworldly beauty.

Shorter began playing soprano saxophone on his last two Davis LPs, *In a Silent Way* and *Bitches Brew*. He continued to play both soprano and tenor saxophones with Weather Report.

Shorter changed his style drastically when he joined Weather Report. Instead of long, melodic phrases, he often played short bursts of notes alternating with long silences and sustained tones. This new style meshed well with the unusual percussion sounds, conversational bass figures, and crackling keyboard ideas which characterized the group. Often Shorter would go several measures without playing. Then, after playing only a note or two, he would become silent again. His was a very difficult role. Instead of creating melodic improvisations, he participated in a collective effort to create textures. The delicate balance achieved in the collective improvisations of Weather Report is due in part to Wayne Shorter's tasteful and very disciplined sense of musical discretion. **He artfully made the difficult transition from jazz soloist in the conventional sense to ensemble improviser** in the new context created by Weather Report. (Listen to "Umbrellas" and "Seventh Arrow" on *Weather Report* and "Surucucu" on *I Sing the Body Electric*.)

Wayne Shorter's recorded work with Miles Davis and with Weather Report is generally very careful playing. However, he can be heard taking more chances within a recorded concert appearance made during the first year he was with Davis: *Live at the Plugged Nickel*. It is as though there are two sides to Shorter, a restrained and reflective side that is most evident in the studio dates he made with Davis (*E.S.P.* and *Sorcerer*, for instance) and a more impassioned and daring side that is most evident in *Live at the Plugged Nickel* and in several of his recorded concert dates with Art Blakey. Most of the albums Shorter made under his own name fit the restrained category, as do his solos and collective improvisations recorded with Weather Report.

Like Lester Young, Shorter sharply curtailed his creative output after a while. Though his composing continued, Shorter's richly imaginative soloing was not heard much after his mid-1960s Miles Davis recordings. Young had burst on the recording scene with an extremely fresh and buoyant style. Then within six years he had stopped creating, though he continued soloing persuasively until his death. Shorter parallels Young in that he appeared with Art Blakey in 1959 playing compelling, original solos and continued that level of creativity with Davis but then receded to a supportive role in Weather Report thereafter. Shorter's peak was the early and mid-1960s with Blakey and Davis. Shorter also parallels Young because he and Young were probably the most melodic of all jazz tenor saxophonists. Furthermore their roots were less detectable than were the roots of most other modern tenor saxophonists. In other words, Young and Shorter were possibly the most original improvisers on their instrument.

Wayne Shorter was one of the key composers of the 1960s and 70s. He wrote extensively for albums of his own and contributed substantially to the repertories of three historically significant groups: Art Blakey's Jazz Messengers (1959–64), the Miles Davis Quintet (1964–69), and Weather Report (from 1971).

Though the details are beyond the nontechnical scope of this book, **Shorter's historical significance is partly determined by the unusual ways that he makes chords move within his compositions.** Some of his tunes place chords in sequences which had never been common to jazz. His compositions are the subject of much study by jazz scholars, and Shorter is one of the most respected of all modern jazz composers. Many feel that his writing constitutes a greater contribution than his saxophone playing.

Shorter was notable for supplying Weather Report with a style for one branch of its repertory: pieces characterized by a pastoral feeling which was achieved by dreamy melodies containing many silences and sustained tones in a relatively slow tempo. The resulting effect was a sense of suspension. (Listen to "Three Clowns" on Weather Report's *Black Market* album and "Harlequin" on their *Heavy Weather* album.) An historic aspect in the performance of some of these pieces is the **reversal of character traditionally assumed by jazz melody and accompaniment, respectively.** Such melodies as "Manolete" and "Non-Stop Home" on Weather Report's *Sweetnighter* album possess clarity and simplicity, whereas the accompaniment is turbulent. (You might remember that, at least as early as the bop era, horn lines had traditionally been more complex than their accompaniments.) This practice continued the manner in which the Miles Davis Quintet had performed Shorter's "Nefertiti" on the 1967 Davis album called *Nefertiti*. (The serene, floating quality of "Nefertiti" had also been present in Zawinul's writing. This was evident at least as early as the 1969 Miles Davis recording of Zawinul's "In a Silent Way" and the 1970 Zawinul recording of "Dr. Honoris Causa." Zawinul had been attracted by the flavor of the Miles Davis "Nefertiti" performance, and historical continuity occurred when Shorter and Zawinul extended this compositional flavor when they teamed up to co-lead Weather Report.)

Another prominent aspect of Weather Report's music that is linked to Wayne Shorter and the original recording of "Nefertiti" is the **extensive repetition of melodic lines within a single rendition while continuous variation of accompaniment figures occurs.** This was not Shorter's idea; it stemmed from the way things were handled by Miles Davis and Tony Williams at the original "Nefertiti" recording session. However, Shorter's composition provided the impetus for this approach, and both Zawinul and Shorter capitalized upon it in the construction of pieces for Weather Report performances. (Listen to "Boogie Woogie Waltz," "Manolete," and "Non-Stop Home" on Weather Report's *Sweetnighter* album. Once you recognize the device, you will soon find yourself identifying it within numerous other Weather Report albums.)

The contributions of Shorter listed above only scratch the surface of his compositional work.* For example, he also wrote a number of engaging themes that are waltzes, as well as pieces for Weather Report that possess a funky, dance-like sound. (Listen to "Port of Entry" on Weather Report's *Night Passage* album and "Mysterious Traveler" on

---

* The following Wayne Shorter compositions have been recorded by leading jazz groups: "Children of the Night," by Art Blakey and by Billy May; "Infant Eyes," by Stan Getz; "Lester Left Town," by Art Blakey and by Stan Getz; "Dear Sir" and "Rio," by Lee Morgan; "One by One," "Sweet 'n' Sour," "This is for Albert," "On the Ginza," "Contemplation," "Mr. Jin," "Free for All," "Hammerhead," "Sleeping Dancers Sleep On," "Noise in the Attic," "Giantis," "Sincerely Diana," "Backstage Sally," "The Summit," "Ping Pong," "Roots and Herbs," "The Back Sliders," "United," "Look at the Birdie," and "Master Mind," by Art Blakey; "Pinocchio," by Miles Davis and by Weather Report; "Plaza Real," "When It Was Now," "Sightseeing," "Port of Entry," "Tears," "Eurydice," "Manolete," "Non-Stop Home," "The Moors," "Surucucu," "Mysterious Traveler," "Blackthorn Rose," "Lusitanos," "Freezing Fire," "Lost," "Elegant People," "Three Clowns," "Harlequin," and "Palladium," by Weather Report; "Dolores," by Miles Davis and by Miroslav Vitous; "E.S.P.," "Footprints," and "Nefertiti," by Miles Davis and many other bandleaders; "Fall," by Miles Davis and by Pat Martino; "Iris," "Limbo," "Vonetta," "Prince of Darkness," "Masqualero," "Orbits," "Paraphernalia," "Sanctuary," "Water Babies," "Capricorn," "Sweet Pea," and "Two Faced," by Miles Davis; and "The Chess Players," by Jimmy Rowles.

their *Mysterious Traveler* album.) Shorter's work for Miles Davis and Weather Report is easy to find because it is on Columbia records and was popular enough to stay in print. However, do not let the stress on his Columbia documentation lead you to overlook the richness that awaits you in the many albums made under his own name for Blue Note records and those made with Art Blakey for Blue Note and other small companies. Many of the compositions that have attracted the attention of jazz musicians and scholars lie in the Blue Note material.

INFORMATION FOR LOCATING CITED ALBUMS

All the albums cited in this chapter were released by Columbia under the name of Miles Davis or Weather Report. In the following list, these albums appear according to the order in which they were cited.

Miles Davis Albums	*Weather Report Albums*
Seven Steps to Heaven PC 8851	*Black Market* PC 34099
Miles in Europe PC 8983	*Heavy Weather* PC 34418
My Funny Valentine PC 9106	*Sweetnighter* PC 32210
Four and More PC 9253	*Night Passage* PC 36793
Nefertiti PC 9495	*Mysterious Traveler* PC 32494
Sorcerer PC 9532	
Filles de Kilimanjaro PC 9750	
Miles Smiles PC 9401	
E.S.P. PC 9150	
Miles in the Sky PC 9628	
In a Silent Way PC 9875	
Bitches Brew PG 26	
Live at the Plugged Nickel C2 38266	

CHAPTER SUMMARY

1) Tenor saxophonist Wayne Shorter contributed a fresh solo style to jazz.
2) Shorter's solos and compositions significantly affected the character of the Art Blakey band, the Miles Davis group, and Weather Report.

3) Shorter was influential in his compositional use of
   a) the interval of a fourth,
   b) sustained tones and silences in melody lines,
   c) melodic construction that suggests a dreamy, floating quality, and
   d) chord sequences previously unusual in jazz.
4) Bassist Ron Carter has a sleek tone and impeccable sense of tempo.
5) Carter has been the most in-demand jazz bassist since 1960.
6) Carter's walking and pedal points furnished a firm foundation for the 1963–68 Miles Davis groups that were exploring explosive accompaniment sounds that were not timekeeping rhythms.
7) Carter sometimes incorporated nonwalking, interactive techniques.
8) Tony Williams, one of the most historically significant drummers in jazz, displayed most of his innovations while playing with Miles Davis between 1963 and 1969.
9) Williams showed great diversity in his accompanying techniques.
10) Williams introduced the jazz technique of sharply snapping the high-hat shut on all four beats of each measure instead of just on the second and fourth. This became the standard practice in jazz-rock.
11) The Hancock-Carter-Williams rhythm section represents possibly the highest evolution of accompanying styles in jazz. Their imagination, sensitivity, versatility, and virtuosity has led them to be the most highly admired unit since the Count Basie rhythm section of the 1930s.

chapter 19

TWENTY YEARS OF JAZZ, ROCK, & AMERICAN POPULAR MUSIC

This chapter is included because the dominant stream of jazz during the 1970s and 80s was jazz-rock and because this was the first jazz style to attain widespread popularity since the swing era. There exists much confusion about what precisely is included in the categories of jazz-rock and fusion. The next few pages are therefore presented to help clarify these terms. The bulk of the chapter then discusses key figures in these styles and outlines their major contributions: Miles Davis, Larry Coryell, John McLaughlin, Don Ellis, Joe Zawinul, and Jaco Pastorius. (The work of several other key figures has already been examined in previous chapters: Herbie Hancock on pages 256–258, Chick Corea on pages 258–262, and Wayne Shorter on pages 304–309.) The group called Weather Report receives lengthy treatment here not just because it was the leading and most long-lived fusion band, but because it made historically significant contributions to methods of simultaneous collective improvisation, and it investigated an enormous range of unusual rhythms and tone colors. Weather Report's members are widely respected jazz musicians who chose to explore nontraditional lines of development after they contributed substantially to the music of several well-established jazz groups.

Jazz and rock share similar roots in gospel music, work songs, and the blues, but they represent the products of two divergent lines of musical evolution (see Figure 19.1). For example, jazz employs aspects of formal European concert music and steers away from vocals, being primarily instrumental music that has intricacy comparable to twentieth-century symphonic music. Rock, on the other hand, emphasizes vocals and sticks largely to elementary compositional forms such as the four-chord, twelve-bar blues. While the rock line became a part of the popular music mainstream, jazz acquired a status like that of classical chamber music because its audience was small and specialized. Blues singers from the first part of the century such as Leadbelly and Bessie Smith are routinely cited in jazz history texts, but it is usually in reference to origins of jazz rather than to the dominant course of jazz itself. The stream which continued from Leadbelly through B. B. King to Jimi Hendrix was already essentially separate from jazz by the 1920s. Although the gospel music that had influenced Bessie Smith continued to influence popular music, as seen in singers of the 1960s such as Aretha Franklin and James Brown, it only occasionally influenced jazz.*

Prior to the 1950s, blues and gospel music were especially influential in the popular music made by black performers who were marketed to black audiences. Ranging from Bessie Smith in the 1920s to Louis Jordan in the 40s, their music comprised the category called "race records." Then, during the 1950s, this category acquired a new name: rhythm and blues (r & b), and it strongly influenced another style of popular music called rock (see Figure 19.1). In addition to its r & b roots, much of rock also reflects the predominantly white musical streams of country music or hillbilly music (one early form of rock being termed rockabilly, Elvis Presley exemplifying this style) and western swing (a form that combines American popular music and jazz with a diversity of ethnic traditions ranging from the dance music of Cajun and Czech peoples to that of Mexican, German, and Polish peoples). Rock is distinctly removed from jazz, being significantly less like jazz than r & b had been. Note, however, that despite differences of players' race, rock and r & b remain similar because of these Afro-American traits:

1) extremely simple melody lines
2) extensive pitch bending
3) reliance upon ostinato
4) strict adherence to steady tempo

Some r & b in the 1960s contained more complicated accompaniment rhythms than rock contained. Then, during the late 1960s, black

---

* What little impact gospel music made on modern jazz was usually felt in only the simplest jazz styles, those containing characteristics similar to the black popular music known as rhythm and blues. These jazz styles were created by commercially successful players who, although possessing jazz skills, remained only on the periphery of important jazz developments: the Earl Bostic and Eddie Vinson bands of the 1940s and 50s; organ and saxophone combinations such as those of Jimmy Smith and Stanley Turrentine beginning in the late 1950s; the piano trios of Les McCann, Ramsey Lewis, and the Three Sounds; the combos led by King Curtis; pianist Ray Charles and the saxophonists he employed, including Hank Crawford and James Clay.

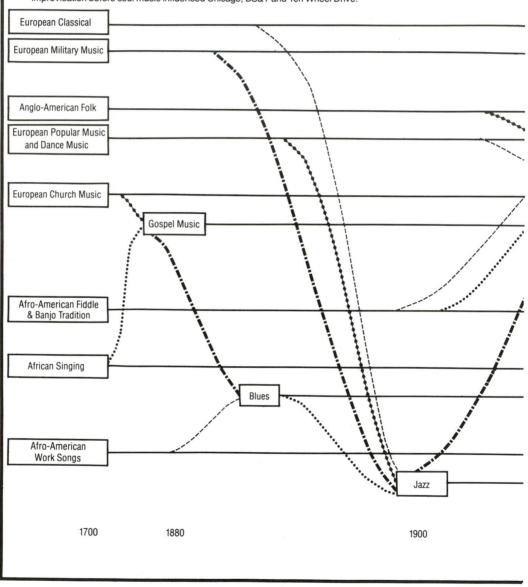

FIGURE 19.1. Chart of Parallel Streams Distinguishing Jazz from Rock and Jazz-Rock

Jazz and rock share a few similar origins, but they are separate styles.

Their origins constitute musical streams that continued by themselves and remain alive today.

Chicago, BS&T and Ten Wheel Drive are offshoots of soul music, more than offshoots of jazz.

Rhythm & Blues evolved into soul music and already had a tradition including jazz improvisation before soul music influenced Chicago, BS&T and Ten Wheel Drive.

European Classical

European Military Music

Anglo-American Folk

European Popular Music and Dance Music

European Church Music

Gospel Music

Afro-American Fiddle & Banjo Tradition

African Singing

Blues

Afro-American Work Songs

Jazz

1700   1880   1900

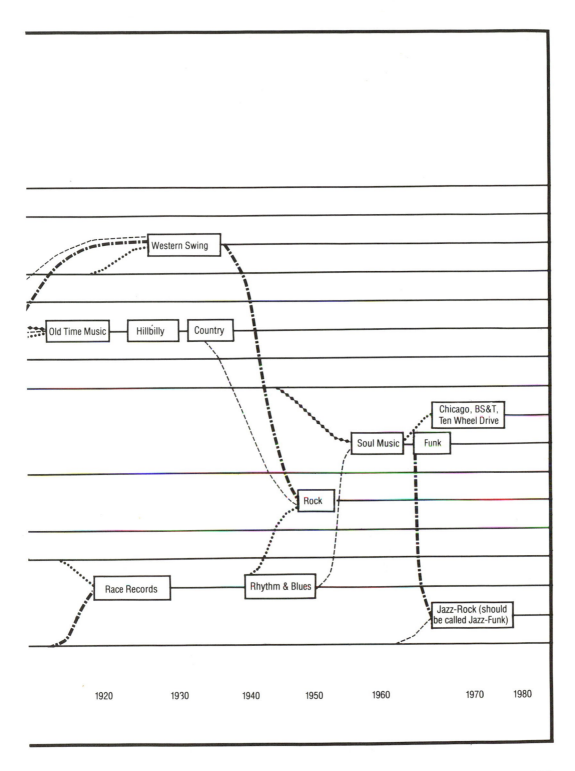

Western Swing

Old Time Music — Hillbilly — Country

Chicago, BS&T,
Ten Wheel Drive

Soul Music — Funk

Rock

Race Records — Rhythm & Blues

Jazz-Rock (should
be called Jazz-Funk)

1920   1930   1940   1950   1960   1970   1980

315

styles which extended r & b became the source for intricately syncopated drum patterns and complementary bass figures. The rhythm section musicians working for Motown recording artists and for singer James Brown, for example, devised accompaniment patterns which were far more complicated than those used by such prominent rock groups as the Beatles and the Rolling Stones. (Listen to the bass figures and drum patterns on the 1967 "Reflections" or the 1968 "Love Child" by Motown's Supremes. Or listen to the 1967 "I Heard It Through the Grapevine" by Motown's Gladys Knight or the 1968 "Cloud Nine" by Motown's Temptations.[1] Then pay close attention to the rhythm section style on James Brown's 1967 "Cold Sweat."[2]) The work of accompanists for Sly Stone during the early 1970s was especially complex, having built upon the Motown and James Brown techniques, stylistically separate from rock. (Listen to Sly Stone's "In Time" from the *Fresh*[3] album.) By this time, the labels "funk" and "soul" had begun replacing the r & b label, which had already replaced the "race records" label. However, this new pair of labels still served the same purpose its predecessors had served: identifying a primarily black form of American popular music. It was this category, not rock, which influenced a number of jazz musicians during the 1970s. Therefore **the jazz-rock label itself is not appropriate for the music that it identifies.** The music ordinarily signified by the term jazz-rock would more accurately be termed jazz-funk or jazz–r & b fusion.[*]

By the middle 1960s, the dominant jazz and rock styles had evolved into uniquely separate idioms, with little in common. Then, during the late 1960s, a partial blending of the soul music-funk stream and the jazz stream occurred and was labeled "jazz-rock" (see Figure 19.1). Some jazz musicians remained unaffected by funk, and many funk groups continued unaffected by jazz. But much of the music produced by jazz groups during the 1970s and 80s demonstrated a larger number of funk characteristics than had previously been used in modern jazz, and some funk groups attempted to incorporate more of the improvisation and advanced harmonies found in jazz.

[1] *The Motown Story* Motown MS 5 726
[2] *Best of James Brown* Polydor 6340
[3] Epic KE 32134
[*] The style which, during the late 1970s and early 1980s, was called disco is a blend of funk and Latin American rhythms played at the tempos most conducive for dancing (most commonly 120 beats per minute, the standard march tempo). It refers mostly to an accompaniment style which has been heard under almost every kind of solo line, from the singing of Donna Summer to swing era melodies to excerpts from Beethoven compositions. This style of music should also be removed from the umbrella category of rock.

DISTIN-GUISHING JAZZ FROM ROCK AND FUNK

Jazz of almost any period can be distinguished from rock and funk in that rock and funk typically have:

1) shorter phrase lengths
2) less frequent chord changes
3) less complexity of melody
4) less complexity of harmony
5) less use of improvisation, especially in accompaniments
6) much more repetition of melodic phrases
7) more repetition of brief chord progressions
8) much simpler drumming patterns
9) more pronounced repetition of drumming patterns
10) more pronounced repetition of bass figures

More of rock and funk performances is preset than it is in the average jazz performance. Not only does jazz ordinarily require solos to be improvised fresh each time they occur, but jazz also requires that the accompaniments for the solos be improvised. Even the accompaniments for the theme statements are often different in each performance of a given tune.

Rhythmic feeling provides another means for distinguishing jazz from rock and funk. Where jazz places emphasis on flexibility and relaxation, rock stresses intensity and firmness. Where jazz attempts to project a bouncy feeling that has a distinct lilt to it, rock and funk seem to sit on each beat instead of pulling it along or leading it as jazz does. Jazz musicians often characterize the time sense of rock and funk musicians as being straight up and down rather than being shuffling or loping as jazz seems to be.

Instrumentation preferred by jazz musicians was different from that ordinarily preferred by rock and funk musicians. From the 1950s through the 80s, rock placed far greater emphasis on electronic instruments and high amplification of ordinary instruments than was usual in jazz.

BLOOD, SWEAT & TEARS, CHICAGO, AND TEN WHEEL DRIVE

Mid-1960s forerunners of the "jazz-rock" approaches include the 1966 band called The Free Spirits[4] with guitarist Larry Coryell and the 1967 quartet of vibraharpist Gary Burton and Coryell.[5] Another less well-known group was The Fourth Way, a 1968–71 band with pianist Mike Nock and violinist Michael White.[6] The greatest acclaim did not go to these groups, however. Instead, it went to a group, first recorded

[4] *Free Spirits* ABC 593
[5] *Duster* RCA 3835, and *Lofty Fake Anagram* RCA 3901
[6] *The Sun and the Moon Have Come Together* Harvest SKA 0423

in 1967, called Blood, Sweat & Tears,[7] an eight-piece band featuring vocals in a James Brown and Ray Charles style with horn work similar to that employed by Brown and Charles. Next was the 1968 group called Chicago,[8] a seven-piece pop band featuring singing (solo voice as well as four- and five-part harmony) and late 1960s Motown-style ensemble figures voiced for trumpet, trombone, and saxophone. Third was the 1970 Ten Wheel Drive,[9] a ten-piece band playing in a style similar to that of the first two. These three groups were identified by music journalists as being "jazz-rock" bands, and they were phenomenally successful with the record-buying public. (Chicago's first album, the 1968 *Chicago Transit Authority*, remained high on the record sales charts longer than any albums other than singer Carole King's extraordinarily successful *Tapestry*. The second album put out by Blood, Sweat & Tears contained the hit song "Spinning Wheel," and had reached the number 1 chart position during 1969.) Chicago's level of musicianship was unusually high for a popular group, and their songs were quite engaging in the way that music of the Mamas and Papas, Jefferson Airplane, and Simon and Garfunkel had been.

When Ten Wheel Drive, Chicago, and Blood, Sweat & Tears emerged, much attention was directed to their use of horns and improvisation. Listeners and journalists assumed that such elements lent jazz character to the music, that such use was innovative, and that it justified the "jazz" part in the label "jazz-rock." Yet, soul singer-composer James Brown had already been using horns and improvisation since the late 1950s, and his 1965 hit "I Got You (I Feel Good)" had made prominent use of saxophone and brass in accompaniment figures and brief interludes. In other words, elements which many journalists presumed to have been contributed to "jazz-rock" by Chicago and Blood, Sweat & Tears, were primarily a reflection of the influence of other styles within popular music, not jazz (see Figure 19.1). These elements had already been previously explored mainly by black popular musicians, and therefore, almost the only element which the three popular "jazz-rock" bands have in common with jazz is the occasional presence of a brief, improvised solo, something that r & b bands had long been known for, and which, furthermore, was not even well-represented by the 1967–68 work of these particular jazz-rock groups. Instead of resembling jazz, their ensemble playing is modeled after the James Brown and Motown brass style in that their predominant subdivision of the beat is straight eighth-notes and sixteenth-notes instead of the swing eighth-notes which characterize jazz. Neither is the singing style a true jazz style; rather, it is patterned after

[7] *Blood, Sweat & Tears* Columbia PC 9720
[8] *Chicago Transit Authority* Columbia PG 8
[9] *Brief Replies* Polydor 24 4022 (or 24 4024)

soul singing. Admittedly, the written ensemble harmonies are more advanced than Motown's and James Brown's, but such sophistication had already been common in some non-jazz pop music and was, therefore, not exclusive to jazz, either.

Another line of reasoning used in applying the jazz label to the most popular "jazz-rock" groups followed the fact that members of the groups were known to have jazz aspirations. This undoubtedly colored the thinking of journalists who overlooked the connections with James Brown and Motown while assuming a primary connection with jazz. Such journalists failed to remember that jazz musicians had frequently toured and recorded with many popular non-jazz groups for decades prior to this; however, their presence had not made those groups into jazz groups any more than the presence of jazz hornmen such as Randy Brecker, Lew Soloff, and Fred Lipsius in Blood, Sweat & Tears made that pop group into a jazz band. Blood, Sweat & Tears is a highly professional and creative group of musicians who have performed several different styles of popular music. However, B, S & T did not necessarily demonstrate a fusion of jazz with rock. The groups which genuinely created a new kind of music by fusing jazz with rock and funk were those of Larry Coryell, Gary Burton, and Mike Nock. The most original fusions were made in the bands of trumpeter Miles Davis and those of some former Davis sidemen during the period between 1968 and 1975.

INTRODUCTION TO COVERAGE OF MAJOR FIGURES IN JAZZ-ROCK

One of the earliest and most adventuresome jazz-rock groups was called Lifetime,[10] led by former Miles Davis drummer Tony Williams and employing guitarist John McLaughlin, bassist Jack Bruce, and organist Larry Young. Another such group was John McLaughlin's Mahavishnu Orchestra,[11] which, in turn, expanded exposure for a number of musicians who also led other prominent "jazz-rock" groups of their own (drummer Billy Cobham, pianist Jan Hammer, violinist Jean-Luc Ponty). One of the most prolific bands was former Davis pianist Chick Corea's Return to Forever,[12] one edition of which spun off into the groups formed by drummer Lenny White, bassist Stanley Clarke, and guitarist Al Dimeola. Finally, there was the longest lasting of all jazz-rock groups, Weather Report, the collective effort of composer-pianist Joe Zawinul and composer-saxophonist Wayne Shorter, both of whom were former Davis collaborators. Several of these bands are described next.

[10] *Once in a Lifetime* Verve VE 2 2541
[11] *Birds of Fire* Columbia PC 31996
[12] *Hymn to the Seventh Galaxy* Polydor 5536 (or 2310283)

TABLE 19.1. A Few of the Many Jazz-Rock Musicians and Bands

Singer-Based Bands

Blood, Sweat & Tears
Chicago
Ten Wheel Drive
Chase

Instrumental Groups and Their Leaders

Lifetime (Tony Williams)
The Head Hunters
    (Herbie Hancock)
Return to Forever (Chick Corea)
Mahavishnu Orchestra
    (John McLaughlin)
Free Spirits (Larry Coryell)
Fourth Way (Mike Nock)
Eleventh House (Larry Coryell)
Blackbyrds (Donald Byrd)
Prime Time (Ornette Coleman)
Spyro Gyra
Word of Mouth (Jaco Pastorius)
The Decoding Society
    (Ronald Shannon Jackson)
Caldera
Oracle
Soft Machine
Jeff Lorber Fusion
The Crusaders
Weather Report (Joe Zawinul
    and Wayne Shorter)
Miles Davis
Bob James

Piano

Herbie Hancock
Chick Corea
Joe Zawinul
Jan Hammer
Jeff Lorber
Milcho Leviev
George Dukes
Bob James

Trumpet

Randy Brecker
Tom Browne
Michael Lawrence
Lew Soloff
Miles Davis

Saxophone

Michael Brecker
Wayne Shorter
David Liebman
Steve Grossman
Grover Washington
Eddie Harris
Ronnie Laws
David Sanborn
John Klemmer

Guitar

Pat Metheny
Al Dimeola
John McLaughlin
Larry Coryell
Steve Khan
Blood Ulmer

Bass

Michael Henderson
Stanley Clarke
Jaco Pastorius
Rick Laird
Jeff Berlin
Jamaaladeen Tacuma

Violin

Michael White
Jerry Goodman
Jean-Luc Ponty
Michael Urbaniak

Vibraharp

Gary Burton
Roy Ayers

Drums

Tony Williams
Billy Cobham
Steve Gadd
Lenny White
Alphonse Mouzon
Leon Chancler
Harvey Mason
Ronald Shannon
    Jackson
Peter Erskine
Al Foster

MILES DAVIS In addition to developing many highly creative extensions of existing jazz styles, the 1964–68 Miles Davis Quintet was one of the first established jazz groups to experiment with mixing the musical devices of rock and funk with those of jazz. Rhythmic styles other than bouncy, swinging jazz patterns appear throughout their records. Straight, repeating eighth notes played by Tony Williams on the ride cymbal, and occasionally the statement of each beat by sharply snapping the high-hat closed, are sometimes coupled with simple, repeating bass figures played by Ron Carter, figures that do not fit traditional walking bass rhythms. All of this bears a marked similarity to the rhythmic feeling of rock. (Listen to these hints of rock in accompanying patterns on "Eighty-One" in the *E.S.P.*[13] album, "Freedom Jazz Dance" on the *Miles Smiles*[14] album, "Masqualero" on the *Sorcerer*[15] album, and "Frelun Brun," "Tout de Suite," and "Filles de Kilimanjaro" on the *Filles de Kilimanjaro*[16] album.) "Stuff," in the 1968 *Miles in the Sky*[17] album, marked the first use of electric piano on a Davis recording, thus creating a tone color associated with rock. One album in particular, the 1968 *Filles de Kilimanjaro* (coming directly after *Miles in the Sky*), strongly indicated a trend away from jazz sound. It not only used electric piano and bass, it also contained the extensive use of military-like drumming patterns that resembled the insistent playing of rock drummers more than they resembled the relaxed and lilting playing of modern jazz drummers.

The next two LPs that Davis recorded became significant in directing modern jazz of the 1970s. For these sessions, Miles drew from a pool of drummers (which included Tony Williams, Jack DeJohnette, Lenny White, Charles Alias, and Jim Riley). His pool of keyboard players included Herbie Hancock, Chick Corea, Joe Zawinul, and Larry Young. Wayne Shorter played tenor and soprano saxophones, Bennie Maupin played bass clarinet, John McLaughlin played guitar, and the bassists included Dave Holland and Harvey Brooks. The records were *In a Silent Way*[18] and *Bitches Brew*,[19] both made in 1969. They contained a variety of musical approaches, but the dominant style was a combination of jazz and rock. Many melodies were reminiscent of the floating, almost motionless feeling of Shorter's "Nefertiti." In fact, a Shorter tune, "Sanctuary," was included on *Bitches Brew*.

In a Silent Way was the beginning of Davis's **partnership with pianist-composer Joe Zawinul**, who had been with the Cannonball

[13] Columbia PC 9150
[14] Columbia PC 9401
[15] Columbia PC 9532
[16] Columbia PC 9750
[17] Columbia PC 9628
[18] Columbia PC 9875
[19] Columbia PG 26

Adderley quintet during the 1960s. Davis's relationship with Zawinul was similar to those he had with Gil Evans in the late 1940s and late 50s, with Bill Evans on *Kind of Blue,* and with Shorter from 1964 to 1969. Davis recorded Zawinul pieces of the "Nefertiti" style: "In a Silent Way" (*In a Silent Way*) and "Pharoah's Dance" (*Bitches Brew*). Miles continued to employ Zawinul's work on later LPs but did not always credit Zawinul on the album labels. (Most Davis recordings made after 1969 list Davis as sole composer in spite of the fact that he was sometimes performing the compositions of others. Zawinul's "Double Image" is properly credited on the Davis *Live-Evil* LP, but his "Orange Lady" which is the last third of "Great Expectations" on the *Big Fun* LP, is credited to Davis.)

The post-1968 music of Davis differed in several respects from his 1963–68 style. **Instrumentation** was altered.

1) Electric piano and organ replaced conventional piano. And Davis often employed two or more electric keyboard instruments at once.

2) Fender electric bass guitar replaced acoustic string bass viol (see page 16 for illustration).

3) Except for George Benson's work on one tune ("Paraphernalia," in the 1968 *Miles in the Sky*), Miles had not previously used guitar. It was an important change when guitarist John McLaughlin appeared on *In a Silent Way, Bitches Brew,* and *Live-Evil.* After that, Davis used quite a few guitarists; at one time, he had three in a single band.

4) The Davis saxophonists of this period spent more time on soprano sax than on any other instrument. The soprano had the potential for penetrating and carrying its sound out over drums and electric instruments, where a tenor might not be able to cut through.

5) Davis usually employed two or more drummers. By the early 1970s, he had settled into the pattern of using one man on conventional drum set and another man on auxiliary percussion such as conga drums, shakers, rattles, gongs, whistles, and a large quantity of instruments native to Africa, South America, and India. On several LPs he used Indian musicians playing the sitar (a stringed instrument) and tabla (drums).

The **rhythm section concept** was another way in which Davis's post-1968 groups differed from his 1963–68 groups. The post-1968 groups featured elaborate configurations of colors and textures, and rhythm section members played with a very high level of activity. The beat was easily detectable, but it was surrounded by a mass of constantly changing sounds, sometimes delicate and gentle, sometimes turbulent.

Miles Davis Band, the jazz-funk group with which Davis ended a five-year retirement in 1981. This photo was taken by Mark Vinci at a 1982 concert with (left to right): soprano saxophonist Bill Evans (his tenor sax is sitting to his right), electric bassist Marcus Miller, Miles Davis (wearing hat, holding trumpet), Mino Cinelu (playing conga drum), Al Foster (drums). Guitarist Mike Stern, a regular member of this group, is not shown.

Textures often seemed to be created for their own sake rather than as accompaniments. The textures on *In a Silent Way* and *Bitches Brew* were as much in the forefront as the written melodies and improvised solo lines. The textures were generated by several electric keyboard instruments (piano and organ), guitar, basses, several drummers, and, on *Bitches Brew*, partly by Bennie Maupin's bass clarinet playing. Bass lines were composed of a blend of rock formulas, the freely improvised nonwalking style of Scott LaFaro, and figures borrowed from Latin American music (see notated rock and Latin bass figures on pages 427 and 428).

Most post-1968 Davis music was centered around a few repeated chords, a repeating bass figure, or a mode, rather than a sequence of frequently changing chords. The tunes reflected Wayne Shorter's composing style and the departures he had made from bop. Complexity was now centered in the rhythm section figures, rather than in the melodies. **Performance format** differed as well. Instead of improvising on a single tune for five to ten minutes, everyone taking his turn solo-ing, and then stopping before going on to the next tune, the post-1968 format accented medleys. Davis conducted the transitions between tunes, and his bassists led the way by changing the patterns of their repeating figures. The bass was the pivot in this music; **bass figures were as essential to the 1970s and 80s style as complex chord changes had been to bop and hard bop.**

Davis often set up a new mood and the harmonies for it by playing chords on an electric keyboard instrument. (He rarely carried a key-board player after 1972.) In this way Davis often dictated the tempo and rhythm that was to persist throughout that next passage. Davis used this scheme to gracefully make transitions between moods within the medleys, and he sometimes continued reinforcing the mood by comping.

In spite of the marked simplification occurring in rhythm section harmonies, **improvising soloists tended to retain the harmonic complex-ity of chord progression-based styles.** The more thoroughly grounded in chord progression-based styles an improviser was, the more variety he could bring to a solo whose accompaniment was extremely repeti-tive. John Coltrane had perfected techniques for spontaneously invent-ing chord progressions while improvising on mode-based forms and repeating bass figures (see pages 426–428 for notations of bass figures). The Davis saxophonists and guitarists used these same techniques. **They had also abandoned bop concepts of phrasing;** none of Parker's or Gillespie's pet phrases could be heard, although many of Coltrane's were evident. Improvisers seemed more intent on creating moods than melodic lines.

Davis's sidemen of this period were highly skilled players. (If they lacked the innovative gifts of such former Davis associates as Gil Evans, Sonny Rollins, John Coltrane, Bill Evans, and Wayne Shorter, they lacked none of the training necessary for keeping up with the demands of this intense music.)

After 1968, Miles led groups whose **personnel** were not as stable as his late 1950s and 1960s bands. During the 1968–73 period, each new LP had new personnel, and the musicians on tour were not always the same as those used in the studio. Coltrane had been with Davis on and off for five years. Shorter had also stayed approximately five years. But after Shorter left, Miles employed more than five different saxophonists in five years.

His rhythm sections were more stable, however. After various com-binations of pianists, bassists, and drummers, he settled for several years with bassist Michael Henderson and drummers Al Foster (con-ventional set) and M'Tume Heath (conga drums and auxiliary per-cussion). After pianist Keith Jarrett left, Miles rarely used a keyboard instrument. He occasionally played organ himself to set harmonies and moods, but usually depended on guitarists Reggie Lucas and Pete Cosey to supply chords.

Fender bassist **Michael Henderson** (b. 1951) was on the road with Davis longer than Ron Carter had been. Although he made recordings with Davis as late as 1968 and 1971, Carter was not a full-time touring member of the group after 1966. Henderson was approaching the length of employment seen by Paul Chambers (1955–63). He was well versed in rock bass playing, having worked with several well-known rock bands before joining Davis. His musicianship was solid and provided a reliable foundation for the Miles Davis sound of the 1970s.

From 1968 to 1975, Davis recorded *In a Silent Way, Bitches Brew, Live at the Fillmore, Jack Johnson, Live-Evil, On the Corner, In Concert, Big Fun, Get Up with It,* and *Agharta.* Some of these LPs were drawn from the recordings of different bands. In other words, some LPs are simply collections of Davis tapes rather than consistent samples of a single group.

For the new jazz-rock idiom, Davis altered his **trumpet style.** He often played fast, sweeping runs in and out of his extreme high register. He wired his instrument to an amplifier and connected electronic attachments which simulated echo (by means of a tape loop device called Echoplex) or created alterations of tone color previously achieved by rubber plunger mutes (by means of the wah wah pedal). He could be quite violent and sound much like a rock guitarist, or he could play in the tender, mournful manner he had displayed on *Porgy and Bess* and *Sketches of Spain.* Sometimes most of the band would become silent while he quietly played with only one other musician, but that was rare. Usually the mood was very outgoing and full of unrelenting tension. The level of musicianship was very high, and the complexity of the music set it apart from rock, but its effect was often quite similar to that of the loud turbulence generated by rock bands of the late 1960s and 70s. Admiration for such rock musicians as Jimi Hendrix and Billy Preston was evident in Miles's music. The post-1968 Davis recordings displayed a blend of the jazz tradition, 1960s and 70s rock, and the music of India and South America. It was infused with the spirit of Charlie Parker and John Coltrane, but the tone colors were those of rock.

JOHN McLAUGHLIN

John McLaughlin (b. 1942) is a British guitarist who had been active in British rock bands and jazz groups since the late 1950s and had collaborated in 1963 with bassist Jack Bruce and drummer Ginger Baker (who later became two-thirds of the well-known rock group called Cream). He first became known to American musicians primarily during the period of 1969–71 when he began playing with Tony Williams's Lifetime and recording with Miles Davis.

McLaughlin is notable for a phenomenally high level of instrumental proficiency, and he has become probably the most influential jazz guitarist since Wes Montgomery. He may also be responsible for some of the rise in musicianship which has characterized rock guitarists since 1970. Despite his being considered a jazz musician, McLaughlin used a tone which was unlike traditional jazz guitar quality. It was hard, not soft, cutting, not smooth, and metallic, not warm. In short, it had the color and texture preferred by rock guitarists, not jazz guitarists. And he frequently altered the size and shape of his tone by use of a wah wah pedal and phase shifter. (The phase shifter produces a subtle swirling of the sound.) Another point of contrast between McLaughlin and the jazz tradition is that most of McLaughlin's improvisations contain far less of the pronounced syncopation and the easy, relaxed, swing feeling that had previously typified jazz. Improvisations in McLaughlin performances were unlike the bouncy conception which was part of the Charlie Christian, Wes Montgomery, and Kenny Burrell styles. McLaughlin performances also lacked the gentle lyricism which was so characteristic of improvisations by Jim Hall.

The syncopations in John McLaughlin's lines were more typical of rock than of jazz. And his solos were often composed of long strings of sixteenth notes which were periodically interrupted by held tones which McLaughlin expressively distorted in waveform and in pitch. The inflections he preferred were refinements of those which had been customary in rock and in blues guitar playing. McLaughlin's rhythmic conception and his melodic conception had more in common with classical music and the 1960s improvisations of John Coltrane than with standard bop practice. In McLaughlin's long lines of sixteenth notes, he often chose sequences which were reminiscent of the patterns used by Coltrane. (Incidentally, both McLaughlin and Coltrane had studied the music of India and had been fond of basing their solos on modes learned from such study.)

During the early 1970s, McLaughlin played a custom-made electric guitar having two necks, one with six and the other with twelve strings. McLaughlin also worked with the vina, an Indian seven-string instrument that has four playing strings and three accompanying strings. Then during the late 1970s, he played another specially built instrument inspired by the vina, with a form like an autoharp's, having a scalloped fingerboard and accompanying strings.

McLaughlin's work in Lifetime and in his own Mahavishnu Orchestra projected unusually high intensity. This effect is partly due to high amplifier settings and a stress on rapid-fire, multinoted themes with extremely busy accompaniment. The interaction and determination displayed by such Mahavishnu albums as his 1971 *Inner Mounting Flame*[20] and his 1972 *Birds of Fire* are due to a high level of co-

[20] Columbia PC 31067

operation and mutual inspiration between drummer Billy Cobham, electric bassist Rick Laird, and electric pianist and synthesist Jan Hammer. Many listeners feel that those recordings remain benchmarks for ensemble cohesion and inspired jazz-rock improvisation. Feeling was so high for this music that *Birds of Fire,* at one time during 1973, reached position number 15 on *Billboard*'s chart in the popular album category. These albums are also distinctive for their use of irregular meters, time signatures which, though common to Indian music, had previously been rare in jazz and rock. Over the years, McLaughlin's groups also offered fine examples of jazz-rock violin playing, first through Jerry Goodman, then, beginning in 1974, with Jean-Luc Ponty, whose recordings with his own group have been among the best selling in all of jazz-rock.

Not all of McLaughlin's 1970s output consisted of high intensity electronic music. He also recorded on hollow body guitar in his 1970 *My Goal's Beyond,*[21] an album which McLaughlin personally lists among his favorite works. It contains a side of overdubbed, self-accompanying, solo guitar improvisations and a side with saxophone, violin, acoustic bass, and drums. There is an expansive and exhilarated feeling in the solo side, especially in McLaughlin's rendering of his original composition "Follow Your Heart." Though leaving the non-electric approach for a few years right after this album, McLaughlin returned to it when touring and recording with Shakti, an Indian music ensemble comprised of violin, tabla, mrindagam, and ghatam. His fondness for the nonelectronic sound also emerged in what many fans consider to contain his best solo: "Rene's Theme," a duet with fellow guitarist Larry Coryell on Coryell's 1970 *Spaces*[22] album. This pairing with Coryell recurred during the 1980s when McLaughlin toured in duo and trio with several guitar giants, all playing hollow body guitar: Coryell, Al Dimeola, Christian Escoude, and Spanish flamenco guitarist Paco de Lucia.

LARRY CORYELL Guitarist Larry Coryell (b. 1943) is especially significant in jazz history because he was one of the first to blend the styles of country music, blues guitar, and rock with established jazz styles. He did this during the mid-1960s while playing in the bands of drummer Chico Hamilton and vibraharpist Gary Burton. And Coryell's own group, The Free Spirits, was active in 1966, which was well before the major onslaught of rock-influenced jazz groups in 1969 and 1970. Burton had been attracted to Coryell's work with The Free Spirits and the possibilities that it suggested for jazz. The 1967 *Duster* album contains several pas-

---

[21] Elektra Musician EL 60031 and Douglas 9 KZ 30766
[22] Vanguard 6558 (79345)

sages in which Coryell solos in a style which is clearly drawn from rock. Burton and his other sidemen follow Coryell's lead and manage to approximate the flavor and intensity of Coryell's work. Burton further pursued this avenue with guitarist Jerry Hahn on a 1968 album called *Country Roads and Other Places,* and then continued to employ excellent guitarists who were interested in combining country music, rock, and jazz, thereby introducing Mick Goodrick and Pat Metheny. (Metheny became one of the two or three most popular jazz guitarists of the late 1970s and early 80s.)

Free Spirits, Foreplay (Coryell's 1969–72 band), and the Eleventh House (a later band) were all jazz-rock groups. However, it is important to note that Coryell was not strictly a rock guitarist. As early as his time with Chico Hamilton, Coryell had proven himself to be an unusually imaginative and technically proficient improviser of jazz lines. He possessed a capability for speed and invention rivaled only by McLaughlin. Coryell's playing could be distinguished, however, in that his note beginnings were more percussive, they had more "pop." Additionally Coryell was given to greater variety in his solos than McLaughlin employed. The twists and turns in his lines suggested more jazz roots in Coryell than in McLaughlin. Fortunately all these comparisons are easy to make because McLaughlin performed on Coryell's *Spaces* album, which documents a time when both guitarists were at a peak in their creativity and technical prowess.

Like McLaughlin, Coryell demonstrated considerable interest in non-rock playing during the late 1970s and the early 1980s. He performed as an unaccompanied solo guitarist, and he played duets with guitarists Philip Catherine, Steve Khan, McLaughlin, and violinist Michael Urbaniak.

John McLaughlin and Larry Coryell became the most influential models for jazz guitarists who were developing styles during the 1970s. Since the rock style was the main kind of popular music during the 1960s and 70s, the vast majority of professional musicians during that period were rock musicians. And because jazz has traditionally drawn from whatever pools of players are present at any given period, a sizable proportion of guitarists who ended up in jazz during the 1960s and 70s had roots in rock. Rock has always been a guitar-dominated music, not saxophone-dominated as jazz has been. Jazz-rock therefore features more guitarists than earlier styles of modern jazz had featured.

DON ELLIS   Don Ellis (1934–1978) was a modern jazz trumpeter, composer, arranger, and bandleader involved in numerous innovative approaches to music. His inclusion in this section only acknowledges the portion of his career which touched on techniques which were important to jazz-rock.

As a leader of large jazz ensembles during the 1960s and 70s,[23] Don Ellis introduced and popularized electronic instruments which had not been especially common to big bands. He also enjoyed a considerable following among big band disciples and jazz educators because of his extensive exploration of irregular meters. His work was influenced by the music of India as well as twentieth-century European compositional approaches of symphonic writers. It is nearly impossible ever to determine who was truly first with a given instrument or particular technique in jazz. But, keeping in mind the limitations of specifying who was truly the first, it is important to note that Ellis has been cited for the initial popularization of

1) big band format for jazz-rock;
2) 1966 use of organ and irregular meters in jazz big band;
3) 1967 use of clavinet and Fender Rhodes electric piano;
4) 1969 use of electric trumpet, echo-plex, quarter-tone trumpet, and ring modulator (all of these except the four-valved, quarter-tone trumpet are devices for altering sounds electronically);
5) 1970 use of electric amplification and tone alteration of entire saxophone section.

JOSEF ZAWINUL

Joe Zawinul (b. 1932) is a pianist and composer who moved from his native Vienna, Austria to the United States in 1959. After playing briefly with the band of trumpeter Maynard Ferguson, he toured as accompanist to singer Dinah Washington from 1959 to 1961. His first great impact was then made with the bands of saxophonist Cannonball Adderley between 1961 and 1970, during which time he authored two of the band's most popular funk hits: "Mercy, Mercy, Mercy"[24] and "Walk Tall." His next great success was the use of his "In a Silent Way" by Miles Davis as the title track for a 1969 album which pioneered the fusion of jazz improvisation with rock instruments and rock accompaniment practices. Davis also included Zawinul's "Pharoah's Dance" in the best-selling *Bitches Brew* album as well as using Zawinul as chief arranger for *In a Silent Way* and *Bitches Brew*.

In 1971 Zawinul founded an innovative jazz-rock band called Weather Report, and it was with this band's 1977 *Heavy Weather*[25] album that he enjoyed his greatest sales since "Mercy, Mercy, Mercy." The album sold more than 400,000 copies and contained Zawinul's "Birdland," an arrangement of catchy, syncopated phrases in extended repetition, inspired by the composer's memories of hearing the Count

[23] *Live at Monterey* Pacific Jazz PJ 10112; *Shock Treatment* Columbia CS 9668; *The New Don Ellis Band Goes Underground* Columbia CS 9889
[24] *Mercy, Mercy, Mercy* Capitol SM 2663
[25] Columbia PC 34418

Basie band at the New York night club called Birdland. The piece epitomizes the danceable, riff-band style favored by Basie, though presented here in a translation to jazz-rock tone colors. It received wide exposure in discotheques and in recordings by the Maynard Ferguson big band and the vocal group called Manhattan Transfer.

Zawinul has made significant contributions in the use of electronic instruments for jazz. He had used the Wurlitzer electric piano on the Adderley recording of "Mercy, Mercy, Mercy," which was recorded in 1966, and he subsequently employed a Fender Rhodes electric piano on tour. Singer-bandleader Ray Charles had previously carried electric piano, as had Sun Ra, but it was not common in jazz until after its appearance with Zawinul. Miles Davis was so taken with the Fender Rhodes when he heard Zawinul playing it in Adderley's band that he required its use by three successive pianists in his own bands (Herbie Hancock, Chick Corea, and Keith Jarrett), thereby influencing subsequent work by those men with their own groups. This soon became the most common keyboard instrument in jazz groups of the 1970s. Even such nonrock-oriented pianists as Bill Evans and Oscar Peterson recorded with the Rhodes. Zawinul was also one of the first musicians to master the Oberheim Polyphonic (exemplified on side one of Weather Report's *Heavy Weather*), the Arp and the Prophet synthesizers, as well as the ring modulator (which he first recorded in 1971 on "Seventh Arrow" in Weather Report's first album, *Weather Report*).[26]

Considered to be one of the leading composers of the 1970s, Zawinul demonstrated creativity and favorite devices which parallel those of Charles Mingus in the 1950s and Duke Ellington in the 1940s. He generated a broader variety of rhythms, in melodic as well as accompaniment figures, than possibly any other jazz composer of the 1970s. Zawinul wrote numerous pieces and touched highly diverse tone colors and moods. Throughout his albums with Weather Report run playful melodies with highly imaginative accompaniments, such as "Man in the Green Shirt" (*Tale Spinnin'*)[27] and "The Juggler" (*Heavy Weather*). His "In a Silent Way" and "Arrival in New York" (both on *Zawinul*)[28] are impressionistic tone poems. Zawinul encouraged the use of a wide assortment of exotic percussion instruments on the part of his musicians. And he himself produced unusual timbres and rhythms by playing African thumb piano (also known as sansa or kalimba), clay drum, tambura, xylophone, and steel drums. Gentle sounds are conjured by ocarina, hollow body guitar, thumb piano, and tambura on his "Jungle Book" (*Mysterious Traveler*).[29] And, during a period of

[26] Columbia PC 30661
[27] Columbia PC 33417
[28] Atlantic SD 1579
[29] Columbia PC 32494

jazz history when electric instruments dominated the sound of most albums, Zawinul used the strains of unamplified piano on the recording of Wayne Shorter's "Blackthorn Rose" (*Mysterious Traveler*), precisely sounding each tone, paced as though to savor its every vibration. He also used it in combination with sustained organ tones in his "Five Short Stories" (*Tale Spinnin'*). And like Ellington, Zawinul arranged wordless vocals, actually using his own voice in this capacity on his "Badia" (*Tale Spinnin'*) and "Jungle Book" (*Mysterious Traveler*), and that of bassist Jaco Pastorius on "Birdland" (*Heavy Weather*). On "The Orphan" (*8:30*),[30] Zawinul combined Wayne Shorter's tenor saxophone tone with the soft texture of a children's choir. The breadth of tonal spectra in Weather Report's work might explain how Zawinul's music found its way on to the turntables of demonstration units in stereo equipment stores. The music of Weather Report had joined symphonic music as a vast source of varied timbres and loudnesses by which to judge the quality of sound systems.

WEATHER REPORT   Joe Zawinul left the Adderley quintet in 1971 and joined saxophonist Wayne Shorter and bassist Miroslav Vitous (b. 1947) to create a remarkable new concept in improvisatory music embodied in the group called Weather Report. It was to outlast all other jazz-rock bands. Zawinul, Shorter, and Vitous were joined by two drummers, Alphonse Mouzon (b. 1948) on conventional set and Airto Moreira playing the exotic instruments for which he had already become known in the bands of Cannonball Adderley and Miles Davis. It should be noted that, despite their being routinely classified with jazz-rock, Weather Report performs in a broad range of original fusions of jazz with non-jazz styles. Only a small portion of their output truly qualifies for the jazz-rock category.

The **collective improvisation of musical textures and the emancipation of rhythm section instruments from conventional roles were significant aspects of the Weather Report approach.** Miroslav Vitous was a bassist uniquely able to improvise melodies as well as or better than the average hornman. He had abandoned the bass timekeeping role in several selections on his *Infinite Search* LP. Vitous had a sophisticated melodic sense; he was in a class with such outstanding bass soloists as Paul Chambers and Scott LaFaro. He was also very capable with bowed bass. Vitous had a keen sense of what to play for the sake of creating interesting rhythmic textures and how to keep his instrument's voice in sensitive musical conversations with other group members. Vitous did not simply break up walking bass lines or play in a decorative two feeling as LaFaro did. **The Vitous contributions to Weather**

---

[30] Columbia PC2 36030

Wayne Shorter (soprano sax), Miroslav Vitous (bass), and Joe Zawinul (piano), founding members of Weather Report and masters of collective improvisation. Pictured here in the early 1970s. (*Courtesy of Bill Smith and CODA*)

Report included fragmented melody statements, bowed sustained tones, and syncopated interjections. He could just as easily bow melody in unison with a sax line as feed rock style bass figures into the group texture. Vitous could play in unison with a rhythm the drummer was stating on ride cymbal or underscore a pattern being played on piano. He could quickly go back and forth, too. Vitous had cast off the restraints of traditional bass playing and become an improviser first and timekeeping bassist second. (His work made sense, too. It was not just the flashy playing of a gifted showoff.)

Airto Moreira brought an imagination of sweeping proportions to his use of Latin American percussion instruments. His rhythms made a compelling combination with those of Vitous and Mouzon.

Eric Gravatt soon took Mouzon's place, and Dom Um Romao took Airto's; these were the first of a long series of personnel changes. By the middle 1970s, even bassist Miroslav Vitous had left, and the only founding members who remained were Shorter and Zawinul.

Weather Report came on the scene with the standard instrumentation of sax, piano, bass, and drums. They also had an auxiliary percussionist, but that was not unusual; many 1950s and 60s jazz groups had employed conga drummers or other auxiliary percussionists to add a Latin American flavor to their groups. But **Weather Report did not use its conventional instrumentation in conventional ways.** It was rare for bassist Miroslav Vitous to walk, or for the drummer to play standard ride rhythms or close the high-hat sharply on the second and fourth beats of each measure. Zawinul usually did not comp for Shorter, and the auxiliary percussionist was not simply restricted to the conga drum. "Eurydice," on Weather Report's first LP,[31] is one of the few pieces which contains walking bass, drummer playing ride rhythms and closing high-hat on second and fourth beats, sax solo followed by piano solo, etc. And even in that conventionally approached performance, there are portions which deviate from the standard bop roles. For example, drummer Alphonse Mouzon often closed his high-hat on all four beats, and interjected musical comments to the point where instead of just keeping time and coloring the sound, he is heard in the forefront of the group. On "Eurydice" Miroslav Vitous often abandons the walking bass role and instead contributes embellishments to the ensemble. Zawinul does not always comp behind Shorter, either. He sets up delicate flourishes, plays counter-melodies, and sometimes lays out. Airto Moreira interjects colorful, speech-like sounds throughout the proceedings with his cuica, an instrument in which the player gently slides his fingers along a stick which in turn alters the tension of a specially connected drumhead and causes it to vibrate.

Collective Improvisation
On their first three LPs (*I Sing the Body Electric*,[32] *Sweetnighter*,[33] *Weather Report*), Weather Report explored an unusual approach to combo improvisation. **Instead of adhering to roles consistent with bop formulas, the instruments in Weather Report were played in highly interactive ways.** Spurts of melody might come from any member, not just from the sax. Rhythmic figures and fills could also be produced by any member, not solely by a drummer.

The kinds of interaction between members were so varied that **in some pieces there was no distinction between soloist and accompanist.** One player's sound might stand out momentarily from the ensemble texture, but it soon blended into the overall texture again. In this situation, every member had to be capable of playing melodically or of simply adding to the overall texture of the group sound. Weather Report's members developed special techniques for managing such tasks. (See pages 15–24 for an explanation of standard jazz solo and accompaniment roles.)

[31] *Weather Report* Columbia PC 30661
[32] Columbia PC 31352
[33] Columbia PC 32210

Solo choruses, as conceived in swing and bop, did not occur on Weather Report's first album. A particular voice (sax, piano, arco bass, etc.) often held the focal point for a few moments. Call the few moments a solo if you wish. But regardless of how you label the event, it maintained much more continuity with the entire piece than conventional jazz solos usually did. Most conventional jazz solos came in sequence with other solos. They adhered to fixed chorus lengths and came strung together, one player directly following another. Each player did his own thing regardless of whether its mood or color continued or developed that of the preceding solo.

In Weather Report, each member's work contributes to the prevailing mood and color. The players do not usually feature themselves, but rather create notes primarily to serve the group sound. This approach helps produce a variety of consistently maintained musical feelings and flavors. There was a greater variety of texture and moods in Weather Report's music than was available to most bop, West Coast, and hard bop groups. Only bands led by such versatile composers as Duke Ellington, Charles Mingus, and Sun Ra had previously succeeded in achieving a comparable range of musical colors. (For greater understanding of improvisational methods, see pages 26–27.)

In Ellington's music, composition played a more important role than improvisation. For Mingus and Sun Ra the relative proportions of composition and improvisation vary considerably from piece to piece. Weather Report employs a certain amount of composition and works out quite a few rhythms and instrument effects in advance also. But much of the balance and distinctive feeling in their music is produced spontaneously. The fact that their spontaneous musical efforts work out so well is a credit to the sensitivity and discretion of Weather Report's members.

Good examples of collective improvisation are "Seventh Arrow" and "Umbrellas," on Weather Report's first album, *Weather Report*, "Surucucu," on *I Sing the Body Electric*, and "125th Street Congress," on *Sweetnighter*. Prewritten figures pop up at the beginning and end and occasionally within the pieces, but otherwise the music seems spontaneous.

Prior to 1970, modern jazz had produced very few recordings of collective improvisation in which solos were of secondary importance. In 1949, Lennie Tristano, Lee Konitz, and their group recorded "Intuition" and "Digression." Occasional attempts at improvised counterpoint were made during the 1950s by Dave Brubeck and Paul Desmond, John Lewis and Milt Jackson, and Gerry Mulligan and Bob Brookmeyer. In 1960 Ornette Coleman, Eric Dolphy, Freddie Hubbard, Don Cherry, et al. recorded *Free Jazz*, which contained moments when all musicians participated in spontaneous, collective improvisation. The 1965 LP, *Ascension*, which included John Coltrane, Pharoah

Sanders, and others, had moments similar to those in *Free Jazz*. Yet in spite of the high-level improvisatory skills possessed by Tristano, Konitz, Coltrane, and others, the quality of their collective improvisations rarely equalled the overall quality produced in noncollective contexts by those same men. But Weather Report's collectively improvised performances stand out as highly successful examples. It was not that Joe Zawinul or Wayne Shorter were improvisers superior to Tristano, Konitz, or Coltrane, but in the context of Weather Report, Zawinul and Shorter have been able to collectively improvise music which, to many listeners, is consistently more successful than the collective improvisations of Tristano, Ornette Coleman, John Coltrane, etc. It is worth noting that the earliest forms of jazz placed great emphasis on the interplay between melodic voices (trumpet, clarinet, trombone). Often no single player had the lead. Over the years, jazz lost its interest in the collectively improvised approach. Weather Report might represent a return to that approach, indicating that jazz has come full circle.

Orchestral Approaches

Although they did not entirely abandon collective approaches, much of Weather Report's work after their third LP, *Sweetnighter*, left collectively improvised approaches in favor of more orchestral techniques, in which repeated, prewritten themes and preset Latin American and rock rhythm section figures dominate the sound. (Weather Report's exploration of Latin American rhythms has been extremely fresh.) Their *Mysterious Traveler, Tale Spinnin'*, and *Black Market*[34] all contain careful mixing of prearranged material and jazz improvisation. Their creative use of both acoustically and electrically produced tone colors achieved as broad a scope as any non-symphonic style rooted in the jazz tradition.

Both Shorter and Zawinul seem attracted to the compositional style of impressionist composers Claude Debussy and Maurice Ravel. This is reflected in sustained tone melodies which seem to float by and conjure up pastoral scenes. Some notable examples occur in "Orange Lady" (*Weather Report*) where Shorter's soprano sax and the bowed bass of Vitous state the melody in unison, "Dr. Honoris Causa" (*Zawinul*) where the soprano sax states a serene melody in unison with flute and trumpet, and "Will" (*Sweetnighter*) where English horn and bass play the theme in unison over Latin American rhythms. Though their music is sometimes reminiscent of Debussy, Ravel, Vaughan Williams, Aaron Copland, or Morton Gould, Weather Report's creations are set off from the works of those classical composers by the complex layers of rhythm patterns underlying the melodic lines.

[34] Columbia PC 34099

Away from Collectively Improvised Textures

With their 1973 *Sweetnighter* album, Weather Report began including more compositions which were constructed of brief phrases repeated continually and accompanied by a more repetitive, funk-influenced rhythm section style. The emphasis on repetition and funk was intended by Zawinul to capture a larger slice of the record-buying market. And, as demonstrated by the construction of his "Boogie Woogie Waltz" on *Sweetnighter*, and that album's increase in popularity over its predecessors, the new strategy led to wider popular acceptance of the band.

Weather Report Significance

In summary, Weather Report is significant in jazz history in many ways.

1) Their first three albums
   a) brought simultaneous collective improvisation to a new level of polish and imagination;
   b) offered collective improvisation that was rhythmically compelling at the same time as it was rich with wide-ranging tone colors;
   c) demonstrated the improvisation of textures more than jazz solo lines and did this in a way that was palatable to far wider audiences than any previous attempts had attracted.
2) Their group concept afforded a unique opportunity for emancipation of the bassist from bop roles.
3) The band evolved a form of jazz-funk that featured more improvisation than most other fusion bands.
4) It was one of the first fusion bands to achieve popular recognition without using vocals.
5) It made more original and extensive use of exotic rhythms than most jazz groups that historically preceded it.
6) The band combined several jazz giants and gave them a fresh and unique platform for creative composing and improvising.

JACO PASTORIUS

In 1976, virtuoso bass guitarist Jaco Pastorius (b. 1951) joined Weather Report. To understand the roles he assumed in the band, it is helpful to note that Joe Zawinul has called upon his bassists to play in four fundamentally distinct ways. First is the standard jazz technique of walking bass, as demonstrated by Miroslav Vitous on "Eurydice" (found in Weather Report's first album). Second is a nonrepetitive, interactive approach which is identified most prominently by Scott LaFaro's work with the 1961 Bill Evans trio and displayed by Vitous in his improvisations within "Waterfall" on Weather Report's first album. This technique demands much imagination as well as requiring that the bassist second guess his colleagues, discreetly omit many notes, and play only when it will do the most good. Third is what is commonly called "funk bass." This is the repetition of highly syncopated bass figures which are often filled with staccato notes. These types of figures were also common in the popular dance music of the 1970s. In this technique, it is not sufficient for the bassist to simply know the proper figures and cleanly execute them. What is crucial is that he play them with a contagion that moves people in a way peculiar to funk music. (This technique was not a specialty for Miroslav Vitous, however it was a specialty for his replacement, Alphonso Johnson.) The fourth role of the bassist in Weather Report was to solo. This was, however, not a high priority demand made on Weather Report bassists until Jaco Pastorius joined the group.

Jaco Pastorius is outstanding in all four of the above bass roles. He walks persuasively, as he proved on "Crazy About Jazz" (contained in Weather Report's eleventh album which has the same title as their first: *Weather Report*). He plays in the nonrepetitive, interactive way, as evidenced on "Dara Factor One" (also on the eleventh album) and "Dream Clock" (*Night Passage*).[35] And, he is a natural funk player, providing the proper rhythmic feeling in accompanying soul singers Sam and Dave on his own album (*Jaco Pastorius*),[36] as well as the dancing feeling he lent Weather Report's "Barbary Coast" (*Black Market*), "Palladium" (*Heavy Weather*), and "River People" (*Mr. Gone*).

Pastorius appreciably altered the character of Weather Report's sound and the rhythmic feeling that went with it. Compare, for example, the sound of *Heavy Weather* (on which he is prominent) with the sound of earlier Weather Report albums, and the difference will quickly reveal itself. The bassist's fluid tone, his use of vibrato at the end of some tones, and his ease of playing all combined with his high energy and playful spirit to propel the band in a light-hearted way that had not been previously identified with the group. In Pastorius, Zawinul found an enticing soloist in addition to a musician with all the qualities which he had originally sought from Miroslav Vitous and Alphonso Johnson. Zawinul additionally discovered a versatile and original composer who contributed "Barbary Coast," "Teen Town," "Havona," "Punk Jazz," "River People," and "Three Views of a Secret" to the Weather Report library.

Weather Report concerts during the late 1970s always featured an unaccompanied Pastorius solo. The bassist drew upon electronic means for altering sound that were reminiscent of Jimi Hendrix. (In fact, Pastorius regularly performed a Hendrix medley in his early 1980s perfor-

---

[35] Columbia JC 36793
[36] Epic PE 33949

mances.) Pastorius used playback echo to provide spontaneous accompaniments for his improvisations. He extracted chords from his bass and capitalized on overtones to orchestrate his performance as though he had an entire band behind him. He demonstrated the same prodigious speed that had impressed listeners who had heard his recording of Charlie Parker's "Donna Lee" (*Jaco Pastorius*), a very difficult line to execute.

In 1982, Pastorius left Weather Report and launched his own unique group called Word of Mouth. Using no keyboard instruments or guitars for chording, Pastorius employed trumpet and saxophone paired with steel drum and his bass to state melody lines. On this band's first album (*Word of Mouth*),[37] he employed the sound of harmonica as well as thick-textured ensemble writing which was sometimes reminiscent of Gil Evans and Thad Jones. Like Zawinul, Pastorius used the gentle sound of children's voices as an additional seasoning in his tonal repertory. On "John and Mary" Pastorius used the same children's choir that Zawinul used on "The Orphan." Diversity was the byword to his presentations. Pastorius not only set the pace for a new generation of jazz bassists, but he also explored a unique spectrum of tonal textures, tapping orchestral music and the music of the Caribbean as well as American pop styles such as soul music.

ESTABLISHED JAZZ GREATS EMBRACE ROCK

Jazz-rock mixed jazz improvisation with the instrumentation and rhythmic conception of r & b. It was the most commonly performed jazz in the 1970s, thereby surpassing Dixieland, swing, bop, and free jazz in the size of its audience and its number of players. It was adopted not only by musicians who were just then developing their own styles, but also by older, established players. Many major figures in modern jazz changed the instrumentation of their rhythm sections by replacing piano with electric piano and synthesizer and by replacing acoustic bass viol ("string bass") with Fender electric bass guitar (see page 427 for notations of rock bass figures). Drummers learned new timekeeping patterns which resembled the materials of r & b as well as Latin American styles. (See page 431 for notations of drumming figures used in recordings by Sly Stone and Herbie Hancock.)

Trumpeter Dizzy Gillespie, one of the bop pioneers, used guitar, bass guitar, and drums, played rock-tinged pieces and recorded *Souled Out*, a funk album. And then to the surprise of many fans, Ornette Coleman, who had been a 1950s pioneer in free jazz, hired a rock-oriented guitarist named James "Blood" Ulmer in 1974. Coleman toured and recorded with a band he called Prime Time, featuring an

[37] Warner Brothers 3535

electric bassist, two electric guitarists, and two drummers, playing in a style which was distinctly unlike that of his quartets which had employed "acoustic bassist" Charlie Haden and drummer Eddie Blackwell.

Not all established jazz figures who embraced rock remained with it, however. For many, the affiliation lasted only through the mid-1970s. Gillespie, for instance, soon returned to conventional jazz swing feeling and instrumentation. By the late 1970s, trumpeter Freddie Hubbard and saxophonist Joe Farrell, two of those previously established jazz figures who had embraced rock the longest and with the most popular recognition, were recording once again in conventional jazz setting. Pianist Chick Corea, whose 1973 *Hymn to the Seventh Galaxy* was strongly influenced by hard rock, later pursued nonrock approaches such as piano concert tours in duet with fellow pianist Herbie Hancock (*An Evening With Herbie Hancock and Chick Corea*) and vibraharpist Gary Burton (*Duet*). In 1982 and 1983 Corea was touring and recording with bassist Miroslav Vitous and drummer Roy Haynes, thus reforming the trio that had made his landmark *Now He Sings, Now He Sobs* of 1968. Herbie Hancock split his time between funk and the jazz approaches he had refined during the 1960s with Miles Davis. During the late 1970s and early 1980s, he toured and recorded with acoustic bands whose personnel was almost the same as that on his classic 1965 album *Maiden Voyage,* and he did all this while his funk albums continued to sell very well. Saxophonist Sonny Rollins seemed to use rock as simply one more alternative to his wide-ranging repertory, and the thirteen-piece band of trumpeter Maynard Ferguson seemed to view rock music much as Rollins did. Ferguson recorded big band versions of Herbie Hancock's funk hit "Chameleon" and Joe Zawinul's disco hit "Birdland," as well as "Hey, Jude" by the Beatles, side by side with the Sonny Rollins jazz standard "Airegin." Since the time jazz began, jazz has always shown the capacity to absorb diverse streams of music. The incorporation of rock and funk demonstrated that this capacity had not been diminished.

MODELS FOR JAZZ-ROCK PLAYERS   Improvising jazz-rock soloists tended to draw from the approach of John Coltrane if they were saxophonists, Freddie Hubbard if they were trumpeters, and from Chick Corea and Herbie Hancock if they were pianists. Bop melodic rhythms were incompatible with many of the jazz-rock accompaniment patterns, but the rhythmic properties of 1960s Coltrane-style lines were not. Pianists and guitarists often adopted repeating accompanying riffs in place of the spontaneous comping which had been customary since the 1940s. Hancock invented widely imitated riffs of this sort, but he also interspersed his playing with standard jazz comping.

Many bassists learned how to play the Fender electric bass guitar and began accumulating the syncopated and staccato figures which drew upon the work of late 1960s players in the Motown bands, groups led by James Brown during the same period, and the work of bassists in the early 1970s groups of Sly Stone (see page 427 for notations). Some jazz bassists carried their bass viol as well as the new bass guitar with them, but many eventually abandoned the bass viol and switched exclusively to bass guitar.

Drummers who served as models for jazz-rock were Tony Williams, Billy Cobham, and, after the mid-1970s, Steve Gadd. Drumming style was very active, with much use being made of the bass drum. The high-hat was often snapped closed sharply on every beat of the measure instead of being closed predominantly on the second and fourth beats of each measure. There was considerably less bounce and lilt than there had been in jazz of the 1950s, and timekeeping was more strictly stated than during the exploratory years of the 1960s. The beats were stated insistently and not always in a manner that alternated tension with relaxation as previous jazz styles had done. To some extent, there was an increase in the use of drums instead of cymbals for timekeeping. Despite the similarities between jazz-rock drumming and funk drumming, jazz-rock drumming could be distinguished by its greater amount of spontaneous variation.

POPULAR APPEAL By the mid-1980s, rock had exceeded the duration of swing's popularity in the mainstream of popular American music. Swing had been strong for about ten years, approximately 1935 to 1945, and a force in popular music for twenty years at most (perhaps late 1920s to late 1940s). Rock had now already been present for thirty years (since the mid-1950s), and jazz-rock had now been popular for more than fifteen of those thirty years. Jazz-rock became the first jazz style since the swing era to gain popular acceptance anywhere near the level accorded to swing, and it lasted at least as long as the swing era.

By incorporating elements of r & b and rock, several established jazz figures achieved popular success that rivaled all the peaks of recognition accorded to jazz players since the end of the swing era's wide appreciation of jazz-oriented band music. For example, despite highly creative and prolific composing and improvising throughout the 1960s, jazz pianist Herbie Hancock found his largest-selling work to occur when, in 1973, he produced the Sly Stone-influenced *Head Hunters*[38] album which, at one time, managed to occupy position number 13 on the *Billboard* chart in the popular album category. It had been extremely unusual for a jazz instrumental to ever be within the

[38] Columbia PC 32731

list of top one hundred best-selling albums; but after the late 1960s, and due largely to jazz-rock, this situation changed dramatically.

Only a few jazz instrumentals had previously reached sales of more than a million copies, yet jazz-rock records now did, with trumpeter Chuck Mangione's *Feels So Good* selling about 2.2 million copies. It had previously been unusual for a jazz album to sell more than 10,000 to 20,000 copies, but jazz-rock albums frequently sold more than 100,000 copies during the 1970s. At the beginning of the 1970s, jazz had about a 3 percent slice of the record market. At the beginning of the 1980s, its share had more than doubled, and, by some accounts, it had tripled. However, the new success for jazz did not depend so much on jazz character as it depended specifically on jazz-rock character. The category seemed to make more of a difference than the quality. As with swing era big band recordings, those jazz-rock pieces which presented the least improvisation tended to enjoy the most acclaim. And, as with the hits of the swing era, jazz-rock hits were identifiable by simple, repeating riffs which were syncopated in a catchy way. Much of what went by the jazz-rock label consisted of little more than funky rhythm vamps, elementary chord progressions, and an improvised solo riding on top of it. (This was the formula for several hits by saxophonist Grover Washington,[39] guitarist Earl Klugh,[40] and the bands of Jeff Lorber[41] and Spyro Gyra.[42]) This music was so popular that, in addition to the "jazz-rock" and "jazz fusion" labels, it also acquired the label of "cross over" music because sales of the records crossed over from the jazz market and entered the popular market.

There are several possible explanations for the new popularity of jazz and that of jazz-rock in particular. First, rock had already been popular for more than fifteen years by the time that *Head Hunters* was released. Perhaps when **jazz adopted the electric instruments and the accompaniment rhythms associated with rock,** it was providing a bridge of similarity for listeners that served to ease them into a kind of music that had otherwise been strange and difficult to listen to. A second possibility is that the **prominence of drums was more inviting to dancers** than modern jazz had previously been. Third is the **relative simplicity of chord progressions** found in jazz-rock. The new music was admittedly more involved than rock had previously been, but it was clearly less complex than most earlier jazz styles. A fourth explanation involves the **extensive use of repetition for a single accompaniment pattern.** This was fundamental to the boogie woogie style of jazz piano playing which was enormously popular during the 1940s, and it

---

[39] *Mr. Magic* Kudu 20 and Motown 175

[40] *Living Inside Your Love* Liberty BN LA 667 G

[41] *Soft Space* Inner City 1056

[42] *Spyro Gyra* Amherst AHM 1014 and MCA 37149; *Morning Dance* Infinity 9004 and MCA 37148

was fundamental to most of the jazz-rock hits of the 1970s. Technically it is known as ostinato, which means that a particular rhythm or brief melodic figure is repeated extensively. In summary, many of the largest-selling recordings in popular music, jazz, and classical music are distinguished by their simplicity, rhythmic vitality, and use of repetition. This combination of features could also account for much of jazz-rock's commercial success.

A fifth possible explanation for the increased proportion of the record market which became aligned with jazz during the 1970s is **the school stage band movement.** During this period, for the first time, there were several hundred-thousand school musicians playing in sixteen- to twenty-piece ensembles which were like swinging concert bands. These groups were common in high schools and colleges, and were even being included in the offerings of many junior high schools. This exposure to jazz might have induced students to buy quantities of jazz records that their nonjazz-educated predecessors had not bought.

CHAPTER SUMMARY

1) Jazz and rock represent different streams in Afro-American music, but they have occasionally overlapped.

2) Jazz differs from rock in its lesser amount of repetition, larger amount of improvisation, greater complexity, and higher level of musicianship.

3) Chicago, Blood, Sweat & Tears, and Ten Wheel Drive probably ought not be called jazz-rock because they demonstrated little improvisation and had more origins in soul music than in rock and roll.

4) These three groups represent amalgamations of existing trends rather than a fresh style.

5) The most genuine fusions of soul music (funk) and jazz occurred in bands of Larry Coryell, Gary Burton, and Miles Davis, and in the bands launched by their sidemen.

6) The two most influential jazz-rock guitarists were John McLaughlin and Larry Coryell.

7) Their tone color and rhythmic conception departed from jazz guitar tradition and drew more from urban blues and rock practices.

8) John McLaughlin plays with phenomenal speed and precision, drawing from the music of India and John Coltrane.

9) McLaughlin led several innovative bands containing musicians who were themselves important jazz-rock bandleaders: drummer Billy Cobham, violinist Jean-Luc Ponty, and pianist Jan Hammer.

10) Pianist Joe Zawinul wrote the funk hits "Mercy, Mercy, Mercy" and "Walk Tall" while with Cannonball Adderley's band.

11) Zawinul's composition "In a Silent Way" and his arrangements formed the basis for the important 1969 Miles Davis jazz-rock albums *Bitches Brew* and *In a Silent Way*.

12) In 1971, Zawinul founded Weather Report, an innovative fusion band which was still playing during the 1980s.

13) Weather Report featured compositions of Zawinul and saxophonist Wayne Shorter, touching impressionistic music, African, Latin American, and classical European traditions.

14) Weather Report originally began with much collective improvisation, in a manner quite unlike those used by Lennie Tristano and Ornette Coleman.

15) Weather Report eventually adopted approaches employing extensive pre-set repetition and the feeling of soul music, culminating in Zawinul's riff-based disco hit "Birdland."

16) Roles for the bassists in Weather Report include walking, funk bass, soloing, and the interactive-nonrepetitive style.

17) Jaco Pastorius was a virtuoso bass guitarist with Weather Report from 1976 to 1982 whose sound and imagination became an important model for bassists.

18) Pastorius was also a composer-arranger, combining such unusual tone colors as harmonica, steel drums, and children's voices in addition to integrating classical music and funk style for his own band, Word of Mouth.

chapter 20
BIG BANDS IN THE 1960s & 1970s

The jazz-oriented big bands which remained on the road almost continuously throughout the 1950s were those of Stan Kenton, Ellington, Basie, Woody Herman, Lionel Hampton, and Harry James, joined by the bands of Don Ellis, Buddy Rich, and Maynard Ferguson in the sixties and seventies. While Ellington and Basie usually had a rather stable personnel, the others tended to experience a high turnover in sidemen and generally employed much younger musicians.

As a commercial force in jazz, the big band was almost extinct by the early 1950s. Then, by 1985 with Don Ellis, Stan Kenton, Harry James, Count Basie, and Duke Ellington dead and no bandleaders filling those vacancies, almost the only modern big band jazz was that preserved by student musicians in schools and colleges.

STAN KENTON One of the few jazz musicians to become widely known by the American public after Louis Armstrong and Duke Ellington was Stan Kenton (1912–1979). That name, unlike Ellington's or Armstrong's, represented a huge number of different composers, arrangers, and soloists. Kenton created a composing and arranging style which owed much to Claude Thornhill, Fletcher Henderson, and Benny Carter. Kenton composed the popular "Eager Beaver" and his well-known theme, "Artistry in Rhythm."[1] He also developed a piano style, influenced, in part, by Earl Hines. However, Kenton was less important as a pianist and arranger than he was as a bandleader. His skill at public relations and his talent for finding and employing creative modern composers

[1] *The Jazz Compositions of Stan Kenton* Creative World 1078

rank among his major contributions to jazz history. It is significant that, because of his band's great popularity during the late 1940s, Kenton became financially free enough to experiment and that he channeled this freedom into hiring relatively unknown writers and encouraging ambitious compositions which had little chance of realizing commercial success. Improvisers had enjoyed these kinds of opportunities throughout jazz history, but composers had not. His bands provided work for hundreds of musicians who may not have otherwise received much exposure. Though he began leading bands in 1941 when the big band era was still flourishing, he continued to lead long after big bands went out of fashion.

Stan Kenton's pattern was to go on tour for eight to twelve months, then disband, get new arrangements, promote another catchy banner such as "Progressive Jazz," "Innovations in Modern Music," or "New Concepts," and then go on tour again with different personnel. Several sidemen reappeared in successive editions, but hundreds of anonymous others filled the sections only briefly. Musicianship was high but individuality was generally low.

Stan Kenton maintained a resident orchestra in Los Angeles from 1964 to 1967, commissioning new works and calling it the Los Angeles Neophonic Orchestra. Then in the early 1970s, he launched an ambitious project to gain direct control over the means of production, marketing, and distribution of his recordings by setting up a mail-order record company. He reissued many of his old albums, licensed from Capitol record company when it had refused to keep them on the market, and he made new records, marketing them himself. His tours concentrated on promotion of "membership" in an enterprise which he called Creative World. By 1973, the operation had a 100,000-name mailing list, a music publishing house which sold primarily to high school and college stage bands, and a promotional scheme that succeeded in filling hundreds of auditoriums with new and old fans.

Just as the feeling projected by the Basie band can be described as easy swinging, the feeling projected by the Kenton bands can be described as massive power and intensity. Whether slow or fast, his pieces are usually massive-sounding. Much of his repertory is solemn and weighty, essentially twentieth-century music scored for trumpets, trombones, and saxophones plus rhythm section. Some of his material also required French horns, tuba, strings, and Latin American percussion instruments. The band's character is based more on elaborate arrangements than on the simplicity and swing associated with Count Basie's approach.

The Kenton bands emphasized composition over improvisation. In fact, some solo improvisations were not solos in the conventional sense, but embellishments of the ensemble sound. One example is the practice of overpowering a soloist in a loud ensemble sound, thereby turning the solo line into an ensemble line which is almost indistinct. Again, a contrast with Basie is helpful. The Basie band of the late 1930s was almost a "big combo" in the sense that solo improvisation was primary, and some of the ensemble backgrounds were almost incidental to the music. The Kenton band approach contrasts markedly in that the ultimate effect was frequently similar to that of a brass choir instead of the jazz produced by a "big combo."

Some of the most impressive work produced by the Kenton bands was nonswinging concert music which vividly exposed rich, modern harmonies. Two and three moving parts were sometimes presented simultaneously. **Pete Rugolo**[*] (b. 1915) helped formulate the Kenton style of the 1940s in works such as "Interlude," and one of the most respected of all modern jazz arrangers, **Bill Holman** (b. 1927), wrote extensively for Kenton. The weighty pieces which Kenton performed by composers Robert Graettinger (1923–1957) ("City of Glass"),[2] Johnny Richards (1911–1968) ("Cuban Fire"),[3] and Russ Garcia (b. 1916) ("Adventures in Emotions")[4] were quite unlike the dance band tradition of big band jazz. Trademarks of these approaches are trumpet parts which are high-pitched, loud, and often block-voiced as five-note chords, and the use of saxophone passages written in long strings of sixteenth notes which come up from the low range of ensemble like fountains or descend like a waterfall. These elements collectively became identified with the Kenton label **"progressive jazz."** (Many listeners mistakenly use that label to identify all modern jazz. Somehow Kenton's label rather than the "cool" label or the "modern" label seems to have been caught by the American public and applied to almost any style which is not swing or Dixieland.)

Although performances by the Kenton bands usually cover a range from the softest of sounds to the loudest, Kenton has a reputation for being the loudest of big bands. This is partly due to the preponderance of brass instruments. It was not unusual, for example, to find five trumpets and five trombones in a Kenton band at the same time as Ellington was carrying only four trumpets and three trombones. Additionally, some Kenton trombonists have doubled on tuba, and one version of his band carried an entire section of mellophoniums (trumpet-French horn hybrids which were specially made for Kenton). The saxophone section has occasionally been called upon to augment the

---

[*] Pete Rugolo's "Mirage" is on *Mirage* in the New World series of albums donated to libraries and colleges by the Rockefeller Foundation (see vol. 216). This volume also contains "Egdon Heath" arranged by Bill Russo for Kenton.

[2] *The City of Glass and This Modern World* Creative World 1006

[3] Creative World 1008

[4] *Stan Kenton Conducts the Los Angeles Neophonic Orchestra* Capitol SMAS 2424

band's massiveness by employing the unusual combination of two baritone saxophones.

The most innovative of all Kenton's soloists was **Lee Konitz,** who played with the band for a little over one year. (See pages 179–180 for more on Konitz.) Other distinctive improvisers who appeared in Kenton bands included alto saxophonist **Art Pepper** (1925–1982) and trumpeter **Conte Candoli** (b. 1927). Known more for his extensive high range than for interesting solo lines, trumpeter **Maynard Ferguson** (b. 1928) was also a standout among Kenton sidemen.[5]

The Kenton band is particularly notable for its glossy trombone sound. For more than three decades, Kenton's soloists invariably preferred high-register work, and graced the beginnings of many tones with long, climbing smears. They used a meticulously controlled vibrato which was initially slow and then usually quickened dramatically near a note's end. Their approach was extroverted, but in the well-manicured way of Tommy Dorsey rather than the rough or guttural way of earlier jazz trombonists. Of Kenton's trombonists, **Frank Rosolino** (1926–1978)[6] had the most influence outside the ranks of Kenton's bands. His technique was excellent, and he played bop lines which considerably extended the concept of jazz trombone from the foundations provided by Jack Teagarden and Tommy Dorsey.

Another contribution of the Kenton bands is an exploration of Latin American music. Although Duke Ellington and Jelly Roll Morton had employed Latin American rhythms in pre-modern jazz, and Dizzy Gillespie's big band had pioneered Afro-Cuban approaches, **Kenton, more than any other bandleader, became identified with Latin American drums and rhythms in modern big band jazz.** (He used one or more Latin American percussionists full-time with the band for several periods in the 1950s and 1970s.)[7]

The question of where to place Kenton's style is a knotty one. You may justifiably place his music in the category of cool jazz because his band was based on the West Coast during the 1950s, many of his players showed the influence of cool jazz founders Lester Young and Miles Davis, and Kenton chose to project a highly controlled feeling with his music which was not especially jumpy. Some listeners prefer to call Kenton's music "big band bop," while others identify his music as "third stream" because it blends the orchestral approaches of symphonic music with jazz improvisation. Otherwise you may choose to label Kenton's output by his own category, **"progressive jazz."**

---

[5] Konitz, Candoli, and Ferguson are all featured on *New Concepts of Artistry in Rhythm* (Creative World 1002).

[6] See footnote 5.

[7] See footnote 3.

WOODY HERMAN

Woody Herman (b. 1913) is one of those rare jazz musicians who has good business sense and great skill at putting together all-star big bands. His band has not only survived the decline of big bands, but featured some of the better improvisers in a field otherwise dominated by Ellington and Basie musicians. Herman is a good swing era clarinetist and a Johnny Hodges-style alto saxophonist. However, his greatest contribution has been a string of modern jazz big bands filled with top-notch improvisers.

The Woody Herman band uses only four saxophones (three tenors and a baritone) instead of the five-man combination used in the Duke Ellington and Count Basie bands. Note that there is no alto saxophone except in rare instances when Herman himself augments the section with his. The saxophone section has a distinctive sound because of this unusual make-up and because, as recently as the 1950s, the players in that section modeled their sound after Lester Young (see pages 132–135 for discussion of the Young style). This is the distinctive quality known as the "Four Brothers" sound,[8] named after the four saxophonists who played together in the band during the 1940s and a piece that had been written for them by Jimmy Giuffre. These musicians included the great bop baritone saxophonist Serge Chaloff and some of the best Lester Young disciples in jazz: Stan Getz, Herbie Steward, and Zoot Sims. Herman continued to fill his saxophone section with Lester Young disciples until the early 1970s when he gained several John Coltrane-Joe Henderson-style players. The saxophonists he used thereafter derived their styles from a variety of sources. Though the band has featured outstanding trumpeters and trombonists, its best soloists have usually been saxophonists.

In 1939, Woody Herman had recorded "At the Woodchopper's Ball," a riff-based twelve-measure blues that became a hit, and in 1948 he did "Early Autumn,"[9] a lush, impressionistic ballad that also became well known. Herman still played them publicly during the 1980s, but despite his repetition of these pieces, Herman led an essentially contemporary band throughout the 1970s and 80s. After the 1950s, the band had lost some uniqueness, but gained a versatility which Maynard Ferguson, Count Basie, and Stan Kenton lacked. Herman began recording tunes by composers as diverse as Horace Silver, Charlie Mingus, Henry Mancini, Herbie Hancock, Keith Jarrett, Chick Corea, and The Beatles. By 1968 the band was using rock-derived material and electric instruments. The Herman band became stylistically varied and remained that way.

Each edition of Woody Herman's "Herd," as his bands have affectionately been called, has showcased outstanding young soloists, and

[8] *Greatest Hits* Columbia PC 9291
[9] *Early Autumn* Capitol M 11034

original compositions and arrangements. The band has retained loose-ness and steered clear of ambitious and exotic orchestral conceptions that attracted Stan Kenton. Herman likes his music to be swinging and direct. In fact he edits out any passages in his men's pieces that he feels are elaborate or unswinging. Herman deserves credit for his stay-ing power as well as his allegiance to a simple and unpretentious big band style. He should also be accorded gratitude for supporting thou-sands of young jazz musicians who have filled his sections and drawn inspiration from him.

MAYNARD FERGUSON

Jazz has known many musicians with astonishing instrumental facility: pianist Art Tatum, bassist Jimmy Blanton, drummer Tony Williams, saxophonist John Coltrane, and others. Some of those men are also known for innovative concepts of improvisation, but spectacular facil-ity is often talent enough.

Trumpeter Maynard Ferguson is known both as an astounding high-note artist and as a leader of several exciting post-bop bands. Maynard's almost freakish mastery of the trumpet extends throughout its entire range. No register is the least bit awkward for him. His fa-cility takes him to B above double high C. What is even more impor-tant is that on most nights he does not simply squeal those incredibly high notes, but actually plays them with good intonation and large tone. Most big band high-note artists play few if any improvised solos, restricting their playing to trumpet-section lead work in order to keep their lips set specifically for those high parts. Maynard amazes brass players by not only playing high-register lead parts, but also impro-vising solos on nearly every tune. In addition to that, his endurance is as phenomenal as his range, and he can switch to trombone or French horn right in the middle of a piece, making an immediate ad-justment to it. In fact, he is a master not only of the trumpet, but of all the brass instruments. He plays most of the reed instruments, too.

By 1950, Ferguson had already led his own bands as well as played in those of Charlie Barnet and Boyd Raeburn. However, his most sig-nificant early exposure came when he played lead trumpet with Stan Kenton[10] from 1950 to 1952 and then, later, as the leader of his own thirteen-piece band formed during 1957.[11] Although his band was characterized by Kenton's emphasis on loud, flashy brass, it had a dif-ferent feel: it swung. The band had a precise, hard-driving style that carried a lot of tension with it. Whereas Basie's effect is a subtle glow and Kenton's a massive brass choir, Ferguson's band was a happy fire, crackling away.

---

[10] Stan Kenton *The Lighter Side* Creative World 1050
[11] *Message from Newport / Newport Suite* Roulette RE 116

The 1957 to 1965 Ferguson band had an instrumentation more compact than the usual big band. Instead of a sax section containing two altos, two tenors, and a baritone, his had an alto, two tenors, and a baritone. They tended to have a biting sound which was almost brassy. Rather than the usual three to five trombones, Maynard had only two. His thirteen-piece band had a tight, polished sound that was filled with raw excitement. It seemed to thrive on fast tempos and loud playing; it had few slow or subdued arrangements.

Unlike Kenton, Maynard gave his sidemen plenty of unhindered solo time. Few of those sidemen became important after leaving Maynard, but many continued to play in road bands and do studio work.

Many written arrangements came from within the Ferguson band. Trombonist Slide Hampton wrote "Frame for the Blues," a dramatic arrangement of well-paced bluesy figures.[12] Trombonist Don Sebesky's arrangement of "Maria"[13] was a gorgeous feature for Maynard's ballad style. Sebesky later achieved recognition writing accompaniments for guitarist Wes Montgomery and alto saxophonist Paul Desmond at A & M Records during the 1960s and 70s. But some of his best work has been for a wide variety of soloists at C.T.I. Records: Freddie Hubbard, Hubert Laws, Milt Jackson, and others.

During the mid-1960s, Maynard was forced to disband. Then during the early 1970s, he formed a new band in England which made several albums of showy, rock-tinged material. Some of their pop tune arrangements, "MacArthur Park," for example, became popular with AM radio disc jockeys, a portion of the media usually unfriendly to jazz. Little by little, what had originally been a band with British personnel now contained more and more American musicians. It eventually became based in the United States, and it toured almost continuously into the 1980s.

Ferguson's 1970s and 80s band was even more compact than his 1957–65 band. At one time, the instrumentation was down to four trumpets (plus Ferguson), two trombones, one alto, one tenor, and one baritone saxophone (see pages 88–89 for explanations and photographs of big band instrumentation). The band sounded like his earlier one to the extent that several old pieces were reworked for it ("L-Dopa," "Airegin," "Got the Spirit," and "Maria"), and it had bright tone colors and high energy. However, his 1970s and 80s band sound was rooted less in modern jazz traditions. Much of the music was like show band writing, and it used electric instruments playing rock and funk style accompaniments. Ferguson's 1970 recording of "MacArthur Park"[14] had opened the popular music market for him,

[12] See footnote 11
[13] *Maynard '62* Roulette R52083
[14] *M. F. Horn* Columbia PC 30466

and his 1972 recording of "Hey, Jude" (by the Beatles) continued that pattern. Ferguson's greatest popularity, however, was accorded to a 1978 recording of "Gonna Fly Now," a Jay Chattaway arrangement of Bill Conti's theme song for the immensely popular "Rocky" movie.[15] Ferguson followed that huge success with numerous recordings of television and movie themes. Most of these recordings contained large amounts of orchestration and small amounts of jazz improvisation. The band also capitalized on the popularity of jazz-rock by recording Herbie Hancock's hit "Chameleon"[16] in 1974 and Joe Zawinul's hit "Birdland" in 1978 (see pages 313–319, 329–330, and 339–341 for more about this style and these particular pieces).

Ferguson received radio airplay for his renditions of popular themes, and he participated extensively in school concerts and jazz clinics for young musicians. He was far better known to young trumpeters during this period than Miles Davis was, even though Davis was a far more innovative player. Davis did not record show tunes during this period, nor did he perform school clinics. Furthermore, Davis played the trumpet in a way that was not acceptable to most school band directors, and the Davis repertory from this period was not as easily adapted to the big bands and marching bands in high schools and colleges as the Ferguson repertory was. So, despite Ferguson's being a far less innovative improviser than Davis, Ferguson influenced more young school trumpeters than Davis did during this period. Another irony is that Ferguson's 1957–65 recordings had the most jazz, but his 1970s recordings enjoyed the most sales. In summary, Ferguson's importance in jazz history is found in

1) his leading distinctive modern jazz big bands that toured almost continuously for about thirty years;

2) his exceptional mastery of the trumpet influencing countless musicians of the 1960s, 70s, and 80s;

3) his providing exposure for composers and arrangers who later occupied significant roles in commercial jazz;

4) his breaking modern big band jazz through to the popular music market by way of "MacArthur Park," "Hey, Jude," and "Rocky," during a period of very low popularity for this particular instrumentation;

5) his being one of the earliest big bands to embrace jazz-rock.

THAD JONES–
MEL LEWIS

Despite the large audience acquired by Kenton, Herman, and Ferguson, many listeners considered the best big band of the 1970s to be one co-led by trumpeter Thad Jones and drummer Mel Lewis. Though

---

[15] *Conquistador* Columbia PC 34457
[16] *Chameleon* Columbia PC 33007

the band toured, it was not a road band in the fifty weeks per year sense that Kenton's, Herman's, or Ferguson's was. The Jones–Lewis band depended heavily on free-lance jazz musicians living in New York. For over ten years, most Monday nights found the band at the small New York night club called the Village Vanguard.

At various times since its formation in 1965, the Jones–Lewis band has featured soloists who were more original improvisers than the Stan Kenton, Woody Herman, or Maynard Ferguson bands were carrying at the same time. One of the earliest editions of the band was especially distinctive because it included several well-established individualists who were veterans of the 1950s and 60s avant-garde bands.[17] Pianist Roland Hanna and trombonist Jimmy Knepper had been with Charles Mingus. Virtuoso bassist Richard Davis had been with Eric Dolphy, and Davis became the first bassist to do in a big band what Charles Mingus and Scott LaFaro had done in combo settings: He improvised accompaniments containing a great variety of melodic and rhythmic figures that vigorously interacted with the solo and ensemble lines instead of just playing walking bass lines (see pages 253–256 and 331–333 for more about these approaches).

Spearheading the band was Thad Jones, another veteran of the explorative Mingus groups. Jones was among the most well respected of all hard bop trumpeters. (Mingus ranked Jones as a musical genius.) He had improvised highly creative and strikingly unorthodox solos on Count Basie records of the 1950s as well as collaborating with Mingus in several innovative recordings. Co-leading the band was drummer Mel Lewis (b. 1929), who had played with the modern big bands of Stan Kenton, Gerald Wilson, and Gerry Mulligan as well as appearing with countless small groups. Musicians consider Lewis to be among the most tasteful and swinging of big band drummers. He is a uniquely flexible accompanist who is perfectly suited for the Thad Jones band conception.

The Thad Jones arranging style was one of the most original to appear since Duke Ellington's. And coincidentally, one of its trademarks was using soprano saxophone in lead position as Ellington had done about thirty years earlier. The lines Jones wrote were often very difficult to play, but his musicians executed them with finesse. The Jones harmonies were rarely ordinary, and they paradoxically managed to be rich without sounding ponderous. There was a pixie-like lightness and humor to his melodic rhythms, and he often maintained a suspended feeling by using unconventional rhythm section accompaniment patterns, frequently shifting densities, and occasionally deleting accompaniment altogether. Much of this manner recalled the strategies pioneered by Charles Mingus during the 1950s.

[17] *Presenting Thad Jones–Mel Lewis and the Jazz Orchestra* Solid State SM 17003 and SS 18003

The Jones–Lewis band was one of the first big bands after the Basie group of the 1930s both to achieve a flexible interaction between improvising soloist and rhythm section and to offer plenty of uncluttered solo space. During certain moments in a performance the Jones–Lewis band sounds like an up-to-date, modern jazz combo, indistinguishable from the quality combos of its period. This poses a striking contrast to the sound of the Kenton, Herman, and Ferguson bands. Those are rooted in earlier styles and usually characterized by both short solos and screaming ensemble figures which regularly engulf the improvising soloists who are trying to play sensitively and be heard.

The band continued to feature strikingly gifted improvisers and first-rate ensemble players for more than ten years. It even managed to retain much of its high regard among musicians after Thad Jones left it and moved to Denmark in 1979. At this time, trombonist Bob Brookmeyer, who had contributed arrangements during the 1960s, now returned to write additional material, thereby filling part of the vacancy caused by the Jones departure. Brookmeyer was a very thoughtful arranger who produced music which sometimes recalled the writing of Gil Evans. (See pages 185–189 for more on Brookmeyer and 215–216 for more on Evans.)

Unfortunately the Jones–Lewis records never sold well, so few were made, and fewer remain available. Few of the best moments for this great band were documented. The band's recorded output is quite slim considering the number of years the band was active and the number of albums that are available to document other big bands of the same period.

CHAPTER SUMMARY

1) There were very few steadily working big bands after the swing era, and aside from Duke Ellington's and Count Basie's, those that were prominent in the 1960s and 70s were led by Stan Kenton, Woody Herman, Thad Jones, and Maynard Ferguson. In the 1980s, the only regularly touring big bands were led by Herman, Basie, Ferguson, and drummer Buddy Rich.

2) Kenton's was an arranger's band, often featuring complex twentieth-century symphonic music with great emphasis on brass.

3) Kenton's arrangements originally drew from the methods of Fletcher Henderson and Claude Thornhill, but eventually the band provided a vehicle for writing by Pete Rugolo, Johnny Richards, Robert Graettinger, and Bill Holman.

4) Kenton's music has been collectively labeled "progressive jazz."

5) Woody Herman's band was swinging and improvisation-oriented, with an emphasis on saxophones.

6) The Herman saxophone section contained the unusual combination of three tenor saxophones and one baritone saxophone, called the "Four Brothers" sound and featured many prominent Lester Young disciples such as Stan Getz.

7) Trumpeter Maynard Ferguson, known for his ultra-high-register playing, has led a string of big bands that sound hard-driving and brass-oriented but place more stress on swinging than Kenton's bands did.

8) The Thad Jones–Mel Lewis band was composed of New York City free-lance jazz musicians, had an emphasis on combo format, and reflected Charles Mingus and Duke Ellington among its sources.

9) Though these are oversimplifications, you might find this list of comparisons helpful for discriminating the prominent big band sounds.

   a) Count Basie's was built on its rhythm section and emphasized tenor saxophone soloists, whereas Stan Kenton's was built on trumpets and trombones.

   b) Maynard Ferguson followed the brass emphasis of Kenton, whereas Woody Herman followed the saxophone emphasis of Basie.

   c) The Thad Jones–Mel Lewis band often saw itself as a large combo in the Basie manner.

   d) Duke Ellington's emphases alternated between composition and improvisation.

   e) Basie, Herman, and Jones–Lewis stressed improvisation, whereas Kenton stressed composition.

   f) The Herman and Basie bands sounded the most relaxed, whereas the Kenton and Ferguson bands sounded the most intense.

appendix

A Very Abbreviated Outline of Jazz Styles—Not strictly chronological; many styles overlap the same time periods, and most have continued long after their inception. Many innovators continued playing for decades after their style emerged.

Time	Style	Hornmen	Pianists	Composers-Arrangers	Rhythm Section Musicians
1920s	Early Jazz	Louis Armstrong, Sidney Bechet, Bix Beiderbecke	James P. Johnson, Earl Hines	Jelly Roll Morton	Baby Dodds, Zutty Singleton, Pops Foster
1930s	Swing	Coleman Hawkins, Roy Eldridge, Johnny Hodges, Benny Carter	Art Tatum, Teddy Wilson	Duke Ellington, Fletcher Henderson, Sy Oliver	Chick Webb, Dave Tough, Sid Catlett, Walter Page, Gene Krupa
Late 1930s	Transition to Bop	Lester Young, Don Byas	Nat Cole		Count Basie Rhythm Section 1937–43, Jimmy Blanton
1940s	Bop	Charlie Parker, Dizzy Gillespie, Dexter Gordon, Stan Getz	Thelonious Monk, Bud Powell, Al Haig	Thelonious Monk, Tadd Dameron, Dizzy Gillespie	Kenny Clarke, Max Roach, Oscar Pettiford
Late 1940s	Transition to Cool & West Coast	Lee Konitz, Miles Davis	Lennie Tristano	Claude Thornhill, Gil Evans	
1950s	West Coast	Gerry Mulligan, Chet Baker, Art Pepper	Dave Brubeck	Gerry Mulligan, Shorty Rogers, Jimmy Giuffre	Chico Hamilton

Period	Style				
1950s	Hard Bop	Clifford Brown Sonny Rollins Thad Jones John Coltrane Cannonball Adderley Miles Davis	Tommy Flanagan Horace Silver Red Garland	Horace Silver Benny Golson Cannonball Adderley Jackie McLean Gigi Gryce	Art Blakey Philly Joe Jones Paul Chambers Sam Jones Wilbur Ware
Late 1950s	Transition to Modal Jazz and Free Jazz	Miles Davis John Coltrane Ornette Coleman	Bill Evans Cecil Taylor	Charles Mingus Miles Davis	
Early 1960s	Coexistence of Hard Bop, Free Jazz, and Modal Jazz	Eric Dolphy	Bill Evans McCoy Tyner Cecil Taylor	John Coltrane Ornette Coleman Wayne Shorter Charles Mingus Don Cherry	Elvin Jones Bill Evans Trio with Scott LaFaro Cecil Taylor with Sunny Murray
Mid-1960s		Freddie Hubbard Joe Henderson Wayne Shorter Don Cherry	Herbie Hancock	Wayne Shorter John Coltrane Herbie Hancock	Miles Davis's 1963–68 rhythm section
Late 1960s	Transition to Jazz-Rock	Miles Davis	Joe Zawinul	Joe Zawinul	Tony Williams
1970s	Coexistence of AACM, Jazz-Rock, and Modal Jazz	AACM players	Keith Jarrett Herbie Hancock Chick Corea Joe Zawinul	Chick Corea AACM Joe Zawinul John McLaughlin	Miroslav Vitous Airto Moreira Jaco Pastorius

ELEMENTS OF MUSIC

In describing the nature of jazz and the characteristics of different styles, several basic musical terms are quite helpful. This chapter is devoted to defining some of these terms, and I urge all readers, including those who are musically knowledgeable, to examine them carefully.

When people think of jazz, they usually think of rhythm first. But because the word rhythm is often used to describe a large variety of musical characteristics, some uses convey inaccurate or contradictory meanings. Much of the confusion can be avoided by first understanding three related terms for which rhythm is often mistaken: beat, tempo, and meter.

Beat Music is often said to have a pulse. The unit of pulse is called a beat. When you tap your foot to music, you are usually tapping with the beat. Here is a visualization of the pulse sequences we call beats.

Tempo Tempo refers to the speed or rate at which the beats pass. If you describe a piece of music as fast, you probably mean it has a rapid tempo, not that it occupies a short time span. When the beats continue at a regular rate, we say the tempo is constant. A clock's ticking is a good example of constant tempo. If the passage of beats is rapid, the speed is called up tempo. Medium tempo means medium fast; down tempo means slow.

Meter The beats in music are rarely undifferentiated. They are usually heard as being grouped. Meter describes the type of grouping. Our perception of grouping results when sequences of beats are set off from each other. This occurs in several ways. Every third or fourth beat may be louder or longer than the others. It may be distinctive because it has a different pitch or tone quality. Those differences are perceived as emphasis or accent. If we hear a sequence of beats grouped in fours, it may be due to a pattern of accents which creates this effect: **ONE** two three four **ONE** two three four. That pattern represents a meter which musicians simply call "four."

If the beats fall into the pattern, **ONE** two three, **ONE** two three, **ONE** two three, musicians say that the music "is in three" or in waltz time.

Meters of four and three are quite common, but there are also meters of five, six, seven, and others. A meter of five might sound like **ONE** two three four five **ONE** two three four five, **ONE** two three four five, with a large accent on the first beat and no other accents. Or there may be a strong accent on the first beat and a smaller accent on the fourth: **ONE** two three FOUR five **ONE** two three FOUR five **ONE** two three FOUR five; or a smaller accent on the third beat: **ONE** two THREE four five **ONE** two THREE four five **ONE** two THREE four five. A meter of six usually feels like **ONE** two three FOUR five six **ONE** two three FOUR five six.

Each group of beats is called a **measure.** When the meter is three, there are three beats in a measure; when the meter is four there are four beats in a measure.

Rhythm In the broadest sense, rhythm simply refers to the arrangement of sounds in time, and therefore encompasses beat, tempo, and meter. But rhythm has come to mean something more specific than these features. In fact, beat, tempo, and meter furnish the framework in which rhythm is described.

Imagine a continuous sequence of beats occurring at a constant tempo, with four beats to a measure. The steady beat which in musical notation is represented by a string of quarter notes can also be visualized as a series of boxes, representing equal amounts of time. Our meter would be called "four." Each beat is called a quarter note, and each unit of four beats constitutes a measure.

The sound within a measure can be distributed in an infinite number of ways, one of which includes "filling" the measure with silence. Rhythm is the description of how that measure or a sequence of measures is filled with sound.

Let us take a few examples, numbering the four parts of the measure one, two, three, and four, respectively. We shall create rhythms by using a single sound mixed with silence. First, divide a measure into four equal parts, filling only the first and third with sound.

We have a rhythm. It is not complex, but it does what a rhythm is supposed to do: it describes the distribution of sound over time. In fact, this is the bass drum part in numerous marches, and it is the string bass part in many slow dance pieces.

Now, instead of taking just one measure, take two measures as a unit of repetition. In other words, the rhythm is two measures long.

Finally, repeat a one measure rhythm to fill two measures worth of time. This might be heard as a two measure rhythm or as two one measure rhythms.

Rhythm is the distribution of sound over time, but rhythm also refers to the way sounds are accented. Usually, the first beat of a measure is accented. An example would be the typical OOM pah pah accompaniment for a waltz. In a measure of four, the first and third beats are often accented, as in the BOOM chick BOOM chick drum pattern used in much popular music.

Examining our use of accents can lend understanding to a rhythmic element called *syncopation*, a crucial aspect of jazz feeling. For example, if we expect to hear a sound on every beat but only hear it in a few odd places, the upset we feel is the result of syncopation. This upset can be very stimulating and contribute a prime component of jazz feeling.

Examine this manner of filling two measures.

Note that the sounds which occur, bordered by silence, in positions other than on the first and third beats seem to stand out. They seem to be self accenting. If we additionally stress these odd positions by making the sounds in those positions louder than the sounds in other positions, syncopation is enhanced: one TWO three four ONE two three FOUR.

The concept of syncopation partly depends on a listener's expectations. For example, if we are expecting to hear *ONE* two THREE four, but we actually hear one *TWO* three FOUR, we are experiencing syncopation. Jazz drummers often keep time by playing boom CHICK boom CHICK (one TWO three FOUR) instead of BOOM chick BOOM chick. This syncopation is part of what makes a performance sound like jazz. Another frequently used syncopation occurs when we hear one two three FOUR when we are expecting to hear ONE two three four. So you see that rhythm involves the arrangement of stresses in addition to just describing the arrangement of sound over time. We have also seen that a phenomenon called syncopation results when the sounds are arranged or stressed in unexpected ways. Of course, what is expected depends on what the listener is accustomed to hearing. Therefore the statement that syncopation consists of unexpected accent is inadequate. Perhaps a more useful definition involves the accent of beats other than the first and, in measure of four beats, also the third beat. Silence can also be syncopating. For example, if we encounter silence at a time when we are expecting to hear ONE, the feeling of syncopation results.

To understand more complex syncopations and another essential element of jazz feeling, the swing eighth note, requires an acquaintance with ways in which beats are divided into smaller units. Here is a measure in four, with four quarter notes to the measure. We can divide each quarter note in half to produce eighth notes.

There are two eighth notes for every quarter note. If we place accents on the eighth notes according to the way we previously accented the measure of quarter notes, we have *ONE* two three four

FIVE six seven eight. The time span for a measure of eight eighth notes is identical to that in a measure of four quarter notes, but keeping track of eight eighth notes is cumbersome. So we express the eighth notes in terms of subdivided quarter notes, saying "and" for the second half of each quarter note (every other eighth note): one and two and three and four and. Each word, whether it is the name of a number or the word "and," represents an eighth note.

Syncopation occurs when any of the "and's" receives more emphasis than the numbered units. Accenting the "and's" is essential to rhythms frequently employed in jazz. The final two beats in a measure are often divided into eighth notes with the last one accented the most: three and four AND (for notations of this and other syncopations, see page 428). Many notes which appear in written form on the first beat of a measure are played on the and of the fourth beat in the preceding measure when given a jazz interpretation. The practice of playing a note slightly before or slightly after it is supposed to be played is a syncopating device which jazz musicians apply to pop tunes in order to lend jazz feeling to a performance.

The quarter note can also be divided into three equal parts to produce what are called eighth-note triplets.

Here, each quarter note is divided into four equal parts, called sixteenth notes.

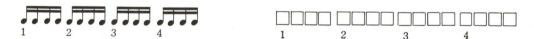

So far we have examined equal divisions of the quarter note. But it is also possible to divide it into notes of unequal value, for instance, a long note and a short note. One such pattern consists of a dotted eighth note followed by a sixteenth note. A dot after a note means that the note receives one and a half times its usual value; therefore the dotted eighth note has the combined value of an eighth note and a sixteenth note.

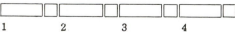

Another long-short pattern is based on the triplet division of the quarter note. The pattern is called a tied triplet figure. Here, the first note has the value of two-thirds of a quarter note, and the second has the value of one-third.

Jazz has one rhythmic quality which, to my knowledge, is not found in any other kind of music: jazz swing feeling. A discussion of it appears in the "What Is Jazz?" chapter, but that discussion hinges on the swing eighth note which is examined next.

Having heard the term swing eighth note, you might wonder how, if an eighth note is simply half the duration of a quarter note, we can have different types of eighth note, swing eighth note being one of them. Strictly speaking, you cannot have different types. An eighth note is an eighth note. Our descriptive language is loose enough, however, that we can use the term to label notes of slightly more or less duration than the eighth note is understood to receive.

This looseness in applying the term eighth note is not exclusive to jazz musicians. Nonjazz musicians often use terms such as **legato,** which means long or slurred together or connected. They use the term **staccato,** which means short, abruptly separated. A legato eighth note equals a full-value eighth note. A staccato eighth note, on the other hand, has variable duration. Its length depends on the style of performance, and its value may actually be less than half that of a legato eighth note. It can be called an eighth note only because it is immediately followed by silence which fills up the remaining time that a full-value eighth note requires. Perhaps a staccato eighth note should be called a sixteenth note, or it should bear some designation that is more precise than the label of "staccato eighth note."

				Quarter notes

								Eighth notes

Eighth note triplets

Tied eighth note triplet figures

Dotted eighth—sixteenth note figures

A wide assortment of eighth note durations and stresses are found in jazz styles. There are no jazz musicians who divide the beat in only one way. But there is a pattern that is more common than any other. It is a long-short sequence which is close, but not identical, to the pattern of durations found in the tied-triplet figures. The tied-triplet figure, you may remember, consists first of a long sound, then a shorter sound which is half the duration of the first sound. The two sounds together fit the duration of a single beat in the manner of a quarter-note triplet. The duration pattern most commonly employed by jazz musicians the **swing eighth-note pattern,** falls somewhere between the tied-triplet figure and a sequence of eighth notes having identical durations. In other words, the first member of the pair is shorter than the first member of a tied-triplet pattern, and the second member is somewhat longer than a triplet eighth note. But neither member's duration is truly equal to an even eighth note, what musicians call "a straight eighth."

The stress patterns for swing eighth-note patterns are distributed differently from player to player. Sometimes within the work of a given player, the stresses are distributed differently from performance to performance, sometimes from passage to passage. Basically, however, the first in a group of such swing eighth notes is louder than subsequent notes which occur on upbeats.

There is considerable confusion about notation of swing eighth notes. Such lack of uniformity exists in this regard that about the only accurate statement is that when reading eighth notes, the desired choice of duration patterns usually depends upon the particular band and the style of arrangement being played. A little history might make this point a bit clearer. In countless written arrangements of jazz-oriented pieces which were published before the 1960s, dotted-eighth sixteenth figures appeared whenever the arranger wanted a swing eighth sound. (The arranger did *not* want true dotted-eighth sixteenth note patterns in which long-short meant the long member sounded three times the duration of the short one.) The notation appeared as even eighths thereafter in most arrangements, but the intention was for those notes to also be played as swing eighths. (If an arranger of this period wanted *truly even* durations, a written message appeared above the notes: "even 8ths." The musician's assumption was to otherwise play all the written eighth notes in a swing rhythm.)

To appreciate the rhythms which typify jazz, we should keep in mind the fact that several rhythms are usually played simultaneously. *Polyrhythm* (meaning *many rhythms*) is very important to jazz. When you listen carefully to a modern jazz performance, you should be able to hear several different rhythms at the same time. These include the rhythm in the melodic line, that of the bassist, the rhythm played by each of the drummer's four limbs, and each of the pianist's two hands.

Polyrhythms are often created by patterns which pit a feeling of four against a feeling of three. In other words, two measures can be played at the same time, with one being divided by multiples of two and the other being divided by multiples of three. In addition to that, the onset of one pattern is often staggered in a way which results in something less than perfect superimposition atop another pattern. Pitting three against four and staggering the placement of rhythms can project the feeling that the rhythms are tugging at each other. The resulting combination of stresses can be extremely provocative, and it can produce new syncopations in addition to those already contained in the separate patterns.

You can now understand why to say that jazz is quite rhythmic is to make an almost meaningless statement. All music has rhythm, and most music has syncopated rhythms. What sets jazz apart from many other types of music is the preponderance of syncopated rhythms, the swing eighth note sequences, and the constant presence of polyrhythm.

SCALES, KEYS, TONALITY, AND MODALITY

Understanding scales is basic to appreciating chord progressions, and an acquaintance with scales and chord progressions aids our knowledge of the rules which guide jazz improvisation. Everyone is familiar with musical scales. No one has been able to live very long without hearing a friend, neighbor, or family member practice "his scales."

Scales comprise the rudiments of beginning practice routines for singers and instrumentalists alike. Even people who cannot read music are familiar with the sequence *do* (pronounced dough), *re* (pronounced ray), *mi* (pronounced mee), *fa, sol, la, ti* (pronounced tee), *do*. Those eight syllables do not represent exact pitches as C, D, E, F, G, A, B, C; they are only the names of acoustic relationships. (Do not let that term, acoustic relationships, scare you. It is one of the simplest concepts in music. It means only that no matter what frequency of so many vibrations per second is assigned to *do*, the remaining seven pitches are determined by set multiples of it, for example twice the frequency, 1½ the frequency, and so forth.)

"*Do re mi fa sol la ti do*" numbers eight elements, the eighth element carrying the same name as the first, *do*. Its relationship to the first is exactly double the frequency of the first. For example, if the first *do* were 440 vibrations per second, the next higher *do* would be 880. It is no more complicated than that. That last *do* ends one sequence and begins another. The relationship between the bottom *do* and the top *do*, the first and eighth steps of the scale, is called an *octave*. The sound of two notes an octave apart is so similar that if they are played simultaneously, you can easily mistake the pair for a single tone. Most naturally produced tones contain an octave as one component of all the frequencies that combine to give a tone its own characteristic color or quality. The octave is called a harmonic or an overtone of the tone's fundamental pitch. That is the reason two tones an octave apart sound like one when they are played at the same time.

Since the interval of an eighth, from *do* to *do,* represents a doubling of frequency, you have probably guessed that those intervals between the first and the eighth must be fractions. You guessed correctly. The ratio of the fifth step (*sol*) to the first step (*do*) is $3/2$, that of the third (*mi*) to the first (*do*) is $5/4$, etc.

The seven note scale has many labeling systems. We have already used three of them: a) do, re, mi, fa, sol, la, ti, do; b) first, second, third, fourth, fifth, sixth, seventh; and c) the frequency ratios: re/do $= 9/8$; mi/do $= 5/4$; fa/do $= 4/3$; sol/do $= 3/2$; la/do $= 5/3$; ti/do $= 15/8$. Next is the system which uses alphabet letters A, B, C, D, E, F and G.

Look at the diagram of the piano keyboard printed here.

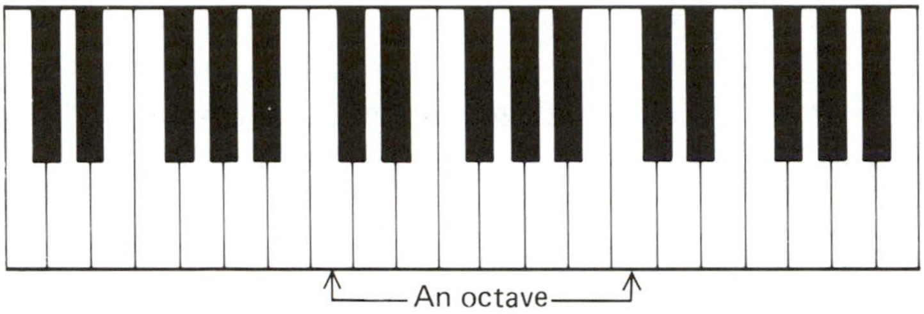

It is constructed so that the pattern of eight white keys and five black keys recurs again and again. The distance, or interval, between the beginning of one pattern and the beginning of the next is called an octave. The scale which beginners usually learn first is the C scale; the C scale is obtained by playing eight of the white keys in succession, starting with the one labeled C. That scale, C, D, E, F, G, A, B, C, contains the same note relationships which we know as do, re, mi, fa, sol, la ti, do. Play the notes of the C major scale in the order in which they are numbered in the diagram.

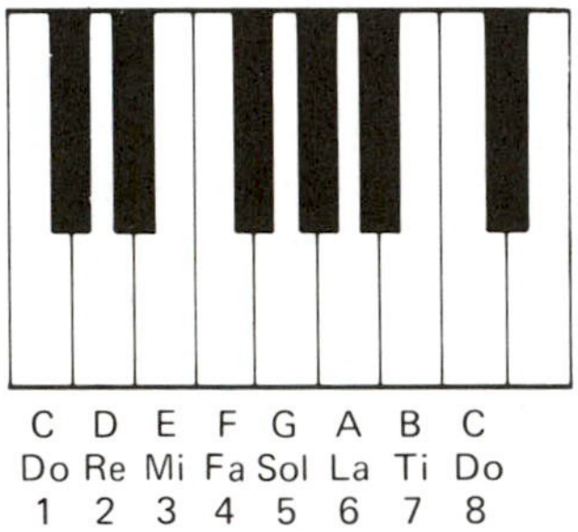

Look again at the piano keyboard.

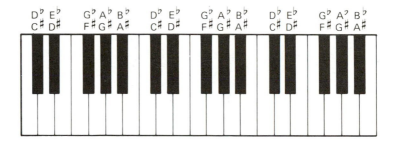

The black keys are known as sharps and flats. Sharp is symbolized ♯ (like the number sign on a typewriter) and flat is symbolized ♭ (like the lower case b on the typewriter). The black keys derive their names from the white keys which are next to them. The black key to the right of A is called A-sharp because it is slightly higher than A. But it is also referred to as B-flat because it is slightly lower than B. If we want only a C scale, going up an octave from C to C, we use none of the black keys. But if we want scales which begin on any note other than C, we have to employ at least one (and sometimes all) of the black keys. For instance, to play a major scale on D, it is necessary to make use of two sharps, F-sharp and C-sharp.

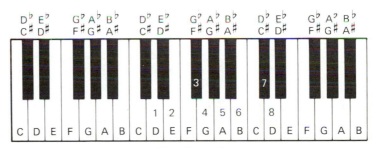

D major scale

A scale may be played starting from any black or white key. Altogether there are twelve such scales. Going up (moving left to right) from C, they are the scales of C, C-sharp, D, D-sharp, E, F, F-sharp, G, G-sharp, A, A-sharp, and B. Or, naming them in descending order, C, B, B-flat, A, A-flat, G, G-flat, F, E, E-flat, D, and D-flat.

When musicians say that a tune is in a certain key, for instance, the key of C, they mean that the song is played with the notes of the major scale beginning on C.

The relationship of the notes of the major scale gives a song a particular kind of sound and structure which is called **tonality.** Although tonality is a complicated idea, it can be understood as the feeling that a song must end on a particular note or chord. A key defines a scale which, in turn, defines that key. If a piece of music has the feeling of reaching for the same note, the key note, or it seems loyal to some note more than to any other, the overall harmonic character of the piece is called *tonal.*

There is another term like the term scale that is not interchangeable with key. The term is **mode**. Like a scale, a mode describes a sequence of acoustic relationships. Some modes even have the same number of elements as the scales we just explored. In fact, the C scale has a mode name: Ionian. But if we use the notes in the C scale and start the sequence on D, we produce another mode, Dorian. In other words, if we go from D to D in the key of C, we have constructed the Dorian mode.

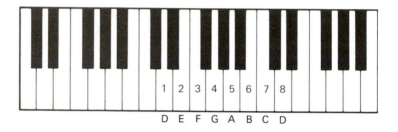

For each of the seven scale steps in a key, there is a corresponding mode. The major scale itself has a mode name: Ionian; beginning on the second step produces the Dorian mode; the third step, the Phrygian mode; fourth, the Lydian mode; fifth, the Mixolydian mode; sixth, the Aeolian mode; and seventh, the Locrian mode. Each has different sound because each has a different sequence of acoustic relationships which results from starting on different steps of the scale. I urge you to find a keyboard and play these modes. The concepts outlined here mean little without the sounds they describe.

We have seen that there are twelve keys, C, C♯ (or D♭), D and so forth. We also know that for each key there is a corresponding seven note scale starting on the note which bears the name of the key (C D E F G A B for the C scale). Within each key there are modes, one mode beginning on each of the seven steps. The mode constitutes an octave of its own. Scales (modes) of fewer than seven notes and **greater than seven notes** also exist (see page 418). The most common scale constructed of more than seven notes is the *chromatic,* simply that sequence of all the piano keys in an octave, white ones and black ones. Scale is a poor name because the chromatic scale is actually just another way of dividing an octave into twelve equal parts. It does not indicate a key as the C scale and the B♭ scale do. The chromatic scale is only a sequence of very small intervals called half steps.

The chromatic scale has twelve steps: C, C♯ D, D♯ E, F, F♯, G, G♯, A, A♯ and B. Unlike the modes, which have to be started on certain scale steps to guarantee their unique qualities, the chromatic scale can be started on any note, proceed through an octave and create the same identifiable chromatic quality no matter what note is chosen for its starting position. That means the C chromatic scale is identical to the C♯ chromatic scale (and all others). Perhaps it should be called "chromatic scale starting on C" or "chromatic scale starting on C♯," specifying exactly what tone is to be the reference note.

The chromatic scale is very important because it expands the number of acoustic relations possible. Given twelve different tones in place of only seven, we have the option of raising and lowering (sharping and flatting) virtually any note we wish. Most Western European music of the past two centuries uses the chromatic scale instead of limiting itself exclusively to notes within one key at a time or, what is even more restrictive, only one mode at a time. Music was produced during the twentieth century which used all twelve tones equally and discarded the feeling of particular keys. Tonal music, you remember, is simply music which seems to be loyal to a certain note, always reaching for that note. Music without tone center is called *atonal*.

Most music has key feeling even when employing all twelve tones in the chromatic scale. This is just another way of saying that most music has tonality. During improvised music, tone centers might shift, but they usually remain long enough for their effect to be perceived. Most jazz employs tone center. It is extremely difficult to improvise without at least implying temporary tone centers and key feelings. The twelve tones are usually employed to enrich the conventional do re mi tonal orientation instead of providing a harmonic orientation all their own, one of atonality. Keep in mind that some music employs more than one key at once, but this type of music is not generally termed atonal. It is called *polytonal* which means many keys.

If you play within the do re mi scale and enrich your melody with chromatic tones, the character of your playing can be partly described by how often you employ certain chromatic tones. Many people consider *bluesy quality* essential to jazz. A central component of bluesy quality is the frequent use of chromatics, three chromatics in particular: the *flat third*, *flat fifth* and *flat seventh* notes of the scale. In other words, chromatic scale tones are employed to enrich the seven tones already available.

In the key of C, the blue notes are E-flat, G-flat, and B-flat. Remember the C scale consists of C, D, E, F, G, A, and B; there are no sharps or flats (none of the piano's black keys). To create a blue note we lower the third step of the scale. In the key of C this means changing E (a white key) to E-flat (a black key). We use both E *and*

E-flat in constructing jazz lines, but the E-flat stands out because it is not one of the notes in the C major scale.

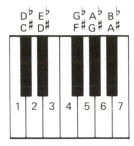

C scale without any blue notes

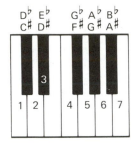

C scale with the flat third blue note

The second most common blue note is achieved by lowering the seventh step of the scale. In the key of C, this means changing B (a white key) to B-flat (a black key). Again we use both B *and* B-flat for our lines, but the B-flat is more distinctive because it is not in the key of C.

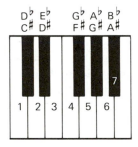

C scale with the flat seventh blue note (B-flat)

Note that the concepts of regular third step and blue third step are like the concepts of major chord and minor chord (the sounds of which you can demonstrate for yourself, using the following keyboard diagram as a guide to positioning your first, third, and fifth fingers).

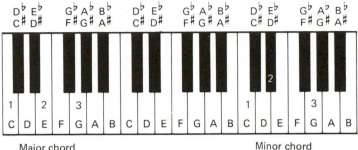

Major chord   Minor chord

The third most used blue note is the lowered fifth. Its use was not frequent until modern jazz began in the 1940s, but thereafter it became a standard device to convey a bluesy feeling, much as the lowered third and seventh had been in early jazz. In the key of C, a flat fifth is achieved by lowering G (a white key) to G-flat (a black key).

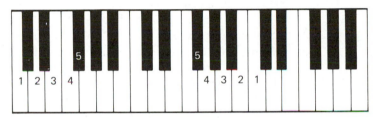

Going up to the flat fifth (G-flat)   Coming down to the flat fifth (G-flat)

BLUE NOTES Some jazz hornmen, especially the earliest ones who made records, occasionally employ a slightly flattened third and seventh degree of the scale. They lower the pitch less than traditional European tuning would consider a half step (a chromatic semitone). Many modern jazz hornmen have moved away from this practice, adopting an in-tune pitch framework instead, with a net result that they are rarely termed bluesy, soulful, or funky players.

Such pitches cannot be produced on the piano, but that does not mean that pianists have not wanted to produce them. (The usual keyboard solution to this problem was to sound two or three neighboring piano keys at the same time, making a major/minor sound and letting the listener's ear resolve the clash by perceiving the resulting sound as bluesy.) The 1970s proliferation of synthesizers in the hands of jazz pianists saw the molding of countless solos employing blue notes because synthesizers are capable of generating pitches that represent fine gradations between those found on the piano. No longer were jazz keyboard players handicapped in the realm of the blue note. (It is also noteworthy that pitch bending had been a favored technique in the work of rock guitarists, rock having been influenced by Afro-American traditions, and that, when using such pitch alterations, the jazz synthesists often sounded like rock guitarists.)

The same motivation might explain the preponderance in jazz of thirds and sevenths which are flatted in a key that ordinarily contains only major thirds and sevenths. For example, in the key of C, there is no E-flat, but jazz musicians are prone to play E-flats in order to sound bluesy.

The attraction that jazz musicians have for out-of-tune thirds and sevenths might be the result of differences between African and European tuning systems. One possibility is suggested here. The European seven-tone scale is not based on equal divisions of the octave. It is a sequence of whole steps and half steps, each half step representing about one-twelfth an octave. (A whole step is the interval between C and D or between E-flat and F. A half step is the interval between B and C or between E-flat and E.) A mix might have occurred with a West African system which uses an equidistant seven-tone scale, some of its pitches coinciding fairly closely to the European seven-tone scale, but with the third and seventh steps being flat relative to their counterparts in the European system. This means that if an African sang his own pitch in a European piece, the third and the seventh would sound blue rather than perfectly in tune.

CHORDS AND CHORD PROGRESSIONS

Familiarity with the concept of scales allows us to explore the concept of chords and chord progressions, which, in turn, is essential to appreciating the harmony that jazz improvisers follow. These concepts are quite simple, but they have far-reaching applications, not only in jazz, but in all music which uses harmony.

A chord is obtained by sounding three or more notes simultaneously. It does not matter what notes are chosen. Any notes will do. Try these:

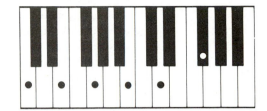

Although chords can be constructed from any tones, they are usually described in terms of scale notes and given Roman numeral names. The most common chord, one alternately described as a tonic chord, a major triad, the key chord, or a I (Roman numeral for 1) chord, employs the first, third, and fifth notes of the scale: *do, mi,* and *sol*. In other words, this chord is produced by simultaneously sounding do, mi, and sol in any key, any register, with any loudness or tone color.

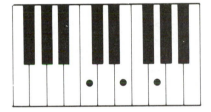

I chord in key of C

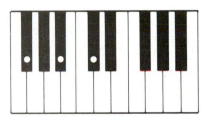

I chord in key of F-sharp

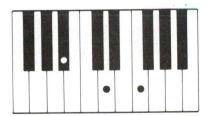

I chord in key of B-flat

Chords are named for the scale step on which they are based. A I chord is based on the first step of the scale, do; a II chord is based on the second step, re; a III chord on the third step, mi; a IV chord on fa; a V chord on sol; a VI chord on la; and a VII chord on ti. This system of naming is very handy for describing chord progressions (see page 415 for notations of chord progressions).

A chord change is simply what it says, changing a chord. If we move from one chord to another, we have executed a **chord change.** We have moved forward, progressed, from one chord to another. In other words, a **chord progression** has been made. If the chords involved are those based on the first and second steps of the scale, respectively, we could describe the chord change as a I-II progression. If we move from a chord based on the first step to a chord based on the fourth, we create a I-IV progression. The reverse of that is a IV-I. If we move from the I chord to the V chord, and then back to the I chord, we create a I-V-I progression.

To hear the sound of a very common chord progression, the I-IV-I-V-I blues progression, find a piano, an organ, an accordion, or any other keyboard instrument and strike all the keys simultaneously, the number of counts (1234, 2234, etc.) indicated in the diagram on page 375. You need not worry about what fingers to place on what keys. In fact, go ahead and use fingers from both hands if necessary. Try to keep a steady rate for striking the keys. If you can keep a steady rate, you may find that you are sounding like you have heard pianists and guitarists in rhythm and blues bands sound.

Chord Voicing   Most music uses chords which have been **voiced.** (For notated examples see page 417). The concept of voicing is a very simple concept. It involves the fact that the keyboard is a succession of repeating octaves.

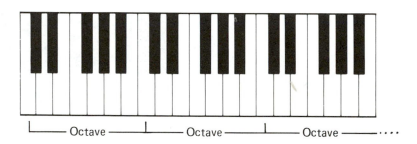

With the resulting repetition of notes available, we can pull each chord note away from the position it holds within a single octave and spread the chord over the range of the keyboard. We can also include additional notes and/or omit some of the original notes. All these manipulations fall under the heading of voicing.

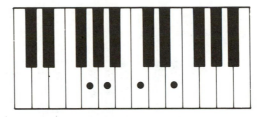

1234 2234 3234 4234 (I chord for 4 measures)

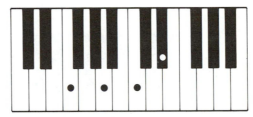

1234 2234 (IV chord for 2 measures)

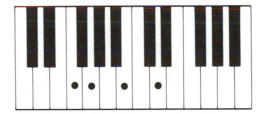

1234 2234 (I chord for 2 measures)

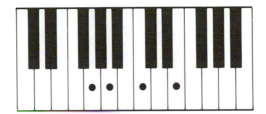

1234 2234 (V chord for 2 measures)

1234 2234 (I chord for 2 measures)

The same chord (three notes) arranged in different positions across the keyboard.

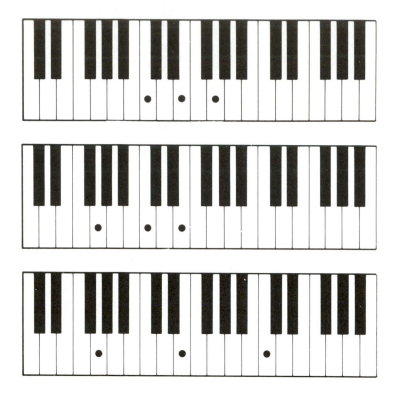

Jazz pianists can often be identified by the way they voice chords, and characteristic preferences in piano voicing are important components of the style in almost every period of jazz. In recent jazz, for example in the work of pianists McCoy Tyner and Chick Corea, **voicing in fourths** is quite common. Voicing in fourths means that chords are made up of notes four steps away from each other. In other words, a chord voiced in fourths might contain do, fa and ti instead of do, mi and sol. (The interval between do and fa is called a perfect fourth. To create a perfect fourth between fa and ti, the ti must be flatted. In building a chord composed of perfect fourths, each successive note is considered do of a new scale and the fourth note, fa, in that scale is used.) You can hear the sound of a chord voiced in fourths by playing this:

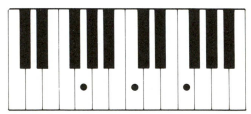

The term voicing also refers to how the notes of a chord are assigned to instruments in an orchestra or band. The ranges of the instruments as well as their tone colors are taken into consideration in voicing chords. Characteristic voicings serve to identify the work of different arrangers. Duke Ellington, for instance, voices chords in a manner distinguishable from Stan Kenton. Both Ellington's chords and his choice of instruments differ.

Voicing is also a term used to identify the instruments playing a melody. For example, we might say Duke Ellington voiced the lead (the melody) for clarinet, trumpet, and tenor sax, meaning that those instruments played a unison passage in a particular Ellington arrangement.

The Blues

The term "the blues" has several meanings. It can describe

1) a sad feeling, or music which projects a sad feeling;
2) a rhymed poetic form;
3) a slow, funky, earthy type of music;
4) a type of chord progression, usually contained in twelve measures, which has certain predictable chord movements in the fifth, seventh, ninth, and eleventh measures;
5) any combination of the above.

Blues poetry is so common in popular music, that a technical description of the positions of accent and rhyme is not necessary in order for you to recognize the form. A single, very characteristic example, can serve to illustrate the structure of blues poetry:

My man don't love me, treats me awful mean. (pause)
My man don't love me, treats me awful mean. (pause)
He is the lowest man I've ever seen.　　(pause)

The I, IV, and V chords are basic elements of harmony used in the blues. In the twelve-bar blues, which is the most common blues form, these chords are distributed over twelve measures in a particular way. Although many variations are possible, the basic form is always the same. The chords and their respective durations are shown in the following chart. Each slash (/) indicates one beat. Perhaps it is helpful for you to think of a chord played on each beat by a rhythm guitarist. Note that the principal chord changes occur in the fifth, seventh, ninth and eleventh measures.

I　　　　　　　　　IV　　　I　　　V　　　I

Although the chord relationships of the fifth, seventh, ninth, and eleventh measures usually hold, the remaining measures are the scene of countless alterations. Modern jazz blues progressions often employ more than one chord in a single measure and at least one change every measure. It is not unusual to have ten to twenty chord changes in the space of twelve measures. Sometimes the principal chords of the fifth, seventh, ninth, and eleventh measures are also altered (see page 416 for typical modern jazz blues progressions). When the blues is sung, the words are often distributed in a standard way over the twelve-bar progression (see page 379).

A blues can be fast or slow, happy or sad. It may have lyrics or it may be a purely instrumental piece, and its chord progressions may be simple or complex. For a piece to be a blues, the only requirement is that the I-IV-I-V-I chord progression or a variant of it be presented in a twelve-measure form.

The Thirty-Two Bar AABA Tune

Another form on which jazz musicians often improvise is the thirty-two-bar AABA tune. The thirty-two bar tune is made up of four eight-measure sections. The opening eight measures, called the A section, is repeated in the second section. The third part is the B section, sometimes referred to as the bridge, release, inside, or channel. The last eight bars bring back the material of the first eight. So the tune falls into what is called AABA form. Thousands of pop tunes composed during the 1920s, 30s, 40s, and 50s were thirty-two bars long in AABA form.

Listening for the Twelve Bar Blues and Thirty Two Bar Forms

To gain a practical familiarity with chord progressions, glance at the list of tunes on page 380. These are categorized as twelve-bar blues or thirty-two-bar tunes in AABA form. Go to a record collection and find performances of tunes on the list, and choose one of them. Listen to approximately the first thirty seconds to determine whether this rendition has an introduction or begins immediately with the tune itself. Also determine how fast the beats are passing. A clue can often be found in the bass playing. If the bass is walking, there is a bass note for every beat, four beats to the measure. Listening to that sound, you should be able to hear the pulse as though the bassist were a metronome. The sound of the drummer's ride cymbal may also be a good indication of where the beats lie.

Having listened long enough to determine the tempo, you will also have discovered whether or not there is an introduction, and the point at which it ends and the tune begins. If you are not sure whether the beginning of the piece is an introduction or part of the tune itself, wait a while and listen for it to recur. If it does not recur it is probably an

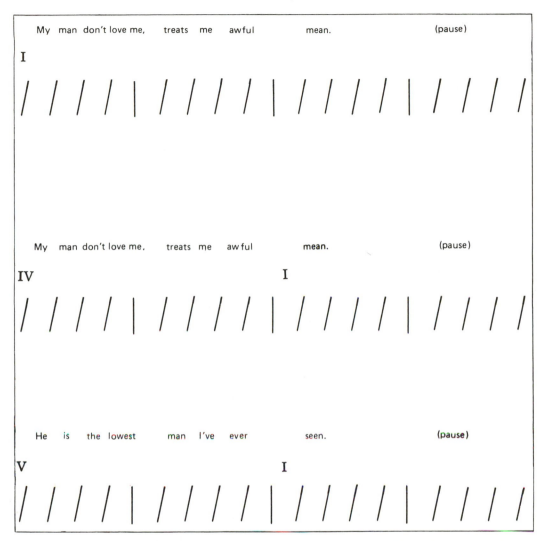

Blues poetic form in relation to the 12-bar blues chord progression.
The lyrics shown are from Billie Holiday's "Fine and Mellow." Copyright:
Edward B. Marks Music Corporation. Used by permission.

Compositions in Twelve-Bar Blues and Thirty-Two Bar A-A-B-A Forms

Twelve-Bar Blues Compositions

"Bags' Groove"
"Barbados"
"Billie's Bounce"
"Bloomdido"
"Bluesology"
"Blue Monk"
"Blues in the Closet"
"Blue 'n' Boogie"
"Blue Trane"
"Cheryl"
"Cool Blues"
"Cousin Mary"

"Footprints"
"Freddie the Freeloader"
"Goodbye Porkpie Hat"
"Jumpin' with Symphony Sid"
"Mr. P. C."
"Now's the Time"
"One O'Clock Jump"
"Sid's Ahead"
"Soft Winds"
"Straight, No Chaser"
"Walkin' "
"Woodchopper's Ball"

Compositions with Thirty-Two Bar A-A-B-A Construction

"Ain't Misbehavin' "
"Angel Eyes"
"Anthropology"
"Birth of the Blues"
"Blue Moon"
"Body and Soul"
"Budo" ("Hallucinations")
"Darn That Dream"
"Don't Blame Me"
"Don't Get Around Much Anymore"
"Easy Living"
"52nd Street Theme"
"Flamingo"
"Four Brothers"
"Good Bait"
"Have You Met Miss Jones"
"I Can't Get Started"
"I Cover the Waterfront"
"I Love You"
"I'm Beginning to See the Light"
"It's Only a Paper Moon"
"I Want to Talk About You"
"Jordu"

"Lady Be Good"
"Lover Man"
"Lullaby of Birdland"
"Makin' Whoopee"
"The Man I Love"
"Midnight Sun"
"Misty"
"The More I See You"
"Moten Swing"
"Move"
"Oleo"
"Over the Rainbow"
"Perdido"
"Robin's Nest"
"Rosetta"
" 'Round Midnight"
"Ruby, My Dear"
"Satin Doll"
"September Song"
"Take the 'A' Train"
"Well, You Needn't"
"What's New?"
"What Is This Thing Called Love?"

introduction. In AABA form the first part, A, is immediately repeated, AA, before a new section, B, occurs. The routine for most twelve-bar blues tunes consists of repeating the entire twelve bars before beginning improvisation. Musicians occasionally use the same music for an ending that they used for the introduction. So if you hear something familiar at the end which does not seem to fit exactly in twelve or thirty-two bars, it may be the introduction attached for use as an ending.

By now you should know both the tempo at which to count beats and the moment to begin counting. Start when the tune itself starts (right after the introduction, in most cases). For a twelve-bar blues count: "1234, 2234, 3234, 4234, 5234, 6234, 7234, 8234, 9234, 10 234, 11 234, 12 234." Listen and count until you can detect the chord changes in measures five, seven, nine, and eleven:

$^\text{I}$//// | //// | //// | //// |$^\text{IV}$ //// | //// |$^\text{I}$ //// | //// |$^\text{V}$ //// |
//// |$^\text{I}$ //// | //// |

If your counting is accurate, you will eventually be able to anticipate these important chord changes. That should provide some insight into harmonies that the jazz musician uses in his improvisation.

Count like this for a thirty-two-bar AABA tune:

	"1234, 2234, 3234, 4234, 5234, 6234, 7234, 8234,
repeat	234, 2234, 3234, 4234, 5234, 6234, 7234, 8234,
bridge	234, 2234, 3234, 4234, 5234, 6234, 7234, 8234,
back to A	234, 2234, 3234, 4234, 5234, 6234, 7234, 8234."

Listen and count over and over until you cannot only hear the bridge and the repeated sections, A-A, when they occur, but anticipate them. Do not become discouraged if you find it necessary to start and stop many times. Counting beats and measures requires practice. It is very important because it may be your only clue to the tune's form once a soloist has begun improvising. Learning to count accurately may take a few minutes, a few hours, or even a few days, but it is essential to an understanding of jazz improvisation. It will be well worth the effort. You might get especially good at anticipating the B section. If you know the tune, or can learn it by listening a few times, try humming it while listening to the soloists improvise on its chord changes. This will help clarify the relationship between the improvisation and the original tune. It will also help you keep your place.

Not all tunes fit into the twelve-bar blues form or the thirty-two-bar AABA form. "I'll Remember April" is a forty-eight-bar ABCDAB form. "I've Got You Under My Skin" is a fifty-six-bar ABACDEF form. Together, the twelve-bar blues form and the thirty-two-bar AABA form probably describe more tunes than any other single form, but they actually describe less than forty percent of all tunes written between 1910 and 1960. Let us examine a few other forms.

The twelve-bar blues is a particular set of chord progressions (I-IV-I-V-I) in a twelve measure package. There are twelve-bar forms which are not blues simply because they do not follow the I-IV-I-V-I progression or any variation of it. For example, Richard Rodgers' "Little Girl Blue" is an AAB form in which each section is twelve bars long, but it is not a blues. It is also not uncommon in pop tunes to find a twelve-bar section which is actually an eight-bar progression with an extra four-bar progression connected to it.

The word "blues" in a song title does not necessarily signify the twelve-bar blues form. Both musicians and nonmusicians use the term "blues" to describe any slow, sad tune regardless of its chord progression. "Birth of the Blues" is a thirty-two bar AABA tune and "Sugar Blues" is an eighteen-bar tune. The "St. Louis Blues" is actually a twelve-bar blues plus an eight-bar bridge and an additional twelve-bar blues. Performers sometimes choose to repeat, delete, and reorder sections of "St. Louis Blues" when they play it.

Some people use the terms "eight-bar blues" and "sixteen-bar blues." Usually the tune they are describing has the I-IV movement in the first five bars and deviates from the twelve-bar I-IV-I-V-I progression thereafter. Some tunes of lengths other than twelve bars sound very much like twelve-bar blues simply because they contain the I-IV-I-V-I progression, but the durations of a few chords may be changed, and certain sections may be repeated. Herbie Hancock's "Watermelon Man," for example, has been called a "sixteen-bar blues."

Unlike the twelve-bar blues the thirty-two bar AABA form is not always based on the same basic chord progression. Many different chord progressions have been used in the AABA form. Fats Waller's "Honeysuckle Rose" and Erroll Garner's "Misty" are both thirty-two-bar AABA tunes, yet they have almost completely different chord progressions.

The form AABA does not always contain thirty-two bars nor does each section necessarily have the same number of measures. In "Girl from Ipanema," which is AABA, the A section has eight bars while the bridge has sixteen. In "Secret Love," another AABA tune, the A section has sixteen bars while the bridge has only eight.

There are also elongated versions of the basic twelve-bar blues and thirty-two-bar AABA forms. Lee Morgan's "Sidewinder" is a twenty-four-bar blues: each chord lasts twice as long as it would in a twelve-bar blues. Another example is the sixty-four-bar AABA form in which each section is sixteen bars long instead of eight. Ray Noble's "Cherokee" and Lerner and Loewe's "On the Street Where You Live" are both sixty-four bar AABA tunes. Charlie Parker's "Ko Ko," is based on the chord changes of "Cherokee"; consequently it is also a sixty-four-bar AABA tune. There are shortened versions of the thirty-two-bar AABA, too. Sonny Rollins's "Doxy" is a sixteen-bar AABA tune; each section is only four bars long.

AABA is not the only common thirty-two bar form for pop tunes. Numerous tunes fit an ABAC form (both the C section and the B section differ from the A section). "My Romance," "On Green Dolphin Street," "Indiana," "Sweet Georgia Brown," and "Out of Nowhere" all fall into a thirty-two bar ABAC form. In addition to the thirty-two bar AABA and ABAC, there is also the thirty-two bar ABAB. "How High the Moon" is an example. There are shortened versions of these, also. "Summertime" is a sixteen-bar ABAC tune. "Autumn Leaves" is a sixteen-bar AABC tune. Each section is four bars long in those tunes.

Hundreds of tunes fit into sixteen measures. "Peg o' My Heart" is a sixteen-bar pop tune. Horace Silver based his "The Preacher" on the sixteen-bar pop tune "Show Me the Way to Go Home." Wayne Shorter has written many sixteen-bar tunes, including "E.S.P.," "Nefertiti," "Prince of Darkness," etc. Some chord progressions are used in sixteen-bar tunes almost as often as the I-IV-I-V-I progression appears in the twelve-bar blues. Certain sixteen-bar progressions have become standard.

Verse and Chorus. It is important to note that the forms we have been examining refer only to chorus length. A large number of tunes consist of two major parts, a verse followed by a chorus. The verse traditionally differs from the chorus in tempo, mood, and harmony:

1) The chorus might be played at a faster tempo than the verse.
2) Verses are often performed freely, with accelerations and decelerations of tempo.
3) The verse might feel as though it is leading up to something, whereas the chorus usually has the stamp of finality to it.
4) There may be little similarity between chord progressions used in the verse and those in the chorus.
5) The key of the verse is sometimes different from that of the chorus.
6) Choruses are repeated, but once a verse is played, it is usually over for the entire performance.
7) The chorus is the section of the tune jazz musicians usually choose as basis for improvisation.

Breaking into Multiples of Two. When you are listening to performances and trying to detect forms, be aware that arrangements of thirty-two-bar AABA, ABAC, and ABAB tunes sometimes depart from strict repetition of those thirty-two bars. Arrangements sometimes contain four-, eight-, and sixteen-bar sections, formed by omitting or adding to portions of the original thirty-two-bar tune. Note also that many tunes, especially pre-1930s Dixieland tunes, have long, elaborate forms similar to those of marches and of nineteenth-century European dance music (such as the quadrille). Forms for many tunes in pre-1920s jazz were derived from march music. A piece might have a series of sections consisting of multiples of eight bars. Designating each section by a letter of the alphabet, a piece might conceivably follow a pattern like this:

A–A– B –B–C–D–E–F–C–D–E–F
16–16–16–16–16–24–32–16–16–24–32.

When listening for form, keep in mind that even in the most intricate pieces, forms can usually be broken down into two-bar segments. So if you are unable to divide a piece neatly into either four-bar or eight-bar sections, try using a few two-bar sections. "Sugar Blues" can be heard as 18 or as 8+10 or as 8+8+2. That form poses problems for the improviser because it tends to break the flow of ideas conceived in four- and eight-bar melodic units. It is like being forced to walk left, right, left, right, left, left, right. The form of the original "I Got Rhythm" is

A — A — B — A + tag
8 — 8 — 8 — 8 + 2 or
8 — 8 — 8 — 10.

When jazz musicians improvise on its chord progression, they omit the two-bar tag. If included, the tag would interrupt the flow of the improvisations and again be like having to take two steps with your left foot before going back to an alternation of right with left. Another popular tune that has an unusual structure is "Moonlight In Vermont." It follows the form:

A — A — B — A + tag
6 — 6 — 8 — 6 + 2.

Modal Forms   During the late 1950s and especially during the 60s and 70s, modal forms practically eliminated the "change" part of "chord change." In modal music, improvisations are based on the extended repetition of one or two chords. Those chords contain so many notes that they either include or are compatible with all the notes in a scale. The term mode is synonymous with scale, hence the term "modal music." Although this is not the definition of modal employed by classical composers and in textbooks on classical music, it is what jazz musicians and jazz journalists have come to mean by "modal" (see page 418 for further discussion of modes). In most instances, jazz musicians also employ notes which are not contained in the mode or in the repeated chords. Some of John Coltrane's work, for example, is not strictly modal, but has the flavor of music which is.

In modal music the entire improvised portion of the performance is often based on a single chord and scale. Usually the chord and its scale are minor, Indian, Middle Eastern, or in some way more exotic-sounding than the chords used in most pop tune progressions. Because it is based on a single scale, the music has no real chord changes, just a drone.

Sometimes a melody containing chord changes of its own precedes the improvised section of a modal performance. John Coltrane's recordings of the Rodgers and Hammerstein tune "My Favorite Things" are a good example. Coltrane played the original melody while his rhythm section played the appropriate chord changes. Then the entire group improvised only on the primary chord of the tune (and of course, the scale compatible with that chord). Near the end of their improvisations, they switched to another chord, which lent the piece a slightly different character. Coltrane could have retained the chord progressions of the tune and used them as the basis for improvisation, but he chose not to.

Some modal music does have chord changes, or "mode changes." One rich chord (or scale, depending on how one cares to conceive it) is the basis for four, eight, or perhaps sixteen measures. Then a different chord is in effect for another similar duration. The Miles Davis tune "Milestones" is based on one mode for the first sixteen bars, a different mode for the second sixteen bars, and a return to the original mode for the final eight bars. The melody has the form AABBA, and each section is eight bars long. Herbie Hancock's "Maiden Voyage" has a thirty-two bar AABA construction; here each mode lasts for four bars. The A section is based on two different modes, each lasting only four bars. The B section makes use of another two modes also lasting four bars each. If each mode were labeled by letter name, "Maiden Voyage" could be described as X-Y-X-Y-Z-W-X-Y. "So What" (on the Miles Davis album *Kind of Blue*) has a melody in thirty-two bar AABA form, and the use of modes corresponds to that form: there are sixteen bars of one mode, eight of another, and a return to the original mode for the last eight bars. John Coltrane's "Impressions" not only takes the same form as "So What" but also uses exactly the same modes. (See page 422 for the modes used in "Milestones," "Maiden Voyage," and "So What.")

Much jazz of the 1960s and 70s was based on infrequent chord changes (another way of saying modal) instead of the frequent chord changes found in most twelve-bar blues and thirty-two-bar forms. Many groups abandoned both the blues form and the thirty-two-bar forms. Some groups used complex melodies and intricate rhythm section figures, yet their improvisations were based almost exclusively on one or a small number of chords ("Freedom Jazz Dance," for example).

The Effects of Form on Improvisation

Song forms of four and eight bar sections tend to break improvisations into small segments of similar length. Divisions of form, in other words, can influence the flow of improvised lines. This is not necessarily a disadvantage, however. The divisions in form can frame well-chosen melodic figures, and they can provide a means of transition from one figure to another. This creates more continuity than a solo might contain without chord progressions. Forms based on single modes sounding indefinitely tend to free the improviser, enabling him to create lines that are as long or short, tense or relaxed as he desires. No preset tension-relaxation devices in the form of chord progressions are there to suggest construction patterns for his improvised lines.

Bridges. The B section of an AABA tune is called the bridge. It bridges the gap between repetition of A sections, and it usually provides a contrast to the material in the A sections. The bridge can break up or lift the mood established by repeated A sections. Many bridges are placed a few keys higher than the A section. A key change can be a boost in any situation, but is especially effective after the repeated A sections.

The bridge is important to improvisers because a good improviser can capitalize on the bridge's natural capacity to provide contrast. Some of the greatest solo segments in jazz are those improvised over the chord progressions of a tune's bridge. The rhythm section also takes advantage of the bridge and is often especially active just before the bridge is entered and just before it is exited. Heightened rhythmic activity can announce the arrival or departure of the bridge.

Combos often use the bridge as a container for solo spots. Sometimes a tune's melody will be played for the final time in the performance, and when the bridge occurs, everyone stops playing except the drummer. It becomes his feature. Then the entire band returns precisely on the first beat of the final A section.

In some jazz tunes the bridge consists only of chord changes. Such pieces require improvisation during the bridge but return to the written melody when the final A section is reached. Sonny Rollins's tune "Oleo" is an example. Many groups also use that approach on "The

Theme," a popular up-tempo number for jazz combos of the late 1950s and early 60s.

Turnarounds. Another important part in the construction of standard tunes is the turnaround (also known as the turnabout or turnback). In many, perhaps in most songs, the seventh and eighth measures of each section are occupied by a single sustained tone or two long tones (see below). That part of the tune might be considered dead space due to the lack of melodic movement, but the jazz musician uses that space. (See page 417 for common turnaround chord progressions.) He fills it with chord changes which lead directly to the beginning of the next section. Jazz musicians are expected to know a variety of chord progressions common to turnarounds. The manner in which they fill that space with chord changes and improvised lines is the art of the turnaround.

Turnarounds in 32-bar A-A-B-A and 12-bar blues.

In 32-bar A-A-B-A form:

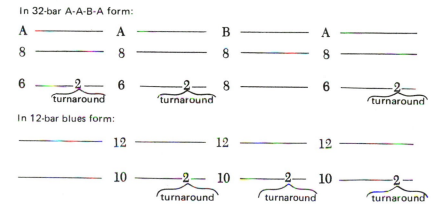

In 12-bar blues form:

The whole combo digs in when a turnaround comes up. Drummers tend to kick more and, thus, tie together the musical statements of one section and bring in the next. Those bassists who almost invariably walk are more likely to vary this pattern in a turnaround. Tension can be built during a turnaround and resolved by the onset of the next section of the piece.

Phrasing in Relation to Form Jazz musicians prior to the mid-1940s tended to improvise phrases which coincided with the tune structure. Most progressions consist of two- and four-bar units, and improvised solos often proceeded in phrases of similar length. Furthermore, soloists tended to make larger silences at or near the end of an A section or B section. They rarely connected tune sections by continuing phrases through the turnarounds. They stopped at or before the turnarounds, and then started anew at the beginning of the next section. They treated the eighth bar line as a barrier. Twelve-bar blues solos often contained phrases which started at the beginning of each chorus regardless of what happened at the end of a previous chorus, thus treating the twelfth bar line as a barrier.

One characteristic of modern jazz (beginning in the 1940s) and the music of the players who most influenced it, was the use of phrases which began somewhere within an eight-bar section and continued into the next section without a pause. There was no lull during the turnaround.

A characteristic of some modern jazz during the 1960s and 70s was the absence of preset chord progressions. That free approach significantly loosened the tendencies of jazz phrasing. Although players retained patterns common to preceding jazz eras, they were free to phrase with greater variety due to the lack of underlying chord movements. Some jazz of this type projects a feeling of expansiveness quite unlike the crowded feeling often projected by modern jazz of the 1940s and 50s.

Some tunes which appeared during the 1960s, especially those of Wayne Shorter, were sixteen or more bars without any repeated sections. The A section was not repeated, there was no bridge, no turnaround. These tunes were "all A." That form enabled improvisers to play with great continuity yet without the crowded, segmented feeling which sometimes characterizes improvisations based on standard AABA and ABAC forms with the usual turnarounds and bridges. Sometimes a free, floating feeling could be projected by improvisers using these "all A" forms.

TONE COLOR   An important element of music, usually the first to be perceived, is tone quality or tone color. The term tone *color* is preferable because quality can imply that a tone is good or bad. But because musical beauty is a subjective perception, the term quality is less appropriate than that of color, a neutral term. This element is also known as timbre (pronounced tamm'burr).

How can you tell the difference between the sound of a flute and the sound of a trumpet if they each play only one note, and it is the same note? The difference is tone color. What is tone color? It is traditionally defined as the spectrum of frequencies generated by each instrument in its own unique way.

This definition is an oversimplification of a complex situation in which many factors come into play.

The spectrum of frequencies produced by an instrument is not fixed. The spectrum varies depending on the pitch and the forcefulness with which it is played. The ways in which a player starts and stops a note, the attack and release, also are important in determining tone color. The attack and release are accompanied by temporary changes in a tone's frequency spectrum.

Another complication arises from our tendency to associate an instrument's tone color with the aggregate effects of all the notes being played on it rather than the spectrum of frequencies present in a single note.

Finally, when sounds come to our ears, they are modified by room acoustics and by recording and playback techniques. The way our ears deal with that variability is quite involved.

Tone color varies greatly from one instrument to another, and there are also especially discernible differences in tone color among jazz musicians playing the same instrument. For example, to speak of the tenor sax tone color of John Coltrane or Stan Getz is to describe sounds so unique that some inexperienced listeners could differentiate them as easily as they could distinguish flute from trumpet. The evolution of jazz tenor saxophone playing reflects not only changes in the phrasing and rhythms, but also changes in tone color.

Tone color is a very personal characteristic of a player's style. Jazz musicians place great emphasis on creating the particular tone colors they want. A jazz musician's attention to tone color is comparable to an actor's concern for costume, make-up, and voice quality combined. Tone color is so important to saxophonists that many spend lifetimes searching for the perfect mouthpiece. They also experiment with different methods of blowing and different ways of altering the vibrating surface of the cane reeds that are attached to their mouthpieces.

Because the tenor saxophone is capable of producing an exceptionally wide variety of tone colors, it is easier to differentiate jazz tenor saxophonists by tone color alone than it is to recognize a particular trumpeter or pianist. That is not to say that differences are absent from trumpeter to trumpeter or from pianist to pianist. The differences are just more subtle.

Two pianists can play the same piece on the same piano and produce quite different sounds. No two pianos have the same tone color, and one piano can produce distinctly different tone colors, depending on how hard the keys are struck. The use of the pedals and a pianist's timing in releasing one key and striking the next are crucial to the sound. A key may be released before, after, or at the same time as the next is struck. When a note is short and ends well before the next note begins, we call it a staccato note. If one key is released after the next is struck, the two sounds overlap in time. Notes played smoothly one after the other are said to be legato. The amount of overlap influences the clarity of attack and the dimension of legato-staccato. Our ears hear sounds in combined form rather than as single tones. Whatever is left in the air from a preceding sound mixes and colors the subsequent sound. The relationship between consecutive sounds, ranging from complete separation to extreme overlapping, are resources which contribute to the personal character of a pianist's style. Count Basie's touch and tone color differ remarkably from Duke Ellington's. Perhaps you will perceive Basie's touch as lighter than Ellington's. No matter how you describe the sound, you will notice a difference if you listen carefully.

Guitarists' interest in tone color is manifested by their search for different types of picks, guitar strings, and amplifiers. Guitar amplifier dial settings are essential to the control of tone color. Bass players are also concerned with many of the same factors.

Trumpeters and trombonists explore available tone colors by experimenting with mouthpiece changes, methods of blowing, mutes, and instruments which represent different manufacturers and models.

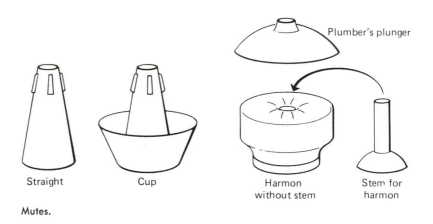

Straight   Cup   Harmon   Stem for
                                without stem   harmon

Mutes.

Intonation is also an important aspect of tone. Intonation refers to playing in tune, playing sharp or flat. Playing sharp means playing at a pitch level somewhat higher than the average pitch of the ensemble. Playing flat refers to playing a pitch somewhat lower than that of the ensemble. Do not confuse the terms sharp and flat with words describing actual note names such as C-sharp and B-flat. These notes are raised (sharped) and lowered (flatted) by a larger amount than is usually the case in out-of-tune playing. That is, the interval between C and C-sharp is greater than the interval between C and that of a performer playing C a bit sharper than his fellow ensemble members. Small deviations of pitch occur all the time even in the best ensembles, but larger deviations lead listeners to comment "someone is playing out of tune."

Why is intonation described in this section on tone color? Intonation affects the tone color of both the soloist and the ensemble as a whole. If a group of musicians played the same piece twice, once without listening or adjusting to each other's pitch (perhaps by pretuning their instruments and then wearing ear plugs for the performance), and then a second time, listening carefully to each other's pitch and continuously adjusting accordingly, you would hear two performances, each having distinctly different tone colors. Ensembles which lack precision tuning have a thicker, rougher sound than precisely tuned ensembles. One element of a slick ensemble sound is careful and consistent tuning.

For tone color reasons, some soloists systematically play a little "high," meaning a bit sharp. Intonation is a musical resource for them. This is common in most types of music, including symphonic, but it is especially true for jazz soloists. A tone cuts through an ensemble if it is a bit sharper than the average pitch of that ensemble. Some jazz soloists seem to play at the average pitch. Others tend to different degrees of sharpness. That is another component of tone color which helps us identify a particular player's work.

GUIDE TO RECORD BUYING

One key to being a happy jazz fan is finding the right albums. This section of the book is directed at explaining numerous short cuts to help you.

Minimizing Risk in Selecting Albums

In seeking record-buying advice, try not to assume that a newspaper, book, or magazine is an authority in itself. We may think their endorsements represent knowledge and understanding somehow greater than that of a single individual. Usually, however, a record review or list of recommended listening reflects only one individual's preferences and his own understanding or lack of understanding.

You may perhaps feel that it is impossible to make good choices without extensive previous knowledge. But the situation is not quite that desperate. Listening to records before you buy them is always a wise practice. Friends, libraries, jazz courses, and radio programs can often help here.

Try to avoid record buying as an impulse purchase. Unless you want a record purely for academic reasons or historical perspective, you might realize too late that you have spent your money on something you do not enjoy. That point might seem elementary, but, unless you can afford to experiment expensively, it is worth keeping in mind. Many albums list musicians and tunes which look great but turn out sounding less than great. Since advance listening will be impossible for many albums, you will have to collect opinions from friends, music teachers, and jazz journalists. If there is a jazz radio station near you, do not hesitate to phone and ask them to play a particular album. (College radio stations not only broadcast more jazz than commercial stations, but they are also more likely to be interested in your requests.) Another strategy is to phone the station just after it has broadcast something you enjoyed, and ask for the album title and record company name. Then decide what records you really want, write down their titles, labels, catalog numbers, and carry that list with you. Then prepare yourself for the frustration, common to jazz fans, of rarely seeing a desired album in the record racks. (Most current jazz albums must be special-ordered, and all out-of-print albums must be obtained through very special sources.)

Those strategies are not guaranteed to always bring records you like. Even if you follow all this advice, you may end up with a record you do not enjoy just because jazz represents an enormous variety of styles, and you may dislike at least one of them. In fact, you may dislike several entire styles plus many players within additional styles. You should also remember that many players had several different periods during their careers. You may enjoy their playing from one period but not from another. (If you do not have access to a comprehensive record collection, your opinion of a particular style or player may be based on only one recording. If that single example is either not stylistically representative or not typical of the quality of improvisation for a given musician, and you dislike what you hear, you run the risk of unintentionally dismissing a larger area of music. Beware!)

Confusing Album Titles

Buying albums with which you are unfamiliar often raises a general problem: Taking album titles seriously. This applies especially to the category of albums bearing titles such as "The Best of ——," "The Indispensable ——," "The Essential ——," and "—— at His Very Best." The biggest drawback is that such a set usually contains only a single record company's recordings, and that particular company may not have recorded the artist during his creative peak. Another company may have. And, of course, both companies may have released LPs called "The Best of ——." We must remember that many artists have had several different styles during their careers and a creative peak for each. They may have been recording for a different company during each important period.

John Coltrane is a case in point. He made important recordings as a bandleader for three different companies (Prestige, Atlantic, and Impulse), and each company documented a different stage in his career. Additionally, some of his best work was recorded under the leadership of Miles Davis for Columbia, a fourth record company. One implication of all this is that an Atlantic record called *The Best of John Coltrane* cannot contain the best Coltrane work from all three periods—although it could sample some of his best Atlantic sessions.

Another point to consider is that many players made some, or perhaps all, of their best recordings as sidemen in other men's bands, not as leaders on their own record dates. Lester Young probably did his best work as a sideman with the 1936–41 combos and big bands associated with Count Basie (reissued by Columbia-Epic and Decca-MCA). His own subsequent combo dates as leader sound unlike the Lester Young of the 1936–41 Basie groups. An Emarcy LP of some 1943–44 sessions called *Pres At His Very Best* is probably not his very best. A Verve LP of 1950s sessions called *The Essential Lester Young* is probably "essential" only to those Lester Young collectors who already have much of his earlier work. Both those LPs contain good playing, but if you are limited to a single album of Lester Young, neither of them would be appropriate. Their titles are misleading.

There are other examples of the confusion arising from album titles and varied careers. In the 1960s, pianist Herbie Hancock and saxophonist Wayne Shorter both made records for Blue Note as leaders of their own recording groups. During much of that time they were also recording for Columbia in the Miles Davis Quintet. Most of their playing on the Davis recordings is superior to that on their own records. But since they were leaders on the Blue Note sessions, those sessions, instead of the Columbia ones, provide the pool for albums titled "The Best of ———." I am not saying that Hancock's or Shorter's Blue Note work is poor. On the contrary, it is excellent music and it also features the beautiful composing that Hancock and Shorter are known for. The point is that, when heard strictly as piano and saxophone improvising, the Hancock and Shorter Blue Note work may not truly represent the absolute best of either man as claimed by an album title. Incidentally, a Columbia album called *The Best of Herbie Hancock* (JC 36309) contains neither his great playing with the 1963–69 Miles Davis groups nor his excellent music and beautiful composing found in his Blue Note work. The album samples yet another facet of Hancock: his jazz-rock material.

Another problem is that the choice of selections usually represents only an opinion, and that opinion is limited by the taste and knowledge of the person in charge, in addition to the dictates of the company. Therefore, even if an artist recorded solely for one company throughout his creative peak, a "Best of ———" album might leave out that artist's best work simply because the person in charge was ignorant of the music.

Another confusing album title is "Greatest Hits." It is usually misleading because, in addition to all the previously mentioned problems, a player's greatest hits measured by sales figures alone may not even appear on an LP titled "———'s Greatest Hits." For example, the largest-selling Miles Davis Columbia recording, his 1969 *Bitches Brew* (GP 26), is not represented on the Columbia album *Miles Davis' Greatest Hits* (PC 9808). Again, by sales figures alone, the 1964 Verve recording of "Girl From Ipanema" was Stan Getz's greatest hit. Yet there is a Prestige LP titled *Stan Getz' Greatest Hits* (Prestige 7337) drawn from 1949 and 1950 sessions. The Prestige material is excellent, perhaps better than the Verve material, yet it does not include his largest selling hits as the album title deceptively implies.

In summary, superlatives are rarely applied accurately in naming jazz records. You might be able to avoid confusion by reading album liner notes, carefully looking for recording dates and personnel, and consulting authorities to determine what companies were recording the artist during critical portions of his career.

How to Locate Records

Many people think certain records are available only in big city stores. But actually, no matter where you live, most records can be obtained by mail. It might be more practical to get records by mail even if you live in or near a big city which is full of record stores, such as New York or Los Angeles. Bus fare, or the price of gas and parking, could amount to a substantial fraction of the price of a record. Even then, a record store often orders your request by mail anyway, which leads to the main point: most of the jazz records mentioned in this book will not be found in average record stores. If they are available to a store, they will probably require a special order. You therefore ought to phone ahead to determine whether traveling an inconvenient distance will be worthwhile. Some stores accept special orders over the phone. You then have only to call the store periodically, and find out whether your order has arrived. (Note that most stores are not interested in your special order business. It is an unprofitable hassle for them. However they will often fail to admit this to you. They will simply take forever or never bother to notify you when they give up trying to find a particular item.) My advice is to forget the stores, and go mail order. Several jazz magazines whose addresses are listed on page 408 will supply you with any currently available jazz record. Out-of-print records can be obtained by getting your name on the mailing lists for jazz record auctions. (Scan the fliers they send, and bid, by mail, on what you want.) The addresses for jazz magazines and specialty record stores on page 399 should be used to begin this process.

About Reissues

Many jazz recordings which have disappeared from catalog listings return later in altered form. This includes the category known as reissues, re-releases, and repackages. Before I discuss them, here is a bit of relevant history. Prior to the widespread use of twelve-inch, 33⅓ rpm (revolutions per minute) LP (long play) records, most jazz was issued on ten-inch, 78 rpm records. (Remember those heavy black discs which almost invariably broke into pieces when you dropped them?) Twelve-inch 33s were not common until the 1950s, so many bop and West Coast style bands—in addition to Dixieland and swing bands—were initially presented on 78s. Several forms of recording material exist including paper, wire, tape, and plastic disc. (In addition to the ten-inch 78s and twelve-inch 33s, there have been twelve-inch 78s, ten-inch 33s, seven-inch 45s, twelve-inch 16s, etc.)

Due to the size of the record and the speed of rotation, most 78s could accommodate only about three minutes of music per side. An album consisted of several records packaged much like a book or a photo album, each record having a separate pocket or sleeve. The set was often bound in leather or cardboard. Then when the LP arrived, many of the three-minute jazz instrumentals originally on 78 were issued again (reissued) on 33⅓ rpm albums. This time, the word album meant a single record containing many selections. All the records in this book's premodern section and a few modern records are to be found in this kind of "reissue." Later on, LPs themselves began to be reissued, re-released, and repackaged. This is the altered form in which you can often find music originally available on records which have "disappeared" from the catalog.

Many albums that are no longer available in the United States are available in foreign countries under the same titles they carried before they went out of print in the United States. During the 1970s, for instance, Japanese distributors began repackaging out-of-print American albums with the album jacket art and liner notes intact. However, relying on imports is not usually that convenient. You ordinarily must match tune titles, personnel, and dates to determine whether a foreign release is the same as the American original you are seeking. A list of importers and their addresses appears on page 399.

Note that jazz groups have frequently recorded several versions of the same tunes, and many players did certain tunes with several different groups. Since you are a jazz fan, your interest lies not necessarily in listening to the tunes themselves but to particular improvisations. You must find the actual performances you want. The improvisation on other versions might not even resemble what you want.

The most common reissue situation is that not only are album titles changed, but material from certain recording sessions is scattered over several different albums. Another common problem is that the original recordings may have belonged to companies which later sold their material. (For instance, one reissue of Charlie Parker recordings originally made for Dial is called *The Dial Masters*.) The original company's name helps you identify reissued material. However, when record companies are bought and sold, sometimes the music is reissued intact, causing you no headaches. (For example, Impulse was bought by ABC, then by MCA, but the 1960s Coltrane classics originally made for Impulse continued to be distributed intact. They have to be sought from MCA, however, not from Impulse.) Another key to locating material in reissued form is that it is often identified by where it was recorded. (For example, the famous Bill Evans–Scott LaFaro music originally made at the Village Vanguard for Riverside record company has been reissued by Fantasy-Prestige-Milestone as *The Village Vanguard Sessions*. Charles Mingus's frequently reissued material from a famous concert at Toronto's Massey Hall, featuring Charlie Parker and Dizzy Gillespie, is sometimes labeled *The Massey Hall Concert*.)

When seeking music that you think is out-of-print, you need complete listing of the musicians on the record date, the tune titles, original album title and record company name, the recording dates, and the original catalog numbers. Personnel listings can be especially useful because material is sometimes reissued under the name of a musician who was a sideman on the original recording session but has now become important enough to warrant a reissue of his work that is packaged as though he were leader at that original session. (For example, a 1956 Tadd Dameron album called *Mating Call* has been reissued under John Coltrane's name and called *On A Misty Night* because Coltrane was a sideman on it but is now in much demand in his own right. Several reissues of Joe Oliver's Creole Jazz Band have come out under Louis Armstrong's name even though Armstrong was a sideman, not the leader, on Oliver's recordings. Much pre-1940 Lester Young is now available in reissues under Young's name despite its having been recorded under Count Basie's leadership.)

You can keep up with what is being reissued by reading jazz magazines and visiting record stores. If you do not want to wait for a particular out-of-print record to be reissued (and some never are), contact importers, rare record stores, and record auctioneers. If you are a serious jazz fan, you will probably have to subscribe to at least one or two of the standard jazz magazines listed on page 408. This will allow you to keep up with material that you will never hear on the radio or see in your local record store. When this book went to press, the magazines that attempted to announce, if not review, most new records and reissues were *Cadence* and *Jazz Times*. Subscription prices were very reasonable, and the magazines' information was indispensable. (It is an enormous job to identify all the albums that come out, but *Cadence* managed to do it, while other magazines only highlighted samples of current product.) If you do not have the patience to wade through hundreds of record listings month after month, but you still want a particular hard-to-find or out-of-print album, write one of the specialty stores. The staffs of these firms are jazz fans who perform location services primarily because they want to share their love for jazz with others and because they know how to help fans who lack the necessary information and contacts. Addresses for these services appear on page 399.

Many Versions of the Same Tune	The problem of a single tune recorded many times by the same artist increased substantially during the 1960s and 70s. This was due to increases in: (1) legitimate reissue programs by major firms, (2) illegitimate releases (called bootleg or pirate records) by numerous small firms, and (3) the discovery, or, in many cases, rediscovery, of a seemingly endless variety of broadcast performances, called air shots or air checks. (Music of the 1930s and 40s, unlike that of the 50s and 60s, is well documented by air checks because most jazz groups made live

radio broadcasts in those days.)

Beginning in the 1960s, record companies began massive distribution of repackaged material. Hundreds of albums with new titles were introduced. Many contained music originally on 78s. Other albums had music originally available on LPs. Some of the albums featured alternate, but originally rejected, versions of tunes. These are called alternate takes. (Some are labeled as alternate takes, but for others, you have to hear both versions to know whether they differ. They sometimes have improvisation equal or superior to the versions originally issued.)

Albums flooded the market from companies, both American and foreign, which operated without the consent of the recorded artists (or of their estates, in the case of deceased artists). Those albums constitute the illegitimate releases mentioned earlier. The companies were small and disappeared quickly. Some of their material had appeared previously on other records, but much of it had never been available before. A lot of it presumably came from homemade recordings of night club appearances and radio broadcasts. Many albums have incorrect tune titles. Few contain complete personnel listings and recording dates. Many display poor sound fidelity. But if you can tolerate all those weaknesses, you might be well rewarded by the music itself. It also may be worthwhile knowing about bootleg recordings because the appearance and distribution of them is a very common phenomenon and likely to continue.

With the bootleg material added to the legitimate releases and reissues, it became possible to own more than eighty albums of Charlie Parker, more than one hundred of Duke Ellington, etc. The record collector might be confronted with five to ten Parker versions of "Confirmation" and "Ornithology" and just as many Ellington versions of "Mood Indigo" and "Sophisticated Lady." Keeping track of recording dates and personnel became essential to discussing particular performances of these frequently recorded tunes.

A few Charlie Parker classics illustrate the usefulness of having personnel, tune titles, recording dates, and original record company name before you begin seeking a particular recording. The much praised music that Parker originally made in the form of 78s for Dial Record Company has been sold in numerous forms, some of them offered by tiny, obscure record companies that worked without the consent of Parker's estate. Take "Embraceable You," for example. Parker recorded many different versions of it. But if you want his famous Dial recording of it, you must remember that he made two different versions at the same session, and you must remember the 1947 recording date, and that the pianist was Duke Jordan, the bassist was Tommy Potter, and the drummer was Max Roach. Any deviation from that particular combination of identifiers signals that you are holding another version of the tune instead of the famous classic version. It is also essential to note the record company name and recording date if you want to locate Parker's famous 1945 "Now's the Time," that was made for Savoy record company with the Miles Davis trumpet solo that was later adapted and recorded by pianist Red Garland on the Miles Davis *Milestones* album. It is especially easy to become confused in this instance because another version of the same tune was also recorded by Parker without Davis in 1953 and released on a Verve album called *Now's the Time*. There are instances in which historic figures recorded only one version of a given tune, but the more you study jazz, the more you will find it beneficial to **keep track of details to ensure you're buying what you originally set out to buy.**

One final example is offered to illustrate the usefulness of having complete information about an improvisation you seek. If you have a transcription of a Miles Davis trumpet solo from a performance of "Joshua," and you want to hear the original or play along with it, you cannot simply run out and buy the correct album, even if you already have the personnel listing and the year of recording. Miles Davis recorded "Joshua" at least three times with saxophonist George Coleman, pianist Herbie Hancock, bassist Ron Carter, and drummer Tony Williams. Two out of the three times were in the same year, 1963. One version was released on *Seven Steps to Heaven*, an album which was issued with two different catalog numbers: Columbia CS 8851 and CL 2051. Another version was released on *Miles Davis in Europe* (Columbia CL 2183 and CS 8983). Then Davis recorded another version in 1964 that was released in *Four and More* (Columbia 9253 and CL 2453).

Rare Record Dealers, Importers, and Auctioneers

Rare Records
417 East Broadway
Glendale, Ca. 91205

Jazz Etc.
P.O. Box 393
Bergenfield, N.J. 07621

The Jazz and Blues
   Record Center
Box 87 Station J
Toronto, Ontario
M4J 4X8 Canada

Cadence Record Sales
Box 345 Route 1
Redwood, N.Y. 13679

Daybreak Express Records
P.O. Box 250 Van Brunt Station
Brooklyn, N.Y. 11215

International Association of
   Jazz Record Collectors
10107 Morgan Meadow Lane
Dallas, Texas 75243
(Write for a membership listing,
then determine who specializes
in the style you seek, and write
that member.)

Import Record Service
P.O. Box 166
Roselle Park, N.J. 07204

Oaklawn
Box 2663
Providence, R.I. 02907

The Smithsonian Institution keeps hard-to-find jazz items in print long after private companies have deleted them from their catalogs. As this book went to press, Smithsonian was carrying rare items by Joe Oliver, Sidney Bechet, Louis Armstrong, Duke Ellington, Art Tatum, Teddy Wilson, Henry "Red" Allen, John Kirby, Freddie Keppard, Fletcher Henderson, and Dizzy Gillespie. When searching for recordings cited in this book, it would be wise to first check the most current Smithsonian listings. You can get a catalog by writing Smithsonian Performing Arts, Washington, D.C. 20560. If you already know what you want, you can order it by phone with their toll-free number 1-800-247-5028.

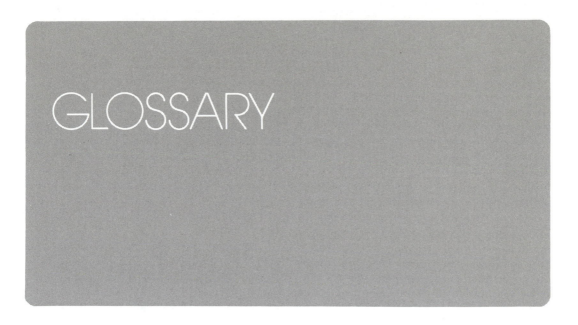

GLOSSARY

antiphonal an adjective describing a common pattern of interaction between improvisers or between sections of a band, taking the form of a question and answer or a call and response.

arco the technique of playing a stringed instrument with a bow.

atonal the character and organization possessed by music that has no key (see page 369 for further explanations and illustrations).

attack the very beginning of a sound (opposite of release).

ballad a slow piece

big band an ensemble of ten or more players.

blue note 1) a pitch somewhere between a major third and minor third or between a major seventh and minor seventh step of the scale (see page 371).
2) minor third or seventh scale step (see page 370).

blues 1) a simple, funky style of black music separate from but coexistent with jazz; beginning at least as early as the turn of the century, probably much earlier; exemplified by such performers as Blind Lemon Jefferson, Leadbelly, Lightnin' Hopkins, Muddy Waters, T-Bone Walker and Robert Johnson. It has

been and continues to be an influence on jazz and rock. The majority of blues compositions employ the I-IV-I-V-I chord progression or a variation of it.
2) a piece characterized by any one or any combination of the following—
a) the I-IV-I-V-I chord progression or some variation of it in a twelve-measure package
b) a sad feeling
c) a slow pace
d) poetry in the form of paired couplets in iambic pentameter
e) many lowered third, fifth, or seventh intervals
(see page 369 for further explanation)

bomb a pronounced accent played by the drummer.

boogie woogie a premodern jazz piano style associated with Meade Lux Lewis and Albert Ammons. It is characterized by a repetitive left-hand bass figure that states almost every beat by dividing it into dotted-eighth sixteenth-note patterns.

bop (bebop) the style associated with Charlie Parker, Dizzy Gillespie, Thelonious Monk, Bud Powell, Dexter Gordon, and Sonny Stitt (see page 143).

break 1) the portion of a piece in which all band members stop playing except the one who improvises a solo. The tempo and chord progressions are maintained by the soloist, but, because the band has stopped, it is called a stop-time. Rarely do such breaks last longer than two or four measures (see page 34 for detailed explanation).
2) the solo itself.

bridge the B part of an A-A-B-A composition; also known as the channel, the release, or the inside (see page 31 for further information).

broken time 1) a style of rhythm section playing in which explicit statement of every beat is replaced by broken patterns which only imply the underlying tempo, exemplified by the 1961 Bill Evans trio with Scott LaFaro and Paul Motian.
2) the manner of playing bass or drums in which strict repetition of timekeeping patterns is not maintained, but constant tempo is; exemplified by the 1960s and 70s playing of Elvin Jones.

chops instrumental facility

chord progression 1) when one chord changes or "progresses" to another chord.
2) a set of harmonies in a particular order with specified durations; for example, the twelve measure I-IV-I-V-I blues progression (see pages 377–379 and 416).
3) the sequence of accompaniment chords intended for a song but used instead as the basis of a jazz improvisation.

chorus 1) a single playing through of the structure being used to organize the music in an improvisation.
2) a jazz solo, regardless of its length.
3) the part of a pop tune performed in constant tempo and repeated several times after the verse has been played, usually the only portion of a tune's original form used by the jazz musician (see page 31 for further explanation).

collective improvisation simultaneous improvisation by all members of a group together.

comping syncopated chording which provides improvised accompaniment for simultaneously improvised solos, flexibly complement-

ing the rhythms and implied harmonies of the solo line (see page 15 for further explanation and page 424 for musical notation).

cool 1) an adjective often applied to describe the subdued feeling projected by the music of Bix Beiderbecke, Lester Young, Claude Thornhill, Gil Evans, Miles Davis, The Modern Jazz Quartet, Gerry Mulligan, Lee Konitz, and Jimmy Giuffre (see pages 177–189).
2) sometimes used as a synonym for West Coast style.
3) sometimes used to denote modern jazz after bop.

counterpoint two or more lines of approximately equal importance sounding together.

Creole- 1) French- or Spanish-speaking individual born in the New World.
2) a person who has mixed French and African ancestry and was born in the New World (also known as "Creole of Color," as opposed to the white-skinned Creole defined above).

decay the very end of a sound; also known as a release. Opposite of attack (see pages 50–52 for discussion).

Dixieland style 1) Chicago combo style that was prominent during the 1920s.
2) a synonym for all preswing-era combo jazz.

double stop sounding two bass strings at the same time.

double-time the feeling that a piece of music or a player is going twice as fast as the tempo, although the chord progressions continue at the original rate.

Fender bass electric bass guitar, used to play bass lines instead of chords; common in jazz rhythm sections after 1970.

fill in general, anything a drummer plays in addition to basic timekeeping patterns; in particular, a rhythmic figure played by a drummer to—
1) fill a silence
2) underscore a rhythm played by other instruments
3) announce the entrance or punctuate the exit of a soloist or other section of the music
4) stimulate the other players and make a performance more interesting.

free jazz an approach associated with Ornette Coleman and Cecil Taylor, in which the music contains improvised solos which are free of preset chord progressions, and sometimes also free of preset meter (see pages 230–231).

front line musicians appearing directly in front of the audience, not blocked from view by another row of musicians. This designation is sometimes used to separate hornmen (because they stand in the front of a combo) from accompanists (who usually appear to the rear of the hornmen).

funky 1) earthy or dirty
2) mean, "low down," evil, or sexy
3) bluesy
4) gospel-flavored
5) containing a predominance of lowered third, fifth, and seventh steps of the scale.
(*Note: During the 1970s this adjective was applied to describe rhythms as well as melody, harmony, and tone color characteristics.*)

fusion a synonym for jazz-rock style (see pages 312–319).

hard bop the jazz style associated with Horace Silver, Art Blakey, and Cannonball Adderley (see page 206 for further explanation).

head the melody or prewritten theme for a piece.

head arrangement a band arrangement that was created extemporaneously by the musicians and is not written down.

high-hat (sock cymbal) an instrument in the drum set which brings two cymbals together by means of a foot pedal (see page 20 for illustration).

horn general label for any wind instrument; sometimes includes stringed and percussion instruments as well (the most general term for all instruments is ax).

jam session a musical get-together where improvisation is stressed and prewritten music is rare (jam means to improvise); may refer to a performance which is formally organized or casual, public or private, for profit or just for fun.

laid back an adjective used to describe a feeling of relaxation, laziness, or slowness; often describes the feeling that a performer is playing his rhythms a little later than they are expected, almost after the beat or "behind" the beat.

lay out to stop playing while other players continue.

legato a style of playing in which the notes are smoothly connected with no silences between them (opposite of staccato).

lick a phrase or melodic fragment.

locked-hands style a style of piano playing in which a separate chord parallels each note of the melody because both hands are used as though they are locked together, all fingers striking the keyboard together; also known as block chording, playing the chord notes as a block instead of one at a time. (See sections on Milt Buckner, Lennie Tristano, George Shearing, Ahmad Jamal, Red Garland, and Bill Evans.)

modal music in which the melody and/or harmony is based on an arrangement of modes. In jazz, the term can mean music based on the extensive repetition of one or two chords or music based on modes instead of chord progressions (see page 418 for further explanation).

mode 1) the manner of organizing a sequence of tones, usually an ascending sequence of an octave.
2) the arrangement of whole steps and half steps common to scales.
(See page 368 for further explanation.)

mute an attachment which reduces an instrument's loudness and alters its tone color (see page 390 for illustrations).

pedal point low-pitched, repeated, and/or sustained tone. It usually retains its pitch despite changes in chords and improvisations occurring around it; common in the 1960s work of John Coltrane and McCoy Tyner.

pitch bending purposeful raising or lowering of a tone's pitch; usually done for coloration or expressive purposes (see pages 40, 51, and 52 for illustrations and explanation).

pizzicato the method of playing a stringed instrument by plucking instead of bowing.

polyrhythm several different rhythms sounding at the same time (see page 364).

progressive jazz music associated with Stan Kenton (see pages 344–347).

ragtime 1) a popular turn-of-the-century style of written piano music involving pronounced syncopation.
2) a label often applied to much pre-1920 jazz and pop music, unaccompanied solo piano styles as well as band styles, improvised as well as written music.
3) the style of music associated with composers Scott Joplin and Tom Turpin.

release 1) the manner in which a sound ends or decays (opposite of attack).
2) the bridge of a tune.

rhythm section the group of players whose band function is accompanying. This role is particularly common for pianists, bassists, and drummers, but it is not exclusive to them (see pages 15–23 for explanations and illustrations, see pages 424, 426, 427, and 430 for musical notations).

ride cymbal the cymbal suspended over a drum set, usually to the player's right, struck by a stick held in the drummer's right hand; used for playing timekeeping patterns called ride rhythms (see page 19 for illustration).

ride rhythm the pattern a drummer plays on the ride cymbal to keep time, the most common being ching-chick-a-ching-chick-a (see notations on page 430).

riff 1) phrase
2) melodic fragment
3) theme.

rim shot the drum stick striking the rim of the snare drum at the same time as it strikes the drum head.

rip an onset ornament in the form of a quick rise in pitch directly preceding a tone. (Listen to Bix Beiderbecke or Louis Armstrong.)

rubato free of strict adherence to constant tempo.

scat singing jazz improvisation using the human voice as an instrument, with nonsense syllables (dwee, ool, ya, bop, bam, etc.) instead of words.

sideman a designation for each musician in a band except the leader.

sock cymbal see **high-hat.**

staccato brief and separated (opposite of legato).

stride 1) left-hand style used by early jazz pianists. It usually employs a bass note on the first and third beats of each measure and a chord on the second and fourth.
2) the piano style of James P. Johnson and Willie "The Lion" Smith.

swing 1) a word denoting approval—"It swings" can mean it pleases me; "to swing" can mean to enjoy oneself; "he's a swinging guy" can mean he is an enjoyable person.
2) the noun indicating the feeling projected by an uplifting performance of any kind of music, especially that which employs constant tempo (see page 5 for further explanation).
3) the feeling projected by a jazz performance which successfully combines constant tempo, syncopation, swing eighth notes, rhythmic lilt, liveliness and rhythmically cohesive group playing (see page 7 for further explanation).
4) the jazz style associated with Count Basie, Duke Ellington, Jimmie Lunceford, Benny Goodman, Art Tatum, Roy Eldridge, and Coleman Hawkins, as in the "swing era" (see page 86).

syncopation 1) stress on any portion of the measure other than the first part of the first beat (and, in meter of four, other than the first part of the third beat), i.e. the second half of the first beat, the second half of the second beat, the fourth beat, the second half of the fourth beat, the second beat, etc.
2) stress on a portion of the measure least expected to receive stress (see page 360 for further explanation).

synthesizer any one of a general category of electronic devices (Moog and Arp, for example) which produces sounds or alters the sounds created by other instruments.

Third Stream a style which combines jazz improvisation with the instrumentation and compositional forms of classical music (see page 158 for further explanation).

tonal inflection   alteration of a tone's pitch or quality, done purposefully at the beginning, middle, or end of a sound (see pitch bending, and see pages 50–52 for illustrations and explanations).

tone color (timbre, tone quality)   the characteristic of sound which enables the listener to differentiate one instrument from another, and, in many cases, one player from another.

tremolo   1) fluctuation in the loudness of a sound, usually an even alternation of loud and soft.

2) a manner of playing a chord by rapidly sounding its different notes in alternation so that the chord retains its character, but also sustains and trembles.

3) the means of sustaining the sound of a vibraharp (see page 159).

4) an expressive technique for use by instruments in which vibrato is very difficult (flute, for example) or in which the variation of pitch necessary for vibrato may not be wanted (some styles of oboe playing, for example).

5) the rapid reiteration of the same note.

turnaround (turnback, turnabout)   a short progression within a chord progression that occurs just prior to the point at which the player must "turn around" to begin another repetition of the larger progression (see page 387 for further explanation and page 417 for musical notation).

two-beat style   a rhythm section style which emphasizes the first and third beats of each four-beat measure, often leaving the second and fourth beats silent in the bass; sometimes called boom-chick style.

vamp   a short chord progression (usually only one, two, or four measures long) which is repeated many times in sequence. Often used for introductions and endings. Much jazz and pop music of the 1960s and 70s used vamps instead of more involved chord progressions as accompaniment for melody and improvisation.

vibrato   the slight fluctuation of a tone's pitch, alternating above and below its basic pitch; used as an expressive device, varied in speed and amplitude by the performer to fit the style and feeling of the music (see page 50 for further explanation).

voicing   1) the manner of organizing, doubling, omitting, or adding to the notes of a chord (see pages 374–376).

2) the assignment of notes to each instrument (see page 377 for further explanation).

walking bass   a style of bass line in which each beat of each measure receives a separate tone, thus creating a moving sequence of quarter notes in the bass range.

West Coast style   the jazz style associated with Gerry Mulligan and Chet Baker during the 1950s (see **cool** and page 182 for further explanation).

SUPPLEMENTARY READING

Biographies

ARMSTRONG, LOUIS. *Satchmo: My Life in New Orleans*. Englewood Cliffs, N.J.: Prentice-Hall, 1954.
Louis Armstrong's autobiography.

CARR, IAN. *Miles Davis: A Biography*. New York: William Morrow, 1982.
An intelligently written and knowledgeable biography of Davis by fellow jazz trumpeter Carr. Contains discography as well as transcriptions of solo improvisations.

CASE, BRIAN, and BRITT, STAN. *The Illustrated Encyclopedia of Jazz*. New York: Harmony Books, 1978.
Over 400 biographical entries.

CHARTERS, SAMUEL B. *Jazz: New Orleans 1885–1963, An Index to the Negro Musicians of New Orleans*. New York: Oak Publications, 1963. (Also Da Capo.)
A valuable source of biographical and musical information on the first jazz musicians.

CHILTON, JOHN. *Who's Who of Jazz: Storyville to Swing Street*. London: Chilton Book Co., 1972.
Available from The Bloomsbury Book Shop, 31–35 Great Ormond Street, London, W.C. 1, England. Biographies of hundreds of musicians born before 1920.

CLAGHORN, CHARLES E. *Biographical Dictionary of Jazz*. Englewood Cliffs, N.J.: Prentice-Hall, 1983.
Profiles of more than 3,400 jazz musicians, composers, vocalists and bands.

DANCE, STANLEY. *The World of Count Basie*. New York: Charles Scribner's Sons, 1981.
Covers Basie and his sidemen in profile and interview formats.

DANCE, STANLEY. *The World of Duke Ellington*. New York: Charles Scribner's Sons, 1970. Also Da Capo paperback.

DANCE, STANLEY. *The World of Earl Hines*. New York: Charles Scribner's Sons, 1977 (hard cover). Da Capo (paperback).
Includes reminiscences by numerous Hines associates, an exclusive chronology of Hines's life, excellent bibliography and discography, plus historical accounts in Hines's own words.

DANCE, STANLEY. *The World of Swing*. New York: Charles Scribner's Sons, 1975. Also Da Capo.
Vignettes of swing era figures, an emphasis on interview material.

ELLINGTON, DUKE. *Music Is My Mistress*. Garden City, N.Y.: Doubleday, 1973. In Da Capo paperback.
Duke Ellington's autobiography.

ELLINGTON, MERCER. *Duke Ellington In Person.* Boston: Houghton-Mifflin, 1978. Also Da Capo paperback.
A biography by Duke Ellington's son, sideman, and road manager.

FEATHER, LEONARD. *The New Encyclopedia of Jazz.* New York: Bonanza, 1960.
Leonard Feather and Ira Gitler's monumental compilation with over two thousand biographies from A to Z.

FEATHER, LEONARD. *The Encyclopedia of Jazz in the Sixties.* New York: Horizon, 1966.
A follow-up to the above, this one including 1400 biographies.

FEATHER, LEONARD, and GITLER, IRA. *The Encyclopedia of Jazz in the Seventies.* New York: Bonanza, 1976.
A follow-up to the above.

FEATHER, LEONARD. *From Satchmo to Miles.* New York: Stein and Day, 1972.
Chapters on Louis Armstrong, Duke Ellington, Count Basie, Lester Young, Charlie Parker, Dizzy Gillespie, Miles Davis and others.

FOSTER, GEORGE MURPHY "POPS." *Pops Foster: The Autobiography of a New Orleans Jazzman.* Berkeley, Calif.: University of California Press, 1971.
Contains numerous details of New Orleans jazz history from the turn of the century plus much on the history of jazz in Chicago. The musical information in the book is indispensable to understanding the history of jazz rhythm section playing, and is not limited to the bass style of its author.

GARA, LARRY. *The Baby Dodds Story.* Los Angeles: Contemporary Press, 1959.
Contains a peek into the techniques used by early jazz drummers. Also has much on New Orleans and Chicago jazz history.

GILLESPIE, DIZZY. *To Be or Not to Bop.* Garden City, N.Y.: Doubleday, 1979.
Reminiscences by Gillespie plus interviews with his colleagues done by Al Fraser.

GITLER, IRA. *Jazz Masters of the Forties.* New York: Macmillan, 1966. Reprinted by Da Capo.
One of the most intelligently conceived jazz history books, it includes musical and biographical discussions of Charlie Parker and the alto and baritone saxophonists, Dizzy Gillespie and the trumpeters, Bud Powell and the pianists, J. J. Johnson and the trombonists, Oscar Pettiford and the bassists, Kenny Clarke, Max Roach, and the drummers, Dexter Gordon and the tenor saxophonists, Lennie Tristano and Lee Konitz, Tadd Dameron and the arrangers.

GOLDBERG, JOE. *Jazz Masters of the Fifties.* New York: Macmillan, 1965. In Collier paperback. Also Da Capo hard cover.
A chapter each on Miles Davis, Thelonious Monk, Gerry Mulligan, Charlie Mingus, John Coltrane, Sonny Rollins, Ornette Coleman, and Cecil Taylor.

HADLOCK, RICHARD. *Jazz Masters of the Twenties.* New York: Macmillan, 1965. In Collier paperback.
A chapter each on Armstrong, Beiderbecke, Earl Hines, Fats Waller, James P. Johnson, Fletcher Henderson, Eddie Lang, and The Chicagoans.

HITCHCOCK, H. WILEY (Ed.). *The New Grove Dictionary of American Music.* London: Macmillan, 1986.
Contains numerous biographies as well as different jazz styles summaries.

JEWELL, DEREK. *Duke: A Portrait of Duke Ellington.* New York: Norton, 1977.
Biography by a British jazz critic who knew Ellington.

PORTER, LEWIS. *Lester Young.* Boston: G. K. Hall, 1985.
A scholarly and technical study of Young done by a fellow saxophonist and jazz historian.

REISNER, ROBERT. *Bird: The Legend of Charlie Parker.* New York: Citadel, 1962. Reprinted by Da Capo Press.
Charlie Parker biography in the form of documents.

RUSSELL, ROSS. *Bird Lives: The High Life and Hard Times of Charlie Parker.* New York: Charterhouse, 1973. In Popular Library paperback.
Charlie Parker biography in the style of a novel.

SHAPIRO, NAT, and HENTOFF, NAT. *Hear Me Talkin' to Ya*. New York: Dover, 1955. Also Peter Smith. Also Greenwood.
Interviews with famous jazz musicians.

SHAPIRO, NAT, and HENTOFF, NAT. *Jazz Makers*. New York: Rinehart, 1957. Also Grove Press, Greenwood, and Da Capo Press.
A chapter each on Jelly Roll Morton, Baby Dodds, Louis Armstrong, Jack Teagarden, Earl Hines, Bix Beiderbecke, Pee Wee Russell, Fats Waller, Art Tatum, Coleman Hawkins, Benny Goodman, Duke Ellington, Charlie Parker, Fletcher Henderson, Count Basie, Lester Young, Roy Eldridge, Charlie Christian, and Dizzy Gillespie.

SIMPKINS, C. O. *Coltrane: A Biography*. New York: Herndon House, 1975.
Contains transcriptions, work sheets, interviews, and analyses in addition to biographical details.

SPELLMAN, A. B. *Black Music: Four Lives*. New York: Schocken, 1966.
Biographical interviews with Ornette Coleman, Cecil Taylor, Jackie McLean, and Herbie Nichols.

STEWART, REX. *Jazz Masters of the Thirties*. New York: Macmillan, 1972. In Collier paperback. Also Da Capo hard cover.
A chapter each on Ellington, Hawkins, Henderson, Basie, Art Tatum, and Benny Carter.

SUDHALTER, R. M., EVANS, P. R., and MYATT, W. D. *Bix, Man and Legend*. New York: Schirmer Books, 1974.
An exhaustive biography of Bix Beiderbecke. Written by fellow trumpeter Sudhalter, this book includes technical analyses, an excellent discography, an almost day-by-day chronology of Beiderbecke's life with explanations for almost every mystery surrounding it. Also contains transcriptions of excerpts from solos.

SUMMERFIELD, MAURICE J. *The Jazz Guitar*. Gateshead, Tyne and Wear, England: Ashley Mark Publishing Company, 1978.
Biographies of almost all the prominent guitarists in jazz history.

TAYLOR, ARTHUR (Ed.). *Notes and Tones*. New York: Perigree, 1982.
Interviews with Miles Davis, Randy Weston, Ornette Coleman, Philly Joe Jones, Don Byas, Ron Carter, Johnny Griffin, Charles Tolliver, Eddie Lockjaw Davis, Leon Thomas, Max Roach, Erroll Garner, Dizzy Gillespie, Carmen McRae, Nina Simone, Tony Williams, Sonny Rollins, Don Cherry, Hampton Hawes, Kenny Clarke, Freddie Hubbard, Richard Davis, Elvin Jones, Kenny Dorham, Art Blakey, Hazel Scott, and Betty Carter.

THOMAS, J. C. *Chasin' the Trane: The Music and Mystique of John Coltrane*. Garden City, N.Y.: Doubleday, 1975. In Da Capo paperback.
Impressionistic biography with quotes from Coltrane's colleagues interwoven. Excellent discography. Includes poetry inspired by Coltrane's music.

ULANOV, BARRY. *Duke Ellington*. New York: Creative Age, 1946. In Da Capo paperback.

WILLIAMS, MARTIN. *Jazz Masters of New Orleans*. New York: Macmillan, 1970. In Collier paperback. Also reprinted by Da Capo.
A chapter each on King Oliver, Jelly Roll Morton, Sidney Bechet, Louis Armstrong, and Original Dixieland Jazz Band.

Jazz Magazines

Coda
Box 87 Station J
Toronto, Ontario
M4J 4X8 Canada

Down Beat
222 W. Adams St.
Chicago, Ill. 60606

Crescendo
122 Wardour St.
London W1V 3LA
England

Jazz Educators Journal
Box 724
Manhattan, Kans. 66502

Cadence
Cadence Building
Redwood, N.Y. 13679

Jazz Journal International
35 Great Russell Street
London WC1B3PP
England

Jazz Times
8055 13th Street Suite 301
Silver Spring, Md. 20910

The Black Perspective in Music
P.O. Drawer I
Cambria Heights, N.Y. 11411

Musician
P.O. Box 1923
Marion, Ohio 43306

Annual Review of Jazz Studies
Transaction Books
Rutgers University
New Brunswick, N.J. 08903

Jazz Index
c/o Norbert Rücker
Kleiststrasse 39
D-6000 Frankfort 1
West Germany

Sources for Information About Jazz Records

Bibliography of Discographies—Volume 2–Jazz (1981) by Daniel Allen
R. R. Bowker Company
1180 Avenue of the Americas
New York, N.Y. 10036

International Association of Jazz Record Collectors
90 Prince George Drive
Islington, Ontario M9B 2X8 Canada
(Become a member, then correspond with others who share your interests.)

Bibliography of Discographies—Journal of the Association for Recorded Sound Collections
Box 1643
Manassas, Vir. 22110

International Association of Sound Archives
Open University Library
Walton Hall
Milton Keynes MK7 6AA
England

Jazz Bibliography (1981) by Bernhard Hefele
K. G. Saur Publishers
Munich, West Germany

Basic Jazz Record Resource Materials

These are discographies, books that tally such things as personnel for particular recording sessions, listings of all the recording sessions for a particular player, listings of all the recording sessions done by a particular company, all the different catalog numbers under which a particular performance has been issued, how many versions were made of a given tune at a given recording session, the day and place of recording, etc.

Jazz Records 1897–1942 by Brian Rust
Storyville Publications and Co. Ltd.
66, Fairview Drive
Chigwell, Essex IG7 6HS
England
(Also available from Oaklawn Books, Box 2663, Providence, R.I. 02907)

Jazz Records 1942– by Jorgen Grunnet Jepsen
(Available from Oaklawn Books; see address above)

Sixty Years of Recorded Jazz 1917–1977 by Walter Bruyninckx
Lange Nieuwstraat 121
2800 Mechelen
Belgium
(Also available from *Cadence*, Cadence Building, Redwood, N.Y. 13679, and from Oaklawn Books, see address above)

Note: Oaklawn Books carries hundreds of discographies, rare jazz books, and imported jazz books. Write them to get on their mailing list.

Texts for Readers Familiar with Musical Notation

HODEIR, ANDRÉ. *Jazz: Its Evolution And Essence.* New York: Grove Press, 1956. In Da Capo paperback.
Technical analyses of various styles and recordings including an essay on trombonist Dicky Wells and one on Ellington's "Concerto for Cootie."

JOST, EKKEHARD. *Free Jazz.* New York: Da Capo Press. Or Vienna, Austria: Universal Edition.
First published in 1975, this text contains technical analyses and notations of work by John Coltrane and Miles Davis (*Kind of Blue*), Charles Mingus, Ornette Coleman, Cecil Taylor, Archie Shepp, Albert Ayler, Don Cherry, The Association for the Advancement of Creative Musicians, Sun Ra, and The Art Ensemble of Chicago.

OSTRANSKY, LEROY. *The Anatomy of Jazz.* Seattle, Washington: University of Washington Press, 1960. Also Greenwood.

SCHULLER, GUNTHER. *Early Jazz: Its Roots and Musical Development.* New York: Oxford University Press, 1968.
Scholarly and quite technical examination of the earliest jazz known, its possible sources in African music and nineteenth-century American popular music. Detailed analysis of Louis Armstrong, Jelly Roll Morton, assorted pre-swing players, Fletcher Henderson, Ellington's earliest recordings, Bennie Moten and bands of Kansas and Missouri during the 1920s and early 1930s.

TAYLOR, BILLY. *Jazz Piano: A Jazz History.* Dubuque, Iowa: William C. Brown, 1983. Reminiscences by a well-known jazz pianist and teacher. Interspersed with musical notations and technical discussion, although the book should be understandable to nonmusicians who wish to ignore them.

Technical References

BAKER, DAVID. *Jazz Improvisation: A Comprehensive Study for All Players.* Chicago: Maher, 1969.
A helpful instruction manual for intermediate and advanced as well as beginning jazz improvisers.

COKER, JERRY. *Improvising Jazz.* Englewood Cliffs, N.J.: Prentice-Hall, 1964.
Excellent explanation of chords, chord progressions, how to swing, and how to improvise melodically.

MEHEGAN, JOHN. *Jazz Improvisation 1. Tonal and Rhythmic Principles.* New York: Watson-Guptill Publications, 1959.

MEHEGAN, JOHN. *Jazz Improvisation 2. Jazz Rhythm and the Improvised Line.* New York: Watson-Guptill Publications, 1962.

MEHEGAN, JOHN. *Jazz Improvisation 3. Swing and Early Progressive Piano Styles.* New York: Watson-Guptill Publications, 1964.
The three volumes by Mehegan provide scholarly instruction series for the serious jazz student who has solid knowledge of the piano. The series is not exclusively for pianists, but any hornmen using it must have some acquaintance with the keyboard. Distributed by Music Sales, P.O. Box 572, Chester, N.Y. 10918; and Songbooks Unlimited, 352 Evelyn St., Paramus, N.J. 07653-0908.

MOST, SAM. *Metamorphosis: Transformation of the Jazz Solo.* Tustin, Calif.: Professional Music Products, 1980.
A very practical guide for the advanced music student who is learning how to develop improvised solo lines.

RIZZO, PHIL. *Creative Melodic Techniques Used in Jazz Improvisation.* Modern Music School, 101 Northfield Road, Bedford, Ohio 44146.
Manual for the beginning improviser.

SUDNOW, DAVID. *Ways of the Hand: The Organization of Improvised Conduct.* Cambridge, Mass.: Harvard University Press, 1978.
A difficult-to-read narrative on how one man learned how to play jazz piano. Filled with useful photographs and drawings of hand positions on the keyboard.

ZINN, DAVID. *The Structure and Analysis of the Modern Improvised Line.* New York: Excelsior Music Publishing Company, 1981.

Available through Theodore Presser Company in Bryn Mawr, Pennsylvania 19010. A very formal, technical instruction manual for musicians. It should also interest music theorists because it represents an intelligent analysis for the construction of melodic lines from rhythmic and harmonic perspectives.

Note: To keep up with the currently available technical references, you might find it helpful to be on the mailing list of Jamey Aebersold, who distributes hundreds of such publications and tests their usefulness at the clinics he runs. Write Jamey Aebersold, 1211-D Aebersold Drive, New Albany, Ind. 47150.

General References

BASCOM, WILLIAM R., and HERSKOVITS, MELVILLE J. (Eds.) *Continuity and Change in African Cultures.* Chicago: University of Chicago Press, 1959.
Contains an excellent chapter on African music by Alan Merriam and several other studies of African art and culture that should be helpful for readers interested in the roots of jazz.

BERLIN, EDWARD A. *Ragtime: A Musical and Cultural History.* Berkeley, Calif.: University of California Press, 1980.
Scholarly evaluation of ragtime. Includes musical notations.

COKER, JERRY. *Listening to Jazz.* Englewood Cliffs, N.J.: Prentice-Hall, 1978.
One of the best guides to appreciating the playing of jazz improvisers. Loaded with insights about how musicians develop solos. Keyed to the *Smithsonian.* Contains numerous, detailed analyses that often require musical background from the reader.

COLLIER, JAMES LINCOLN. *The Making of Jazz.* Boston: Houghton-Mifflin, 1978.
If you can get past the author's attempts at psychoanalyzing musicians, you will find some interesting musical analyses here. This is probably the longest American history of jazz, and it integrates a large assortment of styles in an easy to read manner.

FEATHER, LEONARD. *The Book of Jazz.* New York: Horizon, 1957, 1965, 1976 (hard cover). Dell (paperback).
An instrument by instrument history of jazz plus discussions of the origins of jazz and the nature of jazz improvisation. This book, in all its revisions, remains the best compact guide to jazz and summary of the perspectives of the world's foremost jazz journalist.

SOUTHERN, EILEEN. *The Music of Black Americans: A History.* New York: W. W. Norton, 1971, 1983.
Covers popular music, classical music, folk music, religious music, and jazz.

SOURCES FOR NOTATED JAZZ SOLOS

Transcriptions are promised for every note played by every musician on every recording that is accompanied by the SCCJ designation in this book. The project is a joint effort of the Smithsonian Institution and Schirmer Publishing Company. Information can be obtained by writing Smithsonian Institution, Performing Arts Division, Washington, D.C. 20560. When writing, identify the material as "The Smithsonian Collection of Classic Jazz Scores."

Many jazz books and magazines include notations of jazz improvisations. The Mehegan books, listed here under "Technical References," contain numerous solo transcriptions. *Down Beat* magazine, listed on page 408 under "Jazz Magazines," includes transcriptions or instructional aids in almost every issue. Going through back issues of *Down Beat* can reveal a treasure house of notations.

There are hundreds of books filled with transcriptions of famous jazz improvisations. Catalogs and ordering information for them are available in *Jazz Educators Journal*, the official journal of the National Association of Jazz Educators. You can get back issues from school band directors who belong to the organization. Or you can join the organization yourself by sending them your check. It is only a small fee, and the information they distribute is well worth it. Just write National Association of Jazz Educators, P.O. Box 724, Manhattan, Kans. 66502.

James DaPogny has transcribed several Jelly Roll Morton piano solos and added them to published works and music from the rolls of player pianos for a total of 40 numbers in *Ferdinand "Jelly Roll" Morton: The Collected Piano Music*, published by Smithsonian Institution Press/G. Schirmer.

The most dedicated of all solo transcribers is Andrew White. From him, you can order more than 400 John Coltrane solos, more than 300 Charlie Parker solos, and several Eric Dolphy solos. Just write Andrew's Music at 4830 South Dakota Avenue, N.E., Washington, D.C. 20017.

Jamey Aebersold distributes numerous books of solo transcriptions. One series is by David Baker, and it includes one book each for Clifford Brown, Miles Davis, John Coltrane, Sonny Rollins, Cannonball Adderley, and Fats Navarro. Aebersold also distributes transcription books by Ken Slone and Don Sickler. Slone has prepared a book of Clifford Brown solos. Sickler has one of Joe Henderson's solos. There are also some fairly elaborate transcription books from a series originally published under the auspices of *Down Beat* magazine. It includes *Jazz Styles and Analysis: Guitar* by Jack Petersen (74 solos from 64 guitarists), *Jazz Styles and Analysis: Alto Sax* by Harry Miedema (125 solos from 103 saxophonists), and *Jazz Styles and Analysis: Trombone* by David Baker (157 solos). Aebersold distributes so many more such books, you ought to just send him a letter listing the soloists you seek. Then, with your letter, include a stamped post card addressed to you, and ask Aebersold to return the postcard with the availability and price written on it so that you can order what you want that he has. When this book went to press, Aebersold was carrying books of solos by Stan Getz, Chick Corea, Louis Armstrong, Bill Evans, Horace Silver, Benny Goodman, Art Tatum, J. J. Johnson, Charlie Parker, Thelonious Monk, Bud Powell, Paul Chambers, Dexter Gordon, and others. Simply write Jamey Aebersold at 1211X Aebersold Drive, New Albany, Ind. 47150. (The same advice about the post card applies to dealing with Andrew White. In fact, White has been known to transcribe solos on demand. So if you want to pay for something that is not already in his catalog, consider commissioning it from him.)

Many solo transcriptions can be found in doctoral dissertations. These are books written to earn a doctor's degree. Most are never commercially published. However, when the doctor's degree is granted, most dissertations are automatically deposited with a company called University Microfilms, which permanently retains one copy and then makes and sells additional copies on demand. This has been occurring only since 1956, so do not contact University Microfilms for work completed before then. University of Chicago, Harvard University, and Massachusetts Institute of Technology are among the few institutions that do not contribute to this repository.

To get a dissertation, write University Microfilms International, 300 Zeeb Road, Ann Arbor, Michigan 48106. Tell them the author's name (it helps to have the middle initial), the first two words of the title, the college where the dissertation was done, and the year it was completed. This information, or at least the first two parts of it, help them identify the dissertation when you lack the catalog number. When you correspond with them, tell them your college affiliation because they extend a discount to students and faculty. If you do not want to write them, you can phone them at their toll-free number (1-800-521-3042; from Michigan, Alaska, and Hawaii: 313-761-4700; from Canada: 1-800-268-6090) and you can even order them to bill your credit card.

You will probably come across many titles of books, articles, and dissertations that you just want to glance at and not necessarily own (most cost more than 20 dollars). For that reason, it is handy to know about interlibrary loan services. If you have never used such a service, ask the staff at your college library reference desk. The staff should have a computer that will tell what nearby library is holding the book, article, or dissertation you want. The staff can put in a request, then you need wait only a few days or weeks before your library receives it for you. Then you can check it out just as you would check out one of your own library's holdings. Note that if you want only a single article from a periodical, your interlibrary loan staff can sometimes arrange for a distant library to copy the article and send it for you to keep. (This can be quite convenient when you want a particularly good transcription that lies in an old jazz magazine that no one in town seems to have.)

To keep up with new dissertations that are being added to the literature about jazz, you could scan the music listings in your library's current copies of *Dissertation Abstracts*. This is a periodical that publishes summaries of dissertations that have just been completed.

Here are a few dissertations that have many transcriptions in them:

Charlie Parker: Techniques of Improvisation, by Thomas Owens, 1974, University of California
Catalog Number 75-1992
(Contains about 250 Parker solos)

A History and Analysis of Jazz Drumming to 1942, by Theodore Dennis Brown, 1976, University of Michigan
Catalog Number 77-7881
(Contains numerous drum solos and timekeeping rhythms as well as analyses.)

The Improvisational Techniques of Art Tatum, by Joseph A. Howard, 1978, Case Western Reserve University
Catalog Number 78-16468
(Contains analyses of the "Willow Weep for Me" and "Too Marvelous for Words" solos that are in SCCJ plus 240 more. It also boasts an appendix of the melodies and chord progressions for many popular tunes, a feature that amounts to what musicians ordinarily call a "fakebook.")

Structural Development in the Jazz Improvisational Technique of Clifford Brown, by Milton Lee Stewart, 1973, University of Michigan
Catalog Number 73-24692

John Coltrane's Music of 1960 Through 1967, by Lewis R. Porter, 1983, Brandeis University
Catalog Number 83-18239

Jazz, 1920 to 1927: An Analytical Study, by Launcelot Allen Pyke, II, 1962, State University of Iowa
Catalog Number 62-4988
(Contains transcriptions of 1926 "Perdido Street Blues" with Kid Ory, Johnny Dodds and Baby Dodds, 1923 "Snake Rag" by King Oliver's Creole Jazz Band, 1942 "Down By the Riverside" by Bunk Johnson's Original Superior Band, 1927 "Keyhole Blues" by Louis Armstrong and His Hot Seven, the 1923 Gennett recording of "Dippermouth Blues" by King Oliver's Creole Jazz Band, 1924 "Cake Walkin' Babies" by Armstrong and Bechet, 1926 "Big Butter and Egg Man From The West" by Louis Armstrong and His Hot Five, 1923 "Sweet Lovin' Man" by King Oliver's Creole Jazz Band minus Oliver, 1925 "Papa De-Da-Da" by Armstrong and Bechet, and 1923 "Southern Stomps" by Oliver's Creole Jazz Band.)

FOR MUSICIANS

This section is designed to give musically literate readers a chance to experience some of the musical elements discussed in the text. It is possible to learn more by playing the examples at the piano than by simply reading the attached explanations. After you have played these figures yourself, they will be easier to hear in jazz recordings.

Chords and Chord Progressions

We can imagine chords as being built by tones in major scales (Bb C D Eb F G A Bb or C D E F G A B C or D E F♯ G A B C♯ D). Beginning with a single tone, the chord is made by adding every other tone in the scale. In other words, the first, third, and fifth tones are used when the beginning tone is the key note (first tone of major scale). The second, fourth, and sixth tones are used when the chord is based on the second step of the scale. The third, fifth, and seventh tones are used when the chord begins on the third step of the scale.

If a chord is based on the first tone of the major scale, it is called the "one chord," symbolized by the Roman numeral for one, I. (Roman numerals are used for chord names.) The chord based on the second step of the major scale is a II chord. The labeling system continues through the VII chord.

415

Of course, there is more to it than that. Before you can apply chord knowledge to studying improvisation, you must become acquainted with the construction of many types of chords: dominant sevenths and major sevenths; major, minor, diminished, and augmented chords; chords with added ninths, elevenths, and thirteenths; chords with added fourths and sixths, flat fifths, raised ninths, etc. And there is a collection of different chord labeling systems which also must be confronted.

Twelve-Bar Blues Progressions Though basically a I-IV-I-V-I progression, the twelve-bar blues may contain a huge assortment of chord progressions. Here are three possibilities for a blues in the key of C.

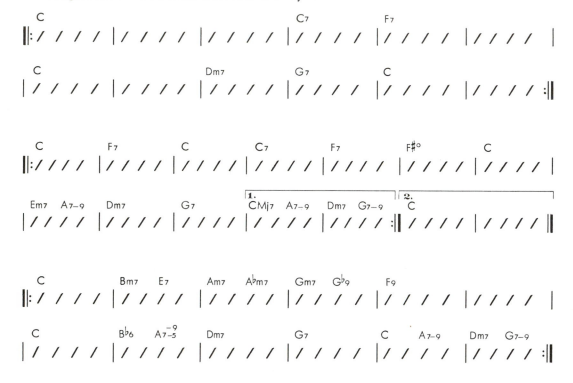

Turnarounds Turnarounds are the chord progressions occurring in the seventh and eighth, fifteenth and sixteenth, thirty-first and thirty-second bars of a thirty-two-bar chord progression, and in the eleventh and twelfth bars of a twelve-bar blues progression. Some turnarounds occupy more or less than two measures, however. Turnarounds provide an opportunity for numerous variations, which depend on the preferences and era of soloist and rhythm section.

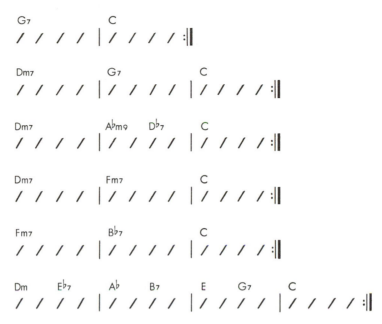

Voicing Rarely is a chord played with its tones contained in a single octave, the root on the bottom, the third in the middle, and the fifth on the top.

Usually chords are voiced. This means that the positions of a chord's tones are scattered over the keyboard; the tones may be altered, doubled, added to, missing, and so forth. Instead of having the root on the bottom and the fifth on the top, a chord might have its root on top and fifth on the bottom.

Or perhaps the third is on the bottom with the fifth next and the root on top.

In some voicings, the root is doubled by being duplicated in different octaves.

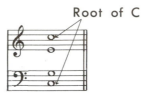

Quite frequently the sixth is added to enrich major triads.

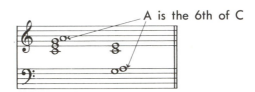

Instead of being voiced in thirds (every other step in a major scale), some chords are voiced in fourths.

There are a great variety of possibilities available in voicing chords. Only a few simple examples have been cited as an introduction. In addition to striking force, phrasing, speed, and precision, an important characteristic of a jazz pianist's style is his preference in voicings. For instance, McCoy Tyner often uses an interval of a fifth in the left hand together with a chord voiced in fourths in the right hand.

Modes   Though used for centuries in classical music, modes just recently became popular harmonic bases for jazz improvisation. Modes are constructed using the tones for the major scale, and different modes are produced by starting on different notes of the scale. Each mode's unique sound is the result of its particular arrangement of whole steps and half steps. For example, in the Ionian mode (also known as the major scale), half steps occur only between the third and fourth tones and the seventh and eighth (an octave up from the first) tones.

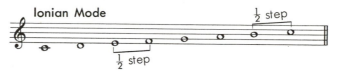

Ionian Mode

The Dorian mode is constructed from the same tones as the Ionian, but it begins on the second tone of the major scale. The Dorian mode has half steps between its second and third and its sixth and seventh tones.

Dorian Mode

There is a mode for each step of the major scale. Each mode has a distinct musical personality because its half steps fall in different places.

Examine the following modes, play them and listen carefully. Find the position of the half steps in each mode. Once you know a mode's pattern of whole and half steps, you should be able to begin it on other notes. Remember that the interval between Bb and C is defined as a whole step as is that between E and F#. Remember also that the interval between B and C is a half step as is that between E and F.

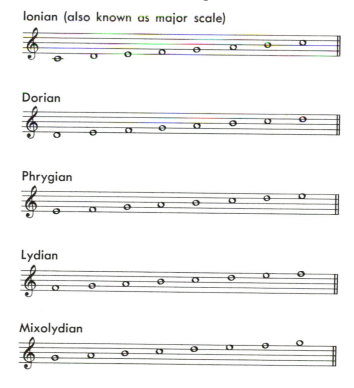

Ionian (also known as major scale)

Dorian

Phrygian

Lydian

Mixolydian

Aeolian (also known as ancient, minor, pure, natural)

Locrian

Arabian

Gypsy

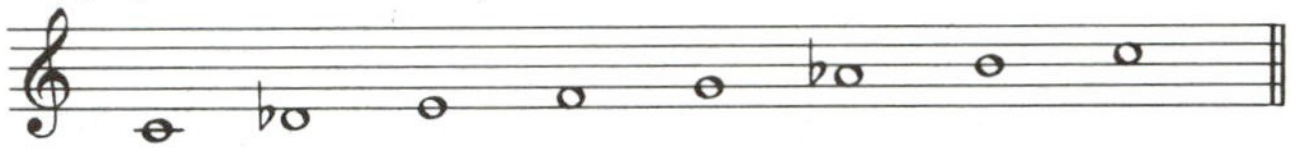

Hungarian

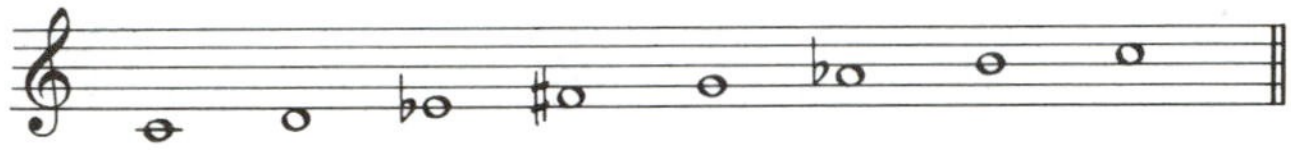

Byzantine

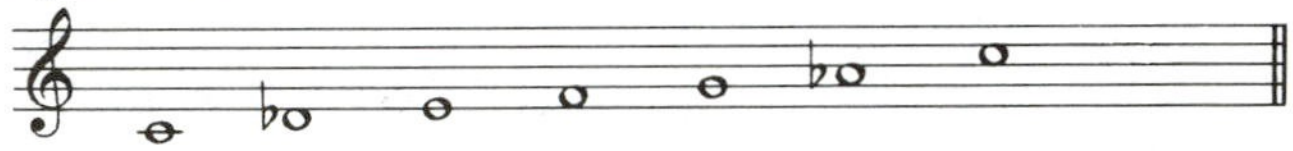

Persian

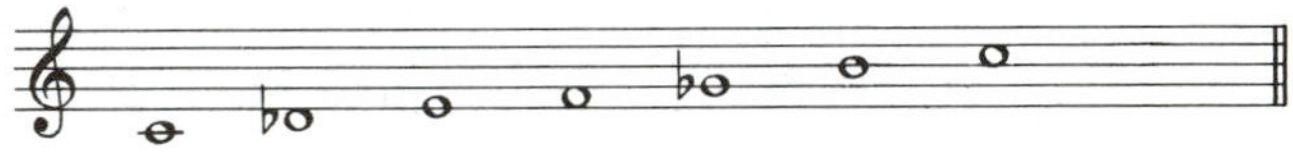

Balinese

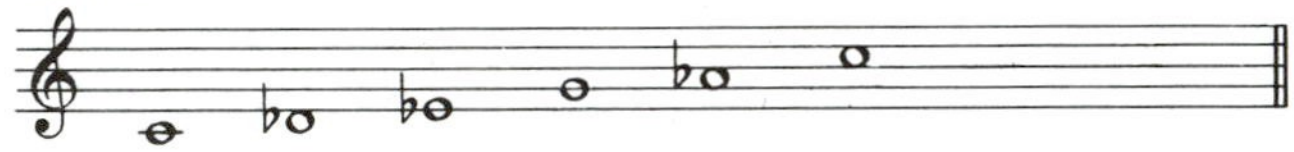

Spanish

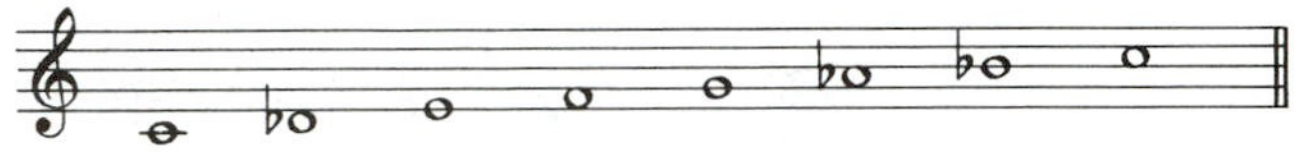

Chinese

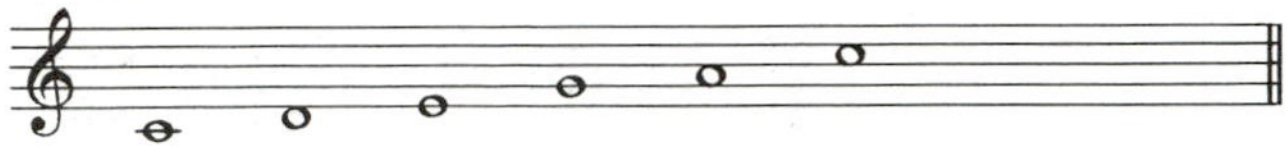

Jewish

Pentatonic

Whole Tone

Diminished

Inverted Diminished

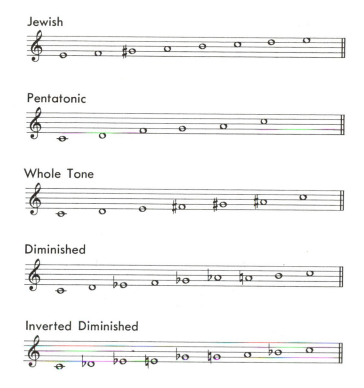

Modal Construction of "All Blues"   The piece "All Blues" on the Miles Davis album *Kind of Blue* follows the modal construction illustrated below. (Note that the piece was mislabeled "Flamenco Sketches" on many copies.)

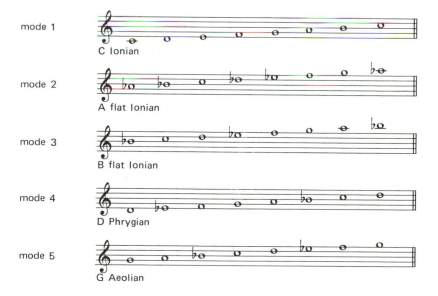

mode 1 — C Ionian

mode 2 — A flat Ionian

mode 3 — B flat Ionian

mode 4 — D Phrygian

mode 5 — G Aeolian

Modal Construction of "Maiden Voyage"

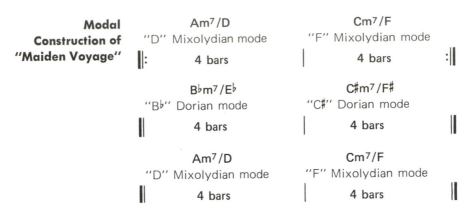

Am⁷/D
"D" Mixolydian mode
‖: 4 bars

Cm⁷/F
"F" Mixolydian mode
4 bars :‖

B♭m⁷/E♭
"B♭" Dorian mode
‖ 4 bars

C♯m⁷/F♯
"C♯" Dorian mode
4 bars ‖

Am⁷/D
"D" Mixolydian mode
‖ 4 bars

Cm⁷/F
"F" Mixolydian mode
4 bars ‖

"D" Mixolydian, first mode for A section of "Maiden Voyage" Am⁷/D

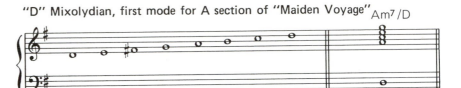

"F" Mixolydian, second mode for A section of "Maiden Voyage" Cm⁷/F

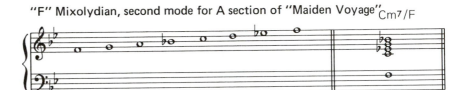

"B♭" Dorian, first mode for bridge of "Maiden Voyage"   B♭m⁷/E♭

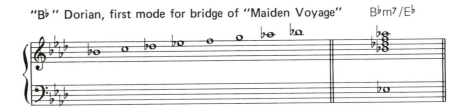

"C♯" Dorian, second mode for bridge of "Maiden Voyage"   C♯m⁷/F♯

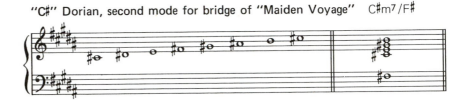

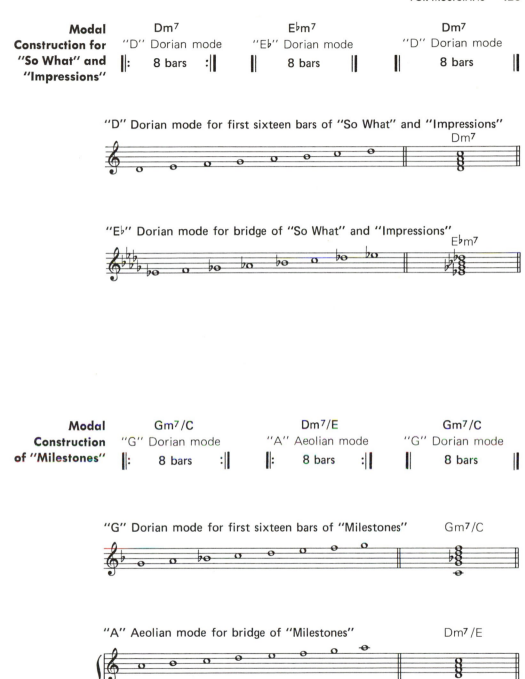

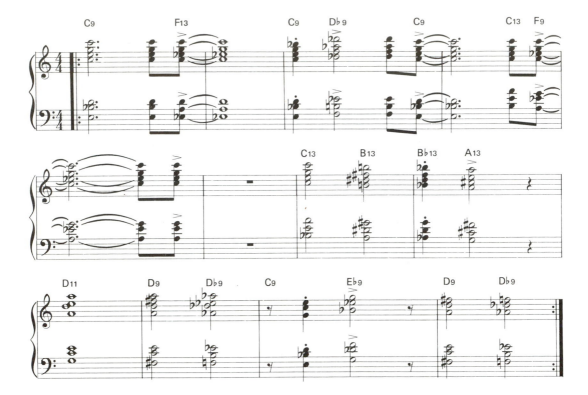

Piano comping for 12-bar blues in the key of C (conceived and notated by Willis Lyman).

Comping Here are two examples of piano accompaniments, or comping, for a modern jazz twelve-bar blues solo. Comping is accompaniment simultaneously composed and performed to fit the style of a piece, and harmonic and rhythmic directions of the solo line. Comping usually contains pronounced syncopation.

Note that these chords have been voiced. Comping involves countless ways to voice chords, alter chord progressions, and design rhythms. But basically, comping is meant to accompany and complement the solo line by producing syncopated, unpatterned bursts of chords. Patterned chording, by definition, cannot flexibly enhance a spontaneously conceived solo line. Prewritten patterns (and accompanying figures which sound prewritten) cannot sensitively interact with solo improvisation. The improvising soloist might just as well be playing with a

Piano comping for 12-bar blues in the key of F (conceived and notated by Jerry Sheer).

big band using written arrangements. (For examples of comping which sensitively interact with and enhance improvised solos, listen to Tommy Flanagan and Herbie Hancock. For examples of accompanying which are not comping in the sense used above but are more like prewritten material, listen to post-1960 Horace Silver and to John Lewis's work with the Modern Jazz Quartet.)

Walking Bass Lines Walking is meant to provide timekeeping in the form of tones chosen for their compatibility with the harmonies of the piece and style of the performance. Ideally, the walking bass complements the solo line.

Three choruses of walking bass are shown here. They display three levels of complexity.

Walking bass lines for the 12-bar blues in the key of C (conceived and notated by Willis Lyman).

Rock Bass Lines Jazz bassists of the 1970s incorporated many devices which were previously used mainly by rock bassists. A number of rock bass figures are notated here to illustrate the material from which many 1970s jazz bassists drew.

Rock bass figures (notated by Richard Straub).

Latin American Bass Line   During performances of many jazz pieces of the 1950s and 60s, including the first eight bars of "On Green Dolphin Street" and "I'll Remember April," bassists employed a figure like the one below which was called a "Latin bass figure."

Syncopations   The rhythms common to jazz contain many syncopations. Here is a collection of examples.

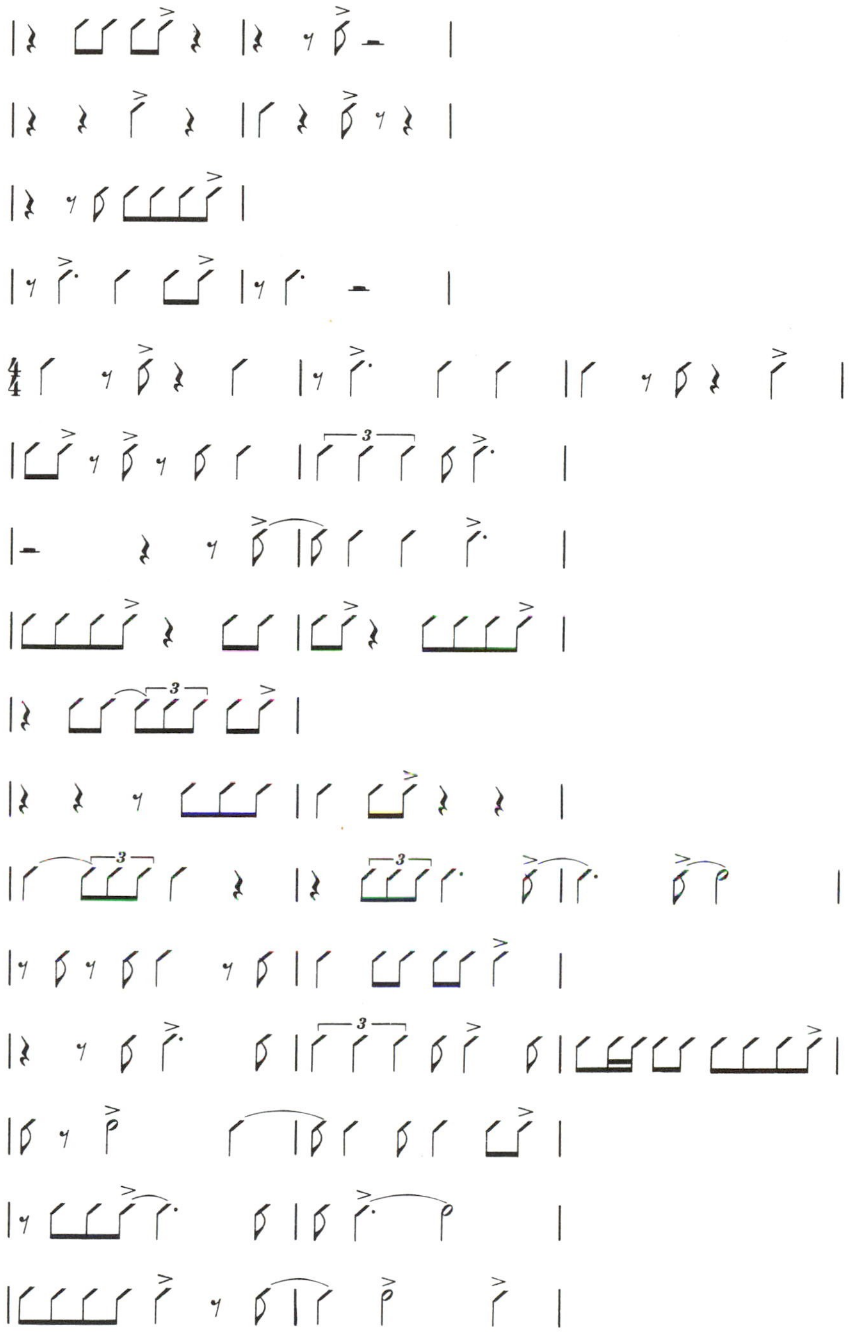
3
4/4

Ride Rhythms Ride rhythms are used by drummers to keep time and propel a performance. These rhythms contribute to jazz swing feeling, accomplishing in the high register (cymbals) what the walking bass does in the low register.

Basic Jazz Ride Rhythm Common in Slow and Medium Tempos (4-Beat Feel)*

Basic Jazz Ride Rhythm Common in Fast Tempos (4-Beat Feel)

VARIATIONS:
Medium Tempos — Elvin Jones

Medium Tempos — Roy Haynes

Fast Tempos — Billy Higgins

Fast Tempos — Roy Haynes

Basic Jazz Ride Rhythm Used to Imply 2-Beat Feel

*NOTE: The 12/8 figures are notated from 4/4 tunes. (Transcribed by Chuck Braman.)

Jazz-Rock Drumming Drummers since the late 1960s learned new timekeeping patterns which resembled the materials of r & b as well as Latin American styles.

Andy Newmark — "In Time" from Sly Stone's *Fresh* 1973

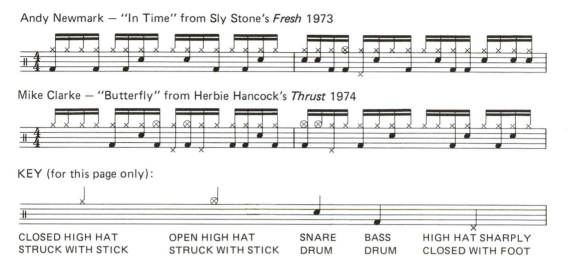

Mike Clarke — "Butterfly" from Herbie Hancock's *Thrust* 1974

KEY (for this page only):

| CLOSED HIGH HAT STRUCK WITH STICK | OPEN HIGH HAT STRUCK WITH STICK | SNARE DRUM | BASS DRUM | HIGH HAT SHARPLY CLOSED WITH FOOT |

(Transcribed by Chuck Braman.)

A SMALL BASIC RECORD COLLECTION*

Louis Armstrong and Earl Hines, 1928 Smithsonian 2002
Sidney Bechet—Master Musician RCA AXM2-5516
The Bix Beiderbecke Story Vol.2—Bix and Tram Columbia CL 845
This Is Duke Ellington RCA VPM-6042
The Best of Count Basie MCA2-4050
Benny Goodman—Carnegie Hall Jazz Concert Columbia OSL-160
Dizzy Gillespie—The Development of an American Artist Smithsonian 2004
The Genius of Bud Powell Verve VE2-2506
Charlie Parker—Bird—The Savoy Recordings Savoy 2201
Thelonious Monk—The Complete Genius Liberty(Blue Note) 579
Woody Herman's Greatest Hits Columbia PC 9291
Miles Davis—The Complete Birth of the Cool Capitol N-16168
First Sessions(Konitz,Tristano) Prestige P-24081
Gerry Mulligan—Freeway Liberty LT-1101
Stan Kenton—New Concepts of Artistry in Rhythm Creative World 1002
Dave Brubeck—The Fantasy Years Atlantic SD2-317 or Fantasy (OJC) 046
Sonny Rollins—Saxophone Colossus and More Prestige P-24050
Clifford Brown and Max Roach Mercury EXPR-1033
Art Blakey and the Jazz Messengers Columbia PC 37021
Charles Mingus—Better Git It in Your Soul Columbia CG 30628
Ornette Coleman—The Shape of Jazz to Come Atlantic SD 1317
Miles Davis—Kind of Blue Columbia PC 8163
John Coltrane—Giant Steps Atlantic SD 1311
Bill Evans—The Village Vanguard Sessions Milestone M-47002
John Coltrane—Live at Birdland MCA(Impulse)-29015
The Heliocentric Worlds of Sun Ra ESP Disk 1014 & 1017
Albert Ayler—Spiritual Unity ESP Disk 1002
Miles Davis—Sorcerer Columbia PC 9532
John Coltrane—Interstellar Space MCA(Impulse)-29029
The Best of Herbie Hancock Liberty(Blue Note) 89907
Miles Davis—Live-Evil Columbia CG 30954
Chick Corea—Now He Sings, Now He Sobs Liberty LN-10057
Cecil Taylor—Fly,Fly,Fly! Pausa 7108
Keith Jarrett—Staircase ECM-2-1090
Weather Report—I Sing the Body Electric Columbia PC 31352
The Smithsonian Collection of Classic Jazz Smithsonian 2100

* This is a list of suggested buys for listeners who want only one good, representative album for a major style. Miles Davis has four entries here not because he is four times as important as anyone else, but because these particular albums do a fine job of illustrating four separate and historically significant group approaches to jazz. The same reasoning applies to the three entries for John Coltrane. The collection comprises a bare minimum introduction to jazz history.

INDEX

A-A-B-A, 31–32, 111, 114, 122, 131, 150, 155, 170, 195, 217, 303, 378, 380, 382, 386–388
AACM, 234, 268–278
Aarons, Al, 133
Abrams, Richard, 273
Adams, Pepper, 192, 194, 249
Adderley, Cannonball, 152, 192, 201, 213, 216–222, 295–296, 322, 329
Adderley, Nat, 67, 192, 212
AFRICA/BRASS, 248
African music, 8, 40–55
Afro-Blue, 292
Afro-Cuban music, 153
AFRO–EURASIAN ECLIPSE, 121
After You've Gone, 96
AGHARTA, 210, 325
A Good Man Is Hard to Find, 79
Ain't Misbehavin', 65
Air Conditioning, 151
Airegin, 200, 339
Akyoshi, Toshiko, 112
Albany, Joe, 147
Ali, Rashied, 240
All about Rosie, 251
All Blues, 218–222, 421
All the Things You Are, 148, 283
All Too Soon, 119
Allen, Henry Red, 58, 87

Allen, Marshall, 240, 272
alto saxophone, 88, 99, 118–119, 183, 192, 201–202, 226–234, 246, 248–249
Altschul, Barry, 239, 260
Ammons, Albert, 66
Ammons, Gene, 135, 147, 168
ANATOMY OF A MURDER, 108, 124
Anderson, Cat, 93, 112, 116
Anderson, Fred, 273
antiphonal style, 88, 401
A.R.C., 239
arco, 16, 401
Armstrong, Lil Hardin, 58
Armstrong, Louis, 45, 57–60, 63, 67–77, 97, 140, 172, 232
Arodin, Sidney, 58
Arp synthesizer, 330
Arrival in New York, 330
Art Ensemble of Chicago, 239, 274–275
Artistry in Rhythm, 344
ASCENSION, 272, 286, 334
Ashby, Harold, 112
Ashby, Irving, 87
ASPHALT JUNGLE, 108
ASSAULT ON A QUEEN, 108
AT THE BAL MASQUE, 124
AT THE GOLDEN CIRCLE, 231
At the Woodchopper's Ball, 348
atonal, 369, 401

attack, 49, 51, 401
attitude of informality, 53
Au Privave, 151
Auld, Georgie, 87
Austin High Gang, The, 57–59
Autrey, Herman, 87
Ayers, Roy, 320
Ayler, Albert, 10, 151, 214, 226, 233–236, 240, 260, 274, 276, 281
Ayler, Don, 240

Bach, J. S., 9
Badia, 331
Bags' Groove, 209
Bailey, Benny, 147, 192
Bailey, Buster, 58, 87
Baker, Chet, 183, 185, 198, 212
Baker, David, 166, 198, 201–202
Baker, Ginger, 325
Baker, Harold Shorty, 87, 108, 112
Bakiff, 122, 124
Ball, Ronnie, 181
ballad, 401
banjo, 46–47, 77, 79, 90
Barbados, 151
Barbarin, Paul, 58
Barbary Coast, 337
Barbieri, Gato, 240, 290, 296
baritone saxophone, 77, 88, 119, 183–185, 192

Barnet, Charlie, 87, 112, 118, 296, 349
Bartók, Béla, 262
Bartz, Gary, 208
Basie, Count, 45, 49, 57, 63, 65, 87, 90, 105, 128–142, 143, 148, 160, 163, 177, 344–346, 349, 352–354
bass clarinet, 271
bass drum, 20, 80, 90, 145
bass guitar, 15–17
bass saxophone, 77–79, 88, 274–275
bass viol, 15–17, 86, 112, 121–122, 160, 183, 192, 204–205, 214, 239–241, 243–250, 253–256, 293, 302–303
bassoon, 271
Bauduc, Ray, 58
Bauer, Billy, 147, 179
Beatles, The, 316
bebop, 401
Bebop, 145
Bechet, Sidney, 45, 52, 57–58, 74, 118, 172, 296
Bedspread, 246
Beiderbecke, Bix, 57, 67, 71–74, 77, 83
Beirach, Richie, 265
Bell, Aaron, 112
Bellson, Louis, 87, 95, 112, 120, 133
Beneke, Tex, 87
Benson, George, 25, 69, 208, 322
Berg, Bob, 196–197
Berger, Karl, 157
Berigan, Bunny, 71, 87, 94, 97
Berlin, Jeff, 320
Berman, Sonny, 147
Bernhardt, Warren, 224, 252
Bernhart, Milt, 183–184
Berry, Chu, 87
Berry, Emmett, 133
Berton, Vic, 58
Best, Denzil, 147
Better Git It in Your Soul, 245
Bigard, Barney, 60, 87, 112–115, 122
big band, 401
big band era, 86–146
big band instrumentation, 88
BIG BAND JAZZ, 93
BIG FUN, 322
Biggest and Busiest Intersection, The, 121
Billie's Bounce, 151
Billy Boy, 214
Bird Calls, 247
Bird Feathers, 151
Bird Gets the Worm, 149
Birdland, 329–330, 339, 351

BIRDS OF FIRE, 326–327
Birth of the Blues, 382
BIRTH OF THE COOL, 181–182, 207, 210, 215
Bishop, Walter, 147, 210
BITCHES BREW, 207, 307, 321–323, 329
Black and Tan Fantasy, 107, 122
Black Artists Group, The, 276
BLACK BEAUTY, 260
Black Bottom Stomp, 63, 79
Black, Brown and Beige, 108, 116
Black Byrds, The, 320
black classical music, 11
BLACK MARKET, 308
Blackthorn Rose, 331
Blackwell, Eddie, 228, 233, 240, 286
Blakey, Art, 28, 195–196, 202–203, 210, 224, 262, 272, 308
Blanchard, Terence, 212
Blanton, Jimmy, 87, 109, 112, 115, 143, 160, 217, 243–244, 246, 253
Bley, Paul, 189, 229, 233, 240, 252, 260, 263
block chording, 102–103
block voicing, 92
Blood, Sweat and Tears, 318–319
Bloomdido, 151
Blue and Sentimental, 136
Blue Cellophane, 120
Blue Devils, The, 132
Blue Horizon, 52, 75
Blue in Green, 208, 217, 223
blue note, 52–54, 115–116, 370–372, 401
Blue Serge, 119
Blue Seven, 199
blues, 41, 313, 377, 380, 382, 401, 416
blues poetry, 377, 379
Blues in C♯ Minor, 96, 101
Blues in Thirds, 65
Blues to Bechet, 75
bluesy quality, 369
Bluiett, Hamiet, 276
Bluing, 36
Blythe, Jimmy, 58
Bobcats, The, 60
Body and Soul, 32, 34, 36, 93, 97, 101, 150
Bojangles, 108
Bolden, Buddy, 58, 60
bombs, 161–162, 401
Bonner, Joe, 293
boogie-woogie, 49, 66, 137, 401
Boogie Woogie Waltz, 309, 336
bop, 401
BOP-BE, 264

Boplicity, 209
Bostic, Earl, 87, 118, 281, 313
Boston, 178
Bothwell, Johnny, 118
Bowie, Lester, 212, 240, 274–275
Boy Meets Horn, 53, 116
Boyd, Manny, 296
Boyd, Nelson, 147
Brackeen, Charles, 233
Brackeen, Joanne, 293
Bradford, Bobby, 233, 240
Brand, Dollar, 157
Braud, Wellman, 58, 87, 112
Braxton, Anthony, 240, 260, 276
break, 402
Brecker, Michael, 296, 320
Brecker, Randy, 197, 212, 319–320
bridge, 31, 378, 386, 402
Brignola, Nick, 192
broken time, 17, 402
Brookmeyer, Bob, 53, 166, 188, 353
Brooks, Roy, 192, 197
Brooks, Tina, 192
Brown, Clifford, 166, 193–194, 197–198, 202–203, 212, 236
Brown, James, 44, 313, 316, 318–319, 340
Brown, Lawrence, 87, 108, 120
Brown, Marion, 233, 240
Brown, Pete, 87
Brown, Ray, 147
Brown, Ted, 181
Brown, Theodore Dennis, 90
Browne, Tom, 197, 320
Brubeck, Dave, 186–188, 334
Bruce, Jack, 319
Brunis, George, 58
brushes, 80–81, 90, 113, 123, 219
Buckner, Milt, 87, 102, 164
Budo, 163
Bud's Bubble, 149
Budwig, Monty, 183
Burns, Ralph, 147
Burrell, Kenny, 194, 205
Burton, Gary, 317, 319, 320, 327–328
Butterfield, Billy, 60
BYABLUE, 264
Byas, Don, 36, 87, 98, 100, 120, 133, 143, 167–169, 193, 232
Bye Bye Blackbird, 208
Byers, Billy, 133
Byrd, Donald, 192, 194, 203, 320

Cables, George, 203, 256

Caceres, Ernie, 87
Cage, John, 10, 276
Cake Walkin' Babies from
    Home, 35, 45, 47, 67, 75
Caldera, 320
California, 178, 182–194
call and response, 45
Callender, Red, 147
Calloway, Cab, 87, 144, 153
Candlelights, 72
Candoli, Conte, 147, 153, 183–
    184, 347
Caravan, 122, 124
Carey, Mutt, 58
Carisi, John, 182
Carmen, 150, 152
Carney, Harry, 108, 111, 112,
    119, 122
Carolina Shout, 61
Carter, Benny, 87, 92, 99, 133
Carter, John, 233
Carter, Ron, 194, 210, 301–306,
    321
Casbah, 157
Casey, Al, 87
Catlett, Buddy, 133
Catlett, Sid, 81, 87, 161
Caution Blues, 65
Celia, 163
Chaloff, Serge, 133, 147, 348
Chambers, Paul, 194, 204, 210,
    212–222
Chameleon, 339, 351
Chancler, Leon, 320
CHANGE OF MIND, 108
CHANGE OF THE
    CENTURY, 236
channel, 31
Charles, Dennis, 240
Charles, Ray, 313, 318, 330
Charles, Teddy, 189, 212
Chasin' the Trane, 281, 286
Chattaway, Jay, 351
chatter, 81, 161–162, 237
Chelsea Bridge, 119, 122
Cherokee, 148, 383
Cherry, Don, 233, 236–237,
    240–241, 274, 286
Chicago, 57–63, 67–68, 74, 81,
    268–278
Chicago Jazz, 61
Chicago style, 59, 71
Chicago Transit Authority, 318–
    319
chops, 402
chord, 372–373
chord progressions, 31–33, 373–
    374, 402, 415
chord voicing, 374–377
chorus, 31, 383, 402
Christian, Charlie, 87, 93, 103–
    104, 143, 205
Christmas Song, 32

Chromatic Love Affair, 119
chromatic scale, 368
Cinelu, Mino, 323
Circle, 260
City of Glass, 9, 346
C-Jam Blues, 116
clarinet, 57–58, 74–76, 88, 109–
    110, 112–113, 134, 145,
    165, 271
Clarinet Lament, 113
Clarinet Marmalade, 47, 80, 82
Clarke, Buddy, 151, 183
Clarke, Kenny, 28, 158, 161–162
Clarke, Stanley, 261, 319–320
Classic Jazz, 61
clavinet, 329
Clay, James, 313
Clayton, Buck, 71, 87, 132–133,
    140
Cleveland, Jimmy, 192
C-Melody saxophone, 25, 73,
    235
Coates, John, 263
Cobb, Arnett, 136
Cobb, Jimmy, 192, 210, 216,
    219–224
Cobham, Billy, 197, 319–320,
    340
Cochran, Michael, 293
cohesive group sound, 6
Cohn, Al, 135, 147, 184
Cohn, Sonny, 133
Coker, Henry, 133
Cole, Cozy, 87
Cole, Nat, 63, 69, 87, 101–102,
    143, 162–163, 165
Coleman, George, 169, 192,
    208, 291
Coleman, Ornette, 10, 36, 151,
    180, 189, 223, 226–236,
    260, 262, 268, 272–276,
    286, 338
Coles, Johnny, 112, 212, 257
collective approach, 45, 57, 70,
    75, 86, 233, 270, 286, 335,
    402
Collette, Buddy, 135, 168, 183
Collins, Johnny, 147
Collins, Shad, 133
Coloratura, 117
Coltrane, Alice, 293
COLTRANE JAZZ, 281
Coltrane, John, 15, 28, 37, 52,
    75, 97, 118–119, 151–152,
    154, 157, 194, 198, 212–
    222, 226, 240, 260, 272,
    275, 279–300, 307, 324,
    385
Comin' Home Baby, 206
comping, 18, 90, 130–131, 138,
    145, 156, 160, 402, 424–
    425
Con Alma, 148, 153, 222, 284

Conception, 165, 210
Concertino for Jazz Quartet and
    Orchestra, 158
Concerto for Cootie, 107, 109,
    116, 122
Concierto de Aranjuez, 216
Condon, Eddie, 58, 60
CONFERENCE OF THE
    BIRDS, 239
Confirmation, 151
Conga Brava, 122
Congeniality, 235, 239
Conners, Bill, 261
constant tempo, 6
Cook, Junior, 192
Cook, Willie, 112
COOKIN', 212
cool jazz, 177–190, 402
Cooper, Bob, 135, 168, 183, 184
Cooper, Buster, 112
Copenhagen, 67
Coquette, 150
Corea, Chick, 28, 157, 195, 210,
    239, 251–253, 266, 293,
    295, 319, 339
cornet, 66–67
Coryell, Larry, 186, 208, 317,
    319, 327–328
COSMIC SCENE, 110, 117,
    120
Cottontail, 110–112, 119
Counce, Curtis, 183
Countdown, 283, 295
counterpoint, 47–48, 138, 160,
    402
COUNTRY ROADS AND
    OTHER PLACES, 328
Country Son, 306
cowbell, 80, 90
Cowell, Stanley, 293
Cox, Kenny, 304
Cranshaw, Bob, 192, 240
crash cymbal, 18–21
Crawford, Hank, 313
Crawford, Jimmy, 87
Crazeology, 149
Crazy about Jazz, 337
Creative World, 345
Creole, 402
Creole Love Call, 110, 116
Creole Rhapsody, 107
Creoles of Color, 39–41
Criss Cross, 156
Criss, Sonny, 147, 152
Crosby, Bing, 71
Crosby, Bob, 60
Crosby, Israel, 87
Crosscurrent, 180
CROSSINGS, 257–258
Crothers, Connie, 181
Crusaders, The Jazz, 320
cry, the, 281
Crystal Silence, 261

CUBAN FIRE, 346
Cubano Be, Cubano Bop, 154
cuica, 333
Culley, Wendell, 133
Curson, Ted, 212, 240, 247
Curtis, King, 313
cymbals, 19–22, 48, 90, 161–162
Cyrille, Andrew, 238

Daahoud, 203
Dameron, Tadd, 147, 153, 157, 193, 285
Dameronia, 157
Dance of the Infidels, 163
Dapogny, James, 61–63
Dara Factor One, 337
Dat Dere, 206
Davenport, 57, 72
Davenport, Cow Cow, 58, 66
Davidson, Wild Bill, 58
Davis, Anthony, 112, 157
Davis, Danny, 240
Davis, Eddie Lockjaw, 119, 133
Davis, Miles, 14, 28, 36, 45, 51, 53, 143, 151, 157, 165–166, 177–178, 181–182, 189, 193, 198, 207–225, 239, 251, 260, 262, 301–311, 319–325, 331, 351
Davis, Nathan, 296
Davis, Richard, 352
Davis, Steve, 289
Day Dream, 124
Dead Man Blues, 79
DeArango, Bill, 147
DEATH AND THE FLOWER, 266
Debussy, Claude, 72–73, 102, 104, 305
decay, 50, 402
Deception, 165, 222
Decoding Society, The, 320
decorative two feel, 254
Dee Dee, 223, 231
Deep South Suite, 125
DeFranco, Buddy, 165
DeJohnette, Jack, 28, 210
DeParis, Sidney, 58
DeParis, Wilbur, 58
Desafinado, 170
Desmond, Paul, 186
Detroit, 194
Dickenson, Vic, 87, 133
Dickie's Dream, 140
Dig, 202
Digression, 180
Dimeola, Al, 261, 319–320
Dippermouth Blues, 45, 53, 66, 74, 81
Dis Here, 206
Dixieland, 57–61, 139, 145, 402
Dixon, Bill, 240

Dixon, Eric, 133
Django, 104, 158
Do Nothin' 'Til You Hear from Me, 116
Doctor Jackle, 202
Dodds, Baby, 59–60, 79–83
Dodds, Johnny, 59–60, 74
Doggin' Around, 90, 136
doit, 52
Dolores, 37, 214, 223, 304
Dolphy, Eric, 152, 186, 198, 233, 240, 248, 276, 352
Donaldson, Lou, 152, 192, 203
Donna, 202
Donna Lee, 149, 151, 338
Don't Get Around Much Anymore, 107
Dorham, Kenny, 147, 151, 153, 192–193
Dorian mode, 368
Dorsey, Jimmy, 61, 87
Dorsey, Tommy, 61, 66, 87, 94, 347
Double Image, 322
double stop, 16, 293, 402
double-time figures, 65
double-timing, 34, 402
Down among the Sheltering Palms, 65
Down South Camp Meeting, 93
Doxy, 195, 200, 383
Dream Clock, 337
Drew, Kenny, 192
DRUM IS A WOMAN, A, 125
drum kit, 22
drums, 17–23, 48, 79–83, 120–121, 129, 161–162, 183, 186, 188, 192, 214–215, 224, 238–239, 255, 290–293, 303
Dual Fuel, 121
Durham, Eddie, 87, 132, 133
Dukes, George, 320
Dunlop, Frankie, 192
DUSTER, 327
Dutrey, Honore, 58, 60

Eager, Allen, 135, 147, 168
Eager Beaver, 344
Early Autumn, 169, 348
early jazz, 56–86
East Coast piano tradition, 57
East St. Louis Toodle-Oo, 110, 116, 122
Easy Does It, 95
Echoes of Harlem, 116
Echoplex, 325, 329
Eckstine, Billy, 87, 143–144
edge, 6
Edison, Harry Sweets, 87, 130, 133
Edwards, Eddie, 58

Edwards, Teddy, 192, 296
eight to the bar, 66
eighth note, 361
eighth note triplet, 362
Eighty-One, 209, 306–307
Eldridge, Roy, 25, 87, 95, 143, 152–153
electric bass guitar, 210, *also see* Fender bass
electric piano, 270
Eleventh House, 328
ELLINGTON AT NEWPORT, 110, 117, 120
Ellington, Duke, 48, 63, 67, 75, 83, 87, 92, 105, 107–127, 131, 155, 158, 182, 215, 217, 243–247, 254, 269, 272, 344
ELLINGTON INDIGOS, 124
Ellis, Don, 53, 158, 328, 344
Emanon, 153
Embraceable You, 36, 150
Empty Ballroom Blues, 75
endings, 35
Enevoldsen, Bob, 183
English horn, 271
Enter Evening, 237
Epistrophy, 155
Erskine, Peter, 320
Ervin, Booker, 192
E.S.P., 209, 304–307
Europe, 98
Eurydice, 333, 336
Evans, Bill, 17, 28, 33, 101, 103, 181, 195, 216–222, 224, 251–268, 291, 301
Evans, Gil, 112, 147, 158, 181–185, 215–216
Evans, Herschel, 87, 130, 132, 133, 136, 167
Evans, Stomp, 58
EVERYBODY DIGS BILL EVANS, 252
Evidence, 156
Exactly Like You, 122
EXPRESSION, 281

Fables of Faubus, 247
Faddis, Jon, 153
fall-off, 50–51
Fantasy on Frankie and Johnny, 102
FAR EAST SUITE, 121
Farlow, Tal, 147, 165
Farmer, Art, 192, 197
Farrell, Joe, 152, 261, 291, 296–297, 303, 339
Favors, Malachi, 239, 240, 274–275
FEELS SO GOOD, 341
Fender bass, 338, 340, 402, 426–427

Fender Rhodes electric piano, 329–330
Ferguson, Maynard, 93, 330, 339, 344, 347, 349–354
FESTIVAL SESSION, 110, 113, 117, 120, 121
Fifty-Seven Varieties, 65
fill, 402
FILLES DE KILIMANJARO, 22
Filthy McNasty, 196
Finnerty, Barry, 208
first take, 217
Fischer, Clare, 112, 252
Fisherman, Strawberry and Devil Crab, 211
Flamenco Sketches, 218–219
Flaming Sword, 124
Flanagan, Tommy, 192, 194, 210
Flashes, 72
flatted fifth, 148, 369, 371
Flory, Med, 152
fluegelhorn, 53, 117, 189, 215
flute, 45, 88, 270–272
Focus on Sanity, 286
Follow Your Heart, 327
Footprints, 306
For Django, 104
Foreplay, 328
Forrest, Jimmy, 133
Fortune, Sonny, 208, 296
Foss, Lukas, 10
Foster, Al, 197, 210, 323
Foster, Frank, 133, 169, 192, 194, 291, 296, 320
Foster, Pops, 58, 60
Four, 208
FOUR AND MORE, 301, 303–304
Four Brothers, 188, 348
Fourth Way, The, 317
fourths, 259, 292, 305
Fowlkes, Charlie, 133
France, 74, 103
Franklin, Aretha, 44, 313
Freddie the Freeloader, 212, 217–218
FREE JAZZ, 36, 226, 233–234, 272, 286
free jazz, 26, 37, 189, 223–224, 226–242, 245, 260, 272, 281, 286, 288, 334, 403
free rhythmic style, 33
Free Spirits, The, 317, 327
Freedom Jazz Dance, 208, 303, 386
Freeman, Bud, 58–60
Freeman, Russ, 183
French culture, 38–43
French Impressionist music, 72, 102, 104, *see* Debussy and Ravel

Frenesi, 95
FRESH, 316
Friar's Society Orchestra, 59
Friedman, Don, 252
Friedman, Izzy, 58
front line, 403
Frustration, 119
Fuller, Curtis, 133, 194, 203–204
Fuller, Gil, 147, 153, 157
funk, 316–317
funk bass style, 337
funk drumming, 431
funky, 403
fusion, 403

Gadd, Steve, 320, 340
Galbraith, Barry, 147
Galper, Hal, 293
Garbarek, Jan, 118, 233, 263, 296
Garcia, Russ, 346
Garland, Red, 102–103, 192, 210, 212–214, 291
Garner, Erroll, 87, 102
Garnett, Carlos, 296
Garrison, Arv, 147
Garrison, Jimmy, 240, 289, 293
Gasca, Luis, 212
Geller, Herb, 183
Gennett record company, 82
Georgia, 77
Getz, Stan, 28, 134, 164, 168–170, 195, 282, 348
Giant Steps, 222, 283–284, 288, 295
GIANT STEPS, 283–285
Gibbs, Terry, 147
Gilberto, Astrud, 170
Gill, Kenny, 293
Gillespie, Dizzy, 25, 28, 96, 99–100, 143–148, 152–155, 157–158, 160, 197, 232, 338
Gilmore, John, 240, 272, 286–288, 292
Gingerbread Boy, 208, 214
Girl from Ipanema, 170, 382
Giuffre, Jimmy, 135, 158, 188–189, 223, 241, 275, 348
Give Me the Simple Life, 32
Gleeson, Patrick, 258
Glenn, Tyree, 87, 112
glissando, 51
Golden Cress, 120
Goldstein, Gil, 293
Golson, Benny, 99, 157, 192, 194, 203
Gomez, Eddie, 254
gongs, 120
Gonsalves, Paul, 28, 112, 119–120, 133

Good Bait, 157
Good Man Is Hard to Find, A, 73
Good Mornin' Blues, 140
Goodman, Benny, 60, 87, 93–95, 128
Goodman, Jerry, 320, 327
Gordon, Bob, 183
Gordon, Dexter, 152, 168, 184, 281
Gordon, Joe, 192
GOUTELAS SUITE, 121
Graas, John, 182–183
Graettinger, Robert, 9, 346
Gramercy 5, 95
Grand Terrace Ballroom, 63
Graves, Milford, 240
Gray, Wardell, 84, 133, 135, 147, 152, 168
Great Expectations, 322
Green, Bennie, 147
Green, Charlie, 58
Green, Freddie, 128–129
Green, Grant, 192
Greer, Sonny, 87, 108, 112–115, 120–121, 123
Grey, Al, 133
Griffin, Johnny, 203
Grimes, Henry, 240
Grossman, Steve, 208, 291, 296, 320
Groovin' High, 149, 153
growl style, 110, 120
Gryce, Gigi, 157, 192
Guaraldi, Vince, 183
Guarnieri, Johnny, 87
guitar, 46, 77, 79, 83, 165, 183, 192, 205, 210, 322
Gumbs, Allan, 293
Gyra, Spyro, 320

Hackett, Bobby, 28, 72
Haden, Charlie, 228, 231, 233, 239–241, 264, 286
Haggart, Bob, 60
Haig, Al, 151, 164
Haitian Creoles, 39, 41
Half Nelson, 157, 199
half-timing, 34
Hall, Edmond, 58
Hall, Jim, 186, 188, 326
Hallucinations, 163
Ham 'n' Eggs, 135
Hamilton, Chico, 185–186, 248, 328
Hamilton, Jimmy, 87, 112, 113
Hamilton, Scott, 119
Hammer, Jan, 28, 252, 320
Hampton, Lionel, 87, 94
Hampton, Slide, 350
Hancock, Herbie, 49, 195, 198, 210, 214, 224, 251–253,

Hancock, Herbie (*continued*) 266, 272–273, 301–306, 339–340
Hand Jive, 36, 214, 223
Handy, John, 246, 290
Handy, W. C., 58
Hanna, Roland, 194, 249
hard bop, 191–206, 403
Harden, Wilbur, 192
Hardman, Bill, 192
Hardwicke, Otto, 108, 112, 122
Harlem, 108
Harlem Air Shaft, 109, 113–116, 120
Harlequin, 308
Harmon mute, 211
Harmonique, 281
harmony, 44
Harper, Billy, 200, 296
Harrell, Tom, 197, 212
Harris, Barry, 192, 194
Harris, Beaver, 240
Harris, Benny, 147, 153
Harris, Bill, 87, 95
Harris, Eddie, 28, 320
Harris, Gene, 192, 195
Harris, Joe, 147
Harrison, Jimmy, 58, 87
Hart, Clyde, 87
Haskins, James, 41
Hasselgard, Stan, 165
Haughton, Chauncey, 108
Hawes, Hampton, 147, 183
Hawk Talks, The, 120
Hawkins, Coleman, 28, 34, 36, 87, 92, 97, 132–136, 146, 150, 167, 232, 280, 282
Hayes, Isaac, 11
Hayes, Louis, 192, 194, 197
Haynes, Roy, 147, 192
head, 403
head arrangements, 131, 403
HEAD HUNTER, 257, 340
Head Hunters, The, 320
Heath, Al, 192, 257
Heath, Jimmy, 152, 192, 194, 208
Heath, M'Tume, 210, 324
Heath, Percy, 158, 194
Hefti, Neal, 133, 147
HELIOCENTRIC WORLDS OF SUN RA, 270–272
Hellhound on My Trail, 41, 44
Hello, Dolly, 70
Hemphill, Julius, 276
Hemingway, Ernest, 25
Henderson, Bill, 293
Henderson, Eddie, 212, 258
Henderson, Fletcher, 67, 73, 80, 87, 96–97, 113, 132, 344
Henderson, Joe, 169, 192, 197, 201, 208, 257, 296, 303
Henderson, Michael, 210, 320, 324–325

Hendrix, Jimi, 313, 325, 337
Henry, Ernie, 147, 152
Herbert, Gregory, 296
Herman, Woody, 87, 95, 112, 118, 143, 184, 344, 348–349
Hicks, John, 293
HI-FI ELLINGTON UPTOWN, 12, 121
Higginbotham, J. C., 77, 87, 95
Higgins, Billy, 233, 240
high-hat, 19–20, 86, 90, 115, 129, 136, 138, 161–162, 222, 303, 403
Hiliare, Andrew, 58, 62
Hill, Andrew, 157
Hines, Earl, 57–58, 63, 67, 74, 87, 101–102, 144, 162, 344
Hino, Terumasa, 212
Hodges, Johnny, 75, 87, 99, 108, 112, 118–119, 246, 280–281, 285, 296, 348
Holiday, Billie, 71
Holland, Dave, 239, 260
Holley, Major, 25
Holman, Bill, 183, 346
Holmes, Charlie, 58
Holmes, Richard Groove, 192, 195
Home Again Blues, 79
Honeysuckle Rose, 32, 65, 148, 382
Honky Tonk Train, 49, 66
Hopkins, Fred, 240
horn, 403
horn-like lines, 65
hot band category, 105
Hot House, 149, 157
Hotter Than That, 71, 83
Howard, Darnell, 58
Howard, Joe, 100
How High the Moon, 149, 383
Hubbard, Freddie, 197–198, 233, 240, 339
Hudson, Will, 87, 93
Humphries, Lex, 192
Humphries, Roger, 192
Hutcherson, Bobby, 290

I Can't Believe That You're in Love with Me, 32, 96, 99
I Can't Get Started, 97, 153
I Don't Know What Kind of Blues I've Got, 119
I Found a New Baby, 93
I Got Rhythm, 32, 36, 99–111, 148–149, 200, 384
I Should Care, 156
I SING THE BODY ELECTRIC, 22, 307
I Want a Little Girl, 134, 140
If You Could See Me Now, 157

I'll Remember April, 382
I'm Beginning to See the Light, 107
I'm Going to Wear You Off My Mind, 82
IMPRESSIONS, 248, 286, 293
Impressions, 288, 423
improvisation, 1, 4, 5, 15, 18, 23–27, 30–32, 36–37, 43–44, 217–224, 226–228, 230–234
In a Country Garden, 150
In a Mellotone, 75, 107
In a Mist, 72
In a Silent Way, 207
IN A SILENT WAY, 210, 307, 321, 329
In the Dark, 72
In Time, 316
IN TRANSITION, 237
India, 248, 293
Indian music, 8, 210, 322, 326
Indiana, 149, 383
INFINITE SEARCH, 331
INNER MOUNTING FLAME, 326
Innovations in Modern Music, 345
inside, the, 31
Inspiration, 246
instrumentalized voice, 110
Interlude, 346
INTERSTELLAR SPACE, 288
intonation, 390–391
introductions, 35
Intuition and Digression, 223
Iowa, 71
Irvis, Charlie, 58
Isham, Mark, 212
I've Got You Under My Skin, 382
Izenzon, David, 240

JACK JOHNSON, 209, 211
Jack the Bear, 109, 113, 122, 217
Jackson, Chubby, 147
Jackson, Milt, 154, 158–160
Jackson, Quentin Butter, 112, 120
Jackson, Ronald Shannon, 233, 320
Jackson, Rudy, 112
Jacquet, Illinois, 87, 133, 136
jam session, 403
Jamal, Ahmad, 102–103, 147, 209, 214
James, Bob, 320
James, Harry, 87, 94, 344
Japanese Sandman, 93
Jarman, Joseph, 233, 240, 274–275

Jarreau, Al, 52
Jarrett, Keith, 25, 28, 33, 203,
    210, 224, 229, 239–240,
    262–267
Jayne, 235
Jazz Age, The, 11, 61
jazz fusion, 341
Jazz Singer, The, 11
jazz swing feeling, 7–8, 70, 363
Jazznocracy, 93
jazz/rock, 49, 207, 312–343
Jazztet, The Art Farmer–Benny
    Golson, 204, 292
jazzy, 6
Jeep's Blues, 75
Jefferson, Eddie, 151
Jefferson, Hilton, 58, 87
Jenney, Jack, 87
Jerome, Jerry, 87, 135
Jitterbug Waltz, 65
Jive at Five, 132
Jive Samba, 206
Johnson, Alphonso, 337
Johnson, Budd, 87, 132
Johnson, Bunk, 60
Johnson, Dewey, 240
Johnson, Gus, 132
Johnson, J. J., 95, 166–167,
    192–193, 203–204
Johnson, James P., 57, 61, 107
Johnson, Lonnie, 60, 83
Johnson, Marc, 254
Johnson, Money, 112
Johnson, Osie, 147
Johnson, Pete, 58, 66, 132
Johnson, Robert, 41, 44
Jolly, Pete, 183
Jones, Carmell, 192
Jones, Eddie, 133
Jones, Elvin, 192, 194, 289–
    293
Jones, Hank, 147, 194
Jones, Harold, 133
Jones, Jo, 87, 90, 129–130, 132–
    133, 138, 140, 161–162
Jones, Jonah, 87
Jones, Philly Joe, 192, 194, 210,
    214–216, 224
Jones, Quincy, 133
Jones, Rufus, 112, 121, 133
Jones, Sam, 204–205
Jones, Thad, 67, 112, 122, 133,
    140, 153, 192, 194, 247,
    249, 351–354
Jones, Wallace, 108
Jones-Smith Inc., 130, 140
Joplin, Scott, 42
Jordan, Clifford, 192
Jordan, Duke, 147
Jordan, Louis, 118, 313
Jordan, Taft, 87, 112
Joy Spring, 194, 222
Juggler, The, 330

Jumpin At The Woodside, 32,
    90, 131
Jungle Book, 330
jungle style, 48
Just A-Settin' and A-Rockin',
    119

Kahn, Tiny, 147
kalimba, 330
Kamuca, Richie, 135, 168, 184
Kansas, 63
Kansas City, 49
Kansas City Five, Six and
    Seven, The, 140
Kansas City style jazz, 131–132,
    150
KANSAS CITY SUITE, 99
Katz, Fred, 186
Kay, Connie, 158
Kelly, Wynton, 28, 192, 210,
    216, 223, 252–253
Kenton, Stan, 9, 87, 158, 184,
    246, 344, 348–354
Kenyatta, Robin, 296
Keppard, Freddie, 58, 60
Kessel, Barney, 147, 183
kettledrum, 271
Khan, Steve, 320
Kikuchi, Masabumi, 260
Kincaide, Deane, 87
KIND OF BLUE, 36, 211–212,
    216–224, 233, 251–252,
    288, 385
King, B. B., 313
King Porter Stomp, 63, 93
Kirby, John, 87, 97
Kirk, Andy, 87, 132
Kirk, Roland, 25, 28, 249–250
Kirkpatrick, Don, 133
Kiss and Run, 199
Klactoveesedstene, 162, 232
Klemmer, John, 200, 296, 320
Klugh, Earl, 341
Knepper, Jimmy, 192, 352
Ko-Ko, 21–22, 120, 148–149,
    202–203, 383
Konitz, Lee, 71, 135, 178–184,
    276, 347
Kotick, Teddy, 147, 251
Krivda, Ernie, 296
Krupa, Gene, 60, 87, 90, 94, 96,
    129
Kuhn, Steve, 252
KULU SE MAMA, 287
Kyle, Billy, 63, 87, 163

LaBarbera, Pat, 200, 296
Lacy, Steve, 154, 240, 295
Ladnier, Tommy, 58
Lady Be Good, 140, 148, 150
Lady Bird, 157

LaFaro, Scott, 233, 240, 253–
    255, 291, 323, 352
La Fiesta, 261
Lagrene, Bireli, 104
laid back, 403
Laine, Papa Jack, 58
Laird, Rick, 320
Lake, Oliver, 233, 240, 276
Lambert, Hendricks, and Ross,
    109
Lamond, Don, 147
Lamphere, Don, 135, 147
Land, Harold, 192, 203, 296
Lande, Art, 265, 304
Lane, George, 248
Lang, Eddie, 83
LaPorta, John, 181
LaRocca, Nick, 59, 71
Lasha, Prince, 233
Lateef Yusef, 25, 192, 194
Latin American bass line, 428
Latin American jazz, 34, 154,
    164, 196, 228, 246, 259,
    323, 335, 338, 345, 347
LATIN AMERICAN SUITE,
    121
LaVerne, Andy, 260
La Virgen de la Macarena, 117
Lawrence, Michael, 320
Laws, Ronnie, 320
Lawson, Yank, 60
lay out, 403
Leadbelly, 313
Lederer, Steve, 296
Lee, David, 240
Lee, George, 132
legato, 403
LEGEND, THE, 99
Leonard, Harlan, 132
Lester Leaps In, 32, 35, 131–
    132, 138–139
Levey, Stan, 183–184
Leviev, Milcho, 320
Lewis, Ed, 130
Lewis, George, 58
Lewis, John, 153, 157, 182, 210
Lewis, Meade Lux, 49, 66
Lewis, Mel, 183–184, 351–354
Lewis, Ramsey, 192, 195, 254–
    255, 313
Leibook, Min, 58
lick, 403
Liebman, David, 203, 290–291,
    296–297, 320
Lifetime, 320, 325
LIGHT AS A FEATHER, 261
Lindsay, John, 62
Lipsius, Fred, 319
lip trill, 198
Liszt, Franz, 9
Litha, 261, 295
Little, Booker, 192
Little Benny, 149

Little Girl Blue, 382
Little Melonae, 202
Little One, 257
LIVE AT BIRDLAND, 22, 291–292, 296
LIVE IN SEATTLE, 281
LIVE AT THE PLUGGED NICKEL, 307–308
LIVE–EVIL, 23, 209–211, 322
Livery Stable Blues, 59
Lloyd, Charles, 186, 262, 290, 296
locked-hands style, 102, 403
Lofton, Cripple Clarence, 58
Lombardo, Guy, 9, 10
Lonely Woman, 236
Lonesome Lullaby, 116
Lorber, Jeff, 260, 320, 341
Los Angeles, 268, 345
Los Angeles Neophonic Orchestra, 345
Lovano, Joe, 296
LOVE SUPREME, A, 289, 295
LOW CLASS CONSPIRACY, 235
Lullaby in Rhythm, 149
Lullaby of Birdland, 165
Lunceford, Jimmie, 87, 93
Lunceford Special, 93
Lush Life, 122
Lyons, Jimmy, 233, 240

Mabern, Harold, 293
MacArthur Park, 350
Macero, Teo, 181
Madness, 223, 257, 301
MAGIC CITY, 270
Mahavishnu Orchestra, The, 326
Maiden Voyage, 385, 422
MAIDEN VOYAGE, 257
Mainstem, 119
major, 370–371
Makowicz, Adam, 100
Mance, Junior, 192
Mangione, Chuck, 203, 341, Man I Love, The, 32, 161
Man in the Green Shirt, 330
Manne, Shelly, 183–184
Manone, Wingy, 58
Manolete, 308–309
Manteca, 154
Maple Leaf Rag, 42, 62
Marable, Fate, 58
Marcus, Steve, 296
Mares, Paul, 58
Margie, 79
Mariano, Charlie, 152, 246
Maria, 350
Marie, 97
Marmarosa, Dodo, 147
Marsalis, Wynton, 197, 212, 203

Marsh, Warne, 135, 179
Marshall, Wendell, 112
Mason, Harvey, 258, 320
Masqualero, 301, 303, 306, 321
Matthews, Ronnie, 293
Maupin, Bennie, 208, 258, 296
Mays, Lyle, 265
McCall, Steve, 240
McCann, Les, 192, 195, 313
McDuff, Jack, 192, 195
McGhee, Howard, 147, 151, 153
McGriff, Jimmy, 192
McIntosh, Tom, 192
McIntyre, Ken, 240
McKibbon, Al, 164, 210
McLaughlin, John, 295, 319–321, 325–328
McLean, Jackie, 202–203, 208, 246
McNeil, John, 212
McPartland, Jimmy, 59–60, 72
McPherson, Charles, 152, 194
McShann, Jay, 87, 132, 144, 150
MEDITATIONS, 281, 295
mellophoniums, 346
Mengelberg, Misja, 157
Mercy, Mercy, Mercy, 206, 329, 330
Merritt, Jymie, 192, 203
Metcalf, Louis, 112
meter, 359
Metheny, Pat, 233, 320, 328
Mezzrow, Mezz, 58, 60
Milenburg Joys, 63
MILES AHEAD, 215
Miles, Butch, 133
MILES IN EUROPE, 211, 301, 304
MILES IN THE SKY, 210, 321
Miles Mode, 287
MILES SMILES, 22, 37, 214, 223, 256, 303–304, 321
Milestones, 208, 213, 222, 288, 385, 423
MILESTONES, 210, 214–215
Miley, Bubber, 110, 112, 116, 122
military bands, 47
Miller, Glenn, 72, 87, 105
Miller, Marcus, 323
MINGUS AH UM, 247
Mingus, Charlie, 28, 63, 112, 158, 160, 240, 243–250, 273–274, 352
minor, 370–371
Minor March, 202
Minority, 195
Mintzer, Bob, 296
Mister Gentle and Mister Cool, 116
Mister J.B. Blues, 122, 254
Misterioso, 155, 160

Misty, 102, 382
Mitchell, Billy, 192, 194
Mitchell, Blue, 192, 197, 212, 258
Mitchell, George, 58, 62, 133
Mitchell, Red, 183–184
Mitchell, Roscoe, 229, 233, 240, 274–275
Mobley, Hank, 192, 197, 203, 208
modal, 384, 403
mode, 368, 403, 418–423
mode-based improvisatory styles, 189, 207, 212–224, 284, 287–288
modern jazz, 143–354
Modern Jazz Quartet, The, 158–160, 173, 178, 265, 275
Moffett, Charles, 240
Mole, Miff, 60, 76
Mondragon, Joe, 183
Monk, Thelonious, 112, 143, 154–157, 160, 283
Monterose, J. R., 192
Montgomery, Wes, 205, 326
Montrose, Jack, 183
Mooche, The, 83
Mood Indigo, 107, 109, 122
Moody, James, 147, 152
Moonlight in Vermont, 170, 174, 384
Moore, Brew, 135, 147, 168
Moore, Charles, 212
Moore, Oscar, 87
Moose the Mooche, 32, 57–58
Morehouse, Chauncey, 58
Moreira, Airto, 210, 331
Morello, Joe, 187–188
Morgan, Lee, 192, 194, 203
Morning Glory, 116
Morton, Bennie, 87, 130–131, 133
Morton, Jelly Roll, 61–64, 74, 79, 243, 247, 269, 347
Mosca, Sal, 181
Moten, Bennie, 87, 132
Moten Swing, 32, 131, 150
Motian, Paul, 240, 252
Motown, 316, 318–319
Mouzon, Alphonse, 320, 331
Moye, Don, 240, 275
Mulligan, Gerry, 28, 147, 181–186, 199, 334
multiphonics, 281
Mundy, Jimmy, 87, 133
Murray, David, 235, 240, 276
Murray, Don, 58
Murray, Sunny, 238
Muskrat Ramble, 76
Musso, Vido, 87
Mussulli, Boots, 147
mutes, 48, 325, 390, 403
MWANDISHI, 258

My Favorite Things, 37, 385
MY FAVORITE THINGS, 287–288, 296
My Funny Valentine, 32
MY FUNNY VALENTINE, 212, 256, 301, 304
MY GOAL'S BEYOND, 327
My Monday Date, 82
My Romance, 383
MYSTERIOUS TRAVELER, 309, 330

Naima, 284–285, 295
Nance, Ray, 108, 112, 116, 123
Nanton, Joe Tricky Sam, 87, 108, 110, 112, 114, 120
Napoleon, Phil, 58
Nardis, 208
Navarro, Fats, 28, 151, 153, 157, 165–166, 193, 197, 236
Nefertiti, 321, 383
NEFERTITI, 37, 210, 214, 223, 301, 303–306
Neidlinger, Buell, 240
Nelson, Oliver, 192
Nestico, Sammy, 133
New Orleans, 38–43, 57–85, 113
New Orleans Jazz, 61–62, 131
New Orleans Rhythm Kings, 59–60
New World a' Comin', 108
New York, 59–60, 65, 67, 76, 131, 178, 268
Newman, Joe, 133
NEWPORT 1958, 113, 117, 120
Newton, Frankie, 87
Nica's Dream, 195–196
Nicholas, Albert, 58, 60
Nichols, Herbie, 157
Nichols, Red, 60, 72, 77
Niehaus, Lennie, 180, 183–184
Night in Tunisia, A, 153
NIGHT PASSAGE, 308–309
Nock, Mike, 317
No Line, 36, 210
No, Papa, No, 81
Non-Stop Home, 308–309
Noone, Jimmie, 60, 74
Norvo, Red, 87
NOW HE SINGS, NOW HE SOBS, 259, 266, 339
Now's the Time, 151
Nuages, 104

Oberheim Polyphonic, 330
oboe, 88, 271
octave, 63, 365, 374
octave voicing, 65
O'Farrill, Chico, 133

Off Minor, 32, 154–155
Okeh record company, 82–83
Ole, 287, 293
OLE COLTRANE, 293
Oleo, 200, 386
Oliver, Joe, 45, 53, 59–60, 67, 74, 83
Oliver, Sy, 87, 93, 95
Ol' Man River, 136
On a Misty Night, 157
On a Turquoise Cloud, 110, 124
On Green Dolphin Street, 208, 251, 383
ON THE CORNER, 22, 210
On the Street Where You Live, 383
One O'Clock Jump, 90, 131, 161
Opus 1, 95
Oracle, 320
Orange Lady, 322, 335
Orbits, 214
organ, 15, 192, 322
Original Dixie Jazz Band One-Step, 79
Original Dixieland Jazz Band, 45, 47, 59, 72, 79–83
Ornithology, 149
Orphan, The, 331
Ortega, Anthony, 233
Ory, Kid, 59–60, 62, 76
Ostrich Walk, 59
Our Delight, 157
OUR MAN IN JAZZ, 236
Out of Nowhere, 383
Owens, Charles B., 296

Page, Oran Hot Lips, 71, 87, 132, 133
Page, Walter, 87, 129, 132, 133
Pagin' the Devil, 134
Paich, Marty, 183
Parenti, Tony, 58
PARIS BLUES, 108, 123
Parish, Avery, 195
Parisian Thoroughfare, 163
Parker, Charlie, 34, 36, 71, 100, 132, 143–153, 156, 160–170, 179–184, 193–194, 199–202, 232, 234, 280–283
Parker, Leo, 147
Parker's Mood, 150–151
Parlan, Horace, 192
Passion, Flower, 118
Pastorius, Jaco, 320, 336–338
Patrick, Pat, 240
Patterson, Don, 192
Payne, Cecil, 192
Payne, Sonny, 133
Peace Piece, 217, 221, 252
Pearson, Duke, 192

pedal points, 284, 403
Peg o' My Heart, 383
Pekar, Harvey, 7, 102, 156, 172, 194, 196, 237
Pell, Dave, 183
Penderecki, Krzysztof, 270, 276
Pent-Up House, 195, 198–199
Pepper, Art, 152, 180, 184, 347
Peraza, Armando, 164
Perdido, 122
Perfume Suite, 109, 117
Perkins, Bill, 168, 184
Perkins, Carl, 183
Perry, Rich, 296
Peter, Paul & Mary, 11
Peterson, Oscar, 14, 25, 100–101, 103, 164–165, 256
Pettiford, Oscar, 112, 147, 160–161
Petrouchka, 150
phase shifter, 326
Pharoah's Dance, 322
Philadelphia, 194
Phillips, Flip, 87, 147
piano, 18, 61–66, 99–103, 107, 128, 155–157, 162–165, 183, 192, 214, 237–238, 251–267, 293
piccolo, 271
Pickin' the Cabbage, 96
Picou, Alphonse, 58
Pierce, Nat, 184
pitch bending, 52, 403
Pithecanthropus Erectus, 245
Pitter Panther Patter, 122, 254
Pittsburgh, 57, 63
pizzicato, 17, 403
Plater, Bobby, 118, 133
playing against the changes, 27
playing inside, 236
playing outside, 27, 236
plunger mute, 110, 116, 120
Polka Dots and Moonbeams, 32
Pollack, Ben, 60
polyrhythm, 49, 364–365, 403
Pomeroy, Herb, 212
Pononmarev, Valerie, 203
Ponty, Jean-Luc, 319, 327
PORGY AND BESS, 53, 211, 216
portamento, 51
Portrait of Bert Williams, A, 108, 116
Portrait of Ella Fitzgerald, A, 108
Portrait of The Lion, 108
Potato Head Blues, 79
Potter, Tommy, 147, 210
Pound Cake, 135
Powell, Benny, 133
Powell, Bud, 63, 100, 143, 154, 157, 163–165, 196, 199, 214, 224, 251, 253, 258, 291

Powell, Mel, 87
Pozo, Chano, 154
Preacher, The, 196, 383
Prelude to a Kiss, 124
Presley, Elvis, 313
Previn, Andre, 183
Priester, Julian, 258, 272
Prima, Louis, 71
Prime Time, 338
Prince of Darkness, 304, 383
PRISONER, THE, 256–257
Procope, Russell, 87, 112
Progressive Jazz, 345, 347, 404
Prophet synthesizer, 330
Punk Jazz, 337

quadrille, 43
quadruple-timing, 34
quarter note, 361
quarter-tone trumpet, 329
Quebec, Ike, 136
Quinichette, Paul, 133, 135

Ra, Sun, 14, 63, 112, 157, 240, 269–278, 286–287, 334
race records, 316
Raeburn, Boyd, 87, 348
rag, 42
Ragas, Henry, 58
ragtime, 42–43, 61, 70, 404
Rainbow, 264
Raincheck, 119
Ramey, Gene, 147
Raney, Jimmy, 147, 165
Rank, Bill, 58
Rappolo, Leon, 58
Ravel, Maurice, 72, 102, 104, 262, 335
Really the Blues, 75
Red Hot Peppers, 62
Redman, Dewey, 25, 233, 240, 264
Redman, Don, 58, 87, 92, 113, 133
reed section, 88
Rehak, Frank, 192
reharmonization, 23
Reinhardt, Django, 87, 103–104
RELAXIN', 210, 212
release, 404
Reminiscing in Tempo, 108, 125
Rene's Theme, 327
Return to Forever, 261, 319–320
Reuben, Reuben, I've Been Thinking, 150
Revelations, 245
Rhapsody in Blue, 9, 54

rhythm, 356–359
rhythm and blues, 316
rhythm changes, 149
rhythm guitar, 90, 113, 128–129, 145
rhythmic lilt, 6
rhythm section, 15, 77–83, 90–91, 210, 224, 253–256, 322–323, 340, 404
Rich, Buddy, 87, 95, 188
Richards, Johnny, 346
Richardson, Jerome, 249
Richman, Boomie, 87
Richmond, Danny, 249
ride cymbal, 18–21, 404
ride rhythm, 18–21, 49, 81, 90, 129, 136, 161–162, 430
riff, 88, 404
riff band style, 131, 138–139
Riley, Ben, 192
rim shot, 404
Ring Dem Bells, 120
Riot, 257
River People, 337
Rivers, Sam, 208, 240
Roach, Max, 21–22, 151, 161–162, 193, 202–203, 210, 272
Roberts, Howard, 183
Robinson, Bill Bojangles, 108
Robinson, Fred, 58
rock, 9, 105, 312–319, 321, 327, 340
rock bass lines, 426–427
Rockin' Chair, 94
Rockin' in Rhythm, 122
Rocky, 351
Rodney, Red, 147, 151, 153
Rodrigo, Joaquin, 216
Rogers, Shorty, 147, 182–184, 212, 215
Roker, Mickey, 192
Rolling Stones, The, 201, 316
Rollini, Adrian, 58, 87
Rollins, Sonny, 97, 147, 193, 198–201, 203, 208, 240, 282–283, 296, 339
Roseland Shuffle, 32
Rosolino, Frank, 147, 183–184, 347
'ROUND ABOUT MID-NIGHT, 210, 212
Round Midnight, 154–155
Rouse, Charlie, 147, 156–157
Royal, Marshall, 133
rubato, 33, 217
RUBISA PATROL, 304
Rugulo, Pete, 346
Ruiz, Hilton, 293
Rumsey, Howard, 183
Russell, Curly, 147
Russell, George, 112, 147, 157
Russell, Pee Wee, 58

Sack o' Woe, 206
Safranski, Eddie, 147
Saheb Sarbib, 233
Saint Cyr, Johnny, 58, 60, 62
Saint James Infirmary Blues, 81
Saint Louis, 276
Saint Louis Blues, 52, 382
Salt Peanuts, 153
Sampson, Edgar, 87
Sanborn, David, 320
Sanctuary, 321
Sanders, Pharoah, 240, 287, 290, 296
sansa, 330
Santamaria, Mongo, 258
Santana, Carlos, 295
Satin Doll, 107
Sauter, Eddie, 87
saxophone, 88–89, 226–236, 274–277, see alto saxo-phone, baritone saxophone, bass saxophone, C-Melody saxophone, tenor saxo-phone
saxophone soli, 111
Sbarbaro, Tony, 79–83
scale, 365–369
scat singing, 404
Schifrin, Lalo, 112
Schildkraut, Davey, 152
Schnitter, David, 203
Schoebel, Elmer, 58
Schoenberg, Arnold, 276
Schuller, Gunther, 158
Scofield, John, 208
scoop, 51
scoring across sections, 109
Scott, Cecil, 58
Scott, Shirley, 192
Scott, Tony, 165
Sears, Al, 112
Sebesky, Don, 28, 350
SECOND SACRED CON-CERT, 121
Secret Love, 382
Sedric, Gene, 58
Señor Blues, 206
Señor Mouse, 262
Sepia Panorama, 122
Serious Serenade, 119
set of traps, 22
SEVEN STEPS TO HEAVEN, 211
Seventh Arrow, 307, 330, 334
SEXTANT, 257
SHADES, 264
Shakti, 327
Shank, Bud, 152, 180, 183–184
Shavers, Charlie, 87, 95–97
Shaw, Artie, 87, 95–96, 158
Shaw Nuff, 148, 151
Shaw, Woody, 197, 203

Shearing, George, 102–103, 147, 164–165, 173, 178
Sheldon, Jack, 184, 212
Shepard, Ernie, 112
Shepherd Who Watches over the Night Flock, The, 108
Shepp, Archie, 119, 233, 240
Shields, Larry, 58
Shihab, Sahib, 152
Shoe Shine Boy, 130–131, 140
Shorter, Wayne, 192, 203, 296–297, 304–311, 319, 323, 332, 383, 388
short-term repetition, 49
Show Me the Way to Go Home, 383
Sickler, Don, 201
sideman, 404
Sidewinder, 206, 382
Sid's Ahead, 212
sight-reading, 29
Signorelli, Frank, 58
SILENT TONGUES, 237
Silver Horace, 28, 101, 165, 195–197, 203, 224, 253, 256, 258
Simeon, Omer, 58, 60, 62
Simmons, Sonny, 233
Sims, Zoot, 135, 147, 180, 183, 191–193, 348
Singin' the Blues, 73, 83
Singleton, Zutty, 60, 80, 82
Sister Sadie, 196
sitar, 210, 322
Sivad, 209–210
sixteenth note, 362
Skating in Central Park, 158
SKETCHES OF SPAIN, 51, 53, 211
SKIES OF AMERICA, 229
Skin Deep, 121
Skip the Gutter, 34, 81
Slinger, Cees, 252
smear, 51, 76, 95
Smith, Bessie, 52, 313
Smith, Bill, 240
Smith, Buster, 87, 132, 150
Smith, Carl, 130, 133, 183
Smith, Jabbo, 58, 87
Smith, Jimmy, 192, 195, 313
Smith, Joe, 58
Smith, Johnny, 147
Smith, Pinetop, 58, 66
Smith, Tab, 87, 118, 133
Smith, Willie the Lion, 58, 87, 108, 112, 118
Smoke Gets in Your Eyes, 32
snare drum, 18–21, 80, 90, 113, 123, 145
Snowden, Elmer, 58
So What, 45, 208, 217–218, 223, 288, 385, 423
sock cymbal, 19, 404

Soft Machine, 320
Solar, 255
Solea, 51, 211, 216
Solitude, 107
Soloff, Lew, 319–320
SOMEDAY MY PRINCE WILL COME, 253
SOMETHING ELSE, 229, 236
Sometimes I'm Happy, 93
Song for My Father, 196, 206
Sophisticated Ladies, 109
Sophisticated Lady, 107, 122, 124
soprano saxophone, 75–76, 88, 262, 295, 322, 335
SORCERER, 210, 252, 256, 307–308, 321
soul music, 316
SOULTRANE, 118, 285
Soultrane, 157
Sousa, John Philip, 47–48
space music, 258, 273
SPACES, 327–328
Spain, 261
Spalding, James, 296
Spanier, Muggsy, 58, 60
Sphere, 154
Spinning Wheel, 318
Spyro Gyra, 320, 341
Squeeze Me, 65
Stablemates, 195
staccato, 404
Stacy, Jess, 87
STAIRCASE, 252, 265
Stampede, The, 92
Stars and Stripes Forever, 47
STEAMIN', 212
Steig, Jeremy, 25
Stein, Gertrude, 25
Stella by Starlight, 211
STEPPIN' ON THE GAS, 47, 80, 83
Stern, Mike, 208, 323
Stevens, Eddie Gale, 240
Steward, Herbie, 135, 147, 168, 348
Stewart, Milton, 198
Stewart, Rex, 53, 87, 108, 112, 116
Stewart, Slam, 25, 36, 100
Stitt, Sonny, 135, 147, 152, 168–169, 193, 208, 281-282
Stockhausen, Karlheinz, 260, 276
Stompin' at the Savoy, 32
Stone, Jesse, 132
Stone, Sly, 258, 316
Stone-style drumming, Sly, 431
stop-time solo break, 34, 65, 138
Story of Love, The, 246
Storyville, 39
Stowaway, 65
Straight, No Chaser, 154–155

Straight Up and Down, 295
Stravinsky, Igor, 145, 150
Strawberries, 53
Strayhorn, Billy, 122–124
stride style, 61, 65, 87, 112, 404
string bass, 15–17, 77, 90, see bass viol
String of Pearls, 72
Strong, Jimmy, 58
Strozier, Frank, 152, 192
Struttin' with Some Barbecue, 74, 76
Stuff, 321
SUCH SWEET THUNDER, 109, 125
Sugar Blues, 382, 384
Sugar Foot Stomp, 82
SUITE THURSDAY, 125
Sulieman, Idrees, 147
Sullivan, Ira, 203
Sullivan, Joe, 58, 60
Summer Sequence, 169
Summers, Bill, 258
Summertime, 75, 117, 216, 383
SUN SHIP, 291
Supersax, 152
Supremes, The, 316
Surman, John, 296
Surucucu, 307, 334
suspended cymbal, 129, 145
sweep, The, 293
sweet band category, 105
Sweet Georgia Brown, 383
SWEET RAIN, 252
SWEETNIGHTER, 22, 308–309, 333–334
swing, 404
swing eighth-note pattern, 9, 86, 363
swing feeling, 5–8, 363
swing music or swing era, 86–146
Swingin' Uptown, 93
syncopation, 7, 44, 360–363, 404, 428–429
synthesizer, 270, 404

Tabackin, Lew, 119, 296
tabla, 210, 322
Tacuma, Jamaaladeen, 233, 320
TAIL SPINNIN', 331
Take Five, 187–188
Take the 'A' Train, 116, 122–124
tambura, 330
TAPESTRY, 318
Tate, Buddy, 132, 133, 135–137
Tatum, Art, 63, 87, 97–101, 143, 146, 164–165, 179, 232
Taxi War Dance, 32, 45, 90, 132, 136–138

Taylor, Art, 192, 210, 224
Taylor, Billy, 112, 147
Taylor, Cecil, 10, 14, 36, 112, 157, 180, 226, 237–238, 241, 268
Taylor, Gene, 192
Tchicai, John, 233, 240
Teagarden, Charlie, 58
Teagarden, Jack, 76–77, 347
Teen Town, 337
tempo, 358
Temptations, The, 316
Tempus Fugit, 163
Ten Wheel Drive, 318
tenor saxophone, 88, 97–99, 119–120, 167–170, 183, 192, 198–201, 306–308
Terry, Clark, 112, 117, 133, 147, 153, 215
Teschemacher, Frank, 58–60, 74
Texas, 63, 77
Theme for Ernie, 118, 285
There Is No Greater Love, 32
Thielemans, Toots, 25
Thigpen, Ben, 87
Things to Come, 153
Third Stream music, 158, 216, 245, 347, 404
Third World music, 227–228, 236–237, 264
Thomas, Joe, 87
Thompson, Lucky, 99, 120, 133
Thornhill, Claude, 143, 181–184, 344
Thornton, Argonne, 147
Threadgill, Henry, 233, 240
Three Clowns, 308
Three Views of A Secret, 337
THRUST, 257
TIA JUANA MOODS, 247
Tiberi, Frank, 296
tied triplet figure, 363
Tiger Rag, 43
Tight Like This, 68, 81
timbre, 388, 405
Timmons, Bobby, 192, 194, 203
TIME FURTHER OUT, 188
TIME OUT, 188
Tizol, Juan, 108, 112, 122
Tjader, Cal, 258
Toccata for Trumpet and Orchestra, 158
TOGO–BRAVA SUITE, 121
tom tom, 17, 19
tonal inflection, 405
tone color, 388, 405
tone quality, 388, 405
Tones for Jones Bones, 259
Too Good to Title, 110
Too Marvelous for Words, 99
top cymbal, 129
Tough, Cy, 181

Tough, Dave, 58–60, 87, 90, 95, 161
Tout de Suite, 321
Towne, Floyd, 58
trading eights, 32
trading fours, 32, 138
traditional jazz, 61
Transbluency, 109–110, 124
tremolo, 50, 65, 405
triplet, 362
Tristano, Lennie, 28, 100, 103, 178–182, 223, 240–241, 253, 334
trombone, 57–58, 76, 95, 112, 120, 166–167, 183, 192, 203–204
trombone section, 88
Trumbauer, Frankie, 25, 73–74
trumpet, 57–58, 66–74, 76, 95–97, 112, 116–117, 165–166, 183, 192, 197–198, 209–212, 236, 323, 349
trumpet section, 88
trumpet-style piano, 64
tuba, 77–78, 90
Tune-Up, 208, 283
turnarounds, 146, 387, 405, 416
Turrentine, Stanley, 192, 313
Turrentine, Tommy, 192
twelve-bar blues, 31
two-beat style, 79, 405
tympani, 120, 271
Tyner, McCoy, 102–103, 194–195, 258, 289, 290–293

Ulmer, James Blood, 233, 320, 338
Umbrellas, 307, 334
Un Poco Loco, 163
Undecided, 32
UNIT STRUCTURES, 36
Urbaniak, Michael, 320
Urso, Phil, 147
UWIS SUITE, 121

Valse Hot, 199
vamp, 405
Varèse, Edgard, 270, 273
Vaughan, Sarah, 52
Venuti, Joe, 58, 60, 83
Ventura, Charlie, 119, 147, 173
verse, 383
vibraharp, 158–160
vibrato, 50, 405
VILLAGE VANGUARD SESSIONS, THE, 254
vina, 326
Vinnegar, Leroy, 183
Vinson, Eddie, 118, 283
Vitous, Miroslav, 260, 331–337
voicing, 405, 417

voicing across sections, 109
voicing in fourths, 376

wah-wah pedal, 325–326
Waldron, Mal, 157
Waller, Fats, 57, 63, 65, 68, 130
Walk Tall, 329
Walker, Junior, 295
Walkin', 208, 301
walking bass, 15–16, 79, 113, 136, 138, 405, 425–426
walking tenths, 65
Walton, Cedar, 192, 203
Waltz for Bill Evans, 253
Waltz for Debby, 253
Ward, Carlos, 233
Ware, Wilbur, 192
Warm Valley, 109
Warren, Butch, 192
Warren, Earle, 130, 133
Washington, Grover, 320, 341
Washington, Jack, 130, 133
Waterfall, 336
Watermelon Man, 257, 382
Watkins, Doug, 192, 194
Watson, Bobby, 203
Wayne, Chuck, 147
Weather Bird, 35, 64, 68, 71
WEATHER REPORT, 333
Weather Report, 17, 49, 305–310
Webb, Chick, 87
Webster, Ben, 28, 87, 108, 111–112, 118–119, 132, 285
Webster, Freddie, 147
Welk, Lawrence, 9–10
We'll Get It, 95
Well, You Needn't, 154–155
Wells, Dicky, 87, 130, 133, 137
Wess, Frank, 133
West Coast style, 178–180, 182–194, 207, 347, 405
West End Blues, 63, 70, 71, 81
Weston, Randy, 157
Wettling, George, 81
What Is This Thing Called Love, 149, 157
What Love, 245, 249
Wheeler, Kenny, 212
When Buddah Smiles, 93
When It's Sleepy Time Down South, 75
When Lights Are Low, 94
WHERE HAVE I KNOWN YOU BEFORE? 259
Whetsol, Arthur, 112
Whispering, 149
White, Andrew, 295–296
White Heat, 93
White, Lenny, 261, 320
White, Michael, 317, 320
Whiteman, Paul, 9, 72, 158

whole tone mode, 73, 156
Wilcox, Eddie, 93
Wild Man Blues, 63
Wilkins, Ernie, 133
Will, 335
Williams, Bert, 108
Williams, Buster, 258
Williams, Clarence, 58, 67
Williams Cootie, 87, 94, 111–116
Williams, James, 157
Williams, Mary Lou, 87, 132
Williams, Tony, 210, 224, 291, 301–303, 319, 321, 325, 340
Williamson, Claude, 183
Williamson, Stu, 183–184, 212
Willis, Larry, 256
Willow Weep For Me, 32, 99
Wilson, Dick, 87
Wilson, Gerald, 93, 105
Wilson, Shadow, 133

Wilson, Teddy, 63, 87, 93, 100–103, 163
Winding, Kai, 147, 166
Windows, 253, 259
wire brushes, 80, 123, 129, 219
Wise One, 285
wood block, 79, 82, 90, 120
Woodchopper's Ball, 90
Woode, Jimmy, 112
Woodman, Britt, 112
Woods, Phil, 152, 192
woodwinds, 88
Woody 'n' You, 153
Woodyard, Sam, 112, 121
Word of Mouth, 338
wordless vocal, 110
Work Song, 206
WORKIN', 210
Workman, Reggie, 157, 192
World Saxophone Quartet, The, 276
World's Greatest Jazz Band, 60

Wolverine Blues, 63
Wolverine Orchestra, The, 72
Wrappin' It Up, 93

Yancey, Jimmy, 58
You Don't Know What Love Is, 249
Young, David, 296
Young, Larry, 319
Young, Lester, 25, 73, 87, 98, 130, 132–140, 143, 146, 150, 167–169, 177, 179, 280–282, 347–348
Young, Snooky, 133
Young, Trummy, 87
You're Driving Me Crazy, 132
Ysabel's Table Dance, 247

Zawinul, Joe, 192, 210, 319–322, 329–338
Zeitlin, Denny, 252